Uses of Criminal Statistics

The International Library of Criminology, Criminal Justice and Penology
Series Editors: Gerald Mars and David Nelken

Titles in the Series:

Uses of Criminal Statistics

Edited by

Ken Pease

University of Huddersfield

Ashgate

DARTMOUTH

Aldershot • Brookfield USA • Singapore • Sydney

Published by
Dartmouth Publishing Company Limited
Ashgate Publishing Limited
Gower House
Croft Road
Aldershot
Hants GU11 3HR
England

Ashgate Publishing Company
Old Post Road
Brookfield
Vermont 05036
USA

British Library Cataloguing in Publication Data
Uses of criminal statistics. – (The international library of criminology, criminal
   justice and penology)
   1. Criminal statistics
   I. Pease, Ken, 1943–
   364′.021

Library of Congress Cataloging-in-Publication Data
Uses of criminal statistics / edited by Ken Pease.
        p.   cm. — (The international library of criminology, criminal
   justice, and penology)
      Includes bibliographical references and index.
      ISBN 1-85521-408-3
      1. Criminology—Research—Methodology.   2. Criminal statistics.
   3. Criminal statistics—Great Britain.   I. Pease, K. (Ken)
   II. Series: International library of criminology, criminal justice &
   penology
   HV6024.5.U69   1996
   364—dc20   95-52117
                                                                                     CIP

ISBN 1 85521 408 3

Printed and bound by Athenaeum Press, Ltd.,
Gateshead, Tyne & Wear.

Contents

PART III   STATISTICS OF CRIMINALITY

PART IV   STATISTICS OF CRIMINAL JUSTICE

Acknowledgements

The editor and publishers wish to thank the following for permission to use copyright material.

A.B. Academic Publishers for the essays: Richard Block (1993), 'A Cross-National Comparison of Victims of Crime: Victim Surveys of Twelve Countries', *International Review of Victimology*, **2**, pp. 183–207. Copyright © 1993 A.B. Academic Publishers; Graham Farrell (1992), 'Multiple Victimisation: Its Extent and Significance', *International Review of Victimology*, **2**, pp. 85–102. Copyright © 1992 A.B. Publishers.

American Sociological Association for the essay: Terence P. Thornberry and R.L. Christenson (1984), 'Unemployment and Criminal Involvement: An Investigation of Reciprocal Causal Structures', *American Sociological Review*, **49**, pp. 398–411.

Barry Rose Law Periodicals for the essay: David P. Farrington and Elizabeth A. Dowds (1984), 'Why Does Crime Decrease?', *Justice of the Peace*, **148**, pp. 506–9.

Council of Europe for the essay: S. Field (1995), 'Economic Cycles and Crime in Europe', *Crime and Economy*, Proceedings of the Eleventh Criminological Colloquium, Council of Europe: Strasbourg, pp. 53, 55, 57–72.

Elsevier Science Limited for the essay: David P. Farrington and Christopher P. Nuttall (1980), 'Prison Size, Overcrowding, Prison Violence, and Recidivism', *Journal of Criminal Justice*, **8**, pp. 221–31. Copyright © 1980 Pergamon Press Ltd.

Guardian News Service Limited for the essays: Observer Magazine (1991), 'Crime: The Facts, The Figures, The Fears', *Observer Magazine*, 17 February, cover page and pp. 23–25, 28–31, 33. Copyright © The Observer; Robert Baxter and Chris Nuttall (1975), 'Severe Sentences: No Deterrent to Crime?', *New Society*, 2 January, pp. 11–13. Copyright © New Statesman & Society.

Her Majesty's Stationery Office for the essays: Pat Mayhew and Natalie Aye Maung (1992), 'Surveying Crime: Findings from the 1992 British Crime Survey', *Home Office Research Statistics Department, Research Findings*, **2**, pp. 1–5. Copyright © Crown Copyright 1992. Published with the permission of the Controller of Her Majesty's Stationery Office. The views expressed are those of the authors and do not necessarily reflect the views or policy of the Home Office, Her Majesty's Stationery Office or any other Government Department; Leslie T. Wilkins (1960), 'Delinquent Generations', *Home Office Studies in the Causes of Delinquency and the Treatment of Offenders*, **3**, pp. 1–19. Crown Copyright © 1960. With the permission of the Controller of Her Majesty's Stationery Office; Debbie Crisp (1993), 'Standardising Prosecutions', *Home Office Research Bulletin*, **34**, pp. 13–17. Crown Copyright © 1993.

Series Preface

The International Library of Criminology, Criminal Justice and Penology, represents an important publishing initiative to bring together the most significant journal essays in contemporary criminology, criminal justice and penology. The series makes available to researchers, teachers and students an extensive range of essays which are indispensable for obtaining an overview of the latest theories and findings in this fast changing subject.

This series consists of volumes dealing with criminological schools and theories as well as with approaches to particular areas of crime, criminal justice and penology. Each volume is edited by a recognised authority who has selected twenty or so of the best journal articles in the field of their special competence and provided an informative introduction giving a summary of the field and the relevance of the articles chosen. The original pagination is retained for ease of reference.

The difficulties of keeping on top of the steadily growing literature in criminology are complicated by the many disciplines from which its theories and findings are drawn (sociology, law, sociology of law, psychology, psychiatry, philosophy and economics are the most obvious). The development of new specialisms with their own journals (policing, victimology, mediation) as well as the debates between rival schools of thought (feminist criminology, left realism, critical criminology, abolitionism etc.) make necessary overviews that offer syntheses of the state of the art. These problems are addressed by the INTERNATIONAL LIBRARY in making available for research and teaching the key essays from specialist journals.

GERALD MARS
Professor in Applied Anthropology, University of Bradford
School of Management

DAVID NELKEN
Distinguished Research Professor, Cardiff Law Schoool,
University of Wales, Cardiff

Introduction

The standard of statistical sophistication in criminology is not high. Many books could be filled with criminological work that eschewed statistical analysis, or used it naively or partially. More could be filled by work which paraded statistic after statistic in turgid succession, with little thought of social (rather than statistical) significance and in the absence of obvious criminologial imagination. Statistics are supposed to reduce complex data to their meaningful minimum. That requires that the writer needs to know, and the reader to be told, what the meaning might be. Statistical analysis, however sophisticated, which does not do this is no more than the self-conscious display of a complex skill, like the child who has just learned to ride a bike and wants to show everyone even though he or she is not actually using the bike to go anywhere.

The essays reproduced in this volume were chosen for their excellence. In their selection, six considerations were to the fore:

1 that the data used came from published criminal statistics or a data set which was generally available;
2 that the conclusions could probably not have been (ethically) reached by any means other than those used;
3 that, in most cases, considerable ingenuity has been brought to bear upon the problem;
4 that the statistics used are not complex – the key issues concern the criminological imagination, not statistical ostentation;
5 that the statistics often oppose settled views about crime and criminality;
6 that the data are either recent or are 'classics', in that they have continuing implications for research or practice.

The Ones That Got Away

This volume was originally to have been called 'Uses and Abuses of Criminal Statistics'. The process of putting together this volume involved sending out requests to reproduce copyright material. In the course of doing that, copyright-holders became aware of the title of the volume. Two of the people chosen for the excellence of their contributions rang in concerned as to whether their essay had been chosen as a use or an abuse. One declined without making contact with me, perhaps for fear of being identified as an abuser of statistics. Without exception, those whose inclusion would have been as statistical abusers declined permission to reproduce their work. For that reason, the volume lacks examples of statistical abuses, although this matters little, as there are so many examples in existence. Nevertheless, this experience has served to highlight the following lessons:

1 People who abuse statistics are typically aware of the fact, but decline to have the fact brought to the public attention.

2 I should have foreseen this.
3 People who do good work worry about problems they may not have dealt with properly. Perhaps it is the ability to see pitfalls that allows them to produce good work in the first place.

In this Introduction I will describe the range and quality of statistical information routinely available in the UK and will bemoan the fact that it is not more often analysed in ways which inform policy. That is followed by a brief account of a problem with official statistics in terms of what they do not cover and how this affects and directs the perception of crime. Then I will discuss two examples where what gets recorded in crime and punishment is inappropriate for policy development. This indicates how important it is to be aware of the assumptions about crime which underpin the exercise of counting crimes.

So Much Data; So Few People Care

The UK is richly served with statistics about its crime problem and its criminal justice system. I will concentrate here on the data as it exists in England and Wales, but equivalent, albeit shorter and somewhat less regular, data sources exist for Scotland and Northern Ireland.

Data about crime victims is drawn from the biannual British Crime Survey. This is a survey of up to 18 000 people carried out to determine which of them have fallen victim to crime, which victims have reported the crimes they suffered to the police, and why (see Mayhew *et al.*, 1993). Crimes known to the police are recorded in the annual *Criminal Statistics*, accompanied by four supplementary volumes dealing with particular aspects of court process. Annual reports produced by the various agencies of criminal justice contain details of cases processed. For example, a separate annual volume of *Prison Statistics* details many aspects of prison use, including the distribution of those admitted to prison by age, offence and criminal history. Prison discipline statistics and medication are also covered. The annual reports of the Parole Board throughout its history have reflected how the system of early release from prison operates, by how many the prison population is reduced as a consequence of early release on parole, and what type of offender seems to be most generously treated by the Parole Board. Annual reports of the Criminal Injuries Compensation Board detail payments made under that scheme. Even the annual reports of the Customs and Excise Department contains some information about criminal proceedings. Some annual reports are notably lacking in statistical information. Of these, the reports of the work of the Crown Prosecution Service are among the most remarkable in terms of their lack of data. It is probably no coincidence that this recent and most contentious of organizations lacks such information.

In addition to the *regular* government departments' publications (primarily of the Home Office) the Home Office series of *Statistical Bulletins* documents some 40–50 matters of particular relevance each year, and reports of Royal Commissions and the like are attended by extensive statistical and other research which is later published. Some of the published reports of the Home Office's Research and Statistics Department include analyses of published data. Most of this material is also now available at the Home Office's web site (http://www.homeoffice.gov.uk).

All in all, there is an immense amount of national and local statistical information available to the public. A digest of information judged to be of greatest interest is also available (see Barclay, 1995) and this provides a superb overview of basic information about crime and responses to it. A somewhat dated review of statistical sources and their use can be found in Bottomley and Pease (1986).

The statistics are themselves a fascinating social document of what is felt to be worth recording about crime. In early criminal statistics, the country was divided not, as now, by police force area. Rather the division was as in Table 1 below, wherein such categories as 'seaports' and 'pleasure towns' are identified. It is hard to avoid the conclusion that this classification originated with a civil servant who disliked sailors and was suspicious of pleasure! Further, the social variables which are quoted include pauperism and marriage. At that time, no social variables were plotted against punishment. Pauperism was seen as relevant to crime, but not to the imposition of imprisonment. In contrast, no personal or social variables are graphed against *crime* in recent Home Office statistics, but the prison population is classified by ethnicity. It seems that a century ago people seemed more confident of the personal factors giving rise to crime and of the irrelevance of those factors to punishment decisions. The opposite may now be closer to the belief held.

As the twentieth century advanced, the role of the motor vehicle in recorded crime rose to virtual pre-eminence, whereas the theft of large domestic animals such as the horse has fallen away. Interestingly, theft from an employer declined enormously over time, presumably as the power of organized labour rose to constitute a disincentive to employers' use of the criminal courts to discipline their workforce. In these and other ways, criminal statistics bear witness to the preoccupations of the era which compiled them.

Gathering statistics about crime is a costly business and cannot be justified solely on the basis of the insights they afford on the society which gives rise to them. Despite the richness of the published statistics, frankly not many of those immediately affected seem to have absorbed even a fraction of what is currently on offer. When they are absorbed, their use is typically unimaginative. Any students able to add up and interested in finding out things no-one has ever noticed would be well advised to look at the Home Office *Statistical Bulletins*. For example, the massacre of children in a Dunblane classroom drew the spotlight of public attention towards arrangements for the issue, refusal and revocation of firearms licences. What had not (and still has not) been incorporated into the debate is the data provided every year in England and Wales on these very matters, as *Statistical Bulletins*. They reveal a number of factors relevant to firearms regulation – namely:

1 that the rates of refusal of renewals of licences are much lower than the rates of refusal of first application;
2 that, over time, rates of refusal (particularly of renewals of firearms licences) have fallen;
3 that police forces vary enormously in the rates at which they refuse to issue firearms licences.

Since Thomas Hamilton, the killer of the Dunblane children, was a long-time holder of a firearms licence, the issue of renewal is of central relevance here. The statistical information may not have been crucial in the debate about firearms, but it certainly sheds light on how the regulation of firearms holders had changed in ways which made the massacre of Dunblane more likely, and should have been put to much greater use in that debate.

Table 1. Crimes Committed in Selected Area Types: England and Wales 1892
(The data are taken from Home Office (1993))

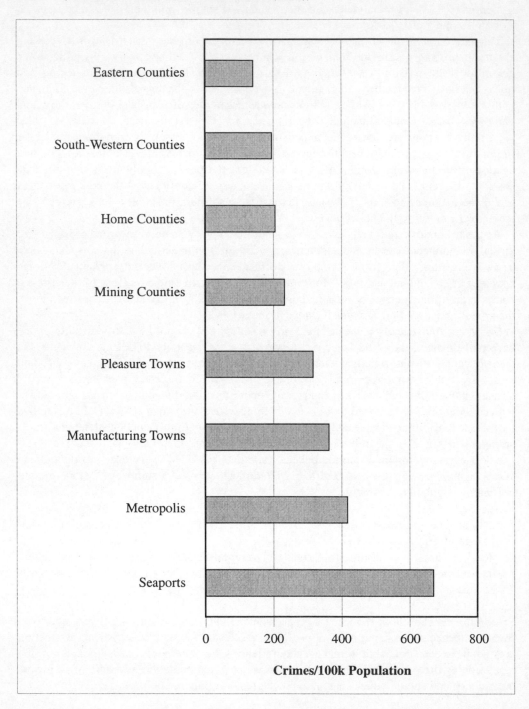

Firearms regulation provides just one example of missed opportunities for using routinely collected data to inform policy. Dramatic trends in the numbers of homes and vehicles burned by arsonists yields another instance among very many of how the maximum use is not made of a plethora of good statistical information. One of the greatest services which could be done to the level of statistical sophistication of those interested in crime would be a far more extensive dialogue with the Home Office's Research and Statistics Department and their counterparts in Scotland and Northern Ireland, together with an imaginative reanalysis of their products.

What Gets Counted Counts

To say that the routine statistical products about crime and justice are valuable far in excess of what would be inferred from their current levels of use is not to say that they are in any sense complete or maximally useful in their depictions. One fundamental point – concerning the basic enumeration of crime – can be used to illustrate this.

What do you understand by the term 'the crime rate'? Clearly, it implies the counting of crimes, but the word 'rate' also suggests that the number of crimes is expressed in relation to some other variable. That variable is usually population. Thus the crime rate is typically the number of crime events per head of population and is expressed as such in criminal statistics. This measure is also referred to as crime incidence. A second measure is termed crime prevalence. This constitutes the number of people against whom crime is committed, however often. In the USA it is thought of as the proportion of people whose lives are touched by crime.

What do both these measures omit? They fail to show how victimization is heavily concentrated on the same people. Prevalence completely ignores this, since a victim is counted simply as a victim irrespective of how many times the person experiences crime. If ten people in a village of 100 people suffer crime, the prevalence is 10 per cent, no matter how many crimes each victim suffers. Incidence counts all the crimes that happen and is indifferent as to who suffers them. In our same village of 100 people there were ten victims. Let's say two of them suffered six crimes each, and the remaining eight suffered one each. The incidence is 20 (total crimes)/100. Incidence rates are really only useful for administrative purposes, such as measuring police workload. They are useless for deciding what to do about crime. The most useful measure for crime control is concentration – the number of crimes/the number of victims. In our village, concentration is thus 20/10. The reason why concentration is a useful measure is that it highlights how effective it is to focus resources on prior victims in preventing crime. Neither incidence nor prevalence gives any clue about what do do about crime. Concentration does. Yet one looks in vain throughout all the volumes of statistics of crime known to the police to obtain data on crime concentration. Only in the most recent reports of the British Crime Survey has this point begun to be addressed. Two essays (by Graham Farrell and Alan Trickett and his colleagues) reproduced as Chapters 8 and 9 of this volume clarify the argument. To restate the basic point, admiration for the professionalism with which official crime statistics are prepared lull us into an acceptance of what is actually counted. The fact that prevalence and incidence predominate over concentration as measures of crime rate exemplifies how the most practically useful measures are often absent.

Another apparently odd example of what is counted when related to the real-life issue of trying to do something about crime is the reconviction rate as an indication of the relative success of different penal sanctions. These statistics are typically of the proportion of those given different sanctions (prison, probation and so on) who are reconvicted within a two-year risk period – that is, two years at liberty. When reconviction rates are compared in this way, the differences between sanctions are typically slight. However, the figures neglect the point at which the risk period starts. For probation, it is immediate. For those given custodial sentences, it only starts after release from custody. For ease of comparison, let us take a group given a one-year prison sentence and another given probation orders. To keep matters simple, we can ignore remission and other early release schemes for prisoners. One year after sentence, many of those given probation will have been reconvicted. One year after sentence, effectively none of those given a year's imprisonment will have been reconvicted. Two years after sentence, even more of those on probation will have been reconvicted. Of the former prisoners, about as many will have been reconvicted as probationers the year before. In short, two years from sentence, fewer prisoners than probationers will have been reconvicted, simply because they were locked up for part of the time. The point here is that, by comparing two-year periods at liberty, the effect of prison in keeping people from committing offences is completely ignored, giving probation a massive advantage. The statistics, as presented, look as though probation is as good as prison in conferring public protection simply because reconvictions only begin to be counted after the incapacitation effect of prison is over. In this example, I would contend that the comparison should be from the point of sentence – that is, that two-year reconviction rates for probation should be the same as two-year reconviction rates dating from the point of sentence. Why is this not done? My speculations are as follows:

1 Because of cost and sentiments of mercy, there is a continuing wish to reduce the use of custody. To clarify its advantage in public protection would not be regarded as helpful.
2 The extent of measured effectiveness required would demoralize the probation service.

These examples should serve as a reminder that the assumptions and perceptions which underpin what gets counted are open to question. In the same way as statistics are not used for policy test and formulation where they could be, so likewise they are not considered in ways which are liable to generate more useful alternatives.

Indifference Bordering on Contempt

We should not neglect the apparently contemptuous abuse of statistics. Political background does determine the perception of crime problems. Danziger (1996) shows that the existence during election campaigns of extensive debate about crime is associated with the perception that crime is rising. In other words, crime is perceived to be rising when there is much discussion about it. This effect may well have occurred during the last few years in England and Wales; during this period, crime has apparently stabilized but its prominence in party political debate means that it is not the public perception. When the political climate influences crime perceptions more than crime statistics, statisticians of crime should start worrying! The general notion of how crime news is managed is a complex one and is well beyond the scope of this Introduction. Those interested should read Surette (1992) as an introduction to the area.

Perhaps one central problem standing in the way of improvement in statistical use is the assumption commonly made that statistics are necessarily a form of deception, so that it is perfectly okay to create whatever impression one wants. As Tufte (1983) notes, 'for many people the first word that comes to mind when they think about statistical charts is 'lie'.

Simple statistics can become distorted, as in Figure 1, modified from the *Daily Mirror* of 15 April 1991. The scales are used by the *Mirror*. An explosion of homicide is manufactured primarily by the use of the scale from 600 to 680 and the use of a tall but narrow graph. This is accompanied by another graph of the same data telling a quite different story. Figure 2 depicts the same data but has a more reasonable scale and, by expressing the murder rate in relation to

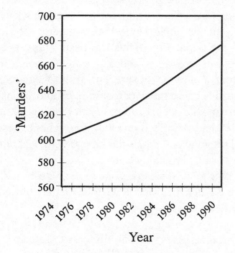

Figure 1: *Daily Mirror*'s 'Death Toll: How the Murder Figures Have Soared'

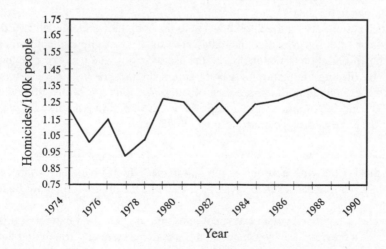

Figure 2: Homicide Risks: The *Mirror* Data Presented Otherwise

the number of people available to be murdered, is fairer as well as more reassuring. A more recent example (8 January 1994) from the same newspaper concerns the relationship between unemployment and crime which is made to look close by the selection of scales. The graph appears under the headline 'Exposed! The Big Tory Lie. Dole and Crime ARE Linked'. In both cases, in the original as it was printed, a human figure is included (a body in the case of the murder graph, an ambiguous burglar/unemployed person in the employment and crime graph). These serve to deflect attention away from the scales and on to the person.

To show how frequently statistical distortion occurs, I decided to include the most mis-leading article in the *Daily Mirror* on crime statistics during the week before writing this. The date now is Thursday 29 May 1997, and on Tuesday 27 May an article appeared entitled 'It's Crime To Do. Straw Pledges More Cops on Street to Fight Shock Rise in Offences'. This reported the International Victimization Survey, which compares the victimization by crime of a representative sample of the population. Thus the basic study is a comparison between countries. However, the headline stresses a 'shock rise in offences'. In fact, the survey contained no data more recent than that of the most recent British Crime Survey, so if the rise was a shock, it shouldn't have been because the data for England and Wales had been in the public domain for a long time. Perhaps the second point worth making is that crime rates over the most recent sweep of the IVS had stabilized or fallen throughout Western Europe, including England and Wales. Indeed, England and Wales did have the highest rates of victimization, but this is very far from being the same as a 'shock rise'.

Impression management by choice of scales is one of the oldest tricks in the book (see Tufte (1983) for a superb and visually beautiful account of the display of quantitative information). He notes other devices as follows:

1   The use of graphics where variations in one dimension reflect the real change, but the graphics are depicted as areas or volumes. Thus if burglary doubles, the picture of two burglars, one twice as tall as the other, would have area differences much greater than 2:1. Tufte calculates the 'Lie Factor', which is calculated as the size of an effect shown in the graphic/its size in the data.
2   Graphic decoration serving to editorialize (as in the body alongside the murder trend).
3   The confusion of design variation and data variation – for example, the non-inclusion of adjustments for inflation or population, or the use of scales which exaggerate the point to be made. By placing the picture of a body alongside, the graph itself becomes tall and narrow, thus exaggerating the impression of steep rise. The use of just three data points (1974, 1980 and 1990) also shows a trend as dramatic and inexorable which fluctuates almost to the point of disappearance when all the data are used.

Lest it be thought that the *Mirror* is being unfairly singled out for unfair criticism, it should be stressed that this is purely because this is the newspaper which I have taken throughout my adult life. Lately, our dog has taken to savaging it as it hits the doormat. Perhaps he has better taste than I do.

Other agencies can get away with statistical nonsense too. The first extract in this volume was to have been a press release by a major communications company which told the story of its initiative in preventing a type of crime with which it was linked. The conclusions it reached were unsustainable on the basis of the evidence given in the press release, but were dutifully reported in the press. A press release is an attempt to gain publicity. It seems to me that a refusal to reproduce such a document is an attempt to withdraw from the public arena material whose publication was sought – at least until its statistical dubiety was pointed out.

Cause by Association

One of the features of crime statistics concerns the variables with which it comes to be associated – popular ones being unemployment and drug use and unpopular ones being rates of meditation and pollution. Simply by looking at variables in the same 'frame' sets up an implication that there is a link. The early local victimization surveys included questions about police accountability alongside crime victimization, giving the impression of a link. Victimization surveys have asked about fear of crime far more often than they have asked about anger about crime, but this has nothing to do with what people feel, simply with what emotions are seen to be appropriate. Academic treatises about crime are self-inventing in the sense that the academic chooses the variables to include. This process is self-perpetuating. If crime were wholly attributable to demonic possession, modern criminology would not notice, simply because demonic possession is not in the repertoire of fashionable explanations for crime. There are indeed associations of crime with meditation and pollution which are at least as impressive as those with the popular variables. Crime rates on Merseyside co-varied with the proportion of members of the Natural Law Party actively engaged in meditation in the area. Levels of violence co-vary with rates of lead pollution in the USA.

The question which should always be asked is 'How is this supposed to work?'. It is the neglect of the mechanism which leads those of us concerned with crime control into trouble – as the recent works of Ray Pawson and Nick Tilley serve to remind us (see Pawson and Tilley, 1997). Let's consider this in relation to the Merseyside meditation issue referred to above. The Natural Law Party claimed that it was the existence of a critical mass of its members in meditation which reduced Merseyside crime and presented a paper to that effect to the British Psychological Society and in a peer-reviewed journal (Hatchard *et al.*, 1996). The claim and the responses to it gained wide publicity. Despite the presence of a highly professional research and analysis department, the police force never really countered the claim other than by a fairly bland assertion of the effectiveness of its own programmes. It would have been relatively easy to test the Natural Law party's claim. Whatever power was deemed to be generated by those meditating, it presumably had a distance decay (otherwise why would not a constant number of meditators change the world). The centre of meditation was the Golden Temple in Skelmersdale. Within Merseyside, some divisions were much further from the Temple than others. There were divisions in forces other than Merseyside which were closer to the Golden Temple than some divisions within Merseyside. It would have been relatively easy to look for a distance decay relationship within Merseyside, and to see whether the population in other police divisions behaved as they should have if meditation were the active ingredient. A similar correlational study links rates of environmental pollution with rates of violent crime (Masters *et al.*, 1997). Plausible as it sounds, this requires research which clarifies links. For example, a polluting accident should have its greatest effect on those just born or just about to be born. Thus rates of criminal violence should be higher in specific birth cohorts if pollution holds the key. If one finds children who have higher levels of lead in their body also to have been officially processed for violent behaviour, that does not tell one much. It could be that such children are less supervised, and hence spend more time on the street, where they pick up more dirt and, in their area, the dirt is polluted by lead. Thus the relationship between lead and violence may in reality be a direct relationship between levels of parental supervision and violence, with levels of lead being merely a marker for lack of parental supervision.

A sad and recent instance of the neglect of mechanism comes from the debate about the reasons for the decline of crime in New York City, which has turned into an unedifying exchange of views between the former Chief of New York Police and academic criminologists. This has practical importance because the notion of zero-tolerance policing which is ascribed to New York is becoming fashionable here. In fact, concentration on mechanism could clarify what happened in New York.

The Presentation of Data about Crime and Justice

An object lesson in how statistical information can be incorporated into press articles about crime comes from the *Observer Magazine* feature reproduced as Chapter 1 of this volume. The scales on the graphs are chosen reasonably, the preponderance of property over personal crime is stressed early in the piece, and changes in crime rates with time are sensibly discussed. The *Observer* extract illustrates the fact that statistical analyses may summarize and sometimes explain sets of data too extensive to comprehend readily.

Chapter 2, by Don M. Gottfredson, addresses some of the issues surrounding the scope of the statistical commentator and the practitioner in criminal justice. While the essay personifies the non-practitioner as researcher rather than statistician, almost all the same considerations apply. Evaluation in criminal justice is usually statistics-based rather than research-based, simply because of the many ethical and practical obstacles to true experimentation in criminal justice. Having read the first two essays in the collection, the reader should have a wary but respectful view of the usability of criminal statistics.

Crime Trends and Patterns

The next five essays are scholarly (but not overly technical) attempts to look at crime trends. The first of these is Gurr's account of historical trends in violent crime (Chapter 3). It is important because of its careful and extensive use of a range of publicly available data and because it counters an impression of a consistent increase in violent crime over centuries. He identifies several general factors which may help account for the 'historically temporary deviations from the downward trend in interpersonal violence'. The second essay in Part II is interesting on account of its analysis of how vulnerable official statistics are to apparently trivial differences in recording practice, as identified by David Farrington and Elizabeth Dowds. It was this vulnerability which led to the development of the victimization survey, wherein a representative sample of the population, not known to be victims, is asked about its crime experiences. The following essay (Chapter 5) summarizes the most recent British national survey of crime victimization, which was carried out in early 1992. While attended by different problems from official statistics (see Sparks, 1981), victimization surveys are an enormously valuable supplement to other official data, and the summary of findings by Pat Mayhew and her colleagues and reproduced here is succinct and fascinating. Chapter 6 by Richard Block then looks at the results of victimization surveys cross-nationally, and comments usefully on some of the methodological problems with such surveys.

The analyses of trends in crime alongside economic indicators carried out by Simon Field (Chapter 7) grapples with the questions of why crime rates change. One of the distinctive features of his analysis is that he measures *change* in crime rates rather than rates themselves. Using this approach, he shows that the economic factors associated with changes in property crime are quite different from those linked with changes in personal crime.

One of the problems with most conventional statistical presentations is that too little attention is paid to how victimization is spread among victims or places. When that issue is addressed, it quickly becomes clear that a minority of people is repeatedly victimized, and when they are victimized this happens quickly. The essay by Graham Farrell (Chapter 8) reviews relevant work and makes it clear that there are profound implications in simply changing the way that victimization is enumerated. The next essay, by Alan Trickett and his colleagues, continues the same theme by looking at the extent to which differences between high and low crime areas is a difference between areas where many people are victimized or few people are victimized, or alternatively whether it is because the same proportion of people are victimized – but more often.

The final essay in Part II, by Larry Sherman and his colleagues, identifies crime 'hot spots'. This is the classic essay on 'hot spots', although it is not the first one to use the phrase.

Statistics of Criminality

Statistics of criminality count criminal people rather than criminal events. These counts are sometimes made in their own right and sometimes in order to understand the social origins or consequences of criminality. The first brief essay in Part III is one of my favourites. Its starting point, showing how one table in criminal statistics could be recalculated to show the prevalence of convictions, is an insight with few parallels in criminology and in which Farrington followed the work of McClintock and Avison, which he cites. This statistic provided the head-line for the *Observer Magazine* essay reproduced as Chapter 1 and has been replicated by other research. It must give comfort that a major piece of criminological information stemmed from a simple observation of this kind.

The rough dimensions of criminal careers appear similar in different countries studied. Chapter 12, by David Farrington and Per-Olof Wikstrom, compares England and Wales with Sweden in the dimensions of the criminal career which can be considered as having four components: participation, duration, frequency and seriousness. Respectively, these refer to the proportion of the population becoming involved in crime, the period of their lives during which they commit crime, how often during that time they commit crime (a rate referred to as lambda in the criminology literature), and how serious those crimes are. Understanding these dimensions of a criminal career is of great potential in understanding how people should be sentenced. For example, there is little crime preventive point in the harsh sentencing of people who have short criminal careers anyway.

Although the criminal career in all its complexity is not yet fully understood, an individual's probability of conviction can be predicted with some accuracy. Humphrey *et al.*'s essay on this topic (Chapter 13) illustrates the development of a predictor of reconviction for people on probation. It is not the best predictor available, but the essay has the virtue of describing the process whereby the predictor was developed in some detail, and of being fairly recent.

The next essay in Part III is reproduced because it is a classic example of how criminological imagination allows data to be looked at in a particular way. Written by Leslie Wilkins and entitled 'Delinquent Generations', it shows how those who were infants during the war years showed a tendency to commit delinquent and criminal acts throughout the following decades. The suggestion was that some aspects of early experience impacted upon their later lives. The work was not conclusive, but research in Denmark (Christiansen, 1963), New Zealand (Slater *et al.*, 1966) and Poland (Jasinski, 1966) giving the same results adds to its persuasiveness. The effect should not be taken to be true (see Rose (1968) for an alternative explanation of the findings) but it has not yet been discounted, and other methods should be brought to bear. The work should also be repeated with more recent cohorts of children in countries which have experienced some similar major interruption of normal life.

Sometimes, particular social factors, such as drug use or unemployment, emerges as the basis for a fashionable theory about why people embark upon a criminal career. The next two essays, by Wilson and Thornberry and Christenson, show, for drug use and unemployment respectively, how such analyses should not be taken at face value. The second of these is by far the most difficult technically in this volume, but should be looked at for its conceptual approach rather than for the details of technique used.

Statistics of Criminal Justice

Parts I to III of this volume contain essays using statistics on crime and criminality. Part IV concerns the operation of the criminal justice system itself. The opening essay by Baxter and Nuttall (Chapter 17) directs itself to the settled judicial belief that one-off deterrent sentences can reduce rates of a crime. It does so by analysing one sentence which was claimed to have such an effect and plotting the rates of the offence in question in the same city and elsewhere before and after the sentence. So much for that settled judicial belief!

In Chapter 18 David Farrington and Trevor Bennett show the effect of the introduction of formal police cautioning on the rate of official processing of juveniles as delinquents. This is, more than any other, the essay which demonstrated the effect of 'net-widening' – that is, the tendency of many reforms to inculpate more people as offenders.

In Chapter 19 (which is included together with the correspondence which it evoked), Nigel Walker criticizes the use of official statistics as evidence of discrimination against women defendants in the criminal justice system. Walker's position is as logical as it is unfashionable.

The following essay, by Debbie Crisp (Chapter 20) concerns the work of the Crown Prosecution Service in discontinuing cases forwarded for prosecution by the police. It is an interesting example of honest statistics which lack the commentary to locate the statistical analysis in a heated debate. The Crown Prosecution Service was introduced to try to remove weak cases from the criminal justice process and to level out area differences in prosecution rates. The essay makes it clear that not only are there still enormous area differences in prosecution rates, but there are also incidental bad effects from the work of the Crown

Prosecution Service, such as the fact that, in one-third of cases, police officers initiating proceedings never hear the outcome of their work. This essay could be used powerfully by a proponent of the abolition of the Crown Prosecution Service. The fact that it has not bespeaks the problem mentioned earlier, that the Home Office often publishes good statistics which could inform public debate, but few people notice and even fewer can see the implications of the data.

A major criminal justice enterprise of the 1970s and 1980s concerned the search for 'alternatives to custody'. This search was grounded in a misunderstanding of the statistics of prison use. Although people sentenced to short periods of imprisonment constitute a majority of those admitted into prison, they are only a small minority of those in prison at any one time. Thus substituting non-custodial sentences for short custodial sentences would have only a small effect on the size of the prison population. Since short-sentence prisoners are also those who are most quickly reconvicted and in the greatest proportions, the effect would be trivial indeed (see Bottomley and Pease, 1986). Nonetheless, criminal justice policy-makers have never let the facts get in the way of a bad policy, and alternatives to custody were introduced in large numbers: community service orders, day training centres, suspended sentences, partially suspended sentences and so on. Chapter 21 by R.F. Sparks is a classic in that it shows that, even if the basic arithmetic had been right, the use made by the courts of the suspended sentence would have subverted the purpose anyway.

The penultimate essay in the volume, by Farrington and Nuttall, deals with the effects of crowding and size of prisons on the rate of reconviction. To me, it is a beautiful example of how routinely collected data can be used to clarify issues of major social importance.

The final chapter, by D.A. Andrews and his colleagues, illustrates a technique of relatively recent origin and substantial importance – namely, the meta-analysis which contrives to combine the results of a variety of disparate research studies to inform a conclusion about the effectiveness of penal treatments. Because it deals with a central issue in criminal justice and because its results are not part of current received wisdom, the analysis assumes great importance.

References

Barclay, G. (1995), *A Digest of Information on the Criminal Justice System*, 3, London: HMSO.
Bottomley, A.K. and Pease, K. (1986), *Crime and Punishment: Interpreting the Data*, Milton Keynes: Open University Press.
Christiansen, K.O. (1963), 'Delinquent Generations in Denmark', *British Journal of Criminology*, 4, pp. 259–64.
Danziger, S.R. (1996), *The Real War on Crime*, New York: Harper.
Hatchard, G.D., Deans, A.J., Cavanaugh, C.I. and Orme-Johnson, D.W. (1996), 'The Maharishi Effect: A Model for Social Improvement. Time Series Analysis of a Phase Transition to Reduced Crime in Merseyside Metropolitan Area', *Psychology, Crime and Law*, 2, pp. 165–74.
Home Office (1993), *Criminal Justice Statistics 1882–1892*, Home Office Statistical Findings 1/93.
Jasinski, J. (1966), 'Delinquent Generations in Poland', *British Journal of Criminology*, 6, pp. 170–82.
Masters, R.D., Hone, B. and Doshi, A. (1997), 'Environmental Pollution, Neurotoxicity and Criminal Violence', in J. Rose (ed.), *Environmental Toxicology*, London: Gordon and Breach.
Mayhew, P., Aye Maung, N. and Mirrlees-Black, C. (1993), *The 1992 British Crime Survey*, London: HMSO.
Pawson, R. and Tilley, N. (1997), *Scientific Realism*, London: Sage.

Rose, G.N.G. (1968), 'The Artificial Delinquent Generation', *Journal of Criminology, Criminal Law and Police Science*, **59**, pp. 370–85.

Slater, S.W., Darwin, J.H. and Ritchie, W.L. (1966), 'Delinquent Generations in New Zealand', *Journal of Research in Crime and Delinquency*, **3**, pp. 140–46.

Sparks, R.F. (1981), 'Surveys of Victimisation: An Optimistic Assessment', in M. Tonry and N. Morris (eds), *Crime and Justice, 3. An Annual Review of Research*, Chicago: University of Chicago Press.

Surette, R. (1992), *Media, Crime and Criminal Justice: Images and Realities*, Pacific Grove CA:Brooks/ Cole.

Tufte, E.R. (1983), *The Visual Display of Quantitative Information*, Cheshire Connecticut: Graphics Press.

Part I
The Presentation of Data about Crime and Justice

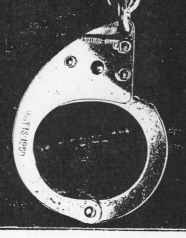

OBSERVER magazine

17 FEBRUARY 1991

Of all British men born in a single month in 1953, one in three had a criminal record by the time he was 30

**THE FACTS
THE FIGURES
THE FEARS**

Is Britain more dangerous and less law-abiding than it was 20 years ago? In this special report, David Rose analyses the evidence, we talk to those at the sharp end and a unique series of regional maps allows you to check your chances of becoming one of crime's victims

CRIME

THE FACTS, THE FIGURES, THE FEARS

TOTAL CRIME PER 100,000

1 Devon and Cornwall
2 Dorset
3 Avon and Somerset
4 Hampshire
5 Wiltshire
6 Gloucestershire
7 Sussex
8 Surrey
9 Thames Valley
10 Warwickshire
11 West Midlands
12 Staffordshire
13 Cheshire
14 Merseyside
15 Kent
16 Metropolitan
17 Hertfordshire
18 Bedfordshire
19 Northamptonshire
20 Leicestershire
21 Derbyshire
22 Greater Manchester
23 Lancashire
24 Essex
25 Cambridgeshire
26 Lincolnshire
27 Nottinghamshire
28 South Yorkshire
29 West Yorkshire
30 North Yorkshire
31 Cumbria
32 Suffolk
33 Norfolk
34 Humberside
35 Cleveland
36 Durham
37 Northumbria
38 South Wales
39 Gwent
40 Dyfed-Powys
41 West Mercia
42 North Wales
43 Dumfries and Galloway
44 Lothian and Borders
45 Strathclyde
46 Central
47 Fife
48 Tayside
49 Northern
50 Grampian

3000 to 4000
4000 to 5000
5000 to 6000
6000 to 8000
8000 to 10000
10000 to 13000

ROBIN HARRIS

MAPS BY STEVE HARRIS

23

CRIME

The next 24 hours will see police in Britain record two murders, 10 rapes, 50 sexual assaults, 50 assaults causing grievous bodily harm, 113 muggings and other robberies, 2,800 burglaries, and 1,200 car thefts. Yet these figures – part of an annual total of about five million recorded crimes – represent only the tip of an iceberg. The true picture is worse.

Crime statistics have come as record levels, accompanied by social and political panic. Each of the three quarters of 1990 for which figures have already been published showed a rise of about 14 per cent on the same period 12 months before. On each publication date, politicians and senior police officers called, according to taste, for more policemen, armed policemen, a return to family discipline or for drivers to be more careful in locking their cars. (The biggest rise last year was in vehicle theft, up 23 per cent for the 12 months to the end of September to 465,000 in England and Wales.)

The latest increases come as a particular disappointment to policymakers, because in 1988 and 1989 the recorded crime rate actually fell. Public debate on the subject, however, remains singularly ill-informed. According to an NOP poll, two-thirds of the population believe that 50 per cent of crimes are violent offences against the person. The true figure is 6 per cent. Small wonder, perhaps, that a Home Office working party chaired by Michael Grade of Channel 4 claimed fear of crime – fuelled by the headline reports of the most sensational crimes – to be as great a problem as crime itself.

It is true, for example, that the elderly most fear crime, especially violent crime, although they are least likely to become victims. (The most dangerous age of all is under one year old, with 28 homicide victims per million

babies. People of more than 70 are far less likely to be murder victims than any adult group, with only eight victims per million. Only children aged 5-15 are safer.)

According to an international survey published last year, Britain's crime rate is lower than the European average, and lower than that of Holland, Germany, Canada and Australia. About 18 per cent of Britons were victims of at least one crime during 1988. In Canada, 28 per cent had experienced a crime, in Holland 26 per cent and in West Germany 22 per cent. At the other end of the scale, Switzerland (15.6 per cent) and Finland (15.9 per cent) had low overall victimisation rates. But safest of all was Northern Ireland: there only 15 per cent of the population experienced a crime in 1988.

The US appeared to live up to its reputation for lawlessness overall, with 28.8 per cent of the population having been a victim of crime. America's murder rate makes ours seem infinitesimal. Nearly twice as many murders (1,051) were committed in the city of New York in the first six months of last year as in England and Wales (627) in the whole of 1989. American homicide, largely the consequence of liberal gun laws, is concentrated in the ghettoes. Black American males have a one in 30 chance of being murdered. In Britain, the odds of a man of any race being the victim of a deliberate killing are 7,000 to one; for women, the figure is 14,000 to one.

Murder illustrates perfectly the difficulty of divining what crime figures really mean. Very few homicides go unreported, which at least makes the raw data numerically reliable. But there are many pitfalls to their interpretation. The claim that society is becoming more violent is a newspaper columnist's cliché. An examination of homicide since World War II appears superficially

to support it: the 1987 record total for England and Wales of 686 dwarfed the low point reached in 1949, when only 298 people were killed. At the same time, the proportion of homicide victims killed by strangers has crept upwards, by 1989, as the graphic (below left) reveals, accounting for a third of all male victims and 12 per cent of women. (As ever, the bulk – 48 per cent – of the 234 murdered women that year were dispatched by their husbands or lovers, although only 10 per cent of men were killed by their wives or girlfriends.)

However, if one compares the present murder rate with that of the nineteenth century, Britain seems a much safer place to live. In 1989, there were 12.5 homicides per million population – almost exactly the same figure as that for 1857, the year that records began. But while 1989 was close to a murder rate peak, 1857 was the bottom of a trough. The next year, 1858, saw 15.8 homicides per million, the total rising to a record 19.6 by 1865 and staying in the high teens for the next 25 years. Not until the end of the century did the homicide rate fall back to a steady average of 10 victims per million per year.

Even then, one must be wary of jumping to the opposite conclusion: that Victorian Britain was altogether more murderous than today. Our firearms laws have spared us the carnage of the US, although gun use has grown steadily in Britain over the past decade. In 1979, firearms were involved in 6,500 offences, but by 1989, this figure was 3,000 higher, with an average annual growth rate of 4 per cent. This rise was accounted for by robberies and criminal damage cases in which guns were used. A gun was actually fired in only 58 per cent of the 9,500 firearms total. Half the firearms crimes involved only airguns; 21 per cent pistols, and 14 per cent the armed robber's standby, the sawn-off or full-barrelled shotgun. Knives and other sharp instruments have remained the favourite murder weapon, employed by about a third of killers. Blunt instruments make up some 12 per cent of cases, while another fifth die from beating and kicking (see left). The problem for historical comparison is that these British ways of death have become much more preventable by surgical techniques. Ambulances bring victims who once would have died to hospital, where slit veins can be sewn, and broken heads mended. A case which once would have been homicide will be subsumed in the much longer list of serious assaults.

If the difficulties in interpreting murder rates begin to be more obvious, the problems with other types of crime figures are far greater. Criminologists refer to crimes never reported to the police, and hence never recorded in their official statistics, as the 'dark figure'. Mind-bogglingly vast, it is also susceptible to unpredictable variations. The improvements in the way that police deal with rape victims, for example, led to a steady rise in the proportion of rapes reported throughout the 1980s, although this is probably still no higher than one-fifth.

There is clear evidence that the proportion of burglaries reported has also increased over the past decade. Here, the reason appears to be the growth in home-ownership. Rental tenants who are burgled may feel there is little point in telling the police because of the scant prospects of catching the perpetrator. They may also lack insurance. But mortgage lenders make buildings insurance a condition of a loan, and having insured bricks and mortar, most homeowners add their contents. Invariably, insurance companies require a police reference number before they will consider a claim. It is no coincidence that the type of theft with the highest reporting rate is vehicle theft, at 86 per cent: legally, ▷ p29

THE WHO AND HOW OF HOMICIDE

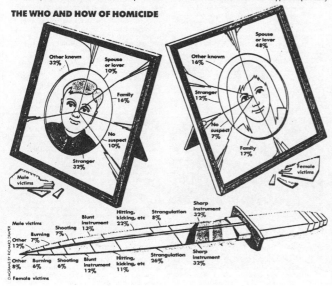

HOMICIDE

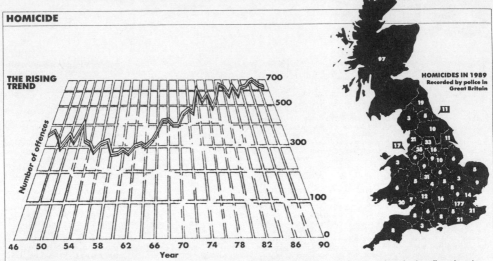

THE RISING TREND

Number of offences

700
500
300
100
0

46   50   54   58   62   66   70   74   78   82   86   90

Year

HOMICIDES IN 1989
Recorded by police in
Great Britain

Detective Superintendent John Jones of the Metropolitan Police recently investigated his 100th murder. Thirty-one years a policeman, he heads one of the Met's 'Area Major Investigation Pools' (AMIPS), specialist squads called out to all but the simplest killings. 'I don't want you to give the impression I'm some kind of Maigret,' he says. 'The old idea of the detective or perhaps two detectives investigating a murder just doesn't happen. I'm a manager, totally dependent on the skills of my team.'

The murder clear-up rate of about 90 per cent is far the highest of any crime, the product of the tremendous resources which homicide inquiries can command. At an AMIP incident room, set up swiftly in the wake of a killing, Mr Jones will use Holmes, the Home Office Large Murder Enquiry System, a sophisticated computer software and database to log and correlate evidence. In theory, says Mr Jones, he must, as an AMIP squad manager, keep an eye on his team's annual budget: a particularly difficult excerise when deal ing with killings close to the start of the financial year. But, as yet, he says, he doesn't know of any case where financial constraint has prevented a 'result'.

Yet behind the managerial exterior, an Inspector Morse lurks: an investigator whose career has not lacked luck, or investigative flair. John Jones distinguished himself as a CID trainee on his first murder in 1965. A man suspected his fiancée was two-timing him. He followed the pair to Harefield, a village on the Met's far northwest-ern rural marches, and as they got out of the man's car, he saw him touch her in a suggestive way. The jealous lover slashed the woman with a knife and stabbed the man in the chest. Called out to the scene that night, the then PC Jones passed a car pulled over at the side of the road. Its driver was hunched over the wheel, weeping. He confessed immediately: 'I've just slashed my girlfriend and killed someone.'

Twenty years later, Mr Jones was at a colleague's retirement party when a subordinate rang to tell him a little girl was missing. 'Children go missing all the time and 99 per cent are found safe and well. But this time I had an instinct that something was up.' He launched an investigation

there and then in circumstances where normally he would have waited. By the time the body was found the next day, the killer was in custody.

Success in an investigation must, he says, be based on missing nothing, no matter how trivial: 'Say you've got a vague description of a vehicle. It can give a start, and you can start eliminating.' Every piece of information will be read by two officers and 'actioned' (considered and given to a team member to follow up). The first 24 hours may be crucial, but it is also important to give witnesses time to settle after this feverish period: 'Early on, they may say something that later doesn't bear examination. If you put that down on paper, you may get misleading details set in

Detective Superintendent John Jones relies on the Holmes computer for help in detecting killers

Total murder and manslaughter offences by region (above). Use the map on page 23 to locate your area. Left: Killing has risen steadily since World War II

stone. It's better to get brief details at first and go back for longer statements after a few days.'

Mr Jones says he is confident he has never put someone away for a killing they didn't commit. He works, he says, on the principle of trying always to have at least three planks of evidence before bringing a case to court, each sufficiently strong to sustain a conviction on its own. He is keenly aware of the difficulties which the Guildford Four case and other recent *causes célèbres* have caused investigators, particularly when it comes to interviews and confessions. Increasingly, the legal adviser almost always present at a murder interrogation will advise a suspect to say nothing.

Like many detectives, Mr Jones believes that the judicial balance, with the protection of subjects provided by the Police and Criminal Evidence Act, has already swung too far against the police without the possible reforms which the May judicial inquiry into the Guildford case may bring. 'Sometimes you get a strong feeling that a person wants to answer your questions,' he says, 'but of course they will always follow their legal advice.'

Having been involved in so many murder inquiries, Mr Jones is unable to come to any conclusions about the type of person who kills. 'There are people who could never generate enough aggression to commit murder, no matter how badly provoked. But killers come from a myriad of backgrounds, and they have a myriad of motives.' There is, he adds, a rage in society that can shock even an experienced investigator: every year, there are two or three killings which start as the most trivial of arguments between drivers in traffic.

John Jones is no Mr Plod. An opera lover and book collector, intensely proud of his Cambridge double blue son, he plans to retire soon to an old watermill in the Pyrenees to write novels. 'I've always tried not to become an effigy of a police-man,' he says. 'There are a lot of things to life other than investigating murder.'   **DAVID ROSE**

CRIME

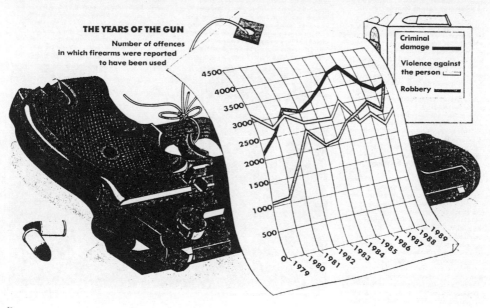

THE YEARS OF THE GUN

Number of offences
in which firearms were reported
to have been used

| Criminal damage |
| Violence against the person |
| Robbery |

4500
4000
3500
3000
2500
2000
1500
1000
500
0

1979 1980 1981 1982 1983 1984 1985 1986 1987 1988 1989

SEXUAL OFFENCES

Dramatic police arrests are a more common sight today than they were a hundred years ago, when juveniles would merely receive a cuff round the ears to admonish them, keeping down the statistics

of course, all vehicle drivers in Britain must be insured.

The best estimate of the size of the dark figure of crime is provided by the British Crime Survey (BCS), a parallel set of statistics compiled at intervals by the Home Office since 1980. The survey, however, is based not on reports of crime to the police, but on lengthy interviews with a representative sample of about 12,000 people. The last BCS, in 1987, found only 41 per cent of the crimes experienced by the sample had been reported, 5 per cent more than in 1981. The police themselves had failed to record in their statistics 36 per cent of the crimes reported to them. The result was that the official statistics contained a mere 27 per cent of the crimes that had taken place. If five million crimes were recorded in Britain last year, therefore, in fact nearly 20 million were committed. The BCS also suggests that the rise in the crime rate is significantly lower than the police figures imply. In the period 1981-87, the police recorded increases of 40 per cent for wounding and 62 per cent for robbery. According to the BCS, the true figures were 12 per cent and 9 per cent. Police figures showed a 40 per cent increase for all crimes in the same period. The BCS found it to be 31 per cent.

In dealing with longer historical spans, crime figures recorded by the police are still less reliable. In 1978, James Anderton, the recently knighted Greater Manchester Chief Constable, began his high-profile media career with a speech in which he spoke of crime as the country's leading 'growth industry'. He cited the fact that the total of recorded crime in England and Wales in 1900 was 77,934; at the time of his speech, it had reached 2.2 million. Geoff Pearson, Professor of Sociology at Middlesex Polytechnic, pointed out in his book *Hooligan* (Macmillan) that the two figures covered periods when the law was enforced so differently that the comparison ▷

In the small interview room in the Kent police force's 'safe house' for victims of sexual abuse there are two sets of anatomically correct dolls: mummy and daddy in one corner, boy and girl in the other. They are impervious to the video cameras on the walls, as are the children (some as young as two and a half) brought into this haven.

The dolls and the boxes of toys downstairs are for the children. The airing cupboard, full of white towels and clean tracksuits, is for the adult victims, victims of rape who will first be taken to the small upstairs examination room before having baths and showers to cleanse them of the dirt and guilt that they associate with the crime.

Since the unit opened just over a year ago, Kent police, who have two further rape suites, have used the house up to four times a week. The majority of interviewees are children. The force received only 97 reports of rape in 1989, and of those, 91.8 per cent were speedily cleared up, the perpetrator known to the victim. 'Rape really doesn't happen as much as people think,' says WPC Jan Bromley, who produced the constabulary's pamphlet on personal safety. 'When it does happen, it generates a lot of publicity.'

Kent, like other forces, was pushed into action after the 1984 TV series on the Thames Valley force highlighted the callous way rape victims were treated. DCI George McQueen, Head of Rochester CID, says: 'They highlighted the macho culture of the police station where nobody believed the victim and would assume the allegation was malicious. That emphasis has reversed since then. We always assume we are hearing the truth, and we try to see that victims are looked after by both women officers and medical staff.'

The Kent safe house is in a residential street and furnished like a home. Male officers confine

The colours represent notifiable sexual offences per 100,000 population in each police area in 1989

themselves to the surveillance room where interviewing can be monitored and, in the case of children, recorded on video. WPC Hazel Donovan, who has dealt with a number of cases says: 'When women come to us, they are frightened, upset and worried about the reception they'd receive at the police station.The house has made a big difference. We are now able to give women a level of care previously denied them, while also providing a comforting atmosphere for the children we bring here. Some of them don't want to leave us afterwards.'
SHYAMA PERERA

A homely environment means that a police interview becomes less of an ordeal for the victims of sexual abuse

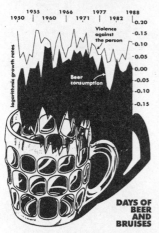

CRIME

**DAYS OF
BEER
AND
BRUISES**

BURGLARY

UNDER 1000
1000 - 1499
1500 - 1999
2000 - 2499
2500 - 2999
3000 AND MORE

This map represents burglaries per 100,000 people per area in 1989. Figures not available for Scotland

made no sense. At the turn of the century, police had far wider powers of discretion, particularly in dealing with juveniles: crimes by youths treated with the traditional cuff around the ears did not appear in criminal statistics. In the nineteenth century, large areas of what are now called inner cities were effectively 'no-go' areas for the police, where only the most serious crimes, like murder, were reported or investigated. Incidents that could not be solved were usually not recorded.

More recent changes in police policy have also had a dramatic effect on crime figures. Until the late 1980s, police called to fights between spouses rarely recorded incidents as crimes, preferring to treat them as 'domestics' in which the law had no place. This is now beginning to change, with inevitable consequences for the number of recorded assaults.

Nevertheless, the three-monthly recorded crime figures do contain useful information. The detailed returns show accurately the uneven distribution of crime – 12 per cent of homes suffer 37 per cent of burglaries, with the greatest risks to the poorest and richest. Overall crime rates are lower in the countryside. But there are many

anomalies. In 1989 the six areas with the highest recorded crime rates were London, Manchester, Humberside, Nottinghamshire, Cleveland and Northumbria (see page 23). In each, there were more than 10,000 crimes per 100,000 people, with the highest rate of all belonging to Northumbria (12,684). The most law-abiding county was Dyfed-Powys, with only 3,817 crimes. But how does one explain Northumbria's burglary rate of 3,463 per 100,000, nearly three times the national average and 700 ahead of its closest rival, Greater Manchester? Why should Humberside's 678 assaults per 100,000 be nearly double that of Merseyside (355), an apparently similar community on the other side of the country?

Despite all the caveats, recorded figures do provide evidence of a genuine long-term increase in crime. When Sir James made his speech in 1978, there were, overall, 4,878 crimes per 100,000 people. By 1989, this had risen to 7,355. The BCS also suggests a real rise in the 1980s. In seeking to understand why, it is easier to state what does not have an influence on crime rates. When figures are published, the Police Federation and Tory MPs routinely call for stiffer sentences. All the evidence suggests that penalties have no effect whatsoever on criminal activity. One study looked at six areas with high mugging rates after a man was given a highly publicised record 20-year sentence for mugging in 1974. The mugging rates were unaffected. In 1976, Canada abolished capital punishment. Not only was the murder rate unchanged, but a poll years later found 50 per cent of Canadians were unaware of this important alteration to the law.

The Home Office last year published a highly significant research pamphlet by Simon Field. He showed convincingly that Labour claims were essentially true: that property crime rose with unemployment and economic recession. He plotted graphs of property crime and consumption 1900-88, finding an exact correlation between falling consumption and theft. To the embarrassment of the Government, Field's work predicted exactly the present rise in property crime. It also showed that violence increased during times of prosperity. Here, he drew another graph, to demonstrate the exact relationship between the amount of beer drunk and violent crime (see above, left). One aspect of violence is that victims and assailants share the same average social profile: both tend to be male drinkers aged 17-24. According to the BCS, people who told the survey they had committed assaults were seven times more likely to become victims.

But, in the longer term, the search for reasons for the rise in crime becomes more difficult. Each time prosperity returns, and theft falls back, it seems to fall to a trough slightly higher than before the slump. Robert Reiner, of the LSE, suggests that one reason may be that there ▷

Intruder alarms, the fastest-growing sector of the security industry throughout the Seventies and Eighties, generated an estimated £70.6 million in UK sales in 1984. The figure more than doubled to £188.8m in 1988.

Brian Cope, managing director of Modern Alarms Ltd, identifies three major reasons for increased demand. 'We find that fear of theft and personal attack, and having more valuable possessions in homes which are unoccupied for longer periods means householders are seeking greater security.' Other influences have been the growth in home-ownership and the tendency of insurers to insist on the installation of an alarm as a condition of cover.

Increasingly sophisticated technology includes infra-red movement detectors, electronic eavesdropping, pressure pads and automatic approach lights. Installation costs depend on whether it is done professionally or DIY, rented or purchased. Prices for the cheaper, more basic professionally installed systems start at around £300.

Meanwhile, insurance payouts for domestic theft continue to escalate. In 1975 the industry paid out £17.9 million; by 1989 the figure had risen to £276.4 million. Ten years ago only one in 20 people holding a home-contents policy made a claim; today it is nearer one in 10. The average sum sought is around £500. The rise is expected to continue throughout the Nineties.

The rise in opportune crime has meant many companies now offer discounts to policyholders who can prove they have met basic security standards. With different ratings given to areas with high and low burglary levels, policyholders in inner cities can expect to pay £22.39 per £1,000 insured if properties are properly secured while policyholders in rural Cornwall can pay as little as £2.54.

Despite the crime explosion, many people still fail to insure the contents of their homes. After the Towyn flooding disaster it was discovered that 40 per cent of the town's houses had no contents insurance. **CHARMAINE SPENCER**

THE CRIME BOOM

Whatever the caveats, as this graph shows crime has shown a relentless increase over the past 40 years

VIOLENT CRIME

ARMED ROBBERIES

Oxfordshire sub-postmaster Alan Atkinson was finishing off the day's business when a masked raider, wielding a long-bore shotgun, marched in and threatened to kill him if he didn't hand over the money in the safe. The 61-year-old, although terrified for his life, told the gunman to think about the consequences of his actions. 'He was just a young lad and if he had been a hardened criminal I would have acted differently.' Mr Atkinson told the raider there was a five-minute time lock on the safe and that by the time it opened someone else would have walked into the post office. The raider ran out and drove away on his motorbike.

The number of armed robberies that have taken place in the past 10 years has increased threefold to 3,390. As a result, banks, building societies and security companies are putting more time and money into finding ways of preventing attacks. Securicor armoured vehicles make about 22 million movements a year, carrying £90 billion in cash, cheques and valuables. An isolated van, carrying more than £1 million in cash and with unarmed guards [Securicor guards are prevented by law from carrying guns], makes a jewel of a target. Home Office figures show there have been 300 to 400 such attacks each year since 1984.

Securicor's managing director Laurie Sinton, admitted that as armoured vehicles become more difficult to penetrate, robbers resort to more violent methods of opening them. Cash cases are fitted with explosive devices which destroy the contents and release foul orange smoke. 'Sometimes the bandits have thrown the case out of a car, rather than put up with the fumes,' said Mr Sinton. Last month, an attempted armed robbery of a security vehicle in London was foiled when bandits picked on one fitted with the latest electronic location-monitoring device which alerted police allowing them to intercept the robbery in progress.

Building societies suffered 581 armed raids in 1989, half of them in London. Jane Jones, under-secretary at the Building Societies Association, believes many are drugs-related. 'The robbers are more often small-time criminals than organised gangs, because at any one time there is very little cash behind the counter,' she says. Most building-society staff are told to comply with robbers. 'There may be bullet-resistant glass between the staff and the robber but in the majority of the attacks there are customers present.'

LAGER LOUTS

It's 11pm on a cold, drizzly Saturday night in Ilkeston, Derbyshire. Young men and women are staggering between the pubs that surround the market square. Policemen are stationed in every available doorway and corner, stamping their feet in a vain attempt to keep warm. There are sparks of expectancy in

Colours represent crimes of violence against the person per 100,000 population in each area in 1989

BELOW 250
250 - 349
350 - 449
450 - 549
550 - 649
650 AND MORE

the air as the elaborate courting ritual takes place in front of police eyes. Girls eyeing up the boys. Boys eyeing up the girls.

Suddenly a police car screeches away. The police and the drinkers charge off in the direction of the Old Wine Vaults where a group of skinheads is on the rampage. With a few split lips and head wounds the police later return to the market square where two drunk youths are arrested. It's 11.20pm and all the cells are full. 11.40: an ambulance is called for yet another casualty of the drinking crisis – a paralytic youth knocked down by a macho male.

'You can plan your duties on Friday and Saturday nights with tedious regularity,' said Chief Inspector Norman Hartshorne of Ilkeston police. 'Between 11pm and midnight you have the fighting and disorder in the market square as everyone empties out of the pubs. Between midnight and 12.30am they smash shop windows on their way home. And from 12.30 you get the domestics .'

Ilkeston, a small market town with a population of 33,000, has a drinking problem. A 1989 Home Office report on drink-related problems in Britain's small towns and villages, *Drinking and Disorder: A study of non-metropolitan violence*, pinpointed unemployment, a rise in the male population and under-age drinking as factors related to the upsurge in rural violence. But police in Ilkeston say unemployment is not the problem – the drinkers are well-dressed and have enough money to pour up to 10 pints of beer down their necks. The police know that they only patrol Ilkeston by consent – if the 500 or so revellers ever decided to make their life difficult there would be nothing they could do. 'We're playing the numbers game,' said Inspector Michael Perry. And it's getting worse. Dr Ralph Lawrence, Ilkeston's police surgeon since 1953 has noticed a steady rise in alcohol-related violence and injuries. 'It's getting uncontainable. The injuries get worse, the fights get worse. It's the tragedy of modern Britain.'   **SARAH LONSDALE**

Small-time criminals rather than organised gangs are responsible for many of the raids on building societies

CRIME

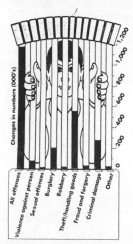

Changes in numbers (000's)

All offences
Violence against person
Sexual offences
Burglary
Robbery
Theft/handling goods
Fraud and forgery
Criminal damage
Other

THE CHANGING FACE OF CRIME

Although Britain's crime rate is still lower than the European average, every category of criminal offence increased between 1980 and 1989

is simply more to steal: more portable valuable objects. But one tends to identify causes according to political prejudice. To Reiner, a Labour supporter, one reason may be the formation of an alienated urban underclass: 'If crime comes down, it will be the by-product of economic and social changes that are desirable for other reasons too.' Right-wingers prefer a nostalgic approach, as Geoff Pearson's book *Hooligan* shows: Conservatives have enthused about a mythical law-abiding society '20 years ago' for decades. Twenty years ago, in fact, they were as worried about crime and disorderly youth as they are now, panicked by hippies in the late Sixties and early Seventies, by Teds in the Fifties and 'Americanised' youth in the Forties.

Shreds of evidence are beginning to emerge, however, that crime-prevention methods – locks, lighting, even neighbourhood watch schemes – may work. From rather different perspectives, the Home Office and Islington's Labour council have produced the results of pilot schemes, claiming big reductions in crime rates on two estates – without simply displacing the crime elsewhere.

The most extraordinary criminal statistic of all suggests that reducing crime will be a long haul. A computerised survey of every person born in a certain month in 1953, revealed that by the age of 30, one in three men had been convicted of a crime. One in 16 had been to prison. Recidivism was not endemic: the 7 per cent who had been convicted of six or more crimes accounted for two thirds of all offences. But this survey did suggest that society may be getting more violent. One in eight men born in 1953 who had been convicted of an offence had committed a crime of violence by the age of 20. For those born in 1963, this proportion had risen to one in five. □

CAR THEFT

The driver of the stolen Sierra, realising he is being followed by a police patrol car, picks up speed until he is doing 84mph in a residential zone. Inspector Noel Wanless shakes his head: 'We're dealing with this sort of incident all the time in Northumbria. So far this year we've had five people killed, including a 10-month-old baby, and several injured – seven of them police officers. We've had more than 30,000 cars stolen and 17,000 are still unaccounted for.'

They call themselves the TWOC gangs in Tyneside. Boys from eight to 18, tooled up with balaclavas and iron bars, steal, race and smash cars with such obsession that police liken it to drug addiction. The TWOCs, an acronym for Taking Without Owner's Consent, are now a feature of the area, their cannibalised wrecks forming bizarre sculptures in the recovery garages.

Kevin, a cocky 12-year-old, is walking home to a housing estate in West Newcastle. TWOC graffiti are on the wall. Does he know what joyriding is? 'Yeah, it's handbrake turns and all that.' Has he ever been in a stolen car? 'Yeah, I was in the back of a car that crashed into a wall. I stayed around till the bizzies [police] came.'

TWOC is a modern phenomenon, not to be confused with joyriding, which people did in the Sixties and Seventies when they missed the last bus home and nicked a car to get across town. TWOC is big business, and Tyneside its corporate headquarters. The local area traffic commander, Chief Superintendent Bob Bensley, elaborates: 'You've got three kinds of thief. The 14-year-olds who take a £30,000 Sierra Cosworth and smash it up, the 16-year-olds who sell the parts and make £800, and the ram raiders who steal two cars, drive one through the window of a shop, steal its contents, and then flee in the second car.'

The number of stolen cars has risen in two years from 18,000 to over 30,000 and the police blame the outbreak on the breakdown of discipline and the redefining of the offence, previously known as 'taking and driving away'. The maximum penalty was reduced from two years custody to six months. Solicitor John Purves, who has represented

▨	3,000 - 4,999
▨	5,000 - 6,999
■	7,000 - 8,999
■	9,000 -10,999
■	11,000 - 12,999
■	13,000 PLUS

FIGURES NOT AVAILABLE FOR SCOTLAND

Northumbria (37) and Manchester (22) have among the highest incidences of car theft per 100,000 cars

hundreds of TWOCers, says: 'TWOC provides an escape from their humdrum existences. They are thrilled by the speed of these flying machines and the more dangerous it gets, the more excited they become. It's an addiction. I had a 14-year-old who admitted five TWOCs and asked for 75 others to be taken into consideration. The press call them deathriders; that's the real thrill.'

Since the death late last year of 10-month-old Richard Hartley, killed when two TWOCers abandoned a moving car to avoid police, community groups have asked the council to install more sleeping policemen. Their living counterparts are unimpressed: 'We've already got them down on some estates and the kids use them as speed ramps. Imagine the buzz of flying off one of those at 90mph.' **SHYAMA PERERA**

Cannibalised shells of stolen cars form a surreal skyline in a breakers' yard. Car theft is an addiction for many

[2]

Research—Who Needs It?*

DON M. GOTTFREDSON

Director, Research Center, National Council on Crime and Delinquency;
Director of Research, National Parole Institutes
Director, Research Service Center, American Justice Institute, 1962-67
Ph.D. (Psychology), 1959, Claremont Graduate School

If the correctional administrator is to do his job of improving his agency's programs on the basis of experience, he will have to adopt some aspects of the scientist's role. To increase his own effectiveness (and that of his agency) he will need a questioning attitude, a determination to test his beliefs or hunches by demanding evidence for and against them, and an ability to plan programs in such a way that he will know at the end whether or not they achieved their missions.

Two general approaches to the problem of program evaluation are described, and their limitations are discussed. Similarly, two methods for evaluating and improving individual case decisions are compared. The methods described all have strengths and weaknesses but can be used together profitably.

A COUPLE OF YEARS AGO, a prison warden told this story:

Once upon a time, there was a Correctional Administrator who was riding a tiger. He maintained a tenuous control over the beast by means of a two-handed grip on its neck, and could do little more than change their mutual direction of travel just the slightest bit. The Administrator's best efforts were not enough to prevent the tiger from taking an occasional nip out of his leg. The tiger found these nips to be both tasty and encouraging.

One day the Administrator and his tiger rode by a decision point where a Correctional Researcher was standing.

The Researcher said, "I see you are riding a tiger," thus demonstrating his keen insight into the Administrator's

problems. At that moment, the tiger turned and took a bite from the Administrator's leg.

The Researcher regarded this action with a solemn expression and presently he issued a finding: "You know, that tiger is biting you and someday he will eat you all gone—unless, that is, you avail yourself of my services."

"Oh," said the Administrator, "you know about riding tigers?"

"Not exactly," replied the Researcher, "but I have made an extensive study of Siamese kittens and I am quite sure the principles are the same."

The Administrator pondered this statement with great respect since he had heard of Correctional Researchers and stood in considerable awe of them. Although he was able to assign only a portion of his decision-making apparatus to the statement, being almost fully absorbed in his efforts to control the tiger, the Administrator soon made an executive decision. Since things were going

* Adapted from an article originally published in *Research Reports*, Washington State Department of Institutions, vol. 2, no. 2, 1969, pp. 11-17.

rather badly at the moment, there appeared [to be] nothing to lose by eliciting the Researcher's aid. "Fine," he said, "come aboard and give me a hand."

"Not so fast," answered the Researcher, "we scientists cannot go slapdash into things. In the first place, we must devise a strategy, and in the second, we must find a quieter tiger. Simply impossible to properly study such a surly creature, you know."

"But this is the only tiger I have," the Administrator said, "and if I let him go he will run around eating a lot of innocent citizens."

"Bosh," replied the Researcher, "you are being a rigid administrator. If you will loosen your grip a little, we can put him into a community of tigers. We will teach him concern for other tigers and then we can form a hypothesis. If we find that he eats fewer citizens after we apply an intervening variable, we will have a result. Of course, if we find he eats more citizens, we will still have a result—opposite direction, naturally. So we can't lose, can we?"

"Well," said the Administrator, who was getting confused by the Researcher's logic, "I'm not at all sure about that. Why don't you just hop up here with me and give a hand with control; then we can start thinking about correction."

"Now, now," answered the Researcher, "you just can't start these things without a systematic study. We must devise an information system and get feedback—from the tiger. Maybe you are not his kind of administrator, and we will need to replace you with an operational research program. Right now, we cannot even describe what you two are doing."

"Chomp," said the tiger.

"All right, all right," said the Administrator, "describe already—do something and hurry up."

"Now, let's see—I would say at the 2 per cent level of confidence that we could have some preliminary results that would point up areas requiring intensive investigation in about five years, plus or minus

2.3 years." The Researcher looked pleased.

"I don't like to be an obstructionist," replied the Administrator, "but I seem to have this problem now and I am not sure I will be around in five plus or minus 2.3 years."

"That is irrelevant to the study," the Researcher said. "You must realize that first we must develop criteria for our subjects. Can't have any tigers that play with kittens, or get high on catnip. That would skew the findings, you know. Besides, we will generate valuable data that will be a great help to the next Administrator."

"Hmmmmmm," hummmmed the Administrator, "that doesn't sound at all practical. However, while you are finalizing it, perhaps you can help me shift my grip a little. Down a ways and a bit to the right should do it."

"Sorry," the Researcher said, "I am fully committed to this overall study of tiger communities I just thought of. However, I can give you a few minutes of consultation concerning your problem. Here, catch these correlational matrices and I will show you how you can optimize your grip."

The Administrator reached out for the research tools, momentarily loosening his grip in the process. The tiger promptly turned and ate him all gone.

The Researcher regarded the scene sadly. "Just when he was coming around to my frame of reference. Well, I told him he was on the wrong tiger. Let's see— what can we do with this empirical data we now have?"[1]

The warden has a point—indeed, several points. But, another story:

Over three centuries ago, Francis Bacon told of a heated argument among friars over the number of teeth in the mouth of a horse. Despite exhaustive searches of the theological

[1] James W. L. Park, "A Tale of Two Tigers," *Correctional Review*, July-August 1965, pp. 3-7.

literature, following traditional methods, they found no answer, and the quarrel continued. When a young and evidently inexperienced friar suggested that they find a horse, look into his mouth, and count his teeth, his colleagues became so angry that they beat him and banished him from the group. It probably seemed quite obvious to them that only the devil could have put this undignified, unprofessional, and unholy idea into the young man's head. They returned to argument and their search of the literature. Still no answer was found, and they concluded that because historical and theological evidence was lacking, the question was unanswerable.[2]

What are the morals to these stories? I think there are several, despite the oversimplified views they give concerning the complexities of administration, research, relationships between administrators and researchers, and science's contribution to the administrator. The stories, of course, are unfair to all concerned, including administrators, researchers, and, if not the horse, the tiger.

Yet some critical problems seem to be highlighted.

Administrators everywhere are beset by immediate, harassing, complex problems which often involve *not* program advances but rather survival and maintenance of the program. The administrator may be as concerned as the research worker with the aims of program improvement; he may be quite aware of the extent of our ignorance about program effectiveness and of our need for more demonstrably relevant classification methods and for experimentation

with new treatment methods. If, however, he is caught up in immediately pressing, difficult management problems, his attention will be drawn more and more toward actions which promise immediate relief and at least the maintenance of the existing program; he will give less and less attention to the problem of changing programs so as to accomplish the treatment aims of the agency more effectively; and he will become more and more apt to regard the title of this paper not as a question but as an answer: Research—who needs it!

Thus the administrators of social agency programs frequently attempt, in the manner of the friars, to answer critical questions about the achievements of their work by argument or by citation of authority.

The administrator himself must learn to look into the horse's mouth. In other words, he can increase his effectiveness by gaining new knowledge about the problems with which his agency deals; this gain can be expected to come when the administrator makes increased use of some of the methods of science in order to evaluate his own effectiveness. The story of the tiger makes it clear that the researcher might benefit by more understanding of the pressures on the administrator; yet, the administrator, too, can gain by adopting as his own some aspects of the researcher's frame of reference.

All administrators (and, incidentally, all judges, probation and parole officers, correctional counselors, parole board members, and various clinical workers) have two things in common. First, they make decisions. Second, *they ordinarily fail to receive systematically any feedback concerning the consequences of the decisions they make.*

---

[2] C. E. Mees, "Scientific Thought and Social Reconstruction," *Electrical Engineering*, 1934, pp. 53, 383-84.

14   DON M. GOTTFREDSON

Careful studies have shown that we do not learn from practice alone. Learning results, instead, from feedback of the *consequences* of practice, that is, from knowledge of the results of our actions. It is evident, therefore, that such feedback is essential to the administrator (or any other agent of change) if he wishes to improve his performance. To improve his decisions, the administrator will have to adopt the role of scientist in looking at his own performance. He must devise procedures which can inform him of the results of his decisions, so that he can identify both his correct decisions and his errors. The methods of the behavioral sciences can provide the necessary tools.

The Administrator's Role as Scientist

The term "science" refers not only to a body of knowledge and a method for gaining knowledge but also to an *empirical attitude*. This attitude suggests it is better to remain without an answer than to accept an inadequate one. It means a desire to deal with facts rather than with opinions and an acceptance of facts even—or especially—when they are opposed to wishes. The word "empirical" refers to an approach which is founded upon observation rather than argument or opinion. There must be room in science, of course, for opinion and interpretation, for differences of opinion and argument; but the solid basis of science is facts collected and observations made.[3] The basis of the administrator's decisions is, at present, more

often untested theory, his own selective experience, or the folklore of his own particular discipline.

"Looking into the horse's mouth"—i.e., making direct observations—is of course only a part of the scientific method; science is, in addition, systematic. It searches not only for facts but for regularity or order and relationships among facts. Therefore, the administrator, in his role as scientist, seeks to discover lawful relationships among the events he observes.

Facts are essential, but they are of little use by themselves. If they are to be helpful, they must be related to one another in ways that yield new laws or principles and in ways that provide guidance to the administrator in future decisions. From these new principles, new facts can be predicted.

This means that facts should be collected according to some plan which is based upon principles already established. This is the research design. Its preparation requires careful planning to ensure that the observations made, or new facts collected, will actually provide the necessary feedback.

If the administrator has planned for it adequately in advance, he can test his "hunches" by comparing his expectations with his actual observations. Those shown wrong can be discarded; those supported by the evidence can be kept. When this process is repeated over and over, new principles can be stated or old ones changed to agree with the observable data.

If the administrator's "hunches" (whether derived from a theory or from looking at known relationships) are to be useful in increasing his effectiveness, they must be stated as *hypotheses*. The word "hypothesis" has a special meaning. It is a statement or proposition, carefully and

---

[3] The term "facts" is used only to refer to events which may be directly observed and replicated by others. This does not imply that "facts" represent any kind of final "truth." In most cases, where the word "facts" is used, the word "evidence" could be substituted.

explicitly stated, which can be tested against observed facts.

Confronted with a reasonable-sounding argument about how he should make his decisions, the administrator with an empirical attitude will reply, "That sounds plausible, but show me the evidence." Too often, at present, he merely says, "That sounds plausible," and then acts. But if he does not follow up to observe the consequences of his action, he is never in a position to discover whether the reasonable-sounding course of action was indeed supported by the later evidence. Without feedback concerning the results, he cannot learn from his experience. Since history provides much evidence that people tend to believe that which supports their own feelings of competence or complacency, we may expect that the administrator in this situation may even begin to believe that the adequacy of his decision is quite obvious. When, on the other hand, he recognizes his hunches as hypotheses to be tested, he will meet his colleagues' arguments in favor of this or that approach with the question, "How do you know?" and more and more of his observations will be made to test these hypotheses. This involves a certain amount of doubt; but if it is accompanied by a determined look for the evidence bearing on the issue, then this can be a healthy skepticism, leading to gains in knowledge.

The administrator, like anyone who makes decisions affecting others, must make these decisions daily, fully realizing the absence of adequate evidence on the probable consequences of his various alternatives. But he is equally aware of the immediacy of his problem and the necessity for prompt action. The clinician confronted with the client who desperately seeks his help cannot turn him away with the explanation that all the data are not yet in. The parole board member knows that a postponement of the parole decision is a denial of parole. The judge knows very well that the convicted offender must be dealt with this morning at ten o'clock, and the correctional administrator knows that "deciding not to decide" on a new program is the same as deciding against it. In short, the problems are there, and administrators must make decisions. It is not possible to call a moratorium on decision-making until these decisions can be made on the basis of empirical study of the problems concerned. However, the administrator can take steps now, as he daily makes decisions, to ensure that his future will not be so shaky.

This requires setting up procedures for testing his hypotheses. Because observations are made in order to test hypotheses, it is especially important that the steps for testing the hypotheses be planned before the observations are made. If these steps are not carefully worked out at the start, the administrator may not be able to test his hypotheses adequately after all. What is needed (before the observations are made) is a statement which clearly defines the problem, states the conditions under which the observations are to be made, and outlines the procedures to be followed in evaluating the results.

A word should be said about the function of a theory in the administrator's role as scientist. Theories have many uses, but they also represent some dangers. Their primary usefulness to the administrator as scientist is that they generate hypotheses which may be tested by making observations. That is, a theory can be particularly useful to the administrator as a guide in selecting those hunches that might most profitably be submitted to the testing procedure. Since he has limited resources for testing hypotheses, but many hunches and unconfirmed beliefs, it is clear that a theory can be useful to him in his evaluation efforts.

Among the dangers of theories is the fact that the term "theory" itself can acquire an almost magical aura, so that the function of hypothesis generation becomes lost and the theory is taken for fact. When the administrator begins to cite the theory as *evidence* for his beliefs, he has abandoned his role as scientist.

The Anatomy of a Decision

It was stated above that one thing administrators have in common is that they all make decisions. To determine how the administrator's decisions may be studied so as to provide the information needed in order to improve them, let us look first at the nature of a decision—at its anatomy.

Any decision has three main components—first, a *goal*, or a set of goals, the administrator would like to accomplish; second, some *information* to guide him in making the decision; third, some *relationship* (we trust) between the information he has to work with and the goals he wishes to achieve.

Administrators spend much time, effort, and money in collecting information and in making decisions. But they have made only scattered attempts to study the effects of the decisions or to learn whether the information gathered is actually useful. For the most part, *relationships* between *information* used to arrive at decisions and the *outcomes* the decision-maker desires are unknown.

The Importance of Stating Objectives

Focusing attention upon administrative decisions and upon the need for increased knowledge of relationships emphasizes the need for explicit statements of the administrator's goals. Before the information which is available for his decisions can be related to his goals, he needs to state exactly what it is that he is trying to accomplish. Similarly, before an agency program can be evaluated, the administrator must know what the program was expected to do. This simple question may not have a simple answer, for organizations, like persons, may have many goals, including some that conflict.

The Value of Describing Programs

At the same time, the administrator will need explicit *descriptions* of his agency programs. He will need to spell out exactly *how* he is trying to reach his goals. Otherwise his attempts to evaluate a program will meet a double disappointment: an inability to state the program's accomplishment and an inability even to describe the program.

Social agency programs are usually changed on the basis of experience gained as the program is developed. Program quality control procedures, therefore, are needed in order to ensure that programs are run in accord with a plan or that, if the program is modified, the plan is modified as well:

Control over quality is not a new concept in research. Research has always shown some concern for quality control. Representativeness of samples, validity, and reliability of measurements are terms which describe the ability of research to maintain a check upon itself. However, the basic concern in an experiment (to investigate the effectiveness of a treatment program in a social agency) is the quality of the intervention and secondarily the quality of the measurement.

Programs, no matter how well designed or sound in theory, are only as good as that which is put into practice. It is the highest of self-deception to inaugurate a program of high-sounding phrases while actually continuing to do business at the same old stand, in the same old way, with the same old procedures. The reverse of this could also be true. It is possible to institute effective innovations in . . . programs without being aware of the nature of their impact.[4]

Without careful record-keeping and documentation of changes in a program plan, the administrator will never be able to assess the impact of the program adequately to provide guidance for future program decisions. Regardless of the program outcomes—whether favorable or unfavorable in terms of his goals—and even with careful follow-up study of these outcomes, he will be unable to describe the program completely enough so that he, or others, can repeat it. If the program was clearly described in advance but changed as it was put into practice, and the changes were not clearly spelled out, then the administrator can only be misled. He will conclude that the program is effective, or that it is ineffective, *when that particular program has never been tried.*

Further Needs in Program Evaluation

As the administrator tries to be more explicit about goals and the methods of trying to reach them, he becomes aware of the need for improved measures of program outcomes, for increased ability to *predict*

these outcomes, and for better ways of classifying the persons a program is intended to change. Improved measures of program outcomes will be needed in order to provide more relevant feedback in terms of the administrator's goals. Prediction methods can play a critical role in helping to evaluate programs; this role will be discussed later. Classification methods are especially important because some programs may be helpful to some persons but not helpful (or harmful) to others. Program decisions will be made blindly until the administrator can describe and compare the *expected* outcomes and those actually *found* when programs are applied to various kinds of persons.

Evaluating Agency Programs

Two ways the administrator, in his role as scientist, can help improve agency program decisions are through analyses of *experiments,* designed to test specific hypotheses, and analyses of *experience,* by a systematic study of "natural variation" among programs and their outcomes. Experiments and experience are not at all the same but suggest two basically different approaches. They can, however, be used profitably together.

EXPERIMENTS

The most rigorous approach to studying the relationship of programs to goals is through an experiment. In simplest form, an experiment is conducted as follows: From a common population, experimental and control groups are designated randomly. This means that each individual in the population has an equal likelihood of being selected for either group. The experimental program is applied to one group and withheld from the other. Since the subjects have been

---

[4] A. Pearl, *Quality Control in Evaluative Research of Correctional Programs,* paper presented at the Ninth Annual National Institute on Crime and Delinquency, Seattle, July 1962.

18   DON M. GOTTFREDSON

assigned at random to the treatment and control groups, it is assumed that they were comparable before the program began, and observed differences in the outcome are attributed to the experimental program.

This approach will be needed to provide crucial tests of the administrator's hypotheses about the effectiveness of treatment. But for the administrator who wishes to evaluate a variety of programs within an agency's operations, this approach alone— despite its power—will not be adequate. Some of the most common problems he will encounter are the following:

1. Selective biases can creep in. After the experiment is run, it may be found that the experimental groups were not originally comparable after all. The rule that all relevant variables except the experimental treatment must be held constant or controlled is a difficult one to follow. For example, a new treatment program in one unit of a prison, jail, or camp may affect the entire institution, including the so-called control group. In any event, a control group in confinement does not receive "no treatment." They receive a *different* treatment, so we are always faced with a comparison of outcomes of program variations.

2. It is not usually possible to arrange to study a representative sampling of *treatments,* and though we may be able to generalize about subjects, we cannot then generalize about treatment. The sampling of *subjects* (i.e., offenders, clients, or patients) may be done carefully, and if truly random (rather than merely haphazard), generalization from the sample to the population from which it was drawn may be justified. In order to generalize about *treatments,* however,

a similar sampling model would be required. That is, a representative sampling of treatments of a given kind should be studied, and this is rarely feasible.

3. There are so many different programs in complex social agencies such as correctional systems, hospitals, educational institutions, or welfare agencies, many actively supported by ardent advocates, that it is usually not administratively feasible to test them all through this kind of research design.

4. An experimental-control group study may be precluded by the nature of the problem which the administrator wishes to study or, in certain cases, by law or by humanitarian or ethical considerations.

SYSTEMATIC STUDY OF EXPERIENCE

The study of decisions offers an additional approach to program evaluation and decision-making when experimental designs are not feasible. In this approach prediction devices may be useful.

Prediction devices for estimating the likelihood of program outcomes are merely summaries, by appropriate statistical methods, of experience with various groups of people. As such, they provide a way of quantifying expectations based upon past experience. After being developed and tested they are applied to each person *before* he is assigned to treatment. When a person has received a specific kind of treatment, we may then ask whether the actual outcome is more or less favorable than *expected* (from past experience with other similar groups). Since we wish to find treatments that improve the chances of success, we will be pleased if the prediction is invalidated by helpful treatment.[5]

If the outcome following treatment can be predicted not only before treatment but *regardless* of treatment, it is very hard to argue that this treatment makes any difference with respect to the specific outcome studied. However, persons assigned to a given treatment may "succeed" (or "fail") significantly more often than expected from their risk classifications. If the validity of the prediction device has been established on other groups, then the observed differences in outcomes must be due to treatment, to factors associated with treatment, or to both.

Further research, using experimental designs, might then be developed to test the administrator's beliefs about the source of the difference. Meanwhile, he can be informed of the relationship—positive, negative, or none—between the program and the outcome.

The study of "natural variation" within an agency is one way for the administrator, using some of the tools of statistics, to obtain helpful feedback when an experiment (in the above sense) is not possible. It requires that he keep records and keep score and that he substitute *statistical* methods of control for the lacking *experimental* controls.

Statistics is not science, but statistical methods are essential tools which the administrator will be unable to do without in his role as scientist. The word "statistics" means, to many, simple enumeration. The number of persons confined in an institution, or the number of escapes, or the number released is usually called "statistics." But counting is only a small part of statistics. The main and potentially more helpful part to administrators in their self-study efforts is a set of methods for *analyzing* numerical data. The methods provide ways to determine the nature and magnitude of *relationships* among sets of information. And they guide our attempts to generalize from observed events to new events.

Statistical methods, therefore, are among the most powerful tools available to administrators; but, surprisingly, they are among the least used. Nearly every social agency keeps track of the number of persons in this or that category. But studies of any *relationships* to be found are rare, and statistical methods are needed in order to measure relationships.

The role that improved measurement can play in the improvement of social programs is suggested by the often quoted words of Lord Kelvin:

> When you can measure what you are speaking about and express it in numbers you know something about it, but when you cannot measure it, when you cannot express it in numbers, your knowledge is of a meagre and unsatisfactory kind.[6]

For proper balance, however, another quotation, from Saint Augustine, should be kept in mind: "For so it is, oh Lord my God, I measure it; but what it is that I measure, I do not know."[7]

[5] L. T. Wilkins, "What Is Prediction and Is It Necessary in Evaluating Treatment?" in *Research and Potential Application of Research in Probation, Parole, and Delinquency Prediction* (New York: Citizen's Committee for Children of New York, Research Center, New York School of Social Work, Columbia University), 1961.

[6] Quoted in Karl Pearson, *Tables for Statisticians and Biometricians, Part I*, 2nd ed. (London: Biometric Laboratory, University College, 1924), p. viii.

[7] Quoted in Ralph G. H. Siu, *T-Thoughts* (Washington, D.C.: National Institute of Law Enforcement and Criminal Justice, Pamphlet No. 4, November 1968), p. 3.

Evaluating and Improving Individual Decisions

The discussion thus far has concerned those decisions which affect agency *programs*. However, the administrator must also make decisions about *individuals*. How will an increased focus on the decision-maker's role as scientist affect his decisions about individuals?

Interviews, clinical impressions, true-false tests, ink blots, subjective feelings, and statistical prediction devices are only a few of the vast array of methods which have been proposed to aid the administrator in evaluating other persons. A whole literature of psychology, psychiatry, and social work deals with these methods; how can we consider briefly their usefulness to the administrator?

It has been suggested that evaluation methods are generally of two types and that each type has special advantages but certain limitations.[8] Cronbach calls the two general approaches to individual evaluations Broad Band (low fidelity), and Narrow Band (high fidelity).

Some procedures, like interviews, psychologists' reports from projective testing, written evaluations prepared by clinical or custodial institution staff, and social history reports, provide a wide variety of information. Each of these "broad-scope" procedures is characteristically unsatisfactory, by any usual standards of reliability and validity, for predicting specific behavior. This means not that they are useless but that the wider coverage is purchased at the price of low dependability (fidelity). What

purposes, then, do these procedures fulfill?

Consider the interview, a wide-scope procedure used by almost all administrators. Evidence that interviews are useful in prediction is preponderantly negative; comparisons have repeatedly shown statistical prediction devices to be more valid. Moreover, interviewers disagree notoriously with one another in their judgments. But even the most forceful advocates of statistical prediction insist on an interview when *they* must make a decision. Why do we persist in interviewing?

The interview allows the administrator to cover or at least touch upon any aspect of the other person's character and life situation: his employment history, his relations with his family, his feelings about authority, his disappointments and expectations, and so on. It may reveal some of his abilities and interests, sexual attitudes, defenses against anxiety, values, and plans. The interview can take any one of innumerable directions to follow leads that a structured objective test or procedure cannot pursue. This is its virtue; by covering a broad range of topics it may provide helpful information for *many different decisions*. Obviously the interview need not bear only on a single problem. It may suggest a further treatment plan, particular areas of weakness to be guarded against, and special potential for favorable adjustment in certain situations.

The broad-scope methods are exhaustive but undependable; that is, they cover more of the ground we wish to know about, but any one prediction from this wide range of information cannot be relied upon to be valid. In contrast, the narrow-range procedures give more accurate

---

8 L. J. Cronbach and G. C. Gleser, *Psychological Tests and Personnel Decisions* (Urbana: University of Illinois Press, 1957). The discussion that follows has largely been abstracted from Cronbach.

information with respect to *one* decision outcome but none at all with respect to decisions in other areas.

The narrow-scope procedures include any objective psychological test with established validity in predicting a single behavioral criterion, parole or probation violation prediction devices, some delinquency prediction scales, certain college aptitude tests, and the like. Compared with the interview and other broad-scope methods, their virtue is their relative dependability (higher fidelity). Their limitation is that they cover relatively little ground; that is, they bear only on that part of the decision concerned with the specific question they help answer.

Though such a device gives a more dependable prediction of outcome than is generally obtained by broad-scope methods, it is relevant only to the *specific* outcome defined for the purpose of study. Unless it has been shown valid also for predicting other specific outcomes of interest to the decision-maker, it provides no guidance for decisions based on expected behavior in other areas. It may tell nothing about appropriate treatment placement.

In general, a narrow-range procedure, such as an objective test, delinquency scale, or parole prediction device, is more reliable (that is, different people will tend to agree on the scores for various others). It is more valid (that is, it predicts better). But it covers only a limited sector of all behavior in which the decision-maker is interested. In short, it has limited range but high fidelity.

How can these two types of methods be profitably combined? We wish to utilize the best features of each—recognizing the limitations of both—

in order to make optimal decisions on the basis of available knowledge.

The optimal use of both will depend upon the nature of the decision problem; i.e., the resources available, the alternative courses of action, and the goals of the decision. Thus optimal procedures for one agency might not be best for others with different resources, alternatives, or goals.

As far as possible, however, it will probably be practical to use wide-scope methods—such as the interview and case history review—as a *first stage* in a decision process. This will provide a further source of hypotheses. Moreover, it will enable use of the fallible information from these methods only to the limited extent deserved by their generally low dependability when it comes to predicting behavior. In the *second stage,* narrow-scope methods, such as the prediction devices mentioned previously, would be used, for these offer the decision maker more dependable help in answering *specific* prediction questions, assuming that these questions are relevant to his decision goals.

When broad- and narrow-scope procedures are used in collaboration, the decision-maker can improve his predictive ability and hence his decisions. He will come upon information he believes could improve the available statistical prediction devices and he should test these hypotheses.

Thus both the subjective and objective aspects of a decision can be combined in a single program for improving individual decisions. Such a program requires that the decision-maker make *explicit* his implicit, perhaps vaguely felt hunches about relevant predictive information; it requires record-keeping, in order to see whether these hunches are right. If they are right, there is a further question: Will the information *improve* the efficiency of existing statistical prediction methods? This, too, can be tested, again by keeping records to provide later feedback concerning "hits" and "misses." A continuous attempt to improve narrow-scope procedures by developing and testing hypotheses from broad-range methods is needed. The main requirement is the empirical attitude of the administrator, his open-minded admission of any hypotheses for testing combined with a dogged demand for evidence.

The Administrator's Three-Legged Stool

The administrator's continuous task of decision-making may be compared to a three-legged stool. One leg is the quality of the information on which his decisions must be based. Another is the goal or set of goals he wishes to achieve. The third is his knowledge of the *relationships* between the information he has to work with and the probable *consequences* of his various decision alternatives. The administrator is required to sit on this stool, because his job is making decisions. But if at present he sits cautiously, it is because he knows that not all three legs of the stool warrant confidence. He is less likely to be floored, however, if he adopts as part of his basic equipment some of the attitudes and methods of science. His role as scientist will eventually enable him to sit more confidently; meanwhile he will know that he is doing what he can to evaluate his own performance in order ultimately to improve it.

Thus research is not an extra for the administrator provided he can still control the tiger; it is a requisite to sound administrative practice.

Part II
Crime Trends and Patterns

[3]

Ted Robert Gurr

Historical Trends in Violent Crime: A Critical Review of the Evidence

ABSTRACT

Recent historical scholarship suggests that the post-1960 increase in violent crime in most Western societies was preceded by a much longer period of decline. In Britain the incidence of homicide has fallen by a factor of at least ten to one since the thirteenth century and the recent tripling of the rate is small by comparison. Evidence of long-term trends in the United States is obscured by the occurrence of three great surges of violent crime which began ca. 1850, 1900, and 1960. The last two upsurges are largely attributable to sharply rising homicide rates among blacks. A number of other Western societies show evidence of nineteenth-century declines in violent crime. The long-term declining trend evidently is a manifestation of cultural change in Western society, especially the growing sensitization to violence and the development of increased internal and external controls on aggressive behavior. Empirical studies of the correlates of violent crime point toward several general factors which help account for the historically temporary deviations from the downward trend in interpersonal violence: warfare, which evidently tends to legitimate individual violence; the stresses of the initial phases of rapid urbanization and industrialization; economic prosperity and decline; and changes in the demographic structure.

It is generally accepted by criminologists and other social scientists that the real incidence of serious crimes against persons and property increased substantially in the United States and most Western European societies during the 1960s and 1970s,

Ted Robert Gurr is Payson S. Wild Professor of Political Science, Northwestern University. Roger Lane, Eric H. Monkkonen, and Michael Tonry provided helpful comments on an earlier draft.

though skepticism remains about the accuracy of official data on the precise magnitude of change. What is less widely recognized is a growing body of historical evidence, some of it examined by Lane in a previous volume in this series (1980), that the incidence of serious crime has traced an irregular downward trend for a much longer period of time, in some places for a century or more. When the historical and contemporary evidence are joined together, they depict a distended U-shaped curve.

The thesis that rates of serious crime in Western societies have traced a reversing U-shaped curve is a simplification of a much more complex reality. It characterizes some but not all offenses. The evidence for it is substantial in some societies, especially the English-speaking and Scandinavian countries, but either lacking or contradictory in others. There are severe problems in the interpretation of official data on crime compiled in different eras. Even where a reversing trend is clearly present, as in England and Wales during the past 150 years, there are substantial short-term deviations around it. For these and other reasons, the U-shaped curve is used here as a hypothesis, not received wisdom, against which to evaluate diverse evidence on trends in violent crime. The first question is whether the evidence from a particular jurisdiction and era is consistent with, qualifies, or contradicts the general model. The subsidiary question is what the evidence suggests about the social dynamics of the long-term trend in violent crime, and of substantial deviations from it.

This essay is limited mainly to evidence about trends in homicide and assault, with occasional reference to robbery. In terms of social importance these offenses are less common than burglary and larceny, but are of greater concern to most people: offenses which inflict bodily harm are and probably have always been more threatening to most people than has property crime. From the perspective of the social and cultural historian, the distribution of these offenses across time, space, and social groups is of particular interest because of what it tells us about interpersonal aggression and the complex of social attitudes toward it. And from a methodological viewpoint, when dealing with data on homicide in particular we can be more confident that trends reflect real changes in social behavior rather than changes in the practices of criminal justice systems.

The first part of this essay comments briefly on what can and cannot be inferred from data on violent crime. The next four parts summarize the statistical evidence on trends in violent crime, both in single jurisdictions and comparatively, for Britain, the United States, and some other Western societies. These parts also refer to evidence and speculation on the social forces responsible for changes over time in the incidence of violent crime, which are then summarized in the final part of the essay.

Some kinds of trend studies are ruled out of close consideration here:

1. Those which examine trends in total or property offenses but not offenses against persons, for example historical analyses by Monkkonen (1981) and Tilly et al. (n.d.).

2. Studies which describe the changing character or incidence of crime over time or among jurisdictions without making use of time-series data, for example Greenberg (1976) and Hay et al. (1975).

3. Microstudies of the characteristics of offenses and offenders in a limited period in a single jurisdiction, for example Baldwin and Bottoms on Sheffield, England (1976), Block on Chicago (1977), Lundsgaarde on Houston (1977), and Stanciu on Paris (1968).

4. Studies of crime trends in third-world societies.

5. Studies of "trends," however statistical, which span less than a decade (of which there are a great many examples).

6. Official reports which table but do not analyze data on crime trends.

To keep the essay within manageable proportions I have also excluded studies of the ways in which the law, police, or courts treat violent offenses and offenders. Finally, I have avoided detailed criticism of the techniques used in trend and correlational analyses, offering only cautionary notes when there are methodological reasons to question a study's findings about trends.

I. Official Data on Interpersonal Violence

This essay begins with the premise that there is some discernible correspondence between trends in some kinds of official data on crimes against persons and real changes in the incidence of interpersonal violence in society. The validity of many of the criticisms of crime statistics is accepted. It is clear, for example, that the reported incidence of many kinds of offenses can be affected by changing degrees of public concern and by changes in the level and foci of police activity. But I contend that it is possible to overcome these limitations of official data by focusing on the most serious offenses and by obtaining converging or parallel evidence on trends in different types of offenses and from different jurisdictions.[1]

Official data on crime pose many threats to the validity of inferences about trends in interpersonal violence. One is the inherent slippage between the occurrence of an offense and the chain of events by which it does or does not enter official records. The closest approximation in official data to information on violent crime is provided by police data on "offenses known." Victimization surveys show that the more serious the offense, the more closely citizen reports correspond with police data (Skogan 1976), which supports the commonly held view that murder is the most accurately recorded violent crime. But offenses known to police have been recorded for only a relatively brief period in most Western societies, and rarely do the records antedate the establishment of modern police forces in the mid to late nineteenth century.

[1] The limitations of contemporary American crime data have been widely discussed, for example by Bloch and Geis (1962, pt. 3); Mulvilhill and Tumin (1969, chap. 2); and Skogan (1975). Detailed discussions of the interpretation of American historical statistics on crime are to be found in Monkkonen's work (1975, 1980, 1981). On the reliability of British historical statistics see Gatrell and Hadden (1972) and Gatrell (1980). My views about what can be inferred from official crime data are spelled out in Gurr, Grabosky, and Hula (1977, chap. I.2).

The alternative sources of information about violent offenses in criminal justice statistics are arrest data and records of indictments or committals to trial, convictions, and sentences. Most studies of nineteenth-century crime, and virtually all earlier ones, use data on indictments/committals or convictions. The slippage between the commission of a felony and the success of private citizens or officials in getting the accused to trial is considerable, and probably was greater before modern police forces were established than since. But because homicide usually has been committed by people known to the victim (as evinced by many microstudies) and in Western societies usually has attracted close official attention, the slippage between act and court record is probably less for homicide than other crimes against persons.

Coroners' records of homicides and death registration data are alternatives to police and court records which have been examined in a number of historical studies (e.g. Brearley 1932; Given 1977; Lane 1979). In principle, data from these sources should be closer to the "true" incidence of homicide than any other, but in fact, as Lane found in his study of nineteenth-century Philadelphia, there may be serious, systematic sources of error in recording the cause of death. And of course death records are of no help in assessing the incidence of other kinds of interpersonal violence.

Official records thus are in varying degrees inadequate for assessing the true incidence of violent offenses, but closer to the mark for homicide than for others. This inadequacy is less a threat to the validity of comparisons across time within jurisdictions than comparisons across jurisdictions, because it is sometimes plausible to assume that the slippage within a given jurisdiction is more or less constant over time. But not always, and there's the rub. Official categories of an offense may change, for example by changes in the inclusion of involuntary manslaughter, infanticide, or attempted murder. This is usually detectable from the sources. More problematic are the results of changes in underlying legal definitions, for example the distinction between murder per se and manslaughter. No distinction was drawn between these two forms of violent death in English criminal procedure until the sixteenth century (see Kaye 1967). Most difficult of all to detect are slow changes in police and prosecutorial procedures. Gatrell observes that English coroners and police became better able to identify death from unnatural causes during the nineteenth century and offers other evidence that homicides were increasingly likely to come to police attention as the century progressed (1980, pp. 247–48). Lane reports on nineteenth-century Philadelphia that "late in the century a number of [manslaughter] cases were prosecuted that earlier would have been tolerated or overlooked" (1979, p. 76).

Lane's observation about lessened tolerance of manslaughter in nineteenth-century Philadelphia is a manifestation of what Soman calls the "sensitization to violence" in Western societies, a process under way for five centuries which was manifest in the gradual "exclusion of most violence from ordinary daily life, and a heightened sensitivity to some of the residual violence" (1980, p. 22). One likely consequence of this shift in values was a growing disposition of private citizens to seek redress for lesser acts of violence, with a parallel increase in officials' disposition to prosecute such cases. The implication for trend analysis is that official data on such offenses as assault and attempted murder could be expected to increase over time (especially before the twentieth century) even if the true incidence of offenses stayed constant.

Because of increased sensitization to interpersonal violence, any long-term upward trend in assault, especially prior to the twentieth century, is prima facie suspect as an indicator of change in social behavior. This is especially so if the trend in assaults runs counter to the trend in homicide. Homicides usually are the result of particularly successful (or unlucky) assaults and it is implausible that the real incidence of serious assaults could increase without a parallel increase in homicide. On the other hand, evidence of long-term statistical *decline* in the incidence of assault has prima facie plausibility because it runs counter to increased public sensitization and official attention. These comments apply to trends observed over a number of decades, not to sharp upward and downward waves in the incidence of assault of a few years' or a decade's duration. Such waves are too brief to be a product of slow change in social values, and, unless they coincide with the creation of modern police forces, are not likely to be an artifact of fluctuating police attention. The same general comment applies also to homicide.

One other artifactual source of long-term variation in assault rates, in the opposite direction from that due to "sensitization," is the shift of cases from higher to lower courts, as happened in early twentieth-century London for example (see Gurr, Grabosky, and Hula 1977, pp. 144–45). I suspect that the following sequence occurred in a number of nineteenth-century jurisdictions: increased public and police attention to minor episodes of violence caused large increases in the numbers of assault cases brought to trial; these soon overloaded the capacity of the higher courts in which most such cases had previously been tried; this overloading led to a shift of most cases, either gradually or abruptly, from higher to lower courts. Gatrell suggests, contrary to my argument about sensitization to violence, that assault rates in England may have declined as drastically as they did between the 1850s and 1914 because of "greater tolerance of petty violence" by the public and police (1980, pp. 289–91). This hypothesis is contrary to most other evidence but warrants attention in future historical research.

The two other main categories of violent crime are sexual assault and robbery. No attempt is made here to assess long-term trends in sexual assault, first because time-series data are sparse, second because it is an offense much more often concealed than reported by the victim: the "dark figure" of reported offenses prior to the use of victimization surveys is unknowably large. Robbery trends, though, may be more reliably estimated and used as a supplemental indicator of changes in interpersonal violence. I regard them as second in reliability only to homicide rates per se, though subject to many of the same questions about validity. Robbery—theft accompanied by the threat or use of force against the victim—has always been regarded as a particularly serious crime in Western societies and usually leaves victims who are more than willing to complain to authorities. I have the impression that robbery's legal definition has not changed appreciably over time in Britain or the United States, and so records of cases brought to official attention should be relatively consistent over time. Robbery is a felony and a relatively uncommon offense and is usually tried before higher courts; it is not likely that any appreciable historical shift of robbery cases from higher to lower courts occurred, although I am prepared to be corrected on both these points by scholars who have done more detailed studies. The most substantial slippage to affect robbery arises from the fact that the offender is usually unknown to the victim, so that court cases (and arrest and clearance rates) are usually much less numerous than offenses, but are likely to have increased—relative to the number of offenses—after the development of modern police systems during the past century. Thus one might expect some artifactual nineteenth-century increase in the number of robbery cases brought to trial, relative to their true or "known to police" incidence. In evidence thereof, the gap between robberies known to police and convictions in London narrowed appreciably between the 1880s and 1930 (see Gurr, Grabosky, and Hula 1977, p. 120). Gatrell asserts that the same principle applies to nineteenth-century English data on indictable crime generally: "the rate of recorded crime crept ever closer to the rate of actual crime" (1980, pp. 250–51).

In summary, I suggest these general guidelines for interpreting long-term trends in violent crime, with special reference to the putative period of decline that ended in the mid-twentieth century. (1) The declining historical trend in *homicide* probably is understated somewhat, because of closer official attention and a stretching of definitions to include more cases of manslaughter. Since the establishment of modern, centralized systems for recording crime and death data, official homicide data are the most accurate of all data on interpersonal violence. A cautionary note: since homicide is a relatively rare offense, it is highly variable over the short run and in smaller localities. Thus homicide rates are best used as an indicator of middle-

and long-run trends in interpersonal violence (see Zehr 1976, pp. 85–86). (2) Data on robberies known are second, albeit a rather distant second, to homicide data in reliability. Long-term trends in trial and conviction data are probably unreliable across those periods in which modern police systems were being established but should be internally comparable before and after that transition. (3) Long-run trends which show increases in assault are suspect because of increasing concern about these offenses. Long-run declining trends in assault are convincing if based on "offenses known," or on trial data for all courts, higher and lower.

Finally, we can be more confident about the underlying trends in interpersonal violence to the extent that there is converging evidence from different studies and different indicators. Conclusions about the directions and magnitude of change in violence are convincing to the extent that they are supported by any of the following kinds of parallel evidence: (1) Similarity in trends of indicators of an offense obtained from two different sources, for example police and coroner's records of homicides. (2) Similarity in trends of indicators of an offense registered at different stages in the criminal justice process, for example offenses known versus committals to trial or convictions. (3) Similarity in trends of indicators of an offense from different cities or regions. (4) Similarity in trends of different offenses, for example homicide and assault, or assault and robbery. Divergence among indicators, especially of types (3) and (4), is not necessarily a threat to validity because the social dynamics of interpersonal violence may vary from region to region, for example, or from one type of offense to another. If they do vary, plausible and testable explanations for the differences must be provided. If this is impossible, then inferences about the social reality underlying the diverging indicators are suspect.

II. Violent Crime in Medieval and Contemporary England

Our knowledge about the general decline of serious offenses against the person in English-speaking countries during the nineteenth century rests first on an analysis of police and court records, which officials collected and aggregated with increasing precision and consistency during the century. Equally necessary to the analysis of trends are accurate population data, without which no reliable estimates can be made of the relative incidence of offenses. Regular population censuses also were largely a nineteenth-century innovation; the first national census in the United States was taken in 1790, in Britain in 1801.

Thus it is difficult to ascertain whether the rates of serious offenses against persons were as high in the eighteenth century and earlier. This question is not entirely a matter of antiquarian curiosity because an unambiguous answer would help us to interpret the nineteenth-century decline and, possibly, the late twentieth-century rise in violent crimes. There are two general possibilities, one developmental, the other cyclical. The developmental possibility is that the nineteenth-century decline in violent crime continued an earlier trend. This would suggest that the decline was due to some fundamental, very long-term social dynamics in the evolution of Western society: perhaps the transition from subsistence agrarian lifeways to town and urban life, or the emergence of more civilized values and nonaggressive modes of personal interaction. The cyclical alternative is that the high level of interpersonal violence of the early nineteenth century was an aberration, the result of a cresting wave that might be analogous to contemporary experience. This would suggest a search for explanation that focuses on such historically discrete processes as the onset of rapid urbanization and industrialization or the impact of war. The two interpretations are not necessarily mutually exclusive: it is possible that violent crime has tended to decline over the long run, subject to short-term reversals, in other words a cyclical pattern of variation around a declining trend.

A. Homicide in Medieval and Early Modern England

Evidence from a handful of historical studies of homicides (and other felonies) in medieval and early modern England helps us choose among these possibilities. A brief characterization of the studies is needed before abstracting their results. First, none is national. Rather they are all based on painstaking analyses of surviving coroners' rolls and court records for specific years in specific jurisdictions, either counties or cities. Second, they are concerned mainly with describing the characteristics of violent crimes: absolute numbers, circumstances in which the crimes occurred, traits of offenders and victims, outcomes of trials, and their relative incidence in different jurisdictions. They are not primarily concerned with estimating rates. Third, the estimates of rates of offenses, or indictments, are subject to substantial error because population data for pre-modern English towns and counties were considerably less accurate than records of violent deaths. One author chooses "to avoid all discussion of rates of crime until, if ever, there is more reliable demographic information for the fourteenth century" (Hanawalt 1979, p. 287). Fourth, all the studies combine data on murder and manslaughter. Finally, few of these studies provide trend information in and of themselves because most are necessarily limited to scattered years by the availability of records (an exception is Beattie 1974). It is only when we juxtapose the results of a number of different studies in different eras that evidence about long-term trends in homicide begins to emerge.

The first systematic records of English homicide are to be found in the thirteenth-century records of the eyre courts, panels of royal justices which visited each county every few years. They had the exclusive prerogative of judging all cases of homicide. Coroners and juries were required to report independently to the court on all violent deaths that had occurred since the previous visit of the court and were penalized for inconsistencies and omissions revealed by comparing their reports. The transcribed records, where they have survived, "portray violent conflict in medieval England with a completeness that is unmatched by the records of any other country in northern Europe in the Middle Ages" (Given 1977, p. 13). Given's study of a wide sample of the eyre rolls shows convincingly that murderous brawls and violent death at the hands of robbers were everyday occurrences in medieval England.

306   Ted Robert Gurr

The average annual homicide rates for five rural counties, based in each instance on eyre rolls covering three to five years at scattered points between 1202 and 1276, are: Bedford, 22 per 100,000 population; Kent, 23; Norfolk, 9; Oxfordshire, 17; Warwickshire, 19 (Given 1977, p. 36). (The comparable rate for England and Wales in 1974 was 1.97 per 100,000). Analysis of the episodes which resulted in violent death shows that most resulted from fights among neighbors, while between 10 and 20 percent were attributed to thieves or bandits—a percentage which increased during the second half of the century. Knives, axes, cudgels, and other implements found in every agricultural community were the typical instruments of death. Usually several assailants were charged in each homicide, another item of evidence that most deaths resulted from brawling among small groups rather than one-on-one attacks.

The medieval English population was more than 90 percent rural and cities were small. Fourteenth-century London had 35,000–50,000 people, Oxford about 7,000, for example. Estimates of urban homicide rates for this period vary enormously. Given (1977, p. 36) reports thirteenth-century rates for London of 12 per 100,000 and for Bristol of 4 per 100,000, considerably lower than the rural rates. On the other hand Hanawalt (1976, pp. 301–2) estimates that London in the first half of the fourteenth century had homicide rates of 36 to 52 per 100,000 per annum (depending on which population figures and which year's homicides are used). Hammer's very thorough study of Oxford for the 1340s shows an extraordinarily high rate of ca. 110 homicides per 100,000, a rate to which scholars contributed no more (as victims or assailants) than might be expected from their proportions in the population. Analysis of the details of cases for Oxford shows that virtually all victims and assailants were males, and except for scholars were almost always of low status. Scarcely any homicides were intra-familial and at least one-third of them involved "strangers," i.e. people having no fixed residence in Oxford (Hammer 1978, pp. 9–19). Unlike the rural pattern, however, very few homicides in Oxford resulted from robbery or burglary.

These early estimates of homicide rates and their contemporary descriptions all sketch a portrait of a society in which men (but rarely women) were easily provoked to violent anger and were unrestrained in the brutality with which they attacked their opponents. Interpersonal violence was a recurring fact of rural and urban life. Had medieval Englishmen been equipped with firearms rather than knives and rustic tools, one can only assume that they would have killed one another with even greater frequency.

The eyre courts largely ceased to function during the fourteenth century and it was not until the late sixteenth century, during the reign of Elizabeth I, that county assize courts left records of indictments in sufficient detail to permit statistical study of serious offenses. These records refer to persons charged with crimes rather than records of offenses per se. Cockburn ventures the opinion that "indictments for homicide probably bear a closer relationship to the actual incidence of violent death than is correspondingly the case with other crimes." He offers these estimates of homicide indictment rates for the period 1559–1603 for three counties, the first two close to London and the other more remote: Essex, 7 per 100,000; Hertfordshire, 16; and Sussex, 14 (Cockburn 1977, pp. 55–56). These figures are noticeably lower than those for the thirteenth and fourteenth centuries.

The difficulties of estimating reliable homicide rates from court records are illustrated by comparing Cockburn's data on homicides in Essex with the results of a more detailed analysis by Samaha (1974). The two authors offer different estimates of homicides and total population. Samaha (1974, p. 20) finds significantly more homicide cases (murder, manslaughter, infanticide) from 1559 to 1603, 215 versus 157 in Cockburn (1977, p. 55), presumably because Samaha uses records from coroners' inquests and lower courts as well as assize records. He also notes that some assize court records are missing, especially for the 1560s (1974, p. 14), hence his numbers of offenses, though higher than Cockburn's, are still underestimated. With respect to population, Cockburn estimates that Essex had 52,000 people but says it is impossible to estimate population changes (1977, pp. 53, 311 n.34). Samaha, citing the same basic source (the Elizabethan muster rolls), estimates that the population increased from 60,000 to 80,000 during the period (1974, p. 33). Despite these considerable discrepancies, the rates calculated from these data for the 45-year period are nearly identical: from Cockburn's data, 6.7 homicides per 100,000 population per annum; and from Samaha's data, 6.8 per 100,000.[2] One other observation from Samaha's study should be noted: the trend in recorded violent crime—especially property offenses—was upward during this period, considerably more so than can be attributed to incomplete early records or to population growth (Samaha 1974, pp. 19–22, 115–16).

There is much other evidence that the interpersonal violence of medieval England had lessened only somewhat in Elizabethan England. To quote Cockburn again (1977, p. 57), few of the killings investigated at assizes during this period resulted from calculated violence. "Rather, they occurred during acts of sudden, unpremeditated aggression and resulted from attacks with a variety of knives and blunt instruments. Fatal quarrels could originate in almost any context—at work, in drink or at play." Handguns, known as "pocket dags," had also come into limited use by this time, and about 7 percent of the violent deaths involved firearms (Cockburn 1977, pp. 58–59). One can also examine the relative proportions of crimes against persons versus property offenses in this period. Of 5,980 indictments in three counties between 1559 and 1603, 12 percent were for offenses against the person (homicide, infanticide, assault, rape, robbery) and 69 percent for offenses against property (other than robbery). This differs from the prevailing twentieth-century pattern, in which more than 90 percent of reported felonies are against property. Moreover the sixteenth-century indictments for homicide were more numerous than those for assault (280 versus 133), not because assault was less

---

[2] Rates calculated by the author of this essay from data reported by Cockburn and Samaha, using 70,000 as the mean population figure for Essex when calculating rates from Samaha's homicide data.

309   Historical Trends in Violent Crime

common, one suspects, but because it was not often thought
serious enough to bring to the assize courts (calculated from
data in Cockburn 1977, p. 55). Samaha excludes assaults entirely from his Essex study because the assault indictments he
examined usually state that the defendant put the plaintiff out
of possession of his land. He concludes that they were not assaults in the ordinary meaning of the term but rather that
plaintiffs were using the criminal law to try civil property disputes (1974, p. 17).

For seventeenth- and eighteenth-century England we can report the results of a study by Beattie, who analyzed statistically
the indictments brought in the higher courts of Surrey and Sussex for a sample of years between 1662 and 1802. The first of
these counties includes London south of the Thames, whereas
Sussex was predominantly rural. Although Beattie does not report fully his calculations of rates for each county and period,
he does give the following rates of murder and manslaughter
indictments per 100,000 population for Surrey (Beattie 1974, p.
61):

1663–65	6.1
1690–94	5.3
1722–24	2.3
1780–84 } 1795–1802	less than 1

A decline was found in both urban and rural parishes of Surrey, and "confirmed in Sussex, where there were on average
between two and three indictments for murder every year in
the seventeenth century and rarely more than one in the
eighteenth" (Beattie 1974, p. 61). Beattie concludes, not surprisingly, that these absolute numbers almost surely reflect a
real decline in killing, not changes in public attitudes or judicial
efficiency. They also bear comparison against trends in the rate
of indictments for assault, which exhibited a pronouncedly different pattern. In both urban and rural Surrey assault rates
traced a wavelike pattern, rising to a very high peak in the
1720s and 1730s, with lesser peaks in the 1760s, 1780s, and at
the beginning of the nineteenth century. In rural Sussex, how-

ever, the assault rates were lower, the peaks of lesser amplitude, and the long-run trend was generally downward, as it was for homicide (pp. 66–69). Beattie attributes the peaks in assault rates to an increased inclination of injured parties to bring cases to court; to the apprehensiveness of authorities about threats to public order, especially in the 1720s; and to real increases in assault (and much greater ones in property offenses) by disbanded soldiers and seamen who periodically flooded London and its environs at the conclusion of wars (of which England was involved in six between 1690 and 1802). There is nothing in Beattie's descriptions of typical assault cases (pp. 62–63) to suggest that any of them were really civil property cases, as Samaha suggests they were in Elizabethan Essex (see above).

B. *Violent Crime in the Nineteenth and Twentieth Centuries*

Beginning in 1805 there are national data on committals to trial for indictable (serious) offenses. At first these were reported only by type of offense, after 1834 by county as well. Generally the data were reported with increasing reliability and detail as the century progressed (see Gatrell and Hadden 1972). The returns provide the basis for a true time-series analysis of English crime rates. The rate of all offenses against persons tried in upper courts was 12.3 per 100,000 in 1836–40, falling to 9.0 in 1896–1900 and 7.7 in 1906–10. Beginning in the 1850s there are series on homicides known to the police, which trace a similar decline from 1.4 per 100,000 in 1856–60 to 0.8 in 1906–10. Common assaults known to police were 408 per 100,000 in the first period, 135 per 100,000 in the last. Gatrell, whose recent study is the source of these estimates, argues trenchantly that the trends cannot be explained away by changes in public attitudes or official practices: they reflect a real decline in interpersonal violence (1980, pp. 282–93). Their cause, he suggests, was not deterrence because impulsively violent offenders are not likely to be deterred by the threat of arrest or punishment. The explanation must be sought in "heavy generalizations about the 'civilizing' effects of religion, education, and environmental reform" (p. 300).

311 Historical Trends in Violent Crime

The national trends are paralleled by the evidence from a study of London beginning in the 1820s. Trends in committals to trial for homicide have been analyzed from 1820 to 1873 for Middlesex County, which included London north of the Thames. Committals for murder varied irregularly throughout the period. In the 1830s, for example, committals ranged from 15 to 35 per year in a county whose population was about 1.4 million. The committals rate for the 1820s and 1830s was about 2 per 100,000, declining irregularly to less than 1 per 100,000 in the 1850s, with temporary upswings in the late 1840s and in the 1860s. Conviction rates were consistently about half the committal rates. Committals to trial for assault declined more sharply during the period. When first recorded in the 1830s and 1840s they ranged from 15 to 25 per 100,000 annually but had declined by 1870 to an average rate of 6 per 100,000 (Peirce, Grabosky, and Gurr 1977, pp. 166–67).

From 1869 through 1931 there are data for all of London (specifically the Metropolitan Police District), which trace a continued irregular decline in rates of homicide. For this period the trend study focuses on convictions. The annual conviction rate for murder and manslaughter gradually declined from about 0.5 per 100,000 in the 1870s to half of that in 1930, while convictions for assault and attempted murder fell from ca. 5 per 100,000 to ca. 1.5 per 100,000 (Peirce, Grabosky, and Gurr 1977, pp. 116–17). Since the 1940s, however, both London and all of England and Wales have experienced increasing rates of violent crime. In London the incidence of homicides known to police has increased from about 0.7 per 100,000 in the 1950s to more than 2.0 in the 1970s. In absolute numbers, the police reported 18 murders and 22 cases of manslaughter in 1950 in London compared with 127 murders and 15 cases of manslaughter in 1974. Indictable assaults increased much more dramatically, from ca. 10 per 100,000 in 1950 to 120 per 100,000 in 1974 (Peirce, Grabosky, and Gurr 1977, pp. 162–64).

The rates of violent crime generally in London since the 1940s have not been substantially higher than those in all of England and Wales. In fact other large English cities tended to have higher rates of indictable crimes against the person in the 1950s than did London. The national trends in violent crime generally parallel the London experience, but as McClintock has noted, the upward trend in these offenses began in London ca. 1950, about ten years later than it became evident in the national statistics (McClintock 1963, chap. 1; see also McClintock and Avison 1968, chaps. 2, 3).

C. Summary: The Long-Term Trend in English Homicide

The comparability of English homicide rates over time is impaired by the fact that only the earliest and most recent studies use data on offenses known to the authorities (the eyre courts in the first instance, the police in the most recent). For the intervening centuries the data refer mainly to committals to trial, which are only roughly comparable. Comparability is further impaired by the lack of reliable population data before 1800 and by the fact that early estimates of rates are available only for a handful of jurisdictions scattered across time and the social landscape. The general trend which emerges from the evidence is nonetheless unmistakable: rates of violent crime were far higher in medieval and early modern England than in the twentieth century—probably ten and possibly twenty or more times higher. The estimates discussed above are displayed graphically in figure 1. Each estimate for a county and city prior to 1800 is represented by a dot, even though the estimate may represent a period of several decades. A speculative trend curve is fitted to these data points. Elizabethan Essex and the period 1820 to 1975 are represented by five-year moving averages.

There are two problematic features of the trends traced in figure 1. One is the extraordinarily high incidence of homicide in fourteenth-century cities by comparison with the preceding century. If the handful of estimates are not grossly in error, there evidently was a tremendous upsurge in violent crime in England (or at least its cities) during the early fourteenth century. Hanawalt suggests as much (1979, p. 260). In general the fourteenth century was more disorderly than the thirteenth. The Hundred Years War, which began in 1337, and the Black

313   Historical Trends in Violent Crime

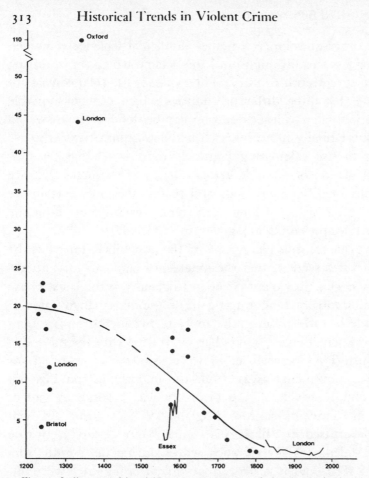

Fig. 1. Indicators of homicides per 100,000 population in England, thirteenth to twentieth centuries. Each dot represents the estimated homicide rate for a city or county for periods ranging from several years to several decades. The sources of the data are referred to in the text, with two exceptions. The estimate of 20 for ca. 1270 is the mean of high and low figures for Bedfordshire, as calculated by Hair (1971, p. 18) using minimum and maximum estimates of population. The estimate for ca. 1550 is the mean of high and low figures for Nottinghamshire for 1530–58, also calculated by Hair (1971, p. 17). Hair's estimates of London homicide rates for the seventeenth through nineteenth centuries, based on the London bills of mortality, are not shown because the source is highly suspect.

Death, which killed perhaps one-third of the population, precipitated social and economic crises of major proportions.[3]

[3] The high urban homicide rates reported by Hanawalt (1979) cannot be attributed to the social disorder which followed the onset of the Black Death because her London and Oxford estimates are for the first half of the fourteenth century whereas the plague arrived in England late in 1348 (see McNeill 1976, p. 166).

314   Ted Robert Gurr

The other question is whether homicidal violence remained more or less steadily high until the decline which set in during the late seventeenth century. The evidence ca. 1600 consists of estimates for three different counties which use questionable population data. Neither question can be definitively answered until substantially more research is done by historians who are willing to risk calculating homicide rates which have a substantial margin of possible error. The more estimates that are available for different periods and places, the more certain we can be of the shape of long-term trends, even if not about the precise rates prevailing at a given time.

The evidence thus clearly favors the possibility, raised at the outset of this section, that the nineteenth- and early twentieth-century decline in violent crime in England was the latest phase in a substantially longer trend. The seemingly high rates of homicide in early nineteenth- and late twentieth-century London were actually very low when contrasted with the more distant historical experience. The possibility of cyclical or wavelike movements away from the underlying trend is not ruled out, however. There probably was a surge in violent crime in fourteenth-century England. Violent crime also evidently increased in Elizabethan times. More certainly, Beattie offers evidence of several such waves during the period from 1660 to 1802, and it is likely that violent crime rates were unusually high in early nineteenth-century London.

Most of the evidence surveyed here relates only to homicide. Did assaults also decline over the long run? For the medieval and early modern period we simply cannot say because the court data on assaults are either nonexistent or unreliable. In Elizabethan times they appear in court records less often than homicide, but a century later assaults were much more numerous. Since most homicides of this period resulted from violent altercations, the real incidence of assault was presumably much higher. The infrequency of assaults in early court records almost surely reflects the fact that it ordinarily was not thought serious enough to warrant indictments unless someone died as a consequence of the assault. The higher assault rates of the period studied by Beattie, from 1660 to 1802, very likely reflect increased concern by victims and courts, not a real long-term increase in assault. During the last 150 years, however, trends and peaks in official data on assault in London and all of England have closely paralleled those for murder and manslaughter. Thus for this period we can be reasonably confident that the incidence of assault, like murder, declined for most of the period but increased after ca. 1950.

III. Trends in Violent Crime in the United States

It would be instructive to be able to compare long-term trends in British homicide with those in North America from seventeenth-century settlement to the present. Unfortunately reliable data and detailed historical studies are largely lacking. The handful of studies which analyze colonial and early republican court records are concerned mainly with the characteristics of offenses, not their incidence. Greenberg (1976), for example, compiled data on all surviving criminal records of New York courts between 1691 and 1775, a total of 5,297 cases, but his analysis focuses on the relative frequency of different kinds of cases, characteristics of the accused, and the distribution of outcomes for the accused. Interestingly, the most common of all categories of offense was crimes of violence against persons which did not result in death, i.e. assaults. These offenses constituted 21.5 percent of the cases; second most frequent were thefts, 13.7 percent.

A. Violent Crime in Nineteenth-Century America

Something about the changing incidence of crime in America up to the Civil War period can be inferred from Hindus's recent study of criminal prosecutions in late eighteenth- and nineteenth-century Massachusetts and South Carolina. Without complete court data for the earlier period, only internal comparisons are possible: for example, that crimes against persons made up 11 to 18 percent of all prosecutions in eighteenth- and nineteenth-century Massachusetts, but over 50 percent—mainly assaults—in South Carolina (1980, pp. 63–65). For Massachusetts he reports time-series data from 1836 to 1873 which show that total number of committals for crimes against persons increased fourfold from 1836 to 1855, declined by half until 1865, and then increases again. Property crime moved up simultaneously and stayed high, except for the Civil War years (1980, p. 72). His data on committals to trial in Suffolk County (Boston) show murder committal rates increasing from 2.1 per 100,000 in 1839–41 to 3.1 twenty years later and then a jump to 7.0 in 1869–70.[4] Assault committals increased from 78 to 293 per 100,000 over the same period (1980, p. 74). This increasing trend is the opposite of England's experience in the same period, but it is based on a study of only two jurisdictions.

A different result is evident in Lane's careful study of homicide in Philadelphia from 1838 to 1901.[5] He begins by diagnosing some of the difficulties of inferring homicide rates from nineteenth-century records. Police arrest statistics in Philadelphia date only from 1857 and even then were a "poor barometer" because some homicides were followed by numerous indiscriminate arrests. Health office figures for homicide also are unreliable because of a "legal-bureaucratic quirk" whereby coroners often failed to indicate that a death was due to homicide. Lane concludes that homicide indictments prepared for grand juries are the best records for Philadelphia but notes that these too pose problems of comparability over time. Such difficulties are particularly true of manslaughter cases: "late in the century a number of cases were prosecuted that earlier would have been tolerated or overlooked" (Lane 1979, chap. 4, quotations from pp. 56, 76). Presumably these or equivalent problems affect the homicide records of other

---

[4] Comparison of Hindus's graphed annual data (1980, p. 72) with tabled data (p. 74) gives rise to the suspicion that the latter may represent two- or three-year rates rather than annual ones. If so, then the rates given in the text are inflated but the *trends* are valid.

[5] An earlier study of Philadelphia examines lower court records from 1791 to 1810 and tabulates, *inter alia*, annual numbers of persons charged with offenses against persons (Hobbs 1943, p. 8). The trend was upward, but, lacking either population data or information on serious offenses against persons, no firm conclusions about changes in rates can be drawn.

317   Historical Trends in Violent Crime

American cities, though few of the authors relying on them
have examined alternative statistics in Lane's painstaking way.

Homicide indictment rates in Philadelphia declined irregularly during the nineteenth century, from ca. 3.3 indictments
per 100,000 population during the two decades before the Civil
War to 2.1 per 100,000 after 1880. The trend was not steadily
downward, however: there were peaks during the 1850s and
again during the fifteen years which followed the Civil War,
analogous to the peaks in Suffolk County. Concealable handguns, which came into use in the 1850s, evidently provided an
upward push against the declining trend but did not reverse it.
Lane excludes from these rates "incidents in which no assault,
aggression, or harm was intended." The data understate the
real decline because study of individual indictments over time
"reveal a further stretching of definitions" of murder over time
(Lane 1979, pp. 70–71). Examination of the races of victims
specified in indictments shows that homicide rates among
blacks in nineteenth-century Philadelphia were considerably
higher than the white rate, 7.5 versus 2.8 per 100,000. In the
twentieth century this gap widened. In the years from 1948 to
1952 the white victimization rate had declined still further, to
1.8 per 100,000, while the black rate had increased to 24.6. In
the early 1970s the white rate was back to its mean nineteenth-
century rate of 2.8 while the black rate was an incredible 64.2.
"As demographic change has made Philadelphia an increasingly
black city, the black homicide rate in itself is enough to account
for the differences between the overall official rates" between
the nineteenth and the late twentieth century (Lane 1979, pp.
112–13). Lane offers the same general explanation for the
nineteenth-century decline in white homicide rates and the
growing discrepancy between black and white homicide rates:
"while the effect of urban-industrial discipline was increasingly
felt among whites, the absence of the same discipline was increasingly evident among blacks" (1979, p. 135).

That homicide rates declined in nineteenth-century Philadelphia is as firmly established as any historical generalization can
be which relies on official American records of offenses. In

318   Ted Robert Gurr

Boston (Suffolk County), by contrast, we have seen from Hindus's data that the trend in the shorter run was upward. Trials
for all categories of crimes against persons, property, morality,
and order in Boston (Suffolk County) began increasing in the
1840s—a period of heavy Irish immigration—and continued
upward into the late 1850s (1980, p. 72). Parallel evidence
comes from Ferdinand's study of Boston's arrest rates for major
offenses from 1849 to 1951: arrests increased sharply during the
1850s for most categories of offenses (1967).

Boston continued to be a violent and disorderly place for a
decade after the Civil War. Robbery, burglary, and larceny arrest rates increased in the aftermath of war. Murder arrests
(Ferdinand 1967) and trials (Hindus 1980) reached their highest
peak in 1869–71. Thereafter, however, the trends turned
downward. Table 1 shows the average arrest rates in Boston
per 100,000 population for offenses against persons in twenty-
year intervals. Overall, murder arrests in 1854–74 averaged 4.7
per 100,000 yearly but declined to about half that rate in
1895–1915. Manslaughter arrests are excluded from these
figures: they averaged about 1.5 yearly per 100,000 with no
evident trend until ca. 1910, when the inclusion of automotive
manslaughter evidently pushed them upward. Thus the
nineteenth-century arrest rates for murder plus manslaughter
fell from ca. 6 to 4 per 100,000 persons, rates that are generally
consistent in magnitude and trend with homicide indictments in

TABLE 1

Boston: Average Annual Arrests per 100,000 for
Offenses against Persons*

Offense	1854–74	1875–94	1895–1915	1916–36
Murder†	4.7	3.0	2.5	2.7
Assault	720	710	460	290
Forcible rape	3.6	3.1	5.4	7.1
Robbery	32	26	24	32

*Estimated from data presented graphically by Ferdinand (1967, pp. 89–95).
†Excluding manslaughter.

319   Historical Trends in Violent Crime

Philadelphia.[6] The incidence of assault arrests in Boston follows
the same downward trend as murder, with some similarity in
fluctuations around the trend. Robbery arrests also show a
slight downward trend in the nineteenth century, followed by a
sharp wave that peaked ca. 1918 and another in the early 1930s.
(Other studies of crime in Boston during this era are Harrison
1934 and Warner 1934.)

Two other studies provide converging evidence about Boston's trends in violent crime in the late nineteenth century.
Lane, using statewide data on court and grand jury cases, and
imprisonments, reports that total commitments for homicide,
rape, armed robbery, and arson declined from 6.8 per 100,000
population in 1860–62 to 2.9 by 1900 (1968). Ferdinand has
analyzed arrests in Salem, Massachusetts, from 1853 to 1966.
Murder and manslaughter were too rare in this smaller city to
permit any analysis of trends, but arrests for simple assault
during the nineteenth and early twentieth centuries were very
similar in incidence, trends, and variations within the trend to
those of nearby Boston (Ferdinand 1972, pp. 579–80).

Powell's study of Buffalo, New York, is also relevant for our
purposes. He traces the trends in arrests from 1854 to 1956,
categorized by type of offense. Arrests for offenses against persons rose very sharply between 1854 and 1874, from about 90
to 1,300 per 100,000 population, in a pattern generally similar
to that in Boston. Most were assaults; in absolute numbers
murders increased from 2 in the former year (or 2.7 per
100,000) to 13 in the latter (or 9.7 per 100,000). Arrests for all
offenses against persons declined steadily thereafter, reaching a
level of 355 per 100,000 in 1893. The decline continued until
about 1905, when a sharp increase began which peaked about
1920 and did not ebb until the 1930s (rates calculated from
data in Powell 1966, pp. 163–64). Powell's general explanation
of this wavelike pattern is to attribute it to anomie, conceived as

[6] A study of murder and manslaughter indictments in predominantly rural New
Hampshire, 1873–1903, yields a substantially lower rate of 1.0 indictments per 100,000
population, with no clear trend discernible over the period (calculated from data in Nutt
1905, pp. 224–25).

the temporary disintegration of the institutional order (Powell 1966, pp. 168–69; 1970, chap. 8).

The broadest evidence for a U-shaped trend in American homicide rates is provided by Monkkonen's study of arrest trends in 23 cities between 1860 and 1920. His main interest is in diagnosing changes in the activities and effectiveness of police. His findings about trends are ancillary to that purpose but highly instructive for ours. The data base includes virtually all cities whose population exceeded 50,000 in the late nineteenth century. The method is to aggregate police data on arrests and population figures for all cities and calculate from them composite arrest rates per 100,000. The aggregate homicide arrest rate had a peak of about 9 per 100,000 during the Civil War years, after which it declined to about 5 during the 1880s. Then there was an upward swing which reached 13 by 1920 (Monkkonen 1981, pp. 76–77). The trend in arrests for drunk and disorderly conduct, estimated in the same way, was different: it moved continuously downward, with only slight deviations, from the 1860s to the 1940s. This was the aggregate pattern; some cities had different trends, notably increases in alcohol-related arrests between 1900 and the onset of Prohibition (Monkkonen 1979). The U-shaped pattern recurs in the trend of total arrests for crimes with victims, a composite in which property offenses bulked large. There was a peak between 1865 and 1876, a decline thereafter, and an irregular movement upward after 1900 (Monkkonen 1981, pp. 74–76). In general Monkkonen regards all these trends as reflections of real changes in social behavior.[7]

B. Violent Crime in Twentieth-Century America

Zahn (1980) has recently made a careful survey of evidence on twentieth-century homicide rates in the United States using both local and national studies. The gist of the evidence is that

[7] Other studies of nineteenth and early twentieth-century trends in property crime, all felonies, and various kinds of petty offenses are synopsized by Monkkonen (1981, app. E).

homicide (excluding auto homicide) tended to increase after 1900 to a peak in the early 1930s. After 1933 the Uniform Crime Reports (UCR) compiled by the FBI show that homicides known to police declined irregularly until the early 1960s, followed by a doubling of the rate in the next fifteen years. The following discussion focuses specifically on the evidence for trends.

Trends in national and urban homicide rates in the early part of the twentieth century were the subject of careful studies by Hoffman (1925, 1928), Sutherland (1925), and Brearley (1932). They relied mainly on death registration data compiled by the federal government from reports of local registrars, but this system was only gradually extended from the New England states to others, which impairs the reliability of trend estimates. Sutherland, using only those states in the "registration area" from 1905 to 1922, found that their annual homicide rates varied little, from 2.22 per 100,000 population in 1905–9 to 2.86 in 1920–22 (summarized in Brearley 1932, pp. 16–17). Hoffman, on the other hand, compiled the death registration records of twenty-eight large cities for 1900–1924 and found that their aggregate homicide rate increased steadily from 5.1 in 1900 to 10.3 in 1924 (summarized in Brearley 1932, p. 16). Brearley, working with data from the entire registration area, reports national rates of 7.5 in 1919 (excluding nine states, three of them southern) and 8.5 in 1929 (excluding only Georgia).

Of equal interest to the aggregate trends are the differences between white and black homicide rates. The former remained virtually constant over the decade at 5.3 per 100,000 in both 1919 and 1927. The rate for blacks, however, increased from 30.5 to 43.8. Moreover, separate figures by states show that every southern state in the registration area experienced an increase over the decade in black homicide rates (Brearley 1932, pp. 19–20). This is consistent with Lane's (1979) observations about an increasing black-white difference in Philadelphia's homicide rates over a much longer time span. A more recent study of homicide arrests in Washington, D.C., from 1890 to 1970, pro-

322   Ted Robert Gurr

vides documentation of the same trend.[8] These are the homicide arrest rates for whites and nonwhites in selected decades, calculated from annual data in Count–van Manen (1977, pp. 200–201):

	Whites	Nonwhites
1890–99	2.9	9.1
1910–19	5.1	20.0
1930–39	6.3	36.1
1960–70	5.0	25.4

Evidence about trends in other kinds of offenses against persons during the first third of the century comes from studies of city arrest data. Sutherland and Gehlke (1933, p. 1127), using arrest data for Baltimore, Buffalo, Chicago, and Cleveland combined, find that robbery declined from 1900 until ca. 1910, then doubled in the next decade and remained at roughly that level through 1931. Wilbach, studying arrest rates for males over 15 in New York City from 1916 to 1936, finds that offenses against the person (mainly assaults) declined from a 1916–18 average of 602 per 100,000 to a 1934–36 average of 289. There was a slight upward trend in robbery arrests, however (Willbach 1938, pp. 69–70, 73). In a parallel study of Chicago from 1919 to 1939 he finds a somewhat different pattern. The rate of arrests for offenses against persons increased by more than half between 1919 and 1927, then declined steadily to 1939, when it was far below the 1919 level. Robbery arrests traced a similar pattern of moderate increase, then substantial decline (Willbach 1941, p. 722). Ferdinand's long-term trend study of arrest rates in Boston, summarized above, shows a sharp increase in robbery arrests from 1900 to ca. 1920, fol-

---

[8] Homicide *mortality* rates by race can be expected to correlate closely with homicide *arrest* rates by race because murder in the United States has always been almost entirely intraracial. In the 1970s there was an increase in big-city robbery homicides in which the assailant was black and the victim was white, but even so, Block's study of criminal homicide in Chicago from 1965 to 1974 shows that victim and offenders were of the same race in 88 percent of cases (Block 1977, p. 40).

lowed by a decline and another peak in the mid-1930s (1967, p. 93). With the exception of New York these studies are generally consistent with the national homicide trends: violent crime tended to increase in the first three decades of the century, then declined.

The UCR national homicide data on offenses known to the police show a decline in rates from about 6.5 in the mid-1930s to a low of 4.8 in the 1950s, interrupted by a temporary increase after World War II. Most scholarly research on homicide in this period consists of microanalyses of characteristics of homicides and their victims in particular cities, both northern and southern. Only Boudouris's (1970) study of Detroit from 1926 to 1968 spans more than a decade. The studies provide a composite picture of homicide that arose mainly out of quarrels between family members, lovers, or two males who knew one another. Murders during robbery were rare. Homicide death rates for black males were much higher than for other groups. Representative figures for Philadelphia, 1948–52 (Wolfgang 1958) and Cleveland, 1946–53 (Hirsch et al. 1973), are: black males, 22.5, 72; black females, 9.6, 16; white males, 2.9, 4; white females, 1, 1.

The increase in violent crime—and property crime—since the 1960s has been so pronounced and so well documented that most scholars have accepted it as a given and focused their attention on explaining rather than debunking it. The national homicide rate was at 4.5 in the early 1960s, increasing to 9.0 in 1978. Increases in a number of cities were higher. In Chicago, for example, the 1960 rate was 10.3, the 1975 rate 25.0 (Block 1977, p. 2). From 1960 to 1978 the UCR rate of aggravated assaults known to police tripled (from 85 to 256 per 100,000) and so did robbery (from 60 to 191 per 100,000) and forcible rape (from 9.4 to 30.8 per 100,000). There was some evidence that rates were peaking out by the late 1970s, however (see Skogan 1979).

The characteristics of homicides which contributed to the increase also are well documented. Block's Chicago study shows that "altercation homicides" between people who know one

324   Ted Robert Gurr

another have increased relatively little compared to the increase in robbery-related homicides in which offender and victim are strangers. In northern cities generally, Zahn concludes, a consistent picture emerges of "an increasing homicide rate in the late 1960s and into the 1970s; an increase in homicides by gun; and an increase in homicides with unknown assailants" (Zahn 1980, p. 123). The only appreciable difference in southern and southwestern cities is that family and acquaintance homicides there remain a major category.

C. Summary: The Long-Term Trend in American Homicide

The composite picture of violent crime in nineteenth-century America is a stable or declining trend with a pronounced upward swing which began shortly before the Civil War and persisted into the 1870s. The evidence is summarized graphically in figure 2. It is limited to cities, mainly on the eastern seaboard and in the Midwest, which may not be representative of what was happening in towns or on the frontier. The trends in violent crime before the Civil War are especially problematic because only Philadelphia and Boston have been studied prior to 1850. After 1900 there was a sustained rise in violent crime to the early 1930s, a thirty-year subsidence, and another increase since 1965. Current national homicide rates are higher than any recorded previously, though only slightly greater than those of the 1920s. They are also greater than any indicated by the fragmentary nineteenth-century evidence.

There is also evidence, summarized graphically in figure 3, that the two waves in twentieth-century homicide rates may be attributable mainly to increases in killings among blacks. White homicide rates have varied much less. The trends in black homicide arrests in Washington, D.C., are especially suggestive in this regard. There is need for careful long-term trend studies on this question which use both homicide and arrest data, distinguished by race, for cities and the nation.

In conclusion, we may ask to what extent the American evidence is consistent with the reversing U-shaped curve proposed at the outset of this essay. The dominant feature of crime

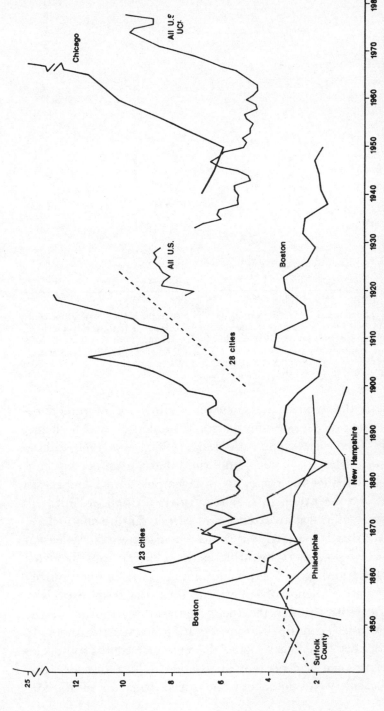

FIG. 2. Indicators of homicides per 100,000 population in the United States, 1840–1980. *Types of data*: indictments: Suffolk County, Philadelphia, New Hampshire; arrests: Boston, 23 cities; homicide registrations: 28 cities, all U.S. 1919–29; offenses known: all U.S. 1933–77, Chicago 1940–75. Sources are given in the text.

326   Ted Robert Gurr

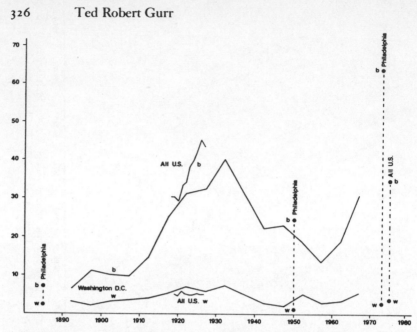

Fig. 3. Differences in homicides per 100,000 by race in the United States, nineteenth century to 1980. *Types and sources of data:* Philadelphia: race of victims in homicide indictments in 1838–1901 (mean), 1948–52, and 1972–74 (Lane 1979); Washington, D.C.: arrests for homicide by race (Count–van Manen 1977); all U.S., 1918–27: homicide mortality rates by race (Brearley 1932); all U.S., 1976: calculated by the author from UCR data on arrests for murder and nonnegligent manslaughter.

trends in the United States is the occurrence of three pronounced upsurges of interpersonal violence which began roughly fifty years apart: ca. 1860, 1900, and 1960. These waves or cycles are of such amplitude that we cannot say conclusively whether the cycles are superimposed on a longer-run decline. To the extent that North America from settlement to industrialization was an extension of British culture and society, I suspect that the underlying trend was downward. At least it was for Anglo-Americans. But as Lane points out (personal communication), non-English immigrants have unquestionably added to the violence of American cities: the Irish, especially from the 1840s through the 1860s; possibly the Italians, in the early twentieth century; and in-migrating blacks throughout. In culturally heterogenous societies the aggregate trends and cycles of interpersonal violence are instructive only about how disorderly society is, not about the social behavior of its con-

stituent groups. The trends-and-cycles problem of understanding homicide in America calls out for social-historical studies which trace the social characteristics of murderers and their
victims over long periods of time.

IV. Correlates of Crime Trends in Britain and the United States

A number of studies, including some of those cited above, have
used time-series crime data to test hypotheses about the causes
of temporal variation in violent crime. This section reviews the
findings of some representative English and American studies.
Correlates of crime trends in other societies are examined in the
following section.

A. *Psychocultural Variables*

Some studies examine the impact of psychocultural variables
on the changing incidence of violent crime. It has long been
observed, for example, that rates of violent crime are higher in
the American South than in the North, and Hackney (1969) has
shown that the differences are only partly accounted for by
differences in socioeconomic and racial characteristics. The
prevailing interpretation is that a distinctive southern subculture sanctions interpersonal violence (Hackney 1969; Gastil
1971; for reviews and reanalyses see Loftin and Hill 1974 and
Jacobson 1975). Jacobson uses a series of cross-sectional comparisons of UCR crime rates between southern and nonsouthern cities between 1951 and 1970 to demonstrate that "the historically observed pattern of higher crime rates in the South
remains today only in vestigial form" (1975, p. 239). The differences remain significant for murder and assault, however:
southern cities continue to have higher rates. Unfortunately
Jacobson does not control for the racial composition of the
urban population. Another test of a psychocultural explanation
is an unpublished time-series study by Dunham and Kiyak
(1975) which correlates "anomie," inferred from national public
opinion poll data, with homicide rates in thirteen cities from
1940 to 1973. Very strong relationships are reported (sum-

marized in Count–van Manen 1977, p. 40). But which way
does causation flow? Does anomie breed violent crime or does
rising urban violence provoke anger and disorientation among
the polled public?

B. Economic Variables

Other time-series studies have focused on the economic correlates of trends in offense rates. Some emphasize the stressful
effects of economic decline, which is assumed to motivate
people, especially those living near the subsistence level, to
crime either from frustration or necessity (see Bonger 1967 for a
review). The method typical of historical work is to compare
graphs of economic conditions and crime. Hanawalt does so for
fourteenth-century England, for example, and finds strong evidence that the total number of cases brought to trial "rose and
fell with the price of grain" (1979, pp. 238–60). A similar pattern is observed between trials and price indexes in Elizabethan
Essex (Samaha 1974, pp. 31–37, 168–69) and, specifically for
property crime, in eighteenth-century Surrey and Sussex (Beattie 1974, pp. 85–95).

As a rough generalization, property offenses are more closely
related to fluctuating economic conditions than are crimes
against persons. Thomas, using data on all England and Wales
from 1857 to 1913, concludes from time-series analysis that offenses against property with violence (including robbery) have
rather strong inverse correlations with the business cycle (when
conditions are good, crime goes down), whereas offenses against
persons are unrelated to changing economic conditions (1925,
pp. 138–41). Studies using twentieth-century American data,
however, detect significant relations between some aspects of
economic conditions and violent crime.

For example, Henry and Short (1954) have correlated
twenty-three time-series of violent crimes against persons
known to police ca. 1929 to 1949 (murder and aggravated assault separately, for various aggregations of city data) with the
business cycle. All but four of the series correlate positively
with economic conditions. Closer examination leads the authors

to conclude not that prosperity causes increased violence but rather that "downward movement of the economic cycle brings with it downward movement of these crimes" (p. 47). They also correlate national data on white and nonwhite homicide rates separately with the business cycle, 1900 to 1940, and find sharply divergent results. White homicide rates increased when the business cycle was low, nonwhite rates decreased when the cycle was low (p. 50). Their interpretation is that blacks, locked into the bottom of the status hierarchy, feel more frustrated and are hence more likely to commit violent acts during good times, when they become increasingly aware of their low status and lack of mobility (pp. 59–62). This is also a plausible explanation for the soaring rate of black homicides during the prosperous 1960s and early 1970s.

As another example, Glaser and Rice (1959) examined the impact of national levels of unemployment on arrest rates for males from 1932 to 1950 nationally and in Boston, Chicago, and Cincinnati. Whereas previous research generally showed little relationship between unemployment and arrest rates in the United States, they argued that the effects should be different for different age groups. And in fact they found that high unemployment was consistently related to high arrest rates for both property offenses and violent crimes for males in their twenties and thirties, but negatively related to juvenile arrest rates.

The most substantial comparative study of the relationship between economic conditions and crime, by Brenner (1976), examines the impact of growth, unemployment, and inflation on national crime statistics ca. 1900 to 1970 in the United States, England and Wales, Scotland, and Canada. Measures of age composition and urbanization also are used. Generally, both growth *and* economic adversity are related to changes in the incidence of property and personal crimes in all four political units, although the relationships vary from one period to another within the larger seventy-year span. Before World War II, cyclical economic fluctuations were the dominant factors, analogous to the more remote historical evidence cited

330   Ted Robert Gurr

above. Since then the effects of economic growth and inflation
are stronger, and—combined with unemployment—account for
90 percent or more of the variation in trends in many offense
categories. (Growth and adversity as measured in this study are
only weakly related. Brenner argues that long-term economic
growth is criminogenic because it causes *comparative* decline in
the socioeconomic status of the lowest income and occupational
groups.) Most important for this essay are findings concerning
changes in violent offenses, estimated by using data on mortality and criminal justice separately:

> crimes of violence are more strongly related to economic
>   growth and adversity after World War II than before;
> the size of the population under age 30 and the gap between
>   their incomes and that of others are strongly related to
>   changing homicide rates since World War II;
> in the period 1920–40 the Great Depression affected the
>   homicide rate somewhat differently than it affected other
>   offenses in that it tended to move upward as employ-
>   ment increased, rather than vice versa, but since World
>   War II "the patterns for both the homicidal and property
>   crimes are identical: they increase sharply during periods
>   of short-term reductions in employment and income"
>   (Brenner 1976, p. 37).[9]

C. Opportunity Theory

Whereas the above studies focus on the stressful effects of
economic change, others attribute increases in property and
other crimes to changes in the opportunities to commit them.
Gould (1969, 1971) uses national data for 1933 to 1965 to show
that the availability of property in the United States has been
curvilinearly related over time to the incidence of property
crime. More exactly, in the 1930s and early 1940s greater
abundance was associated with decreasing property crime, but
thereafter the relationship was positive. The explanation offered
is that the more abundant and less well protected property is,

---

[9] These results are abstracted from a summary paper which does not report any
specific trend or correlation data. The full study has not yet been published.

the easier it is to steal, whether the motives are fun or necessity. A more recent time-series analysis by Cohen, Felson, and Land (1980) of property crime rates in the United States from 1947 to 1977 provides a strong and persuasive test of this "opportunity" theory. A parallel analysis by Cohen and Felson (1979) shows that measures of increased vulnerability of targets (a household activity ratio and the proportion of persons aged 15–24) explain much of the variance over time in homicide and assault rates ($R^2 = .68$ and $.74$, respectively).

D. Correlates of Diverging Crime Trends

The studies cited thus far examine the correlates of crime changes over time in single entities (countries; cities singly or in the aggregate). There are also empirical studies of American cities which try to ascertain why their crime trends differ from one another. Skogan (1977) has examined the differential rates of increase in serious offenses known to police in 32 cities between 1948 and 1970, finding that cities with the greatest levels and rates of suburbanization had the greatest increases in crime. His interpretation is that high suburbanization means the concentration of criminogenic forces in the central city. The most substantial studies of this genre are being carried out as part of the "Reactions to Crime" project at Northwestern University. An initial paper by Jacob and Lineberry (1980) reports an analysis of differential rates of change in crime in 395 cities from 1948 to 1978. They find, for example, that the upward trend in violent crime rates—but not property crime—was considerably higher in cities with declining population than others. With respect to race and crime, the proportion of black population is strongly related to rates of violent crime in 1978 ($r = .65$), but *changes* in the black population from 1950 to 1970 are only weakly related to *changes* in the rate of violent crime ($r = .33$). They also report that changes in the size of the youthful population had very little effect on crime rates over time. Nor did changes in inequality of income over time have any significant effect on crime rates. Finally, in an intensive study of a sample of ten cities, they tested for evidence of police

332   Ted Robert Gurr

or political manipulation of official crime data, and while there
was evidence of such manipulation in a few cities (especially
Newark), a general pattern of manipulation could not be detected.[10] Other papers report on the ways in which trends in
crime rates in the ten-city sample are affected by policing, news
media coverage, and demographic, economic, racial, and lifestyle variables (e.g. Jacob and Rich 1980; Jacob and Lineberry,
forthcoming).

The correlational studies of twentieth-century crime trends
suggest that socioeconomic change is an underlying but indirect
source of variation in violent crime. The dynamics differ so
greatly from one period, place, and social group to another,
however, that we must conclude that contextual and intervening variables determine the specific effects of change. For
example, Henry and Short (1954) distinguished between the
correlates of crime (more exactly, homicide victimization) for
blacks and whites. They found that economic conditions affected black and white homicide rates in different ways. It is
also evident from Count–van Manen's study of determinants of
crime in Washington, D.C. (1977) that the time-series correlates
of homicide mortality and murder arrest rates for blacks are
quite different from those of whites.[11] And Lane's Philadelphia
study shows that the suicide rates for blacks and whites also
have diverged over time, implying that all manifestations of
violence in the two groups are different (Lane 1980, p. 137; and
personal communication). This suggests that quantitative
studies of determinants of crime trends in the United States

[10] Seidman and Couzens (1974) demonstrate the impact of political pressures in
selected American cities on police crime reporting practices using monthly data from
1967 to 1971.
[11] The study is so badly flawed that none of its specific correlation results are worth
mentioning here. A large grab bag of independent variables is used; they are correlated
with the crime-rate data using stepwise regression, so that a different assortment of
variables is to be found in each equation; the data are not de-trended nor are coefficients
corrected for auto-correlation; indeed, no regression coefficients or levels of significance
are reported; and the discussion of results is fuddled. Tables of simple correlations
nonetheless show that the correlates of black and white homicide rates are quite different one from another, and also differ by time-period (Count–van Manen 1977, pp. 139,
141).

333   Historical Trends in Violent Crime

ought to be disaggregated along racial lines. Separate models should be estimated for blacks and whites (using arrest or victimization data) and explanations sought for the observed differences. This follows the suggestion, offered above, that there is much to be learned from examining differential trends in violent crime rates among other kinds of social and economic groups, in the United States and elsewhere. The suggestion is a contemporary twist to an enduring concern among social historians of crime, namely the changing characteristics of offenders and their treatment over time (for example Given 1977; Hanawalt 1979, chap. 4; Lane 1979, pp. 100–14).

V. Violent Crime Trends and their Correlates in Other Western Societies

Here we review the evidence from other European and European-settled societies on long-term trends in violent crime, testing each country's evidence against the U-shaped curve.

A. *The Nineteenth and Early Twentieth Centuries*

I first suggested that there might be a long-term decline in serious crime common to all Western societies on the basis of a comparative study of London, Stockholm and New South Wales. The incidence of murder and assault in the early history of New South Wales (including Sydney) was very high, not surprising in view of the fact that the majority of its male inhabitants through 1840 were convicts and emancipists. Committals to trial for murder between 1819 and 1824 averaged 35 per 100,000 population per annum, for example, compared with ca. 2 per 100,000 in Middlesex County (London) in the same period. The rate dropped sharply after 1830, however: a composite measure of Supreme Court convictions for murder and assault in the colony shows a decline from ca. 45 per 100,000 in the 1830s to ca. 10 in the 1850s and less than 5 in the 1890s. A variety of indicators of serious and lesser offenses against persons show that the decline in interpersonal violence persisted until 1940 (see Grabosky 1976; Gurr, Grabosky, and Hula 1977, pp. 622–25). (Also see Addendum at p. 353.)

334   Ted Robert Gurr

Since New South Wales imported most of its population and
crime problems, as well as its institutions of criminal justice,
from Britain, it is not surprising that its trends in violent crime
paralleled those of the mother country. The most consequential
difference is that the decline in New South Wales was considerably more precipitous once the convict era come to an end. It
is somewhat more surprising to find Scandinavian evidence of a
similar long-term trend. In Stockholm convictions for murder,
manslaughter, and attempted murder combined were ca. 3.5
per 100,000 population in the 1830s, ca. 1.5 in the 1850s, and
less than 1.0 by the turn of the century—although there was a
temporary doubling of the rate in the 1880s. Data on offenses
known to police from 1841 on trace a similar irregular decline.
The rate of known homicides and attempts never exceeded 1
per 100,000 per annum (or five cases annually) from 1920 to
1940 (see Gurr, Grabosky, and Hula 1977, pp. 237–320,
622–24).

France offers the best and most thoroughly studied
nineteenth-century crime statistics of any continental country,
thanks to the publication of annual reports of criminal justice
beginning in 1826. There are several English-language studies
which make use of these data on numbers of persons tried for
various kinds of offenses (Lodhi and Tilly 1973; MacDonald
1910; Zehr 1975, 1976). Zehr's studies are the most thorough,
providing detailed descriptions and time-series analyses of
trends in homicide and serious assault from 1826 to 1913, nationally and in a sample of eight departments. Homicide trials
declined from ca. 3.5 per 100,000 adults in the 1830s to ca. 2 in
the 1860s, then increased and varied between 2.5 and 3 during
the remainder of the century (Zehr 1976, pp. 115–16). The incidence of serious assaults tried before the high courts fell pre-
cipitously (MacDonald 1910, p. 66), but this may simply reflect
a shift of lesser cases to the lower courts. The trend in lower-
court cases of assault and battery was positive: the rates doubled from the 1830s to the first decade of the twentieth century
and were closely correlated over time with per capita wine con-

335   Historical Trends in Violent Crime

sumption but negatively correlated with price indexes (Zehr 1976, pp. 87–110).

Zehr's analysis of the timing of changes in assault rates, and their variable distribution among departments, leads him to the more general conclusion that "most major upswings in violence appear to be relatable to urban-industrial growth or more precisely, to the initial and/or most disruptive stages of the process" (1975, p. 128). In contrast, Lodhi and Tilly make a series of cross-sectional correlation analyses for the 1840s and 1850s, using data on crime rates in departments, and find virtually no relationship between measures of urbanization or industrialization and crimes against persons (1973, p. 311). (They do, however, find strong relationships between the proportion of population urban and property crime.) Since Zehr uses time-series analysis, which is appropriate to testing dynamic arguments, his findings about the economic and other correlates of assault rates carry more weight.[12]

Crime trends in Germany have also been carefully studied from ca. 1882, when the first national data were compiled, to the outbreak of World War I in 1914. Studies by McHale and Johnson (1976, 1977) and by Zehr (1975, 1976) deal particularly with the connections between urbanization, industrialization, and crime in this era. They are less concerned with national trends than with differences in trends, and rates, among regions at different levels of urban and industrial growth. The overall trend in offenses against persons (using court data on persons tried and convictions) shows a 50 percent rise from the early 1880s to the late 1890s followed by a more gradual decline (McHale and Johnson 1977, p. 215; Zehr 1976, pp. 91–94).

[12] Alternatively, the difference in findings may be due to Lodhi and Tilly's use of Assize Court data (1973, p. 300), which includes only the most serious offenses against persons, while Zehr uses data from the lower correctional tribunals on simple assault and battery. Data tabled in MacDonald (1910, p. 66) show that numbers of persons tried for the former averaged about 600 per year compared with 25,000 annually for the latter. Oddly, the rates of serious crimes against persons reported and used by Lodhi and Tilly bear no discernible relationship to rates I have calculated using the data on numbers of persons tried from MacDonald. If nothing else, Tilly and Lodhi are cryptically casual in describing their index. There is no problem reconciling Zehr's index with MacDonald's data.

336   Ted Robert Gurr

But, as in France, the trend was due to changes in the incidence of assault, and as I suggested in an earlier section, upward trends in assaults during the nineteenth century are prima facie suspect because they are more likely a reflection of growing sensitization and closer official attention to assaults than evidence for real increases in interpersonal violence. Indeed, the trend in homicide trials in Germany was downward, declining from an initial rate of about 1.0 trials per 100,000 to 0.76 after 1900 (Zehr 1976, pp. 115–16).[13] Zehr's general observation about France and Germany is that "during the nineteenth century violence became more frequent but possibly less severe" (1976, p. 115). He briefly considers but tentatively rejects the argument that the increase in assault may have been due to more thorough reporting (1976, pp. 88–89).

What of the correlates of trends in crimes against persons in Germany? McHale and Johnson (1977, p. 227) find, as Zehr did for France, that personal crime rates were rather stable in their geographical distribution across time—evidence, in other words, for persisting regional subcultures of interpersonal violence, especially in poorer districts. But levels of personal crime appeared to be unrelated, in any and all cross-sectional comparisons of districts, to urban industrial development (1977, pp. 235–42). This requires modification in light of Zehr's time-series analysis of assault trends in thirteen towns and cities. Though the evidence is mixed, it fits his general thesis that rising assault rates coincided with the initial, not the later stages of urbanization. Once industrial growth and urbanization were well under way, social adjustment set in and interpersonal violence tended to decline (Zehr 1976, pp. 94, 107–14). This fits well with McHale and Johnson's general interpretation of their results, that the incidence of all categories of crime in Germany was highest in regions where social stress was greatest, owing

[13] Zehr also reports graphically earlier homicide data for Prussia alone which show a U-shaped curve with a downslope in the 1850s and a sharp increase in the 1870s (associated with the Franco-Prussian War of 1870–71). Still earlier data for Bavaria from 1835 to 1860 show, at most, a slight upward trend (Zehr 1976, pp. 115–16).

337   Historical Trends in Violent Crime

either to depopulation (in rural areas) or to very rapid population growth (in the swollen urban-industrial centers). As stress increased, then lessened in a particular district, so did crime rise and ebb (1977, pp. 243–44).[14] For a general theoretical analysis of the effects of industrialization and urbanization on crime see Shelley (1981).

B. From World War I to the 1970s

World War I had profound effects on crime in Germany and Austria. The incidence of most kinds of property and personal offenses declined during the war, a pattern widely observed during wartime in other Western societies and readily explained by the fact that the most crime-prone demographic group, young males, were in military service. Immediately after the war, most categories of offenses against persons rose sharply, though more so in Germany (Liepman 1930, pp. 35, 39, 58–59, 77) than in Austria (Exner 1927, p. 24).

The evidence from Germany and Austria is consistent with Sellin's study of postwar murder trends in nine European nations (1926) and with a much broader comparative study by Archer and Gartner (1976) on the impact on homicide rates of a country's participation in war. Archer and Gartner's general procedure is to compare average homicide rates during the five years before the outbreak of war with rates during the first five postwar years. Their comparisons for fourteen of the combatant nations in World War I show postwar increases greater than 10 percent (and averaging 40 percent) in eight of the fourteen; unchanged rates in two; and substantial declines in three. They find even stronger evidence for homicide increases after World War II. Among fifteen combatant nations homicide rates in-

---

[14] These conclusions about the relation of modernization to assault rates are not necessarily invalidated by my suggestion that the upward trend in nineteenth-century assault rates was probably spurious. It is plausible that rapid industrialization and urban growth could cause substantial short-term increases in assault rates in particular jurisdictions, increases superimposed on a longer run decline. It is the upward surge and then subsidence of rates at the onset of modernization that is the essential evidence for arguments advanced by Zehr and McHale and Johnson, not the underlying trend.

338   Ted Robert Gurr

creased substantially in eleven, by an average of 89 percent.[15]
Rates were unchanged in one and lower in three others (Archer
and Gartner 1976, p. 947). The data on these and other nations
which participated in twentieth-century wars are used to test
alternative hypotheses about why war leads so often to increases in homicide. Explanations which focus on social disorganization, economic stress, and the violence of war veterans
are found insufficient to account for homicide increases, and the
authors conclude, without direct test, that the most plausible
explanation is "that wars... tend to legitimate the general use
of violence in domestic society" (1976, p. 958).

Aside from studies of the impact of war on crime, not much
attention has been given to crime trends in Europe from the
1920s through the 1950s.[16] Reference was made above to
studies of Stockholm and New South Wales (Sydney) showing
low and stable rates of offenses against persons for most of this
period (Gurr, Grabosky, and Hula 1977, pp. 282–85, 438–43).
What is strikingly absent from these studies, and those of
British and American crime trends reviewed above, is evidence
of increases in personal crime during the Great Depression of
the 1930s. *Property* offenses evidently increased, especially in
Britain (see Gurr, Grabosky, and Hula 1977, pp. 118–24), but
homicide and assault were at or near their lowest recorded
levels in virtually all countries and jurisdictions. In the United
States, homicide rates *declined* substantially during the depression era (see fig. 2, above).[17]

The "crime waves" in the European countries most affected
by World War II had largely subsided by 1950. The most re-

[15] A study of trends in violent crimes known to police in Japan during and after
World War II provides detailed evidence of these dynamics. Homicides declined
sharply from ca. 2,500 in 1935 to about 1,000 per annum in the early 1940s, then soared
above 3,000 in the early 1950s before beginning a long, gradual decline, falling below
2,000 by the early 1970s. Robbery, an uncommon offense in prewar Japan (less than
2,000 cases annually) increased by 700 percent immediately after the war, and then
declined to 2,000 by the early 1970s (Lunden 1976).

[16] My bibliographic search for trend studies has been confined largely to those published in English. Undoubtedly there are crime-trend studies of continental countries in
other languages which escaped my attention.

[17] This decline may be attributable to the end of Prohibition in 1933. The high
homicide rates of the 1920s were partly the result of conflict over the control of illegal
alcohol (see Zahn 1980, pp. 115–17).

markable subsequent phenomenon is the near universality of rising crime during the period of unprecedented prosperity of the 1960s and early 1970s. The British and North American experience was by no means unique. The late 1940s and early 1950s marked the low ebb of crimes against persons in virtually every English-speaking country. Thereafter the trends were consistently upwards. The same was true of Scandinavia. In Stockholm after 1950 virtually every category of offense against persons and property skyrocketed. Some twenty-year increases in rates of offenses known to police are: murder and attempts, 600 percent; assault and battery, more than 300 percent; rape and attempted rape, 300 percent; robberies, 1000 percent. Stockholm experienced in more serious form a malaise that affected all the Scandinavian countries beginning somewhat later, in the 1960s rather than the 1950s. Elsewhere in continental Europe the trends in personal crimes were somewhat different. The model pattern, evident in convictions data from West Germany, Austria, and France, was one in which offense rates declined from postwar peaks through the 1950s and 1960s but turned sharply upward after 1970. Switzerland is the only European country whose rates of offenses against persons remained steady throughout this period (see Gurr 1977, 1979).

One factor which may help account for the differential timing of increases in personal crimes among Western countries is the shape and timing of the "baby boom" which followed World War II. All records of crime in Western societies, past and present, show that young males are disproportionately represented among offenders. The coming of age of the postwar generation of youths is closely linked to the onset of major increases in personal and property crime in the United States and Britain, as is evident from Ferdinand's study of demographic and crime changes in the United States from 1950 to 1965 (1970) and from the graphs which relate the changing size of the youthful population with offense rates in these two countries in my recent essay (Gurr 1979, pp. 368–69). But the shape and timing of the "age bulge" differ among Western societies. In Britain and the United States, the proportion of the population aged 15 to 29 increased by roughly 50 percent between the mid-1950s and the mid-1970s. Germany and Austria, by contrast, had baby "boomlets" which were smaller than those of the United States and Britain and which began after economic recovery set in during the 1950s. The precise nature of this relationship needs to be specified more precisely and studied longitudinally using demographic and crime data for each Western country. For an exemplary study see Zimring (1979).

The upward trend in violent crime since the 1960s thus seems most pronounced in the English-speaking and Scandinavian countries but it is by no means universal. Among Western democracies it is notably absent in Switzerland, perhaps because of the sociocultural factors specified by Clinard (1978), in Italy, and in Israel (see Gurr 1977, pp. 69–70). Japan has had a steady decline in serious offenses against persons and property since the mid-1950s (see Lunden 1976; Gurr 1977, pp. 69–73), which Bayley (1976) attributes both to policing practices and cultural traits. Last but far from least, the statistical evidence from Eastern European countries, recently summarized by Redo (1980), shows little change in the incidence of violent crime between 1964 and 1977 despite significant increases in the population aged 15–24 in most of these countries.[18]

VI. Some Observations

How well does the U-shaped curve of declining, then rising violent crime fit the evidence reviewed here? The English evidence on homicide covers the longest timespan and is the most convincing in documenting a sustained decline of substantial magnitude. By the same token it makes the post-1960 upturn appear to be a minor perturbation, proportionally no greater than upward swings in homicide rates in Elizabethan times and during the Napoleonic wars—swings which proved to be temporary. In the United States the occurrence of three great surges in violent crime, beginning ca. 1850, 1900, and 1960,

[18] Redo, a Polish scholar, implicitly accepts the accuracy of the official data. There is no prima facie why the homicide and assault data should be misreported for the sake of gilding the official portrait of socialist reality, and even if they are systematically underreported, that should not invalidate the assessment of their trends.

makes it impossible to say whether these increases are superimposed on a long-term decline. My reading of the evidence is that the long-term trend in homicide rates among whites has been generally downward until recently, whereas homicide rates among blacks not only have been higher and more variable but have moved generally upward since the beginning of the twentieth century, perhaps earlier. Declines in homicidal violence also are established for nineteenth-century Stockholm, New South Wales, France, and—beginning late in the century—Germany. In general we have not seen any evidence from any country or jurisdiction that there was a sustained increase in homicides during the nineteenth century—with the important codicil that most of the time-series studies span only the second half of the century. An increase in homicide rates since the 1960s is also a common though not universal phenomenon in Western societies. The exceptions are some continental democracies which began later or avoided the trend entirely. Moreover the increase is specific to Western democracies: Eastern European states and Japan have had steady or declining homicide rates.

The evidence on assault and robbery is more limited but in general parallels the trends in homicide. That is strikingly evident in countries which experienced the post-1960 increase in crime: robbery and assault rates usually increased much more than homicide. In the nineteenth century, however, assault rates moved contrary to homicides in France, Germany, and some American jurisdictions. There is reason to attribute this to increased official attention to minor offenses, not to real and sustained increases in assault.

The discussion of trend evidence has touched on a number of explanations for trends and variations around them. There are two separate questions for which explanation is needed. One is, What social dynamics underlie the long-term decline in violent crime? The other is, What accounts for the big deviations of crime above this trend, especially those sustained upwellings of violence that persist for ten or twenty or more years before subsiding again? I think that there is a simple and singular answer to

342   Ted Robert Gurr

the first question, but multiple and complex answers to the second. I also think that no special, *sui generis* explanation is needed for the late increase in violent crime. Its explanation should follow from an understanding of the dynamics of the long-term decline and of the deviations from it. In other words I propose to regard the upturn of the U-shaped curve as simply the latest, and best-documented, deviation from the underlying trend.

A plausible explanation for the long-term decline in interpersonal violence is what Norbert Elias calls "the civilizing process" (1978) and all that it implies about the restraint of aggressive impulses and the acceptance of humanistic values.[19] By their own accounts, medieval Europeans were easily angered to the point of violence and enmeshed in a culture which accepted, even glorified, many forms of brutality and aggressive behavior (see Given 1977, chap. 1 for a summary; also Elias 1978, pp. 191–205). The progress of Western civilization has been marked by increasing internal and external controls on the show of violence. People are socialized to control and displace anger. Norms of conduct in almost all organized activity stress non-violent means of accomplishing goals. Interpersonal violence within the community and nation is prohibited and subject to sanction in almost all circumstances. The process is in essence a cultural one and like most cultural change had its origins in the changing values of social and intellectual elites. The process, so far as it pertains to violence, contributed not only to the decline in homicide and assault but also to the humanization and rationalization of social policy. It led, for example, to the decline and ultimate abandonment of executions in most Western nations, the end of slavery and the brutalization of wage labor, the passing of corporal punishment in schools and prisons, and many other humane features of contemporary life that are often taken for granted (on the effects of humanitarian thought on criminal justice policies see Gurr, Grabosky, and Hula 1977, chap. V.5).

[19] The following discussion is drawn largely from the conclusion to my 1979 essay on the same topic (Gurr 1979, pp. 365–71).

343   Historical Trends in Violent Crime

The cultural process of sensitization to violence, to use Soman's phrase (1980, pp. 20–23), has not been uniform. It took
root first among the urban upper and middle classes and only
gradually and selectively was promulgated among rural people
and the lower classes. It has been suggested, for example, that
one significant social function of the new nineteenth-century
police forces was to serve as missionaries of upper and middle
class values to the theretofore dangerous lower classes (see for
example Silver 1967 and Monkkonen 1975). Be that as it may,
the thesis that sensitization to violence spread from the social
center to the periphery and from upper to lower classes is in-
trinsically plausible as an explanation of some basic features of
nineteenth-century and contemporary criminality. Interpersonal violence historically may have been higher in rural
than urban areas—the evidence is mixed—because of the persistence there of traditional patterns of interpersonal behavior.
It tended to increase in cities during the early stages of urbanization and industrialization because new immigrants from the
countryside, or from overseas, only gradually assimilated the
lifeways of the city. Violence declined overall during the
nineteenth century and the first half of the twentieth because
Western societies became increasingly urban and formal education became universal. The further down the class and status
ladder, past and present, the more common is interpersonal
violence, because the lower classes did not assimilate and still
have not wholly assimilated the aggression-inhibiting values of
the middle and upper classes. And the black minority in the
United States has far higher rates of interpersonal violence than
the white majority because the barriers of discrimination and
segregation have fostered a subculture which encourages aggressive behavior.

There is one other group that may become *de*sensitized to
violence: youth. The historical process of sensitization to violence must be replicated in the socialization of each new generation of children in each Western society. To the extent that
socialization fails, or is incomplete because it is not reinforced

344   Ted Robert Gurr

by other social institutions, youth are susceptible to other kinds
of values, including those which celebrate violence. This is a
potential factor in the generation of violent behavior which
stands independently of, but is reinforced by, the social fact
that young males are in general more likely to be caught up in
interpersonal violence, as offenders and victims, than any other
demographic category.

The long-run downslope of interpersonal violence is irregular
and some of the irregularities take the form of sharp and sustained increases. I referred above to the evidence, mainly from
studies of France and Germany, that violent crime tends to rise
in the early stages of industrialization and urbanization, though
there is little evidence that the pace of urban growth in general
has affected rates of violent crime. Modernization may have
been one of the sources of high rates of violent crime in early
nineteenth-century England and in the United States in the
1860s and 1870s. But urbanization and industrialization usually
are gradual processes, not likely of themselves to create a single
tidal wave of disorder except in regions and cities experiencing
very rapid change.

The connection between warfare and waves of violent crime
is more precise. In fact, war is the single most obvious correlate
of the great historical waves of violent crime in England and the
United States. Civil and foreign war contributed to the crime
peak of the 1340s (Hanawalt 1979, pp. 228–39). A mid-
eighteenth-century wave of crime coincided with Britain's involvement in a succession of wars from 1739 (war with Spain)
to 1763 (the end of the Seven Years' War). The upsurge of
crime at the onset of the nineteenth century began while Britain
was enmeshed in the Napoleonic wars, from 1793 to 1815, and
continued through the severe economic depression which followed their end. In the United States the peak of urban crime
in the 1860s and 1870s coincides with the social and political
upheavals of the Civil War. The disproportionate fondness for
dueling and less genteel forms of violence among white south-
erners may not have originated with the Civil War (see

Hackney 1969; Gastil 1971), but surely it was reinforced by it. The second high wave of violent American crime crested during the decade after World War I. The third began near the onset of the Vietnam war. Lesser increases in violent crime coincided with or followed both world wars in Britain, the United States, and most continental democracies. We also noted the great increase in violent crime which followed Germany and Austria's defeat in World War I.

War may lead to increased violent crime for a number of reasons, reviewed and tested by Archer and Gartner (1976). I opt for the interpretation, consistent with their evidence, that it does so mainly because war legitimizes violence. It does so directly for young men who become habituated to violence in military service; it does so indirectly for others who find in the patriotic gore of wartime a license to act out their own feelings of anger. The interpretation is difficult to prove. But it is consistent both with the evidence on crime trends and with the social dynamics proposed for the long-run decline in interpersonal violence: if the civilizing process has been accompanied by sensitization to violence, then war, including internal war, temporarily desensitizes people to violence. If there is such an effect it is probably greatest among youth who are at the most impressionable age during wartime. This suggests that the argument could be tested indirectly by careful study of changes in age-specific rates of arrests for violent offenses during periods following war.

Another basic factor that influences the extent of personal crime is the size of the youthful population. If their relative numbers are high in a particular city or era, its crime rates are likely to be higher than in times and places where the population is older. Hanawalt, for example, suggests that some of medieval England's high incidence of homicide may have been due to the fact that it had a relatively youthful population (1979, p. 127). It is also the case that if the relative number of young males increases substantially in a short time, so will crime against both person and property. Such changes have oc-

346   Ted Robert Gurr

curred periodically in Western societies, often as a consequence of socioeconomic change or war. A population boom was underway in England during the first half of the nineteenth century, thanks to better nutrition and higher birth rates. As one result there was a remarkably high proportion of young males in London's population. Over the long run, 1801 to 1971, the changing proportions of males aged 15 to 29 in London's population trace a time-path very similar to, though of much lower amplitude than, the time-path of felonies (Gurr, Grabosky, and Hula 1977, p. 43). The explosion in youth crime in the 1960s and 1970s also is closely linked to substantial changes in the age structures of the United States, Britain, and most other Western societies, as noted in the preceding section.

The strands of this speculative discussion can be brought together by concluding that each great upsurge of violent crime in the histories of the societies under study has been caused by a distinctive combination of altered social forces. Some crime waves have followed from fundamental social dislocation, as a result of which significant segments of a population have been separated from the civilizing institutions which instill and reinforce the basic Western injunctions against interpersonal violence. They may be migrants, demobilized veterans, a growing population of disillusioned young people for whom there is no social or economic niche, or badly educated young black men locked in the decaying ghettoes of an affluent society. The most devastating episodes of public disorder, however, seem to occur when social dislocation coincides with changes in values which legitimate violence that was once thought to be illegitimate. Historically, wars seem to have had this effect. There is also the possibility that other factors, such as the content of popular culture or the values articulated in segmented groups, may have the same consequences.

These conclusions are speculative and imprecise. I will conclude simply by expressing the hope that the next generation of research on trends in violent crimes will be as much concerned with testing these and competing kinds of general explanations as with description.

REFERENCES

Abbott, Edith. 1922. "Recent Statistics Relating to Crime in Chicago," *Journal of Criminal Law, Criminology, and Police Science* 13:329–58.

Archer, Dane, and Rosemary Gartner. 1976. "Violent Acts and Violent Times: A Comparative Approach to Postwar Homicide Rates," *American Sociological Review* 41:937–63.

Baldwin, John, and A. E. Bottoms. 1976. *The Urban Criminal: A Study in Sheffield*. London: Tavistock.

Bayley, David. 1976. *Forces of Order; Police Behavior in Japan and the United States*. Berkeley: University of California Press.

Beattie, J. M. 1974. "The Pattern of Crime in England, 1660–1800," *Past & Present* 62 (February): 47–95.

Block, Richard. 1977. *Violent Crime: Environment, Interaction, and Death*. Lexington, Mass.: Lexington Books.

Bloch, Herbert A., and Gilbert Geis. 1962. *Man, Crime, and Society: The Forms of Criminal Behavior*. New York: Random House.

Bonger, William. 1967. *Criminality and Economic Conditions*, trans. Henry P. Horton. New York: Agathon Press.

Boudouris, James. 1970. "Trends in Homicide, Detroit, 1926–1968." Ph.D. dissertation, Wayne State University.

Brearley, H. C. 1932. *Homicide in the United States*. Chapel Hill: University of North Carolina Press.

Brenner, M. Harvey. 1976. *Effects of the Economy on Criminal Behaviour and the Administration of Criminal Justice in the United States, Canada, England and Wales and Scotland*. Rome: United Nations Social Defence Research Institute.

Clinard, Marshall B. 1978. *Cities with Little Crime*. New York: Cambridge University Press.

Cockburn, J. S. 1977. "The Nature and Incidence of Crime in England, 1559–1625: A Preliminary Survey." In *Crime in England 1550–1800*, ed. J. S. Cockburn. Princeton: Princeton University Press.

Cohen, Lawrence E., and Marcus Felson. 1979. "Social Change and Crime Rate Trends: A Routine Activity Approach," *American Sociological Review* 44:588–607.

Cohen, Lawrence E., Marcus Felson, and Kenneth C. Land. 1980. "Property Crime in the United States: A Macrodynamic Analysis, 1947–1977; with Ex Ante Forecasts for the Mid-1980s," *American Journal of Sociology* 86:90–118.

Count–van Manen, Gloria. 1977. *Crime and Suicide in the Nation's Capital: Toward Macro-Historical Perspectives*. New York: Praeger.

Dunham, H. Warren, and Asuman Kiyak. 1975. "Cultural Change and Homicide: An Interrelationship." Unpublished paper summarized in Count–van Manen 1977, p. 40.

Elias, Norbert. 1978. *The Civilizing Process: The History of Manners.* New York: Urizen. (Originally published 1939.)

Ellwood, Charles A. 1910. "Has Crime Increased in the United States Since 1880?" *Journal of Criminal Law and Criminology* 1:378–85.

Exner, Franz. 1927. *Krieg und Kriminalität in Österreich.* Vienna: Hölder-Pichler-Tempsky; New Haven: Yale University Press.

Ferdinand, Theodore N. 1967. "The Criminal Patterns of Boston since 1869," *American Journal of Sociology* 73:688–98.

———. 1970. "Demographic Shifts and Criminality: An Inquiry," *British Journal of Criminology* 10:169–75.

———. 1972. "Politics, the Police, and Arresting Policies in Salem, Massachusetts since the Civil War," *Social Problems* 19:572–88.

Gastil, Raymond D. 1971. "Homicide and a Regional Culture of Violence," *American Sociological Review* 36:412–26.

Gatrell, V. A. C. 1980. "The Decline of Theft and Violence in Victorian and Edwardian England." In *Crime and the Law since 1850*, ed. V. A. C. Gatrell, B. P. Lenman, and G. Parker. London: Europa.

Gatrell, V. A. C., and T. B. Hadden. 1972. "Criminal Statistics and Their Interpretation." In *Nineteenth Century Society: Essays in the Use of Quantitative Methods for the Study of Social Data*, ed. E. A. Wrigley. Cambridge: Cambridge University Press.

Giffen, P. J. 1965. "Rates of Crime and Delinquency." In *Crime and Its Treatment in Canada*, ed. W. T. McGrath. New York: St. Martin's Press.

Given, James Buchanan. 1977. *Society and Homicide in Thirteenth-Century England.* Stanford: Stanford University Press.

Glaser, Daniel, and Kent Rice. 1959. "Crime, Age, and Employment," *American Sociological Review* 24:679–86.

Gould, Leroy C. 1969. "The Changing Structure of Property Crime in an Affluent Society," *Social Forces* 48:50–60.

———. 1971. "Crime and its Impact in an Affluent Society." In *Crime and Justice in American Society*, ed. Jack D. Douglas. Indianapolis: Bobbs-Merrill.

Grabosky, Peter N. 1976. *Sydney in Ferment: Crime, Dissent, and Official Reaction, 1788–1973.* Canberra: Australian National University Press.

Greenberg, Douglas. 1976. *Crime and Law Enforcement in the Colony of New York, 1691–1776.* Ithaca: Cornell University Press.

Gurr, Ted Robert. 1977. "Crime Trends in Modern Democracies since 1945," *International Annals of Criminology* 16:41–85.

349   Historical Trends in Violent Crime

————. 1979. "On the History of Violent Crime in Europe and America." In *Violence in America: Historical and Comparative Perspectives*, ed. Hugh David Graham and Ted Robert Gurr. 2d ed. Beverly Hills: Sage Publications.

————. 1980. "Development and Decay: Their Impact on Public Order in Western History." In *History and Crime: Implications for Criminal Justice Policy*, ed. James A. Inciardi and Charles E. Faupel. Beverly Hills: Sage Publications.

Gurr, Ted Robert, Peter N. Grabosky, and Richard C. Hula. 1977. *The Politics of Crime and Conflict: A Comparative History of Four Cities*. Beverly Hills: Sage Publications.

Hackney, Sheldon. 1969. "Southern Violence," *American Historical Review* 76:906–25.

Hair, P. E. H. 1971. "Deaths from Violence in Britain: A Tentative Secular Survey," *Population Studies* 25:5–24.

Hammer, Carl I., Jr. 1978. "Patterns of Homicide in a Medieval University Town: Fourteenth-Century Oxford," *Past & Present* 78 (February): 3–23.

Hanawalt, Barbara A. 1976. "Violent Death in Fourteenth- and Early Fifteenth-Century England," *Comparative Studies in Society and History* 18:297–320.

————. 1979. *Crime and Conflict in English Communities, 1300–1348*. Cambridge, Mass.: Harvard University Press.

Harrison, Leonard V. 1934. *Police Administration in Boston*. Cambridge, Mass: Harvard University Press.

Hay, Douglas, Peter Linebaugh, John G. Rule, E. P. Thompson, and Cal Winslow. 1975. *Albion's Fatal Tree: Crime and Society in Eighteenth-Century England*. New York: Pantheon Books.

Henry, Andrew F., and James F. Short, Jr. 1954. *Suicide and Homicide: Some Economic, Sociological, and Psychological Aspects of Aggression*. New York: Free Press of Glencoe.

Hindus, Michael Stephen. 1980. *Prison and Plantation: Crime, Justice, and Authority in Massachusetts and South Carolina, 1767–1878*. Chapel Hill: University of North Carolina Press.

Hirsch, Charles S., Norman B. Rushforth, Amasa B. Ford, and Lester Adelson. 1973. "Homicide and Suicide in a Metropolitan County. I. Long-Term Trends," *Journal of the American Medical Association* 223:900–905.

Hobbs, A. H. 1943. "Relationship between Criminality and Economic Conditions," *Journal of Criminal Law, Criminology, and Police Science* 34:5–10.

Hoffman, F. L. 1925. *The Homicide Problem*. Newark: Prudential Press.

350   Ted Robert Gurr

————. 1928. "Murder and the Death Penalty," *Current History* 28:408–10.

Jacob, Herbert, and Robert L. Lineberry. 1980. "Cities and Crime." Paper read at the 1980 meeting of the Social Science History Association, Rochester, N.Y.

————. Forthcoming. *Governmental Responses to Crime*.

Jacob, Herbert, and Michael J. Rich. 1980. "The Effects of the Police on Crime: A Second Look." Paper read at the 1980 meeting of the Law and Society Association, San Francisco.

Jacobson, Alvin L. 1975. "Crime Rates in Southern and Nonsouthern Cities: A Twenty-Year Perspective," *Social Forces* 54:226–42.

Kaye, J. M. 1967. "The Early History of Murder and Manslaughter," *Law Quarterly Review* 83:365–95.

Lane, Roger. 1968. "Crime and Criminal Statistics in Nineteenth Century Massachusetts," *Journal of Social History* 2:156–63.

————. 1979. *Violent Death in the City: Suicide, Accident, and Murder in Nineteenth-Century Philadelphia*. Cambridge, Mass.: Harvard University Press.

————. 1980. "Urban Police and Crime in Nineteenth-Century America," *Crime and Justice* 2:1–44.

Liepmann, Moritz. 1930. *Krieg und Kriminalität in Deutschland*. Stuttgart, Berlin, and Leipzig: Deutsche Verlags-Anstalt; New Haven: Yale University Press.

Lodhi, Abdul Qaiyum, and Charles Tilly. 1973. "Urbanization, Crime, and Collective Violence in 19th-Century France," *American Journal of Sociology* 79:296–318.

Loftin, Colin, and Robert H. Hill. 1974. "Regional Subculture and Homicide: An Examination of the Gastil-Hackney Thesis," *American Sociological Review* 39:714–724.

Lunden, Walter A. 1976. "Violent Crimes in Japan in War and Peace, 1933–74," *International Journal of Criminology and Penology* 4:349–63.

Lundsgaarde, Henry P. 1977. *Murder in Space City: A Cultural Analysis of Houston Homicide Patterns*. New York: Oxford University Press.

McClintock, F. H. 1963. *Crimes of Violence: An Enquiry by the Cambridge Institute of Criminology into Crimes of Violence against the Person in London*. London: Macmillan.

McClintock, F. H., and N. Howard Avison with G. N. G. Rose. 1968. *Crime in England and Wales*. London: Heinemann.

MacDonald, Arthur. 1910. "Criminal Statistics in Germany, France and England," *Journal of Criminal Law and Criminology* 1:59–70.

McHale, Vincent E., and Eric A. Johnson. 1976. "Urbanization, Industrialization, and Crime in Imperial Germany: Part I," *Social Science History* 1:45–78.

————. 1977. "Urbanization, Industrialization, and Crime in Imperial

351   Historical Trends in Violent Crime

Germany: Part II," *Social Science History* 1:210–47.

McNeill, William H. 1976. *Plagues and Peoples*. New York: Double-day, Anchor Books.

Monkkonen, Eric. 1975. *The Dangerous Class: Crime and Poverty in Columbus, Ohio, 1860–1885*. Cambridge, Mass.: Harvard University Press.

———. 1979. "A Disorderly People? Urban Order in the Nineteenth and Twentieth Centuries." Paper read at the 1979 meetings of the American Studies Association, Minneapolis.

———. 1980. "The Quantitative Historical Study of Crime and Criminal Justice." In *History and Crime: Implications for Criminal Justice Policy*, ed. James A. Inciardi and Charles E. Faupel. Beverly Hills: Sage Publications.

———. 1981. *Police in Urban America, 1860–1920*. New York: Cambridge University Press.

Mulvilhill, Donald, and Melvin Tumin. 1969. *Crimes of Violence, Report to the National Commission on the Causes and Prevention of Violence*. Vol. 11. Washington, D.C.: Government Printing Office.

Nutt, Harry G. 1905. "Homicide in New Hampshire," *Journal of the American Statistical Association* 9:220–30.

Peirce, David, Peter N. Grabosky, and Ted Robert Gurr. 1977. "London: The Politics of Crime and Conflict, 1800 to the 1970's." In *The Politics of Crime and Conflict: A Comparative History of Four Cities*, by Ted Robert Gurr, Peter N. Grabosky, and Richard C. Hula. Beverly Hills: Sage Publications.

Powell, Elwin H. 1966. "Crime as a Function of Anomie," *Journal of Criminal Law, Criminology, and Police Science* 57:161–71.

———. 1970. *The Design of Discord: Studies of Anomie: Suicide, Urban Society, War*. New York: Oxford University Press.

Redo, Slawomir M. 1980. "Crime Trends and Crime Prevention Strategies in Eastern Europe." Paper read to the Sixth United Nations Congress on the Prevention of Crime and the Treatment of Offenders, Caracas.

Samaha, Joel. 1974. *Law and Order in Historical Perspective: The Case of Elizabethan Essex*. New York and London: Academic Press.

Seidman, David, and Michael Couzens. 1974. "Getting the Crime Rate Down: Political Pressure and Crime Reporting," *Law and Society* 10:457–93.

Sellin, Thorsten. 1926. "Is Murder Increasing in Europe?" *Annals of the American Academy of Political and Social Science* 126:29–34.

Shelley, Louise I. 1981. *Crime and Modernization: The Impact of Industrialization and Urbanization on Crime*. Carbondale: Southern Illinois University Press.

Silver, Allan. 1967. "The Demand for Order in Civil Society: A Re-

352   Ted Robert Gurr

view of Some Themes in the History of Urban Crime, Police, and Riot." In *The Police: Six Sociological Essays*, ed. David J. Bordua. New York: John Wiley and Sons.

Skogan, Wesley G. 1975. "Measurement Problems in Official and Survey Crime Rates," *Journal of Criminal Justice* 3:17–32.

———. 1976. "Citizen Reporting of Crime: Some National Panel Data," *Criminology* 13:535–49.

———. 1977. "The Changing Distribution of Big-City Crime: A Multi-City Time Series Analysis," *Urban Affairs Quarterly* 13:33–47.

———. 1979. "Crime in Contemporary America." In *Violence in America: Historical and Comparative Perspectives*, ed. Hugh Davis Graham and Ted Robert Gurr. 2d ed. Beverly Hills: Sage Publications.

Soman, Alfred. 1980. "Deviance and Criminal Justice in Western Europe, 1300–1800: An Essay in Structure," *Criminal Justice History: An International Annual* 1:1–28.

Stanciu, V. V. 1968. *La Criminalité à Paris*. Paris: Centre National de la Recherche Scientifique.

Sutherland, E. H. 1925. "Murder and the Death Penalty," *Journal of the American Institute of Criminal Law and Criminology* 15:522–29.

Sutherland, E. H., and C. E. Gehlke. 1933. "Crime and Punishment." In *Recent Social Trends in the United States*, Report of the President's Research Committee on Social Trends. New York: McGraw-Hill.

Thomas, Dorothy Swaine. 1925. *Social Aspects of the Business Cycle*. New York: E. P. Dutton.

Thorner, Thomas. 1979. "The Incidence of Crime in Southern Alberta, 1878–1905." In *Law and Society in Canada in Historical Perspective*, ed. D. J. Bercuson and L. A. Knafla. Calgary: University of Calgary.

Tilly, Charles, Allan Levett, A. Q. Lodhi, and Frank Munger. n.d. [ca. 1974]. "How Policing Affected the Visibility of Crime in Nineteenth-Century Europe and America." Unpublished paper.

Warner, Sam Bass. 1934. *Crime and Criminal Statistics in Boston*. Cambridge, Mass.: Harvard University Press.

Watts, Reginald E. 1931. "The Influence of Population Density on Crime," *Journal of the American Statistical Association* 26:11–20.

Willbach, Harry. 1938. "The Trend of Crime in New York City," *Journal of Criminal Law and Criminology* 29:62–75.

———. 1941. "The Trend of Crime in Chicago," *Journal of Criminal Law and Criminology* 31:720–27.

Wolfgang, Marvin E. 1958. *Patterns in Criminal Homicide*. Oxford: Oxford University Press.

353   Historical Trends in Violent Crime

Zahn, Margaret A. 1980. "Homicide in the Twentieth Century United States." In *History and Crime: Implications for Criminal Justice Policy*, ed. James A. Inciardi and Charles E. Faupel. Beverly Hills: Sage Publications.

Zehr, Howard. 1975. "The Modernization of Crime in Germany and France, 1830–1913," *Journal of Social History* 8:117–41.

————. 1976. *Crime and the Development of Modern Society: Patterns of Criminality in Nineteenth Century Germany and France*. Totowa, N.J.: Rowan and Littlefield.

Zimring, Franklin E. 1979. "American Youth Violence: Issues and Trends," *Crime and Justice* 1:67–108.

ADDENDUM

After this essay was in proof an exhaustive new study of Australian crime trends came to my attention: Satyanshu K. Mukherjee, *Crime Trends in Twentieth Century Australia* (Sydney: Allen and Unwin, forthcoming in 1981). Using newly compiled data on cases charged before magistrates' courts, the charging rates of various offenses are traced nationally and for each of six states. Offenses against persons, consisting mainly of petty assaults, show a distinctive U or dish-shaped curve from 1900 to 1976, nationally and in most states. The national rate declined from ca. 300 offenses charged per 100,000 population aged 10 years and over at the beginning of the century to a low of ca. 110 in the late 1930s, followed by an increase to ca. 300 again in the mid-1970s. Separate analyses for assaults and rape show the same general reversing trend. Homicides trace a less pronounced, more irregular trend whose increase since the 1950s is due at least in part to automotive manslaughters. Robberies charged had no clear trend until the 1960s, when they began a threefold increase. Time-series correlation analysis shows that offenses against persons in Australia tend to vary positively both with size of the police force (because of proactive policing?) and with economic productivity.

[4]

WHY DOES CRIME DECREASE?

DAVID P. FARRINGTON and
ELIZABETH A. DOWDS*

Traditionally, the annual publication of the Home Office *Criminal Statistics for England and Wales* has been greeted with a mixture of sorrow and anger. The reason for this is easy to see. Like the cost of living, the number of crimes recorded by the police seems to keep on rising inexorably. From 1954, when the number of recorded indictable crimes was 456,000, to the 1982 figure of 3,262,000, the yearly crime figures decreased on only three occasions out of 28. From half a million in 1956, the million mark was passed in 1963, two million in 1975 and three million in 1982. The publication of the 1982 *Criminal Statistics* in October, 1983, showed a 10.1% inflation rate in comparison with the previous year, quite similar to the 10.3% increase seen in 1981. If this rate of increase was maintained throughout the 1980s, the number of recorded offences in 1990 would exceed seven million.

Fortunately, the publication of the 1983 *Criminal Statistics* towards the end of 1984 will show that notifiable crimes *decreased* between 1982 and 1983, by about 0.5% or over 15,000 crimes (according to a Home Office statistical bulletin published in March). Is this marginal decrease merely a temporary aberration, or has crime finally stopped increasing? Unfortunately, another statistical bulletin published in June shows that, in the first quarter of 1984, notifiable crimes increased again, by about 5% in comparison with the first quarter of 1983. However, even if the decline in 1983 does prove to have been temporary, it is still important to try to explain it. Criminologists are used to explaining increases in recorded crime, but decreases present a new challenge.

Of course, crime may have decreased in reality in 1983. However, there are many other possible reasons why recorded crime rates might decrease, such as changes in the law leading to decriminalization, a lower probability of crime reporting by members of the public, or a lower probability of recording by the police. Changes in the law can be ruled out as an explanation for the decrease in 1983. The major legislative change (the Criminal Justice Act 1982, brought into effect on May 24, 1983) did not alter the definition of what is or is not a (notifiable or indictable) crime. In contrast, changes in the law have clearly contributed to past increases in recorded crimes. This was true, for example, of the Theft Act 1968, which converted taking and driving away a

* Mr. Farrington is a Lecturer in Criminology at Cambridge University. Miss Dowds is now a Social Survey Officer at the Office of Population Censuses and Surveys. The research project described here was sponsored by Nottinghamshire County Council. A detailed, technical report of it will be published later this year as a chapter in *Reactions to Crime: the Public, the Police, Courts and Prisons*, edited by David P. Farrington and John Gunn (Chichester: Wiley).

vehicle into an indictable offence, and the Criminal Damage Act 1971, which converted previously non-indictable malicious damage into indictable criminal damage. There was a change in Home Office counting rules between 1982 and 1983, in that two new offences (gross indecency with a child and trafficking in controlled drugs) were included in the 1983 figures, but this would have tended to produce a negligible increase in recorded crimes.

Despite their known limitations (e.g. providing no information about crimes against organizations or victimless crimes, problems of remembering), repeated victim surveys are probably one of the best ways of estimating changes in "real" crime rates. When the latest results of the British Crime Survey are available, they should give some indication about changes in "real" crime between 1981 and 1983. Many reasons could be put forward why "real" crime might decrease, such as the increasing efficiency of the police, the success of community protection schemes such as "neighbourhood watch", or even decreasing prosperity leading to less property available to be stolen (since the majority of crimes are of theft or burglary). However, demographic changes provide a less often discussed but perhaps more plausible explanation.

Demographic changes as a fact in crime rates
The highest rates of detected offending are concentrated among young males aged 14-20. In 1982, there were at least six convictions or cautions for indictable offences per 100 males of each age from 14 to 20 in England and Wales, as opposed to comparable rates of only 2.3 for all males and 0.4 for all females. Males aged 14-20 comprised less than 7% of the population aged 10 or over but accounted for more than 37% of detected offenders. If each offender in this category committed more crimes on average than offenders in other age and sex categories, it is not inconceivable that males aged 14-20 could account for at least half of all crimes committed. Therefore, the overall "real" crime rate is likely to be considerably affected by the number of males of this age in the population at any given time. The number of males aged 14-20 reached a peak of over 2.9 million in 1981-82, increasing steadily from the trough of 2.4 million in 1969-70.

In the past, changes in recorded crime rates have not been highly correlated with demographic changes, presumably because other factors (such as changes in police recording practices) have been more influential. However, if demographic factors influence "real" crime rates, and if police recording practices become more standardized, demographic factors may become more important predictors of recorded crime in the future. The number of males aged 14-20 fell by 0.5 % between 1982 and 1983. By 1986, when the bulge of persons aged 17-18 in 1982 has moved into their 20s, the number of males aged 14-20 will be 5% below the peak, and by the mid-1990s the decrease will exceed 25%. By 1990, when the Home

Secretary should be able to announce the completion of a prison building programme leading to a significant increase in institutional capacity, the number of young males who are most at risk of penal incarceration will be declining fast. By then, we could all be talking about the crisis of prison undercrowding, since the cost per inmate per year rises steeply as prisons become less crowded! (However, the Judges and magistrates may save us from this crisis by increasing the probability or length of incarceration).

The causes of the slight decline in recorded crime between 1982 and 1983 are not immediately obvious, but seem most likely to be related to fluctuations in police practices. The increasing computerization of police forces in the last few years has greatly reduced the scope for "cuffing" crimes (i.e. not recording alleged offences reported by the public). In many forces nowadays, the report of an alleged crime is entered directly from the telephone on to the force computer by a visual display unit operator. This development may be one reason for the large increase in recorded crimes from 1979-1982.

Unfortunately, the massive increase in recorded crimes has created problems for the police in dealing with them and clear-up rates, for example, have declined from 47% in 1973 to 37% in 1982. Therefore, it may be that some forces in 1983 decided to be more selective about the investigation of alleged crimes, concentrating resources on those which are more serious or more likely to be solved. This policy could lead to a reduction in the number of alleged crimes which are recorded as actual crimes by the police and hence sent to the Home Office to be included in the *Criminal Statistics*.

Fluctuations in recorded crime — Nottinghamshire experience
We do not know why recorded crime in the whole country decreased between 1982 and 1983, but we do know why it has been decreasing in one county — Nottinghamshire. Taken at face value, the *Criminal Statistics* for 1981 showed that Nottinghamshire was the most criminal area in the country. For several years, Nottinghamshire, the Metropolitan Police area and Merseyside had the three highest recorded crime rates in the country, and in 1981 Nottinghamshire regained the top position it had last held in 1977. Our research into the puzzling case of the high Nottinghamshire crime rate began in 1982. Between 1981 and 1982, whereas recorded crime in the whole country increased by 10%, in Nottinghamshire it stayed virtually unchanged, leading to a decline in Nottinghamshire's position in the "league table" of crime rates from first to fifth. In 1983, whereas recorded crime in the whole country fell by 0.5%, the decrease in Nottinghamshire was 5%, and in the first quarter of 1984, when crime increased by 5% overall, it decreased in Nottinghamshire by 6%. These decreases will lead to a further decline in Nottinghamshire's relative standing.

The aim of our research was to compare Notting-

508   JUSTICE OF THE PEACE, AUGUST 11, 1984   VOL.

hamshire with two other counties which were similar in many respects — Staffordshire and Leicestershire. According to the chief constables' reports, there were 87 recorded crimes per 100 population in Nottinghamshire in 1981, in comparison with 44 in Leicestershire and 40 in Staffordshire. We wanted to explain why Nottinghamshire was roughly twice as high as the other two counties.

There were basically four possible explanations:

(a)   more crimes were committed (in relation to population) in Nottinghamshire;
(b)   members of the public were more likely to report crimes to the police in Nottinghamshire;
(c)   the police were more likely to discover crimes in Nottinghamshire; and
(d)   an alleged crime which was discovered by or reported to the police was more likely to be recorded in Nottinghamshire.

In order to investigate (a) and (b), a random sample of about 1,000 adults in each county was interviewed and asked about crimes committed against them in the previous year and about whether these crimes were reported to the police. In order to investigate (c) and (d), police discovery and recording practices in the three counties were studied.

The crime survey (whose methodology was based on the British Crime Survey) indicated that the number of crimes committed in each county was far greater than the number recorded by the police: 407 per 1,000 in Nottinghamshire, in comparison with 326 in Leicestershire and 262 in Staffordshire. (These estimates included crimes against organizations and against persons under 16). The proportion of crimes reported to the police was almost exactly the same in each county, at about 40%. This led to an estimate of crimes reported to the police per 1,000 population of 162 in Nottinghamshire, 136 in Leicestershire and 102 in Staffordshire.

Comparing these figures with the recorded crime rates of 87, 44 and 40 (respectively) led to the conclusion that the ratio of recorded to reported crime was far higher in Nottinghamshire (53%) than in Leicestershire (32%) or Staffordshire (39%). If the probability of a crime known to the police being recorded had been 35% in all counties (the average of the Leicestershire and Staffordshire figures), the recorded crime rates per 1,000 population would have been 57 in Nottinghamshire, 48 in Leicestershire and 36 in Staffordshire. The police figures for Nottinghamshire were therefore about 30 crimes per 1,000 population higher than expected on the basis of the other two counties.

The study of police recording practices analyzed a 1% random sample of 1981 crime reports in each county (over 1,600 in all). The main aims of this analysis were to investigate the origin of each recorded crime (e.g. from citizen reports or police investigatory practices) and the characteristics of each (e.g. the value of property stolen). The types of crimes recorded in the three counties were quite similar.

Differences — admissions

One major difference between the counties was in crimes arising from admissions, where a person apprehended for one crime admitted others which had not previously been reported to or recorded by the police. About a quarter of Nottinghamshire's crime reports originated in this way, in comparison with 4% in Leicestershire and 8% in Staffordshire. The difference between the counties in crimes arising from admissions amounted to a difference of 18-20 crimes per 1,000 population.

— and crime seriousness

The second major difference between the counties was in the seriousness of recorded crimes. Nearly half of the crimes of dishonesty in Nottinghamshire involved property worth £10 or less, in comparison with 29% in Leicestershire and 36% in Staffordshire. Crimes arising from admissions were especially likely to involve property worth £10 or less (72%). It seemed likely that the Nottinghamshire police were more willing to record relatively trivial crimes than the other two forces.

Adding together crimes arising from admissions and those involving property worth £10 or less, the rate in Nottinghamshire for crimes in one or both of these categories was 43 per 1,000 population, or about half the county's crime rate. The corresponding figure for the other two counties was 12 in both cases. Therefore, these two effects together accounted for a difference of 31 crimes per 1,000 population between Nottinghamshire and the other two counties — almost exactly the excess identified in the crime survey.

We therefore concluded that, of the difference in recorded crime rates between Nottinghamshire and the other two counties of about 45 offences per 1,000 population, about two-thirds reflected differences in police recording practices, while about one-third reflected real differences in crimes committed.

Since our research began, and possibly in the light of our results, the Nottinghamshire police have changed their recording practices. In particular, they decided to spend less time questioning apprehended offenders about all their crimes, and so nowadays do not record so many trivial crimes arising on admission. This is one of the major reasons why recorded crime in Nottinghamshire decreased between 1981 and 1984. Police practices in Nottinghamshire are now more comparable to those in Leicestershire and Staffordshire.

Revealing the "iceberg" of hidden crime

On the basis of the crime survey, the Nottinghamshire crime rate was nearer the truth, and it could be that the Nottinghamshire police recording practices

(Continued on p.509 post)

(Continued from p.508 ante)
in 1981 were revealing more of the iceberg of hidden crime than those followed in the other two counties. The higher recorded crime rate in Nottinghamshire was not accompanied by a higher public fear of crime or by a lower public esteem for the police. In all three counties, the proportion of people who agreed that "taking everything into account, the police in this area do a good job" was in excess of 90%. Also, the likelihood of the public reporting crimes was virtually identical in all three counties. It seems likely that the police in many areas could greatly increase their recorded crime rate and reveal more of the iceberg of hidden crime by adopting the practices used in Nottinghamshire in 1981.

It is clear that police forces have a considerable ability to increase or decrease recorded crime rates by changing their practices. Such changes may explain not only the small decrease in 1983 but also the large increases seen in the last three decades. Criminologists have spent a great deal of time explaining why crime increases, and they should also attempt to explain decreases — however short-lived. The official statistics of recorded crimes are treated as real by the mass media and politicians and hence can have a real impact on government policy. Changes in them would be better understood if more research projects were carried out in which the results of crime surveys were compared with studies of police practices in the same areas.

[5]

HOME OFFICE RESEARCH AND STATISTICS DEPARTMENT

RESEARCH FINDINGS No.2

SURVEYING CRIME: FINDINGS FROM THE 1992 BRITISH CRIME SURVEY

Pat Mayhew and Natalie Aye Maung

The British Crime Survey (BCS) provides an index of crime in England and Wales to set beside the statistics recorded by the police. Many crimes are not reported to the police, and some that are reported go unrecorded. Recorded crime figures are thus an unreliable guide to the extent of crime. They can also be misleading about trends, as readiness to report crimes to the police varies over time. The BCS avoids this problem by asking people directly about their experience as victims.

KEY POINTS

▶ For those crime types that can be compared, recorded crime figures nearly doubled between 1981 and 1991, but the BCS suggests a lower rise of about 50%.

▶ Since 1987, recorded crime figures for the comparable sub-set of offences have risen particularly steeply - by 39% - whereas BCS crimes have risen by 14%.

▶ Since 1981, burglary and other thefts have risen broadly in line with recorded crime figures, but violent crime has risen more slowly and vandalism has hardly increased at all.

▶ Recorded crime shows a larger rise than the BCS largely because more crimes committed are now reported to the police, perhaps because of wider telephone ownership and insurance cover. For comparable crimes, 36% were reported in 1981 and 50% in 1991.

▶ The BCS estimated a total of 15 million crimes in 1991 against individuals and their property. For BCS crime types which can be compared with police statistics, incomplete reporting and recording mean that only 30% end up in police records.

▶ Vehicles are a very common target: one in five owners were victims of some sort of vehicle offence in 1991. 36% of all BCS crimes involved vehicles.

The BCS has been carried out in England and Wales in 1982, 1984, 1988 and 1992, measuring crime in the previous year. Each sweep interviewed a representative sample of over 10,000 people aged 16 and over. BCS estimates cannot provide a complete count of crime. Many crimes cannot be covered in household surveys, such as fraud, shoplifting, commercial burglary and drug offences. Crime surveys are also prone to various forms of error, mainly to do with the difficulty of ensuring that samples are representative, the frailty of respondents' memories, their reticence to talk about their experiences as victims, and their failure to realise an incident is relevant to the survey. In sum, the BCS does not claim to chart the 'true' level of crime; for some offence categories, however, it provides a better guide to the extent of crime and to trends than recorded crime figures.

BCS CRIMES IN 1992

The survey estimated a total of 15 million crimes in 1991 (see Table A, page 5). The estimates have been derived by applying survey rates to the England and Wales household and adult population. Most of the crimes counted by the survey were against property; 36% involved vehicles, 9% were burglaries and 30% other sorts of theft. Violent crime (wounding and robbery) accounted for 5% of the total, but common assaults, involving little or no injury, accounted for another 12%. Sexual offences have been omitted from results because trend data are unreliable.

REPORTING CRIME

Victims of crime are asked whether they reported what happened to the police. Of all BCS crimes in 1991, 43% were reported. Theft of vehicles and burglaries with loss were generally reported. Vandalism, theft from the person and attempted motor vehicle thefts were much less often brought to the attention of the police. Reporting rates are shown in Table C (page 6).

Crimes went unreported mainly because victims felt that they were not serious enough or that the police would be unable to take any effective action. But not all unreported crimes were trivial. Some involved substantial loss or injury, and were regarded by their victims as serious. Table 1 shows there has been an increase in reporting since 1981.

Table 1
Percentage of crimes reported to the police since 1981
All BCS offences

1981	1983	1987	1991
31%	34%	37%	43%

COMPARING BCS AND POLICE STATISTICS

Some 65% of BCS offences fall into categories which can be compared with crimes recorded by the police. This sub-set excludes common assaults, which are not recorded by the police, and 'other household thefts' and 'other personal thefts', which do not match any police categories. Various adjustments are made to recorded crime categories to maximise comparability with the BCS. (For example, crimes against those under 16 are excluded as they are not covered by the BCS. Recorded vehicle thefts are adjusted to exclude incidents involving commercial vehicles. And the large amount of vandalism against public and corporate

property is also excluded.)

In comparing trends for the comparable sub-set of crime categories, there are three relevant measures:

- The number of offences recorded by the police;
- BCS offences, whether or not reported to the police;
- BCS offences reported to the police (derived from applying the percentage of reported offences to the BCS total).

For various reasons, the police do not record all incidents reported to them. They may not always accept victims' accounts, or may question their interpretation of events. Some incidents may be considered too trivial to warrant a crime report. The BCS estimates that, for the sub-set of offences where direct comparisons can be made, around 60% of reported crimes in 1991 were recorded by the police. This estimate necessarily regards as unrecorded an unknown proportion of incidents defined by the BCS as falling within the comparable sub-set but actually recorded by the police in categories outside of the sub-set.

For the comparable sub-set in total, incomplete reporting and recording means that only 30% of BCS crimes ended up in police records. The figure was much higher for well reported offences such as thefts of vehicles and burglaries with loss, and rather lower, for instance, for vandalism and attempted offences. Figure 1 shows the proportion of BCS crimes recorded by the police for three categories of crime:

Acquisitive crime:	Burglary; all vehicle and bicycle theft; and thefts from the person.
Vandalism:	Against household property; and vehicles.
Violence:	Wounding and robbery.

Figure 1

Recorded and unrecorded crime, 1991

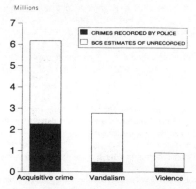

TRENDS SINCE 1981

Figure 2 shows trends in crime for the comparable sub-set of offences, with figures for 1981 indexed at 100. The number of recorded crimes rose by 96% between 1981 and 1991. BCS offences, whether reported or not, rose by 49%. The number of reported offences rose by just over 100%, reflecting partly the underlying growth, and partly an increase in reporting. (For the sub-set, the reporting rate rose from 36% in 1981 to 50% in 1991.) The result is that the dotted line in Figure 2, covering reported offences, shows a trend similar to that of police statistics.

Figure 2

Indexed trends in crime 1981 - 1991 comparable sub-set
(all 1981 rates = 100)

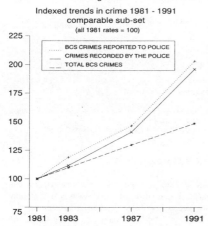

Within sub-groups of offences, the pattern is by no means consistent (Figure 3). Burglary and other thefts have grown since 1981 at a similar rate to recorded crime. Vandalism, on the other hand, and crimes of violence have increased much less rapidly than police statistics suggest, the latter being inflated by increased reporting.

Acquisitive crime

Acquisitive crimes, around two-thirds of the sub-set, have nearly doubled since 1981. Some types of offences have risen steeply, whether measured by the BCS or police statistics. Vehicle thefts of all kinds, including attempts, have more than doubled. Within this group, attempted thefts have risen most rapidly - 395% (BCS) and 336% (police statistics). This suggests not only that car thieves are more active, but that cars have become better protected - whether by manufacturers or owners. Burglary has risen by about three-quarters, according to both sources. Despite the parallel trends in acquisitive crime, the BCS shows that a greater proportion is now being reported. This implies that fewer reported crimes are being recorded, or that they are being recorded as other types of crime, such as vandalism.

Vandalism

Vandalism of private property has shown no significant change in the BCS since 1981, though reporting has increased. Given the small proportion of vandalism which is reported, any rise in reporting translates into a much larger rise in recorded crime. But increased reporting alone cannot fully explain the divergence in trends. The police may now be recording some offences as vandalism which the BCS classifies as attempted burglary, for example, or attempted vehicle theft.

Violence

Robbery and wounding have increased by a fifth since 1981, whilst recorded offences have almost doubled. The BCS suggests that reporting levels have risen, but not enough to account fully for the divergence in trends. One possibility is that the police are now giving higher priority to some types of violent crime, such as domestic violence and street robbery; and where there are two options for classification (for instance between wounding and common assault, or between robbery and theft from the person), they may now choose the more serious.

Figure 3

Indexed trends in different offence groups, 1981 - 1991
(all 1981 rates = 100)

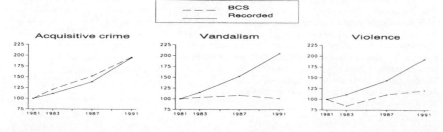

TRENDS SINCE 1987

For the comparable sub-set of offences, recorded crime has risen by 39% since 1987, as against a BCS rise of 14%. Table 2 shows details.

Table 2
Trends in crime 1987-1991

| | % change 1987-1991 | | |
	Crimes recorded by the police	Total BCS crimes	BCS crimes reported to the police
Acquisitive crime	40%	28%	50%
Vandalism	35%	-7%	6%
Violence	34%	9%	22%
Total	39%	14%	39%

EXPLAINING THE INCREASE IN REPORTING

Why has reporting gone up? It has become easier to report, with an increase in telephone ownership from 75% in 1981 to 83% in 1987 and 88% in 1991. Certainly, more victims reported crime by phone in 1991 (58%) than in 1987 (50%). Also, more victims were insured, and this may have affected reporting. In 1991, 50% of theft or damage incidents were covered by insurance as against 37% in 1987.

A final possibility is that the findings on reporting are an artefact of the survey method. It is possible that those who have been often victimised will simply forget more trivial incidents. Also, the interview process may result in either interviewers or respondents rationing themselves to a limited number of incidents. When crime is rising, the effect of these processes would be to reduce the rate of increase in crime indicated by the BCS, and to increase the proportion of more serious incidents, which would typically be reported to the police. Further analysis is planned to assess this.

RISKS OF CRIME

Annual crime rates can be expressed in terms of incidence (the number of *crimes* per head of population) or in terms of prevalence (the number of *victims* per head of population). Prevalence figures are lower than those for incidence as some people are victims more than once over a year. (Of those who were victimised in 1991, 55% were a victim once, 45% twice or more.) The rates for more serious offences in 1981 and 1991 are shown in Table 3. Rates are per 100 households for offences treated by the survey as household crimes (affecting the household as a whole), and per 100 adults for personal offences.

Table 3
BCS crime rates, 1981 and 1991

	Incident rate per 100 households		% households victimised once or more	
	1981	1991	1981	1991
Burglary	4.1	6.8	3.4	5.3
Attempts and no loss	2.1	3.3	1.9	2.7
With loss	2.0	3.5	1.8	2.9
All motor vehicle theft[1]	14.0	25.4	10.8	18.2
Theft from vehicles	10.3	16.0	8.2	11.8
Theft of vehicles	2.3	3.5	2.1	3.2
Attempts of and from	1.4	6.0	1.1	4.8
Bicycle theft[1]	2.8	6.5	2.7	5.5

	Incident rate per 100 adults		% adults victimised once or more	
Wounding	1.3	1.5	1.0	1.0
Robbery and theft from person	1.5	1.5	1.3	1.4

Notes: Sub-categories do not sum to main categories because of rounding and multiple victimisation.
[1] Vehicle and bicycle theft figures are per 100 owners.

WHO IS AT RISK?

Risks of crime are not spread evenly across the population. One important factor is the type of area in which people live. Table B (page 5) summarises the variation in risk between different types of neighbourhood. It uses the ACORN classification, which assigns every home in the country into one of 11 groups according to the demographic, employment and housing characteristics of its immediate area. The 1984, 1988 and 1992 data-sets have been combined to increase the precision of the figures, to show crime risks in relation to the national average. Thus residents in ACORN Group G, comprising the poorest council estates, face a risk of burglary which is 2.8 times the average; in ACORN Group A, agricultural areas, the risk is only a fifth of the average. Like burglary, the risks of vehicle crime vary considerably by area, with those in the highest risk areas facing a risk about double the average. Risks of robbery and theft from the person are also focussed on particular areas - though as these can take place away from home, analysis based on ACORN can be somewhat misleading. Other offences, not shown in Table B, are more evenly spread across areas.

TABLE A OFFENCES IN ENGLAND AND WALES, 1981, 1983, 1987 AND 1991

Figures in 000's	1981	1983	1987	1991	% change 87-91 (2)	% change 81-91 (2)
COMPARABLE WITH RECORDED OFFENCES						
ACQUISITIVE CRIME	3,153	3,823	4,808	6,174	28 **	96 **
VANDALISM	2,715	2,795	2,947	2,730	-7 *	1
VIOLENCE	670	568	743	809	9	21
Vehicle vandalism	1,558	1,708	1,629	1,669	2	7
Household vandalism	1,155	1,089	1,317	1,063	-19 **	-8
Burglary: attempts and no loss	376	461	668	660	-1	76 **
Burglary: with loss	374	454	517	705	36 **	88 **
Theft from motor vehicles	1,287	1,537	2,098	2,400	14	86 **
Theft of motor vehicles	286	284	387	517	34 **	81 **
Attempted thefts of and from vehicles	180	294	430	890	107 **	395 **
Bicycle theft	216	288	389	564	45 **	161 **
Wounding	507	423	566	626	11	23
Robbery and theft from person	596	650	494	622	26	4
OTHER BCS OFFENCES						
Other household theft	1,518	1,543	1,515	1,838	21	21
Common assault	1,402	1,429	1,493	1,757	18	25
Other personal theft	1,588	1,730	1,794	1,744	-3	10
ALL BCS OFFENCES	11,045	11,888	13,000	15,052	13 **	36 **

Notes:
1. **Acquisitive crimes**: burglary, thefts of and from vehicles (including attempts), bicycle thefts, theft from the person. **Vandalism**: household property and vehicles. **Violence**: wounding and robbery.
2. Numbers of 1991 offences were derived by multiplying offence rates by 20,131,000 households in England and Wales (household crimes) and 40,661,000 adults (personal crimes). Multipliers for earlier years differ slightly from ones used previously, so some figures differ from previous results.
3. The statistical significance of changes is calculated on the basis of rates taking population change into account. Double-starred differences are statistically significant at the 5% level. Single-starred differences are significant at the 10% level. Percentage changes based on unrounded numbers.

TABLE B RELATIVE CRIME RATES FOR RESIDENTS IN DIFFERENT ACORN NEIGHBOURHOOD GROUPS (1)

			Burglary	Autocrime around the home	Robbery/theft from person
	A.	Agricultural areas	20	20	50
LOW	B.	Modern family housing, higher income areas	60	70	70
RISK	C.	Older housing of intermediate status	70	100	60
	J.	Affluent suburban housing	70	70	70
	K.	Better-off retirement areas	70	80	70
MEDIUM	D.	Older terraced housing	120	160	100
RISK	E.	Better-off council estates	90	110	120
	F.	Less well-off council estates	150	160	100
HIGH	G.	Poorest council estates	280	240	200
RISK	H.	Mixed inner metropolitan areas	180	190	340
	I.	High-status non-family areas	220	150	250
Indexed national average			100	100	100

Notes:
1. Combined 1984, 1988 and 1992 British Crime Survey results.
2. **'Autocrime'**: thefts of and from vehicles, including attempts, vandalism to motor vehicles around the home. All categories include attempts.

[6]

International Review of Victimology, 1993, Vol. 2 pp. 183–207
0269-7580/93 $10

A CROSS-NATIONAL COMPARISON OF VICTIMS OF CRIME: VICTIM SURVEYS OF TWELVE COUNTRIES[1]

RICHARD BLOCK[2]

Loyola University of Chicago, Lake Shore Campus, 6525 North Sheridan, Rood, Chicago, Illinois 60626, USA

ABSTRACT

Comparison of national crime surveys must be made very cautiously because of differences in sampling, methodology and content. In this report methodological differences between the United States' National Crime Survey and victimization surveys of other countries are examined and survey estimates of victimization are adjusted. It is found that U.S. rates of assault/threat, robbery, and burglary are not extraordinarily higher than those of other eleven other countries or regions. However, U.S. levels of gun use are much higher and U.S. levels of both gun and non-gun lethal violence (using Killias, 1990) far exceed those of other industrialized societies.

INTRODUCTION

The United States is a pioneer in surveying a random population sample to derive a measure of victimization that is independent of police reports. In order to derive a measure of crime that is independent of the citizen's decision to notify the police, the Department of Justice introduced the National Crime Survey (NCS) in 1972. Each quarter, a random sample of U.S. households is surveyed about victimization in the previous six months. The NCS is one of the largest and longest continuing social surveys ever undertaken. For 1987, the year analyzed in this report, 46,000 households, including 93,000 individuals over the age of 12, took part in the survey.

Many countries have followed the U.S. lead, using methodologies and questions that are derived from the NCS model. Each survey asks a random sample of the population whether they have been a victim of crime over a specified time period. Victimization questions have been especially similar in these surveys because of the common need in all of them to convert legal concepts into everyday ideas of criminal acts. Surveys of crime have been completed in many countries and several, the Netherlands, England/Wales, Israel, and Hong Kong have fielded a series of surveys. In early 1989, the International Crime Survey (ICS), was completed in 14 countries of Europe, North America and Australia. A second survey of thirty five countries, (not including the United States) was completed in 1991. The completion of these international projects clearly demonstrates the widespread acceptance of the validity of such research (van Dijk, Mayhew and Killias, 1990).

184

This article attempts to use national surveys for cross national comparison of assaults and threats, robbery, and burglary. Using national victimization surveys rather than ICS, important methodological and sampling differences that limit comparisons are delineated and the fruitfulness of making these cross national comparisons is assessed. The analysis reported here is not based upon published reports. The director of each country's victim survey was asked to supply a questionnaire, information on methodology, and resulting publications. Most countries complied with these requests. After reviewing each country's questionnaire, an identical letter was sent to each project's research coordinator requesting methodological information and a specific set of tables. For most surveys, special computer analysis was necessary. In some cases, this was completed in the U.S. either at Loyola or at the Criminal Justice Archives of ICPSR at the University of Michigan. In other cases, it was completed in the survey country.

A METHODOLOGICAL COMPARISON OF THE NCS AND OTHER NATIONAL VICTIM SURVEYS

The key to any comparison of national victimization surveys is correction for methodological and fielding differences. The research presented here is based upon surveys of twelve countries or regions: Canada, England/Wales, the Federal Republic of Germany (Baden/Wurtenberg), Finland, Hong Kong, Hungary (Barayana), Israel, the Netherlands, Scotland, Sweden, Switzerland, and the United States.

Victimization questions are very similar among the studies. However, fielding and sampling techniques are not. Appendix A presents a methodological summary of each of the surveys used in this report. As can be seen in the appendix, fielding techniques encompass most of the methodologies of survey research, varying from mailed questionnaires, to telephone interviews, with or without computer assistance (CATI) and personal interviews. However, the fielding technique used does not appear to greatly affect the level of victimization. Sample size varies from 2,500 to the nearly 50,000 panels of the NCS, with correspondingly large differences in confidence intervals and error estimates. Response rates vary from 60 to near 100 per cent. Killias has hypothesized that a low response rate will be associated with a high crime rate; only those respondents will agree to participate who have something to report (Killias, 1987). However, the 1989 ICS did not confirm his hypothesis (van Dijk, Mayhew and Killias, 1990). The response rates and samples in these national surveys are on average considerably higher than in the recently completed international crime survey (78.6% vs. 41.3%).

In most countries, respondents are asked about crimes in the last year; however, the NCS panel survey covers only those crimes occurring in the last six months. Some other surveys ask first about all victimizations that ever occurred to the respondent or occurred in the last five years and then narrow the recall period to the last year. The U.S. and Hong Kong surveys interview every member of the household and derive independent reports of victimization. The Israeli survey interviews a single member as a reporter not only for the household but for every member of the household. This sampling method probably results in under reporting of victimizations of family members who were not respondents. The other surveys interview a single respondent in each household. That respondent represents himself or herself for personal crimes and the household for crimes such as burglary or auto theft.

Each of these methodological differences affects the level at which victimizations are reported. Methodological differences may increase or decrease the relative level of victimization across surveys.

In preparation for the National Crime Survey two important methodological problems were recognized and corrected. These corrections are the central problem in comparison of the NCS and other victim surveys (Biderman and Lynch, 1981).

External Telescoping

This may be defined as the incorporation of victimizations occurring outside a time period into a time period. The longer the recall period the less the chance of external telescoping. If respondents are asked about crimes occurring in their life time external telescoping is impossible. If respondents are asked about crimes occurring in the last month, the likelihood of external telescoping is very high. All surveys except the NCS are bounded only by the respondent's memory. Most surveys question respondents in January about occurrences in the last year. The NCS is a quarterly survey occurring throughout the year. Most external telescoping will occur at the earliest point of the recall period. Respondents will bring incidents that occurred before the time period into it. In addition crimes occurring after the reference period may also be brought into it. For example, respondents may include post New Year crimes as crimes occurring in the previous year.

The bounding technique used in the NCS is designed to eliminate external telescoping. An address is included in the NCS panel for seven cycles (3.5 years). The panel's first survey sets a bound for the second survey, but is not included in the calculation of victimization rates. Analysis of the NCS first time panel addresses (unbounded survey), and the second administration addresses indicate that external telescoping is a very substantial problem (Turner, 1984; Cantor, 1989). Comparisons of unbounded to bounded surveys result in unbounded rates for specific crime rates that are fifty to sixty percent higher than bounded rates. The bounding technique of the NCS successfully reduces external telescoping. However, it also reduces the level of victimization in the U.S. in comparison to other countries that do not use this technique.

186

Recency Bias (Memory Decay and Internal Telescoping)

A problem of all retrospective surveys is that more distant events tend to be forgotten. Recalled events will tend to cluster toward those most recent in time. More contemporary crimes are easily remembered, but those occurring even a few months earlier are often forgotten. The greater the length of a recall period, the greater the problem of recency bias. As a result the longer the span of recall of a victimization survey, the greater the recency bias (or memory decay). As Bushery (1981) has shown in the United States, more crimes will be reported in a three month recall than in a six month recall, and more in a six month recall than a one year recall period. If Bushery's findings are correct for other surveys, then memory decay should be greater in these surveys than in the NCS.

Internal telescoping may also lead to the bunching of recalled events to the more recent points in the recall period. Thus, November's crimes may be moved in memory to December. The methodology of the NCS is no better able to handle internal telescoping than the other victimization surveys. If only respondents interviewed in January for the NCS are considered, then victimizations tend to bunch in December, just as in the other surveys. However, because the NCS is administered each quarter during the year, internal telescoping is distributed evenly throughout rather than disproportionately near the end of the year. In all surveys, the net effect of internal telescoping for a year's estimate is zero. Surveys other than the NCS typically sample respondents in January. Thus, December of the previous year is the most recent month. Unfortunately, December is typically a high month for victimization of both property crimes and violence. It is impossible to separate recency bias in these surveys from internal telescoping and crime seasonality. Due to memory decay and internal telescoping, the most recent month is that with the highest victimization level. However, due to seasonality, the real level of victimization may also be high in December.

External telescoping and recency bias have opposite effects. A shorter time period reduces recency bias but increases external telescoping. The NCS solution to these problems is to create a panel of addresses, an absolute bound to reduce telescoping[3], and a compromise recall period of six months. An address is maintained in the interview panel for three and a half years. The first interview is used only for bounding. Interviews two through seven are referenced on the preceding interview for crimes occurring in the last six months.[4] While this technique rigorously addresses the known problems of retrospective surveys, it is extremely expensive and represents a long term commitment that no other country has been willing to finance.[5]

Figures 1 and 2 are schematic models of telescoping, recency bias and memory decay over a year's survey for the United States National Crime Survey (Figure 1) and for national surveys that use a one year recall bounded in the respondent's memory (Figure 2). Column One represents a real victimization level. Columns two, three and four represent the effect of recency bias/memory decay, internal and external telescoping. Column five represents the survey estimate of victimization. While external telescoping, internal telescoping, and memory decay are depicted separately in these models, it is not possible to measure them independently.

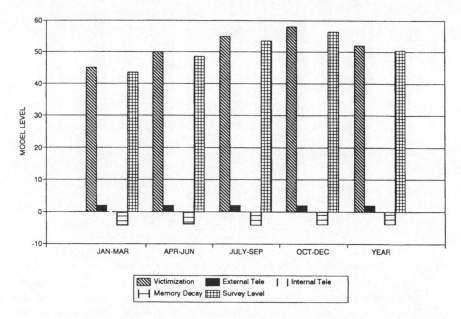

FIGURE 1.   Schematic Model of Methodology Effects for the US National Crime Survey

The National Crime Survey model (Figure One) suggests small, constant levels of external telescoping and recency bias, and no internal telescoping. External telescoping is limited by the NCS technique of bounding each survey by a previous survey. Recency bias is limited by a six month period of recall and by surveying respondents throughout the year. A respondent who was victimized in December may be questioned about the crime in a survey administered in January through May. The NCS methodology is designed to correct for external telescoping, recency bias and memory decay. Therefore, survey levels are close to a real but unmeasured victimization level.

In other surveys (Figure 2), high levels of external telescoping result from the lack of a fixed bound. However, their higher level of memory decay results from a longer recall period. Internal telescoping tends to move an incident closer to the date of survey administration. The relationship between real levels and survey levels vary over the year. Survey levels are on the average considerably higher than the real but unmeasured level of victimization.

188

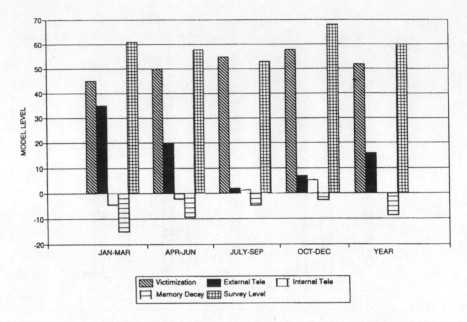

FIGURE 2.   Schematic Model of Methodology Effects for Surveys Outside the United States

While these problems may exist in victimization surveys administered at a single point in time, they are only important in comparison to surveys, such as the NCS, that use a different methodology. As estimated in the following section, comparison of these models suggests an upward adjustment to the NCS is necessary for comparison to other national surveys.

ADJUSTING FOR BOUNDING AND RECENCY BIAS/MEMORY DECAY

The NCS solutions to these two methodological problems of telescoping and recency bias/memory decay have prevented direct comparisons between it and other victim surveys. The US design is a panel survey of addresses. Each address is interviewed seven times about crimes occurring in the last six months. The first interview at the address serves as a bounding interview. It only delineates the time span of the re-interviews and is not included in calculation of crime rates. The other victim surveys interview respondents only once about crimes occurring in the last year. There is no formal bounding survey. For bounding purposes these surveys either occur soon after the New Year or are bounded only by the respondent's memory.

Because surveys of other countries ask respondents about the past year and the NCS asks about the last six months, recency bias/memory decay is likely to be substantially greater in the other surveys than in the NCS. This will result in a serious under counting of crimes relative to the United States. On the other hand, as has been previously shown, there is a very substantial fall off in estimated victimization from the bounding survey to the first re-interview of the NCS (Biderman and Cantor, 1984). For comparative purposes, the first NCS interview is methodologically most similar to the other surveys of this project than the second and later follow ups.

Table 1 is an attempt to derive multipliers for the effect of the NCS bounding technique. For this table, separate unweighted rates were calculated for bounded and unbounded surveys and a ratio of the bounded/unbounded was calculated using the NCS/VRS survey of 1983.[6] For less serious crimes, assault/threat with no injury and illegal entry where nothing is stolen, unbounded rates are more than double bounded rates.[7]

TABLE 1

The Effect of Bounding on the United States National Crime Survey (VRS)[8]

	Unweighted Data Age 16+		
	UNBOUND RATE	BOUND RATE	UNBOUND/BOUND bound multi
Assault/threat	24.92	12.40	2.01
with injury	3.08	2.05	1.50
no injury	21.84	10.35	2.11
Burglary	26.20	17.70	1.48
stolen	21.73	15.30	1.42
no stol	5.42	2.40	2.26
Number of cases	persons	households	
bounded	18214	9081	
unbounded	4831	2510	

Tables 2 and 3 demonstrate possible corrections for differential recency bias for assault/threats and burglary. As can be seen in the tables, especially for assault/threat, the U.S. bounded/six month recall fielding technique, combined with the administration of interviews throughout the year, results in a substantially smoother distribution of crimes over the year than in four surveys that ask the respondent to recall crimes over a year with a less precise bound.[9] In the four non-U.S. surveys, the percentage of crimes reported as occurring in the most recent six months is very substantially greater than in the earlier six months. For example, while in the NCS 47% of all assaults and threats are reported to occur in the first six months of the year, Table 2 shows that in England 30%, in Scotland

190

TABLE 2

The Derivation of Bounding and Memory Decay Estimates and a Correction Factor for Assault/Threat

	Percent Distribution of Assaults over Quarters of Year				
	U.S.	Eng.	Scot.	Neth.	H.K.
Jan–Mar	20.80	12.90	18.50	10.94	18.0
Apr–Jun	25.70	17.10	12.40	22.40	21.6
Jul–Sept	26.20	26.90	34.30	31.25	18.7
Oct–Dec	27.80	43.10	34.70	35.42	41.7
Jul–Dec/Jan–Jun = Decay					
	1.16	2.33	2.23	2.00	1.53

Avg Assault Decay other than US *2.02*

Ratio Assault Decay in Other/US = 1.74
Therefore, must multiply rate in first six months by 1.74 to derive a comparable rate to U.S.
Approx Multiplier over the year *1.37*

U.S. Bound effect Assault: the Ratio of Bounded to Unbounded Assault Rates (Table One) *2.01*

Ratio US Bound Multiplier/Avg Memory Decay Multiplier = 1.47

TABLE 3

The Derivation of Bounding and Recency BiasMemory Decay and a Correction Factor for Burglary

	Percent Distribution of Burglaries over Quarters of Year				
	U.S.	Eng.	Scot.	Neth.	H.K.
Jan–Mar	21.10	24.60	30.80	16.99	19.30
Apr–Jun	25.10	18.80	11.90	25.49	26.70
Jul–Sept	27.00	28.50	25.30	24.84	26.00
Oct–Dec	26.80	28.10	32.00	31.37	28.00
Jul–Dec/Jan–Jun = Decay					
	1.16	1.30	1.34	1.32	1.17

Avg Burg Decay other than US *1.29*

Ratio Burglary Decay in Other/US = 1.10
Therefore, must multiply rate in first six months by 1.10 to derive a comparable rate to U.S.
Approx Multiplier over the year *1.05*

U.S. Bound Affect Burglary (From Table One) *1.48*

Ratio US Bound Multiplier/Avg Memory Decay Multiplier = 1.48

31%, in the Netherlands 33%, and in Hong Kong 40% are reported between January and June.

As Table 3 illustrates, variation in burglary across seasons of the year is less systematic than for assaults (memory decay is less). Respondents are both less likely to forget or telescope burglary than assault. For burglary (1.29) the average ratio of the last six months of the year in comparison to the first six months is less than for assault. Both the memory decay correction and the bounding correction (Table 1) are smaller.

If the difference in percentage between the NCS and the other surveys is totally a result of differential recency bias/memory decay, than the other surveys would tend to understate crime rates relative to the U.S. for the January to June period. The average ratio of other country/U.S. assault decay is 1.74. That is, the ratio of assaults in the July–December six months to the January to June six-months in four countries compared to the United States is 1.74. This is a multiplier for other countries relative to the U.S. rates for the earlier six months. Averaged over a year, this memory decay/recency bias multiplier would be 1.37.

An estimate of the combined effects of bounding which relatively decreases U.S. crime rates and memory decay which relatively increases U.S. crime rates in comparison to any other countries is given by the ratio of the bounding correction/memory decay correction. Thus, NCS crime rates for assault should be multiplied by an estimated 1.47 to derive rates that are methodologically similar to those of four other surveys. Similarly, the burglary ratio is 1.41. Therefore, NCS crime rates for burglary should be multiplied by an estimated 1.41 to derive rates that are methodologically similar to those of the four other surveys.[10] These ratios – 1.47 for assault and 1.41 for burglary – are applied to the NCS as adjustment factors in Figures 3 and 4.

ASSAULTS AND THREATS, ROBBERY, AND BURGLARY

Table 4 presents a summary of the coverage of each of these crimes as used in this report. For those countries that ask separately about robbery, the questions are very consistent. For assault and burglary, as the crime moves from more serious to less serious, the consistency of inclusion declines. Particularly significant differences are in the inclusion or exclusion of attempted crimes and in the inclusion of threats and robberies as assaults.

Several countries exclude attempted burglaries or burglaries where nothing is stolen. In the Netherlands, Sweden, and Israel, robbery is included as another form of assault. Hong Kong includes only serious assaults. Switzerland excludes assaults by persons living in the household. Perhaps the most consistent comparisons would include only attacks (either armed or unarmed) and completed burglaries of primary residences. However, for this report a wider range of crimes are included in each category.

192

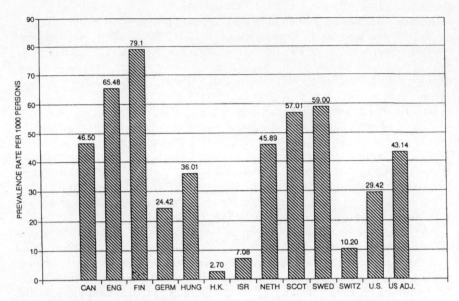

FIGURE 3.   Assault/Threat Prevalence
            Comparative Victim Survey Estimates

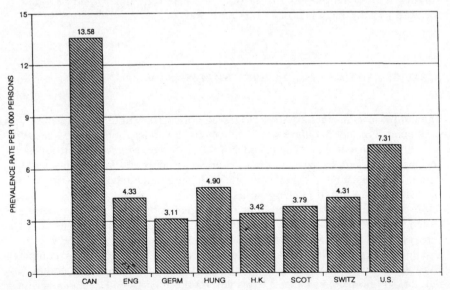

FIGURE 4.   Robbery Prevalence
            Comparative Victim Survey Estimates

193

TABLE 4

Summary Comparson of Attacks & Threats

	Attacks		Includes		Threats	
Country	Armed	Unarmed	Robbery	Rob Inj	Armed	Unarmed
Canada	Y	Y	N	N	Y	Y
England/Wales	Y	Y	N	N	Y	Y
Germany (Baden/Wurt)	Y	Y	N	Y	N	N
Finland	Y	Y	Y	Y	Y	Y
Hong Kong	Y	Y	N	N	Y	Y
Hungary (Barayana)	Y	Y	N	Y	N	N
Israel	Y	Y	Y	Y	Y	Y
Netherlands	Y	Y	Y	Y	N	N
Scotland	Y	Y	N	N	Y	Y
Sweden	Y	Y	Y	Y	Y	Y
Switzerland	Y	Y	N	N	Y	Y
United States	Y	Y	N	N	Y	Y

Summary Comparison of Robbery

	Force		Threat	
Country	Comp	Attempt	Comp	Attempt
Canada	Y	Y	Y	Y
England/Wales	Y	Y	Y	Y
Germany (Baden/Wurt)	Y	Y	Y	Y
Hong Kong	Y	Y	Y	Y
Hungary (Barayana)	Y	Y	Y	Y
Scotland	Y	Y	Y	Y
Switzerland	Y	Y	Y	Y
United States	Y	Y	Y	Y

Summary Comparison of Burglary

	House		Garage		Other	
Country	Comp	Attmpt	Comp	Attmpt	Comp	Attmpt
Canada	Y	Y	Y	Y	N	N
England/Wales	Y	Y	Y	Y	Y	Y
Germany (Baden/Wurt)	Y	Y	Y	Y	Y	Y
Hong Kong	Y	Y	Y	Y	N	N
Hungary (Barayana)	Y	Y	Y	Y	Y	Y
Israel	Y	Y	N	N	N	N
Netherlands	Y	N	Y	N	N	N
Scotland	Y	Y	Y	Y	Y	Y
Sweden	Y	N	Y	N	Y	N
Switzerland	Y	Y	Y	Y	Y	Y
United States	Y	Y	Y	Y	Y	N

194

For consistency, younger respondents (<15) were eliminated from the United States survey and comparisons are of prevalence per 1,000 individuals or households rather than incidence. In other words, the question asked is how many respondents per 1,000 were victims of at least one assault or threat in the reporting period and not how many assaults were committed per 1,000 respondents in the reporting year.[11] Because prevalence rather than incidence is counted, all surveys use the same rule for counting serial offenses (repeated victimizations against the same person and of the same crime type) – they are counted as one victimization.[12]

A PRELIMINARY COMPARISON OF RESULTS

Figures 3 and 4 represent a preliminary comparison of prevalence rates of victimization for assault, threat and robbery. Both unadjusted and adjusted U.S. rates are presented. U.S. rates are adjusted for the effects of bounding and telescoping.

Assault, Threat and Robbery

Rates of violent crime vary substantially across countries (Figure 3). The rate of assault, threat, and robbery prevalence estimate in Finland (79.1) is 29 times higher than that in Hong Kong (2.70). However, the low rates in Hong

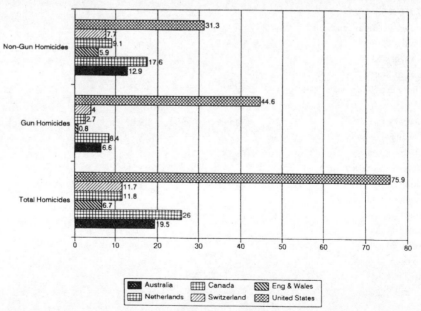

FIGURE 5. Weapon Use in Homicide: Six Nation Comparison
           Average Annual Homicides Per Million 1983–1989. Source, Killias (1990)

Kong, Israel, and Switzerland probably result from differences in question or method. The survey of Hong Kong only includes serious assault; however, serious threats are included. The survey of Switzerland excludes assaults by household members, and the survey of Israel probably underestimates personal crime because a household respondent is asked to recall crimes against other members of the family.

Previous research has shown rates of violence in England and Scotland to be higher than in the U.S. Dutch assault rates have increased over time and were in 1986 very similar to those of other Northern European countries and to the U.S. and Canada. Finnish and Swedish rates are taken from a survey that concentrates heavily on violent crime. Dutch, Swedish, and Finnish assault rates include robberies and, therefore, slightly overstate a rate comparable to the U.S. and the other surveys. With the exception of the German survey, fielding and question differences may account for some of the difference between surveys in violence prevalence rates.

Demographically, U.S. assault and threat per 1,000 respondents are, as Table 5 shows, very similar to the average of the other surveys. U.S. rates for males (51.26) and females (31.21) are quite similar to those for other countries (47.68 and 25.18). The decline in assault and threat rates from the youngest respondents to the oldest respondents is equally dramatic. Assault and threat rates for respondents over age 60 are similar in the U.S. and the average of other surveys. While injury is less common in assault and threat in the U.S. survey (28.12%) than the average of the other surveys (47.60%), weapons are more commonly present in the U.S. assault (29.27%) than the average of the other surveys that asked the question (19.74%). Guns represented 15.9% of weapons used in assault in the three surveys that explicitly asked about the presence of firearms. In the U.S. survey, a gun was present 40.90% of weapon assaults. Thus, not only were weapons more likely to be present in U.S. assaults than in other countries, but guns were more likely to be present in victimizations with a weapon.

TABLE 5

U.S. Assaults and Threats Compared to the Average of Other Surveys

Prevalence Rates per 1000	United States	Other Survey Average
Male	51.26	47.68 (8)*
Female	31.21	25.18 (8)
Under 20	144.92	116.80 (7)
Over 60	10.07	10.46 (6)
Percent of Incidents		
Injury	28.12	47.60 (6)
Weapon	29.27	19.4 (4)
Gun or Weapon	40.90	15.91 (3)

* Number of Countries with Information Available

196

Robbery

In all countries investigated, rates of robbery (Figure 4) are far lower than those of assault or burglary. The Canadian rate is highest (13.58). However, the United States prevalence rate of robbery (7.31 per 1,000) is probably higher than that of the other countries that explicitly asked about robbery (avg. 4.01 per 1,000). Question coverage is nearly identical in the surveys. While it was not possible to adjust for recency bias and bounding, the adjustment is not likely to be large because of the seriousness of the crime. Serious crimes are both less likely to decay or to be effected by bounding. U.S. robbery rates for both males (8.75) and females (6.09) are higher than the average of the other countries (5.56 and 4.77). The fall off in risk of robbery with age is very similar in the U.S. and the average of other countries (Table 6).

TABLE 6
U.S. Robberies Compared to the Average of Other Surveys

Prevalence Rates per 1000	United States	Other Survey Average
Male	8.75	5.56 (5)*
Female	6.09	4.77 (5)
Under 20	13.66	15.29 (5)
Over 60	2.92	1.77 (5)
Percent of Incidents		
Injury	37.44	43.73 (4)
Weapon	46.26	32.87 (4)
Gun or Weapon	39.04	15.30 (3)

* Number of Countries with Information Available

The robbery pattern of injury and weapon use is similar to that in assault. While the rate of injury to U.S. robbery victims is not exceptionally high, the rate of weapon use (46.26%) and especially the rate of gun use (18.06%) is much higher than the average of the other countries that asked the question (32.87% weapon use, 2.56% gun use). Thirty-nine percent of all weapons used in robbery in the U.S. were guns compared to 15.30% of all weapons used in three other countries.

The relatively small differences in violence between the United States and other industrialized societies in these survey comparisons contradicts common sense. Common sense, however, may be derived from studies of lethal violence, a crime that is never included in victim surveys. As reported by Killias (1990), using police reports (Figure 5), U.S. rates of homicide far exceed those of other countries. Of the six nations studied, the average U.S. homicide rate from 1983–1986 was three times as high as Canada's and eleven times that of England and Wales. Attributing this solely to the availability of guns is incorrect. While the U.S. gun homicide rate far exceeds that of the other countries, the U.S. non-gun homicide rate is greater than the total homicide rate of any of the other five countries. Combining the current research and that of the ICS with Killias' work on homicide, it appears that the U.S. reputation for criminal violence is primarily derived from lethal violence and that these high levels of lethal violence include both gun and non-gun inflicted deaths.

Burglary

United States' burglary prevalence rates are among the highest in the survey (Figure 6); however, several countries have nearly equivalent rates. Of countries with lower rates, some cover fewer types of crime (eg. the Netherlands), others (eg. Switzerland) may cover more crime types. How might variation between countries be explained? Perhaps there is cultural variation in opportunities and guardianship. While many U.S. burglaries occur during the day in unguarded homes, in other countries, where women are less likely to be paid workers, homes are more likely to be guarded. Similarly, while second homes are included in several surveys, it is likely that fewer Hungarians own a second home than do Swedes.

The distribution of burglary risk is somewhat different in the United States and the other countries surveyed. In all countries, the risk of burglary is greatest in the most urbanized areas (Figure 7). However, in the United States, the relationship between urbanization and burglary risk is weaker than in other countries. Suburban (59.84) areas and areas outside urban areas (SMSAs) (63.99) have about the same rate of burglary. In other countries, especially England and Scotland, burglary risk is very strongly related to living in the city centre.

NOTIFICATION OF THE POLICE

Victimization surveys count both those crimes of which the police are aware and those that they are not. Therefore, most surveys ask the respondent whether or not they notified the police. The likelihood of notification of the police may be affected both by legal and cultural differences, the availability of other helping institutions, trust in the police, the definition of what is police business, and by crime seriousness. For example, a small legal change, the introduction of registration cards, resulted in a dramatic increase in the likelihood of police notification of pick-pocketing in Hong Kong. In some countries, violence occurring at home is not considered to be police business (indeed, it was excluded from the Swiss survey). In general, the probability of the police finding out about more serious crimes is greater than less serious crime. The probability of police notification of assaults is lower than robberies. Therefore, they are analyzed separately.

Table 7 includes all incidents reported in the survey. The police are more likely to learn about an assault in Hong Kong (49.19%) than in other surveys. However, the Hong Kong survey reports only on serious assaults. Of the other surveys, the

198

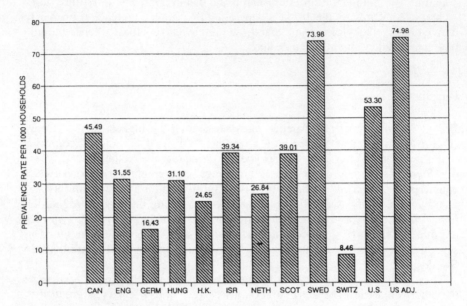

FIGURE 6. Burglary Prevalence
Comparative Victim Survey Estimates

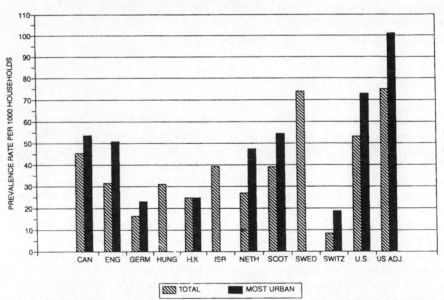

FIGURE 7. Burglary Prevalence & Urbanization
Comparative Victim Survey Estimates

TABLE 7

Notification of the Police

Contry	Assault	Robbery	Burglary
Canada	30.04	31.91	70.45
England/Wales	36.16	44.44	62.89
Germany	30.36	43.85	52.50
Hungary	18.18	33.33	61.25
Hong Kong	49.19	43.95	32.65
Israel	32.00	N.A.	52.50
Netherlands	33.94	N.A.	89.11
Scotland	36.05	66.67	56.71
Switzerland	30.34	84.15	82.76
Average	32.95	49.97	62.13
United States	44.64	56.61	51.31

Hungarian survey (18.18%) reports an exceptionally low rate of notification. The police are more likely to be notified about violence in the United States (44.64%) than the average of the other surveys (32.9%). The higher rate of notification in the U.S. survey may result from the greater prevalence of weapons in U.S. violence than in other countries.

Notification of robbery varies from 31.91% in Canada to 84.15% in Switzerland. The U.S. rate of robbery notification was 56.6% in comparison to an average of 50.5% for other countries. However, the number of robberies against residents of countries other than the U.S. in their native country is very small and statistical variation has a large component of error. Only burglaries where the criminal entered a home are included in the Dutch survey; therefore, it is not surprising that police notification is higher in the Netherlands (89.11%) than other countries. The rate of police notification in the U.S. (51.31%), is slightly below that for the average of other countries which include both completions and attempts (63.71%). Variation in notification may result from differences in insurance coverage or the proportion of attempts and completions. Some of these differences could be analyzed using the available surveys.

SUMMARY

Although all victim surveys have the same origin – the National Crime Survey of the United States – and ask similar questions, comparisons between surveys are difficult and must be made with extreme caution. Comparison of the United

200

States' NCS and other national victim surveys is especially difficult. Among the differences that make comparison difficult are the following.

Methodological Differences

Sample size

These varied from 2,500 to more than 60,000. Estimates made from smaller samples have much greater confidence intervals and standard errors for rate and percentage estimates than larger samples. An advantage of the International Crime Survey is that sample sizes are approximately the same; however, all are small.

Period of recall

The NCS asks about victimization in the last six months. Most other surveys ask for victimizations in the last year. This results in recency bias or memory decay that tends to over estimate U.S. victimization rates in contrast to those of other countries.

Bounding method

The NCS has an absolute bound, each address being included in a panel for three and one-half years. Victimizations are bounded by the most recent previous survey. Other surveys are bounded only in the respondent's mind and sometimes by the New Year. The less precise bounding of the other surveys tends to result in external telescoping that over-estimates victimization rates in other countries in comparison to the U.S.

Sampling Frame

Who is to be excluded and included, while not a major topic of this report, may affect rates of victimization. The NCS includes residents of institutions such as dormitories, has both English and Spanish versions, and includes both citizens and non-citizens. All of these groups are excluded from some of the surveys. They may have higher levels of victimization than persons included in the sampling frame. For this project, only respondents aged 15 or 16 and older are included.

201

Question Differences

Coverage

This concerns both the range of crimes that are included and those acts that are excluded. While in general questions appear similar, significant differences exist between countries. For example, among possible inclusions or exclusions in burglary are attempted break-ins, commercial crime, crimes in garages and other out-buildings, crimes in second homes, and successful break-ins during which nothing was stolen.

Language and Translation

The cultural meaning of the same act may vary from country to country. U.S. common usage does not differentiate between robbery and burglary. The NCS is careful to include victimizations which result from screening questions other than the one intended, but other surveys are not (Dodge, 1985). English and Scottish surveys, on the other hand, using a very complex set of coder decisions, are very careful in defining specific crime categories.

CONCLUDING REMARKS

Any comparison of United States' victimization rates based upon the National Crime Survey and the national crime surveys of other countries must be made very cautiously; however, U.S. robbery rates are probably higher than most other countries. Household burglary rates are high, but so are those of several other countries. U.S. prevalence rates of assault and threat are relatively low in comparison to countries that have similar coverage. However, both for assault and robbery, U.S. levels of weapon use, especially of guns, is much higher than that of the few other countries that asked the question. Based on Killias, United States' rates of lethal violence far exceed those of other countries. The U.S. rate of either gun or non-gun lethal violence exceeds the total rate of lethal violence for the other countries studied.

It is possible to control for some methodological, language and questionnaire differences in national victim surveys. In this report, bounding and recall, age of respondent, and the handling of series victims were taken into account. It is also possible to control for or at least be aware of differences in coverage.

Having worked through many comparative problems, I have concluded that comparison of national surveys other than the NCS may be possible if great caution is taken to insure similarity of coverage and fielding techniques. However, comparison of the United States NCS and that of other countries requires too many assumptions and adjustments. While it is possible to make these

202

adjustments, the resultant comparisons may be believable only in a very wide range. The best comparison of victimization experience is between identical surveys with identical methodologies. These surveys have twice been successfully completed, however, the relatively small number of respondents to each survey and the differential response rates of the surveys limit comparison.

APPENDIX A

Methodological Summary of the Surveys Used for this Analysis

Country: Canada
Survey Title: General Social Survey
Administration History 1 Cycle
Year Used 1987
People Interviewed 9870
Households Interviewed 9870
Response Rate 83%
Fielding Techniques cati
Period Covered 1 year
Bounding Technique Jan/Feb interviews

Country: England/Wales
Survey Title: British Crime Survey
Administration History 1981, 1983, 1987, 1990
Year Used 1987
People Interviewed 5146
Households Interviewed 5146
Response Rate 74%
Fielding Techniques in house interview
Period Covered 1 year
Bounding Technique Jan/Feb interview

Country: Federal Republic of Germany (BADEN/WURTENBERG)
Survey Title: Comparative German-American-Hungarian Vict. Survey
Administration History once
Year Used 1981
People Interviewed 2252
Households Interviewed 2252
Response Rate 64%
Fielding Techniques mailed
Period Covered one year
Bounding Technique from date of interview

Country: Finland
Survey: Title Safety of Finnish Life
Administrative History 1980, 1988
People Interviewed 14,000
Households Interviewed Not Applicable
Response Rate 87%
Fielding Technique
Period Covered one year
Bounding Technique from datc of interview

Country: Hong Kong
Survey Title: Crime and its Victims in Hong Kong 1989
Administration History 1978, 1981, 1986, 1989, 1991
Year Used 1986
People Interviewed 55437
Households Interviewed 17819
Response Rate 99%
Fielding Techniques house to house
Period Covered 1 year
Bounding Technique early January inter.

Country: Hungary (BARAYANA)
Survey Title: Concealed Victimization in Barayana (Hungary)
Administration History Once
Year Used 1981
People Interviewed 2446
Households Interviewed 2446
Response Rate 73%
Fielding Techniques mailed
Period Covered 1 year from int date
Bounding Technique from date of survey

Country: Israel
Survey Title: Victimization of Households in Israel
Administration History 1979, 1981, 1987
Year Used 1987
People Interviewed 5964 Non-Jewish households excluded
Households Interviewed 5964 Representing 20496 individuals
Response Rate unknown
Fielding Techniques in house interview
Period Covered 1 year
Bounding Technique from date of interview

204

County: The Netherlands
Survey Title: Victims of Crime
Administration History Annual/Bi-annual since 1975
Year Used 1986
People Interviewed 9502
Households Interviewed 9502
Response Rate 63%
Fielding Techniques in house interview
Period Covered 1 year
Bounding Technique given in Jan/Feb

Country: Scotland
Survey Title: Scottish Crime Survey
Administration History 1981, 1988
Year Used 1981
People Interviewed 5031
Households Interviewed 4255
Response Rate 81%
Fielding Techniques in house interview
Period Covered 1 year
Bounding Technique Jan/Feb interview

Country: Sweden
Survey Title: Annual Survey of Living Conditions
Administration History Yearly since 1975
Year Used 1988
People Interviewed 11841
Households Interviewed 11841
Response Rate 83%
Fielding Techniques In house interview
Period Covered 1 year
Bounding Technique one year from interview

Country: Switzerland
Survey Title:
Administration History 1984 Fr. 1986 Ger/It
Year Used 1984 French/1986 Ger/It
People Interviewed 6500
Households Interveiwed 6500
Response Rate 65%
Fielding Techniques CATI
Period Covered 1 year/life/6 years
Bounding Technique Jan interview

205

Country: United States
Survey Title: National Crime Survey (NCS)
Administration History Continuous from 1973
Year Used 1987
People Interviewed 97600
Households Interviewed 48400
Response Rate 93%
Fielding Techniques in pers/tele/cati
Period Covered 6 months
Bounding Technique since last panel

NOTES

1. This project is funded under Bureau of Justice Statistics Contract OJP-89-M-014. The project reflects the author's analysis not that of the Bureau of Justice Statistics or that of the many agencies and individuals who supplied information for the comparison.
2. A project involving studies of so many countries would not be possible without the help of many collaborators. I would like to thank the following, my co-workers for this comparison.
   Data Coordinators and Researchers:
   Canada, Roger Boe; England/Wales, Patricia Mayhew and Wesley Skogan; Germany, Harald Arnold; Hong Kong, K.S. Lau; Hungary, Lazlo Korinek; Israel, Giore Rahav; The Netherlands, Marianne Junger; Scotland, Douglas Payne; Sweden, Joachim Vogel and Lars Hall; Finland, Kauko Aaroma; Switzerland, Martin Killias; The United States (ICPSR), Spencer Pricenash and Victoria Schneider.
   Translators:
   Venezuela, Jesus Gonzalez; France and Switzerland, Michelle Pagnol; Hungary, Lia Hoffman-Irwin.
   Assistance at Loyola:
   Gayle Hoopaw, Jing Xhang, David Gabrovich.
   Finally, thanks go to Wesley Skogan for his continued support and to Carol Kalish of BJS for suggesting that I undertake the project.
3. The difference between a bounded and unbounded household is not absolute. A household is considered bounded if the address is bounded. However, over three and a half years, occupants of many addresses change. The surveys of new residents are considered to be bounded although they in fact are not as clearly indicated by the much higher levels of victimization reported by these respondents in their first interview. See Roman and Sliwa (1980) and Cantor (1989).
4. An additional advantage of the NCS panel interview methodology is a smoother distribution of crimes throughout the year in comparison to countries where a survey is asked only during a limited time period. Recency bias is greatest for the last month. If that month can occur in any quarter of the year, the monthly distribution will be smoother than if all questionnaires were administered during the same two or three weeks.
5. *Panel bias*: The reduction in reported crimes with each re-interview was an unexpected problem created by the NCS technique. Either behavioural changes or conditioning to the survey results in the number of crimes reported declining with each re-interview.
6. Included as unbounded surveys were those new to the panel and those old addresses with a new household.
7. While calculated somewhat differently, these are very similar to Murphy and Cowan (1976).

206

8. These estimates are based on the surveys administered in February 1985 covering the pre-vious six months. All addresses not included in the survey before and all households not sur-veyed before are considered to be unbounded.
9. The surveys used for this analysis are the 1981 England/Wales and Scottish surveys, NCS/VRS survey, and the Dutch survey of 1984.
10. No correction was possible for robbery because of the few number of occurrences of this crime outside the United States.
11. Prevalence rates were not available for Hong Kong for this preliminary report.
12. Because of the treatment of series crimes, estimates presented here will differ from those of published reports.

BIBLIOGRAPHY

Biderman, A.D. and Cantor, D. (1984). A Longitudinal Analysis of Bounding, Respondent Condi-tioning, and Mobility as Sources of Panel Bias in the National Crime Survey. *Proceedings of the Section on Survey Research Methods* pp. 708–713, *American Statistical Association.*

Biderman, A.D. and Lynch, J.P. (1981). Recency bias in data in self-reported victimization. *Proceedings of the Social Statistics Section* pp. 31–40, *American Statistical Association.*

Bureau of Justice Statistics (1988). *Criminal Victimization in the United States, 1987.* Department of Justice; Washington D.C., 15.

Bushery, J.M. (1981). Recall bias for different reference periods in the National Crime Survey. *Proceedings of the Section on Survey Research Methods* pp. 238–243. *American Statistical Association.*

Cantor, David. (1989). Substantive implications of longitudinal design features: the National Crime Survey as a case study. In *Panel Surveys* (D. Kasprzyk et. al, eds.) pp. 25–51. John Wiley & Sons; New York.

Cantor, David (1985). Operational and Substantive Differences in Changing the NCS Reference Period. Proceedings of the Social Statistics Section pp. 128–137. American Statistical Associ-ation.

Dodge, Richard W. (1985). *Response to Screening Questions in the National Crime Survey.* U.S. Department of Justice, Bureau of Justice, Statistics Technical Report.

Killias, Martin (1987). New methodological perspectives for victimization surveys: lessons from Switzerland, National Crime Survey. The American Society of Criminology 39th Annual Meeting, Montreal, Quebec, Canada; November 1987.

Killias, Martin (1990). Gun ownership and violent crime: the Swiss experience in international perspective. *Security Journal,* **1**, 1169–174.

LaVange, Lisa M. and Folsom, Ralph E. (1985). Regression Estimates of National Crime Survey Operations Effects: Adjustment for Non-Sampling Bias p. 109–114. Proceedings of the Social Statistics Section, American Statistical Association.

Murphy, Linda R. and Cowan, Charles D. (1984). Effects of bounding on telescoping in the National Crime Survey. *The National Crime Survey: Working Papers, Volume II: Methodological Studies.* Dept. of Justice, Bureau of Statistics, Washington D.C.

Roman, A.M. and Sliwa, G.A. (1982). *Final Report on the Study Examining the Increased Use of Telephone Interviewing in the National Crime Survey*) (Memorandum dated August 9, 1982). U.S. Bureau of Census; Washington, DC.

Saphire, Diane Griffin (1984). Estimation of Victimization Prevalence Using Data From The National Crime Survey. Springer-Verlag; New York.

Turner, Anthony G. (1984). The effect of memory bias on the design of the National Crime Survey. *The National Crime Survey: Working Papers, Volume II: Methodological Studies.*

van Dijk, Jan J.M., Mayhew, Pat and Killias, Martin (1989). First Findings from the 1989 Multinational Victimization Survey. Annual Meeting of the Society of Criminology, Reno, Nevada, November 1989.

van Dijk, Jan J.M., Mayhew, Pat, and Killias, Martin (1990). Experiences of Crime Across the World: Key Findings of the 1989 International Crime Survey. *Kluwer Law and Taxation Publishers; Deventer, The Netherlands.*

[7]

CRIME AND ECONOMY

11th Criminological
Colloquium
(1994)

ECONOMIC CYCLES AND CRIME IN EUROPE

by
Mr S. FIELD
Research and Statistics, Home Office,
(United Kingdom)

INTRODUCTION

This paper describes an empirical study of crime and economic trends in European countries. Previous research has established a strong association between crime and the business cycle in England and Wales. The aim of this paper is to compare crime trends and the business cycle in a number of European countries using the same approach.

BACKGROUND

The idea that crime is partly determined by economic circumstances is one of the perennial themes of criminology. One of the earliest references to the theme was offered by Von Mayr (1867) who showed that property crime tended to be more prevalent in Bavaria during periods when the price of rye (a staple food) was higher.

More recent work has covered the relation between a wide variety of economic factors and crime, but it has given particular attention to poverty, unemployment and inequality. Belknap (1989) offers a recent, and fairly comprehensive review of such research. However the extent of research on the business cycle as such, (necessarily involving time series analysis) as opposed to the more general effects of economic circumstances on crime has been fairly limited. Among relevant time series studies are those by Cook and Zarkin (1985), Cantor and Land (1985), Land and Felson (1976), Danziger and Wheeler (1975) and Wolpin (1978). The findings of these studies have been far from consistent, and many of the studies undertaken a decade or more ago would not pass muster in relation to modern time series techniques. Many of the reported findings may therefore be questioned on methodological grounds.

Theoretical discussion on crime and economic circumstances reflects two basic ideas. First, wealth may cause crime because wealth generates more targets for crime. When people have money they purchase goods such as cars and televisions, all of which represent opportunities for theft. Second, wealth may prevent crime because when people have money in their pockets they have less need to steal. Stealing goods is much harder work than just going out to buy them. So the wealth of the population may both cause and prevent crime.

The double effect of wealth on crime makes theory difficult to test. It can be argued both that an increase in wealth should cause crime to rise, and that it should cause crime to fall. For these reasons cross-sectional studies of wealth and crime are open to an ambiguous interpretation.

Much of the literature simply elaborates one or other of the two strands of thought regarding wealth and crime. For example, under the economic theory of crime developed by Becker (1974) and others, it is argued that potential criminals allocate their time to a mix of legitimate and illegitimate activities depending on the risks and rewards associated with each. Legitimate rewards will depend on wage rates. Illegitimate rewards will depend in part on the goods available to steal. Both wage rates and available goods will depend on the state of the economy.

Long term and short term effects: the role of the business cycle

Recorded crime has risen in almost every European country in the period since the second world war. It seems likely that the growth of the European economy is in some way tied to this development, most obviously in relation to crimes which have grown in line with the number of suitable targets, such as car theft. Testing such hypotheses is difficult, since reliable comparative international data on the growth in actual (as opposed to recorded) crime is elusive in the period before victim surveys.

57

This paper is concerned with a different issue — the short term effects of the business cycle. While these are far from independent of long term effects, they are likely to be different in nature. In any case, time series data, of the type employed in this study, are a less appropriate tool for exploring long term effects than are cross-sectional data.

THE STUDY OF CRIME AND THE BUSINESS CYCLE IN ENGLAND AND WALES

A systematic study of crime and the business cycle in England and Wales was published in Field (1990). Field examined the post second world war period in relation to a wide variety of other factors, including not only economic factors, but also criminal justice and other social variables.

His main finding was of a very strong link between the business cycle and most types of crime. Trends in property crime were strongly and inversely associated with the business cycle, as indicated in figure 1.

Figure 1

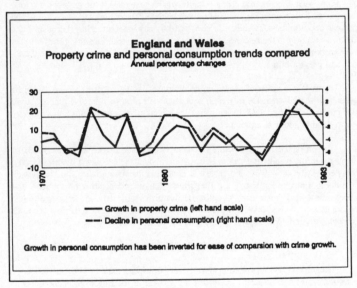

58

This relationship is apparent in a wide variety of different offences undertaken for gain, including theft, burglary, robbery and fraud. Although it is at its strongest in the last 20 years, it can be traced back to the time of the first world war.

In good years for the economy, when spending is rising fast, property crime tends to rise more slowly or even fall. Conversely, during recessions, when spending is falling, property crime rises rapidly. In good years for the economy, when spending is rising fast, property crime rises slowly, or even falls. Property crime was therefore found to have a counter-cyclic relation to the business cycle.

Although the immediate effect of consumption growth is to hold down property crime, there is a tendency for property crime to 'bounce back' a few years later. There is no long run association between consumption growth and property crime. This can be proved by looking at five year periods: since the beginning of this century, there has been no association at all between the rate of growth of consumption in five year periods and crime growth in the same periods.

Quite the opposite pattern was observed with 'personal' crimes not undertaken for gain — assaults and sexual offences. During favourable periods for the economy, when consumption is growing rapidly, growth in the number of such crimes tends to accelerate. Personal crime therefore has a *pro-cyclic* relation to business cycle in England and Wales. The relation is not nearly as strong as in the case of property crime.

EXPLANATIONS

At the outset, the double effect of wealth on crime was described. Wealth may cause crime because wealth generates more goods available to steal; we might call this the *opportunity* effect. Alternatively, wealth may prevent crime because wealthier people have less need to steal; this may be called the *motivation* effect.

In England and Wales, the immediate effect of an economic recession tends to be an acceleration in property crime. The motivation effect therefore appears to be dominant, at least in the short term. In the longer run it appears to be balanced by the opposing opportunity effect.

There are two possible reasons why the motivation effect is sometimes dominant in the short run. First, effects on motivation occur through a relatively small group — the young males who are responsible for most recorded crime. In practice, the business cycle has a disproportionate impact on the economic circumstances of this group, since they are unlikely to be in settled employment. This means that the effects of the business cycle are amplified.

Second, on the other side, the opportunities for crime are not determined by current purchases of goods, but by the stock of goods available for theft. This will be determined by purchases made in the last few years. For example, the number of cars on the street — all potential targets of theft — is the affected by the economic situation over the last few years; not by the 1994 economic situation. In other words the effect of the economy on the opportunities for crime is delayed.

The result is that the short term effect of consumption growth is to hold down crime, but this is balanced by a longer term, reverse effect.

Finally, there is yet a third effect of consumption on crime. In the last fifteen years the routine activity theory of crime has been developed extensively, stemming from a paper by Cohen and Felson (1979). Central to this theory has been the idea that people are more vulnerable to crime — particularly crimes of violence and sexual offences, when they are away from their homes. We now have a lot of empirical evidence to support this view.

This theory has an economic dimension. People tend to spend less time out and about, whether earning or spending, during economic recessions. Staying at home and watching television is cheap. Staying at home and watching television also tends to reduce the level of crime. This is a third effect of consumption on crime. Although it has some effect on property crime, its strongest effects are felt on violent crime and sexual offences. This routine activity effect almost certainly explains the pro-cyclic relation between personal crime and consumption in England and Wales.

The choice of economic variable

The analysis of data for England and Wales, repeated here using European data, uses personal consumption as the main economic variable for analysis. This approach is unusual, and the theoretical basis deserves explanation.

Under the modern economic theories of consumption (as for example in Ando and Modigliani, 1963) it is argued that current levels of personal consumption are primarily determined by the expected lifetime stream of income and wealth, rather than by current income. The idea behind this is that people do not have to match current consumption to current income. In any one year, they can choose to spend less than their income and save the rest, or borrow in order to spend more than their income. However in the long term people have to limit their spending to that permitted by their lifetime wealth and income. With this constraint in mind, people will limit their current consumption according to their expected income in the long term. A person expecting a legacy may happily run up debts, while someone approaching retirement without a pension may save heavily. It follows that current consumption tends to reflect long term income expectations, and a change in consumption reflects a change in those long term expectations. In a real sense, therefore a change in consumption reflects a much more fundamental reassessment of economic circumstances than does a change in disposable income, which might, for example, reflect adverse circumstances which are known to be temporary.

Although both consumption and unemployment are indicators of the business cycle, the two factors can be distinguished. In England and Wales, Field showed that consumption is far more closely associated with crime trends than is unemployment, and that once the effect of consumption is taken into account, unemployment has no additional power to explain crime trends. To examine whether the same result might apply in other European countries, unemployment data were also examined.

DATA FOR THE EUROPEAN STUDY

Data on crime and economic trends were collected from a number of European countries for comparison with economic data. The main source of data was Interpol crime statistics, but two auxiliary crime data sets were also employed.

Data were extracted form the Interpol publications which collate figures for recorded crime from many different countries from around the world. Data were extracted for as many European countries as possible. Interpol attempt to collect data in categories which are so far as possible common to all the different countries. In practice, the different systems of criminal law, and different means of data collection mean that there are great difficulties in comparing the level of crime in one country with that in another country using the Interpol measure. In the period up to 1976, Interpol published crime data in seven categories and in thirteen categories in the period since 1976. A time series for the whole period was constructed using the crime categories of the early period, associating the crime categories as indicated in table 1.

Table 1:   Interpol Crime Categories

Crime category in period up to 1976	Crime category in period since 1977
Murder	Murder
Sex offences	Sex offences (including rape)
	Rape
	Serious Assault
	Theft (all kinds of theft)
Minor larceny: all other kinds of larceny	Aggravated Theft
	Theft of motor cars
	Other thefts
Major larceny: robbery and burglary	robbery and violent theft
	Breaking and entering
Fraud	Fraud
Counterfeit currency offences	Counterfeit currency offences
Drugs offences	Drug offences
Total number of offences	Total number of offences

Given the large number of gaps in the data, an interpolation procedure was used to estimate data points where one or two years' data were missing. Where one year's data were missing, the crime figures for the year were estimated as being the average of the preceding and the following year. Where two years data were missing, the crime figures were again estimated as being intermediate between the years for which data are available, on the assumption that crime displayed a linear trend during the three years between the two points in time for which data were available.

61

Finally, inspection of the data revealed that there were nevertheless some breaks in the data series at 1976-77, (when the definitional changes in Interpol data were introduced). Where these were clear, the data were 'spliced', so that the annual growth rate for 1976-77 was treated as the average of the growth rates in 1975-76 and 1977-78.

Applying this approach yielded crime statistics covering a number of types of crime for the following countries:

Austria	Italy
Belgium	Luxembourg
Denmark	Norway
England and Wales	Spain
Finland	Sweden
France	The Netherlands
Greece	West Germany

It was decided to abandon data for Luxembourg, since they are too patchy for a sensible analysis. Data were analysed for the other 13 countries.

Recording and reporting

This study is based on crimes recorded by the police; many crimes, however, are not reported, and some reported crimes are not recorded. Figures for recorded crime therefore measure reporting and recording practices as well as actual crime. This raises the question of the extent to which trends in recorded crime reflect trends in recording and reporting rather than trends in actual crime.

While no direct evidence on this point was assessed across European countries, there are some reassuring points. The evidence from the United States, where a reasonably long time series of victim surveys is available, is that annual changes in crime rates are reasonably well correlated as between victim surveys and recorded crime. The link between reported crime the economic cycle in England and Wales does not seem to be an artefact of reporting and recording practice, for the link was at its strongest in well-reported crimes such as car theft, and average theft loss data yielded no evidence of a business cycle effect on the propensity to report smaller losses. This leaves us with some reason to believe that the results of the present study relate to actual, as well as recorded crime trends.

Economic data

Data on personal consumption and on total unemployment were collected for the same time periods for these countries from OECD compendia of economic data (OECD, 1988, 1992, 1993).

62

METHOD

Most crime rates show a relatively steady long run rate of growth, such that their growth rates do not show a long term tendency to drift in one or other direction although they do fluctuate from year to year. In this respect they are similar to unemployment and consumption data. In the past, a common statistical pitfall in time series analysis was to directly compute the correlation between two variables displaying time trends, report a statistically significant result (which reflected no more than the fact that time trends were common to both variables) and draw the inference that the two factors were causally related.

To avoid this difficulty, time trends were removed from the data before beginning the analysis. This was achieved by analysing the data in terms of the annual percentage growth rates of crime and economic variables, rather than in terms of the level of crime. (It is, of course, also possible for there to be time trends in growth rates, as well as in levels, but inspection of the data yielded little evidence of this phenomenon).

Initially each crime variable was regressed first against a constant and consumption growth and second against a constant plus unemployment growth. Associated with each regression are a set of three 'mis-specification' tests — normality, heteroscedasticity and serial correlation. These tests are designed to ensure that the assumptions on which the regression models is based are valid. The test for normality is also a useful means of testing the stability of the dataset under analysis, since it will identify outliers — anomalous years for the growth of crime which might equally well be attributed to a change in data definitions or collection procedures.

The main regression models were therefore:

$$\Delta Cijt = \beta_o + \beta_1 * \Delta Sjt$$
$$\Delta Cijt = \beta_o + \beta_1 * \Delta Ujt$$

where:

$\Delta Cijt$ is the annual percentage change in the number of crimes of type i in country j in year t.

ΔSjt is the annual percentage change in personal consumption in country j in year t.

ΔUjt is the annual percentage change in the number of unemployed persons in country j in year t.est la variation annuelle en pourcentage du nombre de chômeurs dans le pays j pour l'année t.

β_o and β_1 are coefficients.

Further regressions were then conducted, adding a lagged dependent variable and two additional lags to the economic variable to the regressors, to test for the relevance of lagged effects. Very little additional information of any significance emerged from these additional regressions and they have not been reported here.

63

RESULTS

Table 2:   Serious theft, robbery and burglary

CONSUMPTION	Estimated coefficients and t-ratios		Diagnostic statistics				
	Intercept	Consumption growth	R-squared	Standard error	Normality	Heterosce dasticity	Serial cor-relation
Austria	5.7 (4.0)	-.5 (1.1)	.01	10.7	fail		
Denmark	6.5 (2.1)	.0 (.6)	.00	9.4			
England and Wales	8.4 (1.5)	-1.1 (0.3)	.35	7.2			
France	9.1 (1.9)	-0.3 (0.3)	.03	9.0			fail
Netherlands	13.2 (2.6)	-0.3 (0.7)	.01	9.5			
Sweden (1974-1990)	2.3 (1.7)	-0.4 (0.4)	.07	6.8			
UNEMPLOYMENT	Estimated coefficients and t-ratios		Diagnostic statistics				
	Intercept	unemployment growth	R-squared	Standard error	Normality	Heterosce dasticity	Serial cor-relation
Denmark	6.8 (1.9)	.0 (.0)	.06	9.4			
England and Wales	4.9 (1.7)	.00 (.01)	.01	8.9			
France	6.4 (2.0)	0.3 (0.1)	.15	8.7			
Netherlands	11.6 (2.1)	.1 (0.1)	.04	9.7			
Sweden (1974-1990)	20.1 (10.5)	-0.17 (0.10)	.20	5.7			
	Shaded area indicates estimated coefficient significantly different from zero at the .05 level.						

The results for serious theft, burglary and robbery are given in table 2. Usable data were only available for 6 countries. Only in the case of England and Wales and France were economic factors found to be relevant.

Table 3   Minor theft

CONSUMPTION	Estimated coefficients and t-ratios		Diagnostic statistics				
	Intercept	consumption growth	R-squared	Standard error	Normality	Heterosce dasticity	Serial cor-relation
Denmark	7.1 (2.4)	-0.6 (0.7)	0.02	11.2	fail		
Finland	5.2 (2.9)	0.5 (0.7)	0.02	9.7			
France	8.9 (3.2)	-0.3 (0.5)	0.01	15.4	fail		
West Germany	3.0 (2.3)	-0.5 (0.6)	0.02	6.9	fail		
UNEMPLOYMENT	Estimated coefficients and t-ratios		Diagnostic statistics				
	Intercept	unemploy-ment growth	R-squared	Standard error	Normality	Heterosce dasticity	Serial cor-relation
Denmark	6.4 (2.3)	.0 (.0)	.00	11.7	fail		
Finland	7.1 (2.0)	.0 (.1)	.00	10.0			
France	6.2 (1.7)	0.2 (0.1)	.12	7.3	fail		
West Germany	1.2 (1.5)	.03 (.03)	.03	7.2	fail		
	Shaded area indicates estimated coefficient significantly different from zero at the .05 level.						

Table 3 gives the results for less serious theft, on which data were available for 5 countries. In no case was there significant evidence that economic factors were affecting the crime rate.

Although tables 2 and 3 yielded few significant associations, some evidence emerges from the overall pattern of results that consumption growth is negatively correlated with the growth of theft offences in most countries. Five out of six countries show negative correlations in the case of serious theft, and three out of four in the case of minor theft.

65

Table 4   **Fraud**

CONSUMPTION	Estimated coefficients and t-ratios		Diagnostic statistics				
	Intercept	consumption growth	R-squared	Standard error	Normality	Heterosced asticity	Serial cor-relation
Belgium (1977-1990)	-0.2 (20.3)	3.6 (8.3)	.02	49.0	fail		
Denmark	3.8 (5.0)	-0.5 (1.5)	.00	22.9			fail
England and Wales	.1 (1.7)	-0.4 (0.3)	.05	8.1			
France	7.6 (3.9)	0.6 (0.6)	.00	18.7	fail		
Greece (1974-1990)	22.3 (10.3)	-7.5 (3.9)	.20	27.2			
Norway	4.7 (2.8)	-1.0 (0.8)	.06	11.3			
West Germany	7.8 (1.5)	-2.1 (0.4)	.45	4.7			

UNEMPLOYMENT	Estimated coefficients and t-ratios		Diagnostic statistics				
	Intercept	unemploy-ment growth	R-squared	Standard error	Normality	Heterosced asticity	Serial cor-relation
Belgium (1977-1990)	7.9 (13.9)	-0.4 (1.2)	.01	49.3	fail		
Denmark	3.9 (4.5)	-.07 (.07)	.04	22.8			
England and Wales	4.5 (1.4)	.00 (.01)	.01	7.3			
France	10.3 (4.3)	.00 (0.3)	.00	19.0			
Greece (1974-1990)	5.5 (3.3)	.12 (.34)	.01	30.4			fail
Norway	2.5 (2.5)	.01 (.07)	.04	12.1			
Sweden (1974-1990)	47.0 (28.1)	-0.4 (0.3)	.17	15.3	fail		
West Germany	1.3 (1.1)	.06 (.02)	.20	5.7			

Shaded area indicates estimated coefficient significantly different from zero at the .05 level.

The fraud results, as outlined in table 4 are striking in that no country displayed any association between economic factors and fraud except West Germany, where the association was extraordinarily strong. Once again, despite a general lack of statistical significance at the individual country level, there was some overall tendency for fraud offences, like theft offences, to behave counter-cyclically: five of the seven countries display inverse associations between fraud and consumption growth.

The case of West Germany was so striking that the data were plotted in figure 2.

Figure 2

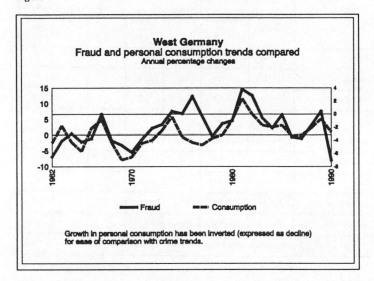

The unemployment regressions are not tabulated here but they show no association with fraud except in the case of West Germany where the association was much less strong than in the case of consumption growth.

Tables 5 and 6 give results for murder and sexual offences. Murder is a particularly relevant crime in that the recorded crime figures may be less subject to the effects of recording and reporting variations than in the case of other offences. No relation with the business cycle emerged in the case of either type of offence, save for sexual offences in England and Wales.

No results were tabulated for drug offences or for counterfeiting, since data from very few countries were adequate for analysis.

Table 5:   **Murder**

CONSUMPTION	Estimated coefficients and t-ratios		Diagnostic statistic				
	Intercept	consumption growth	R-squared	Standard error	Normality	Heterosce dasticity	Serial cor-relation
Austria	-1.6 (5.4)	1.0 (1.5)	.02	14.3			
Denmark	12.6 (6.2)	-1.2 (1.8)	.02	28.6			fail
England and Wales	3.5 (2.1)	0.1 (0.4)	.01	9.9			
France	4.2 (1.5)	-0.3 (0.2)	.05	7.1			
Greece	14.8 (8.6)	-2.3 (3.2)	.03	22.8			
Netherlands (1962-1983)	7.3 (3.3)	0.6 (0.7)	.03	10.1			
Spain	10.1 (8.6)	-1.1 (1.9)	.01	31.9			
Sweden (1974-1990)	5.6 (2.0)	0.7 (0.5)	.13	8.1			
West Germany	0.7 (2.3)	0.70 (0.66)	.04	7.1			

Shaded area indicates estimated coefficient significantly different from zero at the .05 level.

Table 6:   **Sexual offences**

CONSUMPTION	Estimated coefficients and t-ratio		Diagnostic statistics				
	Intercept	consumption growth	R-squared	Standard error	Normality	Heterosce dasticity	Serial cor-relation
Denmark	-0.4 (2.9)	-0.7 (0.8)	.02	13.1			fail
England and Wales	-0.2 (0.9)	0.63 (0.16)	0.35	4.1			
France	2.2 (1.0)	-0.13 (0.16)	.03	4.9			
West Germany	0.3 (1.4)	-0.7 (0.4)	.10	4.2			fail
Norway	4.4 (3.2)	-0.4 (0.9)	.01	13.0			
Netherlands	1.8 (1.7)	-0.3 (0.4)	.02	6.0			
Sweden (1974-1990)	4.2 (2.4)	0.3 (0.6)	.02	9.9			

Shaded area indicates estimated coefficient significantly different from zero at the .05 level.

These results provide little evidence of any general association between crime and economic trends. However there were significant difficulties with the data under examination. Some of the data was unusable because of dramatic changes in the level of crime which appear from year to year or because of gaps in the data. It might be that the data set as a whole is flawed by these difficulties. As a cross check on this possibility two further data sets were examined carefully. Additional analysis was therefore conducted on a data set for the 1950-1981 period prepared by Statistics Sweden, and on a second data set prepared for an earlier Council of Europe study covering the offences of wounding, motor vehicle theft and all crimes in France, Germany, England and Wales between 1964 and 1982 (Statistics Sweden, 1983; Council of Europe, 1985).

A full set of regressions was prepared using these data sets. However their results do not yield anything which goes beyond that revealed in the correlation matrices for growth rates, which are reported below in Table 7.

Two main results emerge from this table. First, rape offences in Norway and Sweden appear to rise more rapidly when unemployment falls — so that rape offences have a pro-cyclic relation to the economy This finding is consistent with that for sexual offences in England and Wales, although unemployment rather than personal consumption appears to exert the dominant influence in Scandinavia.

Second, motor vehicle theft has a pro-cyclic relation to the business cycle in West Germany. This is the opposite finding to that reported for England and Wales in the earlier study (which does not quite emerge as significant in the more limited data summarised in the table above).

Of other findings, the results for assaults in Finland can be discounted as a variety of legislative and statistical changes have probably rendered the data unstable. Although the results here show that unemployment, rather than consumption is more closely associated with motor vehicle theft, Field (1990) showed that consumption is the dominant economic factor over a long time period.

Table 7: **Correlations between annual percentage changes in recorded crime and in indicators of the business cycle**

SCANDINAVIA 1950-1981

		Murder	Rape	Assault	Theft	Robbery
CONSUMPTION	Denmark	-0.31	0.08	-0.38	-0.24	-0.42
	Norway	0.20	0.12	-0.11	-0.15	-0.29
	Sweden	0.14	0.13	0.20	0.15	0.16
	Finland	-0.10	0.19	0.57	0.03	0.26
UNEMPLOYMENT	Denmark	-0.10	0.09	0.15	-0.15	0.04
	Norway	0.14	-0.50	0.09	0.23	0.42
	Sweden	0.02	-0.46	-0.38	0.00	0.14
	Finland	0.11	-0.27	-0.52	0.22	-0.10

FRANCE, WEST GERMANY AND ENGLAND AND WALES, 1964-1982

		Wounding	Motor vehicle theft	Total crimes
CONSUMPTION	France	0.01	0.06	-0.01
	Germany	-0.13	0.57	-0.20
	England and Wales	0.34	-0.28	-0.76
UNEMPLOYMENT	France	0.09	0.14	0.09
	Germany	-0.04	-0.23	0.33
	England and Wales	-0.28	0.56	-0.04

▒▒▒▒▒	Shaded correlation coefficients are statistically significant at .05 level.

70

CONCLUSIONS AND DISCUSSION

In Europe, with the notable exception of Britain, the relationship between the business cycle and crime appears weak. Only in isolated contexts, such as in the case of rape in some Scandinavian countries, or fraud and vehicle theft in West Germany, are clear relationships evidence.

At the same time, the results do seem to confirm that crime-business cycle links, where they exist, usually take the form observed most clearly in Britain. Rape in Scandinavia and fraud in West Germany both obey this rule. Moreover, although the individual results were not statistically significant, there does appear some overall tendency for property crime to behave counter-cyclically, as indicated in the negative coefficients on the consumption variables in tables 2-4. This rule, that property crime tends to rise during recessions, while personal crimes including assaults and sexual offences tend to fall has been observed in a number of contexts, and has been remarked on by Bonger (1916) and Radzinowicz (1971).

However the results are surprising in that a very strong and clear relationship in one country has no parallels elsewhere in Europe. This suggests that the driving forces connecting crime to economic trends in England and Wales are distinctive of that country. It would be fruitless to speculate on the answer to such a complex question, which clearly requires further research. Such research would have to examine what elements in the British business cycle are relatively distinctive of that country. One element deserving of examination is the British housing market, which bears a more intimate relationship with the business cycle in Britain than in many other countries.

At the same time, the British results are certainly not unique. Fraud offences in West Germany are very closely tied to the business cycleIt would be intriguing to place these results in a wider international context. There are some indications, noted in Field (1990), that aggregate crime trends in the United States and Japan are also counter-cyclic, (reflecting trends in numerically predominant property crime).

There is no evidence for any association between murder and the business cycle in Europe. This is consistent with results from the U. S. (Cook and Zarkin, 1985). On the theoretical grounds advanced at the outset, there are in fact few reasons to connect murders to the business cycle. Since a large proportion of recorded murders are domestic, they cannot be tied to time away from home in the same way as many recorded assaults.

Finally, the limitations of this exercise deserve to be re-emphasized. It has concerned itself with the short term impact of fluctuations in economic circumstances only. Even where crime trends are independent of the business cycle, it by no means follows that crime is independent of economic circumstances. The longer term effect of economic change deserves separate assessment.

BIBLIOGRAPHY

Ando, A. and Modigliani, F. (1963). 'The 'Life Cycle' hypothesis of saving: aggregate implications and tests' *American Economic Review* vol 53, pp. 55-84.

Becker, G. (1974). 'Crime and punishment: an economic approach' in *Essays in the Economics of Crime and Punishment* New York: National Bureau of Economic Research.

Belknap, J. E. (1989). 'The economics-crime link'.

Bonger, W. (1916). *Criminality and Economic Conditions.* Chicago: Little and Brown.

Cantor, D. and Land, K. C. (1985) 'Unemployment and crime rates in the post-world war II United States: a theoretical and empirical analysis' *American Sociological Review* vol 50, pp. 317 - 332.

Cohen, L. E., and Felson, M. (1979) 'Social change and crime rate trends: a routine activity approach' *American Sociological Review*, vol 44, pp. 588-608.

Cook, P. J. and G. A. Zarkin (1985). 'Crime and the business cycle'. *Journal of Legal Studies* 14: 115-128.

Council of Europe. *Economic Crisis and Crime* (1985). European Committee on Crime Problems. Strasbourg: Council of Europe.

Danziger, S. and D. Wheeler (1975). 'The economics of crime: punishment or income redistribution'. *Review of Social Economy 33, 2: 113-131.*

OECD. (1988, 1992) *Labour Force Statistics.* 1966-1986; 1970-1990. Paris: OECD.
OECD. (1993) *Main Economic Indicators. Historical Statistics: prices, labor and wages.* Paris: OECD.

Orsagh, T. and Witte, A. D. (1981) 'Economic status and crime: implications for offender rehabilitation'. *Journal of Criminal Law and Criminology* vol 72, No. 3, pp. 1055-1071.

Radzinowicz, L. (1971). 'Economic pressures' in Radzinowicz, L. and Wolfgang, M. (Eds.), *Crime and Justice* vol 1, London: Basic Books.

Statistics Sweden. (1983). *Nordic Criminal Statistics.* Stockholm: Statistics Sweden.

Thomas, D. A. (1925). *Social Aspects of the Business Cycle.* London: Routledge.

Wolpin, K. I. (1978). 'An economic analysis of crime and punishment in England and Wales 1894-1967' *Journal of Political Economy* vol. 86, 5, pp. 815-40.

Von Mayr (1867) ''Statistik der gerichtlichen Polizei im Konigreiche Bayern', cited in Mannheim, H. (1965). *Comparative Criminology vol 2.* London: Routledge.

[8]

International Review of Victimology, 1992, Vol. 2, pp. 85–102
0269-7580/92 $10
© 1992 A B Academic Publishers—Printed in Great Britain

MULTIPLE VICTIMISATION: ITS EXTENT AND SIGNIFICANCE

GRAHAM FARRELL

Department of Social Policy and Social Work, Manchester University, M13 9PL, UK

ABSTRACT

The extent and significance of multiple and repeat victimisation have gone largely unrecognised. The literature is explored with respect to demonstrating that multiple victimisation is robust across crime types and method of study. Nine different research methods suggest a similar pattern of the distribution of victimisation; a small proportion of the population experience a large proportion of all crime. In the British Crime Survey, 70% of all incidents were reported by the 14% of respondents who are multiple victims (a conservative figure). With respect to significance, victimisation should not be studied without fully accounting for multiple victimisation. Many areas of policy and practice may be affected by a recognition of the importance of multiple victimisation. For crime prevention policy, if repeat or multiple victimisation can be prevented, a large proportion of all crime might be prevented. Crime prevention strategy developed through responses to victimisation should be spatially and temporally focused.

INTRODUCTION

It has long been suggested that some offenders repeatedly offend, (recidivist offending) and account for a disproportionately large amount of all offences committed. However, it has barely been recognised that some people, households, or other targets however defined, may, through being 'recidivist' or repeat victims, account for a large proportion of all offences experienced. (This is not necessarily to suggest a link between the two phenomena.) Despite the growth of victimology in the past two decades, there is an absence of substantive research into multiple victimisation. This is reflected in most crime-related activities. Recognition of the importance of repeat victimisation may have implications for several spheres, for example: crime prevention strategy, other aspects of the criminal justice system, health services, insurance industries and security industries.

The bulk of the paper is concerned with demonstrating that similar patterns of multiple victimisation can be found regardless of type of crime or method of study and analysis. To give a clearer structure, the paper is divided into a general literature section, followed by three specialised sections on the British Crime Survey (BCS), evidence from a local crime

86

survey which generated the present writer's initial interest in multiple victimisation, and a section on repeat victimisation and crime prevention. The accompanying discussion of the theoretical and policy implications in the concluding section is by no means exhaustive.

The term multiple victimisation is used in this paper to refer to multiple criminal incidents experienced by either a person or place. It is also called repeat victimisation, recidivist victimisation, or multi-victimisation. This definition will be developed as the paper progresses.

One area of influence for multiple victimisation might be upon crime prevention strategy. This is used as a practical illustration throughout, and provides a useful backdrop for the paper. Multiple victimisation is a complex social phenomenon, and there is a great difference between types of crime. Opinion will probably remain divided on the potential of multiple victimisation for general crime prevention strategy. However, this should not detract from recognition of the importance of multiple victimisation.

If a summary of the potential for developing a general crime prevention strategy around multiple victimisation had to be given, it might take the form given below, split into three parts;

(i)   Reason: If multiple victimisation (using the broadest definition), could be prevented, most crimes would be prevented. That is, if a small proportion of the population are repeatedly victimised so that they experience a large proportion of **all** criminal offences, then preventing repeat victimisation would prevent a large proportion of **all** offences from being committed[1,2].

(ii) Illustration: The information gathered by the 1982 British Crime Survey suggests that over 70%, or over seven in ten, of the offences it covered, were experienced by just 14% of the total population.

(iii) Method: The prevention of multiple victimisation might be developed through responses to victimisation.

Agency responses, the last part of the summary, are not the subject of this paper. They are touched on briefly in the concluding section. Before this aspect can be developed further, the extent and significance of multiple victimisation needs to be established.

Within sections, the review of the literature is presented in an approximate chronological order, to demonstrate how discussion of multi-victimisation is still in a very early stage of development. It would be difficult to claim that this is an exhaustive review since multiple victimisation is often hidden within, or secondary to, another subject of study. The individual studies and sections each contribute to the overall picture of multiple victimisation, so that they provide a more comprehensive and persuasive argument when considered as a whole.

REVIEW OF LITERATURE

In 1973, Johnson *et al.* published a monograph entitled *The Recidivist Victim; A Descriptive Study*. The study attempted to describe the social, medical and criminal characteristics of victims and recidivist victims of gunshot and stabwounds from the records of a US hospital. The study emerged due to the authors' personal experiences of the same people returning to the hospital time and again, as repeat victims of these types of violence. Case histories were constructed which showed that some victims, whilst not always 'frequently' returning to the hospital, did so every year or every other year throughout the 1960s. Since it can be supposed that only a small proportion of all violence reaches hospital records, most going unreported, the study might be seen to suggest that some people live with violent repeat victimisation as part of their everyday lives, in some cases over their lifetimes. The purpose of the study was to try to increase awareness of repeat victimisation, though it appears to have been largely overlooked. The paper suggests that criminal justice procedures might be different for multi-victims, for example, in terms of compensation and insurance. In the conclusion, crime prevention policy is implicit when it suggests: 'A suicide or a battered or abused child is automatically reported for investigation, why not a recidivist victim?' (1973; p.75).

Perhaps the earliest work to use a victim survey and concentrate on repeat victimisation is that of Eduard Ziegenhagen, *The Recidivist Victim of Violent Crime* (1976). Ziegenhagen used statistical tests to try to predict any outstanding characteristics of repeat-victims of types of violence. He suggested that they may be of lower socio-economic status than single incident victims and found that repeated assaults were more likely to take place 'inside [a] neighbour's home or other building' (1976; p.549), whereas repeat robberies took place outside, near the home. With respect to gender, Ziegenhagen found that 'males are more likely to be recidivist victims . . . than females probably because of social roles which emphasise violence as an acceptable and in some cases preferred solution to disagreement' (1976; p.545). Whilst this may in part explain why males are more likely to be violent offenders, it does not suffice as an explanation of multi-victimisation, primarily because crimes against women will be under-reported (Ziegenhagen acknowledged that domestic violence will be largely excluded from the survey). Ziegenhagen concludes that for repeat victims of violence, 'expectations that they will be treated worse than others by the police may preclude their participation in crime prevention efforts as well as in police related programs designed to aid victims of crime' (1976; p.550). These findings may suggest either that policing might need to adapt to respond to violent repeat victimisations, or that a different orientation, perhaps with the emphasis on alternative agencies, should be developed for crime prevention efforts aimed at interpersonal crime. This will be discussed at greater length in the context of more recent developments.

The two studies so far mentioned have limited their definition of repeat victimisation. Both looked only at violent crime. Johnson *et al.* (1973) restricted their study to only some of the more serious types of violence, and then only if they were on hospital records. Ziegenhagen (1976) selected interviewees based on police records, which have reporting and recording limitations, and then only studied assault and assault with robbery. Both studies use the phrase 'recidivist' victim, which suggests that the victim is in some way to blame for the repeat victimisation. The phrase 'recidivism' is useful in drawing an analogy with recidivist offending, but unfortunate in that it implicitly blames the victim.

One of the major studies recognising repeat victimisation is also commonly accepted as one of the 'classics' of victim-survey based studies in victimology. *Surveying Victims* by Sparks *et al.* (1977), was based on work conducted in three London boroughs, from which Sparks went on to write a series of articles in the early 1980s (eg. Sparks, 1981), and upon which Genn's article 'Multiple victimisation' (1988) is based. The 1977 book used mathematical modelling to observe the highly skewed distribution of victimisation through their sample. They found that a small percentage of the population, because they were repeatedly victimised, accounted for a substantial proportion of all types of crime in the survey. Initially they attempted to fit the spread of repeat victimisation to a Poisson distribution. The data did not fit this model, which suggested that repeat victimisation was not caused by 'bad luck', that is, it did not correspond to a chance distribution of independent, single-incident, victimisations in a population sampled with replacement. With the further dismissal of a 'contagion' effect Poisson model of victimisation, the attempt was made to fit a heterogeneous model. This was an attempt to fit a Poisson model to different sub-groups of the population characterised by, for example, socio-demographic characteristics such as age, sex and ethnicity, or by type of crime. Whilst this was found to be more accurate than the standard Poisson model, it was "far from perfect".

Hindelang *et al.* devoted a chapter of their 1978 book, *Victims of Personal Crime* (1978) to the analysis of multiple victimisation. They used data from eight US cities and over 165,000 interviews. The book is mainly known for developing the lifestyle/exposure theory of victimisation, which may have overshadowed their work on multiple victimisation. They established certain patterns of multiple victimisation which they summarised as follows:

'First, both once victimised persons and once victimised households were more likely to have suffered subsequent victimisation than were members of the population (persons or households respectively) selected at random. For personal victims, this is accounted for – but only in part – by the finding that repetitive victims were more likely than one-time victims to be victimised by persons known to them. Second, persons living in households in which another household member had been personally victimised had a greater risk of personal victimisation than persons living in households in which no other household member had been personally victimised. Third, persons living in households that had been victimised by a household crime had a higher risk of personal victimisation than persons living in households that had not been victimised by a household crime' (1978; p.149). For Hindelang *et al.*, the implications of multiple victimisation were primarily to provide support for their lifestyle model of victimisation.

Since these three studies, other attempts have been made to investigate repeat victimisation through mathematical and statistical techniques. Albert Reiss (1980), using data from the US National Crime Survey (NCS) wrote:

'Evidence of repeat victimisation makes it clear that victimisation is not a random occurrence...Moreover, in repeat victimisation, there is a proneness to repeat victimisation by the same type of crime' (1980; p.52).

This was a finding echoed by Fienberg (1980), though using different methods of analysis. The two articles are complementary and were published in the same volume. Reiss constructed a crime-switch matrix to explore the difference between observed repeat victimisation as reported in the NCS, and repeat victimisation which would be expected due to random chance. Fienberg used a semi-Markov model to observe the likelihood that a repeat victimisation was of the same or a different crime-type to a prior victimisation. The Markov-chain method has been used in criminology in the study of criminal 'careers' to observe the likelihood that recidivism is by the same or different crime-type (see, for example, Stander *et al.*, 1989). As will be more explicitly developed in section 5, the recognition that one victimisation incident may be followed by another of the same type has direct implications for crime prevention.

The United States NCS, when analysed, excluded 'series' of crimes reported. A series of crimes are crimes which an interviewee deemed to be related (whether rightly or wrongly), so that they appeared as a 'series'. These are potentially of great importance as a prime example of repeat victimisation. According to Albert Reiss (cited in Skogan (1981; p.9)):

'including series incidents (for analyses of the NCS) would increase the estimated number of crimes in the United States by 18 percent.'

Multiple victimisation is mentioned, again all too briefly, in the report of the first Islington Crime Survey (ICS) (Jones *et al.*, 1986; p.84). The survey showed that for all crimes, 47% of households reported multiple victimisation, and that multiple victimisation was most likely for assault (38%), followed by vandalism (37%) and burglary (24%). Much lower rates of repeat victimisation were reported for theft from the person (17%), as might be expected for a relatively 'anonymous' crime, though no

90

information is provided with respect to repeat robbery. The apparently low frequency (15%) of repeat sexual offences reported can probably be put down to the fact that those sexual assaults which are reported may be much more likely to be 'stranger violence', with sexual assaults by men who are known, and which may be more likely to be repeated, going largely unreported. The higher rate of multiple victimisation for all crime than for any of the individual types, again suggests multiple victimisation can be by different types of crime as well as by the same type of crime.

Repeat victimisation may be of particular relevance in the study of racial attacks and racially motivated crime. In the London borough of Newham, a recent crime survey (London Borough of Newham, 1987) showed that 116 ethnic minority victims reported 1,550 incidents of victimisation, though these were not neccessarily all racially motivated. In addition, an ongoing Manchester University project studying violent crime has found that on an estate in the east end of London racial attacks are one of the major problems, as well as being one of the crimes most likely to be repeated (Sampson and Phillips, forthcoming). In this instance, the offenders often know, or can easily find out the address of the ethnic minority victims, and so the opportunity is great for repeated victimisation within a local community.

Genn (1988) provides a shift away from the conventional definition of repeat victimisation used so far in this paper. She provides a critique of victim surveys which impose a strict definition of 'a crime' and 'a victim' upon the interviewee. Most victim surveys have only a one year reporting period, limit the number of crimes which can be reported, and impose an artificial limit on those reported, before computer analysis. Genn suggests that, in particular for certain types of crime such as domestic violence, some people are forced to live with almost continual victimisation as part of their everyday lives. Based upon the findings of a victim survey (Sparks *et al.*, 1977) and the extent of victimisation in some households, Genn returned to the research site to conduct some follow-up interviews. Genn's participant observation study of multiple victimisation included spending several months with a group of victims on a high crime estate in north London. Genn reports that 'after some months of association with this group of people, I no longer found it surprising that a structured questionnaire administered to one household should uncover some thirteen incidents of "victimisation"' (1988; p.93). Genn argued that for some households, victim surveys aften picked up only a fraction of the total incidents. Similar limitations of existing sources of knowledge about victimisation are suggested by Stanko (1988), who argues that most violence remains 'hidden' from official agencies like the police, as well as from victim surveys. This, it is argued, is one of the factors behind the commonly held belief, perpetuated by the media, that violence is usually between strangers. There is an increasing volume of literature to suggest that the majority of violence may take place between familiars, that is, people who know each other, whether as partners, neighbours, relatives, workplace acquaintances, 'friends' or known others (for example, Stanko 1988, 1990; and Smith, 1989 give an overview of some of the literature on domestic violence). The literature draws attention to the fact that a large proportion of familiars' violence is against women. The prevention of violent crime may, therefore, not necessarily be based solely upon recorded crime information from the police, as it might be with burglary (burglary is usually reported for insurance purposes), but has to look at hidden violence against women. Violence by men against women constitutes a large proportion of all violence, and might also be the most likely to be repeat victimisation. Violence between familiars is more likely to be recurrent (for reasons of opportunity at the very least); the most obvious example of this is domestic violence.

Sherman *et al.* (1989) studied the spatial distribution of calls reported to the police. They found that in a major city in the US, 50% of all calls to the police for some types of crime came from 3% of locations. An analogy can be drawn between their locational 'hot-spots of predatory crime', and the phenomenon of repeat victimisation of certain people and households, with a similar potential for focusing crime prevention strategies.

Providing an additional quantitative perspective to the phenomenon of repeat victimisation, Trickett *et al.* (1991), using BCS data, suggest that repeat victimisation is more intense in 'high crime' areas. They broach the important question of whether certain areas have 'high' crime rates because more people are victimised, or because there is greater multiple victimisation of the same people. They suggest a positive correlation between the overall incidence of crime and the extent of repeat victimisation, from which it might be inferred that crime prevention may become more efficient as it becomes more 'focused'. Focusing on repeat victimisation within 'high crime' areas may be more efficient in terms of crimes prevented (as well, therefore, as per unit of labour and expenditure), even than focusing on repeat victimisation across all areas. This first foray into the phenomenon of repeat victimisation from a sociological perspective may suggest that more widespread social differences between areas are the primary determining factors in repeat victimisation, rather than the characteristics or actions of individuals. Suggesting that multiple victimisation is due to area rather than individual characteristics, and that victim-orientated crime prevention strategies can be appropriately focussed in high crime areas is preferable to arguments which blame the victims of crime.

MULTIPLE VICTIMISATION AND THE BRITISH CRIME SURVEY

In 1984, Michael Gottfredson, in writing a Home Office report analysing aspects of the 1982 BCS, included a separate two and a half page appendix

92

'Multiple victimisation' (Gottfredson 1984; pp.41–3). Whilst reducing it to
an appendix has the effect of marginalising the issue, the extent of multiple
victimisation in the BCS is evident:
    'of the victims of personal crime in the BCS, 72% were one time
    victims while 28% were repetitively victimised. For all crimes in the
    survey, the corresponding percentages are 56% one-time victims and
    44% multiple victims...' (1984; p.42).
    Further analysis of the data which Gottfredson presents suggests that
over 70% of all criminal incidents reported by the 1982 BCS were
experienced by multi-victims, who made up only 14% of the population.
This is despite the fact that, as will be discussed later in this paper, the
crimes against women which are under-represented in the BCS (see, for
example, Stanko, 1983), may also be those most likely to result in repeat
victimisation. The distribution of victimisation for 'all offences' in the 1982
BCS is shown in Table 1 below, calculated from Gottfredson (1984; p.41).

TABLE 1

Distribution of victimisation for all offences: 1982 British Crime Survey.

Number of times victimised	Respondents (%)	Incidents (%)
0	68.1	0.0
1	17.8	29.1
2	6.2	20.3
3	3.1	15.2
4	1.8	11.8
5 or more	2.9	23.7
	99.9*	100.1*

* total percent not equal to 100 due to rounding

Table 1 shows the highly skewed distribution of victimisation revealed
by the BCS. This is itself an extremely conservative estimate, given the
current limitations of the BCS for the study of multiple victimisation
(Genn; 1988). Those people who reported having been victimised on two
or more occasions, that is with 'number of times victimised' between 2 and
'5 or more' (left hand column) make up 14% of the population (summing
the four corresponding percentages in the middle column). This 14% of
the population who are multiple victims, in the year covered by the survey,
reported 70.9% of all the incidents reported (summing the four percentages in the right hand column). Similar patterns of the distribution of
victimisation for household offences and personal offences can also be
generated.

93

Some inferences about the extent and nature of multiple victimisation might be made from Hough (1986). Hough presented both incidence and prevalence rates of victimisation for violent crimes (1986; p. 124). In his paper, the incidence rate represents the estimated average number of incidents per 100 respondents, here expressed as a percentage. The prevalence rate represents the estimated percentage of respondents who are victims. For all violent offences in the 1982 BCS, there is a prevalence of 4.5%, and an incidence of 8.02%, suggesting almost twice as many incidents as victims. There are variations within types of violence. The most prevalent crimes are not necessarily those with the highest average number of victimisations per victim. Thus the most prevalent crimes may not necessarily be those with the highest rates of repeat victimisation. (Sexual assaults are excluded here, which, as with other violence between familiars and against women, is largely unreported.) The rankings of incidence and prevalence are the same, with common assault the highest for each, followed by threat of assault, wounding and robbery. However, from the ratio of incidence to prevalence (which is, as discussed below, not a totally unambiguous indicator), robbery appears the most likely type of violence to be repeated. This is followed by assault, threat of assault and wounding. The suggestion is, therefore, that whilst a person is unlikely to be robbed, once robbed they may be the most likely to be robbed again in comparison to the recurrence of other types of violence. Further work is needed to reveal the nature of these relationships. For all types of violence, the ratio of incidence to prevalence for all types of crime is higher than would be expected if it were a sum of the individual types of crime. This suggests that victims report more than one type of violence. Multiple victimisation can therefore be by different types of violent crime as well as by the same type.

Incidence rates are always higher than prevalence rates, with there being more criminal incidents than victims. This is because some people are multiple victims. Presented side by side, incidence and prevalence rates do suggest the existence of multiple victimisation; however they serve as little more than an indicator and a generalisation. They fail to attribute any importance to multiple victimisation, and do not demonstrate the distribution of victimisation within the victimised population, even to the extent of Table 1 above. This is an observation of the way that most of the previous literature has presented victimisation, though there has been a progression from the times when only incidence rates were presented as 'the' victimisation rate. The difficulties which multiple victimisation might provide for criminological study, in particular for computer-coded victim surveys, is not sufficient reason for it to remain marginalised.

Amongst the limitations of the BCS is the fact that interviews are only conducted with persons aged over 16 years. There is very little evidence about the victimisation of young people. The recent Edinburgh survey of

94

the victimisation of young people (Anderson *et al.*, 1990) showed that the victimisation of young people, commonly portrayed primarily as offenders, is widespread. There would as yet appear to be little information available about the extent of multiple victimisation of young people.

EVIDENCE FROM A LOCAL CRIME SURVEY

The project of which the local victim survey was part was the catalyst for the writer's initial interest in multiple victimisation. The project was based on a 'high crime' estate in a British city, and the importance of multiple victimisation became apparent through every different aspect of the project, from the victim survey to police crimes and incident logs (calls from the public), in fieldwork and in the referrals made to the *Victim Support* scheme on the estate. A report by Alice Sampson (1991), presents information about multiple victims referred to the 'high crime' estate-based *Victim Support* scheme which mirror the patterns of repeat victimisation from victim surveys. Sampson found that out of 289 referrals to the scheme over two years, 46 households or residents (16%) were victims of more than one reported crime, and that '(t)hese victims accounted for 38% of the crimes' (1991; p.6). In addition, 20 of the multi-victim households suffered from both property and personal crimes, 20 from at least two property crimes, and 8 people were victims of interpersonal crime only. Of the 46 multi-victims, 'in 10 cases it is not known if the incidents were related or unrelated; in 23 cases the (victim support) workers thought they were unrelated; and in 13 cases the incidents were related (they were either domestic attacks, neighbour disputes or the offender was known but did not live in the same flat or next door)' (1991; pp.6–7). The victim survey on which the present writer worked, carried out on the estate on which the *Victim Support* office was based, found similar patterns of multiple victimisation (Sampson and Farrell, 1990; Farrell, 1990). These findings are valid in their own right, but when viewed in the light of the works already reviewed, lend weight to many of the findings. Six hundred people were interviewed in the survey. Multiple victims accounted for 78.8% of all crimes reported. This finding corresponds with the findings from the BCS where multiple victims accounted for 70% of all crimes. In addition, the higher rate of multiple victimisation on the 'high crime' estate corresponds with the findings of Trickett *et al.* (1991) that repeat victimisation is more intense in high crime areas. The survey also suggested that 5% of the respondents reported 62% of the personal crimes. Of the victims of personal crime, a third were multi-victims of personal crime, and one in six had experienced at least two different types of personal crime in the last year (corresponding with the suggestions from the re-analysis of Hough (1986)). A person or household reporting a burglary or attempted burglary was more than twice as likely to report a personal crime. The suggested link between personal and property crime found both in the survey and in the referrals to the *Victim Support* workers is also recognised by Hindelang *et al.* (1978) and by Gottfredson (1984). The intensity of victimisation of certain people may be even greater than this paper has suggested so far. In the 'high crime' estate victim survey, 15 people (2.5% of respondents) reported 141 incidents (30% of total incidents). The 1982 BCS data shows that 2.9% of the respondents reported 23.7% of the total incidents (see Table 1 above).

PREVENTING MULTIPLE AND REPEAT VICTIMISATION

Whilst some of the implications of multiple victimisation for crime prevention policy have already been mentioned (Trickett *et al.*, 1991), the only existing application of these practices is the Kirkholt Burglary Prevention Project (Forrester *et al.*, 1988a) which aimed to reduce burglary on a council housing estate in Rochdale, in the north west of England. The initial research phase combined interviews with known (detained) burglars, with burglary victims and their neighbours, and analysis of available burglary data, to find that,

'once a house had been burgled, its chance of further victimisation was four times the rate of houses that had not been burgled at all'
(Forrester *et al.*, 1988b; p.2289)

The strategy was developed to implement a combined package of opportunity reduction and situational crime prevention measures at those households which were burgled during the course of the project. These were the houses that were predicted to be the most likely victims in the near future, and the package of measures effectively stopped repeat victimisation. The final report of the project (Forrester *et al.*, 1990) states that burglary was reduced by 75% within three years. In addition, the project also implemented social crime prevention measures, such as initiatives in the local schools, to try to reduce the future levels of offending in the area. The project has been 'returned to the community' with the intention that its members will work to maintain its practices. As a crime prevention project, this provides the most persuasive indications to date that the targeting of repeat victimisation may be a successful, focused and economically viable means of general crime prevention. The perceived attractions of the prevention of repeat victimisation as a general strategy of crime prevention are summarised in Pease (1991; p.76):

' – Attention to dwellings or people already victimised has a higher 'hit rate' of those likely to be victimised in the future.
– Preventing repeat victimisation protects the most vulnerable social groups, without having to identify those groups as such, which can

96

> be socially divisive. Having been victimised already probably
> represents the least contentious basis for a claim to be given crime
> prevention attention.
> – Repeat victimisation is highest, both absolutely and proportion-
> ately, in the most crime-ridden areas (Trickett *et al.*, 1991), which
> are also the areas that suffer the most serious crime (Pease, 1988).
> The prevention of repeat victimisation is thus commensurately
> more important the greater an area's crime problem.
> – The rate of victimisation offers a realistic schedule for crime
> prevention activity. Preventing repeat victimisation is a way of
> "drip-feeding" crime prevention.
> – Even from the unrealistic view that crime is only displaced,
> avoiding repeat victimisation at least shares the agony around
> (see Barr and Pease, 1990).'

Whilst the Kirkholt project focused solely on burglary prevention, Pease
argues that its theoretical base provides a foundation for crime prevention
of a general nature. This is not necessarily to argue that the opportunity
reduction and situational measures used in the Kirkholt project are
generally applicable – these were tailored for the specific project – rather
that crime prevention in general might concentrate upon the phenomenon
of repeat victimisation. The 'drip-feeding' of crime prevention is an
analogy created to suggest that targeting repeat victimisation is more
practically viable – it is spread through time, and hence less labour
intensive and easier to maintain. Obviously the main motivation underlying the prevention of repeat victimisation is the social benefit to the
victim(s) and the community, but other positive externalities would
include such as police-labour saved for crimes prevented (no crime
reports, no follow-ups).

The main objection to the prevention of repeat victimisation as it has
so far been discussed might be that crimes perceived to be 'prevented'
might instead be displaced. Barr and Pease (1990) suggest that whilst much
of the literature on displacement is inconclusive, it is unlikely that all crime
'prevented' in one place will occur elsewhere, and that even if it does this
may result in a more egalitarian distribution of crime.

The time interval between a victimisation and a further victimisation
has significant implications for crime prevention policy. The work on the
likelihood of repeat victimisation, pioneered by Reiss (1980) has been
furthered by Polvi *et al.* (1990) using recorded burglaries for the whole of
Saskatoon city in Canada for 1987. They showed a similar pattern to
Forrester *et al.* (1988a, 1988b) about the likelihood of repeat burglaries.
Across the city, dwellings were nearly four times as likely to be burgled
following a first burglary. The importance of Polvi *et al.*'s work lies in the
time-course analysis, where it was found that:

> 'following a first burglary...the disporportionate risk is primarily
> encountered in the month following the first victimisation, and within

that month in the first days following the first break-and-enter offense' (1990; p.11).

Along similar lines, Farrell and Pease (1991) looked at the extent of crimes reported in 1990 by thirty three schools in an area of Merseyside. Seven schools reported only one crime, and the most victimised school reported 28 crimes in 1990. Of the total of 296 crimes reported, 263 (97.6%) were repeat crimes. Of these, 208 or 79% were revictimisations occuring within one month of a prior victimisation. The implication for crime prevention is that responses to victimisation must be immediate, but that the necessary duration for a prevention strategy may be relatively short in order to prevent a large proportion of repeat victimisation.

A prevention strategy based upon repeat victimisation must have sources of information about crime. With respect to sources of information, property and personal crimes can again be contrasted. A large proportion of burglaries and car thefts are reported to the police (Hough and Mayhew, 1985), not least for insurance purposes. However, as already mentioned, much violence goes unreported. In order to have any chance of preventing repeat victimisation, knowledge of the occurrence of crime must be increased beyond that of recorded crime. Existing sources of information must be explored, and potential sources developed. One alternative to recorded crimes is police incident logs or message pads (which are mainly telephone calls to the police from the public). To give one concrete example, an ongoing Manchester University project researching violence has found that on one estate in Merseyside of about 1300 houses, there were (the least estimate) 143 calls to the police about domestic violence in 1990 (Stanko, 1991). These calls came from 86 different addresses. One household made at least 15 calls! A similar distribution of calls to the police were found by the present writer whilst working on a 'high crime' inner city estate, where, for example, one household made fifty calls to the police in less than two years, which ended when one partner murdered the other (Farrell, 1990). It is important to note that these are only incidents which, when received by the police are 'coded' as domestic violence; it is possible for domestic violence to go unrecognised when it is logged as a disturbance or assault. With respect to repeat victimisation, these findings must also be taken in the context of the suggestion that a woman who calls the police has, on average, been the victim of 35 previous beatings by a male partner (cited in Horley, 1988; p.2).

Other potential sources of information about the nature of repeat victimisation might include hospital casualty departments (Shepherd, 1990) or General Practitioners' surgeries (Stanko, 1991). In a survey of victims of assault at an accident and emergency hospital in Bristol, Shepherd (1990) found that 43% of victims were multi-victims of assault. Of these, 27% reported involvement in more than two assaults, and 7% reported having been assaulted more than ten times! This distribution of

98

violence mirrors the skewed distribution of crime found in other studies. Shepherd also studied social factors, and suggested that multi-victims of assault are more likely to be unemployed, with 58% of unemployed respondents as multi-victims, compared to 38% of employed victims. In addition, the suggestion is made that unemployed victims are twice as likely as employed victims to have experienced more than two previous assaults; 44% compared to 22%.

CONCLUSIONS: LOOKING TO THE FUTURE

Some patterns of the nature of repeat victimisation begin to emerge from the literature. The most obvious of these is that a relatively small proportion of the population seems to experience a large proportion of all crime. There is a highly skewed distribution of crime in the population which is not due to chance. This observation would appear to hold up to rigorous testing from a variety of different sources. In this paper, nine different research methods have generated similar patterns in the distribution of victimisation. Similar patterns of multiple victimisation have emerged from: hospital records (Johnson *et al.*, 1973); interviews generated from recorded crime (Zeigenhagen, 1976); local victim surveys (Sparks *et al.*, 1977; Jones *et al.*, 1986; Farrell, 1990); national victim surveys (Gottfredson, 1984; Hough, 1986; Trickett *et al.*, 1991); international victim surveys (Hindelang *et al.*, 1978; Reiss, 1980; Fienberg, 1980); a survey of hospitalised victims of assault (Shepherd, 1990); participant observation (Genn, 1988); victim referrals to a *Victim Support* scheme (Sampson, 1991); police recorded crimes (Forrester *et al.*, 1988, 1990; Polvi *et al.*, 1990; Farrell and Pease, 1991), and police incident logs (Stanko 1991; Farrell 1990).

A multiple victim may experience many different types of crime. In addition, and not in contradiction, there is the suggestion of repeat victimisation by the same type of crime. These two phenomena might be termed inter-crime and intra-crime, or across crime-type and within-crime type multiple victimisation respectively. Some emerging patterns are currently unexplained; for example, the apparent connection between property and personal crimes suggested by the fact that they are often both reported by the same victim (though the lifestyle model affords one explanation). In addition, the degree of skew in the distribution of victimisation is such that the two or three percent of respondents to victim surveys who are the most victimised report between a quarter and a third of all incidents. The existing work on the time-course of repeat victimisation would appear to generate similar patterns. The likelihood of repeat victimisation is much greater in a short period after victimisation, the majority of repeat victimisation within the first month, and within that month skewed heavily towards the day of the prior victimisation (Polvi *et al.*, 1990; Farrell and Pease, 1991).

The Kirkholt project (Forrester *et al.*, 1988a, 1988b, 1990; Pease, 1991) suggests that a combined package of opportunity reduction and situational and community crime prevention measures can be used to effectively reduce repeat household burglary in high crime areas, with comparatively low rates of displacement. By preventing repeat burglary through immediate response to victimisation, the vast majority of all burglaries were prevented. The most obvious implications from this project are the prevention of repeat instances of other types of property crime and preventing repeat burglary of business and other non-residential premises. This could possibly be extended to such as the prevention of car theft and other motor vehicle crime; other possibilities for target hardening. The Kirkholt burglary project concentrated only on one estate. It is possible that its practices can be extended to different and wider areas. There is currently a project similar to Kirkholt being undertaken in Northern Ireland by the Extern organisation (McCreadie, 1991). Further work into the time-course of repeat victimisation with respect to crime prevention strategies is continuing to be explored by Ken Pease and his colleagues.

The prevention of multiple victimisation might be developed through agency responses to victimisation. This is not to suggest that all crimes can be addressed through the same approach. Responses to victimisation will need to vary with agency, type of crime, circumstance, and the characteristics and resources of different areas. The intention in this paper is to draw attention to multiple victimisation. The intention is not to make different crimes into sub-groups of multiple victimisation, which they are not. Agencies which might address responses to a first-known victimisation may be as diverse as Police Crime Prevention Officers, women's refuges, *Victim Support*, and Police Domestic Violence Units, through to General Practitioners, hospitals and housing departments. Both *Victim Support* and Crime Prevention Officers, for example, at present respond to crimes as if they are single, discrete events. Many of the response strategies could be simple, requiring relatively small adjustments to existing working methods. Pease (1991) suggests that if domestic properties experience a heightened likelihood of repeat burglary within a short time period, security and insurance firms might develop the leasing of alarms on a short term basis. This might be possible for some other crimes – for example, for households victimised by racist attacks, though this is to assume the households have resources to cover the expense. An alternative might be for an agency such as the housing department to have a pool of alarms which can be made available. As another possibility, information already gathered by the police, both recorded crimes and incident logs as discussed earlier, might be collated so that repeat calls to individual households can be monitored. In this way, repeat calls made by a woman beaten by a male

100

partner, even though these may not be 'crimed' by the police, could result, at the very least, in the provision to women victims, of information regarding opportunities and support agencies available.

Bringing together the existing evidence provides a fuller picture of the importance of repeat victimisation. The tentative findings from each individual study provide a more comprehensive and persuasive argument when presented and considered as a whole. What becomes apparent from the literature are not only the crime prevention possibilities, but also the fact that criminology/victimology should only approach the study of victimisation when taking account of multiple victimisation. The perceived definition of 'victimisation' implicit in many criminological studies should adjust to include the phenomenon of multi-victimisation. Whilst incidence and prevalence rates are now being increasingly used together, they do little more than suggest the existence of multiple victimisation. Perhaps quantitative studies should portray the distribution of victimisation within the victimised population. There are many studies in which the absence of detail of multiple victimisation may affect the emphasis of the results, with subsequent influence upon policy. The most obvious and available data source which can be studied with respect to multiple victimisation is the BCS. Qualitative study is needed into the phenomenon of multiple victimisation. Other theoretical implications may arise if multiple victimisation is recognised as significant. As well as questioning the accepted definitions of 'a victim' and 'a crime', these include implications for the study of fear of crime, and lifetime experiences of victimisation. For example, the disparity between reported fear of crime and reported experiences of crime may be a combination of hidden crime (Stanko, 1988) and past experiences of crime not picked up by the one year reporting period of victim surveys. Gender differences in fear might be linked to childhood victimisation experiences which, with the exception of the Edinburgh survey, remain marginalised. Sentencing policy and criminal injury compensation might need to take account of the perspective of the multiple victim.

ACKNOWLEDGEMENTS

Thanks to Alice Sampson and Ken Pease, at the very least for advice and comments on earlier drafts, and thanks to Coretta Phillips, Betsy Stanko, Gloria Laycock and Adrian Moss. An earlier version of this paper formed a chapter in Barr *et al.* (1991).

NOTES

1. The summary used here generalises across types of crime, and assumes known and accepted (that is, often those used in law,) definitions of what constitute 'a crime', 'a victim', and consequently a multiple victim.

2. The main reservation to crime prevention may be crime displacement, which will be touched on later.

REFERENCES

Anderson, S., Kinsey, R., Loader, I. and Smith, C. (1990). *Cautionary Tales: A Study of Young People and Crime in Edinburgh: Summary of Findings*, Unpublished paper, Centre for Criminology and the Social and Philosophical Study of Law, University of Edinburgh.

Barr, R. and Pease, K. (1990). Crime placement, displacement and deflection. In: *Crime and Justice: An Annual Review of Research* (M. Tonry and N. Morris, eds.) Vol. 12, pp. 277–315. University of Chicago Press; Chicago.

Barr, R., Farrell, G., McCready, F. and Pease, K. (1991). *Multiple Victimisation in Northern Ireland*. Unpublished report to the Northern Ireland Office, March 1991.

Farrell, G. (1990). *Multivictimisation*. Unpublished dissertation. University of Surrey; England.

Farrell, G. and Pease, K. (1991). *School Burglary, Criminal Damage and Other School Crime*, Unpublished report to Mersyside Police. August 1991.

Fienberg, S.E. (1980). Statistical modelling in the analysis of repeat victimisation. In *Indicators of Crime and Criminal Justice: Quantitative Studies* (S.E. Fienberg and A.J. Reiss, eds.) US Dept. Bureau of Statistics.

Forrester, D., Chatterton, M. and Pease, K. with the assistance of Brown, R. (1988a). *The Kirkholt Burglary Prevention Project, Rochdale*. Home Office Crime Prevention Unit Paper no. 13. HMSO; London.

Forrester, D., Chatterton, M. and Pease, K. (1988b). Why it's best to lock the door after the horse has bolted. *Police Review*, 4 November 1988, 2288–2289.

Forrester, D., Frenz, S., O'Connell, M. and Pease, K. (1990). *The Kirkholt Burglary Prevention Project: Phase II*. Home Office Crime Prevention Unit Paper no. 23. HMSO; London.

Genn, H. (1988). Multiple victimisation. In: *Victims of Crime: a new deal?* (M. Maguire and J. Pointing, eds.) pp. 90–100. Open University Press; England.

Gottfredson, M.R. (1984). *Victims of Crime: The Dimensions of Risk*. Home Office Research Study 81. HMSO; London.

Hindelang, M., Gottfredson, M.R. and Garofalo, J. (1978). *Victims of Personal Crime: an Empirical Foundation for a Theory of Personal Victimisation*. Ballinger; Cambridge, Mass.

Horley, S. (1988). *Love and Pain: A Survival Handbook for Women*. Bedford Square Press; London.

Hough, M. and Mayhew, P. (1985). *Taking Account of Crime: Key Findings from the 1984 British Crime Survey*. Home Office Research Study 85. HMSO; London.

Hough, M. (1986). Victims of violent crime, findings from the British Crime Survey. In *From Crime Policy to Victim Policy; Reorienting the Justice System* (E.A. Fattah, ed) pp. 117–132. Macmillan; Canada.

Johnson, J.H., Kerper, H.B., Hayes, D.D. and Killenger, G.G. (1973). The Recidivist Victim: A Descriptive Study. *Criminal Justice Monograph Vol IV. No. 1*. Institute of Contemporary Corrections and The Behavioural Sciences, Sam Houston State University; Huntsville, Texas.

Jones, T., Maclean, B. and Young, J. (1986). *The Islington Crime Survey; Crime, Victimisation and Policing in Inner-City London*. Gower; London.

London Borough of Newham (1987). *Crime in Newham: the Survey*. London Borough of Newham.

102

McCreadie, F. (1991). Burglary in the Lisburn Sub-division. In *Multiple victimisation in Northern Ireland* (R. Barr, G. Farrell, F. McCreadie and K. Pease, eds) pp. 47–69. Unpublished report to the Northern Ireland Office.

Pease, K. (1991). The Kirkholt Project: Preventing Burglary on a British Public Housing Estate. *Security Journal*, Vol. 2, No. 2, 73–77.

Polvi, N., Looman, T., Humphries, C. and Pease, K. (1990). Repeat break-and enter victimisation: time course and crime prevention opportunity. *Journal of Police Science and Administration*, 17, 8–11.

Reiss, A.J. (1980). Victim proneness in repeat victimisation by type of crime. In *Indicators of Crime and Criminal Justice: Quantitative Studies* (S.E. Fienberg and A.J. Reiss, eds). US Dept. Bureau of Statistics.

Sampson, A. (1991). *Lessons from a Victim Support Crime Prevention Project.* Home Office Crime Prevention Unit, Paper No. 25. HMSO; London.

Sampson, A. and Farrell, G. (1990). *Victim Support and crime prevention in an Inner City setting.* Home Office Crime Prevention Unit Paper No. 21. HMSO; London.

Sampson, A. and Phillips, C. (1991). *Multiple Victimisation: Racial Attacks on an East London Estate*, forthcoming Home Office Crime Prevention Unit Paper. HMSO; London.

Shepherd, J. (1990). Violent crime in Bristol; an accident and emergency department perspective. *British Journal of Criminology*, 30, 289–305.

Sherman, L.W., Gartin, P.R. and Buerger, M.E. (1989). Hot spots of predatory crime: routine activities and the criminology of place. *Criminology*, 27, 27–55.

Skogan, W.G. (1981). *Issues in the Measurement of Victimisation.* US Department of Justice, Bureau of Justice Statistics.

Sparks, R., Genn, H. and Dodd, D. (1977). *Surveying Victims.* Wiley; London.

Sparks, R. (1981). Multiple victimisation: evidence, theory and future research. *Journal of Criminal Law and Criminology*, 72, 762–778.

Stander, J., Farrington, D.P., Hall, G. and Altham, P.M.E. (1989). Markov chain analysis and specialisation in criminal careers. *British Journal of Criminology*, 29, 317–335.

Stanko, E.A. (1983). Hidden fears. *The Guardian*, 5th September 1983.

Stanko, E.A. (1988). Hidden violence against women, In *Victims of Crime: a new deal?* (M. Maguire and J. Pointing, eds) pp. 40–46. Open University Press; England.

Stanko, E.A. (1990). When precaution is normal: a feminist critique of crime prevention. In *Feminist Perspectives in Criminology*, (L. Gelsthorpe and A. Morris, eds) pp. 173–183. Open University Press; England.

Stanko, E.A. (1991, unpublished) *Public Violence.* Summary of research findings, violent crime reduction project.

Trickett, A., Osborn, D.K., Seymour, J. and Pease, K. (1991). What is different about high crime areas? *British Journal of Criminology*, 32, 81–89.

Ziegenhagen, E. (1976). The recidivist victim of violent crime. *Victimology: An International Journal*, 1, 538–550.

[9]

BRIT. J. CRIMINOL.   VOL. 32   NO. 1   WINTER 1992

WHAT IS DIFFERENT ABOUT HIGH CRIME AREAS?

ALAN TRICKETT,* DENISE R. OSBORN,* JULIE SEYMOUR,** and KEN PEASE†

This note reports secondary analysis of the 1982 British Crime Survey. It ranks sampling points by total crime experienced, and identifies differences between high and low crime areas. These differ in 'vulnerability', measured as the ratio of crimes to victims. This reveals that the number of victimizations per victim rises markedly as area crime rate increases. Thus a strategy of crime prevention which concentrated on the prevention of repeat victimization would focus on the most vulnerable people and places.

Some areas are chronically high in crime incidence. This is one of the original and enduring issues in criminology. Looked at in terms of offenders, high crime incidence may be attributed to a lot of offenders committing a few crimes each, or a few offenders committing many crimes each. An appropriate penal strategy depends upon knowing which applies. For example, the observation that a few offenders are responsible for many crimes has meant that incapacitation has been considered as a potentially attractive strategy (see Cohen 1986).

Just as a crime rate can be considered from a perspective which concentrates on offenders and their appropriate disposition, so it can be considered in terms of victims. Defining prevalence as the proportion of people who become victims and vulnerability as the number of victimizations per victim, then an area's crime incidence is a product (literally, in the arithmetical sense) of crime prevalence and vulnerability. In other words, just as an area may suffer much crime because of a few very active offenders or many less active offenders, so an area may suffer much crime because many people become victims once or because a few people are repeatedly victimized.

Knowing the reason for the differences between areas is of crucial importance for crime prevention strategy. Take two simple extremes: if high crime areas are so because the proportion of residents who become victims of crime is high, the problem of crime prevention is predominantly that of attempting to prevent a non-victim from becoming a victim. If high crime rates occur because of repeat victimization, crime prevention should correspondingly focus on preventing people who have already been victimized from being victimized again. In many ways, the latter is a less daunting prospect, notably because crime prevention effort may be focused on a smaller proportion of people and places.

Recognition of the phenomenon of multiple victimization and its significance for crime prevention strategy has developed over the last fifteen years (see Sparks *et al.* 1977; Sparks 1981; Forrester *et al.* 1988; Barr and Pease 1990). Yet the question of how

* Department of Econometrics and Social Statistics, University of Manchester.
** Department of Sociology, University of Manchester.
† Corrections Canada and University of Saskatchewan.
Thanks are due to Margaret Irivine for her considerable work in making the British Crime Survey data usable. Financial support is acknowledged from the Leverhulme Trust, the Economic and Social Research Council, and the Department of Econometrics and Social Statistics, University of Manchester. We would also like to thank two anonymous referees and the editor of this journal for their very constructive comments on the first draft of this paper.

ALAN TRICKETT *ET AL.*

multiple victimization contributes to area differences has not, to the authors' knowledge, been posed in the way in which we seek to do it here. This is not to say that there has been little secondary analysis of victimization surveys, and in particular the British Crime Survey; there has been a good deal. Previous analysis has concentrated on the role of personal or area characteristics, including lifestyle indicators (Gottfredson 1984; Hope and Hough 1988; Maxfield 1987*a*, *b*; Sampson and Groves 1989). The matter which we deal with is the simple, related, but separable one of the relative contributions that victim prevalence and repeat victimization make to area differences in crime experience. We report below a descriptive decomposition of area crime incidence, together with some statistical analysis, with the purpose of clarifying that issue.

Method

Data are taken here from the 1982 British Crime Survey[1] (see Hough and Mayhew 1983, Wood 1983). The 1982 Survey had an effective sample of 10,905 adults in England and Wales, interviewed between February and April 1982. Within the main questionnaire of the Survey, screening questions identified crime victimization experience since January 1981. Those questions catalogued all such experience to determine whether more detailed questions on crimes experienced should be asked using a 'victim form'. The screening questions are ideal for our purposes. They provide a convenient summary of all crime said to have been suffered, rather than the somewhat reduced set which is represented in the victim form of the Survey.[2]

Sampling took place in 238 of the 552 parliamentary constituencies in England and Wales (see Wood 1983). Metropolitan inner-city areas were deliberately over-sampled; otherwise constituency selections were made systematically with probability proportional to electorate. Within the selected constituencies, in one half of cases a ward was selected with probability proportional to electorate; in the second half two polling districts were selected, again with probability proportional to electorate. Every nth address of an elector was selected, starting from a random number less than n, to yield a total of sixty addresses per ward and thirty addresses per polling district. Within each address, the interviewee was chosen in effect randomly from among those aged 16 or over who were resident there.

The unit of analysis in what follows is a sampling point, of which there were 358. Each of these comprised either a ward or a polling district. For the present purposes, none of the weighting procedures devised for the Survey was employed. The implications of this will be discussed towards the end of this paper.

Area crime rates were considered in three forms: total crime, personal crime, and property crime. Personal crime here consists of those incidents where the victim came into direct contact with the criminal. By this definition, thefts from the person are classified as personal crime; however, thefts of, or damage to, unattended personal possessions are classified as property crimes. Attempted crimes are included.

In what follows, the incidence rate is the number of crimes reported divided by the

[1] At the time of writing, similar analyses are being undertaken of the 1984 Survey and plans are in hand to repeat the study from the 1988 Survey.

[2] Not all crimes committed against a victim were recorded on the victim forms. This was partly because a maximum of four victim forms were completed per respondent (although one form can refer to a 'series' of incidents). Some alleged incidents may be discounted in the victim forms due to inconclusive evidence as to whether a crime actually occurred.

WHAT IS DIFFERENT ABOUT THE HIGH CRIME AREAS?

number of respondents: in other words, it is the average number of crimes per respondent. The number of crimes has been obtained by a simple aggregation of the numbers of occurrences reported by respondents in the main questionnaire. However, milk stolen from outside a dwelling has been omitted from our analysis.

The prevalence rate is the proportion of respondents victimized once or more. Finally, vulnerability is the number of crimes reported, on average, by each victim.

Based on total crime reported, sampling points were ranked from the one with the lowest crime incidence to the one with the highest. To obtain groupings of sampling points large enough to enable significant conclusions to be drawn, ranked sampling points were split into deciles, i.e. the 10 per cent of areas with the lowest total crime incidence, the 10 per cent with the next lowest, and so on up to the 10 per cent with the highest. All subsequent analysis was carried out by aggregating information to the decile level. Hereafter, whenever we refer to area, our figures are based on this decile aggregation.

Descriptive Results

The first, perhaps unsurprising, result was that the ordering of deciles for total crime was precisely reflected in the ordering for property crime and almost exactly for personal crime. The latter result is more notable, since personal crime is less common than property crime.

Taking the lowest decile as a base with a value of 100, Figure 1 presents the incidence rates in each decile for crimes against property and against the person separately. Rescaling to a base of 100 has been undertaken to facilitate comparisons. The incidence of

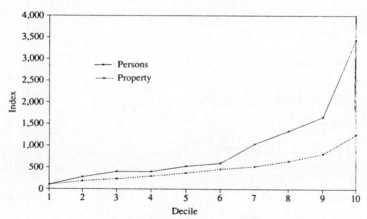

FIG. 1   Incidence of crime (base: decile 1 = 100)
Source: British Crime Survey 1982.

property crime exhibits approximate linearity up the seventh decile, after which the upward trend becomes steeper, in particular between the ninth and tenth deciles. Crime against the person increases more steeply from the sixth decile, dramatically so between the last two deciles. How that high incidence is reached in terms of prevalence versus vulnerability is a central question to be addressed.

ALAN TRICKETT *ET AL.*

The pattern is presented in the way judged to be most visually accessible in Figures 2 and 3. Again taking the lowest decile as 100, the two figures present the increase in prevalence and vulnerability respectively. (The reader's attention is drawn to the vertical scales of the two figures: different scales have been used to accommodate the differing rates of increase in prevalence and vulnerability over deciles.)

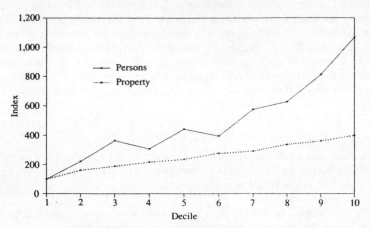

FIG. 2   Prevalence (base: decile 1 = 100)
Source: British Crime Survey 1982.

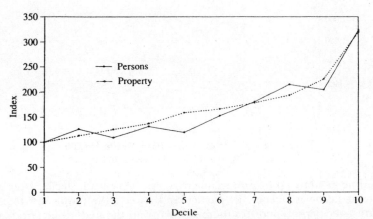

FIG. 3   Vulnerability (base: decile 1 = 100)
Source: British Crime Survey 1982.

84

WHAT IS DIFFERENT ABOUT THE HIGH CRIME AREAS?

The feature which emerges most dramatically from Figure 2 concerns the prevalence of offences against the person. This is around eleven times as large in the worst (highest) decile than in the best (lowest) decile. Making the same comparison for property crimes, prevalence is around four times as large. The vulnerability of victims with respect to both personal and property offences is slightly more than three times as high in the worst as in the best area (see Figure 3). In other words, when people are victimized, they experience about three times as many crimes on average in the highest crime areas compared to the lowest.

Returning briefly to Figure 1, the values there represent the multiplicative interaction of prevalence and vulnerability. Thus, for example, the incidence rate for personal crime in the highest crime decile is more than 34 times that of the lowest. Figures 2 and 3 decompose this, with prevalence being about eleven times and vulnerability about three times the low crime area rate. On the other hand, prevalence and vulnerability make roughly equal contributions to the less dramatic increase in property crime incidence demonstrated in Figure 1.

The most prominent distinguishing characteristic of the high crime area when compared with the low crime area, therefore, is the relatively widespread extent of personal victimization. While property crime gets worse in the high crime area, what gets very much worse is the probability of any citizen falling victim to a personal crime. More specifically, a person is about four times as likely to experience one or more property crimes in the highest crime area compared to the lowest; they are, however, about eleven times as likely to be a victim of personal crime. This is, of course, not to say that the likelihood of falling victim to a personal crime is as high as the likelihood of experiencing a property crime. It is not. But neither is it to say that the pattern observed means that multiple victimization is not extensive enough to allow for focused crime prevention efforts.

Statistical analysis

As already discussed, Figures 2 and 3 show observed prevalence and vulnerability by decile. These values are reported once again in Tables 1 and 2; here, however, they are not re-scaled to a base of 100. In addition, these tables present expected prevalence and vulnerability figures for all areas. Expected prevalence represents the anticipated proportion of people who would be victims if the victim of each crime were selected randomly. Expected vulnerability is then obtained as the average number of crimes that the randomly chosen victims would experience. Both of these expected values take the number of crimes in a decile, and hence the incidence, as given. Note that since the expected vulnerability figures are derived from the expected prevalence ones, we apply a statistical test for the difference between observed and expected only to the prevalence rates. (Statistical details are contained in the appendix.)

We find that observed and expected prevalence rates differ significantly from each other for almost all deciles, and do so more dramatically the worse the crime experience of the area. That is, consistently fewer people are victimized than would be anticipated if crime were random; indeed, as a proportion of the expected prevalence, the actual rate tends to decrease as the crime rate rises. Since the incidence rate is taken as given for this analysis, fewer victims implies that those victimized must suffer crime more

ALAN TRICKETT *ET AL.*

TABLE 1   *Actual and Expected Value Comparisons: Property Crimes*

Decile group	Prevalence			Vulnerability	
	Observed	Expected	p-value	Observed	Expected
1	0.1286*	0.1500	0.0270	1.2632	1.0830
2	0.2065**	0.2559	0.0001	1.4313	1.1545
3	0.2409**	0.3177	0.0000	1.5866	1.2028
4	0.2784**	0.3833	0.0000	1.7353	1.2605
5	0.2999**	0.4522	0.0000	2.0060	1.3304
6	0.3548**	0.5252	0.0000	2.0986	1.4176
7	0.3741**	0.5707	0.0000	2.2591	1.4809
8	0.4315**	0.6520	0.0000	2.4447	1.6181
9	0.4618**	0.7325	0.0000	2.8538	1.7993
10	0.5085**	0.8714	0.0000	4.0314	2.3524

Notes:
1. The p-value relates to testing whether or not the actual prevalence rate is significantly different from that expected under random victimization.
2. * denotes significantly different from expected at the 5 per cent, but not the 1 per cent level. ** denotes significantly different from expected at the 1 per cent level.
3. Significance tests are applied only to prevalence rates; see text for discussion.

TABLE 2   *Actual and Expected Value Comparisons: Personal Crimes*

Decile group	Prevalence			Vulnerability	
	Observed	Expected	p-value	Observed	Expected
1	0.0164	0.0192	0.2614	1.1765	1.0092
2	0.0362*	0.0524	0.0100	1.4865	1.0267
3	0.0596	0.0738	0.0314	1.2857	1.0384
4	0.0500**	0.0745	0.0010	1.5455	1.0387
5	0.0723**	0.0971	0.0026	1.4125	1.0515
6	0.0643**	0.1092	0.0000	1.7975	1.0585
7	0.0942**	0.1815	0.0000	2.1250	1.1030
8	0.1027**	0.2286	0.0000	2.5263	1.1349
9	0.1331**	0.2746	0.0000	2.4118	1.1686
10	0.1745**	0.4849	0.0000	3.8000	1.3674

Notes:
1. The p-value relates to testing whether or not the actual prevalence rate is significantly different from that expected under random victimization.
2. * denotes significantly different from expected at the 5 per cent, but not the 1 per cent level. ** denotes significantly different from expected at the 1 per cent level.
3. Significance tests are applied only to prevalence rates; see text for discussion.

frequently. For the worst decile, once someone falls victim to personal crime, an average of three further such victimizations will occur during the year. Much the same is true for property crimes.

Once again, the most striking comparison concerns personal crime. In the highest crime decile, only about a third of the expected number of victims actually suffer crime: therefore, victims experience, on average, nearly three times as many crimes

WHAT IS DIFFERENT ABOUT THE HIGH CRIME AREAS?

as expected with random victimization. We have already commented on the increase over deciles in the observed prevalence rate for personal crime (shown in Figure 2). Table 2 brings out a different aspect of this: the actual increase in prevalence over deciles is, in fact, a great deal less than expected with random victimization.

With fewer people than expected victimized, our results in Tables 1 and 2 show the importance of multiple victimization. This means that the probabilities strongly support those among the police who put in place prevention of detection aids after a first victimization: a number of further crimes are likely soon to be attempted (see Polvi *et al.* 1990). The focus on the prevention of repeat victimizations becomes more potentially profitable the worse the incidence of crime in an area. Of course, the practical problems involved in mobilizing such communities presents the real challenge. None the less, the data presented in this paper demonstrate clearly the scope for the prevention of repeat victimizations in such crime-ridden areas.

Discussion and Conclusions

On a purely descriptive level, the data presented here are of interest. Rates of property crime incidence rise dramatically in the worst compared with the best areas; the components, prevalence and vulnerability, each contribute roughly equally to this increase. Rates of personal crime rise even more dramatically, with prevalence here rising much faster than vulnerability. However, despite the spectacularly greater prevalence of personal victimization, these victims suffer between three and four times the number of offences of low crime areas; they also suffer about three times the number of offences compared with random personal crime. This high rate of mutiple victimization means that the prevention of such repeat crimes is an exercise with some appeal.

The prevalence observed in high crime areas implies that a strategy of preventing repeat crimes would require many first-time victims to be focused on every year. On the other hand, the high number of repeat victimizations means that investment in such a programme would more predictably address future events, compared both with other kinds of intervention in high crime areas and with similar initiatives in low crime areas. Additionally, such a strategy would mean optimal resource utilization, a prime concern in times of scarce policing resources.

The nature of the sampling of the Survey means that the shape of the curves presented here may not be representative of areas generally, because inner cities are over-sampled. If inner-city areas are high in crime incidence, then we have a larger proportion of high crime areas than we would without over-sampling (and vice versa if they are low in crime incidence): this influences where the dramatic rise of the incidence curve begins, but not its basic shape. Therefore, the inner-city over-sampling does not affect the major conclusions of this research; nevertheless, replication on other data and in other ways would be valuable.

Our approach has an advantage over much previous analysis of the British Crime Surveys in that it does not require possibly pejorative statements about people and their lifestyles: we simply address the pattern of crime over areas, with no necessary reference to victim blame. In other words, our approach avoids the thorny problem of whether victims 'cause' crime through their lifestyle or other characteristics.

ALAN TRICKETT *ET AL.*

References

BARR, R., and PEASE, K. (1990), 'Crime Displacement', in M. Tonry and N. Morris, eds., *Crime and Justice*. Chicago: University of Chicago Press.

COHEN, J. (1986), 'Research on Criminal Careers: Individual Frequency Rates and Offence Seriousness', in A. Blumstein *et al.*, eds., *Criminal Careers and Career Criminals*, vol. 1. Washington, DC: National Academy Press.

FORRESTER, D., CHATTERTON, M. R., and PEASE, K. (1988), *The Kirkholt Burglary Prevention Demonstration Project, Rochdale*, Crime Prevention Paper no. 13. London: Home Office.

GOTTFREDSON, M. R. (1984), *Victims of Crime: The Dimensions of Risk*, Home Office Research Paper no. 81. London: HMSO.

HOPE, T., and HOUGH, M. (1988), 'Area, Crime and Incivilities: A Profile from the British Crime Survey', in T. Hope and M. Shaw, eds., *Communities and Crime Reduction*. London: HMSO.

HOUGH, M., and MAYHEW, P. (1983), *The British Crime Survey: First Report*, Home Office Research Study no. 76. London: HMSO.

KENDALL, M. G., and STUART, A. (1977), *The Advanced Theory of Statistics*, vol. 1, 4th edn. London: Charles Griffin & Co. Ltd.

MAXFIELD, M. G. (1987*a*), 'Lifestyle and Routine Activity Theories of Crime: Empirical Studies of Victimization, Delinquency and Offender Decision Making', *Journal of Quantitative Criminology*, 3: 275–82.

—— (1987*b*), 'Household Activity, Routine Activity and Victimization: A Comparative Analysis', *Journal of Quantitative Criminology*, 3: 301–20.

POLVI, N., LOOMAN, T., HUMPHRIS, C., and PEASE, K. (1990), 'Repeat Break and Enter Victimisation: Time Course and Crime Prevention Opportunity', *Journal of Police Science and Administration*, 17: 8–11.

SAMPSON, R. J. (1987), 'Personal Violence by Strangers: An Extension and Test of the Opportunity Model of Predatory Victimization', *Journal of Criminal Law and Criminology*, 78: 327–56.

—— (1988), 'Local Friendship Ties and Community Attachment in Mass Society: A Multilevel Systematic Model', *American Sociological Review*, 53: 766–79.

SAMPSON, R. J., and GROVES, W.B. (1989), 'Community Structure and Crime: Testing Social-Disorganisation Theory', *American Journal of Sociology*, 94: 774–802.

SAMPSON, R. J. and WOOLDREDGE, J. D. (1987), 'Linking the Micro- and Macro-Level Dimensions of Lifestyle-Routine Activity and Opportunity Models of Predatory Victimisation', *Journal of Quantitative Criminology*, 3: 731–93.

SPARKS, R. F. (1981), 'Multiple Victimization: Evidence, Theory, and Future Research', *Journal of Criminal Law and Criminology*, 72: 762–78.

SPARKS, R. F., GLENN, H., and DODD, D. J. (1977), *Surveying Victims*. London: Wiley.

WOOD, D. S. (1983), *British Crime Survey: Technical Report*. London: Social and Community Planning Research.

APPENDIX: STATISTICAL METHODOLOGY

Denote the respondents in an area, or decile, as $i = 1, \ldots, N$. Then, for the type of crime being analysed (property or personal), we define two variables:

$$V_i = \begin{cases} 1 & \text{if respondent } i \text{ is a victim} \\ 0 & \text{if respondent } i \text{ is not a victim} \end{cases}$$

88

WHAT IS DIFFERENT ABOUT THE HIGH CRIME AREAS?

and C_i, number of crimes suffered by respondent i. Consequently, $C_i = 0$ if $V_i = 0$, while $C_i > 0$ if $V_i = 1$. Using these variables, we have:

$$\text{Incidence} = \frac{\Sigma C_i}{N}$$

$$\text{Prevalence} = \frac{\Sigma V_i}{N}$$

$$\text{Vulnerability} = \frac{\Sigma C_i}{\Sigma V_i}.$$

All summations here are over $i = 1, \ldots, N$. In what follows, N and ΣC are treated as given while ΣV is a random variable.

If each respondent is equally likely to be selected as the victim for each crime captured by the survey, the probability of respondent i being the victim is $1/N$. If selection is independent for each crime (sampling for crime is random), then the probability of any one respondent *not* being a victim for any of the ΣC crimes is

$$\Pr\{V = 0\} = \left(1 - \frac{1}{N}\right)^{\Sigma C} = \left(\frac{N-1}{N}\right)^{\Sigma C}.$$

Therefore, on these assumptions, the probability of being a victim is

$$\Pr\{V = 1\} = \left[1 - \left(\frac{N-1}{N}\right)^{\Sigma C}\right].$$

Our expected value of prevalence is then the proportion of victims we would expect under these assumptions, namely $\Pr(V = 1)$.

The theoretical distribution of the number of victims is bionomial, with the probability of a 'success' being $\Pr(V = 1)$ with N 'trials'. Therefore, the expected number of victims is

$$E(\Sigma V_i) = N \Pr(V = 1).$$

We test the random sampling hypothesis by comparing the observed number of victims with that expected: the number of 'trials' is certainly large enough for the normal approximation to work very well in this case. The p-values quoted in Tables 1 and 2 are the (one-sided) probabilities of obtaining a statistic at least as large as the one we obtain, under null hypothesis. This test statistic applies also to prevalence, since this is defined as $\Sigma V/N$ with N given.

The expected number of victims has also been used to obtain expected vulnerability. Our measure here is

$$E(\text{Vulnerability}) = \frac{\Sigma C_i}{E\{\Sigma V_i\}}.$$

We have used this definition to ensure that the product of expected prevalence and expected vulnerability yields the observed incidence rate: that is, we have decomposed observed incidence in terms of expected values. It may be noted that this does not yield the true expected value of vulnerability, which is $\Sigma C \, E(1/\Sigma V)$ for the given number of crimes ΣC. Since, however, $E(1/\Sigma V) \geqslant 1/E(\Sigma V)$ (Kendall and Stuart 1977, exercise 9.13), our measure understates the true expected value.

[10]

HOT SPOTS OF PREDATORY CRIME: ROUTINE ACTIVITIES AND THE CRIMINOLOGY OF PLACE*

LAWRENCE W. SHERMAN
University of Maryland

PATRICK R. GARTIN
University of Maryland

MICHAEL E. BUERGER
Rutgers University

A leading sociological theory of crime is the "routine activities" approach (Cohen and Felson, 1979). The premise of this ecological theory is that criminal events result from likely offenders, suitable targets, and the absence of capable guardians against crime converging nonrandomly in time and space. Yet prior research has been unable to employ spatial data, relying instead on individual- and household-level data, to test that basic premise. This analysis supports the premise with spatial data on 323,979 calls to police over all 115,000 addresses and intersections in Minneapolis over 1 year. Relatively few "hot spots" produce most calls to police (50% of calls in 3% of places) and calls reporting predatory crimes (all robberies at 2.2% of places, all rapes at 1.2% of places, and all auto thefts at 2.7% of places), because crime is both rare (only 3.6% of the city could have had a robbery with no repeat addresses) and concentrated, although the magnitude of concentration varies by offense type. These distributions all deviate significantly, and with ample magnitude, from the simple Poisson model of chance, which raises basic questions about the criminogenic nature of places, as distinct from neighborhoods or collectivities.

Is crime distributed randomly in space? There is much evidence that it is not. Yet there are many who suggest that it is. In a leading treatise on police innovations, for example, Skolnick and Bayley (1986: 1) observe that "we feel trapped in an environment that is like a madhouse of unpredictable violence and Quixotic threat." People victimized by crime near their homes

---

* This article was supported by grant 86-IJ-CX-0037 from the National Institute of Justice to the Crime Control Institute. Points of view or opinions expressed in this article do not necessarily represent the official position of the U.S. Department of Justice. We wish to thank Anthony V. Bouza, David Dobrotka, Albert J. Reiss, Jr., David Weisburd, and Robert Wasserman. We also wish to thank Robert Dell'Erba, Nancy Beatty, and Debbie Linnell of the Crime Control Institute for their assistance.

28   SHERMAN, GARTIN AND BUERGER

often feel that there are no safe places and that danger lurks everywhere (Silberman, 1978: 15–16). Even many police we know, who acknowledge that some areas are more dangerous than others, often assume a random distribution of crime within areas. For them, the practical question is not whether crime is concentrated in space, but how much.

Such analysis of variation across space is one of the basic tools of science. Many clues to the environmental causes of cancer, for example, have been revealed by the discovery of carcinogenic "hot spots": locations with extremely high rates of cancer mortality (Mason et al., 1985). Similarly, many factors associated with automobile fatalities (such as low population density and distance from emergency medicine) have been highlighted by the discovery of rural western counties with death rates 350 times higher than those in such eastern states as New Jersey (Baker et al., 1987). The methodological history of such analyses can be traced to the moral statistics tradition (Guerry, 1831; Quetelet, 1842) and the sociology of crime and deviance, which pioneered the analysis of variation in behavior across space. Durkheim's *Suicide* (1951) and Shaw et al.'s *Delinquency Areas* (1929) are two classic examples. More recently, sociologists have tested income inequality and other structural theories of crime with variation in crime rates across collectivities, at the levels of nation-states (e.g.,, Krahn et al., 1986; Messner, 1980), regions (e.g., Gastil, 1971; Loftin and Hill, 1974; Messner, 1983), and cities or metropolitan areas (e.g., Blau and Blau, 1982; Messner, 1982; Sampson, 1986).

COLLECTIVITIES, COMMUNITIES, AND PLACES

A common problem of spatial analysis is pinpointing the locations of events. The ecological tradition in criminology has been confined to relatively large aggregations of people and space, which may mask important variation and causal properties within those aggregations. This may be especially important for within-city spatial variation.

Unlike the boundaries of nation-states and cities, the boundaries of within-city crime reporting districts do not correspond to theoretically or empirically defined collectivities, such as local communities or ethnic areas (Reiss, 1986: 26). Nor, as Reiss (1986) also points out, do official statistics on communities include many of the variables on collectivity characteristics needed to test theories of crime. The inability of community data to measure those characteristics creates major problems for community crime research (just as it does for this analysis) and leaves it vulnerable to what one sympathetic observer describes as a claim that there is little more here than an "atheoretical exercise in the mapping of criminal phenomena" (Bursik, 1986: 36).

Even if collectivity characteristics can be measured at the level of community areas, those characteristics may have very different meanings and causal

HOT SPOTS OF PREDATORY CRIME   29

properties at the level of places. An independent variable like per capita alcohol consumption per hour, for example, means something very different at the street-corner level than it does at a 2-mile-square neighborhood level. It is clearly subject to a much wider range at the place level than it is at greater aggregations, with all of the effects of higher levels of consumption being concentrated on behavior in that microsocial space. Focusing on variation across smaller spaces opens up a new level of analysis that can absorb many variables that have previously been shunned as too obvious or not sufficiently sociological: the visibility of cash registers from the street, the availability of public restrooms, the readiness of landlords to evict problem tenants.

The increased range of such independent variables at a micro-place level also means that variation in crime within communities is probably greater than variations across communities (Robinson, 1950). The very meaning of the concept of a bad neighborhood is an open empirical question: whether the risk of crime is randomly or evenly distributed throughout the neighborhood, or so concentrated in some parts of the neighborhood that other parts are relatively safe.

Some recent policy research hints at the latter answer. Taylor and Gottfredson (1986: 410) conclude that there is evidence linking spatial variation in crime to the physical and social environment at the subneighborhood level of street blocks and multiple dwellings (e.g., Jacobs, 1961; Newman, 1972; Newman and Franck, 1980, 1982; but see Merry, 1981a, 1981b). Some 40 years ago, Henry McKay himself made the unpublished discovery that even within high-crime Chicago neighborhoods entire blocks were free of offenders (Albert J. Reiss, Jr., personal communication).

Other findings suggest microlevel variation within blocks for the predatory stranger crimes of burglary, robbery, and auto theft. Salt Lake City houses with well-tended hedges were found to be less likely than other houses in the same neighborhood to be burglarized (Brown, 1983). Tallahassee apartments near the complex entrance and not facing another building were more likely to be burglarized than apartments inside the development facing other buildings (Molumby, 1976). And apartments in building with doormen were also less likely to be burglarized than other apartments (Repetto, 1974; Waller and Okihiro, 1978).

Microspatial variations in robbery rates also suggest nonrandom distributions. Convenience stores near vacant land or away from other places of commerce were more likely to be robbed than those in dense commercial areas (Duffala, 1976). Over a 5-year period in Gainesville, Florida, 96% of all 47 convenience stores were robbed, compared with 36% of the 67 fast-food establishments, 21% of the 71 gas stations, and 16% of the 44 liquor stores (Clifton, 1987). Conversely, over a 10-year period in Texas, gas station workers were murdered at a rate of 14.2 per 100,000 workers per year, compared with a rate of 11.9 for convenience-type store workers and 5.1 per

30   SHERMAN, GARTIN AND BUERGER

100,000 per year for all retail workers (Davis, 1987). Tallahassee convenience stores with the cashier visibly stationed in the middle of the store were
three times more likely to have a low robbery rate as stores with the cashier
set less visibly off to the side (Jeffrey et al., 1987). Convenience stores with
two clerks on duty may be less likely to be robbed than stores with only one
(Clifton, 1987; Jeffrey et al., 1987; but see Chambers, 1988).

Similar microspatial findings are reported in England. English parking lots
with attendants had lower rates of auto theft than unattended parking lots
(Clarke, 1983: 239). Pedestrian tunnels in downtown Birmingham, England,
accounted for a negligible portion of all public space, but they produced 13%
of a sample of 552 criminal attacks on persons (Poyner, 1983: 85).

Traditional collectivity theories may be appropriate for explaining commu-
nity-level variation, but they seem inappropriate for small, publicly visible
places with highly transient populations. Nor is it necessary to give up the
explanatory task to the competing perspectives of rational choice (Cornish
and Clarke, 1986) and environmental design (Jeffrey, 1971; Newman, 1972).
A leading recent sociological theory can address these findings, but only with
a clearer definition of its unit of analysis. The routine activities approach of
Cohen and Felson (1979) can be used to develop a criminology of *places*,
rather than its previous restrictions to a criminology of *collectivities* or of the
life-styles of victimized *individuals* (Hindelang et al., 1978; Messner and
Tardiff, 1985; Miethe et al., 1987) and *households* (Massey et al., 1987).

ROUTINE ACTIVITIES AND PLACE

In their original statement of the routine activities approach, Cohen and
Felson (1979: 589) attempt to account for "direct contact predatory violations," or illegal acts in which "someone definitely and intentionally takes or
damages the person or property of another" (Glaser, 1971: 4). They propose
that the rate at which such events occur in collectivities is affected by "the
convergence in space and time of the three minimal elements of direct-contact
predatory violations: 1) motivated offenders, 2) suitable targets, and 3) the
absence of capable guardians against a violation" (Cohen and Felson, 1979:
589). The theory thus integrates several different vast bodies of literature:
the factors affecting the supply of "motivated" offenders (e.g., Wilson and
Herrnstein, 1985), the opportunity perspective on the supply of stealable
property (e.g., Gould, 1969), the life-style perspective on the supply of persons vulnerable to victimization (Hindelang et al., 1978; Miethe et al., 1987),
the policy research on physical "target-hardening" (e.g., Jeffrey, 1971), and
the literature on the deterrent threat of official and unofficial policing (e.g.,
Sherman, 1986) implied in the concept of guardianship.

The most important contribution of routine activities theory is the argument that crime rates are affected not only by the absolute size of the supply

of offenders, targets, or guardianship, but also by the factors affecting the frequency of their convergence in space and time. The theory claims roots in social and physical ecology, and it explicitly cites Hawley's (1950: 289) space-time concepts of (1) rhythm, the regular periodicity with which events occur; (2) tempo, the number of events per unit of time, "such as the number of violations per day on a given street" (Cohen and Felson, 1979: 590); and (3) timing, the coordination of different interdependent activities, "such as the coordination of an offender's rhythms with those of a victim" (Cohen and Felson, 1979: 590)—presumably, again, at a specific place.

The major limitation of the evidence for the theory, however, is the lack of testing with ecological data on actual places where offenders, targets, and weak guardians converge. As Miethe et al. (1987: 185) point out, most tests of routine activities theory lack independent measures of the life-styles in question and substitute presumed demographic correlates for them. Although Cohen and Felson (1979: 595) do provide data on the personal risks of victimization in different places, they do not link those individual risks to variations in the amount of time individuals spend in different types of places. Rather, they explain national crime trends with national trends in presumed place of routine activities. And although Miethe et al. (1987) do measure the kinds of places in which victims and nonvictims spend their time, they take the individuals as the unit of analysis rather than the places. Given Cohen and Felson's emphasis on the spatial and temporal ecology of crime, the most appropriate unit of analysis for the routine activities approach would seem to be places.

In this article we can go no further than prior research in testing the causal properties explaining variation in crime across places, nor do we attempt tests. Rather, our purpose is to provide a more complete description of the variation in crime across places than has been previously available in order to suggest future directions for developing a sociological criminology of place.

THE SOCIOLOGY OF PLACE

The concept of place lies at the nexus of the physical and social environments, providing a unit of analysis rich in both symbolic content and social organization. We do not mean *place* in the sense of social position in a group (Goffman, 1971), nor in the broader geographical sense of a community (Cobb, 1975). Our more precise geographic concept of place can be defined as *a fixed physical environment that can be seen completely and simultaneously, at least on its surface, by one's naked eyes.*

Although the perceptual boundaries of geographic place are often ambiguous and subject to dispute, centuries of human efforts have been devoted to lessening that ambiguity through such tools as maps, surveys, and street

32   SHERMAN, GARTIN AND BUERGER

names and addresses. The variability in the social institutions of place is suggested by the absence of consecutive street addresses in Japan (Bayley, 1976: 15–16), where houses are given numbers in the order in which they are built. The geographic concept of place embraces an extraordinarily heterogeneous range of environments, from 1-room cottages to 3,000-unit hotels, from street intersections to waterfalls, from farmyards to nightclubs and banks.

The sociological concept of place can be defined as *the social organization of behavior at a geographic place*. Although a place can be coterminous with a collectivity, such as a law firm, nuclear family, or a church in a single building, the human population at places is usually too transient to constitute a collectivity. That transiency does not, however, prevent places from acquiring such variable social organizational properties as customary rules of interaction, financial wealth, forbidden and encouraged activities, prestige rank, moral value, patterns of recruitment and expulsion, legal rights and duties, and even language spoken. Compare, for example, an airport lobby and a homeless shelter, a roadside motel and a university boathouse, a hospital and a liquor store.

Human societies have long invested certain places with moral or spiritual significance. Most cultures designate holy or sacred places for religious rituals. They also create disvalued places as symbols and centers of deviance, as in "What's a nice girl like you doing in a place like this?" The "spirit of place" (or *genius loci*) is a common colloquial image with both positive and negative moral meanings. It appears in a Baptist hymn (Akers, 1965), in a magazine advertisement for an expensive Adirondack resort (Adirondack Life, 1987), in E.M. Forster's (1947: v–vii) account of how he came to write his first story, and more ominously, in a modern story of a murderously haunted house (Anson, 1977). Hawthorne's (1913) *The House of the Seven Gables* is devoted to the avenging place spirit of a house that has a "life of its own" (1913: 42–43).

The social organization of places has been the subject of both novels and social science literature. Bennett's *Imperial Palace* (Ayer Co. Publications, 1976) and Baum's *Grand Hotel* (Amereon Ltd., 1976), for example, richly describe the many different social systems and rules of order existing simultaneously in large luxury hotels, from the boiler room to the different guest rooms. Cavan (1966) describes behavior in bars, and Liebow (1967) portrays the social organization of a black slum street corner. Police research (e.g., Rubinstein, 1973: 162–169) has also described street corner organization from the police perspective. Bittner (1970: 90) implies the strong social order of places when he describes how some police know "the shops, stores, warehouses, restaurants, hotels, schools, playgrounds, and other public places in such a way that they can recognize at a glance whether what is going on within them is within the range of normalcy."

Places, like persons, can be seen to have routine activities subject to both formal and informal regulation. Their formal regulation has become a major arena of social and legal conflict, especially in modern America. Recent examples include historic preservation efforts to prevent demolition of buildings, community activist efforts to prevent renewal of a bar's liquor license, zoning battles over proposals to increase the human density of places through taller buildings, the "not in my back yard" (NIMBY) opposition to halfway houses for convicts and treatment centers for infants with acquired immunodeficiency syndrome (AIDS), and police attempts to stop visible street corner drug dealing. The participants in these conflicts evidence little doubt that the routine activities of places produce important aesthetic and social consequences for the quality of life in adjoining places, including crime.

Despite its conceptual richness and precedent, place has received little systematic attention. Most lacking is quantitative analysis of the causal relationships among various social and physical characteristics of place, such as the relationship of alcohol sales to vandalism controlling for the intensity of lighting, density of place population, price of alcohol, and the socioeconomic status of the patrons. The systematic study of place as a unit of analysis has been left to environmental psychologists, architects, urban planners, and "space doctor" consultants who intervene in problem-plagued public places (Hiss, 1987a, 1987b). Yet few attempts have been made to describe systematically, let alone explain, variation across different kinds of places in such behavior as crime.

There is little point in examining variation in crime by place, of course, if such variation is merely random. Criminal opportunities, it has been argued, are in some sense ubiquitous (Reiss, 1986: 6). Although previous research shows concentrations of crime in space, such concentrations could occur merely by chance—just like throwing darts at a target while blindfolded (Kinley Larntz, personal communication, 1987). The implied premise of routine activities theory is that such concentrations are not random, which some might think is obvious. But to our knowledge, that premise has never been examined across an entire city with place as the unit of analysis.

This article examines that premise. Using street addresses and intersections as an operational definition of urban places, we assess police call data as a measure of place crime in Minneapolis. We describe the distribution of crimes by place and test for the randomness of that distribution. We then consider the implications of the results for further development of a routine activities criminology of place.

POLICE CALL DATA: STRENGTHS AND WEAKNESSES

Of the three traditional methods used for measuring crime, only one is currently appropriate for measuring crime by specific place, and even that is

34   SHERMAN, GARTIN AND BUERGER

beset with major difficulties. Neither victimization surveys (HIndelang, 1976) nor self-report studies (Hindelang et al., 1981) provide data on the exact street addresses of crime, although they could be designed to do so. Only police crime reports provide exact descriptions of location of occurrence, and even they are rarely programmed to be sorted by address. Moreover, official crime reports suffer from the well-known problem of frequent police decisions not to record many crimes that citizens report to them (Black, 1970).

A new source of data on crime has recently become available. With the growth of centralized police dispatching systems, three-digit emergency telephone numbers (911), and the attendant increases in calls to police, administrative data on calls to police provide a reliable indicator of time and place variations in crime (Pierce et al., 1984). Call data are relatively so precise and cast so wide a net that they some day may provide a third major indicator of crime trends—supplementing official crime reports and victimization surveys. One can even imagine a new series of federal crime statistics derived from local call data, the "Uniform Telephone Reports (UTR)." But these data have substantial limitations as well as strengths.

LIMITATIONS

Traditional measures of crime are subject primarily to underreporting, but police call data are subject to both underreporting and overreporting. Calls about crimes may either be made in error or as intentional lies, much like false fire alarms. In other cases, a single criminal event may generate more than one call. Or, if the call record is updated by additional information to the dispatcher from the police at the scene, the update may be recorded as a separate call (referred to as a "mirror") rather than as replacing the earlier call.

Even a great advantage of call data—precision as to the time and place of the crime—has major limitations. There may often be a lag of many hours between the time of the crime and the computer-recorded time of the call (Kansas City Police Department, 1977; Spelman and Brown, 1981). Moreover, the Minneapolis Computer-aided Dispatch (CAD) system has data entry fields for only two locations: the location from which the call is made and the location to which a police car is to be dispatched. There is no provision for the third and most important address—the location of the event's occurrence. Moreover, a fourth location—the residence address of the caller—may sometimes be entered into one of the two available fields.

Places vary in the extent to which they suffer underreporting or overreporting. Hospitals, police stations, and public locations (e.g., gas stations and convenience stores with phone booths), to which crime victims may go in the aftermath of a crime, may suffer overreporting. This problem appears to have

HOT SPOTS OF PREDATORY CRIME 35

been compounded by rising phone bills since telephone deregulation, which police in Minneapolis and elsewhere say has caused more poor people to give up home telephone service. The locations where those crimes actually occurred suffer underreporting. This pattern is augmented by intentional lying to police dispatchers about the location of crimes by representatives of places attempting to avoid losing a license to do business, such as bars or teenage dance halls (see, e.g., Sanchez and Horwitz, 1987).

While certain commercial locations with phones may suffer overreporting of crimes, a different problem often causes underreporting from those locations. Slight variations in the descriptions of the names of commercial locations, added to the street address, are often entered into the computer. Misspellings, omission of some words (e.g., "Moby Dick's Bar" vs. "Moby's"), using the street address only, and other variations produce several distinct data files for calls at the same address—thus undercounting the total crime at that location.

STRENGTHS

Despite these substantial limitations, police emergency telephone records do provide the widest ongoing data collection net for criminal events in the city. Unlike official crime reports, call data are virtually not screened. Police telephone operators are monitored by a continuous audio tape of all transactions, and they cannot safely fail to enter a clearly stated crime report from a clearly stated location. Comparison of the 1986 call data presented below with 1986 Uniform Crime Reports (Federal Bureau of Investigation, 1987: 85) data on Minneapolis, for example, shows that official crime reports were filed for only 66% of calls about robberies (although the Dallas police in 1986 filed reports on virtually 100% of robbery calls, which that city's officers probably reclassify from the scene more conscientiously).

For whatever error they entail, call data in some cities arguably capture many events that neither official crime reports nor victimization surveys would capture. In some cases, for example, a bystander may call about a crime in progress, yet the victim does not want to file a report. Or by the time the police arrive, the victim may be gone or refuse to provide any evidence, so no report is filed. When later asked about victimization events by a Census Bureau surveyor, the victim does not mention the crime. Thus, the criminal event is lost to all other records systems—but not from police call data.

The reliability of police call data is suggested by at least one report of a very high geographic correlation between call data and reported crimes. Data from a 1979–80 multistage stratified cluster sample of 63 street blocks in 12 Baltimore City neighborhoods found several types of reported crimes to be highly correlated with related calls for service. Calls about crimes of violence

36 SHERMAN, GARTIN AND BUERGER

to persons, for example, were correlated with official aggravated assault reports at about r = .80 (Taylor et al., 1981).

As a measure of the concentration of predatory crime at specific places, the errors of overreporting appear to be counterbalanced by the errors in underreporting. Because there are no offense reports listing location of occurrence for the vast majority of all calls, we cannot even estimate how much overreporting there is by location, nor can we estimate the amount of underreporting without inspecting almost 70,000 listings of addresses that generated calls. But knowing that the two sources of error work in opposite directions gives us greater confidence in findings of high concentration than if the errors all increased overreporting.

We can also generally assume that call data about places are immune to being swamped by one-man crime waves, those occasionally visible bursts of activity by street criminals often concentrated in a small area (e.g., Iverem, 1988; Sanchez, 1988). The anecdotal evidence about such crime sprees is that they are usually spread out over several addresses, even when the offender is on foot.

As Biderman and Reiss (1967) suggest, there is no "true" count of crime events, only different socially organized ways of counting them, each with different flaws and biases. Calls to the police provide the most extensive and faithful account of what the public tells the police about crime, with the specific errors and biases that that entails.

DATA COLLECTION

Unfortunately, few if any police departments can provide researchers, or even police chiefs, with a year-long call data base ready to analyze. Computer-aided dispatch systems are designed for operational purposes, so they do not have large storage capacities. The Minneapolis system, for example, can store only about 7,000 call records on line, so the calls must be removed from the mainframe computer about once a week and stored on tape. To construct a single data file for police calls covering 1 year or longer, researchers must generally provide their own computer into which the police backup tapes are read.

Using that procedure in Minneapolis, selected data elements from each complete call record were read from all the available tapes covering the period from December 15, 1985, to December 15, 1986. Missing data were discovered for 28 days, distributed throughout the year in four blocks of about 7 days each. A total of 323,979 call records were copied into a microcomputer, after fire, ambulance, and administrative record calls from police (e.g., out to lunch) were deleted. The findings presented below are derived from those data as well as from a less precise estimate of the number of street addresses and intersections in the city.

ESTIMATING THE DENOMINATOR

Although some data already exist on the distribution of crime by different types of places (Felson, 1987: 922–925; Hindelang, 1976: 300), they have been uncontrolled by any estimate of the relevant denominator: the number of such places at which crimes could possibly occur. We are unable to classify types of places, but we are at least able to estimate the total number of addresses to which crimes could possibly have been attributed.

All police calls in Minneapolis are dispatched to street addresses, intersections, or several hundred "special locations," such as parks, hospitals, and City Hall. Determining the total number of such places in a city requires great caution. The original estimate of 172,000 addresses and intersections supplied by one official source was used for a year of preliminary analysis (Sherman, 1987) until further checking revealed it to be incorrectly based on dwelling units (including individual apartments).

Further checking also revealed different estimates from different sources. The Manager of Inspections Administration for the City of Minneapolis (interview with Erin Larsen, 1987) estimates that there are 107,000 buildings in the city, plus or minus 10,000. The tax assessor's office (interview with Richard Hanson, 1987) reports that there are about 115,000 parcels of land, and about 111,000 parcels with a building on them—some of which parcels are condominium units within multiple-unit buildings. Some of the vacant lots are addresses at which crimes could be reported, but others are slivers of land between a sidewalk and a curb; the counts do not distinguish. The Administrative Engineering Service (interview with Brian Lokkesmoe, 1987) reports that there are about 100,000 locations for garbage pickup.

The number of intersections is more consistently estimated. The Traffic Engineering Office (interview with staff, 1987) reports that a 1973 study found 6,320 intersections. A separate department, Administrative Engineering Services, reports 24,000 corners, or about 6,000 intersections. Using the estimate of 6,000 intersections, and a rough averaging of the estimated number of street addresses at 109,000, we estimate the total number of places in the city to be 115,000.

In Tables 2, 3, and 4, the data presented below have been corrected by deleting from the numerators, but not the denominators, two high-volume places at which the crimes were clearly just being reported, not occurring: City Hall, and the Hennepin County Medical Center.

HOT SPOTS OF CRIME

The analysis reveals substantial concentrations of all police calls, and especially calls for predatory crime, in relatively few "hot spots." Just over half (50.4%) of all calls to the police for which cars were dispatched went to a mere 3.3% of all addresses and intersections (Table 1). A majority (60%) of

38   SHERMAN, GARTIN AND BUERGER

all addresses generated at least one call over the course of the year, but about half of those addresses produced one call and no more. The top 5% of all locations generated an average of 24 calls each, or 1 every 2 weeks.

Table 1. Distribution of all Dispatched Calls for Police
          Service in Minneapolis, by Frequency at Each
          Address and Intersection, December 15, 1985—
          December 15, 1986

No. of Calls	Observed No. of Places	Expected No. of Places	Cumulative % of Places	Cumulative % of Calls
0	45,561	6,854	100%	—
1	35,858	19,328	60.4	100.0
2	11,318	27,253	29.2	88.9
3	5,683	25,618	19.4	81.9
4	3,508	18,060	14.4	76.7
5	2,299	10,186	11.4	72.4
6	1,678	4,787	9.4	68.8
7	1,250	1,929	7.9	65.7
8	963	680	6.8	63.0
9	814	213	6.0	60.6
10	652	60	5.3	58.4
11	506	15	4.7	56.3
12	415	4	4.3	54.6
13	357	1	3.9	53.1
14	297	0	3.6	51.7
15 $\geq$	3,841	0	3.3	50.4

mean = 2.82 X^2 = 301,376   df = 14   p < .0001

The number of calls per location ranged as high as 810 at a large discount store near a poor neighborhood, followed by 686 calls at a large department store, 607 calls at a corner with a 24-hours-a-day convenience store and a bar, and 479 calls at a public housing apartment building (data not displayed). To test the premise that these concentrations are not merely random clusters, we calculated a simple Poisson model of the expected frequency of locations with each level of call volume. The simple Poisson model assumes that (1) the probability of a dispatched call to police is the same for all places and (2) the probability of a call does not depend on the number of previous calls (Nelson, 1980). For a sample of 115,000 places, the frequencies of repeat calls expected by chance are significantly lower than the observed frequencies, with a maximum of 13 calls expected (and 810 observed) at any one location (Table 1).

Some of the chronic locations for calls to police are probably quite safe for the public. Twenty-four retail stores, for example, produced a total of 2,444

HOT SPOTS OF PREDATORY CRIME   39

calls to arrest a shoplifter apprehended by store personnel, or 68% of all calls for that reason in the entire city. Other high-volume call addresses primarily generated calls about such noncriminal matters as traffic accidents, car lockouts, parking disputes, or noise complaints.

The hot spots of predatory crime are best described in Table 2, which shows the distributions of three types of predatory crime generally committed in public places: criminal sexual conduct (rape, molesting, and exposing, designated hereafter as rape/CSC), robbery, and auto theft (also aggregates of several distinct call codes, including attempts and alarms).[1] Taken separately, each of the predatory crimes shows even greater geographic concentration than all calls for service: all 4,166 robbery calls were located at only 2.2% (against a possible 3.6%) of all places, all 3,908 auto thefts at 2.7% (against a possible 3.4%), and all 1,729 rape/CSCs at just 1.2% (against a possible 1.5%) of the places in the city. Thus, robbery had the greatest magnitude of concentration, with a 39% relative reduction in actual locations from the possible number; auto theft had a 21% relative reduction, and rape/CSC had a 20% relative reduction. There were, for example, 113 places with five or more robberies in 1 year, 35 places with five or more auto thefts, and 14 places with five or more rape/CSC calls. Conversely, 95% of the places in the city were free of any of these crimes in a 1-year period.

When the three general offense types are combined in the same places, there are 230 hot spots with 5 or more of any of the three offenses, and 54 locations with at least 10. The 6,212 actual locations with any of the three offenses constitute a relative reduction of 37% from the 9,803 possible number of places if there were no repeat offenses. There is also a high conditional probability of an additional offense once one has occurred, as illustrated in Figure 1. Under the simple Poisson model, each place in the city has only an 8% chance of suffering one of these crimes. But the risk of a second offense given a first shows the observed probability increasing sharply to 26%. Once a place has had three of these offenses, the risk of recurrence within the year exceeds 50% and stays above that level at each higher level of call frequency. The exact day and time of recurrence cannot be predicted, but the fact of recurrence, given three offenses, becomes highly predictable. This predictability exceeds, for example, the 33% to 59% annual likelihood

---

1. Tables 2 and 3 combine different dispatcher identifications of the same address, which the city's computer treats as different addresses if there is any variation in the description following a colon after the street address (e.g., 1414 Bouza Street: Moby's Bar). Colons and descriptions are quite rare among all addressees, but fairly common among the hot spots. The combinations were made by searching all places with 50 or more calls of all types (n = 799 places) for addresses with descriptions following a colon and then for each such address searching all 69,439 data records on places with any calls, for any other record beginning with the same address. (Up to six separate records were found for one address.) This procedure was unable, however, to detect misspellings of street names.

40   SHERMAN, GARTIN AND BUERGER

Table 2.   Distribution of Dispatched Police Calls for Rape,
           Robbery, Auto Theft, by Frequency at Each
           Address and Intersection in Minneapolis, December
           15, 1985—December 15, 1986

No. of	Robbery		Rape/Criminal Sexual Conduct		Auto Theft		Combined	
Crimes	Observed	Expected	Observed	Expected	Observed	Expected	Observed	Expected
0	112,446	110,883	113,612	113,275	111,923	111,136	108,786	105,605
1	1,825	4,048	1,161	1,714	2,574	3,795	4,629	8,993
2	434	69	167	11	345	69	942	380
3	122	0	34	0	85	0	269	12
4	58	0	11	0	36	0	142	0
5	34	0	5	0	15	0	65	0
6	30	0	3	0	6	0	31	0
7	14	0	3	0	2	0	38	0
8	10	0	3	0	6	0	25	0
9	6	0	0	0	0	0	17	0
10	4	0	0	0	3	0	16	0
11	2	0	0	0	1	0	4	0
12	2	0	0	0	0	0	6	0
13	2	0	0	0	1	0	6	0
14	1	0	0	0	0	0	3	0
15	1	0	0	0	0	0	6	0
16	1	0	0	0	0	0	2	0
17	0	0	0	0	0	0	0	0
18	0	0	0	0	1	0	2	0
19	0	0	0	0	0	0	0	0
20>	6	0	0	0	0	0	9	0
Max.	28	2	8	2	18	2	33	3
$\bar{x} =$	.036		.015		.034		.085	
$x^2 =$	3,174		2,391		1,502		8,549	
df =	27		7		17		32	
p<	.0001		.0001		.0001		.0001	

N of places = 115,000.
Note: Table does not include calls dispatched to Hennepin County Medical Center or
City Hall.

of an arrested offender being rearrested for an index offense while free (Blumstein et al., 1986: 58).

Table 2 also tests the possibility that the concentrations of predatory public
crimes have occurred by chance. The simple Poisson models again show significantly lower expected frequencies of repeat offense concentrations than are
actually observed. Where the Poisson distribution predicts a maximum of 2
robberies in any one place, for example, the observed maximum is actually
28.

HOT SPOTS OF PREDATORY CRIME   41

Figure 1   Conditional Probability of k + 1 Calls Given k Calls for Rape/
Criminal Sexual Conduct, Robbery, and Auto Theft in
Minneapolis (December 15, 1985—December 15, 1986)

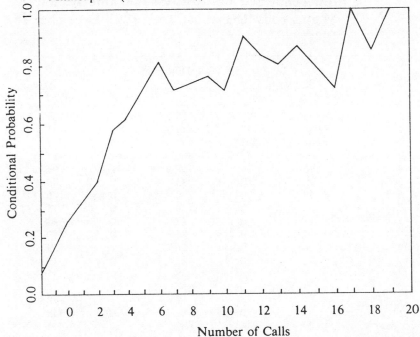

The hot spot pattern of concentration is not limited to crime in public places. Similar patterns were found for three types of crime commonly committed indoors (Table 3). Although their greater frequency produces somewhat less absolute concentration, domestic problems and assaults are actually more concentrated relative to the possible number of places at which those events could have occurred. All 24,928 domestic disturbances were recorded at 9% of all places (although each address can include many apartments), a 59% relative reduction from the possible locations without repeats. All 17,225 assaults were concentrated in 7% of all places, a 55% relative reduction. All 15,901 burglary calls were concentrated in 11% of the estimated 109,000 street addresses, a 27% relative reduction.

The distributions of "inside" crime are also far from random. All three observed distributions in Table 3 are significantly more concentrated than the simple Poisson model of a random pattern of crime occurrence. And as seen in Table 4, every crime we have analyzed differs from a theoretical distribution without repeat locations by a magnitude that varies from moderate to substantial.

42   SHERMAN, GARTIN AND BUERGER

Table 3.   Distribution of Dispatched Police Calls for
            Burglary, Domestic Disturbance, and Assault, by
            Frequency at Each Address and Intersection in
            Minneapolis, December 15, 1985—December 15,
            1986

No. of Crimes	Burglary Observed	Burglary Expected	Domestic Disturbance Observed	Domestic Disturbance Expected	Assault Observed	Assault Expected
0	97,449	94,198	105,158	92,564	106,954	98,946
1	9,032	13,745	5,519	20,090	5,245	14,870
2	1,664	1,003	1,790	2,174	1,394	1,116
3	465	44	866	161	497	58
4	170	10	468	11	293	11
5	92	0	293	0	170	0
6	55	0	208	0	86	0
7	26	0	156	0	73	0
8	13	0	97	0	43	0
9	7	0	86	0	50	0
10	6	0	56	0	29	0
11	6	0	41	0	19	0
12	1	0	48	0	17	0
13	4	0	33	0	8	0
14	1	0	18	0	8	0
$15\geq$	7	0	161	0	112	0
Max.	20	4	62	4	136	4
N =	109,000		115,000		115,000	
x^2 =	8,442		34,423		17,499	
df =	14		14		14	
p<	.0001		.0001		.0001	
$\bar{x}$ =	.145		.217		.150	

Note: Table does not include calls dispatched to Hennepin County Medical Center or
City Hall.

ARE DANGEROUS COMMUNITIES
GENERALLY SAFE?

The data also suggest great variation in predatory crime within communities, regardless of variation across communities. This finding is based on the
5% of all places that had any predatory public crime over the course of a
year, and the estimated 20% of the places in the city that are located in what
local residents define as high-crime neighborhoods (interview with Alva
Emerson, 1987). Assume that all of the 6,212 places with at least one rape/
CSC, robbery, or auto theft were located among the 23,000 high-crime-area
places (which they are not). Even then, the vast majority of places in those

Table 4. Magnitude of Concentration by Location of Six
Offenses Reported to Police in Minneapolis by
Telephone, December 15, 1985—December 15, 1986

| | % of City Addresses | | Percent Reduction |
Offense	Without Repeats	Actual	
Domestic Disturbance	21	8.6	59
Assault	15	7	55
Robbery	3.6	2.2	39
Burglary	14.6	10.6	27
Auto Theft	3.4	2.7	21
Rape/Criminal Sexual Conduct	1.5	1.2	20

areas—15% of the city among the high-crime 20% of the city, or 73% of those high-crime neighborhoods—would still be free of predatory public crime over 1 year.

We do not claim that hot spots are completely unrelated to each other. To the contrary, they are clearly bunched on major thoroughfares, at least in Minneapolis. They are also bunched near each other. Linnell (in press) found that the mean distance between robbery hot spots was 888 feet, and that 90% of them were located on 7 main avenues. In designing a patrol experiment affecting clusters of hot spot addresses, Sherman and Weisburd (1988) found 420 clusters of addresses of three or more hard crime calls, totaling 20 such calls, located within one-half block of each other. Moreover, 72 of those clusters had to be eliminated from the research design because they were located within two blocks of each other and would have violated the necessary independence of treatment. Yet, there were still many addresses in between those clusters about which no police calls had been received.

To be sure, most of the absence of crime by place is due to crime's overall rarity, rather than its concentration. A separate address for each of the crimes would still leave 57% of places in high-crime neighborhoods free of major predatory crimes, rather than the 73% after the actual concentration into hot spots. The relative magnitude of the concentration, then, may not be that substantial, depending on one's view of a 28% relative increase (73% over 57%) in the chance of being free of major predatory crime (assuming incorrectly, again, that all crimes are in high-crime areas). Whether from rarity or concentration, however, the general safety of places in the city's "dangerous neighborhoods" further suggests the theoretical and policy significance of the criminology of place, as distinct from the traditional criminology of neighborhoods or areas.

44   SHERMAN, GARTIN AND BUERGER

THE CRIMINOLOGY OF PLACE

ADJUSTING FOR EXPOSURE PERIOD AND POPULATION

Our findings must be interpreted with great caution, largely because of the enormous heterogeneity across places of both the size of the population and the periods of time at risk. The wide range of risk levels is suggested by capsule qualitative descriptions of the places with highest raw frequencies of predatory crime calls, presented in Table 5.

The nonrandom distribution of crime by place may simply be due to the nonrandom distribution of people. Geographers have long recognized the day-to-day clustering of people residing over a wide area into small "nodes" of activity (Brantingham and Brantingham, 1984: 235). If crime is concentrated in direct proportion to the concentration of people, then there may be nothing particularly criminogenic about those places. It may make sense for police to concentrate their efforts at those nodes, as an experiment in Minneapolis is now attempting to do (Sherman and Weisburd, 1988), but there is no increased per capita risk of crime for people to worry about or for theory to explain.

Two cases in point illustrate the population issue. A Dallas hotel we analyzed looked much like the worst hot spots in Minneapolis. It had a high place rate of predatory crime, with 1,245 crime reports over a 2-year period, 41 of them for violent crimes against persons. Yet the hotel covered 48 acres and had an estimated mean daily population of 3,000 guests, employees, and visitors. The per capita robbery rate was 76% lower than the per capita robbery rate for the entire city (Sherman, 1988).[2] In contrast, the bar on the Minneapolis hot spot list (Table 5) with the highest raw frequency of predatory crime also had very high per capita rates of crime. With 25 robberies in 1 year, and an estimated mean daily population of no more than 300, Moby Dick's Bar had a robbery call rate of 83 per 1,000 persons—seven times higher than the call rate of 12 per 1,000 for the city's entire 1986 estimated population of 362,000. With 81 assaults, the per capita assault rate at the bar was 270 per 1,000, or more than 1 assault for every 4 persons in the bar over the year. Such an environment can reasonably be labeled as a dangerous place, in which individuals face substantially higher personal risks of criminal victimization than in the "average" place.

The estimates of per capita crime risk by place are further complicated by

---

2. One possible cause for the actual "coolness" of this apparently hot spot was the much higher level of guardianship at the hotel. The ratio of patrol officers (including the hotel's security officers) to population was three times higher at the hotel than in the city as a whole, and the density of patrol presence per acre was 63 times higher at the hotel than city wide. As Felson (1987: 927) points out, growing inequality of security is characteristic of the modern metropolis. This inequality has arguably made many people into virtual prisoners of their private spaces, or "modern cliff dwellers" (Reiss, 1987: 42).

HOT SPOTS OF PREDATORY CRIME 45

Table 5. Hot Spots In Minneapolis, December 15, 1985—
December 15, 1986, with 10 or More Predatory
Crimes (adjusted data before aggregation of multiple
address listings)

Rank/Description		Robberies, Rapes, Auto Thefts	All Types
1.	Intersection: bars, liquor store, park	33	461
2.	Bus Depot	28	343
3.	Intersection: homeless shelters, bars	27	549
4.	Downtown Mall	27	445
5.	Intersection: adult bookstore, bars	27	431
6.	Bar	25	510
7.	Intersection: theater, mall, record store	25	458
8.	Hotel	23	240
9.	Convenience Store	22	607
10.	Bar	21	219
11.	Intersection: drugstore, adult theater	18	513
12.	Intersection: restaurant, bar	15	445
13.	Apartment Building	15	177
14.	Department Store	15	449
15.	Intersection: Burger King, office bldg.	15	365
16.	Shopping Mall	15	305
17.	Hotel	14	121
18.	Bar	14	244
19.	Towing Company	14	113
20.	Movie Theater	14	251
21.	Department Store	14	810
22.	High-rise Apartment Building	14	479
23.	Intersection: drugstore, adult bookstore	13	290
24.	Convenience Store	13	113
25.	Intersection: high concentration of bars	13	206
26.	Parking Lot	13	31
27.	Loring Park	13	212
28.	Restaurant	13	25
29.	Apartment Building	12	142
30.	Restaurant	12	198
31.	Homeless Shelter	12	379
32.	Detached House	11	190
33.	High-rise Apartment Building	11	125
34.	Apartment Building	10	233
35.	Intersection: high residential area	10	156
36.	High-rise Apartment Building	10	92
37.	Restaurant	10	122
38.	Intersection: apartments, gas stations	10	197
39.	Intersection: supermarket, liquor store	10	94
40.	Lake Harriet	10	171
41.	Bar	10	107
42.	Apartment Building	10	142
	Totals	661	11,760

46   SHERMAN, GARTIN AND BUERGER

the varying time at risk. One reason the convenience stores in Gainesville had six times greater prevalence than the liquor stores of at least one armed robbery per location (Clifton, 1987) may be that the liquor stores were open for less than half the hours per week of a 24-hour, 7-day convenience store. Just as plane and automobile crash fatalities are computed per passenger mile traveled, the conceptually appropriate indicator for place crimes against persons may be crimes per person-minute spent on the premises. Property crimes would require different adjustments for time at risk. Commercial burglary, for example, should be standardized by the number of hours per week an establishment is closed, and auto theft rates might be standardized by the number of hours each car is present at a place. The violent Minneapolis bar would be even more violent if the annualized violence rates were adjusted for the limited hours per day it was occupied.

ARE PLACES CRIMINOGENIC?

The basic theoretical problem for the criminology of place, however, is not just to account for variation in raw frequencies of place crime, or per unit/period crime target risks. The more fundamental issue is whether the routine activities of places, given their physical environment, are actually criminogenic. Do places vary in their capacity to help *cause* crime, or merely in their frequency of *hosting* crime that was going to occur some place inevitably, regardless of the specific place? Are the routine activities of hot spots criminogenic *generators* of crime, or merely more attractive *receptors* of crime? If a crime hot spot is somehow incapacitated from producing its routine activities, would there be a corresponding net decline in total criminal events, or merely a hydraulic displacement of the same events to the next most appropriate locations?

DISPLACEMENT

A routine activities criminology of place hypothesizes that crime cannot be displaced merely by displacing motivated offenders; the offenders must also be displaced *to* other places with suitable targets and weak guardianship. The findings presented above support that view. If the distribution of crime hot spots was determined solely by the concentration of offenders, then how can we explain the complete 1-year absence of predatory crimes from 73% of the places in high-crime crime areas in Minneapolis (compared with the expected absence from only 57%)?

Cohen and Felson (1979) support the criminogenic role of place by demonstrating temporal correlations between time spent away from home and collectivity crime rates. Other evidence suggests that variations in area-level guardianship are associated with little displacement of offending from better

HOT SPOTS OF PREDATORY CRIME 47

to more poorly guarded areas (Hakim and Rengert, 1981). The entire problem of planned reductions in criminal opportunity unintentionally producing *displacement* of crime may have been exaggerated by policymakers pessimistically resigned to the perseverance of evildoers (Clarke and Mayhew, 1988; Cornish and Clarke, 1987). But as an empirical question, the generator-versus-receptor problem is far from being resolved.

It seems likely, for example, that the criminogenic influence of place varies by type of offense. Crimes arising out of intimate or market relationships may be much less dependent on place than predatory stranger crimes. The concentration of domestic disturbance calls may simply indicate that certain buildings are receptors for the kind of people most likely to experience, or at least call police about, domestic problems; such calls might occur at the same rate no matter where they lived. Some market-driven offenses, like the street sale of prostitution and illegal narcotics, may occur independently of the routine activities of places. As the recent failed crackdown on drugs in the District of Columbia suggests (Reuter et al., 1987), market crimes may create their own routine activities in otherwise relatively unorganized public places.

Yet all the literature on robbery discussed above suggests that cash business places open at night generate opportunities for robbery, the absence of which could well mean fewer robberies. The concentration of exposers in Minneapolis parks (7 of the 25 top-ranked places for sex crimes) suggest that there might be fewer exposures if there were fewer places providing both a desirable audience and abundant opportunities for concealment. Predatory stranger offenses, in particular, seem dependent on places where offenders converge with vulnerable victims and low surveillance.

Yet even predatory stranger offenses vary substantially by type of offense, as Table 4 shows, with respect to the magnitude of concentration they display relative to the number of possible locations. One can avoid robbery twice as effectively by staying away from certain places than one can avoid sex crimes or auto theft. If routine activities of places are criminogenic, they appear to be more powerfully so for some kinds of offenses than others.

CHANGING PLACES, NOT PEOPLE

Ironically, Cohen and Felson (1979) concluded their original analysis with an emphasis on individual life-styles as the primary aspect of routine activities affecting crime, implying the inevitability of higher crime with a more mobile life-style (cf. Hindelang et al., 1978). Focusing on the routine activities of places rather than of individual life-styles produces a different conclusion, as Felson (1987) has recently implied. On a place-specific basis, targets may be made less suitable, guardianship may be increased, and the supply of potential offenders may be reduced. Successful efforts to do so might produce net reductions in crime, holding constant the absolute size of the populations of

48   SHERMAN, GARTIN AND BUERGER

offenders and targets. The routine activities of the person who goes to bars or convenience stores late at night does not have to change for such places to be made less criminogenic.

Many recent examples of such attempts can be found. Local ordinances passed in the late 1980s in Ohio, Florida, and New Jersey require convenience stores to have two or more clerks on duty, for the explicit purpose of reducing armed robbery through better guardianship (Clifton, 1987). A 1987 editorial in the *American Journal of Public Health* recommends that the U.S. Occupational Safety and Health Administration regulate workplace environments to reduce target suitability for robbery-homicide by requiring bulletproof barriers to protect taxi drivers and store clerks and better placement of cash registers to increase surveillability from the street (Dietz and Baker, 1987). The mother of a boy murdered in a 1985 Orlando, Florida, convenience store robbery attempted to create a Mothers Against Drunk Driving (MADD)-type organization called Victims of Interstate Convenience Enterprises (VOICE) to fight for better convenience store security (Lawrence, 1986). New York police developed an Operation Padlock program to close up businesses with repeated crime problems. As part of the developing problem-oriented approach to reinventing police strategies (Eck and Spelman, 1987; Goldstein, 1979), police in Minneapolis have sought to reduce convergence of offenders and targets under weak guardianship by revoking the liquor licenses of two violent bars, based in part on the data analysis presented above (Sherman et al., 1988). Citizens in Detroit have gone as far as buying up and renovating vacant houses to prevent them from becoming crack houses (Wilkerson, 1988b), and citizens in both Detroit and Miami have burned down crack houses, with an acquittal on arson charges by one Detroit jury (Wilkerson, 1988a).

Whether such measures can produce net reductions in crime (without displacement) may be impossible to determine, given the difficulty of holding constant the collectivity supply of motivated offenders—or even of defining adequately who they are (Massey et al., 1987). But controlled experimentation may be the best means for determining the extent to which routine activities of places can be made less criminogenic. Random assignment of a large sample of clusters of hot spot addresses to different levels of guardianship by police patrol, for example, could determine (1) whether guardianship affects place crime and (2) whether crimes reduced in one place are matched by crimes increased in nearby places (Sherman and Weisburd, 1988). The convenience store industry could experiment with numbers of clerks and other guardianship measures and examine potential displacement of armed robbery to other nighttime commercial establishments in nearby jurisdictions.

At the same time, the criminology of place can be enhanced by longitudinal analysis of the characteristics associated with onset, frequency rates, seriousness, and desistance of crime in places (Blumstein et al., 1986; Wolfgang et

HOT SPOTS OF PREDATORY CRIME 49

al., 1972). For example, from 1945 (the birth year of the first Philadelphia cohort) to 1988, one liquor store in Northeast Washington under the same family management experienced 16 robberies and burglaries and 4 robbery-homicides (Mintz, 1988). How does that compare with other liquor stores? How will it compare with future rates under new management? How do liquor stores compare with other types of retail outlets, or other types of places? Such research on the "criminal careers" of places could help to specify the fertile, but still too general, routine activities concepts of target suitability, motivated offenders, and guardianship.

Like the criminology of individuals, a criminology of place could fall prey to the facile notion that getting rid of the "bad apples" will solve the problem. Neither capital punishment of places (as in arson of crack houses) nor incapacitation of the routine activities of criminal hot spots (as in revocation of liquor licenses) seems likely to eliminate crime. But since the routine activities of places may be regulated far more easily than the routine activities of persons, a criminology of place would seem to offer substantial promise for public policy as well as theory.

REFERENCES

Akers, Doris
　　1965　Sweet, Sweet Spirit. New York: MANNA Music.

Anson, Jay
　　1977　The Amityville Horror. New York: Francis Hall.

Baker, Susan P., R.A. Whitfield, and Brian O'Neill
　　1987　Geographic variations in mortality from motor vehicle crashes. New England Journal of Medicine 316: 1,384–1,387.

Baldwin, John
　　1979　Ecological and areal studies in Great Britain and the United States. In Norval Morris and Michael Tonry (eds.), Crime and Justice: An Annual Review of Research. Vol. 1. Chicago: University of Chicago Press.

Bayley, David H.
　　1976　Forces of Order: Police Behavior in Japan and the United States. Berkeley, Calif.: University of California Press.

Biderman, Albert D. and Albert J. Reiss, Jr.
　　1967　On exploring the "dark figure" of crime. Annals of the American Academy of Political and Social Sciences 374: 1–15.

Bittner, Egon
　　1970　The Functions of the Police in a Modern Society. Bethesda, Md.: National Institute of Mental Health.

Black, Donald
　　1970　Production of crime rates. American Sociological Review 35: 733–748.

Blau, Judith R. and Peter M. Blau
　　1982　The cost of inequality: Metropolitan structure and violent crime. American Sociological Review 47: 114–129.

50   SHERMAN, GARTIN AND BUERGER

Blumstein, Alfred, Jacqueline Cohen, Jeffrey A. Roth, and Christy Visher (eds.)
    1986   Criminal Careers and "Career Criminals." Vol. 1. Washington, D.C.:
            National Academy Press.

Brantingham, Paul J. and Patricia L. Brantingham
    1975   Spatial patterning of burglary. Howard Journal of Penology and Crime
            Prevention 14: 11–24.
    1982   Environmental Criminology. Beverly Hills, Calif.: Sage.
    1984   Patterns in Crime. New York: Macmillan.

Brown, Barbara
    1983   Ph.D. dissertation, Department of Psychology, University of Utah. Cited in
            The New York Times, November 17: C11.

Bursik, Robert J., Jr.
    1986   Ecological stability and the dynamics of delinquency. In Albert J. Reiss, Jr.
            and Michael Tonry (eds.), Communities and Crime. Chicago: University of
            Chicago Press.

Cavan, Sherri
    1966   Liquor License: An Ethnography of Bar Behavior. Chicago: Aldine.

Chambers, Ray W.
    1988   Gainesville convenience store security measures ordinance: A review and
            analysis. Unpublished manuscript.

Clarke, Ronald V.
    1983   Situational crime prevention: Its theoretical basis and practical scope. In
            Michael Tonry and Norval Morris (eds.), Crime and Justice: An Annual
            Review of Research. Vol. 4. Chicago: University of Chicago Press.

Clarke, Ronald V. and Pat Mayhew
    1988   The British gas suicide rate story and its criminological implications. In
            Michael Tonry and Norval Morris (eds.), Crime and Justice: An Annual
            Review of Research. Vol. 10. Chicago: University of Chicago Press.

Clifton, Wayland, Jr.
    1987   Convenience store robberies in Gainesville, Florida: An intervention strategy
            by the Gainesville police department. Paper presented at meeting of the
            American Society of Criminology, Montreal, November.

Cobb, Richard
    1975   A Sense of Place. London: Duckworth.

Cohen, Lawrence E. and Marcus Felson
    1979   Social change and crime rate trends: A routine activity approach. American
            Sociological Review 44: 588–608.

Cornish, Derek B. and Ronald V. Clarke
    1986   The Reasoning Criminal: Rational Choice Perspectives on Offending. New
            York: Springer–Verlag.
    1987   Understanding crime displacement: An application of rational choice theory.
            Criminology 25: 933–948.

Davis, Harold
    1987   Workplace homicides of Texas males. American Journal of Public Health
            77: 1,290–1,293.

HOT SPOTS OF PREDATORY CRIME 51

Dietz, Park Elliott and Susan P. Baker
1987   Murder at work. American Journal of Public Health 77:273–274.

Duffala, Dennis C.
1976   Convenience stores, armed robbery, and physical environmental features. American Behavioral Scientist 20: 227–246.

Durkheim, Emile
1951   Suicide: A Study in Sociology. 1897. New York: Free Press.

Eck, John and William Spelman
1987   Problem-Solving. Washington, D.C.: Police Executive Research Forum.

Federal Bureau of Investigation
1987   Crime in the United States, 1986. Washington, D.C.: Government Printing Office.

Felson, Marcus
1987   Routine activities and crime prevention in the developing metropolis. Criminology 25: 911–932.

Forster, Edward M.
1947   Introduction. In The Celestial Omnibus and Other Stories. New York: Alfred A. Knopf.

Gastil, Raymond D.
1971   Homicide and a regional culture of violence. American Sociological Review 36: 412–417.

Glaser, Daniel
1971   Social Deviance. Chicago: Markham.

Goffman, Erving
1971   The insanity of place. In Relations in Public: Microstudies of the Public Order. London: Penguin.

Goldstein, Herman
1979   Improving policing: A problem-oriented approach. Crime and Delinquency 25: 236–238.

Gould, Leroy
1969   The changing structure of property crime in an affluent society. Social Forces 48: 50–59.

Guerry, A.M.
1831   Essai Sur la Statistique Morale de la France. Paris: Chez Corchard.

Hakim, Simon and George F. Rengert (eds.)
1981   Crime Spillover. Beverly Hills, Calif.: Sage.

Hawley, Amos
1950   Human Ecology. New York: Ronald Press.

Hawthorne, Nathaniel
1913   The House of Seven Gables. Boston: Houghton-Mifflin.

Hindelang, Michael
1976   Criminal Victimization in Eight American Cities. Cambridge, Mass.: Ballinger.

Hindelang, Michael, Michael Gottfredson, and James Garofalo
1978   Victims of Personal Crime. Cambridge, Mass.: Ballinger.

SHERMAN, GARTIN AND BUERGER

Hindelang, Michael, Travis Hirschi, and Joseph Weis
    1981   Measuring Crime. Beverly Hill, Calif.: Sage.

Hiss, Tony
    1987a   Experiencing Places-I. The New Yorker, June 22: 45—68.
    1987b   Experiencing Places-II. The New Yorker, June 29: 73–86.

Iverem, Esther
    1988   A teen-age addict is held in the killings of 5 in East Harlem. The New
            York Times, January 10: 1.

Jacobs, Jane
    1961   The Death and Life of Great American Cities. New York: Vintage.

Jeffery, C. Ray
    1971   Crime Prevention through Environmental Design. Beverly Hills, Calif.:
            Sage.

Jeffery, C. Ray, Ronald Hunter, and Jeffrey Griswold
    1987   Crime analysis, computers, and convenience store robberies. Appendix D to
            Wayland Clifton, Jr., Convenience store robberies in Gainesville, Florida:
            An intervention strategy by the Gainesville police department. Paper
            presented at meeting of the American Society of Criminology, Montreal,
            November.

Kansas City (Mo.) Police Department
    1977   Response Time Analysis. In 4 vols. Kansas City.

Krahn, Harvey, Timothy F. Hartnagel, and John W. Gartrell
    1986   Income inequality and homicide rates: Cross-national data and criminologi-
            cal theories. Criminology 24: 269–295.

Lawrence, Donna
    1986   Mad Mother Fights For Tighter C-Store Security. C-Store Digest, October
            20: 1.

Liebow, Elliot
    1967   Tally's Corner: A Study of Negro Streetcorner Men. Boston: Little, Brown.

Linnell, Deborah
    In   The Geographic Distribution of Hot Spots of Robbery, Rape, and Auto
    Press   Theft in Minneapolis. M.A. Thesis, University of Maryland, Institute of
             Criminal Justice and Criminology.

Loftin, Colin and Robert Hill
    1974   Regional subculture and homicide: An examination of the Gastil-Hackney
            hypothesis. American Sociological Review 39: 714–724.

Mason, T.J., F.W. McKay, R. Hoover, W.J. Blot, and J.F. Fraumeni, Jr.
    1985   Atlas of Cancer Mortality for U.S. Counties: 1950–69. DHEW Publication
            (NIH) 75-780. Bethesda, Md.: National Cancer Institute.

Massey, James L., Marvin D. Krohn, and Lisa Bonati
    1987   The routine activities of individuals and property crime. Paper presented at
            meeting of the American Society of Criminology, Montreal.

Merry, Sally E.
    1981a   Defensible space undefended: Social factors in crime prevention through
             environmental design. Urban Affairs Quarterly 16: 397–422.

HOT SPOTS OF PREDATORY CRIME 53

1981b   Urban Danger: Life in a Neighborhood of Strangers. Philadelphia: Temple University Press.

Messner, Steven
1980   Income inequality and murder rates: Some cross-national findings. Comparative Social Research 3: 185–198.
1982   Poverty, inequality and the urban homicide rate. Criminology 20: 103–114.
1983   Regional differences in the economic correlates of the urban homicide rate: Some evidence on the importance of cultural context. Criminology 21: 477–488.

Messner, Steven and Kenneth Tardiff
1985   The social ecology of urban homicide: An application of the "routine activities" approach. Criminology 23: 241–267.

Miethe, Terance D., Mark C. Stafford, and J. Scott Long
1987   Social differentiation in criminal victimization: A test of routine activities lifestyle theories. American Sociological Review 52: 184–194.

Mintz, John
1988   NE store owners retiring with stock of memories. The Washington Post, October 17, 1988: C1.

Molumby, Thomas
1976   Patterns of crime in a university housing project. American Behavioral Scientist 20: 247–259.

Nelson, James F.
1980   Multiple victimization in American cities: A statistical analysis of rare events. American Journal of Sociology 85: 870–891.

Newman, Oscar
1972   Defensible Space: Crime Prevention through Urban Design. New York: Macmillan.

Newman, Oscar and K.A. Franck
1980   Factors Affecting Crime and Instability in Urban Housing Developments. Washington, D.C.: Government Printing Office.
1982   The effects of building size on personal crime and fear of crime. Population and Environment 5: 203–220.

Pierce, Glen L., Susan A. Spaar, and LeBaron R. Briggs IV
1984   The character of police work: Implications for the delivery of services. Center for Applied Social Research, Northeastern University, Boston.

Poyner, Barry
1983   Design against Crime: Beyond Defensible Space. London: Butterworth.

Quetelet, L. Adolphe J.
1842   A Treatise on Man and the Development of His Faculties. Edinburgh: Chambers.

Reiss, Albert J., Jr.
1986   Why are communities important in understanding crime? In Albert J. Reiss, Jr., and Michael Tonry (eds.), Communities and Crime. Chicago: University of Chicago Press.
1987   The legitimacy of intrusion into private space. In Clifford D. Shearing and Philip C. Stenning (eds.), Sage Criminal Justice Systems Annual Series. Vol. 23: Private Policing. Newbury Park, Calif.: Sage.

54   SHERMAN, GARTIN AND BUERGER

Reppetto, Thomas A.
    1974   Residential Crime. Cambridge, Mass.: Ballinger.

Reuter, Peter, John Haaga, Patrick Murphy, and Amy Praskac
    1987   Drug use and policy in the Washington metropolitan area: An assessment.
              Draft. — RAND, Washington, D.C.

Robinson, William S.
    1950   Ecological correlations and the behavior of individuals. American Sociologi-
              cal Review 15: 351–357.

Rubinstein, Jonathan
    1973   City Police. New York: Farrar, Straus & Giroux.

Sampson, Robert
    1986   Crime in cities: Formal and informal social control. In Albert J. Reiss, Jr.,
              and Michael Tonry (eds.), Communities and Crime. Chicago: University of
              Chicago Press.

Sanchez, Rene
    1988   Suspect in rape arrested: 5 assaults occurred near Dupont Circle. The
              Washington Post, January 8.

Sanchez, Rene and Sari Horwitz
    1987   Transcript disputes go-go assault account: 911 caller, police differ on
              stabbing site. The Washington Post, November 18: C1.

Shaw, Clifford R., Henry D. McKay, Frederick Zorbaugh, and Leonard S. Cottrell
    1929   Delinquency Areas. Chicago: University of Chicago Press.

Sherman, Lawrence W.
    1986   Policing communities: What works? In Albert J. Reiss, Jr., and Michael
              Tonry (eds.), Communities and Crime. Chicago: University of Chicago
              Press.
    1987   Repeat Calls to Police in Minneapolis. Crime Control Reports. No. 5.
              Washington, D.C.: Crime Control Institute.
    1988   Violent stranger crime at a large hotel. A case study in risk assessment
              methods. Unpublished manuscript. Crime Control Institute, Washington,
              D.C.

Sherman, Lawrence W. and David Weisburd
    1988   Policing the hot spots of crime: A redesign of the Kansas City preventive
              patrol experiment. Unpublished manuscript. Crime Control Institute,
              Washington, D.C.

Sherman, Lawrence, Michael E. Buerger, and Patrick R. Gartin
    1988   Beyond dial-a-cop: Repeat call address policing. Unpublished manuscript.
              Crime Control Institute, Washington, D.C.

Silberman, Charles
    1978   Criminal Violence, Criminal Justice. New York: Simon and Schuster.

Skolnick, Jerome and David Bayley
    1986   The New Blue Line. New York: Free Press.

Spelman, William and Dale K. Brown
    1981   Calling the Police: Citizen Reporting of Serious Crime. Washington, D.C.:
              Police Executive Research Forum.

HOT SPOTS OF PREDATORY CRIME   55

Taylor, Ralph B., Steven D. Gottfredson, and S. Brower
   1981   Informal Social Control in the Residential Urban Environment. Center for
           Metropolitan Planning and Research. Baltimore, Md.: Johns Hopkins
           University Press.

Taylor, Ralph B. and Steven Gottfredson
   1986   Environmental design, crime, and prevention: An examination of commu-
           nity dynamics. In Albert J. Reiss, Jr., and Michael Tonry (eds.),
           Communities and Crime. Chicago: University of Chicago Press.

Waller, Irvin and Norman Okihiro
   1978   Burglary: The Victim and the Public. Toronto: University of Toronto
           Press.

Wilkerson, Isabel
   1988a   Crack house fire: Justice or Vigilantism? The New York Times, October 22:
           1.
   1988b   Detroit citizens join with church to rid community of drugs. The New York
           Times, June 29.

Wilson, James Q. and Richard Herrnstein
   1985   Crime and Human Nature. New York: Simon and Schuster.

Wolfgang, Marvin E., Robert Figlio, and Thorsten Sellin
   1972   Delinquency in a Birth Cohort. Chicago: University of Chicago Press.

Lawrence W. Sherman is Professor of Criminology at the University of Maryland, College Park, and President, Crime Control Institute, Washington, D.C. He has recently completed the Milwaukee Domestic Violence Experiment, the RECAP experiment in problem-oriented policing at high-call addresses, and has begun (with David Weisburd) an experiment testing the effects of increased police presence at hot-spot address clusters.

Patrick R. Gartin is a doctoral candidate and a National Institute of Justice Fellow at the Institute of Criminal Justice and Criminology at the University of Maryland, College Park. He is also Director of Data Management and Analysis at the Crime Control Institute in Washington, D.C., where he is completing a reanalysis of the Minneapolis Domestic Violence Experiment.

Michael E. Buerger is a doctoral candidate and Sonn Fellow at the Rutgers University School of Criminal Justice in Newark and Director of the Minneapolis office of the Crime Control Institute, where he is managing the Hot Spots Patrol Experiment.

Part III
Statistics of Criminality

[11]

BRIT. J. CRIMINOL.　Vol. 21　No. 2　1981

THE PREVALENCE OF CONVICTIONS

David P. Farrington (*Cambridge*)*

As Walker (1974) pointed out some years ago, little is known about the prevalence of convictions in England and Wales. " Prevalence " in this context refers to the proportion of an age group convicted at some time in their lives. It can be distinguished from " incidence " of convictions, which refers to the proportion of an age group convicted in one year. The purpose of this note is to point out that, if present trends continue, the prevalence of convictions for non-motoring offences in England and Wales will exceed 50 per cent. for males in the foreseeable future. In other words, unconvicted males will be deviant in a statistical sense.

The annual Home Office *Criminal Statistics* do not provide information about the prevalence of convictions. Nor, for that matter, do they provide information about the incidence of convictions. They do show the number of persons convicted each year per 100,000 in each age group, but this is not the number of different persons. For example, Table 5.12 of the 1979 *Criminal Statistics* (Home Office, 1980) shows that the peak age for convictions of males for indictable (or triable-either-way) offences was 18, with 6,695 convictions per 100,000 persons; for females, the peak age was 17, with 1,007 convictions per 100,000 persons.

Perhaps the best method of estimating the prevalence of convictions is to follow up a sample in a longitudinal survey. The only national estimate of prevalence obtained in this way was reported by Wadsworth (1979). For males born in England, Scotland and Wales in 1946, the prevalence of convictions or cautions for indictable offences was 12·9 per cent. up to the twenty-first birthday. For females, the corresponding figure was 2·03 per cent. It is unfortunate that prevalence was not given for convictions alone. However, for this particular cohort, the number of cautions for indictable offences would have been very small. These figures are perhaps under-estimates rather than over-estimates, since Wadsworth's sample excluded all multiple births and all illegitimate births, both of which may have an above-average prevalence of convictions.

Rather than following up a cohort prospectively, it would be possible to establish prevalence by following up a cohort retrospectively if national statistics were available showing the incidence of first convictions for each age in each year. Unfortunately, they are not. As an example of this kind of an analysis, Little (1965) studied the prevalence of arrests for indictable offences in the Metropolitan Police District of London for persons born in 1942. He did this by adding up first arrests of eight-year-olds in 1950, nine-year-olds in 1951, and so on up to 20-year-olds in 1962. The prevalence of arrests for indictable offences up to the twenty-first birthday came to 11·25 per cent. This rate is for males and females combined, since the statistics did

* Institute of Criminology, University of Cambridge.

DAVID P. FARRINGTON

not show them separately. In those days, about 90 per cent. of arrests of persons in the Metropolitan Police District were followed by findings of guilt, so the prevalence of convictions for this London cohort would have been about 10 per cent. up to the twenty-first birthday.

While it is impossible to use the national *Criminal Statistics* to obtain a longitudinal estimate of the prevalence of convictions, it is sometimes possible to obtain a cross-sectional estimate based on one year's figures. If the proportion of people in each age group who are convicted for the first time in that year is known, these figures can be added up over all age groups to show what the prevalence of convictions would be if the conviction rate for that year persisted over a long period.[1] The old *Supplementary Statistics* used to provide information about first convictions at each age, but this was discontinued after 1963 because of doubts about its accuracy.

What are apparently the only official data on the incidence of first convictions published since 1963 can be seen in Table 10.2 of the 1978 *Criminal Statistics* (Home Office, 1979). This table is based on a random sample of about 9,000 persons convicted in 1977 of (non-motoring) standard list offences. The estimated numbers of first convictions shown in it can be related to the population in each age group in 1977 derived from Table 5.11 of the 1977 *Criminal Statistics* (Home Office, 1978), to obtain a national estimate of prevalence.

In estimating prevalence, ideally what is needed is the percentage first convicted at each age. However, it is only possible to estimate the percentage first convicted in each age range. In order to obtain cumulative percentages, it is necessary to multiply by the number of years in the age range. For example, 0·66 per cent. of males aged 10, 11 and 12 were first convicted in 1977. Assuming constancy over the years, in any given cohort 0·66 per cent. would be first convicted at age 10, 0·66 per cent. at age 11, and 0·66 per cent. at age 12, making a total of 1·98 per cent. convicted up to age 12.

This analysis shows 11·70 per cent. of males convicted up to the seventeenth birthday, 21·76 per cent. up to the twenty-first birthday, and 43·57 per cent. at some time in their lives. For females, the corresponding figures are 2·10, 4·66 and 14·70 per cent. The estimates for life-time prevalence are much higher than McClintock and Avison's (1968) figures, based on first convictions for standard list offences in 1965. It does not seem unreasonable to predict that, if the Home Office would publish figures to enable a similar analysis to be carried out in 1989, the life-time prevalence estimate for males would then exceed 50 per cent.

Of course, these figures do not show that 43 per cent. of males dying now have convictions for standard list offences. The present prevalence is certainly much lower. What they do show is that, if 1977 conviction rates continue, the life-time prevalence of convictions among males will eventually reach 43 per cent. Is this prospect to be welcomed? I think not. For a number of reasons, such as that first convictions are followed by increased offending and by

---

[1] It might be better to base such an analysis on the proportion of *unconvicted* people in each age group convicted for the first time, but national figures showing this proportion have never been published.

THE PREVALENCE OF CONVICTIONS

increased antagonism towards the police (*e.g.* Farrington, 1977), efforts should be made to limit the net of social control.

TABLE 1

Prevalence of Convictions in England and Wales (1977 data)

	Population	Number first convicted	First convicted per 100	X Years at risk	Cumulative	1965 estimate
Males						
age 10–12	1,244	8·2	0·66	1·98	1·98	3·06
13–14	833	16·6	1·99	3·98	5·96	7·33
15–16	799	22·9	2·87	5·74	11·70	10·82
17–18	751	22·2	2·96	5·92	17·62	14·04
19–20	728	15·1	2·07	4·14	21·76	16·71
21–24	1,392	16·7	1·20	4·80	26·56	20·40
25–29	1,767	13·0	0·74	3·70	30·26	23·62
30–39	3,170	17·5	0·55	5·50	35·76	27·28
40–49	2,818	10·2	0·36	3·60	39·36	29·37
50+	6,980	9·7	0·14	4·21	43·57	31·33
Total	20,410					
Females						
age 10–16	2,729	8·1	0·30	2·10	2·10	2·03
17–20	1,416	9·0	0·64	2·56	4·66	2·98
21–24	1,322	5·2	0·39	1·56	6·22	3·63
25–29	1,747	5·7	0·33	1·65	7·87	4·32
30–39	3,101	8·3	0·27	2·70	10·57	5·49
40–49	2,774	4·6	0·17	1·70	12·27	6·51
50+	8,759	7·1	0·08	2·43	14·70	7·87
Total	21,848					

Notes

Population in 1977 in thousands, from Table 5.11 (1977).

Number first convicted in 1977 (of non-motoring standard list offences) in thousands, from Table 10.2 (1978).

X Years at Risk = Percentage first convicted multiplied by years at risk. The upper boundary for the 50+ age group is set at 80, for consistency with McClintock and Avison (1968). It might be better to set it at the current life expectation, but this would not lower the final figure substantially.

1965 Estimate — from McClintock and Avison (1968), Table IV.3, also based on first convictions for standard list offences (data supplied by the Statistical Branch of the Home Office).

REFERENCES

FARRINGTON, D. P. (1977). " The effects of public labelling." *British Journal of Criminology,* **17,** 112–125.

HOME OFFICE (1978). *Criminal Statistics, England and Wales,* 1977. London: HMSO.

HOME OFFICE (1979). *Criminal Statistics, England and Wales,* 1978. London: HMSO.

HOME OFFICE (1980). *Criminal Statistics, England and Wales,* 1979. London: HMSO.

LITTLE, A. (1965). " The ' prevalence ' of recorded delinquency and recidivism in England and Wales." *American Sociological Review,* **30,** 260–263.

McCLINTOCK, F. H. and AVISON, N. H. (1968). *Crime in England and Wales.* London: Heinemann.

WADSWORTH, M. (1979). *Roots of Delinquency.* London: Martin Robertson.

WALKER, N. (1974). " CAUTION: some thoughts on the penal involvement rate." In Blom-Cooper, L. (Ed.) *Progress in Penal Reform.* Oxford: Clarendon Press.

[12]

CRIMINAL CAREERS IN LONDON AND STOCKHOLM: A CROSS-NATIONAL COMPARATIVE STUDY

David P. Farrington, Per-Olof H. Wikstrom

ABSTRACT. The main aim of this paper is to compare two cohorts of working-class males born in 1953, from London and Stockholm, on criminal career features between ages 10 and 25: prevalence, individual offending frequency, continuity, onset, desistance and duration. In addition, the relationship between age of onset and other criminal career features, and characteristics of chronic offenders, are reported for both cohorts. Before describing the results, the criminal career approach and cross-national comparisons are discussed, and then the two longitudinal surveys and steps taken to increase the comparability between them.

Criminal Careers and Cross-National Comparisons

THE CRIMINAL CAREER APPROACH

A "criminal career" is defined as the longitudinal sequence of offences committed by an individual offender, with no necessary suggestion that offenders use their criminal activity as an important means of earning a living. The criminal career approach is not a criminological theory but a framework within which theories can be proposed and tested (see Blumstein et al., 1986; Blumstein and Cohen, 1987). A criminal career has a beginning (onset), an end (desistance) and a career length in between (duration). Only a certain proportion of the population (prevalence) has a criminal career and commits offences. During their careers, offenders commit offences at a certain rate (individual offending frequency). For offenders who commit several offences, it is possible to investigate how far they specialize in certain types of offences and how far the seriousness of their offending escalates over time, but these questions are not addressed here.

The criminal career approach emphasizes the need to investigate such questions as why people start offending (onset), why they continue offending (persistence) and why people stop offending (desistance). The factors influencing onset may differ from those influencing other criminal career features such as persistence and desistance, if only because the different processes occur at different ages. Indeed, Farrington and Hawkins (1991) in London found that there was no relationship between factors influencing prevalence (official offenders versus non-offenders), those influencing early versus later onset, and those influencing desistance after age 21; and Loeber et al. (1991) in Pittsburgh reported no relationship between factors influencing onset and those influencing escalation.

65

E. G. M. Weitekamp and H.-J. Kerner (eds.),
Cross-National Longitudinal Research on Human Development and Criminal Behavior, 65–89.
© 1994 Kluwer Academic Publishers. Printed in the Netherlands.

66

Offending is commonly measured using either official records of arrests or convictions or self-reports of offending. The advantages and disadvantages of official records and self-reports are to some extent complementary. In general, official records include the worst offenders and the worst offences, while self-reports include more of the normal range of delinquent activity. Self-reports have the advantage of including undetected offences, but the disadvantages of concealment and forgetting. The key issue is whether the same results are obtained with both methods. Generally, the worst offenders according to self-reports (taking account of frequency and seriousness) tend also to be the worst offenders according to official records (e.g., Farrington, 1973; Huizinga and Elliott, 1986). The predictors and correlates of official and self-reported offending are very similar (Farrington, 1992c).

The results obtained in criminal career research depend on the methods of defining and measuring crime that are adopted. Most criminal career researchers focus on official records of arrests or convictions for relatively serious offences rather than on self-reports of relatively trivial infractions. Most criminal career results quoted in this paper are based on official records. With official records (in comparison with self-reports), the measured prevalence and frequency of offending are lower and the age of onset of offending is later. In principle, there is no reason why the criminal career approach could not be applied to self-reports of relatively trivial offences. In comparing official records and self-reports of the same behaviour, the underlying criminal career parameters (such as the individual offending frequency) might remain the same in each analysis, but the relationship between these parameters and the observed behaviour (e.g., convictions or self-reports) would vary.

One of the distinctive contributions of criminal career research has been to demonstrate the high cumulative prevalence of arrests and convictions of males (for a review, see Visher and Roth, 1986). For example, in Philadelphia, Wolfgang et al. (1987) found that 47% of males were arrested for a non-traffic offence up to age 30, including 38% of whites and 69% of non-whites. In London, Farrington and West (1990) reported that 37% of males were convicted for criminal offences up to age 32, when these were restricted to offences normally recorded in the Criminal Record Office. In the Orebro project in Sweden, Stattin et al. (1989) showed that one-third of males (and 7% of females) were officially registered for non-traffic offences by age 30. This paper is concerned with the criminal careers of males.

An important focus of criminal career research is the relationship between age and crime. It is well known that the aggregate age-crime curve increases to a peak in the teenage years and then declines. The age-crime curve obtained by following up a cohort of people over time (the same people at different ages) is often different from the cross-sectional curve seen in official statistics (which reflects different people at different ages; see Farrington, 1990), showing the need for longitudinal data on the same individuals. Farrington (1986) proposed a mathematical model for the age-crime curve, with three parameters. The first determined the speed of increase of the curve up to the peak, the second determined the speed of decrease of the curve after the peak, and the third determined the height of the peak.

Since the pioneering research of Blumstein and Cohen (1979), much criminal career research has been concerned to estimate the individual offending frequency of active offenders during their criminal careers (for a review, see Cohen, 1986). For example, based on American research, Blumstein and Cohen concluded that the average active Index (more serious) offender committed about 10 Index offences per year free, and that the individual offending frequency essentially did not vary with age. Furthermore, the average active Index offender accumulated about one arrest per year free.

Criminal career research seeks to investigate whether aggregate career features are the same as or different from individual features (Blumstein et al., 1988). A key issue is to determine how far aggregate changes with age or during the course of a criminal career reflect changes within individual offenders as opposed to changes in the composition of the offending population. For example, the aggregate peak in the age-crime curve may reflect either changes in the prevalence of offenders at each age (the proportion of individuals who offend, out of the population) or changes in the frequency of offending (by those who are offenders at each age) or some combination of these. The British and American studies reviewed by Farrington (1986) indicated that the individual offending frequency did not vary greatly with age or during criminal careers. Therefore, the flat age-crime distribution for individual offending frequency is quite different from the peaked distribution for prevalence and from the peaked aggregate age-crime curve.

More recently, however, Loeber and Snyder (1990) concluded that individual offending frequency increased during the juvenile years up to age 16, and Haapanen (1990) found that it decreased during the adult years. Furthermore, Wikstrom (1990) in Stockholm showed that frequency peaked at age 15-17, and in retrospective self-report research with Nebraska prisoners Horney and Marshall (1991) concluded that it varied over time within individuals. Since there are several contrary studies indicating that frequency is stable with age (e.g., Home Office Statistical Bulletin, 1987; Le Blanc and Fréchette, 1989), more research is clearly needed to establish the conditions under which it is relatively stable or varying with age.

In London, Barnett et al. (1987) found that models assuming that all offenders had the same frequency of offending were inadequate. Hence, they proposed that there were two categories of offenders, termed "frequents" and "occasionals". The data showed that both categories incurred convictions at a constant (but different) rate during their active criminal careers (excluding periods when they were not at risk because of incarceration or death). With the Philadelphia cohort data, Barnett and Lofaso (1985) also concluded that offending frequencies stayed relatively constant over time. The best predictor of the future offending frequency was the past offending frequency.

Generally, there is significant continuity between offending in one age range and offending in another. Farrington (1992b) in London reported that nearly three-quarters (73%) of those convicted as juveniles at age 10-16 were reconvicted at age 17-24, in comparison with only 16% of those not convicted as juveniles. Nearly half (45%) of those convicted as juveniles were reconvicted at age 25-32, in comparison with only 8% of those not convicted as juveniles. Furthermore, this continuity over time did not merely reflect continuity in police reaction to crime. Farrington (1989) showed that, for 10 specified offences, the significant continuity between offending in one age range and offending in a later age range held for self-reports as well as official convictions.

Other studies (e.g., McCord, 1991) show similar continuity. For example, in the Orebro project in Sweden, Stattin and Magnusson (1991) reported that nearly 70% of males registered for crime before age 15 were registered again between ages 15 and 20, and nearly 60% were registered between ages 21 and 29. Also, the number of juvenile offences is an effective predictor of the number of adult offences (Wolfgang et al., 1987).

Criminal career research on onset using official records generally shows a peak age of onset between 13 and 15. For example, in the United States, Blumstein and Graddy (1982) found that

68

the age of onset curve for arrests of both white and non-white males peaked at age 15. There has been less research on desistance or career length. The true age of desistance from offending can only be determined with certainty after offenders die.

Barnett et al. (1987) proposed a mathematical model designed to explain time intervals between convictions and desistance probabilities after each conviction in the London data. They found that the frequents had an average career length of 8.8 years and the occasionals had an average career length of 7.4 years. Hence, the frequents and occasionals did not differ much in their average career lengths, although they differed considerably in their individual offending frequencies. Barnett et al. (1989) also carried out a predictive test of their model. The model was developed on conviction data between the 10th and 25th birthdays and tested on reconviction data between the 25th and 30th birthdays. Generally, the model performed well, but it seemed necessary to assume that there was some intermittency (desisting and later restarting) in criminal careers. Some of the frequents ceased offending at an average age of 19 and then restarted again after a period of 7-10 years with no convictions. Hence, an offender might have one criminal career, then a gap, and then another criminal career.

It is generally true that a relatively early onset of antisocial behaviour predicts a long and serious antisocial career (Loeber and Le Blanc, 1990). For example, Le Blanc and Fréchette (1989) in Montreal showed that, according to both self-reports and official records, the duration of criminal careers increased with decreasing age of onset. While an early age of onset foreshadows a long criminal career (Home Office Statistical Bulletin, 1987; Farrington, 1992b), it is less clear whether it also foreshadows a high frequency of offending. Hamparian et al. (1978), in a study of violent juveniles in Ohio, reported that there was a (negative) linear relationship between the age of onset and the number of offences. Neglecting the possibility of desistance, this suggests that the offending frequency may be tolerably constant between onset and the 18th birthday. However, Tolan (1987) found that the frequency of current self-reported offending was greatest for those with the earliest age of onset.

In the Philadelphia cohort study, Wolfgang et al. (1972) discovered that the probability of reoffending (persistence as opposed to desistance) increased after each successive offence. This probability was .54 after the first offence, .65 after the second, .72 after the third, and it reached an asymptote of .80 after 6 or more arrests. Several other researchers have replicated these results by showing the growth in the recidivism probability after each successive offence (see Blumstein et al., 1985).

Wolfgang et al. (1972) also showed that 6% of the males (18% of the offenders) accounted for 52% of all the juvenile arrests, and labelled these 6% the "chronic offenders". The chronics accounted for even higher proportions of serious offences: 69% of all aggravated assaults, 71% of homicides, 73% of forcible rapes, and 82% of robberies. Frequency and seriousness of offending are generally related. Other researchers have essentially replicated these results. For example, Farrington (1983) in London found that about 6% of the males (17% of the offenders) accounted for about half of all the convictions. Furthermore, when convictions of all family members (fathers, mothers, sons and daughters) were added together, it was discovered that less than 5% of the families accounted for half of all the convictions (West and Farrington, 1977).

Rather than reporting that X% of cohort members account for Y% of crimes, Fox and Tracy (1988) suggested using the Lorenz curve (relating the cumulative percentage of crimes to the cumulative percentage of cohort members) and the Gini coefficient to summarize this relationship.

The Gini coefficient is basically the area between the Lorenz curve and the diagonal, scaled to be 0 when offences are perfectly evenly distributed over cohort members and 1 when the distribution is maximally unequal. In the Philadelphia cohort study, the Gini coefficient was .82 for the whole cohort and .47 for offenders only. Wikstrom (1991b) in Stockholm reported even greater Gini coefficients: .94 for the whole cohort and .71 for offenders only. In fact, only 1% of cohort members (6% of all offenders) accounted for half of all the crimes. Hence, offending was even more narrowly concentrated in a small number of people in Stockholm than in Philadelphia and London.

CROSS-NATIONAL COMPARISONS

There have been relatively few systematic comparisons of crime rates and characteristics of crimes in different countries, and even fewer attempts to compare offenders in different countries. The main justification for cross-national comparisons is to establish the generalizability of theories and results and the boundary conditions under which they do or do not hold. It would be desirable to search for universal findings that can be replicated in different contexts. For example, Hirschi and Gottfredson (1983) argued that the aggregate age-crime curve was invariant over different places, times, crime types and so on. If cross-national differences are discovered, the challenge is to explain them by identifying the "active ingredients" (e.g., social, cultural, legal or criminal justice processes in different countries) that cause them. It is desirable to discover theories and results that have a wide range of applicability.

Cross-national comparisons of crimes, crime rates or offending are not easy to carry out, because of differences between countries in laws, legal processes, criminal justice systems, and other conditions (see e.g., Shelley, 1981). Comparative research may be carried out by the "safari" method or through collaboration. In the safari method, a researcher visits another country, reviews relevant literature and statistics, talks to key persons, and then goes home and writes a comparative study between his or her own country and the country visited. The collaborative method (used in the present paper) involves cooperation between at least one researcher from each country.

The collaborative method is most satisfactory, in overcoming language barriers and possible misunderstandings. As Klein (1989, p.5) argued, "at this point we don't need more brief incursions into each other's territories as much as planned and shared, long-term collaborative cross-national journeys." There are many aspects of criminological data from any country that may be misunderstood by a researcher from outside that country. There are many pitfalls for the unwary even in criminological data from one's own country, and it is important to know about these and to avoid mistakes of interpretation. The easiest cross-national comparison is between two countries, involving one researcher from each.

As an example, Farrington and Langan (1992) compared published victim survey data, police and court records and prison statistics in England and the United States, to compare the flow of offenders through recording, detection, conviction and imprisonment. McClintock and Wikstrom (1990), using police records, compared violent crimes in Scotland and Sweden, and later McClintock and Wikstrom (1992) compared violent crimes in Edinburgh and Stockholm. All these papers contain detailed discussions about the comparability of laws and criminal justice systems in these different countries.

The most recent large-scale cross-national comparison in criminology is the International Victim

70

Survey (Van Dijk et al., 1990), conducted in 14 countries. At the present time, an international self-reported offending survey is also being carried out (see Junger-Tas et al., 1992).

No existing published cross-national research focusses specifically on criminal career features. However, Pulkkinen (1988) carried out a replication study. She analysed her data from Finland to see how comparable its criminal career features were to the London data reported by Farrington (1983, 1986). Pulkkinen followed up 196 males and 173 females from age 8-9 (in 1968) to age 27. She found that 28% of males were convicted for relatively serious offences (excluding traffic offences and drunkenness) by age 24, that the peak age for the prevalence of offending was 17, and that 4% of the males accounted for half of all the convictions. After reviewing several other similarities between her results and Farrington's, she concluded that "the regularities obtained in the two longitudinal studies imply that the phenomenon of male delinquency is structurally similar in different communities" (1988, p.194).

The London and Stockholm Projects

THE CAMBRIDGE STUDY IN DELINQUENT DEVELOPMENT

The Cambridge Study in Delinquent Development is a prospective longitudinal survey of the development of offending and antisocial behaviour in 411 London males. At the time they were first contacted in 1961-62, these males were all living in a working-class area of London. The sample was chosen by taking all the boys who were then aged 8-9 and on the registers of 6 state primary schools within a one-mile radius of a research office that had been established. Hence, the most common year of birth of these males was 1953. In nearly all cases (93.7%), their family breadwinner at that time (usually the father) had a working-class occupation (skilled, semi-skilled or unskilled manual workers). Most of the males were white in racial appearance and of British origin. The study was originally directed by Donald J. West, and it has been directed since 1982 by David P. Farrington, who has worked on it since 1969. The major results can be found in four books (West, 1969, 1982; West and Farrington, 1973, 1977), and in more than 60 papers listed by Farrington and West (1990).

A major aim in this survey was to measure as many factors as possible that were alleged to be causes or correlates of offending. The males were interviewed and tested in their schools when they were aged about 8, 10, and 14, by male or female psychologists. They were interviewed in a research office at about 16, 18, and 21, and in their homes at about 25 and 32, by young male social science graduates. At all ages, it was possible to trace and interview a high proportion of the target sample: 389 out of 410 still alive at age 18 (94.9%) and 378 out of 403 still alive at age 32 (93.8%), for example. The tests in schools measured intelligence, attainment, personality, and psychomotor skills, while information was collected in the interviews about living circumstances, employment histories, relationships with females, leisure activities such as drinking and fighting, and offending behaviour.

In addition to interviews and tests with the males, interviews with their parents were carried out by female social workers who visited their homes. These took place about once a year from when the male was about 8 until when he was aged 14-15 and was in his last year of compulsory education. The primary informant was the mother, although many fathers were also seen. The parents provided details about such matters as family income, family size, their employment histories, their child-rearing practices (including attitudes, discipline, and parental agreement), their degree of supervision of the boy, and his temporary or permanent separations from them.

The teachers completed questionnaires when the males were aged about 8, 10, 12, and 14. These provided information about their troublesome and aggressive school behaviour, their school attainments, and their truancy. Ratings were also obtained from their peers when they were in the primary schools, about such topics as their daring, dishonesty, troublesomeness and popularity.

Searches were also carried out in the central Criminal Record Office in London to try to locate findings of guilt of the males, of their parents, of their brothers and sisters, and (in recent years) of their wives and cohabitees. The minimum age of criminal responsibility in England is 10. The Criminal Record Office contains records of all relatively serious offences committed in Great Britain or Ireland. In the case of 18 males who had emigrated outside Great Britain and Ireland by age 32, applications were made to search their criminal records in the 8 countries where they had settled, and searches were actually carried out in four countries. Since most males did not emigrate until their twenties, and since the emigrants had rarely been convicted in England, it is likely that the criminal records are quite complete.

Convictions were only counted if they were for offences normally recorded in the Criminal Record Office, thereby excluding minor crimes such as common assault, traffic infractions and drunkenness. The most common offences included were thefts, burglaries and unauthorised takings of vehicles, although there were also quite a few offences of violence, vandalism, fraud and drug abuse. In order not to rely on official records for information about offending, self-reports of offending were obtained from the males at every age from 14 onwards.

The Cambridge Study in Delinquent Development has a unique combination of features:

(a) Eight personal interviews with the males have been completed over a period of 24 years, from age 8 to age 32;

(b) The main focus of interest is on offending;

(c) The sample size of about 400 is large enough for many statistical analyses but small enough to permit detailed case histories of the boys and their families;

(d) There has been a very low attrition rate, since 94% of the males still alive provided information at age 32;

(e) Information has been obtained from multiple sources: the males, their parents, teachers, peers, and official records;

(f) Information has been obtained about a wide variety of theoretical constructs, including intelligence, personality, parental child-rearing methods, peer delinquency, school behaviour, employment success, marital stability, and so on.

This paper is based on the official records of convictions. The recorded age of offending is the age at which an offence was committed, not the age on conviction. There can be delays of several months or even more than a year between offences and convictions, making conviction ages different from offending ages. Offences are defined as acts leading to convictions. One court appearance can be for several different offences, and it is sometimes a matter of chance whether two different offences lead to two different court appearances or to only one.

An analysis based only on recorded offences would overestimate the number of separate offending events, since one event can lead to two recorded offences (e.g., when an apprehended burglar is convicted both of burglary and of going equipped to steal). In order to yield the closest

72

approximation to the number of offending events, offences are only counted in this paper if they are committed on different days. Where two offences were committed on the same day, only the most serious was counted. This occasionally led to the under-recording of separate offending events on the same day. However, most court appearances arose from only one offending day; the 683 recorded offences up to age 32 corresponded to 613 separate occasions of conviction.

The most relevant information about the criminal careers of the males up to age 31 was published by Farrington (1990, 1992a, 1992b). The cumulative prevalence of convictions was 37%. The peak age for the number of offences and for the number of different offenders was at 17. The median age of conviction was lowest for theft and burglary and higher for violence, vandalism, drugs and fraud. Onset peaked at 14 and again at 17. An early age of onset predicted a long criminal career and a large number of offences.

PROJECT METROPOLITAN IN STOCKHOLM

The two major Swedish longitudinal studies focussing on offending are the Orebro project (see Magnusson, 1988) and Project Metropolitan in Stockholm. (For a review of other Swedish longitudinal studies, see Janson, 1984.) As originally planned, Project Metropolitan was to be launched simultaneously in 1964 in Stockholm, Copenhagen, Oslo and Helsinki, and all four sites were to have similar and coordinated data collection efforts. However, in the event, major studies were launched only in Stockholm and Copenhagen. The Copenhagen researchers aimed to follow up all 12,270 males born in Copenhagen in 1953. They completed a school questionnaire study in 1965 and an interview with the mothers in 1968; subsequent data collection included police records but was limited by funding difficulties (see Hogh and Wolf, 1981, 1983). These Project Metropolitan surveys are two of only 13 major longitudinal studies of offending conducted outside the United States (Farrington, 1988).

From now on, "Project Metropolitan" will refer to the Stockholm longitudinal survey, which has been directed by Carl-Gunnar Janson since its inception in 1964 (see Janson, 1981, 1984). This is a follow-up of all children born in 1953 and living in Stockholm in 1963, comprising 7,719 males and 7,398 females. The major findings have been published in over 30 research reports from the University of Stockholm Department of Sociology.

Project Metropolitan aimed to investigate social stratification and social mobility, residential mobility, leisure activities, partner selection and deviance (crime, addiction and mental illness). A school questionnaire study was completed in 1966 with 13,450 children, and 4,021 mothers were interviewed in 1968. All other data have been collected from registers, including hospital birth records, school records, census records, draft board records, Child Welfare Committee records and police records. Data collection continued until 1983, when the sample reached the age of 30. At that point, all identifying information was removed from the records, so it is not possible to follow up this sample after age 30.

The age of criminal responsibility in Sweden is 15, but police records of offences counted as cleared up and believed to have been committed by members of this sample are available from 1966, when sample members became 13. Child Welfare Committee records of offending are available for 1960-65 (See Janson, 1977), but it is unlikely that many of the sample would have an offending record before age 10. The Child Welfare Committee records used here are not available for separate years (only for the 1960-65 time period), are available only for Stockholm, and specify only that the person has offended (not the number of offences). The police records are available for each year, cover the whole of Sweden, and specify the number and types of offences committed by each offender (see Janson, 1982; Wikstrom, 1987). All analyses of offending referred to and carried out in this paper have used offending data up to and including 1978, when sample members became 25. However, later offending data have been collected up to 1983. Up to 1978, 100 of the males (1.3%) had died, and 69 (0.9%) had left Sweden and not returned.

Several analyses have established the correlations between offending and such topics as social class (Janson, 1982), family structure (Smith, 1991), housing tenure (Wikstrom, 1991a), intelligence (Reichel, 1989) and psychiatric diagnoses (Janson, 1989). Wikstrom (1985) completed a special study of violent offenders, while Torstensson (1987, 1990) carried out special analyses of drug abusers and female offenders. However, the most relevant analyses for the present paper are the studies focussing on age and crime by Wikstrom (1987, 1990).

Wikstrom (1987) reported that 31% of males and 6% of females were recorded as offenders up to age 25. The age of onset of offending peaked in 1966, the first year with available police records, and declined subsequently. The median age of onset was relatively early for males, working class children, and for theft and vandalism (as opposed to violence, drugs and fraud). Wikstrom (1990) found that there was a marked peak in the number of offences, and in the individual offending frequency, but that the number of offenders did not vary greatly with age.

CROSS-NATIONAL COMPAPABILITY

From now on, the Cambridge Study sample will be referred to as the London Cohort, and the Project Metropolitan sample will be referred to as the Stockholm cohort. Both cohorts were born in or around 1953, were predominantly of Northern European white ethnicity, and were living in a Northern European capital city at age 8-10. For this paper, both cohorts were followed up at age 25. However, the Stockholm offending data are for calendar years rather than for ages. The Stockholm cohort was followed up to the end of 1978, when the average age of the cohort was 25.5, whereas the London cohort was followed up to the end of their 25th year. In any given "age" comparison, the London cohort are 0.5 years older. For example, for Stockholm offences committed in 1966 ("age 13"), the average age of the average offender in the middle of 1966 would be 13.0. For London offences committed at age 13 (between the 13th and 14th birthdays), the average age of the average offender would be 13.5.

To some extent, the two projects have complementary strengths and weaknesses. The Stockholm project is based on a large representative sample but relies largely on data that could be collected from registers. The London project is based on small area sample, but includes a wide variety of data from many different sources. Since the London males were overwhelmingly drawn from working-class families, only the 3190 Stockholm males (41.3% of Project Metropolitan males) living in working class families at age 10 are studied in this paper. The definition of "working-class" is quite comparable, being based on skilled, semi-skilled or unskilled manual occupations of heads of households.

The records of offending are very complete in both London and Stockholm. Dead males (6) are excluded from the London figures as not at risk of offending after death. Dead males are not excluded from the Stockholm figures, but this has only a minimal effect on the findings. The London records are of convictions, but the Stockholm records are of known (or suspected) offenders. Specifically, if a Stockholm offender was caught for one offence and admitted four others, he would be recorded for five offences. If a London offender was caught for one offence

74

and admitted four others, it is likely that he would be convicted only for one offence (and have the other four "taken into consideration"). Hence, the Stockholm records of offending are more comprehensive. Under age 18, most recorded Stockholm offenders were not prosecuted, because of legal restrictions. From age 19 onwards, more than 90% of recorded Stockholm offenders were convicted or paid a summary fine to avoid a court appearance.

In the interests of achieving comparability of legal categories, the present analyses are restricted to theft (including burglary and receiving), violence (including robbery), vandalism (including arson), drugs and fraud offences only. Other offences (e.g., motoring, sex, possessing an offensive weapon, going equipped to steal) are excluded. The included offences are quite comparable in London and Stockholm, except that violence in Stockholm is more comprehensive, because the English records exclude offences of minor assault. The included offences comprise 89.7% of all recorded London offences and 74.9% of all recorded Stockholm offences between ages 10 and 25. The difference is largely attributable to the proportion of recorded traffic offences in Stockholm (17.1% of all recorded offences).

Criminal Career Features

PREVALENCE, FREQUENCY, CONTINUITY

Figure 1 shows the cumulative prevalence of recorded offending in London and Stockholm up to age 25. The Stockholm curve begins at age 12 because the Child Welfare Committee data do not make it possible to determine the exact year of offending. Generally, the cumulative prevalence curves are very similar. Up to age 25, 1023 of the 3190 Stockholm males (32.1%) and 134 of the 411 London males (32.6%) were recorded offenders. The London cumulative prevalence data at each age were corrected to take into account dead males not at risk of offending, and the corrected data are shown in Figure 1. However, this correction made virtually no difference to the results. The cumulative prevalence up to 25 came to 32.7% rather than 32.6%.

Figure 1

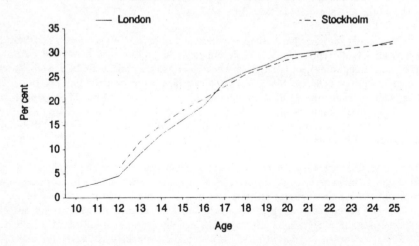

Cumulative Prevalence of Offending

Figure 2 shows the aggregate rate of offending (the number of offences per 100 males) at each age. The Stockholm curve begins at age 13 because the Child Welfare Committee data do not specify the number of offences (only the number of offenders). The Stockholm curve has a greater magnitude than the London curve, because Stockholm offenders had more recorded offences on average. The 969 Stockholm males recorded as offenders by the police from age 13 onwards had 9708 recorded offences, or an average of 10.0 each. The 134 London recorded offenders had 516 recorded offences, or an average of 3.9 each. There were 3.0 offences per sample member in Stockholm and 1.3 in London.

Figure 2

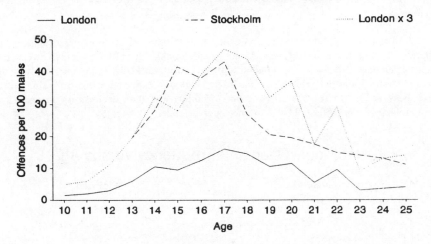

Figure 3

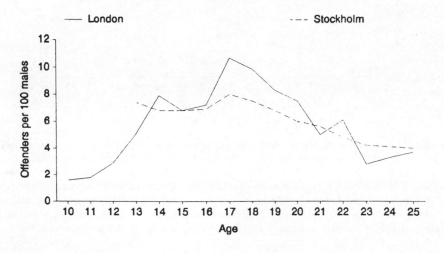

76

In order to make the shapes of the London and Stockholm curves more readily comparable, the London rate is also shown multiplied by 3 in Figure 2. When this is done, it can be seen that the aggregate rate curves for London and Stockholm are quite similar, increasing to a peak at age 17 (of 43.0 offences per 100 males in Stockholm and 15.6 in London), and then decreasing. The Stockholm rate at age 15 is almost as great as the age 17 rate, and proportionally greater than the London rate at age 15. This may be because 15 is the age of criminal responsibility in Stockholm, and there may then be a decrease in police inhibitions against recording offenders and offences.

Figure 3 shows the prevalence of offenders at each age. In London, the prevalence of offenders rises to a clear peak at age 17 (10.5 offenders per 100 males) and then declines. In contrast, the Stockholm curve is much flatter, although it also peaks at 17 (8.0 offenders per 100 males) and then declines.

Figure 4 shows the individual offending frequency (the number of offences per offender) at each age. There is a clear difference between London and Stockholm in this criminal career feature. Individual offending frequencies in London do not vary markedly with age and are always between 1 (the minimum possible value) and 2. In Stockholm, the individual offending frequency rises to a peak at age 15 (of 6.2 offences per offender) and then declines up to age 19, after which it is tolerably constant, at about 3 offences per offender.

Figure 4

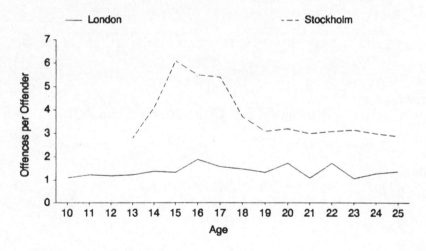

It is important to speculate about alternative explanations for this difference. One possibility is that the use of convictions in London masks the true relationship between the individual offending frequency and age, because most offenders are convicted for only one offence at any given age. However, it is theoretically possible to be convicted for several offences at one age; for example, one offender was convicted for 8 offences at age 14, another for 5 offences at age 18, and another for 5 offences at age 20. It would be useful to investigate whether the individual offending frequency remained constant in London after including offences taken into consideration.

Self-report data on prevalence and number of offences committed were available for 8 specified crime types in London at ages 15-18, 19-21 and 22-24 (Farrington, 1983). However, when the number of offences was divided by the number of offenders to estimate the individual offending frequency, the variations with age were not consistent. For example, between ages 15-18 and 19-21, the individual offending frequency decreased for assault (from 4.4 to 1.8 offences per year), stayed constant for burglary (2.6-2.7 offences per year), and increased for vehicle theft (from 2.4 to 7.4), shoplifting (from 7.3 to 9.8) and vandalism (from 2.5 to 3.6). While these comparisons were affected by small numbers, there was no clear tendency for the individual offending frequency to vary with age.

It might be argued that the individual offending frequency should not be calculated simply by dividing the number of offences by the number of offenders, because some offenders who are in their criminal career may nevertheless have no recorded offences at a particular age. However, when Blumstein et al. (1988) corrected the London conviction data to take account of this, the individual offending frequency was still tolerably constant at different ages. It might also be argued that the neglect of time incarcerated depresses the individual offending frequencies, but Barnett et al. (1987) took account of this in their calculations and still found that the individual offending frequency was constant.

Turning to the Stockholm cohort, it might be argued that the aggregate peak in frequency during the teenage years does not necessarily mean that individuals show a similar peak. The aggregate peak could be caused by different populations of offenders at different ages who all have constant (but different) individual offending frequencies. However, this argument would require that the peak was largely caused by an influx of high-frequency offenders with short criminal careers, whereas it seems more plausible that high frequency offenders would have relatively long criminal careers. Actually, in London, frequent and occasional offenders had similar career lengths (Barnett et al., 1987).

Another possibility is that the Stockholm peak in frequency in the teenage years is a function of changes in methods of official processing of offenders with age. It has already been noted that, from age 19 onwards, recorded offenders in Stockholm were convicted or fined, whereas before age 18 they were not normally prosecuted. It is conceivable that detected teenage offenders might be more willing to admit other offences than older detected offenders, because of the lesser consequences in the teenage years. This might have created the teenage peak.

Table 1 shows the types of offences committed in different age ranges. It can be seen that the percentage of offences that were thefts decreased steadily with age in both London and Stockholm, whereas the percentages of violence, drugs and fraud offences increased with age. Overall, the distributions of types of offences in London and Stockholm were quite similar, although there were proportionally more violent offences in London (despite the more wide-ranging definition of violence in Stockholm) and proportionally more drugs offences in Stockholm.

78

Table 1
Types of Offences at Different Ages

Age	Per Cent					Total
	Theft	Violence	Vandalism	Drugs	Fraud	
London						
10 - 12	96.8	3.2	0.0	0.0	0.0	31
13 - 16	89.4	6.8	1.2	0.0	2.5	161
17 - 20	71.0	13.1	5.1	4.7	6.1	214
21 - 25	61.8	19.1	2.7	4.5	11.8	110
Total	76.4	11.8	3.1	2.9	5.8	516
Stockholm						
13 - 16	89.4	2.1	4.3	2.3	1.8	4011
17 - 20	71.8	9.9	3.9	7.6	6.7	3517
21 - 25	49.2	14.8	5.6	12.2	18.2	2180
Total	74.0	7.8	4.5	6.5	7.3	9708

Table 2 shows the continuity in offending between different age ranges. For example, in London, 47 out of 72 recorded offenders at 13-16 (65.3%) were offenders at 17-20, whereas only 43 out of 337 non-offenders at 13-16 (12.8%) were offenders at 17-20. Two males who died between 17 and 20 were excluded from this comparison. The odds ratio for this comparison is the odds of offending at 17-20 for those who were offenders at 13-16 (47/25) divided by the odds of offending at 17-20 for those who were non-offenders at 13-16 (43/294), which comes to 12.85. Roughly speaking, being an offender at 13-16 increased the risk of offending at 17-20 by about 13 times. The odds ratio measures the strength of the relationship or degree of continuity.

Table 2
Continuity in Offending Between Different Ages

Cohort	Age 1	Age 2	R2 / R1	R2 / NR1	Odds Ratio
London	10 - 12	13 - 16	73.7	15.3	15.49
	10 - 12	17 - 20	66.7	19.9	8.03
	10 - 12	21 - 25	52.9	12.9	7.61
	13 - 16	17 - 20	65.3	12.8	12.85
	13 - 16	21 - 25	48.6	7.5	11.71
	17 - 20	21 - 25	40.9	7.3	8.85
Stockholm	10 - 12	13 - 16	54.3	15.0	6.72
	10 - 12	17 - 20	47.7	14.8	5.24
	10 - 12	21 - 25	38.2	10.8	5.12
	13 - 16	17 - 20	46.1	10.7	7.14
	13 - 16	21 - 25	32.7	8.2	5.43
	17 - 20	21 - 25	41.7	6.5	10.26

Notes: R2 / R1 = Percentage Recorded at age 2 out of those recorded at age 1

R2 / NR1 = Percentage Recorded at age 2 out of those not recorded at age 1

Table 2 shows that there was considerable continuity in offending in both London and Stockholm, although the odds ratios were generally higher in London than in Stockholm. It might be expected that odds ratios for adjacent age ranges would be greater than those for non-adjacent age ranges, and this was indeed true in Stockholm. It was not invariably true in London, although two out of the three adjacent comparisons yielded the two highest odds ratios. It might also be expected that the two most widely separated age ranges (10-12 versus 21-25) would yield the lowest odds ratio, and this was true in both London and Stockholm. However, even in these cases the odds ratios (7.61 in London and 5.12 in Stockholm) indicated remarkable continuity in offending over this long time period.

ONSET, DESISTANCE, DURATION

Figure 5 shows the onset rate (the number of first offenders per 100 males) at each age. The London distribution has two marked peaks, at 14 and 17 (4.4 first offenders per 100 males), while the Stockholm distribution steadily declines from the onset rate at 13 (5.0 first offenders per 100 males). The Stockholm males who had a first recorded offence between 10 and 12 (199, or 6.2 per 100 males) cannot be shown on Figure 5 but are taken into account in calculating the number of first offenders between 13 and 25. (An offender between 10 and 12 would not be counted as a first offender between 13 and 25.) London non-offenders who are dead at each age are excluded from these onset rate calculations. It would be possible to calculate the hazard rate (including only males who have not yet had an onset in the denominator of the rate calculation: see Farrington et al., 1990) rather than onset rates, but this would not materially affect the comparisons between London and Stockholm.

Figure 5

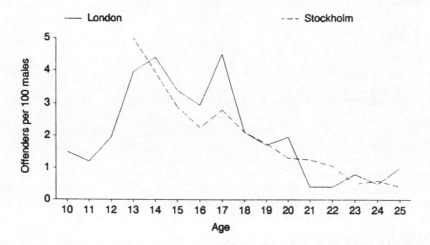

Generally, the London and Stockholm onset curves are similar, except for the relatively high onset rate at age 17 in London. This could have been caused by the fact that juveniles became

80

legally adults at age 17 at this time. The lower inhibitions that the police had against arresting adults (in comparison with juveniles) could have caused the increased onset rate at 17 in London. Setting aside age 17 in London, it would not be unreasonable to conclude that the onset rate peaked at 13-14 in both London and Stockholm and then declined.

Figure 6 shows the "desistance" rate (the number of offenders per 100 males committing their last offence at each age). The word "desistance" is placed in inverted commas because the age of the last offence up to 25 is not necessarily the age of desistance. For example, it would be implausible to suggest that all those who had their last offence at age 25 were desistors. Figure 6 shows an interesting difference between London and Stockholm. Whereas Stockholm "desistance" rates are tolerably constant with age (excluding the artefactual increase at age 25), London "desistance" rates are relatively low up to age 17 and then relatively high. "Desistance" rates at each age could be expressed in relation to the number of males who had begun offending but not desisted before that age, but the rates would then be rather misleading because much of the desistance was "false" according to Barnett and Lofaso (1985). For example, on this basis, the "desistance" rate would be 100% at age 25.

Figure 6

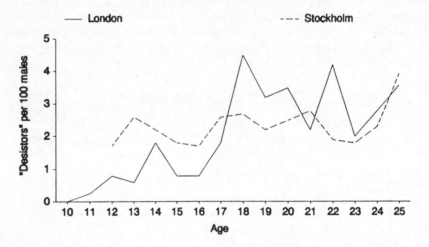

"Desistance" Rate versus Age

—— London   - - - Stockholm

An estimate of false desistance can be obtained by using the London follow-up data to age 32. As expected, the percentage who reoffended between ages 26 and 32 tended to increase with the age of the last offence up to 25. It was 11.5% (3 out of 26) for those last convicted at 10-17, 19.4% (6 out of 31) for those last convicted at 18-19, 26.1% (6 out of 23) for those last convicted at 20-21, 44.0% (11 out of 25) for those last convicted at 22-23, and 40.0% (10 out of 25) for those last convicted at 24-25. It may be that conclusions about "desistance" drawn at age 25 are premature, or that an early age of desistance may be followed after a gap by the restarting of the criminal career.

Figure 7 shows the distribution of criminal career lengths (the number of years between the first and last offence). These distributions are very similar in London and Stockholm. Approximately half of the offenders (38.5% in London, 44.2% in Stockholm) have a career length of zero, since they offend only at one age (London) or in one year (Stockholm). However, the distribution of other career lengths (1-13) is surprisingly flat.

Figure 7

Distribution of Career Lengths

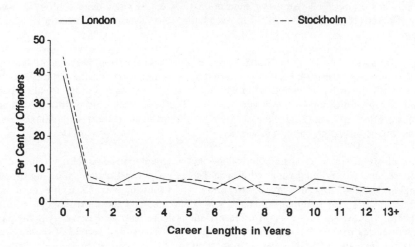

Table 3
Predictability of Age of Onset

Age of Onset	N	Mean Age of "Desistance"	Mean Career Lengths (Years)	Mean No. of Offences
London				
10 - 12	17	10.8	8.1	7.2
13 - 16	58	20.2	5.3	4.6
17 - 20	42	20.1	1.5	2.1
21 - 25	13	23.8	0.0	1.1
Total	130	20.5	3.9	3.7
Stockholm				
10 - 12	199	18.0	6.0	14.5
13 - 16	449	18.5	4.3	11.8
17 - 20	257	19.9	1.7	4.8
21 - 25	118	22.9	0.5	2.4
Total	1023	19.2	3.5	9.5

Note: Dead males were excluded from the London figures

82

ONSET VERSUS OTHER CAREER FEATIURES

Table 3 shows how the mean age of "desistance", the mean career length, and the mean number of offences in the criminal career varied according to the age of onset. Clearly, the mean career length and the mean number of offences decreased with increasing age of onset. At least for ages of onset up to 20, this decrease is probably not caused artefactually by the truncation of the measurement period at age 25, since the mean age of the last offence is at 18-20. The mean age of "desistance" of those with an onset between 21 and 25 is probably misleading. The mean career lengths in London (3.9 years) and Stockholm (3.5 years) were quite similar, as were the mean ages of onset (16.6 in London, 15.7 in Stockholm) and "desistance" (20.5 in London, 19.2 in Stockholm).

Interestingly, for ages of onset up to 20, about one offence was recorded per year of the criminal career in London and about 2.5 offences were recorded per year of the criminal career in Stockholm. In other words, in both London and Stockholm, the frequency of offending per year of the criminal career did not vary with age of onset. The greater number of offences committed by early onset offenders was a function of their longer criminal careers and did not reflect a higher frequency of offending during this career.

An estimate of the effect of the truncation of the measurement period at 25 on criminal career features can be obtained by comparing the data in Table 3 with the London follow-up data to age 32 (Farrington, 1992b). Up to age 32, the mean age of onset was 17.5, the mean age of "desistance" was 23.3, the mean career length was 5.8 years, and the mean number of offences was 4.5. (These figures are based on all offences, not just the restricted range used for purposes of comparison in this paper.) It is only to be expected that the first and second of these quantities, at least, would increase with the age on truncation of the measurement period. Rather than calculating mean or median ages of onset and desistance, it might be better to report percentile ages based on the whole cohort. Assuming that a rule for establishing "desistance" could be developed (e.g., no offence during a five-year period), these percentiles should be independent of the age on truncation.

CHRONIC OFFENDERS

Figure 8 shows how the probability of reoffending increased with each successive offence. This Figure is based on the 969 Stockholm offenders who were recorded by the police, since the number of offences of those recorded only by the Child Welfare Committee was not known. The growth in recidivism probabilities up to the third offence was similar in London and Stockholm. In London, the probability of a first offence was .33, of a second offence given a first was .64, and of a third offence given a second was .72. The corresponding probabilities in Stockholm were .30, .62 and .76. After the fourth offence, these recidivism probabilities reached an asymptote over .90 in Stockholm and around .80 in London. (In London, the probabilities were more erratic because the numbers were smaller. In Stockholm, since more than one offence could be committed on one day, these probabilities may overestimate the probability of offending on one day being followed by offending on a later day.)

In London, 24 males (5.8% of the sample and 17.9% of the offenders) accounted for just over half of all the offences (265 out of 516, or 51.4%). In Stockholm, 66 males (2.1% of the sample and 6.8% of the offenders) accounted for just over half of all the offences (4947 out of 9708, or 51.0%). These males are here termed the "chronic offenders" for purposes of comparison with other studies. The London chronics each had a minimum of 8 recorded offences, while the Stockholm chronics each had a minimum of 35 recorded offences. Clearly, there were more offenders in Stockholm with large numbers of recorded offences. The most persistent offender had 331 recorded offences in Stockholm and 17 in London. Indeed, 13.9% of Stockholm offenders (135) had more than 17 recorded offences. Offending appears to be more concentrated in Stockholm because the Stockholm data concern police-recorded offences whereas the London data concern offences leading to convictions.

Figure 8

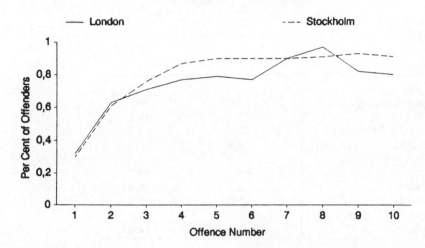

Recidivism Probabilities

Table 4 summarizes differences between chronic and non-chronic offenders. Interestingly, the mean age of onset, mean age of "desistance" and mean career length of chronics were almost identical in London and Stockholm. However, the mean number of offences committed by chronics was far greater in Stockholm (75, as opposed to 11 in London). As expected, chronics had an earlier age of onset, a later age of "desistance", and longer criminal careers than non-chronics in both London and Stockholm. However, there was no marked tendency for chronics to include a higher proportion of more serious (violent) offences in their criminal careers. Indeed, in Stockholm the criminal careers of chronics included a lower proportion of violent offences than the criminal careers of non-chronics, on average.

While the chronics did not include a particularly high proportion of violent offences, they did include a high proportion of violent offenders. Table 5 shows the percentage of cohort members who had committed violent offences in relation to their number of non-violent offences. Clearly, the probability of being a violent offender increased with the number of non-violent crimes committed in both cohorts. Indeed, Farrington (1991) in London concluded that violent offences occurred almost at random in criminal careers, and that violent offenders were essentially equivalent to frequent offenders. The percentage of cohort members who had committed violent offences was similar in London (37 out of 405, or 9.1%) and Stockholm (313 out of 3190, or 9.8%). In both cohorts, there were very few specialist violent offenders who had committed no non-violent offences (only 8.1% of violent offenders in London and 22.4% in Stockholm).

84

Table 4:
Comparison of Chronic and Non-Chronic Offenders

	Chronics	Non-Chronics
London		
Number of Offenders	24	110
Mean Age of Onset	13.4	15.7
Mean Age of "Desistance"	22.4	18.5
Mean Career Length (Years)	9.0	2.8
Mean No. of Offensces	11.0	2.3
% Theft	74.3	78.5
% Violence	12.5	11.2
% Vandalism	1.9	4.4
% Drugs	3.8	2.0
% Fraud	7.5	4.0
Stockholm		
Number of Offenders	66	903
Mean Age of Onset	13.5	16.1
Mean Age of "Desistance"	22.4	19.1
Mean Career Length (Years)	8.9	3.0
Mean No. of Offensces	75.0	5.3
% Theft	83.5	64.2
% Violence	4.9	10.8
% Vandalism	3.3	5.7
% Drugs	4.8	8.3
% Fraud	3.6	11.0

Note: Dead males in London were not excluded from these analyses, because two became chronics before they died and the other four clearly would not have become chronics even if they had survvived.

Table 5:
Violent and Non-Violent Offences

Cohort	No. of Non-Violent Offences	N	% Violent
London	0	278	1.1
	1	52	15.4
	2 - 3	36	22.2
	4 - 7	21	38.1
	8+	18	55.6
Stockholm	0	2291	3.1
	1	344	10.5
	2 - 5	255	20.8
	6 - 20	189	39.2
	21 - 34	51	64.7
	35+	60	78.3

Note: Dead males were excluded from London figures. The chronics in London included 4 Males with 4-7 non-violent offences. The chronics in Stockholm included 6 males with 21-34 non-violent offences.

85

In both cohorts, the majority of chronic offenders were violent offenders (63.6% in London and 77.3% in Stockholm). In Stockholm, despite the fact that chronics included a lower proportion of violent offences than non-chronics, chronics tended to be persistent violent offenders. The majority of Stockholm chronics (59.1%) had committed two or more violent offences, and half of those in the whole sample who had committed 6 or more violent offences (17 out of 34) were among the tiny majority of chronics. Hence, the chronics tended to be the most serious offenders in both cohorts.

Conclusions

There are similarities and dissimilarities in criminal career features in London and Stockholm. The cumulative prevalence of recorded offending is very similar. The shape of the curve for the aggregate offending rate is very similar, reaching a peak at age 17, although the Stockholm curve has a greater magnitude. Interestingly, the peak in the aggregate offending rate largely reflects a peak in prevalence in London and a peak in individual offending frequency in Stockholm. It is ironic that the relationship termed "invariant" by Hirschi and Gottfredson (1983) is the source of the most important difference between the London and Stockholm cohorts. The distributions of types of offences in London and Stockholm are similar, and there is a high degree of continuity in both cohorts between offending in one age range and offending in another.

The curve for the onset rate in London and Stockholm peaks at age 13-14 and then decreases. However, in London there is a second peak at age 17, possibly caused by the legal boundary between juvenile and adult offending. The curve for the "desistance" rate is different, since it is tolerably constant with age in Stockholm but greater at later ages in London. The distribution of career lengths is similar in both cohorts.

In both cohorts, the mean career length and the mean number of recorded offences decreases with increasing age of onset, and there is a constant frequency of offending per year of the criminal career. Also, there is a similar growth in recidivism probabilities in London and Stockholm. Chronic offenders in London and Stockholm have similar ages of onset, ages of "desistance", and career lengths, but Stockholm chronics are much more persistent offenders. Chronics tended to be violent offenders in both cohorts.

The differences between criminal career features in London and Stockholm might be attributed partly to the different criterion for an "offence" (a conviction in London as opposed to a police-recorded offence in Stockholm), which meant that there were many more offences per offender in Stockholm. They might also depend partly on the different legal systems in the two countries, and in particular on the legal boundaries for criminal responsibility in Stockholm at 15 and for adult court in London at 17.

Overall, the cross-cultural replicability of our criminal career results in London and Stockholm is quite impressive. However, our cross-national study is in many respects only a starting point. Further research is needed to establish the effects of different methods of measuring offending on criminal career features. Ideally, coordinated longitudinal studies of criminal careers in different countries are needed, including comparable self-report and official record measurements at different ages. Such studies would help to determine the extent to which criminal career results were truly universal and replicable, and they would also help to locate the sources of any observed differences: in individual characteristics or in social, cultural, legal or criminal justice processes.

86

References

Barnett, A., Blumstein, A. & Farrington, D.P. (1987) Probabilistic models of youthful criminal careers. *Criminology*, 25, 83 - 107

Barnett, A., Blumstein, A. & Farrington, D.P. (1989) A prospective test of a criminal career model. *Criminology*, 27, 373 - 388

Barnett, A. & Lofaso, A.J. (1985) Selective incapacitation and the Philadelphia cohort data. *Journal of Quantitative Criminology*, 1, 3 - 36

Blumstein, A. & Cohen, J. (1979) Estimation of individual crime rates from arrest records. *Journal of Criminal Law and Criminology*, 70, 561 - 585

Blumstein, A. & Cohen, J. (1987) Characterizing criminal careers. Science, 237, 985 - 991

Blumstein, A., Cohen, J. & Farrington, D.P. (1988) Criminal career research: Its value for criminology. *Criminology*, 26, 1 - 35

Blumstein, A., Cohen, J., Roth, J.A. & Visher, C.A. (1986, Eds.) *Criminal careers and "career criminals"*. Washington, D.C.: National Academy Press

Blumstein, A., Farrington, D.P. & Moitra, S. (1985) Delinquency careers: Innocents, desisters and persisters. In M. Tonry & N. Morris (Eds.) Crime and justice, vol.6 (pp. 187 - 219). Chicago: University of Chicago Press

Blumstein, A. & Graddy, E. (1982) Prevalence and recidivism in index arrests: A feedback model. *Law and Society Review*, 16, 265 - 290

Cohen, J. (1986) Research on criminal careers: Individual frequency rates and offence seriousness. In A. Blumstein, J. Cohen, J.A. Roth & C.A. Visher (Eds.) Criminal careers and "career criminals", vol.1 (pp. 292 - 418). Washington, D.C.: National Academy Press

Farrington, D.P. (1973) Self-reports of deviant behaviour: Predictive and stable? Journal of *Criminal Law and Criminology*, 64, 99 -110

Farrington, D.P. (1983) Offending from 10 to 25 years of age. In K.T. Van Dusen & S.A. Mednick (Eds.) Prospective studies of crime and delinquency (pp. 17-37). Boston: Kluwer-Nijhoff

Farrington, D.P. (1986) Age and crime. In M. Tonry & N. Morris (Eds.) Crime and justice, vol.7 (pp.189 - 250). Chicago: University of Chicago Press

Farrington, D.P. (1988) Advancing knowledge about delinquency and crime: The need for a coordinated programme of longitudinal research. *Behavioural Sciences and the Law*, 6, 307 - 331

Farrington, D.P. (1989) Self-reported and official offending from adolescence to adulthood. In M.W. Klein (Ed.) Cross-national research in self-reported crime and delinquency (pp.399 - 423). Dordrecht, Netherlands: Kluwer

Farrington, D.P. (1990) Age, period, cohort, and offending. In D.M. Gottfredson & R.V. Clarke (Eds.) Policy and theory in criminal justice: Contributions in honour of Leslie T. Wilkins (pp. 51 - 75). Aldershot: Avebury

Farrington, D.P. (1991) Childhood aggression and adult violence: Early precursors and later life outcomes. In D.J. Pepler & K.H. Rubin (Eds.) The development and treatment of childhood aggression (pp.5 - 29). Hillsdale, N.J.: Erlbaum

Farrington, D.P. (1992a) Criminal career research: Lessons for crime prevention. Studies on *Crime and Crime Prevention*, 1, 7 - 29

Farrington, D.P. (1992b) Criminal career research in the United Kingdom. *British Journal of Criminology*, 32, 521 - 536

Farrington, D.P. (1992c) Juvenile delinquency. In J.C.Coleman (Ed.) The school years (2nd ed.) (pp. 123 - 163). London: Routledge

Farrington, D.P. & Hawkins, J.D. (1991) Predicting participation, early onset, and later persistence in officially recorded offending. *Criminal Behaviour and Mental Health*, 1, 1 - 33

Farrington, D.P. & Langan, P.A. (1992) Changes in crime and punishment in England and America in the 1980s. *Justice Quarterly*, 9, 5 - 46

Farrington, D.P., Loeber, R., Elliott, D.S., Hawkins, J.D., Kandel, D.B., Klein, M.W., McCord, J., Rowe, D.C. & Tremblay, R.E. (1990) Advancing knowledge about the onset of delinquency and crime. In B.B. Lahey & A.E. Kazdin (Eds.) Advances in Clinical Child Psychology, vol.13 (pp. 283 - 342). New York: Plenum

Farrington, D.P. & West, D.J. (1990) The Cambridge study in delinquent development: A long-term follow-up of 411 London males. In H-J. Kerner & G. Kaiser (Eds.) Criminality: Personality, behaviour, life history (pp. 115-138). Berlin: Springer-Verlag

Fox, J.A. & Tracy, P.E. (1988) A measure of skewness in offence distributions. *Journal of Quantitative Criminology*, 4, 259 - 274

Haapanen, R.A. (1990) *Selective incapacitation and the serious offender.* New York: Springer-Verlag

Hamparian, D.M., Schuster, R., Dinitz, S., & Conrad, J.P. (1978) *The violent few.* Lexington, Massachusetts: Heath

Hirschi, T. & Gottfredson, M. (1983) Age and the explanation of crime. *American Journal of Sociology*, 89, 552 - 584

Hogh, E. & Wolf, P.(1981) Project Metropolitan: A longitudinal study of 12,270 boys from the metropolitan area of Copenhagen, Denmark (1953-77). In S.A. Mednick & A.E. Baert (Eds.) Prospective longitudinal research (pp. 99 - 103). Oxford: Oxford University Press

Hogh, E. & Wolf, P. (1983) Violent crime in a birth cohort: Copenhagen 1953-1977. In K.T. Van Dusen & S.A. Mednick (Eds.) Prospective studies of crime and delinquency (pp. 249 - 267). Boston: Kluwer-Nijhoff

Home Office Statistical Bulletin (1987) Criminal careers of those born in 1953: *Persistent offenders and desistance.* London: Home Office

Horney, J. & Marshall, I.H. (1991) Measuring lambda through self-reports. *Criminology*, 29, 471 - 495

Huizinga, D. & Elliott, D.S. (1986) Reassessing the reliability and validity of self-report measures. *Journal of Quantitative Criminology*, 2, 293 - 327

Janson, C-G. (1977) *The handling of juvenile delinquency cases.* Stockholm: University of Stockholm Department of Sociology

Janson, C-G. (1981) Project Metropolitan: A longitudinal study of a Stockholm cohort (Sweden). In S.A. Mednick & A.E. Baert (Eds.) Prospective longitudinal research (pp. 93 - 99). Oxford: Oxford University Press

Janson, C-G. (1982) *Delinquency among metropolitan boys.* Stockholm: University of Stockholm Department of Sociology

Janson, C-G. (1984) *Project Metropolitan: A presentation and progress report.* Stockholm: University of Stockholm Department of Sociology

Janson, C-G. (1989) Psychiatric diagnoses and recorded crimes. In Crime and delinquency in a metropolitan cohort (pp. 31 - 55). Stockholm: University of Stockholm Department of Sociology

88

Junger-Tas, J., Klein, M.W. & Zhang, X. (1992) Problems and dilemmas in comparative self-report delinquency research. In D.P. Farrington & S. Walklate (Eds.) Offenders and victims: Theory and policy (pp.83-103). London: British Society of Criminology and Institute for the Study and Treatment of Delinquency

Klein, M.W. (1989) Introduction. In M.W. Klein (Ed.) Cross-national research in self-reported crime and delinquency (pp.1-13). Dordrecht, Netherlands: Kluwer

Le Blanc, M. & Fréchette, M. (1989) *Male criminal activity from childhood through youth.* New York: Springer-Verlag

Loeber, R. & Le Blanc, M. (1990) Toward a developmental criminology. In M. Tonry & N. Morris (Eds.) Crime and justice, vol.12 (pp. 375-473). Chicago: University of Chicago Press

Loeber, R. & Snyder H.N. (1990) Rate of offending in juvenile careers: Findings of constancy and change in lambda. *Criminology,* 28, 97 - 109

Loeber, R., Stouthamer-Loeber, M., Van Kammen, W.B. & Farrington, D.P. (1991) Initiation, escalation and desistance in juvenile offending and their correlates. *Journal of Criminal Law and Criminology,* 82, 36 - 82

Magnusson, D. (1988) *Individual development from an interactional perspective.* Hillsdale, N.J.: Erlbaum

McClintock, F.H. & Wikstrom, P-O.H. (1990) Violent crime in Scotland and Sweden: Rate, structure and trends. *British Journal of Criminology,* 30, 207 - 228

McClintock, F.H. & Wikstrom, P-O.H. (1992) The comparative study of urban violence: Criminal violence in Edinburgh and Stockholm. *British Journal of Criminology,* 32, 505 - 520

McCord, J. (1991) Family relationships, juvenile delinquency, and adult criminality. *Criminology,* 29, 397 - 417

Pulkkinen, L. (1988) Delinquent development: Theoretical and empirical considerations. In M. Rutter (Ed.) Studies of psychosocial risk (pp.184-199). Cambridge: Cambridge University Press

Reichel, H. (1989) The intelligence-criminality relationship. In Crime and Delinquency in a metropolitan cohort (pp.7-29). Stockholm: University of Stockholm Department of Sociology

Shelley, L.I. (1981) Introduction. In L.I. Shelley (Ed.) Readings in comparative criminology (pp. xix - xxxiv). Carbondale, Illinois: Southern Illinois University Press

Smith, W.R. (1991) *Social structure, family structure, child rearing and delinquency.* Stockholm: University of Stockholm Department of Sociology

Stattin, H. & Magnusson, D. (1991) Stability and change in criminal behaviour up to age 30. *British Journal of Criminology,* 31, 327 - 346

Stattin, H., Magnusson, D. & Reichel, H. (1989) Criminal activity at different ages: A study based on a Swedish longitudinal research population. *British Journal of Criminology,* 29, 368 - 385

Tolan, P.H. (1987) Implications of age of onset for delinquency risk. *Journal of Abnormal Child Psychology,* 15, 47 - 65

Torstensson, M. (1987) *Drug abusers in a metropolitan cohort.* Stockholm: University of Stockholm Department of Sociology

Torstensson, M. (1990) Female delinquents in a birth cohort: Tests of some aspects of control theory. *Journal of Quantitative Criminology,* 6, 101 - 115

Van Dijk, J.J.M., Mayhew, P. & Killias, M. (1990) *Experiences of crime across the world.* Deventer, Netherlands: Kluwer

Visher, C.A. & Roth, J.A. (1986) Participation in criminal careers. In A. Blumstein, J. Cohen, J.A. Roth & C.A. Visher (Eds.) Criminal careers and "career criminals", vol.1 (pp.211 - 291). Washington, D.C.: National Academy Press

West, D.J. (1969). *Present conduct and future delinquency.* London: Heinemann

West, D.J. (1982). *Delinquency: Its roots, careers, and prospects.* London: Heinemann

West, D.J., & Farrington, D.P. (1973). *Who becomes delinquent?* London: Heinemann

West, D.J. & Farrington, D.P. (1977) *The delinquent way of life.* London: Heinemann

Wikstrom, P-O.H. (1985) *Everyday violence in contemporary Sweden.* Stockholm: National Council for Crime Prevention

Wikstrom, P-O.H. (1987) *Patterns of crime in a birth cohort.* Stockholm: University of Stockholm Department of Sociology

Wikstrom, P-O.H. (1990) Age and crime in a Stockholm cohort. *Journal of Quantitative Criminology,* 6, 61 - 84

Wikstrom, P-O.H. (1991a) Housing tenure, social class and offending: The individual-level relationship in childhood and youth. *Criminal Behaviour and Mental Health,* 1, 69 - 89

Wikstrom, P-O.H. (1991b) *Urban crime, criminals and victims.* New York: Springer-Verlag

Wolfgang, M.E., Figlio, R.M. & Sellin, T. (1972) *Delinquency in a birth cohort.* Chicago: University of Chicago Press

Wolfgang, M.E., Thornberry, T.P. & Figlio, R.M. (1987) *From boy to man, from delinquency to crime.* Chicago: University of Chicago Press

[13]

Br. J. Social Wk. (1992) **22**, 33–46

A Reconviction Predictor for Probationers

CHRISTOPHER HUMPHREY, PAULINE CARTER
and KEN PEASE

Chris Humphrey is a Lecturer in Accounting at Manchester University most of whose research and publications in recent years have concerned performance measurement in the public sector. In particular, he closely monitored and reported on the Financial Management Initiative and its implementation in the Greater Manchester Probation Service. He is currently involved in a study of audit expectations.

Ken Pease is Professor of Criminology at Manchester University. He also holds an appointment with the Correctional Service of Canada. He was formerly Principal Research Officer in the Home Office Research Unit and Head of the School of Sociology and Social Policy at Ulster Polytechnic.

Pauline Carter, a graduate of North Staffordshire Polytechnic, was formerly Assistant Warden of a voluntary organization after-care hostel. She was research assistant on a project funded by the Institute of Chartered Accountants in England and Wales to look at performance measurement in the probation service.

SUMMARY

This paper reports the development of a predictor of reconviction suitable for use with probationers. The predictor, based on the Burgess method of prediction, was developed using a sample of 750 probation cases and a prediction period of three years. Its predictive power is substantial, being of the same order as that of the parole predictor (see Nuttall *et al.*, 1977; Ward, 1988).

Despite the increasing emphasis on offence-focused work in the probation service, the work of the service is not routinely or comprehensively measured in terms of its alteration of criminal careers. By detailing the development of the predictor, and welcoming experimentation with it amongst individual area probation services, it is hoped that this paper will encourage a more focused consideration of the effect of probation supervision on offending behaviour, and therein facilitate the incorporation of broader service quality issues within performance evaluation.

Correspondence to Ken Pease, Professor of Criminology, University of Manchester, Faculty of Economic and Social Studies, Manchester M13 9PL.
The authors gratefully acknowledge the financial support of the Institute of Chartered Accountants in England and Wales (ICAEW) and The Nuffield Foundation, which facilitated the preparation of this paper.

34   C. HUMPHREY, P. CARTER AND K. PEASE

A RECONVICTION PREDICTOR FOR PROBATIONERS

At the simplest and most obvious level, effectiveness is related to an offender not committing further offences.

(Sainsbury, 1985, p. 36)

Simple and obvious are not adjectives frequently used to describe either the nature or the measurement of probation effectiveness. Ambiguous, complex, contradictory, even 'messy' (Thomas, 1985, p. 61) seem more appropriate. It was not always so. Ambiguity in evaluation came with the questioning of the most obvious criterion of penal efficacy, the rate of reconviction. The decade between 1975 and 1985 marked the heyday of a 'nothing works' perspective on correctionalism. What is less often remarked is that 'working' in the sense of this over-used phrase refers specifically to the prevention of reconviction or measures of change which can serve as proxies for that. When effectiveness in those terms was called into question, evaluation got messy. Confidence in the capacity to effect personal change in offenders which altered the course of their criminal careers was the professional sheet anchor of the probation service. Cut adrift from that, the service floats with the wind and tide of political pressure.

The 'nothing works' view of corrections (see Brody, 1976; Lipton *et al.*, 1974) has been subsequently called into question (for example by Gendreau and Ross, 1987). Even had a 'nothing works' perspective been fully justified by the evidence, its unintended consequence for the probation service is now seen to have been a collapse of confidence. The change occurred at a time when the *Zeitgeist* of the social sciences had moved strongly towards structural determinism, or rather when the generation of new and recent recruits to the probation service had been intellectually weaned on the sociological determinism of the late 1960s and early 1970s. It is scarcely surprising that those who had been taught to appreciate criminality as a kind of primitive revolutionary struggle would fall prey to a 'nothing works' perspective. Pease (1985) contended that the change occurred more amongst academics and was disproportionately influential in Home Office circles, while the experienced practitioner remained a closet correctionalist. For McWilliams (1987), the subsequent emergence of the managerial ideal, and the pursuit of custodial diversion policies, whilst appealing to pragmatic economists, were demotivating and burdensome for mainline service deliverers (McWilliams, 1987, p. 115).

A RECONVICTION PREDICTOR FOR PROBATIONERS 35

One of the influential policy documents spawned by the new pragmatism was the Statement of National Objectives and Priorities in Probation (Home Office, 1984). Seven years on from the National Statement, there remains a diversity of view about service morale. Whilst Davies (1990) reports high levels of professional pride and satisfaction amongst probation officers, May (1991) regards the probation service as being under siege, Tuck (1988) notes the loss of confidence in correctional policies, and Humphrey and Pease (1992) report a rather demoralized 'view from the troops'. The continuing psychological grip of the 'nothing works' syndrome (and the appropriateness of Jones's (1981) warnings against the cancerous, self-fulfilling nature of misplaced pessimism) is evidenced by the continuing stream of critical articles still seeking to exorcize penal pessimism from probation thinking (see Roberts, 1990; Thornton, 1987).

What can be said with confidence, however, is that, if the alteration of criminal careers is the objective of probation work, or even one objective of probation work in the 1990s, the work of the Service is not routinely or comprehensively measured in those terms. Humphrey and Pease (1992) showed, in a study of one metropolitan area service, how the notion of probation effectiveness had been captured by input, court-based measures. The number of reports written, the number of orders granted, the types of offenders on orders (classified by gender, age, employment and housing status, seriousness of offence etc.) were seen to dominate any consideration of the outcome and effect of supervision. Such findings are not unique to the area service studied. The Audit Commission (1989, p. 2), for instance, concluded:

While there is a striking variety of probation schemes in operation involving much vision, creativity and imagination, schemes must be evaluated and their impact on offending behaviour assessed. It is unsatisfactory that, at present, considerable sums are spent with relatively little understanding of the effects achieved.

The intention of this paper is to encourage more focused consideration within the probation service of the effect of supervision on offending behaviour. Most basically, by detailing our development of a predictor of reconviction suitable for use with probationers, the paper should serve to set aside the arguments of those cautioning against the development of service quality measures on the grounds of complexity or data inaccessibility. More fundamentally, it is hoped that experimentation with the predictor by individual probation services will encourage the establishment of notions of service quality within their performance evaluation and resource allocation processes. There is also clear evidence (as in the debate over electronic tagging) that the Home

36   C. HUMPHREY, P. CARTER AND K. PEASE

Office and others are already asking crude questions about rates of
reoffending of those on probation—a particularly insidious practice if
the probation service continues to be required to deal with offenders
more likely to reoffend. Without having any baseline in the form of
expected reconviction rates, the probation service will appear to be
ineffective. Therefore it seems essential for the Service to promote
measures closely related to its own professional criteria, rather than
leaving the Home Office or other monitoring agencies to take control
through the development (however understandable) of crude, pragmatic measures, more reflective of the professional criteria and dispositions of civil servants and/or cost-accountants (see Humphrey and
Pease, 1991). A brief reading of the latest proposals concerning possible
systems of cash limits for the probation service (Home Office, 1990)
should serve as salutary for those managers advocating a reactive role
for probation staff.

    It has been put to us that the introduction of a reconviction predictor
would 'de-skill' probation officers. We reject that view. In contrast to
input-based, risk of custody predictors, which have rapidly proliferated
in the Probation Service in recent years[1] (and have become in danger of
turning officers into 'second-guessers' of the minds of the magistracy),
the usage of a reconviction predictor can serve to highlight neglected
supervision skills of officers. Probation officers performing effectively
(in terms of reducing reconviction rates amongst their clients) do not
receive appropriate credit—primarily, as noted earlier, because performance measurement within the Service is principally input-based.
Even if the Service sought to measure officer performance by reference
to changes in criminal careers of probationers, there is no adequate
instrument presently available. The predictor of reconviction described
below would serve to facilitate the identification of officers whose clients
persistently showed lower than expected levels of reconviction. Since it
may well be that officers are effective with different client groups, and
since the characteristics of those officers impacting significantly on probationers' reconviction rates may inform training to improve the work
(and organizational supervision) of those who are not, we see the tool as
being for the short-term benefit of 'effective' officers, and for the long-
term benefit of all officers.

    The first section of the paper examines notions of prediction and
establishes the methodological roots of our predictor. The second
delineates the process by which the predictor was developed. The final
section of the paper assesses the explanatory power of the predictor and

---

[1] A development (see Audit Commission, 1989) which also suggests that the Service does
not have an unconditional antipathy to statistical prediction.

its components. The paper concludes with a consideration of potential applications and possible refinement of the predictor.

CRIMINOLOGICAL PREDICTION

Prediction in criminology is definitively reviewed by Farrington and Tarling (1987) and the interested reader is referred to their work. What follows is a brief introduction to the topic. Prediction instruments have been used for a variety of purposes in criminology, of which perhaps the two most important are providing a sensible baseline for the evaluation of programme effectiveness, and aiding equity of treatment for similar offenders.

The classic study of Mannheim and Wilkins (1955) illustrates a predictor used for the first purpose. This showed that different types of Borstal regime differed in the rates of recidivism of those who experienced them, *after* taking account of prior differences in the likelihood of reconviction. The control made possible by the availability of expected reconviction rates enabled the evaluation of penal treatments to take place on a more even playing field. It remains a paradox of criminology that random allocation between treatments is only ethically supportable when the treatments are very similar. Thus, it is deemed acceptable to allocate randomly to intensive and standard probation, but not to probation and prison. We thus have the situation that comparisons are generally only possible when their outcomes are uninteresting (Pease, 1983). Evaluation of penal treatments relative to a statistical baseline of expectation is the only feasible way of avoiding this difficulty.

The second purpose of criminological prediction is to ensure equity. A good example of this may be found in the work of Nuttall *et al*. (1977). They found that different prisons were recommending for parole differing proportions of prisoners. By applying a statistical predictor of reconviction, it was possible to establish that this was not a function of the dissimilar propensity to reoffend of prisoners in the various establishments, but of the decision-making process. A parity mechanism was introduced into parole procedures which served to reduce the effect of this disparity and which remains in place at the time of writing.

The purpose intended for the probation predictor described below lies closer to the former—specifically, to provide a statistically valid baseline for assessments of the effectiveness of probation staff in reducing reconviction rates of probationers.

38   C. HUMPHREY, P. CARTER AND K. PEASE

THE CONSTRUCTION OF A RECONVICTION
PREDICTOR FOR PROBATIONERS

Criminological predictors can be developed in a variety of ways. The one chosen was the Burgess method. This has the advantage of simplicity. In the Burgess method, the overall split on the dependent variable (in this case reconviction) is used as a benchmark for the effect of the other variables (like age, employment status or previous convictions). These variables are assigned points according to the level of reconviction characteristic of a sub-group relative to that of the group as a whole.

All predictors lose some power when applied to groups other than that on which they were constructed. The more sophisticated the construction process, the greater the degree of 'over-fitting' of the predictor, yielding more 'shrinkage' of predictive power when applied to any other data set. The Burgess method, being simple, has consistently yielded lower levels of shrinkage of predictive power than more complex techniques such as those based on multiple regression techniques (see Farrington and Tarling, 1987). A highly successful instance of the Burgess approach is to be found in the predictor of reconviction developed for British parole research and evaluation (see Nuttall *et al.*, 1977). The predictive power of this instrument has declined only trivially over twenty years (see Ward, 1988). It is upon this instrument that the present predictor has been modelled, including the choice of many of the independent variables.

The intended approach was to develop the reconviction predictor using 1000 successive probation orders imposed in 1985 in one metropolitan area service. Information applying to each probationer as at the date of sentence was collected from area probation records and from Criminal Records Office information.[2] However, given the timescale of the project and limitations in the recording systems relied upon, it proved possible to obtain data on only 750 people. The primary problem lay with the service's recording system.

The final sample of 750 is below the number which would ideally be recommended for an enterprise like this, and is likely to lead to the developed predictor having less power than could otherwise have been achieved. However, the effect of this shortfall in cases is not likely to be of major importance, since the predictor relies primarily on the *relationships* between the independent variables and the dependent, reconviction variable. For the shortfall to subvert the predictor in any significant

[2] Thanks are due to Terri Humphries for her hard work and to CRO staff for their help.

A RECONVICTION PREDICTOR FOR PROBATIONERS   39

way, we would have to believe that the independent variables in the missing cases bore a different *relationship* to reconviction than those in the non-missing cases. To undermine the predictor, it is not sufficient that the missing cases were different from the others in their distribution on any of the variables. For instance, let us imagine that the missing cases contained more people with long criminal records, and more of the long-term unemployed. This is irrelevant to the predictor unless these variables bore a different relationship to reconviction in the missing cases. The predictor would only be undermined if, in the missing cases, long records were associated with low rates of reconviction (for the opposite was so in the cases we analysed). Given the predictor's current reflection of well-founded criminological relationships (for example, as instanced by Nuttall *et al.*, 1977; Ward, 1988) such reversals are in the highest degree improbable. In consequence, access to the missing cases can be expected to have produced only minor amendments to scorings on the various independent variables, and a slight increase on what will be seen below to be an already high level of predictive power.

The period of prediction chosen was three years. This was the longest period which the data made it possible to examine. Length was maximized because it gives a 'cleaner' estimate of change of lifestyle when applied for the purposes set out above. That is to say, it will identify those circumstances in which an offender has been changed over a significant period of his or her life, rather than those for whom a transient effect has been obtained. The three-year prediction period also minimizes the confusion which attends the interpretation of very swift reconviction, which may be for offences committed before probation began (or even before the offence for which the probation order was imposed). In fact the variables which predict reconviction at three years are substantially and unsurprisingly those which predict reconviction at one or two years, and the predictor developed would have been materially the same whatever risk period was selected.

In order to develop the predictor, it was first necessary to divide the cases randomly into two sub-samples of equal size, which would then be used for the construction and validation of the predictor respectively. These will subsequently be referred to as the construction and validation samples. The construction of the predictor rests on the analysis of the construction sample. Comparisons of the reconviction rate associated with each segmented independent variable (gender, age, employment status, etc.) are made with the overall rate of reconviction of the cases in the construction sample, and point scores assigned according to deviations from it. Thus, for the construction sample, the overall rate of reconviction was 61·8 per cent within three years of the date of

40 C. HUMPHREY, P. CARTER AND K. PEASE

sentence. In relation to gender, for example, it was found that 67·3 per cent of men were reconvicted, as compared with 45·6 per cent of women. For each five per cent away from the overall rate of reconviction, a point was assigned. As men were reconvicted five per cent (but less than 10 per cent) more than probationers generally, a points score of +1 was assigned to men. Women were reconvicted over 15 per cent (but less than 20 per cent) less than the overall figure, so a score of −3 was assigned. This procedure was repeated for each variable. Wherever a sub-group did not deviate by at least five per cent from the overall rate, no points were assigned. Then the points for each probationer were accumulated (so a probationer would get −3 for being a woman, +4 for having a first conviction at age 12, and so on).

When each case had a total points score, the next step was to see the relationship between total points score and the proportion of people with that points score who had been reconvicted within three years of the imposition of the probation order. Before doing this, the points scores were banded into the lowest 10 per cent of cases, next lowest and so on up to the highest. Thus banded, the correlation between the points score and the proportion reconvicted was +·92. This correlation is artificially high because the points scores were arrived at using the data in the construction sample. This is the reason for separating the data into construction and validation samples. The crucial test of the predictor was how well it predicted the outcome of interest (in this case reconviction) in the validation sample. For a predictive instrument to have meaningful application in practice, it must have predictive power on samples other than that on which it was constructed. Running the validation sample yields a correlation of +·83. This means that the predictor accounts for more than 70 per cent of the variation in probationer rates of reconviction. At first blush, this is a very good performance, with power of the same order as that of the parole predictor. It is a very much better predictor than we expected, given the sample size and the vicissitudes of life which make reconviction in part a matter of chance. One standard measure of predictive power is the mean cost rating (see Inciardi *et al.*, 1973). For the predictor in question, the mean cost rating is ·484. By historical standards, this is very substantial and is a potential benchmark by which competing predictors could be judged.

The points scores which go up to make the predictor are presented as Annex A, together with the percentage reconviction rate associated with each band of scores. Thus, for example, 18 per cent of those with a points score of −31 or below were reconvicted within three years. This conversion from points to percentages is based upon all of the 750 cases. It should of course be used with appropriate caution. Changing the points score boundaries would somewhat change the percentages given.

For example, placing the band boundary at −29 instead of −31 would increase the percentage of those in the lowest band who were reconvicted, and decrease the percentage of those reconvicted in the next lowest band. The basic relationship between points scores and reconviction seems well-founded, but it would be foolish to be literal about the percentages. An alternative mode of presentation is possible, whereby a line of best fit is presented, such that a points score could be read off to indicate a probability of reconviction, but this would not change the fundamental fact that the predictor is good but approximate.

It will be noted that the familiar aspects of criminal record (age at first conviction and number of previous convictions) make their expected contributions, as do current age and living arrangements. Many of the factors contribute much as they do in the parole predictor (see Nuttall *et al.*, 1977; Ward, 1988). The basic pattern is repeated with early criminality and chronic criminality presaging further criminality. Take and drive away and drug-related offences are also associated quite strongly with reconviction.

THE PREDICTOR AND THE FUTURE

By making the predictor available to area probation services, we hope that it will help to give due recognition to the supervision skills of probation staff and to allow such output-related issues a clearly identified role in (enhancing) officer training programmes, case allocations and staff evaluations. It is fair to anticipate that re-directing attention in this manner to an issue that has served (albeit often unjustly) to engender considerable demoralizing effects within the probation service, could well be perceived as threatening. We recognize such concerns but believe that it remains strongly in the Service's interests to give greater attention to those issues that reside at the heart of a criminal justice agency's *raison d'être*. We also believe that such fears are often overstated and are too frequently used as an excuse for inaction. Indeed, during our recent research in the probation service (see Humphrey and Pease, 1992) we have met with little opposition amongst probation officers to the concept of a predictor of reconviction, with the vast majority of probation officers regarding it as a refreshing change from the area management or Home Office initiated cost-based numbers games in which they saw themselves as increasingly being caught up.

It nevertheless is appropriate to warn against seeing predictors of reconviction as the oracle whose consultation would by itself solve some of the Service's problems. Being neither a denial of, nor a substitute for, professional skill and judgement. the predictor is but a complementary tool, capable of enhancing and promoting such attributes. In this respect, it is worth emphasizing a number of the predictor's technical limitations. First, because the predictor is constructed solely on those given probation, it is not suitable for comparing the relative effectiveness of different sentences. Second, the variables chosen for inclusion in a predictor, whilst well supported by existing criminological literature, remain capable of further refinement. Third, there is the additional problem of declining predictive power over time, although experience with the parole predictor shows the extent of the decline to have been slight.

Aside from such technical considerations, however, for ourselves, and the above mentioned officers, the greatest danger with the predictor is that, as with any other performance measure, it can be mis-used and generate unintended, dysfunctional consequences (see Humphrey, 1991*a*; 1991*b*). This is particularly so in a service whose structure dictates the promotion of a small minority of maingrade probation officers, and where a predictor could become a management tool that is, or is seen to be, used to punish the inadequate but to do little, if anything, to reward the excellent or encourage practice development. In particular, given the predominant current emphasis on court based activities, we fear, and strongly wish to caution against, its use as a court-referenced tool, to control input of people on to probation orders, rather than to assess and improve the quality of probation work in changing the course of criminal careers.

In concluding, we believe it is appropriate to classify the present predictor as a crude, albeit robust, usable and much needed, start. It is entirely possible to refine the predictor so that it accommodates frequency and seriousness of offending, thereby allowing a reduction in these aspects of criminal career to be taken into account in assessing performance relative to expectation. We would also wish to encourage the development of the scale with data from other probation areas. We would be equally happy to see the progress of the Cambridgeshire Scale of Risk of Reconviction (see Merrington, 1990) in similar ways. Ultimately, it will be fascinating to see how such performance measures are developed and changed (subverted?) by other managerial considerations, such as concerns with court credibility, or how cost might drive attention elsewhere even when effectiveness measures exist for immediate use. The implementation of a predictor of reconviction will perhaps be the acid test of both the Service's willingness to address comprehensively the issues of offender change, and of the Home Office's willingness to create a facilitative environment wherein attention to wider output/quality of service issues is actively encouraged.

REFERENCES

Audit Commission (1989) *Promoting value for money in the probation service*, London, HMSO.

Brody, S. R. (1976) *The effectiveness of sentencing: A review of the literature*, Home Office Research Study 35, London, HMSO.

Davies, M. (1990) 'Work satisfaction in probation and social work', *British Journal of Social Work*, **20**, pp. 433–43.

Farrington, D. P. and Tarling, R. (1987) *Criminological prediction*, Albany, State University of New York Press.

Gendreau, P. and Ross, R. R. (1987) 'Revivication of rehabilitation: Evidence from the 1980s', *Justice Quarterly*, **4**, pp. 349–407.

Home Office (1984) 'Probation service in England and Wales: Statement of national objectives and priorities', London, Home Office.

Home Office (1990) 'Formulae for cash limiting probation specific grant', London, Home Office.

Humphrey, C. G. (1991*a*) 'Accountable management in the public sector', in Ashton, D., Hopper, T. and Scapens, R. W., *Issues in management accounting*, London, Prentice Hall, pp. 169–92.

Humphrey, C. G. (1991*b*) 'Calling on the experts: The financial management initiative (FMI), private sector management consultants and the probation service', *The Howard Journal of Criminal Justice*, **30**, pp. 1–18.

Humphrey, C. G. and Pease, K. (1991) 'After the rainbow', *Local Government Studies*, July/August, pp. 1–5.

Humphrey, C. G. and Pease, K. (1992) 'Effectiveness measurement in probation: A view from the troops', *The Howard Journal of Criminal Justice*, in press.

Inciardi, J. A., Babst, D. V. and Koval, M. (1973) 'Computing mean cost ratings (mcr)', *Journal of Research in Crime and Delinquency*, **10**, pp. 22–8.

Jones, H. (1981) 'A Case for Correction?', *British Journal of Social Work*, **11**, pp. 1–17.

Lipton, D., Martinson, R. and Wilks, D. (1974) *The effectiveness of correctional treatment*, New York, Praeger Publishers.

McWilliams, W. W. (1987) 'Probation, pragmatism and policy', *The Howard Journal of Criminal Justice*, **26**, pp. 97–121.

Mannheim, H. and Wilkins, L. T. (1955) *Prediction methods in relation to borstal training*, London, HMSO.

May, T. (1991) 'Under siege: The probation service in a changing environment', in Reiner, R., and Cross, M. (eds.) *Beyond law and order: Criminal justice policy and politics*, Milton Keynes, Open University Press, in press.

Merrington, S. (1990) *The Cambridgeshire Risk of Reconviction Scale: 1990 progress report*, Huntingdon, Cambridgeshire Probation Service.

Nuttall, C. P. *et al.* (1977) *Parole in England and Wales*, Home Office Research Study 38, London, HMSO.

Pease, K. (1983) 'Penal innovations', in Lishman, J. (ed.) *Evaluating social work effectiveness*, Aberdeen, University of Aberdeen Press.

Pease, K. (1985) 'A five-year plan for probation research', in Senior, P. (ed.) *Probation: Direction, innovation and change in the 1980s*, London, NAPO.

Roberts, C. (1990) 'Nothing works re-assessed: The effectiveness of forms of probation supervision on subsequent criminal careers'. Paper given to the Conference of the Association of Chief Officers of Probation (ACOP) Finance and Resources Group, Blackpool, 2 May.

Sainsbury, E. (1985) 'Measures of effectiveness in probation practice', in Sainsbury, E. (ed.) *Research and information in the probation service*, Sheffield, Midlands Regional Staff Development Office of the Probation Service.

Thomas, C. (1985) 'The present state of the probation service', in Sainsbury, E. (ed.)

44   C. HUMPHREY, P. CARTER AND K. PEASE

Research and information in the probation service, Sheffield, Midlands Regional Staff
    Development Office of the Probation Service.
Thornton, D. (1987) 'Treatment effects on recidivism' in McGurk, B., Thornton, D. and
    Williams, M. (eds.) *Applying psychology to imprisonment*, London, HMSO.
Tuck, M. (1988) Address to the Australian Bicentennial International Congress on Cor-
    rective Services, London, Home Office Research and Planning Unit.
Ward, D. (1988) *The validity of the reconviction prediction score* (Home Office Research
    Study, No. 94), London, HMSO.

ANNEX A

PREDICTOR POINTS

PREDICTIVE VARIABLE	*Points*
TYPE OF OFFENCE	
Burglary	+2
Theft, Receiving	−1
Fraud, Forgery, Deception	−1
Assault, Public Order, Threats	−1
Take and Drive Away	+5
Drink/Drug Offences (inc. Drunk Driving)	+5
Sexual Offences	−1
Other	−2
OTHER OFFENCES TAKEN INTO CONSIDERATION (TICS):	
There are TICs	+1
AGE AT OFFENCE:	
18 or less	+3
19–21	+1
26+	−2
EMPLOYMENT STATUS AT DATE OF OFFENCE:	
Employed (inc Student and Unfit for Work)	−3
IF UNEMPLOYED, LENGTH OF TIME UNEMPLOYED:	
Less than 10 Months	+2
TIME IN LAST JOB:	
6 Months or More	−2
LIVING ARRANGEMENTS AT OFFENCE:	
With friends/siblings	+2
With partner	−3
With parents	+1

A RECONVICTION PREDICTOR FOR PROBATIONERS   45

PREDICTIVE VARIABLE	*Points*
MARITAL STATUS AT OFFENCE:	
Married/cohabiting	−4
Widowed/separated/divorced	−2
Single	+1
NO. OF PREVIOUS PROBATION/SUPERVISION ORDERS:	
1	+1
2+	+2
NO. OF PREVIOUS PROBATION/SUPERVISION ORDERS BREACHED:	
1	+1
2+	+3
AGE (IN YEARS) AT FIRST PROBATION ORDER:	
Up to 21	+3
22–25	−1
26–30	−2
31+	−6
NUMBER OF PREVIOUS CUSTODIAL SENTENCES:	
0	−1
2+	+3
AGE AT FIRST ACTIVE CUSTODIAL SENTENCE:	
Up to 19	+4
26+	−6
LONGEST ACTIVE CUSTODY (IN MONTHS):	
4–6	+5
7–12	+1
13+	+2
NUMBER OF PREVIOUS DISPOSALS OF ANY KIND:	
0	−2
1	−3
2	−2
3	+1
4–5	+2
6+	+1
AGE AT FIRST DISPOSAL:	
Up to 14	+4
15–16	+1
19–25	−3
26+	−6
NUMBER OF SUSPENDED SENTENCES:	
2+	+2

46   C. HUMPHREY, P. CARTER AND K. PEASE

PREDICTIVE VARIABLE	*Points*
NUMBER OF COMMUNITY SERVICE ORDERS (CSOs):	
0	−1
1+	+4
DID OFFENDER RECEIVE SUPERVISION ORDER AS A JUVENILE?:	
Yes	+5
No	−1
GENDER:	
Male	+1
Female	−3
LENGTH OF CURRENT PROBATION ORDER	
Under 12 Months	−1

SCORE CONVERSION

ACCUMULATED PREDICTOR SCORE	PERCENTAGE RECONVICTED IN 3 YEARS (%)
−31 or below	18
−30 to −25	32
−24 to −21	38
−20 to −17	42
−16 to −7	57
−6 to −1	64
0 to +8	66
+9 to +15	69

[14]

LESLIE T. WILKINS

DELINQUENT GENERATIONS

Statement of the Problem

1. It has long been the opinion of many social workers and sociologists that evacuation and other disturbances of the lives of young children during the 1939–45 war would have a lasting effect upon the behaviour of these children. So far as is known this has not been confirmed statistically.

2. Some theories of child development lead to an expectation of a greater frequency of behaviour defects in the later lives of children born during years of stress involving abnormal family circumstances. For example, the conditions which Bowlby[1] described as "maternal deprivation" applied to some of those born during the war while the circumstances classified by Andry[2] as "paternal deprivation" applied to many more. Although Andry and Bowlby differ in the parent selected and in the age of the child at the period they believe to be critical, both these writers and many others would agree that those who were young children in war time would be more likely to behave abnormally in later life. In war time the family circumstances of a large proportion of the population are abnormal and this proportion may be large enough for the effects of such conditions to be noticeable in certain national statistics at a later date.

3. Delinquency is a manifestation of behaviour abnormality which (so far as it is detected) is well documented, and the criminal statistics are now available for a period long enough to justify an attempt to discover whether the war time conditions did in fact have a disturbing effect upon those who were then young children. Unfortunately it is not a simple matter to identify the presence or absence of any such effect. The birth rate directly affects the numbers of persons who in any subsequent year are exposed to the risk of committing offences, and thus a greater number of offenders found guilty in any age group in any year may mean only that there were more persons in that age group.

4. The research reported in this paper began as an examination of factors which might assist in making forecasts of the future demand for different penal treatment facilities. The main factor considered was the "bulge" in the birth rate. The "bulge" is often regarded as beginning in 1946 or 1947, but in fact 1947 was the peak year and births were high for some years before and after this.

5. It was clear that the provision of accommodation for offenders should be estimated in terms of the "bulge". But this was not all. Part of the "bulge" occurred before the end of the war and it had been suggested that children born during the war might be more crime-prone than others. Any such effect of the conditions in the year of birth would be superimposed on the effect of the "bulge" in the birth rate, so that estimates of crime based only on the birth rate would be too low.

6. *The main object of this paper is to examine and test the theory that children born in certain years (for example, during war-time) are more likely to commit offences than others, and that this tendency remains from childhood to early adult life.*

1

A*

Data Available

7. Criminal statistics were, at the time of carrying out this study, available in a form suitable for the analysis proposed, from 1946 to 1957. The lowest age of criminal responsibility is age eight. Thus those born in 1938 were first exposed to the risk of being found guilty of offences at some time during 1946. Similarly those born in 1939 became first exposed to this risk during 1947. It was possible to examine statistics of the numbers of persons found guilty of indictable offences for the years 1946 to 1957 for each of the birth years 1925/6 to 1948/9. This period covers the war years and a short time beyond the peak of the "bulge". It is convenient to display these figures in a rectangular table with the ages of the offenders at the top and the years in which they were found guilty down the side. Table 1* reproduces these data from Criminal Statistics.

Method of Analysis

8. It is, of course, not possible by simple direct comparison of crime rates to say whether some birth years are delinquency prone. Several factors obscure the effect, if any, of year of birth. In dealing with problems of this kind it is conventional to postulate that the effect does *not* exist, and to set up a system of analysis such that, in that case, the figures derived will not differ very much from zero. If the resulting figures differ widely from zero, the proposition (that there is no effect) is not sustained. Before this type of analysis can be carried out there are a number of considerations that must be examined. These will first be taken singly and later their joint effect will be dealt with. Some specific birth groups also will be examined, and a general solution will follow.

Considerations

(a) Numbers at risk

9. The numbers of offenders are, of course, in some measure a reflection of the numbers of persons exposed to risk. This factor may be eliminated by relating the numbers found guilty to the population involved. For this purpose the mid-year population estimates published by the Registrar-General for ages eight to twenty-one years seem to be the best basis for the calculation of rates. Rates are expressed for 100,000 of the population of each age. The mid-year population figures are reproduced as Table 2* and the rates per 100,000 (Table 1 figures divided by Table 2 figures times 100,000) are shown in Table 3*; in the remainder of this paper these rates are referred to as "crime rates".

(b) Numbers and rates

10. Before the general effect of the relationship between numbers and rates is dealt with it is interesting to examine the crime rate for eight year old offenders over the years 1946–1957 (first columns of Tables 1 and 3). It will be seen that it has fallen quite sharply in recent years. This fall in crime rates has taken place

---

* *See* Appendix I.

at the same time as the rise in the population in this age group. The two sets of figures are given below:

Year	8 year old offenders crime rate (male)	Population of 8 year old males
1946	426	295
1947	435	295
1948	517 (largest)	288
1949	487	272 (smallest)
1950	488	294
1951	479	322
1952	377	339
1953	368	336
1954	291	341
1955	228 (smallest)	439 (largest)
1956	246	392
1957	290	365

The tendency for crime rates in this age group (eight year old males) to fall as the population at risk increased is interesting ($r = -0.94$), and further study is being made of this phenomenon. For the purpose of the present analysis, however, this interaction, whatever its explanation, is only a disturbing factor that must be removed before other factors, which it masks, may be clearly seen. It is, in any event, only a post-war feature related to the "bulge" in the birth rate; there is a tendency for the correlation to drop as the birth year moves away from the "bulge" and it shows a tendency to be in the reverse (i.e., positive) direction for those born before 1939.*

11. This phenomenon may be the result of one of several factors or of a combination of factors. As an example, one factor might be that people who were having large families after the war, differed in some manner associated with delinquency, such as social or economic status, from those who were having large families before the war. There may be some other possible and equally acceptable explanation or several independent factors may be concerned.

12. The fact that for some birth years the crime rate is negatively correlated with the numbers at risk, whereas in other birth years the correlation is positive, raises a technical point to which it will be necessary to refer later when a general solution is attempted.

Specific Birth Groups

13. Before going into a general solution it is possible to illustrate the nature of the apparent birth group effects by considering two specific birth years. It is interesting to note that in 1948 eight year old boys showed the worst crime rate for that age in any of the years studied (rate 517—*see* Table 3) and in 1957 seventeen year old boys showed the highest crime rate for that age (1,780—*see* Table 3)—and *that these boys represent the same birth years.* If the influences affecting the crime rate for eight year old boys were serious influences acting on the personality of the young then the effect should be observable also at later

---

* The change in the pattern of the correlations, as here suggested, is a smooth trend. At present, only an analysis based on approximations is available, and more work needs to be done before this further research is published. No matter what results may emerge from further study, the work reported in this paper will not be affected.

ages. In fact this birth group shows a fairly consistent tendency to be associated with high crime rates at all ages. For eight year old males the average rate over the twelve years was 386 but this birth group recorded 517. At age nine, the average rate was 773, but the rate for this birth group was 949. These results are shown in the following analysis for all ages up to seventeen years.

Age	Crime rate at the age stated for males 8 years old in 1948	Average rate for all birth groups at the stated age	Percentage above or below average
8 . . .	517	386	34
9 . . .	949	773	23
10 . . .	1,399	1,113	26
11 . . .	1,734	1,411	23
12 . . .	1,908	1,688	13
13 . . .	1,926	1,976	− 3
14 . . .	1,975	2,143	− 8
15 . . .	1,451	1,628	− 12
16 . . .	1,509	1,521	− 1
17 . . .	1,780	1,396	27

14. In only two years did this birth group show a crime rate much below the twelve year average for the age through which they were passing.

15. A similar result is obtained for the boys born a year earlier, namely, those who were nine years old in 1948. An analysis similar to the one above traces this birth group:

Age	Crime rate at the age stated for males 9 years old in 1948	Average rate for all birth groups at the stated age	Percentage above or below average
8 . . .	435	386	13
9 . . .	990	773	28
10 . . .	1,284	1,113	15
11 . . .	1,667	1,411	18
12 . . .	2,102	1,688	24
13 . . .	2,270	1,976	15
14 . . .	2,115	2,143	− 1
15 . . .	1,404	1,628	− 16
16 . . .	1,324	1,521	− 15
17 . . .	1,434	1,396	3
18 . . .	1,617	1,117	45

16. Both these birth groups were better than average during their 15th and 16th year, but reverted to their more usual pattern at seventeen or eighteen years of age. This is a very odd fact for which there is no obvious explanation. We may, however, look at this result in a different way. The 15th and 16th years during which these birth groups were less involved in crime than the average for the twelve years, were years when the total crime rate for *all* age groups from 8–20 was below the average. It is possible that *in relation to the lower total level of crime in these years, these birth groups were still worse than average.*

4

Standardisation by Crime Patterns

17. If an allowance is made for the general crime rate for the years when crime rates in all age groups were less than average for the twelve years, the two birth groups discussed above do show crime rates above average throughout—from their 8th to 17th/18th year of age. This observation in these specific cases seems likely to be a general effect, thus it will be necessary to make a general adjustment for purposes of a general solution. Accordingly all analyses for age groups will be related to figures which make an allowance for the different volume of crime cleared up in different years by using the total of persons found guilty in the age range 8–20 years inclusive. This seems logical because it may be argued that variations in the total amount of crime detected and related to offenders of different ages may be due to factors outside the range of the problem to which this analysis is directed. For instance, the different level of juvenile crime in different years may, in part, be due to different proportions of crime recorded and cleared up, and this in turn be due in part to variations in police activity. In the current analysis these fluctuations, whatever their cause, may obscure the evidence of age differences and birth group differences.

General Solution (Males, England and Wales)

18. As was noted in the specific case of two birth groups, both age and the general crime pattern over different years affect the analysis; earlier the effect of different numbers of persons in different ages exposed to risk was allowed for by using crime rates. A general solution requires that these three factors are taken care of simultaneously. There is one further consideration: the crime rate is not independent of the population at risk (*see* paragraph 8). This fact makes it necessary to standardise by the use of rates instead of the numbers of persons. A slightly different result not affecting the general conclusions is obtained by this method from that which would have been obtained by the use of the more usual techniques of calculating averages ("expectations").* The method of standardisation used is described in Appendix II.

19. The general solution for males in England and Wales is given in Table 4 (Appendix I). In this table the crime rate expected after allowing for the disturbing influence of the factors discussed above (namely, age, population, crime pattern, age × population interaction) is made equal to zero, and accordingly it is possible to show crime rates in excess of the expected rate as positive and crime rates below the expected rate as negative figures. To further simplify presentation the difference has been expressed as a percentage based on the expected rate.

20. In accordance with the method outlined in paragraph 8, if all birth groups were similarly prone to crime, the plus and minus figures in Table 4 would be unsystematically arranged (i.e., at random). Some variation would be expected due to chance factors, but chance is not systematic in its effects. An inspection of Table 4 reveals marked patterns of plus and minus signs, clearly non-random. All the rates in the whole bottom left hand corner of the table are below "expectation". We accordingly conclude that some birth groups are less crime prone than others.

21. It will be realised that the diagonal cells of Table 4 represent a particular birth group. For example, the first cell in the first row (8 years of age in 1946),

---

* For this reason the overall sum of the O–E tables is not zero.

and the second cell in the second row (9 years of age in 1947) refers to the same birth group. A person born on the first of January, 1939, would be eight years of age (last birthday) for one year up to 31st December, 1947, and a person born on the 31st December, 1939, would be eight years old during 1948. It is possible to re-write Table 4 to relate to birth years, but due to the fact that birth may occur at any time during a year and the age at finding of guilt during a year may relate to any time during the year, exact single years of birth cannot be given. To indicate this point in Table 5* the birth years are stated in pairs.

22. The block of plus signs noted in Table 4* is now seen to relate to persons born between 1935/6 and 1941/2. These are followed by a block of minus signs for those born after 1941/2. This is very unlikely to be due to random factors and this result alone suggests that an explanation is necessary.

General Solution (Females, England and Wales)

23. Before an interpretation is sought it is instructive to examine the pattern of female crime in the same age range for the same years. The total pattern of female crime differs considerably from that for males and the crime rate is very much less. Variations due to chance influences on small numbers are likely to have a much greater effect in the analysis of female crime rates. Detailed workings (which it has been considered unnecessary to reproduce in this report) lead to the results shown in Table 6* which shows percentage differences between the observed and expected rates. It will be noted that the picture is very similar to that for males. There are, however, some interesting exceptions to the general rule and these will be discussed later.

General Solution (Males, Scotland)

24. It is known that the pattern of juvenile offences in Scotland differs considerably from that in England and Wales. The criminal code also differs. If these analyses are revealing anything of fundamental significance the same features might be revealed by a similar analysis of the Scottish statistics.† Unfortunately the Scottish figures cannot readily be obtained for any year prior to 1949. The basic rates which it has been necessary to use for Scotland relate to crimes and offences and thus cover a wider range of delinquency than the category "indictable offences" used for our analysis for England and Wales. Table 7* shows the basic figures and Table 8* the analysis comparable with Table 5* for England and Wales.

25. It will be noted that the pattern of crime and offences by age groups shows that in Scotland youths of seventeen years of age are the most delinquent —three years older than in England and Wales. Why the age peak in Scotland should be later than in England is not known, and the reason cannot now be explored. The age pattern may be different only because the analysis includes different offences, but for our present purpose it is unnecessary to explore further. In view of this basic difference in age pattern it is perhaps surprising to find that after standardising the age, population and total crime in the same way as for England and Wales, the same basic patterns of birth-group delinquency again appear (*see* Table 8).

---

* *See* Appendix I.

† We gratefully acknowledge the co-operation of the Scottish Home Department for tabulating their figures and for permission to publish their results.

Comparison of General Solutions

26. We may now collect together the results of the birth group analysis for the three sets of data, males and females in England and Wales, and males in Scotland. For certain birth years only one or two figures are available on which to base the calculation of above or below average delinquency and it is convenient to use the method of moving averages to smooth out any chance variation. A conventional period is the seven year moving average. This period has the additional advantage that it is the same length as World War II. Averaging (over seven years) the figures from Tables 5*, 6* and 8* the following is derived:

Seven year moving average of differences between percentage observed and expected rates

Year of Birth	England and Wales		Scotland
	Males	Females	Males
	%	%	%
1925/6 to 1931/2 . . .	− 4·6	+ 2·9	Not available
1926/7 to 1932/3 . . .	− 3·8	− 0·8	Not available
1927/8 to 1933/4 . . .	− 4·6	− 3·6	Not available
1928/9 to 1934/5 . . .	− 5·3	− 5·0	− 8·7
1929/30 to 1935/6 . .	− 4·2	− 4·4	− 5·8
1930/1 to 1936/7 . . .	− 2·6	− 3·2	− 2·0
1931/2 to 1937/8 . . .	− 1·0	− 1·2	+ 1·9
1932/3 to 1938/9 . . .	+ 2·5	+ 1·7	+ 4·4
1933/4 to 1939/40 . .	+ 5·4	+ 4·4	+ 6·8
1934/5 to 1940/1 . . .	+ 7·9	+ 7·3	+ 7·8
1935/6 to 1941/2 . . .	+ 8·6 (Peak)	+ 8·7 (Peak)	+ 8·3 (Peak)
1936/7 to 1942/3 . . .	+ 7·5	+ 7·7	+ 6·7
1937/8 to 1943/4 · . .	+ 5·1	+ 5·0	+ 4·2
1938/9 to 1944/5 . . .	+ 2·8	+ 3·0	+ 1·5
1939/40 to 1945/6 . .	− 1·1	− 0·3	− 2·5
1940/1 to 1946/7 . . .	− 7·5	− 9·0	− 8·3
1941/2 to 1947/8 . . .	− 13·7	− 16·9	− 12·3
1942/3 to 1948/9 . . .	− 18·7	− 21·1	− 14·3

27. The similarity between the three sets of figures is remarkable. The peak agrees almost exactly in amount as well as in period. The one difference between males and females—for the first noted birth group—may be due to the fact that these figures are based on fewer items than those towards the centre of the table. Unreliability could be expected at the lower end of the table for the same reason.

The Effect of War Period

28. Perhaps the most noteworthy fact revealed by this tabulation is that the peak excess criminality characterises those born in the seven-year period 1935/6 to 1941/2. The war began in September, 1939, and by the middle of 1945 the main effect on this country was over. The main war effect would thus be expected for the years 1940–1945, and for the two-year overlapping periods with which we have to work in this study 1939/40 to 1945/6, but births during this period

---

* *See* Appendix I.

7

show a rate slightly below the twelve-year average. It requires an addition of four years to the years 1935/6–1941/2 to give exactly 1939/45–1945/6. This suggests a different form of analysis to study when the effect of the war was most evident in these data. We may collect figures together so that we have in each group the greatest number of children passing through a given year of age during the war and note the rates for crime that have since characterised these groups. For example, we collect together the greatest number passing through their first year of life during the war by summing births during the period 1939/40 to 1945/6, since by this means the whole war period is included for all cases. Similarly collecting other figures for other ages, the following analysis is derived:

Average percentage by which the observed crime rate differs from that expected when the number of children passing through the war at different ages is maximised

Maxima passing through	England and Wales		Scotland
	Males	Females	Males
First year of life (0–1 year). ⎤	− 1·1	− 0·3	− 2·5
Second year . . .	+ 2·8	+ 3·0	+ 1·5
Third year . . .	+ 5·1	+ 5·0	+ 4·2
Fourth year . . .	+ 7·5	+ 7·7	+ 6·7
Fifth year . . .	+ 8·6 (Peak)	+ 8·7 (Peak)	+ 8·3 (Peak)
Sixth year . . .	+ 7·9	+ 7·3	+ 7·8
Seventh year . . .	+ 5·4	+ 4·4	+ 6·8
Eighth year . . .	+ 2·5	+ 1·7	+ 4·4
Ninth year . . . ⎦	− 1·0	− 1·2	+ 1·9

(bracketed with label: during the 1939–45 war)

29. The greatest "crime-proneness" is thus found to be associated with that birth group who passed through their fifth year during the war. This is the year immediately preceding school attendance except for the small percentage who attend nursery schools prior to compulsory primary school attendance. Whether this means that disturbed social conditions have their major impact on children between the age of four and five is not proved, but this is a likely hypothesis. It is not clear how any hypothesis which relates the greatest impact of disturbed social conditions to a much earlier age could be consistent with these results.

Critical Ages

30. It is unsafe to make inferences regarding the exact age at which the incidence of the war had most effect because a 1939 birth may have taken place at any time during the year and a 1946 conviction at any time during 1946 and similarly for all birth and conviction years. It is clear, however, that the average crime-proneness rises from a negative figure when the number born during the war is a maximum (i.e., when we have collected together the greatest number of war-time births) to a peak when the maximum relates to those who were between four and five years old during the war. After five years of age the crime-proneness figures drop, reaching again a negative value for those passing through their eighth or ninth year during the war. A large number of theories may equally fit these observations.

8

31. It is of further support to this result to note that a previous crime-prone group was born in the years 1926/7, 1927/8. The data are, however, limited to a few years. None the less, the addition of four or five years brings this birth group to coincide with the worst part of the depression of the 1930's. The concomitance of these two results seems unlikely to be due to chance. There appears to be something particularly significant in social disturbances occurring in the fourth and fifth year of a child's life.

32. Perhaps the deprivation of mothers is important in very early life and paternal deprivation later, say between four and five years of age? But the depression did not deprive children of parents. Perhaps the simple explanation is that the behaviour of children is influenced by factors in the family and social situation only when they are old enough to recognise social situations as such for themselves and to seek (consciously) to manipulate them. Before the results of this analysis were known this age was assessed to be about four years for the normal child. Prior to $3\frac{1}{2}$ years of age children will play in the same room as their " friends" but not play *together*. Communication of a socially effective kind does occasionally develop before four years and occasionally after four, but these are normal individual differences.[3] War-time and economic depression effects could thus be related to the age at which social communication was beginning to be effective.

General Conclusion

33. Any theories regarding the lasting effects of war-time and other disturbances of the lives of young children must, it seems, accommodate the fact that children *born* during the 1939–45 war have not as yet shown any tendency towards excess criminality. None the less the general theory that some birth years are associated with excessive criminality is sustained by the current analysis. It has been shown that this tendency has applied to both sexes, has remained persistent in the groups concerned from eight to twenty years of age, and applied also in exactly the same way in Scotland, although the pattern of recorded offences was very different from that of England and Wales. Moreover, it seems that disturbances of social or family life had the most marked effect on subsequent criminality if they occurred when the children concerned were passing through their fifth year.

34. There may be many theories explaining the reasons for these observations, but no theory derived from macroscopic statistical data of this kind can be proved by the same statistics as give rise to the theory or cause it to be considered in this connection.

Exception to the General Case

35. It would be unsatisfactory to leave this report at this stage without comment on the exception to the general rule of birth group effects and the agreement between the pattern for males and females. The main exception relates to males who are now between seventeen and twenty-one years of age.

36. One of the most disturbing features of the pattern of post-war criminal statistics is the recent crime wave amongst young adult males between seventeen and twenty-one years of age. The crime wave among males has been associated with certain forms of dress and other social phenomena. It is true that this age group was born before the war (1935/6 to 1938/9) and passed through their

9

critical ages during the war, but this does not explain the recent trend in their crime pattern. As Tables 5 and 6 show (averages given in last row of table) they are expected to be more crime prone than other age groups and the girls behave according to this expectation. For males, however, the expected proneness, based on their earlier years, is greatly exceeded in 1956 and 1957 when they became young adults. In particular the birth group 1935/6 (nineteen years of age in 1955 and twenty years of age in 1956) were only a little worse than average when they were between eight and sixteen years of age, but in 1956 showed a crime rate 40 per cent above expectation. In 1957 the three birth groups 1936/7 to 1938/9 were particularly crime-prone (+ 30 per cent; + 22 per cent; + 31 per cent). This is far in excess of expectation. The beginning of the young male adult crime problem seems from Table 4 to have been in 1954 when the differences between expected rates and those observed changed from negative (1953) to positive (1954).

37. It seems that this pattern is an example of a wave of a different type from those seen earlier in this birth group, for other birth groups and for females. This seems to indicate that the recent crime wave phenomenon among young males cannot be dismissed as "only to be expected in view of their childhood experiences".* Some increase in criminality might have been expected, but not to the extent found to occur.

Limitations of Study

This study raises more problems than it solves, but this perhaps, is to be expected of most studies at this stage of development in criminology. Many theories could be put forward suggesting explanations of various kinds and many of these theories could be conflicting. It is hoped that some critical tests can be made of some of these at a later date.

References

(1) BOWLBY, J. Maternal Care and Mental Health. W.H.O. Geneva (1951).

(2) ANDRY, R. Delinquency and Parental Pathology. Methuen, London (1960).

(3) This follows from the theories of that school of sociology which stresses the importance of communication, e.g., BERNSTEIN, Basil " A Public Language ". B.J. Soc. *x* (4), pp. 311–325.

(4) LODGE, T. S. A Comparison of Criminal Statistics of England and Wales with those of Scotland. Brit. J. Delinquency (1950).

* It would, of course, be possible to postulate a latent period for the effects of childhood disturbance which are expected to show in behaviour disorder during late adolescence. If this theory could explain also the difference for boys and girls it would not be inconsistent with the present results, but there is no other evidence to support it.

10

APPENDIX I

TABLE 1

Numbers of male persons 8–20 years of age, found guilty of indictable offences in the years 1946–1956, England and Wales

Year	8	9	10	11	12	13	Age 14	15	16	17	18	19	20	Totals
1946	1,257	2,379	3,333	3,928	4,280	4,734	4,280	5,045	5,023	4,525	3,122	2,688	2,530	47,124
1947	1,283	2,393	3,156	3,668	4,315	4,755	4,067	4,366	4,593	4,144	2,832	2,675	2,466	44,683
1948	1,489	2,900	3,943	4,790	5,474	6,093	6,339	5,011	4,630	4,194	3,035	2,723	2,900	53,521
1949	1,325	2,733	3,762	4,586	5,157	5,601	6,005	5,197	3,926	3,381	2,786	2,232	2,414	48,105
1950	1,435	2,674	4,014	4,885	5,504	6,009	6,494	4,281	3,849	3,565	2,565	2,376	2,460	50,111
1951	1,543	2,828	3,822	5,046	6,200	7,122	7,747	5,144	4,383	4,074	2,988	2,519	2,836	56,252
1952	1,279	2,599	3,531	4,551	5,532	6,697	7,365	5,104	4,624	4,201	2,921	2,573	2,707	53,684
1953	1,238	2,354	3,250	3,864	4,482	5,586	6,219	4,334	3,996	3,650	2,571	2,132	2,324	46,000
1954	991	2,030	2,911	3,510	4,133	4,808	5,629	4,073	3,685	3,361	2,582	2,069	2,140	41,922
1955	1,000	1,962	3,000	3,732	4,452	5,001	5,542	4,135	3,840	3,593	2,881	2,433	2,362	43,933
1956	965	2,140	2,929	3,879	4,957	5,943	6,388	4,356	4,285	4,144	3,446	2,934	2,901	49,267
1957	1,059	2,292	3,636	4,338	5,474	6,898	7,827	5,404	4,918	5,090	4,673	3,772	3,427	58,808
Total	14,864	29,284	41,287	50,777	59,960	69,247	73,902	55,450	51,752	47,892	36,402	31,126	31,467	593,410
Mean	1,239	2,440	3,441	4,231	4,997	5,771	6,158	4,621	4,313	3,991	3,033	2,594	2,622	49,451

11

TABLE 2

Population estimates (mid-year) for the same age groups and years as Table 1, England and Wales

(All figures × 1,000)

Year	8	9	10	11	12	13	14	15	16	17	18	19	20	Totals
1946	295	287	282	279	274	277	288	294	294	295	275	246	307	3,693
1947	295	296	288	283	280	275	278	288	294	293	275	244	300	3,689
1948	288	293	294	287	282	279	273	277	290	297	274	240	295	3,669
1949	272	288	293	294	286	282	278	272	277	291	278	239	298	3,648
1950	294	271	287	293	294	286	282	278	272	276	272	248	299	3,652
1951	322	294	271	291	295	294	287	281	277	270	266	237	294	3,679
1952	339	321	294	271	290	295	294	287	282	277	248	237	289	3,724
1953	336	339	321	294	271	290	294	294	287	282	249	231	277	3,765
1954	341	339	341	322	293	268	285	290	290	285	263	218	275	3,810
1955	439	341	338	340	322	292	268	285	290	290	276	234	281	3,996
1956	392	439	341	338	340	322	292	267	284	209	283	243	230	4,060
1957	365	391	438	340	338	340	321	293	268	286	289	260	256	4,185
Total	3,978	3,899	3,788	3,632	3,565	3,500	3,440	3,406	3,405	3,431	3,248	2,877	3,401	45,570
Mean	331	325	316	303	297	292	287	284	284	286	271	240	283	3,797

Footnote.—In the years immediately following the war the Registrar-General did not show the population serving in H.M. Forces overseas separately from the total population. An adjustment has been made in the above figures (but not on the Criminal Statistics for these years) based on the proportion overseas for the nearest years, for which the separate figures were available.

12

TABLE 3

Rates (per 100,000 of the related population) for males aged 8–20 years of age found guilty of indictable offences in the years 1946–57, England and Wales

Year	\multicolumn{13}{c}{Age}	Average Rate	Rate directly calculated
	8	9	10	11	12	13	14	15	16	17	18	19	20		
1946	426	829	1,182	1,408	1,562	1,709	1,486	1,716	1,708	1,534	1,135	1,093	824	1,278	1,276
1947	435	808	1,096	1,296	1,541	1,729	1,463	1,516	1,562	1,404	1,030	1,096	822	1,215	1,211
1948	517	990	1,341	1,669	1,941	2,184	2,322	1,809	1,597	1,412	1,108	1,135	983	1,462	1,459
1949	487	949	1,284	1,560	1,803	1,986	2,160	1,543	1,417	1,162	1,002	934	810	1,315	1,319
1950	488	987	1,399	1,667	1,872	2,101	2,303	1,540	1,415	1,292	933	958	823	1,368	1,371
1951	479	962	1,410	1,734	2,102	2,422	2,699	1,831	1,582	1,509	1,123	1,063	965	1,529	1,529
1952	377	810	1,201	1,679	1,908	2,270	2,505	1,778	1,640	1,517	1,178	1,086	937	1,453	1,442
1953	368	694	1,012	1,314	1,654	1,926	2,115	1,474	1,392	1,294	1,033	923	839	1,234	1,222
1954	291	599	854	1,090	1,411	1,794	1,975	1,404	1,271	1,179	982	949	778	1,121	1,100
1955	228	575	888	1,098	1,383	1,713	2,068	1,451	1,324	1,239	1,043	1,040	841	1,145	1,099
1956	246	487	859	1,148	1,458	1,846	2,188	1,631	1,509	1,434	1,218	1,207	1,261	1,269	1,213
1957	290	586	840	1,275	1,620	2,029	2,438	1,844	1,835	1,780	1,617	1,451	1,339	-1,456	1,405
Average	386	773	1,113	1,411	1,688	1,976	2,143	1,628	1,521	1,396	1,117	1,078	935	1,320	

13

TABLE 4

Percentage by which the observed crime rate for males for each age and each year was greater or less than the expected rate for that age and year, England and Wales

Year	Males aged												
	8	9	10	11	12	13	14	15	16	17	18	19	20
1946	+ 13·9	+ 10·8	+ 9·7	+ 3·1	− 4·3	− 10·6	− 28·4	+ 8·9	+ 16·0	+ 13·5	+ 5·0	+ 4·8	− 9·0
1947	+ 22·5	+ 13·6	+ 7·0	− 0·2	− 0·8	− 4·9	− 25·8	+ 1·2	+ 11·6	+ 9·3	+ 0·2	+ 10·5	− 4·5
1948	+ 21·1	+ 15·7	+ 8·8	+ 6·8	+ 3·9	− 0·2	− 2·2	+ 0·3	− 5·2	− 8·7	− 10·4	− 4·9	− 5·1
1949	+ 26·8	+ 23·2	+ 15·8	+ 11·0	+ 7·3	+ 0·9	+ 1·2	− 4·9	− 6·5	− 16·5	− 9·9	− 13·0	− 13·0
1950	+ 22·0	+ 23·2	+ 21·3	+ 14·0	+ 7·1	+ 2·7	+ 3·7	− 8·7	− 10·2	− 10·7	− 19·4	− 14·2	− 15·1
1951	+ 7·2	+ 7·5	+ 9·4	+ 6·1	+ 7·5	+ 5·9	+ 8·7	− 2·9	− 10·2	− 6·7	− 13·1	− 14·8	− 10·9
1952	− 11·3	− 4·7	− 2·0	+ 8·1	+ 2·7	+ 4·4	+ 6·2	− 0·7	− 2·0	− 1·2	− 4·1	− 8·4	− 8·9
1953	+ 1·9	− 3·9	− 2·7	− 0·4	+ 4·9	+ 4·3	+ 5·6	− 3·1	− 2·0	− 0·8	− 1·0	− 8·3	− 4·0
1954	− 11·3	− 8·7	− 9·6	− 9·1	− 1·5	+ 6·9	+ 8·5	+ 1·5	− 1·6	− 0·6	+ 3·6	+ 3·7	− 2·0
1955	− 31·9	− 14·2	− 8·0	− 10·3	− 5·5	− 0·1	+ 11·2	+ 2·8	+ 0·4	+ 2·3	+ 7·6	+ 11·2	+ 3·7
1956	− 33·7	− 34·5	− 19·6	− 15·3	− 10·1	− 2·7	+ 6·3	+ 4·3	+ 3·3	+ 6·9	+ 13·5	+ 16·5	+ 40·4
1957	− 31·9	− 31·3	− 32·4	− 18·1	− 13·0	− 6·9	+ 3·1	+ 2·7	+ 9·4	+ 15·6	+ 31·3	+ 22·0	+ 29·9

14

TABLE 5

Percentage by which the observed crime rate for males for each year (1946–1957) was greater or less than the expected rate for the birth group years, England and Wales
(Table 4 re-arranged by birth groups)

Males born in the years

Year	1925/26	1926/27	1927/28	1928/29	1929/30	1930/31	1931/32	1932/33	1933/34	1934/35	1935/36	1936/37	1937/38	1938/39	1939/40	1940/41	1941/42	1942/43	1943/44	1944/45	1945/46	1946/47	1947/48	1948/49
1946	−9·0	+4·8	+5·0	+13·5	+16·0	+8·9	−28·4	−10·6	−4·3	+3·1	+9·7	+10·8	+13·9											
1947		−4·5	+10·5	+0·2	+9·3	+11·6	+1·2	−25·8	−4·9	−0·8	−0·2	+7·0	+13·6	+22·5										
1948			−5·1	−4·9	−10·4	−8·7	−5·2	+0·3	−2·2	−2·2	+3·9	+6·8	+8·8	+15·7	+21·1									
1949				−13·0	−13·0	−9·9	−16·5	−6·5	−4·9	+1·2	+0·9	+7·3	+11·0	+15·8	+23·2	+26·8								
1950					−15·1	−14·2	−19·4	−10·7	−10·2	−8·7	+3·7	+7·1	+14·0	+21·3	+23·2	+22·0								
1951						−10·9	−14·8	−13·1	−6·7	−10·2	−2·9	+8·7	+5·9	+7·5	+6·1	+9·4	+7·5	+7·2						
1952							−8·9	−8·4	−4·1	−1·2	−2·0	−0·7	+6·2	+4·4	+2·7	+8·1	−2·0	−4·7	−11·3					
1953								−4·0	−8·3	−1·0	−0·8	−2·0	−3·1	+5·6	+4·3	+4·9	+6·9	−1·5	−3·9	+1·9				
1954									+2·0	+3·7	+3·6	−0·6	−2·0	−0·8	−3·1	−1·6	−9·1	−9·6	−8·7	−11·3				
1955										+3·7	+11·2	+7·6	+2·3	+0·4	−1·6	+1·5	−0·1	−5·5	−10·3	−8·0	−14·2	−31·9		
1956											+40·4	+16·5	+13·5	+6·9	+3·3	+4·3	+6·3	−2·7	−10·1	−15·3	−19·6	−34·5	−33·7	
1957												+29·9	+22·0	+31·3	+15·6	+9·4	+2·7	+3·1	−6·9	−13·0	−18·1	−32·4	−31·3	−31·9
Average	−9·0	+0·2	+3·5	−1·1	−2·6	−3·9	−13·1	−9·9	−5·3	−1·0	+6·0	+7·8	+8·3	+11·4	+10·9	+11·6	+4·3	−2·1	−8·7	−8·6	−15·8	−32·9	−32·5	−31·9

Maximum group born 1935–1941/2

15

TABLE 6

Percentage by which the observed crime rate for females for each year (1946–1957) was greater or less than the expected rate for the birth group years, England and Wales

Year	Females born in the years																							
	1925/26	1926/27	1927/28	1928/29	1929/30	1930/31	1931/32	1932/33	1933/34	1934/35	1935/36	1936/37	1937/38	1938/39	1939/40	1940/41	1941/42	1942/43	1943/44	1944/45	1945/46	1946/47	1947/48	1948/49
1946	+16·9	+12·3	+13·2	+ 1·7	− 3·4	− 7·5	−13·5	−12·6	−12·2	+ 2·9	+ 1·3	+10·9	+36·8											
1947		+16·4	+ 9·6	+ 5·0	− 3·2	+ 2·1	− 2·1	−16·8	− 6·1	− 8·7	+ 6·3	+11·3	− 4·0	+ 5·0										
1948			+ 4·9	− 9·2	+ 1·9	− 8·6	− 9·1	− 4·6	+ 1·8	+ 0·0	+ 6·9	+ 9·9	+10·6	+13·8	+29·2									
1949				− 2·2	− 8·1	− 4·1	− 8·3	− 5·0	+ 0·6	− 2·2	− 1·7	+ 9·1	+ 6·5	+16·9	+29·2	+35·0								
1950					− 0·7	− 9·1	−10·7	− 8·1	− 1·1	+ 2·2	− 9·6	− 2·3	− 0·7	+ 5·4	+13·9	+22·0	+35·0							
1951						−12·1	− 8·5	−11·0	− 9·0	− 5·0	− 4·0	+ 0·5	+ 7·9	+16·4	+10·9	+28·2	+26·4	+ 9·1						
1952							−16·7	− 3·8	−13·0	− 1·4	− 4·3	− 1·0	+ 4·2	+11·5	+12·0	+10·4	+13·5	− 3·6	− 8·7					
1953								−11·2	− 2·9	− 3·8	+ 7·9	+ 4·7	− 1·1	− 4·1	+ 3·3	+ 7·9	+ 0·0	− 3·7	− 2·0	− 4·8				
1954									− 3·0	+ 4·4	+ 5·3	+ 3·9	+ 5·0	+ 1·1	+ 8·8	+ 4·1	− 6·3	−17·0	−23·7	+ 0·0	−36·8			
1955										+ 3·2	+10·0	+ 8·8	+ 6·5	+ 3·0	+ 0·6	+ 4·7	+ 3·1	−15·0	−16·0	−18·1	−15·9	−38·9		
1956											− 4·0	+ 4·8	+ 4·4	+ 8·4	+ 4·8	+13·9	+ 0·0	− 5·0	− 8·3	− 3·0	−11·3	−40·9	−33·3	
1957												+12·4	+ 5·5	+ 7·4	+15·2	+10·8	+ 4·4	− 7·0	− 3·4	− 8·9	−22·7	−46·8	−46·9	−20·0
Average	+16·9	+14·4	+ 9·2	− 1·2	− 2·7	− 6·6	− 9·8	− 9·1	− 5·0	− 0·8	+ 3·0	+ 6·1	+ 6·9	+ 7·7	+12·8	+15·2	+ 9·5	− 6·6	−10·4	− 7·0	−21·7	−42·2	−40·1	−20·0

Maximum group born 1935/6–1941/2

16

TABLE 7

Rates (per 100,000 of the related population) for males aged 8–20 years of age found guilty of crimes or offences in the years 1949–1957, Scotland

Year	8	9	10	11	12	13	14	15	16	17	18	19	20	Total
1949	1,118	2,256	3,105	3,581	4,602	5,589	6,235	6,403	7,427	8,710	7,225	5,742	6,543	68,535
1950	1,253	2,175	3,438	3,849	4,800	5,537	6,425	6,547	7,668	9,018	7,564	6,087	6,737	71,098
1951	1,068	2,372	3,098	3,918	4,924	5,530	6,501	6,829	7,661	9,019	7,334	7,044	6,649	71,947
1952	1,026	1,990	2,939	3,614	4,763	5,359	6,523	6,509	7,748	8,818	7,484	7,029	7,000	70,802
1953	1,035	1,879	2,650	3,309	4,143	5,435	6,260	6,791	7,958	8,468	7,409	7,213	7,802	71,432
1954	852	1,869	2,507	3,135	3,785	4,935	6,328	6,637	7,698	9,396	8,756	7,670	8,134	71,702
1955	755	1,702	2,607	2,885	3,657	4,845	6,187	6,726	7,925	9,599	9,512	8,439	8,685	73,524
1956	826	1,385	2,283	2,916	3,652	4,871	6,000	6,448	8,268	10,016	11,046	9,564	9,765	77,040
1957	1,020	1,695	2,170	2,919	3,726	5,017	6,125	6,529	8,472	11,551	12,806	11,493	11,200	84,723
Average	995	1,925	2,755	3,347	4,228	5,235	6,287	6,602	7,869	9,511	8,793	7,809	8,066	73,423

17

TABLE 8

Percentage by which the observed crime rate for males for each year (1948–1957) was greater or less than the expected rate for birth group years, Scotland

Year	1928/29	1929/30	1930/31	1931/32	1932/33	1933/34	1934/35	1935/36	1936/37	1937/38	1938/39	1939/40	1940/41	1941/42	1942/43	1943/44	1944/45	1945/46	1946/47	1947/48	1948/49
1949	−13.1	−21.2	−12.0	−1.9	+1.1	+3.9	+6.2	+14.4	+16.6	+14.6	+20.7	+25.5	+20.3								
1950		−13.7	−19.5	−11.2	−2.1	+0.6	+2.4	+5.5	+9.2	+17.2	+18.8	+28.9	+16.7	+30.1							
1951			−15.9	−7.9	−14.9	−3.2	−0.6	+5.6	+5.5	+7.8	+18.9	+19.5	+14.7	+25.8	+9.5						
1952				−10.0	−6.7	−11.7	−3.8	+2.1	+2.2	+7.6	+6.2	+16.8	+12.0	+10.6	+7.2	+7.0					
1953					+0.4	−5.1	−13.4	+2.3	+3.9	+5.7	+2.3	+6.7	+0.7	+1.6	−1.2	+0.3	+6.9				
1954						+3.3	+0.6	+2.0	+1.2	+0.2	+2.9	+3.1	−3.5	−8.3	−4.1	−6.8	−0.6	−12.3			
1955							+7.5	+7.9	+8.0	+0.8	+0.6	+1.7	−1.7	−7.6	−13.6	−13.9	−5.5	−11.7	−24.2		
1956								+15.4	+16.7	+16.7	+0.4	+0.1	−6.9	−9.0	−11.3	−17.7	−17.0	−21.0	−31.4	−20.0	
1957									+20.3	+27.5	+22.3	+5.3	−6.7	−14.3	−15.6	−17.0	−23.6	−24.4	−31.7	−23.7	−11.1
Average	−13.1	−17.5	−15.8	−7.8	−4.4	−2.0	−0.2	+6.9	+9.3	+11.2	+10.3	+12.0	+5.1	+3.2	+4.2	−8.0	−8.0	−17.4	−29.1	−22.3	−11.1

Maximum group born 1935/36–1941/42

18

APPENDIX II

METHOD USED FOR CALCULATING EXPECTED RATES

The expected rate for any age-group (j) in any year (i) was assumed to be given by:

$$E_{ij} = \frac{\sum\limits_{i=1}^{m} r_{ij} \ \sum\limits_{j=1}^{n} r_{ij}}{\sum\limits_{i=1}^{m} \ \sum\limits_{j=1}^{n} r_{ij}}$$

When i = year
m = no. of years
j = age-group
n = no. of age-groups
in Table 3

The formula is equivalent to:

$$E_{ij} = \frac{\text{Average rate for year i (all ages)}}{\text{Average rate for all years (all ages)}} \times \frac{\text{Average rate for age-groups}}{\text{(all years)}}$$

It is derived as follows:

Rate for age-group j in year i $= r_{ij}$

Average rate for all age-groups in year i $= \dfrac{\sum\limits_{j=1}^{n} r_{ij}}{n}$.   .   .   .   . (1)

Average rate for age-group j in all years $= \dfrac{\sum\limits_{i=1}^{m} r_{ij}}{m}$.   .   .   .   . (2)

Average rate for all age-groups in all years
(either the average of (1) for m years or $= \dfrac{\sum\limits_{i=1}^{m} \ \sum\limits_{j=1}^{n} r_{ij}}{mn}$.   .   .   . (3)
the average of (2) for n age-groups

$$E_{ij} = \frac{(1) \times (2)}{(3)} = \frac{\sum\limits_{i=1}^{m} r_{ij} \ \sum\limits_{j=1}^{n} r_{ij}}{\sum\limits_{i=1}^{m} \ \sum\limits_{j=1}^{n} r_{ij}}$$

Example:

Age 19 in 1955
Average rate for age 19 $= 1{,}078$
Average rate for 1955 $= 1{,}145$ $\left.\right\}$ from Table 3
Average rate for whole table $= 1{,}320$

$$E = \frac{1{,}078 \times 1{,}145}{1{,}320} = 935$$

O = Actual rate $= 1{,}040$

$$\text{Excess} = \frac{O - E}{E} \times 100 =$$

$$= \frac{1{,}040 - 935}{935} = 100 = +11 \cdot 2$$

as in Table 4

(in actually calculating the table, of course, intermediate averages were not used; the formula was used as it stands.)

The expected number of offenders could have been obtained by a similar calculation from Table 1, and the expected rate could have been derived by relating this to the actual population given in Table 2.

19

(85799) Wt. 2598/R/45 K.16 7/62

[15]

James Q. Wilson

Drugs and Crime

The essays in this volume share a common assumption—that the sale and possession of certain drugs, in particular heroin and cocaine, will continue to be illegal. The authors of these essays made that assumption because they were asked to. I do not know whether any of them favor the legalization of these drugs, but I do know that some people who read this book will favor it. It is important, therefore, to be clear as to the arguments for and against legalization. To do so, one must distinguish between the good and bad reasons for controlling the use of drugs.

Some people argue that we must "stamp out" drug abuse in order to reduce crime, break up criminal gangs, and improve public health. But there is no reason to believe that vigorously enforcing the drug laws will achieve any of these goals and many reasons to think that they may make these matters worse.

Consider crime: there is no doubt a strong association between the use of drugs and aggressive behavior, but, as Jeffrey Fagan points out in his essay, it is far from clear that this correlation amounts to a cause. People who become aggressive after drinking alcohol or using cocaine usually turn out to be people who were aggressive before consuming these substances. Personality factors and social setting seem to have a large, perhaps dominant, effect in determining whether getting high will lead to aggression, moody introspection, or quiet gaiety. Heroin seems to induce in its users euphoria, drowsiness, and sexual impo-

James Q. Wilson is a professor in the Graduate School of Management at the University of California, Los Angeles.

tence, but not aggression. There is a good deal of anecdotal evidence
suggesting that using phencyclidine (PCP) or amphetamines or smoking crack will cause violent behavior, but so far not much systematic
evidence supports this theory.

There is also a strong association between drug use and street crime,
and here the research shows that, for at least certain drugs, their use—
or more accurately, their purchase—does cause higher rates of income-
generating crime. During periods when heroin addicts are using the
drug heavily, the rate at which they commit crimes is much higher than
it is during periods when they are relatively abstinent. The reason is
that the illegality of heroin produces a black market in which price rises
to the point where many addicts can only support their habits by theft
or prostitution.

Though the search for drugs may cause criminals to increase the rate
of their criminality, it is not a desire for drugs that leads people to
criminality in the first place. Jan and Marcia Chaiken suggest in this
volume that many heavy drug users were committing crimes before
they turned to drugs; they began spending money on drugs in part
because crime had produced money for them to spend and in part
because criminality drew them into a social setting in which drug use
was common and expected.

For all these reasons, it is not clear that enforcing the laws against
drug use would reduce crime. On the contrary, crime may be caused
by such enforcement because it keeps drug prices higher than they
would otherwise be.

Or consider criminal gangs: tough law enforcement may break up
those criminal enterprises that traffic in drugs, but it may also make
such enterprises more skilled, more ruthless, and more dangerous. The
more profitable drug sales are, the greater the incentive dealers have to
protect their profits by arming themselves against rivals, forcibly maintaining discipline among subordinates, and corrupting or otherwise
resisting the criminal justice system. Critics of drug enforcement often
compare the effects of our drug laws to those prohibiting the sale of
alcohol: any effort to suppress the use of a popular substance will create
rich and powerful criminal syndicates.

Or consider public health: injecting drugs, such as heroin or cocaine,
can lead to hepatitis or AIDS if contaminated needles are used, and
such needles are more likely to be used if the drugs are consumed
surreptitiously. Over half the AIDS victims generally contracted the
disease through intravenous drug use. Drugs sold illegally are beyond
the reach of the pure food and drug laws; as a result, many addicts use

heroin that has been "cut," or adulterated, with harmful substances. When marijuana is grown illegally, it may be produced in fields sprayed by the police with dangerous herbicides or covered by the growers with harmful fertilizers. And even when a drug is free of poisons, its strength is often unknown, so that a user may unwittingly take a fatal overdose. Mislabeling a drug is not a crime to those who sell drugs illegally.

In short, attempting to suppress the use of drugs is costly—very costly. This fact has led many people to call for their legalization, either totally or under some form of government regulation. The readers of this volume may wonder why its authors have spent so much effort exploring the law-enforcement strategies when the "obvious" thing to do is to eliminate all the costs of law enforcement by repealing the laws that are being enforced. The result would be less crime, fewer and weaker gangs, and an opportunity to address the public health problems in a straightforward manner.

But there is another side to the story. Legalizing drugs would also entail costs. Those costs are much more difficult to measure, in part because they are to a large degree moral and in part because we have so little experience with legalized drugs that we cannot be certain how great those costs would be.

The moral reason for attempting to discourage drug use is that the heavy consumption of certain drugs is destructive of human character. These drugs—principally heroin, cocaine, and crack—are, for many people, powerfully reinforcing. The pleasure or oblivion they produce leads many users to devote their lives to seeking pleasure or oblivion and to do so almost regardless of the cost in ordinary human virtues, such as temperance, fidelity, duty, and sympathy. The dignity, autonomy, and productivity of many users, already impaired by other problems, is destroyed.

There are, to be sure, many people who only experiment with drugs or who use them regularly but in a "controlled" way. Citizens—including the contributors to this volume—differ in how seriously they view such use. Some will argue that if users can maintain their moral character while consuming drugs, no social problem exists. Moreover, a national survey suggests that drug use by casual or controlled users has been declining in recent years. The proportion of Americans saying that they currently use any drug has dropped significantly since 1985 (Office of National Drug Control Policy 1989, p. 1). The essays here, however, are primarily concerned with the heavy user of the most dangerous drugs—heroin and cocaine. And for that group, the news is

524   James Q. Wilson

bad. The same survey shows that the proportion of cocaine users who
consume it frequently (i.e., weekly or more often) has doubled since
1985 (Office of National Drug Control Policy 1989, p. 3). In this group,
the moral costs of drug abuse are undeniable.

But there are some people who deny that society has any obligation
to form and sustain the character of its citizenry. Libertarians would
leave all adults free to choose their own habits and seek their own
destiny so long as their behavior did not cause any direct or palpable
harm to others. But most people, however willing they may be to
tolerate human eccentricities and support civil liberties, act as if they
believed that government, as the agent for society, is responsible for
helping instill certain qualities in its citizens. This is one reason (indeed, it was the original reason) for mandatory schooling. We not only
want to train children to be useful, we want to train them to be decent.
It is the reason that virtually every nation that has been confronted by a
sharp increase in addiction to any psychoactive substance, including
alcohol, has enacted laws designed to regulate or suppress its use. (The
debauch produced by the sudden arrival of gin in eighteenth-century
England led to debates not very different from the ones we are having
today about cocaine.) Great Britain once allowed physicians to prescribe opiates for addicts. The system worked reasonably well so long
as the addicts were middle-class people who had come by their dependence as a consequence of having received painkillers in hospitals. But
as soon as oblivion-seeking youth became heroin addicts, Britain ended
the prescription system, replacing it at first with a system of controlled
dispensation from government clinics and then with a system of substituting methadone for heroin coupled with the stringent enforcement
of the laws against the latter.

Even if we were to decide that the government had no responsibility
for character formation and should only regulate behavior that hurt
other people, we would still have to decide what to do about drug-
dependent people because such dependency does in fact hurt other
people: a heroin addict dreamily enjoying his euphoria, a crack smoker
looking for that next high, a cocaine snorter eager for relief from his
depression—these users are not likely to be healthy people, productive
workers, good parents, reliable neighbors, attentive students, or safe
drivers. Moreover, some people are directly harmed by drugs that they
have not freely chosen to use. The babies of drug-dependent women
suffer because of their mothers' habits. We all pay for drug abuse in
lowered productivity, more accidents, higher insurance premiums, bigger welfare costs, and less effective classrooms.

The question is whether the costs of drug use are likely to be higher when the drug is illegal or when it is legal. In both cases, society must pay the bill. When the drug is illegal, the bill consists of the law-enforcement costs (crime, corruption, extensive and intrusive policing), the welfare costs (poorer health, lost wages, higher unemployment benefits, more aid to families with dependent children, and various treatment and prevention programs), and the moral costs (debased and degraded people). When the drug is legal, the bill will consist primarily of the welfare costs and the moral costs.[1] Which bill will be higher?

The answer chiefly depends on how many people will use the drug under the two scenarios. We have a rough idea of how many people regularly use heroin and cocaine under the present illegal scenario. How many will regularly use it under the legal scenario?

No one knows for certain, but it will almost surely be many more people than now use it. The free-market price of cocaine is probably no more than 5 percent of its present black-market price. The consumption of a widely desired, pleasure-inducing substance will, without question, increase dramatically if the price is cut by 95 percent (Kaplan 1988; Moore, in this volume). But suppose that the government levies taxes on the legal cocaine, either to raise revenue, discourage use, or both. The higher the government sets the tax on, and thus the price of, the drug, the less will be consumed, but the greater the incentive the drug user will have to steal (in order to pay the high price) or to manufacture the drug illegally (in order to undercut the government price). Either way, high taxes get us right back where we started. There is no such thing as an optimal price of cocaine because there is no such thing as an optimal mix of two radically opposed goals—to reduce drug use and to prevent drug-related crime.

Moreover, the true price of the drug is the monetary price plus the difficulty and inconvenience of the search for it and the risk associated with consuming a product of unknown quality. Though drugs are sold openly on the streets of some communities, for most people— especially for novice, middle-class users—they are hard to find and are

---

[1] There will also be law-enforcement costs when the drugs are legal, if we assume—as do most proponents of legalization—that the drugs would not be sold to minors. As we know from our experience with alcohol, it is neither easy nor cheap to keep forbidden things out of youthful hands. Moreover, it is almost inevitable that such drugs would be taxed, partly to pay for the welfare costs associated with their use and partly because "sin taxes" are a politically popular way of raising general revenues. The higher the tax, the greater the incentive to evade it; hence, the government will have to invest in enforcing payment of the tax.

526   James Q. Wilson

often found only in unattractive and threatening surroundings. Legalizing the drugs, *even if the price is not cut*, will make the drug more attractive by reducing the costs of searching for the product, negotiating a transaction, and running the risk of ingesting a dangerous substance. The combined effect of lowered market prices and lowered transaction costs will be very great.

Just how great cannot be known without trying it. And one cannot try it experimentally, for there is no way of running a meaningful experiment. The increase in drug use that would occur if people in one neighborhood or patients at one clinic were allowed to buy the drug at its market cost can give us no reliable information on how many people would use it if the drug were generally available in all neighborhoods and at any clinic.

The experience of other countries confirms that ease of availability is associated with large increases in use. When Great Britain allowed private physicians to prescribe heroin and young people began to avail themselves of this source, the number of known addicts (many more were unknown to the authorities) increased *thirtyfold* during a fifteen-year period. It was because of this increase that the British government changed the law. After a brief period in the 1970s when the number of known heroin addicts stabilized, a new storm broke. Between 1980 and 1985, the number of newly notified heroin addicts increased *fivefold*. Geoffrey Pearson (1990) estimates that by the mid-1980s Great Britain had some 15,000 registered drug addicts and probably ten times as many unregistered ones; this in a country whose "system" some people once thought should be a model for the United States. The increased availability of heroin in Europe, a continent once generally free of addicts, has been followed by a sharp increase in the number of addicts.

Even if legalization increases the number of addicts, would it not dramatically decrease the number of crimes committed by addicts? Not necessarily. No doubt the average number of crimes *per addict* will fall (few people would have to steal in order to buy drugs at market prices), but the increase in the number of addicts would mean an increase in the number of people leading such deviant lifestyles that occasional crime might be their only (or their preferred) means of support. Thus the *total number* of crimes committed by drug users might not fall at all.

Because we cannot know what our level of drug use would be under a legalized regime (though we can be certain it would be much higher than today) and because people disagree about many of the costs— especially the moral costs—of drug use, the debate over legalization will never be resolved. However, being aware of these issues will help people focus the debate on the right question. That question is this: how can we minimize the sum of the law-enforcement, moral, and welfare costs of drug use? If we want drugs to be illegal, it is because we believe that the very high law-enforcement costs will be offset by lower moral and welfare costs. If we want drugs to be legal, it is because we believe that the higher moral and welfare costs will be offset by the lower law-enforcement costs. In making this choice, we are making an estimate of how large the drug-using population will be in each case, and we are assigning a value to the tangible but real moral costs.[2]

I. Designing a Strategy

Assuming that heroin and cocaine will be illegal because of the moral and welfare costs associated with their use, we want to design a rational control strategy that will minimize those costs for a given level of effort. In doing so, we want to know where the marginal dollar can most effectively be invested.

In answering that question, it is customary, and correct, to distinguish between the demand for drugs and the supply of those drugs. It is also customary, but wrong, to consider demand-reduction strategies as involving prevention, education, and treatment and to think of supply-reduction strategies as involving law enforcement and foreign policy. Demand reducers are the nice guys—teachers, doctors, scientists, publicists; supply reducers are the tough guys—detectives, customs inspectors, and crop eradicators. Much of the debate over the relative budget shares that should go to demand or supply reduction reflects an ideological predisposition to choose either the tender-minded or the tough-minded approach.

There is some truth in this distinction, but not much. Law-enforcement efforts can reduce demand as well as supply. Prevention and education programs can reduce supply as well as demand. The

[2] Having stated the issue in what I trust is an evenhanded way, let me be clear about my own views: I believe that the moral and welfare costs of heavy drug use are so large that society should bear the heavy burden of law enforcement, and its associated corruption and criminality, for the sake of keeping the number of people regularly using heroin and crack as small as possible. I also believe that children should not be raised in communities in which heroin and cocaine are sold at the neighborhood drugstore. Obviously, there is some point at which the law-enforcement costs might become too great for the gains they produce, but I do not think we are at that point yet. I set forth my arguments at length in Wilson (1990).

reasons are explained in the essays by Mark Moore, Dana Hunt, and Mark Kleiman and Kerry Smith.

Demand reduction occurs when for any reason drugs become less attractive. If an education or prevention program persuades young people not to seek out drugs, demand is reduced. If the police make it very hard for a first-time or novice user to find a willing seller of drugs, supply is reduced—but so also is demand. The reason is that first-time, novice, or occasional users will abandon the search for drugs if that search is difficult, dangerous, or costly. By the same token, if law enforcement results in the commitment of the user to a mandatory treatment program that the addict would not have voluntarily entered, law enforcement may contribute to demand reduction. Indeed, the chief reason we have laws against possessing (and in some states, using) drugs is to reduce demand. They work—up to a point.

Similarly, if a treatment program successfully eliminates the desire for drugs on the part of a junkie, demand will have been reduced. But if that junkie is also a drug dealer who no longer feels he must deal in order to feed his own habit, then the treatment program has also removed a source of supply. Of course, a reformed supplier may be quickly replaced with an unreformed one, in which case there has been no supply reduction at all. But sometimes the reformed dealer sold to a circle of occasional users who did not know any other "connection"; when their friend/dealer is gone, their drug supply drops.

Drug use, in its early stages, tends to be a social activity occurring among—and often with the encouragement of—friends and associates. Whatever interdicts that network, whether it be a program labeled "prevention," "treatment," or "law enforcement," constitutes demand reduction. Deeply dependent addicts, by contrast, often use drugs in a more individualistic and isolated manner; their demand is much harder to reduce, whether by treatment or law enforcement.

The ambiguity of the distinction between prevention and law enforcement is illustrated by the case of drug testing. There is good evidence that drug testing in the military reduced drug use by curbing demand. Such testing may—no one yet knows for certain—reduce drug demand in civilian occupations. Is drug testing an example of prevention or of law enforcement? If the tests are conducted by doctors in a treatment program, we call it prevention. If they are conducted by probation officers desirous of knowing whether probationers have observed the terms of their freedom, we call it law enforcement. But the tests are identical in the two cases. The consequences for the person tested may also be identical if he is in the treatment program as an alternative to incarceration.

The failure of policymakers to understand that demand reduction is not synonymous with treatment or law enforcement with supply reduction has led them to make funding decisions based on such false identities. The debate over the Omnibus Drug Abuse Act of 1988 was in large measure a debate over whether 50 percent or 60 percent of the federal antidrug budget should be earmarked for prevention, treatment, and education in the belief that these activities, and only these activities, will reduce demand.[3]

The essays in this book try to avoid this artificial distinction. Moore and Kleiman and Smith explain how demand may be reduced somewhat by street-level law enforcement aimed at breaking up vulnerable dealing systems. Eric Wish and Bernard Gropper suggest ways in which random testing for drug use, using either urine or hair samples, may reduce demand. Douglas Anglin and Yih-Ing Hser, in evaluating the effectiveness of drug treatment programs, point out that, the longer drug users spend in such programs, the higher their chances of success. But left to their own devices, users tend to drop out of most programs. Legal coercion can keep these users in programs longer and thus increase their chances of successfully reducing drug use.

II. The Problem

No one should underestimate the difficulty of reducing drug abuse no matter what methods are used. Relatively modest law-enforcement and prevention efforts may be successful with many novice or occasional users, but the persistent heavy user presents a formidable challenge. In the essays by Dana Hunt, Jan and Marcia Chaiken, and Bruce Johnson and his colleagues, we encounter the urban underclass in all its refractory and frightening complexity. Persistent, heavy users have almost every personal and social problem one can imagine: they tend to be poorly schooled, unemployed (except in drug sales), deeply involved in criminality, and lacking any semblance of a normal family life. Some are homeless. They often use many drugs, not just one; if heroin becomes costly or frightening, they shift to barbiturates. They will use amphetamines, PCP, and crack almost interchangeably as circum-

---

[3] The final split was 55 percent for "demand reduction" (by which was meant treatment and education) and 45 percent for "supply reduction" (by which was meant law enforcement).

stances require. They often drink alcohol to excess, alone or in combination with other drugs.

Drug use and crime do not follow one another in some neat sequence; rather, both—as well as many other social pathologies—arise from deeply rooted causes, some symptoms of which appear in early childhood. Casual drug users, like occasional or low-rate lawbreakers, are quite unlike heavy drug users or high-rate offenders. Whether one looks at drugs or crime, the key distinction to make among people involves the *rate* at which misconduct occurs.

The great increases in high-rate users in the United States occurred during three periods. As Bruce Johnson and his colleagues show, heroin became a major problem between 1965 and 1973, so much so that a sizable proportion (though still a minority) of all inner-city blacks and Hispanics who reached the age of eighteen during this period became addicted. This was the "heroin generation." It was followed by a cocaine epidemic in 1975–84. Heroin addicts continued to exist, but the new recruits into the drug culture preferred cocaine to heroin. Unlike heroin before it or crack after it, cocaine snorting was commonplace among many affluent people. Starting around 1984–85, "rock," or crack, appeared—an inexpensive form of cocaine that quickly spread, especially among low-income users. Today, urine testing in jails shows that cocaine, in any of its various forms, is by far the most common drug used by arrestees, more common than opiates (including heroin) by a factor of at least three to one in most large cities. (Washington, D.C., is unusual in having a high proportion of PCP users among its jail population.)

Although heavy drug users typically lead hectic, disorderly, dangerous lives, the organizations that distribute the drugs have become, in many communities, important sources of power, wealth, and social status. The willingness of some crack-distributing gangs to employ violence using automatic weapons is well known.

Given the great appeal of drugs, the disorganized lives of many of their heavy users, and the existence among these users of all manner of social disabilities, no one should suppose that we are capable of achieving, by plan and at any reasonable cost, a dramatic reduction in the extent of current use. We can, perhaps, curb the spread of these drugs to new users and reduce, marginally, their use among some current consumers.

But changes do occur. At one time, heroin seemed to present an insoluble problem, with the number of addicts growing at what appeared to be an exponential rate. Then, in the mid-1970s, that growth slowed and even stopped. Why? We are not certain, but several factors—some planned, some unplanned—were probably involved. Turkey ceased being a source of illegal opium, and France ceased being a haven for illegal heroin laboratories; the temporary—but acute—shortage of heroin drove many addicts into treatment programs. The hazards associated with injecting heroin became so well known as to reduce its use. The glamour associated with heroin use by artists, musicians, and athletes faded as the would-be user began to confront the sorry reality of the typical user—poor, homeless, diseased, wretched. The availability of a heroin substitute—methadone—helped many addicts end their dependence on heroin with its cycle of euphoric highs followed by painful and frightening lows and brought them into a long-term relationship with counselors who helped them lead better lives. It is possible that similar forces will some day stop the growth of cocaine and crack. But that day is not yet here.

III. Reducing the Supply

In his essay, Mark Moore evaluates the likely effect of present and additional efforts to reduce the importation of dangerous drugs. His conclusion is that, while it is desirable to interdict smuggling networks and eradicate crops, we should not expect much gain from even sharply increased efforts along these lines. It is a view shared by many top federal law-enforcement officials.

The reasons are well understood. Eradicating opium poppy and coca crops overseas is difficult to do because such fields can be developed in regions where there is either no effective government at all or one that is hostile, or at best indifferent, to U.S. interests in these matters. There were large, albeit temporary, gains from reducing the Turkish poppy crop in the early 1970s, but Turkey is a nation with an effective government sympathetic to U.S. concerns and prepared to invest in alternative programs (e.g., poppy cultivation methods that greatly reduced the likelihood of an illegal diversion of the product to heroin traffickers). No government at all exists in the Golden Triangle of Southeast Asia; no friendly government exists in Iran; a friendly government does exist in Colombia, but with respect to the drug trade, it was until 1989 barely a government at all: its key officials are regularly exposed to the terror of murderous gangs and the hostility of coca farmers. Mexico is, at the highest levels, committed to reducing the drug trade, but the central authorities find it difficult to impose great costs on their own population (by, e.g., suppressing poppy cultivation) when they confront corrupt local officials and a public unsympathetic to American demands when it is American demand for drugs that has fueled the drug trade in the first place.

Interdicting drug shipments as they cross the U.S. border is desirable and politically essential, but the effect of even major increases in such interdiction is likely to be small. That is because low-volume, high-profit drugs, such as cocaine and heroin, can enter the United States by so many diverse routes and in such easily concealed bundles that even a very large increase in successful interdiction will capture only a small proportion of the smuggled drugs. Moreover, smuggling costs account for only a small fraction (perhaps 10 percent) of the final price of cocaine. Low transportation costs and the ease of substituting new routes for discovered routes combine to make interdiction a poor tool with which to raise drug prices and reduce drug supplies. Peter Reuter and his colleagues at RAND (Reuter, Crawford, and Cave 1988) have estimated that doubling the proportion of drugs intercepted would increase the total cost of getting drugs to the final consumer by only 10 percent. Though these estimates rely on arguable assumptions and imperfect data, there is some clear evidence supporting a pessimistic conclusion: despite substantial increases in antismuggling efforts and massive increases in the amount of cocaine seized, cocaine imports have continued to rise, and its street price has continued to fall during the 1980s (Reuter, Crawford, and Cave 1988).

Even scholars most skeptical of the marginal product of additional investments in crop eradication and smuggling interdiction believe that such efforts must continue at some level. Interdiction has some effect, especially on bulky drugs such as marijuana. It has made a difference, though not a long-lived one, on the availability of heroin. It sends a signal to other nations that the United States is serious about the drug problem. It gives force to our commitment to various international treaties banning drug smuggling. And it responds to popular demands that all parts of the drug-dealing chain confront risks and sanctions (Reuter 1988; Reuter, Crawford, and Cave 1988).

On the international front, Moore argues that immobilizing high-level trafficking networks that operate across national boundaries may be more valuable than going after crops or smugglers. These networks corrupt governments, use violence to defeat competitors, and manipulate large amounts of cash earned from illegal transactions. Breaking up such groups may have some value in reducing drug availability and will certainly be valuable in reducing the power of organized crime.

Mark Moore and Mark Kleiman and Kerry Smith (in this volume) argue that additional money for supply reduction may be more usefully spent on the city streets than overseas or at our borders. Since this is contrary to what many people believe, it is important to understand the reasons. First, the retail markets for drugs are highly localized; if disrupted, not only can the supply of drugs be reduced, but also the demand (at least among those users who are highly sensitive to search costs). Second, the operation of local markets often relies on personal contacts (dealers and users who know each other). Personal contacts can be made more risky, and thus the number of transactions produced by these contacts made fewer if some dealers and users are undercover police officers or "righteous" dealers and users are observed by watchful patrol officers. Third, disrupting local markets can improve the conditions of neighborhood life by reclaiming the streets for honest citizens and emboldening them to assert social control over dealing. Fourth, visible police efforts to reduce local dealing reassure the public that the police have not been corrupted; ignoring local dealing encourages the public to suspect that corruption is the reason.

But if increases in supply-reduction efforts should be directed more at local markets than at international smuggling, what tactic should be used? Kleiman and Smith list five possibilities. While admitting that no one has made a systematic evaluation of any of them, they supply some plausible reasons for thinking that tactics aimed at specific neighborhoods ("focused crackdowns") and at controlling known users who are also predatory criminals or drug sellers are more likely to be helpful than efforts at arresting "Mr. Big" or making citywide dealer arrests ("street sweeps"). Arresting Mr. Big is very costly in law-enforcement resources, and the benefits may not be commensurate since rival Mr. Bigs usually stand ready to take over from the Mr. Big who has gone to jail. (Indeed, many Mr. Bigs are arrested because their competitors have leaked information to the police.) Citywide street sweeps often have too little impact on any one neighborhood to make a difference; Kleiman and Smith compare this tactic to picking up 10 percent of the trash in every city park instead of picking up all the trash in one park. Gang suppression is a more ambiguous case. Sometimes a gang that colonizes a city (e.g., a Jamaican gang that enters a new "market" in Kansas City) brings with it a more sophisticated drug-distribution system, thereby increasing the supply of drugs. But sometimes gangs arise after crack is already abundant; their presence makes street life more

534   James Q. Wilson

dangerous, but their absence would not measurably reduce the amount of crack on those streets.

The uncertainty as to the best local supply-reduction tactic is evident from the variety that exists among the methods now employed in big cities. New York City combines a major effort to catch Mr. Big with heavy reliance on focused crackdowns, such as Operation Pressure Point on the Lower East Side. Detroit tends to emphasize street sweeps. Los Angeles carries out street sweeps and gang suppression efforts, supplemented by a major demand-reduction program involving police officers in the schools—Project DARE.

Kleiman and Smith's support for focused crackdowns is challenged by some who argue that drug dealing and crime are not actually reduced; they are merely displaced to other neighborhoods. No firm answer can be made to this criticism, but Kleiman, Moore, and others (see Sherman 1990) have given us good reasons for thinking that under many circumstances, displacement is a good deal less than 100 percent. Thus, there is a net benefit.

IV. Demand Reduction

I believe that every contributor to this volume agrees that significant reductions in drug abuse will come only from reducing the demand for those drugs. Supply-reduction efforts must continue (and, in the case of heroin, they have had some good results), but the marginal product of further investments in supply reduction is likely to be small, especially at the international level. Bigger reductions may come from well-designed local enforcement efforts, but we have as yet next to no systematic evidence about which efforts produce what effects under what circumstances.

Some enthusiasts for sending the marines to occupy Bolivia may dismiss the scholarly consensus about the importance of demand reduction as springing from the customary softheadedness of intellectuals. Let me say, then, that I know of no serious law-enforcement executive who disagrees with this conclusion. Typically, police officials tell interviewers that they are fighting either a losing war or, at best, a holding action.

There are only two ways of reducing demand: altering the subjective state of potential drug users (through prevention and treatment programs) or altering the objective conditions of potential drug users (by increasing the costs of drug use).

A. *Altering Subjective States*

Everyone agrees we need more prevention and treatment programs. By "prevention" we mean primary prevention—that is, reducing the percentage of young people who use drugs for the first time. By "treatment" we mean reducing the rate at which active drug users continue to use those drugs. The problem is to discover what kinds of prevention and treatment programs work, for what people, and at what cost. This is a good deal harder than the political advocates of prevention and treatment imagine.

1. *Prevention.* Some progress has been made. After many failed efforts and false starts, there is evidence that certain prevention programs may actually reduce the number of young people who begin drug use. Gilbert Botvin's essay reviews the false starts and shows how little we have gained, in terms of lessened drug use, from mass-media campaigns, scare tactics, informational lectures, and the display of role models such as athletes who decry drug use. These efforts have been based on the assumption that drug users are unaware of the bad effects of drugs; once they learn of these effects, they will stop using them.

But ignorance is not what leads some adolescents—the primary target of prevention programs—to become heavy drug users. During their teenage years, people assert their independence from parental authority and begin to conform to the expectations of peers. For most young people, this transfer from family-centered to peer-centered lives occurs with only a few bumps and bruises, including some experiments with drugs. But for some, it takes the form of a wholesale rejection of parental authority and a desire to emulate the behavior of peers who are most defiant of adult standards. Among the characteristics of many of the more defiant and deviant young people are impulsiveness, poor school performance, low self-esteem, and a desire for new experiences. Using drugs is only one way—and usually not the first way—in which deviance is expressed. Heavy drug users also tend to be sexually promiscuous, to smoke and drink (often to excess), and to be truant. Although there is nothing inevitable about the process, it is striking that heavy drug use is typically preceded by "light" drug use (smoking marijuana, swallowing an occasional amphetamine), which in turn is often preceded by smoking cigarettes and drinking alcohol.

To such persons, hearing the facts about drug use is almost irrelevant. Young people, as Botvin notes, have a sense of their own invulnerability and value the opinion of their peers more than the advice of their teachers. Two decades of prevention efforts foundered on the rocks of these stubborn facts.

Then a glimmer of hope appeared from efforts to reduce cigarette smoking. The new strategy was based on teaching junior high school (and in some cases even younger) students how to recognize and cope with peer pressure. It is often called "resistance skills training." A broader version—broader in that it attempts to improve the social competency of the young people—is called "social skills training" (see also Bell and Battjes 1985). The essence of these approaches (though not their full complexity) is captured by the slogan, "learning to say 'no.' " The instructors in these programs are sometimes school teachers, sometimes (as in Los Angeles and a few other cities) police officers, and sometimes other teenagers.

Evaluations of these strategies suggest that they slow the rate at which people begin smoking and reduce the proportion of a given group that ever smokes. But will an approach that reduces smoking also reduce drug use? There is evidence that skills training can reduce alcohol use and may even reduce teenage pregnancy, and there is at least one study (see Botvin, in this volume) that finds a reduction in drug use. Many more carefully evaluated experimental projects will have to be carried out before we can be confident that this psychosocial strategy is truly effective in discouraging drug use, but for the first time there are at least grounds for hope.

2. *Treatment.* The evidence that treatment works is stronger than the evidence that prevention works. Anglin and Hser (in this volume) summarize this evidence; other reviews, already available in the literature, concur with this assessment (Tims and Ludford 1984).

The phrase "treatment can work" does not mean that drug users can be "cured"—that is, that, after the treatment, they will live drug-free lives. Drug dependency cannot be fixed as if it were akin to a broken leg. It is more like a chronic disease that requires long-term management and in which we measure gains, not by the proportion of people who are fully cured, but by the relative improvement in the quality of their lives. There are benefits from treatment even when no cure occurs. Those benefits include a reduction in the *rate* of drug abuse and the personal and social costs associated with it (such as poor health, drug-related crime, and low labor productivity).

There are at least four major kinds of treatment programs. Detoxification involves short-term medical help to end immediate drug use and enable the patient to overcome the pains and hazards of withdrawal. Drug-free outpatient centers rely on counseling and training to help users resist drugs while living in the community. Maintenance programs supply heroin users with a legal opiate, methadone, that when taken orally in stable doses produces no "high" of its own and can block the high produced by heroin. Properly administered, methadone, though addictive, can reduce the craving for heroin and prevent the withdrawal pains associated with ending heroin use "cold turkey." Therapeutic communities (TCs) are residential programs in which drug users are exposed to systematic and continuous efforts to get them to confront their addictive lifestyles and alter their personalities so that they can lead drug-free lives.

All of these programs can reduce drug abuse *if* the patients stay in them. Retention in a program, rather than the characteristics of the programs themselves, appears to be a consistently important factor in explaining success. What, then, explains retention?

The answer to that question is not entirely clear. The characteristics of the drug user explain some of the differences. Anglin and Hser believe therapeutic communities do better with young polydrug users who have poor employment records. These people have the worst problems and the poorest prospects, and so the demanding and all-encompassing nature of a TC is more likely to produce retention than more permissive outpatient programs. Methadone maintenance, by contrast, seems to work better with older addicts who have fewer personal and family problems and are already motivated to seek help. Young polydrug users who are black or Hispanic seem, in some studies, to drop out of programs sooner than persons with different characteristics. But there are practitioners (DeLeon 1984) who believe that there are few, if any, obvious patient characteristics that explain retention (though there may be more subtle psychological states that do explain it).

There is one factor that may affect retention, and that is legal compulsion. Persons who enter community-based treatment programs as a condition of probation or parole, if those conditions are effectively monitored and enforced, tend to stay in programs longer than those who enter without such compulsion. As a consequence, they benefit from the treatment as much as clients who stay in the program without compulsion. The best evidence of this comes from the careful long-term studies of the California Civil Addict Program (CAP) (Anglin 1988). This program, sometimes called "civil commitment," involved sending drug users first to a residential treatment center and then re-

538   James Q. Wilson

quiring the users, as a condition of release back into the community, to become part of an outpatient service in which their drug use was monitored, and they were supplied with a variety of services.

In evaluating CAP, researchers for several years followed both heroin users whom the courts had put into the mandatory outpatient program and a similar group of users who had also been required to enter it but, because of procedural errors, had been released after a minimal exposure. While in the residential facility, both groups reduced their drug use. After release, those who were required to stay in the CAP outpatient service showed lower rates of drug use than those who were allowed to drop out, a difference that persisted for over a decade. Anglin concluded that "civil commitment has an important and dramatic effect in suppressing daily heroin use by narcotics addicts" (Anglin 1988, p. 11). But scholars studying civil commitment programs in New York and in the federal government found no such effects (Inciardi 1988).

The reason for the different outcomes was the difference in the programs. In California, supervision in the community was close, was done by specially trained parole officers having small case loads, and entailed frequent urine tests to detect drug use. Enforcement was strict: resuming drug use often led to reincarceration. The slogan was "You use, you lose."

In New York and in parts of the federal program, the supervision was less close and done by social workers, testing was less frequently used, and penalties for relapse were less regularly enforced (Anglin 1988; Inciardi 1988; Anglin and Hser 1989). (An exception was that part of the federal civil commitment program administered by the U.S. Bureau of Prisons. It seems to have worked as well as the California program, apparently because the Bureau's personnel, like their California counterparts, were experienced law-enforcement professionals.)

Much of the research on drug treatment has focused on programs that enroll heroin users. We know much less about how to treat cocaine or crack users. And one treatment program—methadone maintenance—has almost no relevance for cocaine. Methadone is useful because it prevents the withdrawal pains that follow a cessation in heroin consumption. But stopping cocaine use, while it can induce a deep emotional depression, does not produce withdrawal pains. There cannot be a cocaine version of methadone.

That does not mean that there can be no chemical treatment for cocaine and crack users. There are, in fact, several exciting leads about the value of giving cocaine abusers drugs that are used to treat depression, epilepsy, and Parkinson's disease.[4] The use of these medications has arisen out of basic research that has begun to identify the way in which drugs affect the brain cells.

Addiction, after all, is a disease of the brain. Different kinds of drugs affect the brain differently. Cocaine seems to interfere with the way in which one brain cell communicates with another. Though the actual processes are far more complex (and less well understood) than this lay summary will imply, the key mechanism seems to involve a neurotransmitter called dopamine (and possibly others as well). A neurotransmitter is a chemical messenger that is especially important in certain brain cells found in those parts of the brain (such as the ventral tegmental area) that produce pleasurable sensations. When the brain is operating normally, dopamine is released by one cell to "turn on" an adjacent cell; then the dopamine is carried back to the first cell to await another signal and the adjacent cell "turns off." Cocaine apparently blocks this return flow, probably by interfering with the transporter molecules. The result is that excess dopamine continues to excite the adjacent cell, leading the cocaine user to experience a prolonged period of intense pleasure (Ritz et al. 1987; Gawin and Ellinwood 1988; Koob and Bloom 1988). The brain tells us we are having a wonderful time even when we are just sitting in a chair. The moderating tendencies in normal brain chemistry are upset.

As more is learned about this basic neurochemical process, we will learn more about how other benign drugs can be used to block the ability of cocaine to upset the regular dopamine transport system. We may also learn why some people are more likely than others to use cocaine in an uncontrolled manner (Kozel and Adams 1985).

In all the political debate about how best to mount (and pay for) a drug-control program, not much is heard about neurochemistry and neurobiology. Yet these disciplines are the ones that will probably

---

[4] These drugs include desipramine, bromocriptine, carbamazepine, imipramine, and buprenorphine, among others. No chemical is likely to be a "magic bullet" that will "cure" drug dependency, if for no other reason than the fact that cocaine users find the drug so pleasurable that they do not wish to become abstinent. Moreover, many drug-dependent people suffer from a host of other problems. Chemical treatment can, however, help addicts function normally while undergoing other forms of counseling and therapy. In time, basic research may reveal ways of using pharmacology to prevent drug experimentation in the first place.

540   James Q. Wilson

provide us with the best understanding and the most effective treatments for drug abuse. Funding this basic research ought to be a major federal priority. So far, it is not.

B. Changing Objective Conditions

Changing the subjective state of drug users is obviously the most desirable goal, because people who no longer crave a drug can be left free in the community with fewer risks to themselves and to others. But it is not necessary to change the preferences of people to change their behavior. We understand that when we make racial discrimination illegal: people may continue to have racist attitudes, but they are less likely to commit racist acts because the costs of doing so have gone up. We also understand this when we rely on the criminal justice system to deter crime. Whatever their preferences, would-be criminals must take into account to some degree the costs of crime.

We have already seen how law enforcement can indirectly reduce demand, at least among casual or novice users, by making drugs harder to find and buy. We can also use sanctions directly to reduce demand by making it more risky to be identified as a drug user. This is the potential role of drug testing.

There is no question that drug testing, properly done in the appropriate setting, can reduce drug use. The experience of the armed forces during and since the war in Vietnam provides ample evidence of this. The U.S. Navy's program, summarized in the essay by Wish and Gropper, is the most extensive. The testing is roughly at random, with the average person experiencing three tests per year. Almost 2 million urine samples (each taken under direct observation to eliminate substitution) are examined each year. At the first sign of drug use, the person is brought into a treatment program. If that person tests positive a second time, he or she is ordinarily declared unfit for service and discharged. The navy asserts that, in 1981, 48 percent of all enlisted personnel under the age of twenty-five were users; by the late 1980s, that proportion was less than 5 percent. Other studies are consistent with the view that testing in the military has been a deterrent to drug use.

Testing is now being employed by various courts as a way of helping judges make decisions about whom to release while awaiting trial and as a way of helping control the drug usage of convicted offenders who are on probation or parole. The civil commitment program and its kin, Treatment Alternatives to Street Crime (TASC) (Bureau of Justice

Assistance 1989), are examples of this latter function. We do not yet know, however, whether the mere use of random drug testing as a condition of release, absent any other treatment interventions, will deter drug use, but it ought to be possible to find out. Some efforts along these lines are now underway at various sites around the country. Preliminary results suggest that, as with the civil commitment program, testing alone will not be enough. The most serious abusers have so many problems and so deviant a lifestyle that many may skip the tests. Only testing coupled with sufficient supervision and the willingness of the supervisor to revoke probation or parole and reincarcerate may be sufficient to reduce drug use and attendant criminality.

No one knows whether testing can serve as an effective deterrent in settings less disciplined than the military or less powerful than the criminal justice system. It is not obvious, however, that it has no place in civilian occupations. The penalties of failing a test may be less among civilian workers than among probationers, but the typical civilian drug user probably has a less serious problem than the typical probationer and so might be more easily deterred. Suppose, for example, that drug tests were routinely used to screen people applying for the reinstatement of a driver's license after it had been suspended for driving while intoxicated and for people seeking employment in a wide range of occupations where safety and reliability are of paramount concern. By sharply constricting the range of activities open to frequent drug users, the costs of drug use to all but the most addicted would obviously go up and the disadvantages of entering a treatment program would go down. Under these circumstances, the demand for drugs ought to decline. Moreover, the existence of a widespread testing program would presumably have a tutelary effect: young people would observe that society was serious about drug abuse and thus, perhaps, be less inclined to regard drug use as a pro forma evil—something perfunctorily condemned but actually tolerated. Whether the theory is correct will depend on evidence that no one has yet tried to collect.

I am assuming here that drug tests can be made reliable and inexpensive.[5] That is a large but not unreasonable assumption. More difficult to solve are the ethical and legal issues involved in testing. To some,

---

[5] Wish and Gropper review the evidence on reliability and cost. They suggest that cheap urine tests can be used for screening and more expensive tests for confirming or rejecting initial positive results. The combined probability of both tests being in error (unless the urine sample has been adulterated) is very low. Hair samples are expensive to test (as of now) but are hard to adulterate.

542   James Q. Wilson

testing is an invasion of privacy and intolerable for that reason. That surely cannot be the case in the military or the criminal justice system where far greater invasions of privacy—and of liberty—are necessary and commonplace. In other, less restrictive settings, privacy is a value that must be balanced against other values, such as public safety. Automobile drivers are exercising state-controlled privileges that can expose them to, among other things, the obligation to stop at police roadblocks and submit to tests for sobriety. Adding tests designed to detect drug use does not clearly invade an established right, especially if the tests can be done in ways that are not intrusive and embarrassing (as may be possible if hair or saliva tests can be made as economical and reliable as the urine tests).

The courts have yet to settle the issues involved in testing, nor can they settle them wisely unless careful real-world experiments are carried out. Ultimately, the courts will probably defer to some degree to popular views: to the extent society makes it clear that reducing the demand for drugs is extremely important, the courts will take that into account in striking a balance between public safety and personal privacy.

V. Conclusions

In reading the essays of this book, I am struck both by what we know and what we do not know. We know drug trafficking is driven by the demand for drugs and that reducing that demand, to the extent that it is feasible and fair to do so, will have a greater effect on the drugs-crime connection than reducing the supply. We know that demand reduction, to be effective, must involve elements of both therapy and coercion; a demand-side strategy cannot be purely a medical, an educational, or a law-enforcement strategy. We know that various treatment programs will help reduce demand—if people can be induced to remain in them. We suspect that some primary prevention programs will work, but we are not certain of this. Neither do we know the kinds of persons for whom they will work, nor for how long.

We do not know as much about reducing cocaine use as we know about reducing heroin use. We do not know what kind of street-level enforcement efforts are most effective in reducing either the demand for or the supply of drugs, though we think that the street is where the principal law-enforcement effort must be made.

Above all, we do not know how to alter the moral climate so that drug use is regarded as loathsome. A large number of young people still try drugs; many, though perhaps somewhat fewer than was once the case, go on to use them regularly. Public officials can and should decry drug use and make clear the moral, as well as the practical, grounds for it being wrong. But government statements are not likely to be as effective in shaping the moral climate as the efforts of neighborhood associations, community groups, and literary and artistic figures. Statements from these sources may not have any direct preventive effect, but their cumulative, long-term effect in shaping the ethos within which standards of personal conduct are defined may be great. There is no way to test that assumption, but there can be little harm in acting as if it were true. One of the advantages of making certain drugs illegal and enforcing the laws against their possession is that these actions reinforce the social condemnation of drug use and the social praise accorded temperate behavior.

I have watched several "wars on drugs" declared over the last three decades. The wars typically begin with the statement that the time for studies is past and the time for action has come. "We know what to do; let's get on with it." In fact, we do not know what to do in any comprehensive way, and the need for research is never more urgent than at the beginning of a "war." That is because every past war has led, after brief gains, to final defeat. And so we condemn another generation to risk.

We certainly know enough to begin, if not a "war," then a reasonable array of programs. In our urgency to get on with what we do know, it is important that we organize some of those efforts—in prevention, treatment, and supply reduction—in a frankly experimental manner so that, before the next war is declared, we will have improved our knowledge of what works. Moreover, some of the most urgently needed research is basic research on such questions as the biological basis of addiction, the ability of chemicals to block the euphoric effects of drugs and thereby reduce the craving for them, the presence or absence of biological markers that will help us identify the individuals most at risk for addictive behavior (Braude and Chao 1986), and the early childhood and familial processes that increase the likelihood of young people allowing their impulsiveness, search for thrills, and desire for independence to lead them into self-destructive behavior.

544   James Q. Wilson

REFERENCES

Anglin, M. Douglas. 1988. "The Efficacy of Civil Commitment in Treating Narcotic Addiction." In *Compulsory Treatment of Drug Abuse: Research and Clinical Practice*, edited by Carl G. Leukefeld and Frank M. Tims. National Institute on Drug Abuse Research Monograph no. 86. Rockville, Md.: Department of Health and Human Services, National Institute on Drug Abuse.

Anglin, M. Douglas, and Yih-Ing Hser. 1989. "Legal Coercion and Drug Abuse Treatment: Research Findings and Social Policy Implications." Unpublished manuscript. University of California at Los Angeles, Drug Abuse Research Group, March.

———. In this volume. "Treatment of Drug Abuse."

Bell, Catherine S., and Robert Battjes, eds. 1985. *Prevention Research: Deterring Drug Abuse among Children and Adolescents*. National Institute on Drug Abuse Research Monograph no. 63. Rockville, Md.: Department of Health and Human Services, National Institute on Drug Abuse.

Botvin, Gilbert J. In this volume. "Substance Abuse Prevention: Theory, Practice, and Effectiveness."

Braude, Monique C., and Helen M. Chao, eds. 1986. *Genetic and Biological Markers in Drug Abuse and Alcoholism*. National Institute on Drug Abuse Research Monograph no. 66. Rockville, Md.: Department of Health and Human Services, National Institute on Drug Abuse.

Bureau of Justice Assistance. 1989. *Treatment Alternatives to Street Crime (TASC): Resource Manual*. Washington, D.C.: U.S. Department of Justice, Bureau of Justice Assistance.

Chaiken, Jan M., and Marcia R. Chaiken. In this volume. "Drugs and Predatory Crime."

DeLeon, George. 1984. "Program-based Evaluation Research in Therapeutic Communities." In *Drug Abuse Treatment Evaluation: Strategies, Progress, and Prospects*, edited by Frank M. Tims and Jacqueline P. Ludford. National Institute on Drug Abuse Research Monograph no. 51. Rockville, Md.: Department of Health and Human Services, National Institute on Drug Abuse.

Fagan, Jeffrey A. In this volume. "Intoxication and Aggression."

Gawin, Frank H., and H. Ellinwood. 1988. "Cocaine and Other Stimulants: Actions, Abuse, and Treatment." *New England Journal of Medicine* 318:1173–82.

Hunt, Dana. In this volume. "Drugs and Consensual Crime: Drug Dealing and Prostitution."

Inciardi, James A. 1988. "Some Considerations on the Clinical Efficacy of Compulsory Treatment: Reviewing the New York Experience." In *Compulsory Treatment and Drug Abuse: Research and Clinical Practice*, edited by Carl G. Leukefeld and Frank M. Tims. National Institute on Drug Abuse Research Monograph no. 86. Rockville, Md.: Department of Health and Human Services, National Institute on Drug Abuse.

Johnson, Bruce D., Terry Williams, Kojo A. Dei, and Harry Sanabria. In this volume. "Drug Abuse in the Inner City: Impact on Hard Drug Users and the Community."

Kaplan, John. 1988. "Taking Drugs Seriously." *Public Interest* 92:32–50.

Kleiman, Mark A. R., and Kerry D. Smith. In this volume. "State and Local Drug Enforcement: In Search of a Strategy."

Koob, George F., and Floyd E. Bloom. 1988. "Cellular and Molecular Mechanisms of Drug Dependence." *Science* 242:715–23.

Kozel, Nicholas J., and Edgar H. Adams, eds. 1985. *Cocaine Use in America: Epidemiological and Clinical Perspectives*. National Institute on Drug Abuse Research Monograph no. 61. Rockville, Md.: Department of Health and Human Services, National Institute on Drug Abuse.

Moore, Mark H. In this volume. "Supply Reduction and Drug Law Enforcement."

Office of National Drug Control Policy. 1989. *National Drug Control Strategy*. Washington, D.C.: U.S. Government Printing Office.

Pearson, Geoffrey. 1990. "Drug Control Policies in Britain: Continuity and Change." In *Crime and Justice: A Review of Research*, vol. 14, edited by Michael Tonry and Norval Morris. Chicago: University of Chicago Press (forthcoming).

Reuter, Peter. 1988. "Can the Borders Be Sealed?" *Public Interest* 92:51–65.

Reuter, Peter, Gordon Crawford, and Jonathan Cave. 1988. *Sealing the Borders: The Effects of Increased Military Participation in Drug Interdiction*. Report no. R-3594-USDP. Santa Monica, Calif.: RAND.

Ritz, Mary C., R. L. Lamb, Steven R. Goldberg, and Michael J. Kuhar. 1987. "Cocaine Receptors on Dopamine Transporters Are Related to Self-Administration of Cocaine." *Science* 237:1219–23.

Sherman, Lawrence. 1990. "Police Crackdowns: Initial and Residual Deterrence." In *Crime and Justice: A Review of Research*, vol. 12, edited by Michael Tonry and Norval Morris. Chicago: University of Chicago Press.

Tims, Frank M., and Jacqueline P. Ludford, eds. 1984. *Drug Abuse Treatment Evaluation: Strategies, Progress, and Prospects*. National Institute on Drug Abuse Research Monograph no. 51. Rockville, Md.: Department of Health and Human Services, National Institute on Drug Abuse.

Wilson, James Q. 1990. "Against the Legalization of Drugs." *Commentary* 89:21–28.

Wish, Eric D., and Bernard A. Gropper. In this volume. "Drug Testing by the Criminal Justice System: Methods, Research, and Applications."

[16]

UNEMPLOYMENT AND CRIMINAL INVOLVEMENT: AN INVESTIGATION OF RECIPROCAL CAUSAL STRUCTURES*

TERENCE P. THORNBERRY   R. L. CHRISTENSON

University of Georgia

Current etiological theories of criminal behavior are unidirectional in structure; positing that crime is caused by a variety of social factors, these theories tend to ignore the reciprocal causal influence of crime on those factors. The present paper assesses the theoretical and empirical consequences associated with unidirectional explanations of criminal involvement. Using a linear panel model approach, it also examines the advantages of reciprocal causal structures by estimating a nonrecursive model of the relationship between crime and one other variable, unemployment. Results indicate that a reciprocal model is far more accurate than a traditional, unidirectional one; unemployment and crime appear to mutually influence one another over the individual's life span. Implications of these findings for etiological theories of criminal behavior are discussed.

Current sociological approaches to the etiology of crime and delinquency[1] can be subsumed under one of four theoretical perspectives (Kornhauser, 1978:21). They are: social control theory, which treats the absence of controls over the person's conduct as the basic cause of crime; strain theory, which posits that structurally induced strain is the primary causal factor; social learning theory, which attributes criminal behavior to the development and reinforcement of deviant values; and integrated models, which combine elements of two or more of these theories into a more general body of explanatory principles.

While these four approaches stress different causal factors as being responsible for criminal involvement, all adopt a *unidirectional* or asymmetrical causal structure. Asserting that various social factors cause criminal involvement, they ignore the possibility that crime and its presumed causes are embedded in a reciprocal causal structure, mutually influencing one another over the person's life span. The present paper shows, however,

that reciprocal structures are both logically consistent with existing theories and provide a more accurate specification of the causal processes actually involved in the genesis of criminal behavior. To do so, it first evaluates the theoretical difficulties posed by asymmetrical models and then illustrates the advantages of reciprocal structures by estimating a nonrecursive model for the relationship between unemployment and crime.

THE CONSEQUENCES OF UNIDIRECTIONAL STRUCTURES

The unidirectional structure of etiological theories is evident in the causal paths they include and exclude. In social control theory, for example, such factors as attachment to parents, success in school and work, and belief in conventional values all exert a negative effect on criminal involvement (Hirschi, 1969). Yet, as currently specified, the theory does not include causal paths from delinquency to any of these factors. Other etiological theories adopt the same underlying structure, a point well illustrated in the causal models and diagrams presented in works that integrate control, strain and social learning theories (e.g., Johnson, 1979:67; Elliott et al., 1979:10; Weis and Sederstrom, 1981:35). None of these models allows for reciprocal causal influences from crime to other variables.[2]

Such unidirectional causal structures are not

* Direct all correspondence to: Terence P. Thornberry, Research Center in Crime and Delinquency, University of Georgia, Athens, GA 30602.

This project was supported in part by the National Institute of Mental Health (Grant No. MH13,664) and by the Research Center in Crime and Delinquency of the University of Georgia. The authors would like to thank Drs. Robert A. Ellis, James Massey, Jorge Mendoza, Robert A. Silverman, Abraham Tesser and Stewart Tolnay for commenting on earlier drafts of this paper.

[1] For our purposes there are no substantive differences between delinquency and crime and the two forms of criminal involvement are treated synonymously in this paper.

[2] While these models allow for some reciprocal effects among the causal variables—e.g., holding delinquent values and having delinquent friends may influence one another over time—the "causal" variables remain uninfluenced by delinquent conduct.

UNEMPLOYMENT AND CRIMINAL INVOLVEMENT   399

necessarily invalid so long as they provide an accurate reflection of the behaviors they are designed to model. When causal relationships are reciprocal, however, unidirectional models are misspecified and impede an accurate understanding of the causal processes at work precisely because they ignore potentially important causal paths. The empirical consequence of such misspecification is that results from recursive statistical models,[3] typically used to test unidirectional theories, can be incomplete and misleading. Such findings are incomplete since estimates for reciprocal paths simply cannot be obtained. More importantly, recursive tests can produce misleading results since estimates of unidirectional effects obtained from them may be in substantial error. Conceivably, recursive tests could indicate a unidirectional relationship between two variables, i.e., X→Y, when the actual relationship (as estimated from a nonrecursive model) could indicate either that the variables are reciprocally related, i.e., X ⇄ Y, or that the direction of causality is actually reversed, i.e., X←Y[4] (see Heise, 1975:191–93; Hanushek and Jackson, 1977:79–86).

Combined with the apparent implausibility of asserting that criminal behavior does not influence family relationships, success in school and work, choice of deviant or nondeviant peers, and so forth, these potential limitations are serious enough to warrant reexamination of the appropriateness of unidirectional models of crime causation. Indeed, when available evidence is assessed, reciprocal models seem far more appropriate.

CRIME AS A RECIPROCAL CAUSAL INFLUENCE

Although relatively little research has investigated reciprocal causal influences of criminal involvement, there are both theoretical and empirical grounds for adopting such an approach. Theoretically, Greenberg and Kessler (1981:4–5) identify three types of causal relationships that should not be assumed, a priori, to be unidirectional. They are relationships between: (1) a person's behaviors and beliefs, e.g., beliefs about conventional morality and criminal behavior; (2) different

behaviors of the person, e.g., association with delinquent peers and criminal behavior; and (3) behaviors of different individuals, e.g., delinquent behavior and reactions of parents and teachers to it.

The theoretical appropriateness of reciprocal models is also suggested by societal reaction and social disorganization theories, both of which include reciprocal effects. Unlike etiological approaches, societal reaction theory focuses attention on the consequences of criminal involvement. When criminal behavior is officially labeled it alters the person's self-image and public identity, thereby reducing associations with nondeviant peers and access to conventional roles and activities (Becker, 1963; Matza, 1969). These variables, basic causes of crime in etiological theories, are thus viewed as consequences of crime and its labeling in societal reaction theory. Although incorporating reciprocal effects, societal reaction theory does not by itself resolve the difficulties raised by unidirectional causal structures. First, labeling theory tends to ignore the antecedents of crime, (see Lemert's discussion of "primary deviance," 1967:40–41); and second, reciprocal effects are mediated entirely through official labels, downplaying the causal importance of criminal involvement. Nevertheless, the labeling tradition does indicate the importance of explicitly considering reciprocal causal influences in theories of criminal involvement.

Reciprocal relationships are also suggested by social disorganization theory, an important precursor to current etiological theories. Crime is viewed as a product of social disorganization, but once manifested in delinquent subcultures, criminal behavior feeds back upon and becomes a causal factor in the perpetuation of disorganization (Kornhauser, 1978:26, 58). Thus, crime is both cause and effect; generated by the disorganized social life of the city, crime also contributes to the level of disorganization.

In addition to these theoretical works, some empirical studies also suggest the plausibility of reciprocal models. In their investigation of delinquency and dropout, Elliott and Voss find delinquency at time one to be associated with academic failure, parental rejection, alienation from home and school, and delinquent associates, all measured at a later time (Elliott and Voss, 1974:135, 154, 159). Similarly, Paternoster et al. (1983:476) report that prior delinquency is inversely correlated with several social control variables: belief in the moral validity of conventional rules; involvement in and commitment to conventional activities; and attachment to parents and peers. Among college students, marijuana use is significantly

---

[3] Even theories that allow for some nonrecursive relationships among the causal variables tend to be tested in completely recursive models. Compare, for example, the theoretical model presented by Elliott et al. (1979:10) and their test of the model (Elliott et al., 1982).

[4] See Paternoster et al. (1982) and Paternoster et al. (1983) for a discussion of just such an outcome with respect to deterrence research.

related to later association with peers who use marijuana and to a reduction in psychological distress, but not to commitment to conventional institutions (Ginsberg and Greenley, 1978:29). It should be noted that in all these studies, extensive involvement in criminal behavior, whether or not it led to official labeling, had the reciprocal effects noted (see, e.g., Elliott, 1978:467).

In brief, these theoretical and empirical works all indicate the appropriateness of reciprocal causal structures and lead to the central thesis of this article: namely, that criminal behavior is best viewed as part of an interactional nexus, influenced by, but also exerting a causal influence on, other social factors over the person's life span. Since this perspective represents a substantial departure from the unidirectional structure of current etiological theories, it requires detailed specification and testing.

UNEMPLOYMENT AND CRIME

As an initial effort to this end, the present paper examines the reciprocal relationship between crime and only one of its presumed causes, unemployment. The variable of unemployment is well suited for illustrating the advantages of reciprocal models for the following reasons. First, studies based on individual-level data report consistent evidence that these variables are correlated in the expected direction, an important precondition for examining the issue of causal structure (Glaser and Rice, 1959; Glaser, 1964; Pownall, 1969; Cook, 1975; Sickles et al., 1979; Thornberry and Farnworth, 1982; Davis, 1983). Second, unemployment, like criminal activity, is not an enduring status of the individual but occurs at intermittent intervals over time. Thus, it possesses measurement properties conducive to an analysis of reciprocal effects. Finally, and most importantly, the hypothesis that unemployment influences crime is explicitly developed in most etiological theories of crime, while the reciprocal hypothesis, that crime also influences unemployment, is implicit in and can be derived from these same theories. Three theoretical models are used to illustrate the last point.

Social Control Theory

The hypothesis that unemployment influences criminal involvement is easily derived from a consideration of the bonding elements of commitment and involvement (Hirschi, 1969:21–22). Commitment, the "rational component in conformity," reduces criminal involvement by increasing the costs associated

with deviance. As individuals invest time and energy in conventional activities, criminal behavior is avoided so as not to jeopardize investments already made. Involvement, the behavioral counterpart of commitment, posits that persons "engrossed" in conventional activity cannot, at the same time, devote considerable effort to unconventional or deviant behavior. "The assumption, widely shared, is that a person may be simply too busy doing conventional things to find time to engage in deviant behavior" (Hirschi, 1969:22). Since employment is clearly the predominant form of conventional activity for adult males, the hypothesis that unemployment should increase criminal behavior is explicitly developed within a control model.

The reciprocal hypothesis, that crime influences unemployment, is only implicit in these models. Nevertheless, the assertion that criminal activity reduces both involvement in and commitment to conventional activity, including employment, can be developed within the framework of the theory. The argument with respect to involvement is straightforward: if involvement in conventional activity precludes deviance, involvement in deviance should, by the same token, preclude conventional activity. The argument for commitment, the rational element of the bond, is as follows. Individuals committed to conventional society are unlikely candidates for crime since they wish to maintain investments already made. The greater those investments, the stronger the inertia to remain conventional. But if, for whatever reason, the person engages in criminal activity, the commitment is attenuated. Precisely because crime is unconventional, involvement in crime represents a reduction in the person's investment in conventional society (Kornhauser, 1978:49). Moreover, extensive and prolonged criminal careers should have a greater negative effect on involvement and commitment than isolated, individual criminal acts. This should be particularly applicable to offenders who are officially labeled, but the hypothesis holds even for those who engage in repeated criminal activity without receiving official sanctions.

Strain Theory

Strain theory argues that criminal involvement should be relatively high whenever legitimate opportunities to achieve success are closed to the individual (Merton, 1957; Cohen, 1955; Cloward and Ohlin, 1960). Since the occupational realm is the primary legitimate opportunity structure for adults, it follows that unemployment ought to be positively associated with criminal involvement.

On the other hand, involvement in criminal behavior should influence the availability or openness of legitimate opportunities. Indeed, it is quite reasonable to expect that activities in the world of crime, or in Cloward and Ohlin's term, the illegitimate opportunity structure, ought to create additional barriers to legitimate avenues to success. Employers, for example, ought to be less willing to provide jobs to current and former offenders (see Schwartz and Skolnick, 1962, for empirical support). Thus, illegitimate activities should reduce the availability of such legitimate opportunities as employment.

Economic Theory

Finally, since unemployment is essentially an economic variable, a recent economic model of crime causation can be examined. Based on utility maximization, this model predicts that involvement in licit activities, both in terms of employment and the economic return one receives from employment, will reduce criminal activity. If returns from licit activities are sufficiently large, such activity will be chosen over illicit activities because the latter are both more uncertain and entail higher costs associated with apprehension (see Ehrlich, 1973: Cook, 1975; and Orsagh and Witte, 1981).

Utility theory is also logically consistent with the reciprocal hypothesis that crime influences future levels of unemployment. First, it posits that persons engaged in illicit activity reduce the amount of time allocated to licit activities since, in this model, time allocated to these two activities is unity (Ehrlich, 1973:530; Orsagh and Witte, 1981:1056). Second, like strain theory, utility theory considers the effect that prior criminal involvement has on the availability of licit opportunities. In general, the model asserts that involvement in crime continues, and as the return one receives from crime increases, opportunities in licit activities become less available and less attractive to the person.

Thus, when the hypothesis that unemployment and crime are reciprocally related is treated explicitly, it is found to be consistent with a number of etiological theories of criminal involvement. Indeed, it is precisely for this reason that the relationship between unemployment and crime is selected for analysis. The purpose of the analysis, however, is not to test the relative validity of these different theories. Quite the contrary, the purpose is to demonstrate the potential utility of shifting from static, unidirectional models to more dynamic, reciprocal ones in a variety of different theoretical approaches. Since the relationship between unemployment and crime is embedded in many of these theories, it is an appropriate relationship to examine for this heuristic purpose.

METHODS

Data to examine this issue come from a ten percent sample of the 9,945 members of the Philadelphia birth cohort of 1945 (Wolfgang et al., 1972; Wolfgang et al., forthcoming). Juvenile and adult arrest histories, collected from the files of the Philadelphia police and the Federal Bureau of Investigation, are available for all subjects to age 30, and interview data were collected at age 25. Although an attempt was made to interview all 975 members of the sample, successful interviews were completed with 62 percent, or 567, subjects. The issues of response bias and of weighting the data for nonresponse have been thoroughly investigated, and results suggests that the bias is not sufficient to distort correlational analysis or to alter appropriate conclusions concerning statistical significance (Wolfgang et al., forthcoming; Singer, 1977; Thornberry and Farnworth, 1982). Race, which will be held constant, is the only variable to have a substantial impact on nonresponse, with blacks having a lower completion rate than whites. In general, therefore, difficulties raised by nonresponse are not substantial, and are clearly offset by the analytic advantages that panel designs provide in testing reciprocal causal models (Greenberg and Kessler, 1981:6).

Variables for Analysis

The measure of unemployment is based on an interview item in which each subject traced his employment history from high school until the time of the interview. Unemployment is defined as any period of time the person was not employed, a full-time student, or in the armed services, i.e., any time the person was not involved in conventional activities. Subjects also estimated the month and year each of these periods began and ended. These dates were keyed to the subject's birthdate so that unemployment histories are based on annual intervals.[5] For each year, both the number of times and the proportion of time the subject was un-

---

[5] Although recall no doubt affects the accuracy of these dates, they appear quite suited to estimating the frequency of unemployment at *annual* intervals. Since the subjects were 25 at the time of the interview, most had not experienced a large number of occupational shifts and appeared to be able to trace their occupational careers with relative ease.

employed were determined. Both yield similar results and the proportion of time spent unemployed is used in this analysis.[6]

Criminal involvement is represented by the number of times the subject was arrested at each age. Arrests were weighted for seriousness, producing no substantial differences in results, so only frequency counts are used. Self-reported data, although collected in the interview, are not used since they cannot be divided into annual periods.[7]

Finally, since race, social status of origin and the subject's record of juvenile delinquency are related to both unemployment and adult criminal involvement, separate models are estimated for each group. Race is a dichotomous variable with the sample divided into white and black subjects. Social status is represented by the occupation of the subject's father while the subject was in high school, with occupations divided into white-collar and blue-collar categories based on the U.S. Census classification scheme. Finally, subjects are dichotomized into delinquents, those having one or more official police contacts prior to age 18, and nondelinquents.

The unemployment and arrest data are arrayed to create a four-wave panel design covering the subjects' twenty-first through twenty-fourth years of age. The upper limit was selected since subjects interviewed at age twenty-five could not provide complete unemployment information for that year. Twenty-one was selected as the lower limit for two reasons. First, prior to twenty-one a substantial portion of the employed category is composed of full-time students, while after that age the proportion of students declines substantially. Second, Shannon (1982) reports a positive relationship between unemployment and delinquent activity for the late teenage years. Although this effect may be spurious, produced by the common antecedent of school failure, the present analysis is delayed until twenty-one to avoid this potentially biasing effect.

Model Specification

Figure 1 presents a reciprocal model of the relationship between unemployment (U) and crime (C) for a four-wave panel. At time 1 crime and unemployment are exogenous variables and their relationship is presented as a zero-order correlation; at later times unemployment and crime are endogenous variables. The model allows for cross-correlations among error terms, but does not allow for serial correlation among the errors.[8]

Parameters labled a_i and b_i in Figure 1 are stability coefficients for unemployment and crime, respectively. They measure the relative change, or lack of it, in the same variable across time. Parameters labeled d_i are cross-coefficients representing the effect of unemployment on crime, while those labeled e_i refer to the reciprocal effect of crime on unemployment. All coefficients are expected to be positive.

For both unemployment and crime, stability effects from $t-1$ to t are hypothesized to be significant. The volume of crime (or unemployment) at time t will be affected by the volume of crime (or unemployment) in the preceding year. Longer stability effects are not expected to contribute significantly to the fit between model and data.

With respect to the causal effect of unemployment on criminal involvement, we hypothesize strong instantaneous effects, that is, effects during the same year. Since unemployment reflects reduced levels of integration with conventional activities and the closing of legitimate opportunities, it should increase the level of criminal activity. Yet available theories do not suggest that unemployment at one age should have a strong effect on crime in later years unless there is continued unemployment. If unemployment at time t is followed by employment at $t + 1$, then the person's integration with conventional society is reestablished, a factor that should attenuate lagged effects from previous unemployment. Cook

---

[6] Six subjects are excluded from analysis because of extensive missing information on their employment histories. Seven subjects who report being incarcerated during the study period are also excluded since imprisonment is both an indicator of unemployment and a direct result of criminal involvement. Including the imprisoned subjects in the analysis did not alter results. Nevertheless, they are excluded and analysis is based on a total of 554 subjects.

[7] This is not a substantial problem for this analysis since Thornberry and Farnworth (1982) have demonstrated a substantial level of concordance for official and self-report measures for these subjects.

[8] The present data were tested with first-order, positive, serial correlation, which can be brought about by important excluded exogenous variables, measurement errors, or an improper functional form. The presence of serial correlation would cause overestimation of stability effects and underestimation of cross-coefficients (Kessler and Greenberg, 1981). Results indicate very little difference between the models with and without serial correlation. There were slight changes in the stability effects but virtually none in the cross-coefficients, the ones of major theoretical importance. Since results and substantive interpretations are not affected by serial correlation, it has been excluded from the present analysis.

UNEMPLOYMENT AND CRIMINAL INVOLVEMENT   403

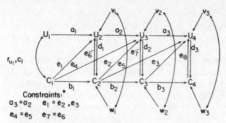

Constraints:*
$a_3 = a_2$ $e_1 = e_2, e_3$
$e_4 = e_5$ $e_7 = e_6$

* The term on the left is free to vary.
Figure 1. Reciprocal Causal Model of Unemployment and Crime

(1975:51) provides empirical evidence consistent with this specification. Thus, the link from unemployment to crime is represented by instantaneous effects.

For the reciprocal effect of crime on unemployment, current theories suggest that both instantaneous and lagged effects are of importance. Since criminal behavior reduces one's integration with conventional society, it should have an instantaneous positive effect on the likelihood of unemployment. Criminal behavior should also have lagged effects on unemployment since the attenuated integration with conventional society and the increased barriers to legitimate activities brought about by crime can have behavioral manifestations, such as unemployment, even without additional criminal involvement. This is in part due to a "criminal record" effect and is consistent with labeling theory's view that the criminal label is a "master status" (Becker, 1963). Thus, the present model specifies both instantaneous and lagged effects for the relationship from crime to unemployment.

Model Identification

The four-wave, two-variable model presented in Figure 1, generally described as a linear panel model, is reflective of a system of linear structural equations. For crime these structural equations are:

$$C_2 = b_1C_1 + d_1U_2 + w_1 \quad (1.1)$$
$$C_3 = b_2C_2 + d_2U_3 + w_2 \quad (1.2)$$
$$C_4 = b_3C_3 + d_3U_4 + w_3 \quad (1.3)$$

and for unemployment they are:

$$U_2 = a_1U_1 + e_6C_2 + e_1C_1 + v_1 \quad (2.1)$$
$$U_3 = a_2U_2 + e_7C_3 + e_2C_2 + e_4C_1 + v_2 \quad (2.2)$$
$$U_4 = a_3U_3 + e_8C_4 + e_3C_3 + e_5C_2 + v_3 \quad (2.3)$$

The problem of identification is that of finding enough empirical information to identify uniquely all parameters. For every parameter to be just identified, the same number of normal equations as there are parameters to estimate must be present (Kessler and

Greenberg:1981). Six parameters in equations (1.1), (1.2) and (1.3) are to be estimated (b's and d's), and in using U_1 and C_1 as instrumental variables six normal equations can be constructed. However, by the same process only six normal equations can be used in calculating the eleven parameters (a's and e's) presented in equations (2.1), (2.2) and (2.3). To identify the parameters in this model, therefore, at least five constraints, appropriately distributed in each wave of the model, are required.

Three types of constraints may be applied. First, a parameter may be fixed at a certain nonzero value, indicating that the actual value is known from the theoretical specification. Second, a parameter may be fixed at zero, a less restrictive assumption. Third, two or more parameters of the same type may be constrained to be equal, the least restrictive constraint available. The characteristic of interactive linear panel models that often leads to a problem of underidentification also leads to the plausibility of consistency constraints among parameters. Thus, consistency constraints have been placed on the following parameters: $a_3 = a_2$; $e_4 = e_5$; $e_1 = e_2, e_3$; and $e_7 = e_6$. If these constraints are too restrictive the goodness of fit statistics will reflect that fact. The model is estimated using LISREL (Jöreskog and Sörbom, 1981) since it allows for jointly dependent endogenous variables, equality constraints, and correlation among error terms, all of which are needed to estimate the model in Figure 1.

RESULTS

The central hypothesis of this study is that unemployment and crime are reciprocally related and that neither can be viewed entirely as a cause or an effect of the other. Figure 1 presented a theoretical model of the reciprocal relationship between these variables; Table 1 and Figure 2 present the empirically supported model.

Results indicate considerable support for the reciprocal effects predicted by the theoretical specification. Overall, there is an adequate fit of the model to these data. Although the chi-square goodness-of-fit statistic is significant ($\chi^2 = 38.49$, d.f. $= 14$, $p < .05$), this is not unexpected for large samples and should not be used as the final arbiter of fit. In such cases Wheaton et al. (1977:99) suggest examining the ratio of chi-square to degrees of freedom and both Bentler and Bonett (1980:591) and Long (1983:75) suggest comparing the expected and observed covariance matrices. Both criteria suggest acceptable fits for these data: the ratio of chi-square to degrees of freedom is 2.75 and the average difference between entries in the

Table 1. Effect Parameters for Reciprocal Model of Unemployment and Crime[a]

Relationship	Parameter	Unstandardized Coefficient	Standard Error	Standardized Coefficient
Unemployment Stability Coefficients	a_1	.621	.042	.559**
	a_2	.493	.043	.519**
	a_3	.493	.043	.523**
Crime Stability Coefficients	b_1	.287	.025	.472**
	b_2	.012	.058	.010
	b_3	.134	.049	.106**
Unemployment to Crime	d_1	.194	.105	.126*
	d_2	.685	.150	.351**
	d_3	1.261	.144	.485**
Crime to Unemployment	e_1	.062	.020	.157**
	e_2	.062	.020	.101**
	e_3	.062	.020	.128**
	e_4	.069	.010	.184**
	e_5	.069	.010	.119**
	e_6	−.021	.092	−.033
	e_7	−.021	.092	−.041
	e_8	.138	.063	.359**
Goodness of Fit	χ^2	38.49**		
	d.f.	14		
	χ^2/d.f.	2.75		
	n	544		

[a] For this model and the ones presented in the following tables, correlations among the residuals and the additional goodness-of-fit statistics are presented in the Appendix.

* $p < .10$.
** $p < .05$.

covariance matrices is .002 and between correlation matrices is .022.[9]

Stability Coefficients

Parameters labelled a_i (Figure 1 and Table 1) estimate the stability effects for unemployment and all three are significant. The level of unemployment at time t−1 affects the level of unemployment at t. The b_i coefficients estimate the stability effects for crime, and in this case two of the three effects are significant. Moreover, the magnitude of the stability coefficients for crime drops considerably over time; the standardized coefficient for b_1 is .472, for b_2 it is .010 (n.s.), and for b_3 it is .106. Thus, the lagged endogenous value of crime appears to be age-specific, declining in magnitude over

[9] Other goodness-of-fit indicators, such as the coefficients of determination, adjusted goodness-of-fit index and root mean square residual have recently been developed for LISREL. These values are presented in Table A-1 but not discussed in the text since the distributions for these statistics are unknown. As such, they are best used to indicate model weakness but not to gauge the goodness of fit of the model. The more familiar chi-square test, with its known distribution, and differences in the covariance and correlation matrices are relied upon to assess goodness of fit.

time. Such a finding suggests that the variance in criminality is increasing as these subjects mature.

Cross-Coefficients

Traditional criminological theory posits a strong instantaneous effect from unemployment to crime. This specification is supported by the data since all first-order derivatives for lagged coefficients are close to zero, indicating that the relationship from unemployment to crime is adequately expressed by the instantaneous paths. The three instantaneous parameters, d_1 to d_3, are positive, as expected, but the effect of unemployment on crime is neither as consistent nor as strong as traditional theories would predict. The first parameter, d_1,

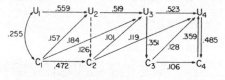

Figure 2. Significant Effects for Reciprocal Model of Unemployment and Crime (Standardized Regression Coefficients)

Table A-1. Ancillary Statistics for Estimated Models

	Correlations Between Exogenous Variables and Between Residuals						
		Delinquency Status		Race		Social Status	
						Blue Collar	White Collar
	Total	Delinquent	Nondelinquent	Black	White	Blue Collar	White Collar
r_{u1c1}	.255**	.285**	.227**	.089	.361**	.198**	.551**
r_{v1w1}	−.035	.138	−.273**	−.143	−.139	−.190	.009
r_{v2w2}	−.193	−.271	−.269	−.589	−.062	−.232	−.883**
r_{v3w3}	−.408**	−.292*	−.667**	−.486*	−.693**	−.342**	−.953**
	Goodness-of-Fit Indicators[a]						
R^2	.292	.245	.557	.688	.285	.356	.636
Adjusted Goodness-of-Fit Index	.852	.067	.843	.806	.643	.768	.461
Root Mean Square Residual	.003	.005	.003	.013	.003	.005	.003

[a] Distributions for these statistics are not available.
* Significant at .10.
** Significant at .05.

is only significant at the .10 level[10] (t = 1.852), and, overall, the parameters increase substantially with age: d_1 = .126, d_2 = .351 and d_3 = .485. Thus, while unemployment does have an instantaneous effect on criminal involvement, the effect is more age-specific than anticipated.

The reciprocal relationship from crime to unemployment appears to operate primarily through lagged effects. All five lagged coefficients are significant while only the last instantaneous effect attains significance. Although the observation that the reciprocal effect is primarily a lagged one is of interest, the most important conclusion is the more general one: these data offer strong support for a causal link from crime to unemployment. Figure 2 indicates that the level of unemployment at time t is dependent upon the level of unemployment at t−1 and also the level of criminal involvement at t−2, t−1 and, for the last wave, at time t.

Table A-1 presents correlations among the residuals; only one correlation is significant (r_{v3w3} = −.408) and the other two are quite small. Although these correlations do not suggest major problems of misspecification, they point to the possibility that excluded variables may well have a significant impact on these variables. This is not an unexpected outcome given our decision to highlight the appropriateness of reciprocal models by concentrating on only two variables.

Summary

These results suggest strong support for a reciprocal model of crime and unemployment.

[10] Significant effects at both the .05 and .10 levels are reported since reciprocal causal structures have not been frequently specified or tested in the past.

Instantaneous effects from unemployment to crime are present, albeit not as consistently as anticipated given the unidirectional focus of traditional theory. On the other hand, the reciprocal effect from criminal involvement to unemployment is strong and consistent, as indicated by one significant instantaneous, and all significant lagged effects. It appears, therefore, that unemployment exerts a rather immediate effect on criminal involvement, while criminal involvement exerts a more long-range effect on unemployment.

CONTROLLING FOR OTHER VARIABLES

Results of the linear panel analysis provide support for a reciprocal relationship between unemployment and criminal involvement for males during the early adult years. Analysis now examines whether a reciprocal relationship is also observed for major demographic and social subgroups. Juvenile delinquency, race, and social status of origin, important correlates of both employment status and adult criminality, are held constant while the theoretical model presented in Figure 1 is reestimated. In general, the fit of the model is much better for less socially advantaged groups— delinquents, blacks and subjects from blue-collar backgrounds—than it is for more-advantaged groups—nondelinquents, whites and subjects from white-collar backgrounds.

Less-Advantaged Groups

Results for delinquent, black and blue-collar subjects are presented in Table 2 and Figure 3. Goodness-of-fit statistics suggest a close fit between the model and the data for these groups. Each of the chi-square values is rela-

Table 2. Standardized Effect Parameters for Reciprocal Model of Unemployment and Crime for Less-Advantaged Subjects[a]

Relationship	Parameter	Delinquent	Black	Blue-Collar Family
Unemployment Stability Coefficients	a_1	.489**	.718**	.589**
	a_2	.546**	.434**	.539**
	a_3	.609**	.448**	.568**
Crime Stability Coefficients	b_1	.544**	.416**	.446**
	b_2	−.094	−.041	.081
	b_3	.147**	.044	.165**
Unemployment to Crime	d_1	−.167	.078	.079
	d_2	.419**	.461**	.207**
	d_3	.568**	.557**	.522**
Crime to Unemployment	e_1	.193**	.111	.054
	e_2	.102**	.080	.032
	e_3	.140**	.141	.031
	e_4	.177**	.157**	.187**
	e_5	.104**	.118**	.118**
	e_6	−.050	.145	.193
	e_7	−.061	.246	.177
	e_8	.257	.650*	.295*
Goodness-of-Fit Statistics	χ^2	34.97**	8.63	21.96*
	d.f.	14	14	14
	χ^2/d.f.	2.50	.62	1.57
	n	166	108	343

[a] Unstandardized coefficients and standard errors are available on request.
* $p < .10$.
** $p < .05$.

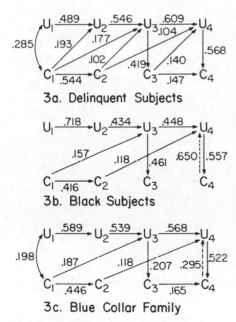

3a. Delinquent Subjects

3b. Black Subjects

3c. Blue Collar Family

⟶ $p < .05$ ---⟶ $p < .10$

Figure 3. Significant Effects for Reciprocal Model of Unemployment and Crime, Less-Advantaged Groups (Standardized Regression Coefficients)

tively low: for blacks it does not attain statistical significance, and for blue-collar subjects it is significant only at the .10 level. Ratios of chi-square to degrees of freedom are also low, ranging from .62 to 2.50, and other goodness-of-fit statistics are acceptable. Overall, it appears that the theoretical model provides a reasonable reflection of the relationship between unemployment and crime for groups with the highest incidence of these behavioral patterns.

Significant effects for these groups are displayed in Figure 3 and, in general, these models are similar to the model based on all subjects. Stability effects for unemployment are significant for all three groups. For crime, the stability effects are considerably weaker, which is also true in the total model. For blacks, only the effect from time 1 to time 2 is significant, while for delinquent and blue-collar subjects the first and third effects attain significance, but with decreasing magnitudes.

As compared to the total model, the effect of unemployment on crime for these groups is more pronounced during the later time periods. The instantaneous effect is not significant at time 2 but attains significance at each of the last two periods. Moreover, the magnitude of the effect becomes stronger at the older ages.

The reciprocal effect from crime to unemployment varies somewhat from group to group but, as was the case with the total sample, is primarily evident in the lagged effects

UNEMPLOYMENT AND CRIMINAL INVOLVEMENT

Table 3. Standardized Effect Parameters for Reciprocal Model of Unemployment and Crime for More-Advantaged Subjects[a]

Relationship	Parameter	Nondelinquent	White	White-Collar Family
Unemployment Stability Coefficients	a_1	.551**	.356**	.410**
	a_2	.444**	.511**	.334**
	a_3	.413**	.486**	.325**
Crime Stability Coefficients	b_1	.395**	.491**	.761**
	b_2	.183**	.124**	−.225**
	b_3	−.036	.100**	.103
Unemployment to Crime	d_1	.365**	.193	−.004
	d_2	.264**	.097	.862**
	d_3	.423**	.238**	.290**
Crime to Unemployment	e_1	.157**	.145	.106**
	e_2	.127**	.085	.089**
	e_3	.138**	.065	.203**
	e_4	.168**	.200**	.224**
	e_5	.126**	.111**	.183**
	e_6	.125	.014	.077
	e_7	.146	.012	.180
	e_8	.650**	.636**	.986**
Goodness-of-Fit Statistics	χ^2	82.97**	97.29**	79.26**
	d.f.	14	14	14
	χ^2/d.f.	5.93	6.95	5.66
	n	388	446	211

[a] Unstandardized coefficients and standard errors are available on request.
* $p < .10$.
** $p < .05$.

and the instantaneous effect at the last time period. For delinquents, both one- and two-year lagged effects are significant, while for blacks and blue-collar subjects, the last instantaneous effect and the two-year lagged effects attain significance. Thus, while the timing of the effect from crime to unemployment varies somewhat across groups, significant effects from crime to unemployment still operate in all three groups.

More-Advantaged Groups

Results for more-advantaged groups—nondelinquents, whites, and subjects from white-collar backgrounds—represent the largest departure from the theoretical model. Goodness-of-fit statistics are presented in Table 3; chi-square values are significant and the ratios of chi-square to degrees of freedom are high. Overall, the fit of the model for these groups is poor. Given these results, effect parameters are presented, but they must be interpreted with appropriate caution.[11]

Although the fit of the model is poor for these groups, the pattern of significant effect parameters (Figure 4) is quite similar to the one already observed for the total sample and

[11] Given these results, models that allowed for serial auto-correlation among the error terms were estimated but they did not improve the fit.

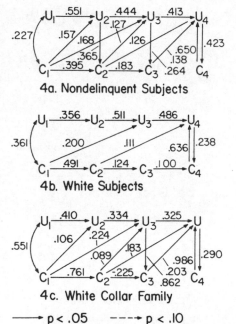

4a. Nondelinquent Subjects

4b. White Subjects

4c. White Collar Family

⟶ p < .05   ---⟶ p < .10

Figure 4. Significant Effects for Reciprocal Model of Unemployment and Crime, More-Advantaged Groups (Standardized Regression Coefficients)

less-advantaged groups. The instantaneous effects from unemployment to crime are stronger at later periods and the reciprocal relationship from crime to unemployment is primarily evident in lagged effects and the instantaneous effect at the last period.

Summary

Holding constant race, status of origin and delinquency has resulted in one major difference in the results. Namely, the theoretical model presented in Figure 1 is more appropriate for less-advantaged groups than for more-advantaged groups. Indeed, the fit for more-advantaged groups is poor, while the fit for the less-advantaged groups, where there is considerably more variation in both unemployment and criminal involvement, is quite strong.

Although results vary by social background, effect parameters do not suggest major departures from either the structure of the theoretical model (Figure 1) or the empirically supported model for all subjects (Figure 2). In each model presented in this section there are significant effects from unemployment to crime and significant effects from crime to unemployment.

DISCUSSION AND CONCLUSION

Contemporary theories of criminal involvement are unidirectional in structure. Based on the premise that various social factors, among them unemployment, cause criminal behavior, they ignore the reciprocal possibility that crime causally influences those factors. Consistent with this approach, traditional theories interpret significant relationships between social factors and crime as evidence of the unidirectional causal influence of those factors on criminal involvement, despite the fact that alternative interpretations are equally plausible.

The central thesis of this paper is that such a perspective is too limited to model the causal processes actually at work. A more accurate reflection of these processes is a reciprocal one in which criminal involvement and a variety of other process variables mutually influence one another over time. To examine the plausibility of this approach the present article investigated the relationship between crime and one other variable, unemployment, and attempted to "decompose" the correlation between them into its reciprocal causal components.

Results offer strong support for a reciprocal model of crime causation. Consistent with our theoretical specification, unemployment has significant instantaneous effects on crime and

crime has significant effects, primarily lagged effects, on unemployment. Moreover, unidirectional models from unemployment to crime and from crime to unemployment were estimated and in neither case could an adequate fit be obtained. Chi-square statistics are well over one hundred and first-order derivatives indicate that reciprocal effects, such as the ones modeled here, are required to attain an acceptable fit. (Results not presented.) This finding is not anticipated by traditional, unidirectional theories of criminal involvement and underscores the pitfalls of imputing directionality on the basis of recursive relationships.

These results suggest, therefore, that the development of reciprocal models of criminal involvement incorporating additional variables may be quite fruitful. Two prefatory points to that development can be discussed. The first concerns the identification of variables likely to be reciprocally influenced by criminal activity, and the second concerns the role of structural variables in reciprocal models.

At the outset it should be noted that reciprocal structures are logically consistent with etiological theories of crime causation such as social control, strain, and other models. Indeed, as indicated earlier, reciprocal relationships can easily be incorporated into these models and tend to enhance rather than reduce their face validity. Thus, developing more refined theoretical models by considering additional reciprocal relationships is logically acceptable and, if present results are replicated when analysis is extended to other variables, necessary.

Many of the central causal variables in criminological theories, such as attachment to parents, success in school, choice of delinquent peers, beliefs about conventional values, aspirations toward and success in the occupational realm, and so forth, are processual.[12] Indeed, it is precisely the processual nature of these variables that is used to explain the initiation and maintenance of criminal behavior. As attachment to parents weakens, as success in school deteriorates, etc., delinquent conduct is likely to follow.

Thus, criminological theory relies upon the mutability of these variables to explain crimi-

---

[12] Process variables are defined by their interactional nature; their values and saliency change over the person's life cycle as they are influenced by other variables. They are distinguished from structural variables which are relatively unchanging statuses of the person. See also Rosenberg's (1968:14–16) distinction between property variables and dispositional variables.

UNEMPLOYMENT AND CRIMINAL INVOLVEMENT   409

nal conduct. Having recognized their mutability, however, criminological theory has failed to examine systematically the manner in which criminal involvement influences these variables. It has also failed to examine, therefore, how criminal involvement and these variables mutually influence one another to produce either higher or lower rates of criminal activity. Such a failing is puzzling since it seems self-evident to assert that criminal involvement, especially prolonged criminal involvement, influences relationships with parents, success in school, choice of delinquent peers and the like. Nevertheless, criminological theory has yet to examine these relationships systematically and the present findings suggest it may well be wise to do so.

Present results also suggest the importance of including structural variables in a reciprocal model of criminal involvement. Age, for example, specified the effect of unemployment on criminal involvement, with the relationship becoming stronger at later ages. It would appear, therefore, that as employment becomes more salient, following the completion of school and likely changes in marital status, position in the employment sector has greater consequences in other behavioral realms such as criminal involvement. Such a view is consistent with a developmental theory of crime (Elliott et al., 1979; Elliott et al., 1982), and suggests that the salient *causes and consequences* of criminal involvement will vary with age.

The varying salience of these variables over time also suggests that the reciprocal model presented in Figure 1 is somewhat misleading. That model is an amplifying one; the two variables are positively related and therefore amplify one another over time, an inherently unstable situation (Heise, 1975). If reciprocal relationships vary in salience over time, however, other process variables, e.g., educational success or family patterns, can alter the relationship between the two initial variables. Thus, the amplifying structure of Figure 1 is produced somewhat artificially since only two variables, taken out of the more general interactive context in which they operate, have been considered in this illustrative investigation.

Finally, the better fit of the model for less-advantaged groups can be discussed. Although this outcome was not anticipated in the model specification, it is not inconsistent with the theoretical perspectives used in the specification. In control theory, for example, if it is assumed that persons with weak bonds in one element, e.g., commitment, have weak bonds in other elements (Wiatrowski et al., 1981), then the stronger relationship between unemployment and crime observed for these groups is interpretable. In essence, other elements of the bond are too weak to reduce the reciprocal impact of increased unemployment or increased criminal involvement for these subjects. For more-advantaged subjects, however, other elements of the bond may well be strong enough to serve as buffers to reduce the effect of failings in any one area. According to strain theory, less-advantaged subjects may be particularly vulnerable to such reciprocal effects precisely since they are, relative to more-advantaged subjects, ill prepared to succeed in the legitimate opportunity structure. Indeed, it is their tenuous hold on legitimate avenues to success that renders them vulnerable to increased levels of unemployment and crime, in the first place, and in turn, to the feedback effects of each variable on the other (see Anderson, 1976).

If this or a similar process is actually at work it highlights the necessity of incorporating structural variables into a complete theory of criminal involvement. Structural variables would appear to affect both initial values of the process variables as well as their interaction over time.

Although inclusion of developmental and structural variables is clearly required in a complete interactional theory, their absence should not detract from the basic finding of this investigation. Namely, for at least the variables of unemployment and criminal involvement, a reciprocal causal structure is more appropriate than a traditional, unidirectional one. Crime does not appear to be a simple product of unemployment; rather, these two variables appear to influence one another mutually over time. If this basic finding is replicated when analysis is extended to other variables then the structure of criminological theory will require substantial revision. Criminal behavior can no longer be viewed as an outcome of social processes; it would have to be viewed as an integral part of those processes, influenced by but also influencing other variables over the person's life span.

REFERENCES

Anderson, Elijah
  1976   A Place on the Corner. Chicago: University of Chicago Press.
Becker, Howard
  1963   Outsiders. New York: Free Press.
Bentler, P. M. and Douglas G. Bonett
  1980   "Significance tests and goodness-of-fit in the analysis of covariance structures." Psychological Bulletin 88:588–606.

Cloward, Richard A. and Lloyd E. Ohlin
1960 Delinquency and Opportunity: A Theory of Delinquent Gangs. Glencoe: Free Press.
Cohen, Albert K.
1955 Delinquent Boys: The Culture of the Gang. Glencoe: Free Press.
Cook, Phillip J.
1975 "The correctional carrot: better jobs for parolees." Policy Analysis 1:11–34.
Davis, James R.
1983 "The relation between crime and unemployment—an econometric model." Paper presented at the annual meetings of the American Society of Criminology.
Ehrlich, Isaac
1973 "Participation in illegitimate activities: a theoretical and empirical investigation." Journal of Political Economy 81:521–65.
Elliott, Delbert S.
1978 "Delinquency and school dropout." Pp. 453–69 in Leonard D. Savitz and Norman Johnston (eds.), Crime in Society. New York: Wiley.
Elliott, Delbert S., Suzanne S. Ageton and Rachelle J. Canter
1979 "An integrated theoretical perspective on delinquent behavior." Journal of Research in Crime and Delinquency 16:3–27.
Elliott, Delbert S., David Huizinga and Suzanne S. Ageton
1982 Explaining Delinquency and Drug Use. The National Youth Survey, Project Report No. 21. Boulder, CO: Behavioral Research Institute.
Elliott, Delbert S. and Harwin Voss
1974 Delinquency and Dropout. Lexington, MA: D.C. Heath.
Ginsberg, Irving J. and James R. Greenley
1978 "Competing theories of marijuana use: a longitudinal study." Journal of Health and Social Behavior 19:22–34.
Glaser, Daniel
1964 The Effectiveness of a Prison and Parole System. Indianapolis: Bobbs-Merrill.
Glaser, Daniel and Kent Rice
1959 "Crime, age and employment." American Sociological Review 24:679–86.
Greenberg, David F. and Ronald C. Kessler
1981 "Panel models in criminology." In James Fox (ed.), Mathematical Frontiers in Criminology. New York: Academic Press.
Hanushek, Eric A. and John E. Jackson
1977 Statistical Methods for Social Scientists. New York: Academic Press.
Heise, David R.
1975 Causal Analysis. New York: Wiley.
Hirschi, Travis
1969 Causes of Delinquency. Berkeley: University of California Press.
Johnson, Richard E.
1979 Juvenile Delinquency and Its Origins. Cambridge: Cambridge University Press.
Jöreskog, Karl G. and Dag Sörbom
1981 LISREL V: Analysis of Linear Structural Relationships by the Method of Maximum Likelihood. Chicago: National Education Resources.

Kessler, Ronald C. and David F. Greenberg
1981 Linear Panel Analysis: Models of Quantitative Change. New York: Academic Press.
Kornhauser, Ruth R.
1978 Social Sources of Delinquency. Chicago: University of Chicago Press.
Lemert, Edwin M.
1967 Human Deviance, Social Problems, and Social Control. Englewood Cliffs, NJ: Prentice-Hall.
Long, J. Scott
1983 Covariance Structure Models: An Introduction to LISREL. Beverly Hills: Sage.
Matza, David
1969 Becoming Deviant. Englewood Cliffs, NJ: Prentice-Hall.
Merton, Robert K.
1957 Social Theory and Social Structure. Glencoe: Free Press.
Orsagh, Thomas and Ann D. Witte
1981 "Economic status and crime: implications for offender rehabilitation." Journal of Criminal Law and Criminology 72:1055–71.
Paternoster, Raymond, Linda E. Saltzman, Theodore G. Chiricos and Gordon P. Waldo
1982 "Perceived risk and deterrence: methodological artifacts in perceptual deterrence research." Journal of Criminal Law and Criminology 73:1238–58.
Paternoster, Raymond, Linda E. Saltzman, Gordon P. Waldo and Theodore G. Chiricos
1983 "Perceived risk and social control: do sanctions really deter?" Law and Society Review 17:457–79.
Pownall, G. A.
1969 Employment Problems of Released Offenders. Washington, D.C.: U.S. Department of Labor.
Rosenberg, Morris
1968 The Logic of Survey Analysis. New York: Basic Books.
Schwartz, Richard and Jerome H. Skolnick
1962 "Two studies in legal stigma." Social Problems 10:133–42.
Shannon, Lyle W.
1982 "Assessing the relationship of adult careers to juvenile careers: a summary." Washington, D.C.: U.S. Department of Justice.
Sickles, Robin C., Peter Schmidt and Ann D. Witte
1979 "An application of the simultaneous Tobit model: a study of the determinants of criminal recidivism." Journal of Economics and Business 31:166–71.
Singer, Simon I.
1977 "The effect of non-response on the birth cohort follow-up survey." Unpublished. Center for Studies in Criminology and Criminal Law, University of Pennsylvania.
Thornberry, Terence P. and Margaret Farnworth
1982 "Social correlates of criminal involvement: further evidence of the relationship between social status and criminal behavior." American Sociological Review 47:505–18.
Weis, Joseph G. and John Sederstrom
1981 The Prevention of Serious Delinquency: What to Do? Washington, D.C.: U.S. Department of Justice.

UNEMPLOYMENT AND CRIMINAL INVOLVEMENT   411

Wheaton, Blair, Bengt Muthen, Duane F. Alwin and
    Gene F. Summers
  1977   "Assessing reliability and stability in panel
         models." Pp. 84–136 in David Heise (ed.),
         Sociological Methodology 1977. San Fran-
         cisco: Jossey-Bass.
Wiatrowski, Michael D., David B. Griswold and
    Mary K. Roberts
  1981   "Social control theory and delinquency."
         American Sociological Review 46:525–41.

Wolfgang, Marvin E., Robert M. Figlio and Thorsten
    Sellin
  1972   Delinquency in a Birth Cohort. Chicago:
         University of Chicago Press.

Wolfgang, Marvin E., Terence P. Thornberry and
    Robert M. Figlio
  forth- From Boy to Man—From Delinquency to
  com-   Crime: Follow-up to the Philadelphia Birth
  ing   Cohort of 1945.

Part IV
Statistics of Criminal Justice

New Society 2 January 1975

Severe sentences: no deterrent to crime?

Robert Baxter and Chris Nuttall

Can a severe sentence on an individual deter others from crime? A survey of one case shows that special police measures have more effect.

The idea of general deterrence—the belief that people will not commit an offence because of fear of punishment—has an important place in criminal justice. It also attracts strong support from many members of the judiciary and the general public. There are frequent demands for its efficacy to be measured by research, but this would create enormous difficulties. So, using a small-scale study, we have tested one particular proposition about general deterrence that is sometimes advanced—the idea that individual sentences can deter criminal activity.

During 1972, mugging—ie, attacks on, and robberies from, individuals in the open—attracted much public anxiety. There was concern that, in some of the major cities in England, this crime was running at a significantly higher level than in previous years and both MPs and the press reflected public disquiet. The Home Office consulted chief constables and later issued an advisory circular to them on the problem. By late 1972, the police forces in the most seriously affected cities had already started to take special measures, and in March 1973 a dramatic decision came from the judiciary when the Crown Court in Birmingham sentenced Paul Storey, a 16 year old youth, to 20 years' detention while his two accomplices got ten years. Storey was charged with attempted murder and robbery, but the offence was popularly seen as mugging. It produced banner headlines in most national papers such as "Twenty years for the mugger aged 16" (*Sun*) and "Boy of 16 gets 20 years for mugging" (*Guardian*). The court decision attracted enormous publicity from press and television—indeed it was probably one of the most publicised sentences in recent years.

Though the sentence was seen in many quarters as being intended to have a deterrent effect, the trial judge, Mr Justice Croom-Johnson, made it clear in passing the sentence that he was primarily concerned with individual factors, as was the Court of Appeal. Lord Chief Justice Widgery, commenting on the offenders, said: "No trace of mental illness is discoverable in any of these three young men, and absolutely no kind of motivation or reason at all in their background, history or any other source is to be found. If they can do acts of this kind in those circumstances once, obviously there is a danger they will do them with equal lack of excuse again, and the safety of the public and the protection of the public from similar incidents is a factor which has to be in the forefront of the sentencing exercise." He went on to discuss at length the problem of predicting the future behaviour of the offenders, especially Storey; and expressed his view, in confirming the sentence, that 20 years was justifiable on the understanding that the Home Secretary would consider the possibility of early release. He also expressed the hope that the Home Secretary would not feel bound by the practice, normal in adult cases, of reviewing the possibility of release only after one third of the sentence had been served. The Home Office gave the court an assurance on this point.

Despite the judges' views, the sentence was widely presented to the public by the press as an exemplary sentence which was meant to have a general deterrent effect. Some members of parliament and representatives of the police saw it in this light and their views were publicised. The *Daily Mirror* headlined such a view from a spokesman for the Police Federation; and the *Daily Mail* reported similar views from a police officer ("If this doesn't frighten them, nothing will") and from a member of parliament ("We must have sentences of this sort to strike real fear into the young thugs and criminals"). In an editorial under the headline "A terrible deterrent," the *Mail* went on to comment that, "Only as a deterrent can society contemplate such terrible punishment. Mugging, the trendy term for a crime as old as sin itself, is in vogue with young thugs. The law should make it known, by every propaganda means at its disposal, that deterrent sentences are in vogue too." The *Daily Telegraph* adopted a similar attitude in its editorial. Virtually every newspaper, from the *Financial Times* and the *Guardian* to the *Daily Mirror* and the *Sun*, headlined the 20 year sentence for mugging. From the terms used, the 20 year sentence was obviously presented as a *general*, rather than an *individual* deterrent.

If the sentence was effective as a general deterrent, one would expect the mugging rate to decline after the trial. Because of the publicity, the impact might reasonably be expected to be immediate, even if it declined after memory of it faded from people's minds. Judging from the public concern at the time, the mugging rate was popularly supposed to be running at a high level (interestingly the level of robbery offences in 1973 was below that of 1972—in some cases the drop was very substantial). However, no matter what was happening to the rate before the trial, one might anticipate that it would drop significantly after the sentence on 19 March 1973 and perhaps rise again as the effects of the sentence began to wear off. It was to find out whether this did happen that we examined the robbery rate for 1972 and 1973.

No satisfactory definition of mugging exists and as the Home Office police department's request for information in October 1972 had produced figures from chief constables based on differing definitions of the crime, the only way of obtaining consistent information was to collect figures of offences categorised as "robbery or assault with intent to rob." This created the problems that crimes other than mugging were included within the category, but the benefit of having comparative and reliable figures seemed reasonable compensation.

Mugging is generally regarded as a youthful exer-

Robert Baxter and Chris Nuttall are research officers in the Home Office

New Society 2 January 1975

Sentencing as a deterrent: number of robberies by week, 1972–73

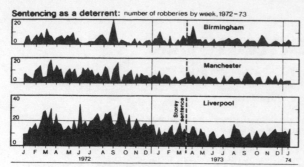

cise; around half of all offences in the robbery category are committed by people under 21, and around three quarters by people under 25. Information was sought only from the large, completely urban police areas outside London as the offence is almost entirely a city crime. Six authorities were approached—Birmingham, Bristol, Liverpool and Bootle, Manchester and Salford, Sheffield and Rotherham, and the West Midlands. Leeds and the two London forces were not included because of problems in collecting data. The information which was obtained—a weekly breakdown of the offences reported for 1972 and 1973—showed that only in Liverpool and possibly in Manchester were there sufficient numbers to suggest that the comparative incidence of this offence was exceptionally high.

Although the 20 year detention sentence was passed in Birmingham as a result of a crime there, that city's robbery rate remained relatively low throughout the two relevant years (the average number of robberies was 4.8 a week in 1972 and 4.4 a week in 1973). The neighbouring West Midlands police area, with weekly averages of 4.0 for 1972 and 2.4 for 1973, and Sheffield, whose weekly averages for 1972 and 1973 were 2.3 and 2.0 respectively, experienced similarly low offence rates. In Bristol, the numbers of such crimes were also very low (less than 1.3 in 1972 and 1.0 in 1973).

In none of the police areas studied did the sentence have the anticipated impact on the number of reported robberies. In Birmingham, where the original offence was committed and the sentence passed, the pattern in the offence rate continued uninterrupted—the number of offences had already started to rise and reached a peak a few weeks after the trial (see figure 1). This is similar to the two previous peaks, which also lasted about five weeks. In Manchester there was no particular pattern (see figure 2). The offence rate had begun to increase shortly before the sentence, as it had in Birmingham, and it continued to do so afterwards though it remained below the level of January 1973. The level remained constant in Liverpool (figure 3) and, again, does not seem to have been influenced by the sentence.

Lack of any apparent general deterrent effect of severe sentences was predictable from various studies carried out in both Europe and the United States. In his research, *Deterrents and Incentives to Crime among Boys and Young Men aged 15-21 years*, H. D. Willcock found that punishment for an offence was rated only fourth by his respondents as a consequence of committing a crime. Ten per cent placed it first, whereas 49 per cent thought that the reaction of their family would be their

chief worry. Professor Johannes Andenaes said in his historical review (*The General Preventive Effects of Punishment*) that fear of apprehension was considerably more important as a deterrent than any possible punishment. Indeed, the California Assembly Committee on Criminal Procedure has taken the same view, remarking that "there is no evidence that more severe penalties deter crime more effectively than less severe penalties" and that "we can find no evidence that crime can be reduced by increasing time served." The committee agreed with the view that the severity of punishment was less significant as a deterrent to crime than the certainty of detection. This opinion was shared by some members of the British police with regard to mugging.

One chief constable pointed out the effect on deterrence of the low risk of apprehension, when he responded to Home Office inquiries about the problem in his city. He remarked that muggers did not have to be very bright to realise how low the chances of detection were and that only an obvious police presence was likely to deter them. This is quite a serious objection to the imposition of deterrent sentences and it was made in November 1972 —some months in advance of Storey's trial. The robbery rate in this chief constable's area was very high; and he put down the low detection rate of around 26 per cent to factors such as the surprise nature of an attack, the darkness making identification by the victim difficult, and the random element brought about by the attacks being motivated by hooliganism. It was hard for the police to obtain reliable evidence that would lead to an improvement in detection, but it was open to them to take preventive steps.

By March 1973, several police forces had already began to take measures in this direction. The Liverpool police force estimated that the monthly average for mugging in their area had risen from 78 for July to December 1971, to 130 for January to June 1972. They noted that this coincided with a substantial growth in all recorded crime during the blackouts caused by the electricity power cuts during the industrial conflict early in 1972. The power cuts may well have aided criminal activity but, at least with regard to robbery, the association between visibility and the crime rate did not last long. The rate continued at a high level throughout the summer and began to fall in autumn, despite the darker evenings. The Liverpool police were fairly specific in the information they gave about the measures they introduced to combat mugging. On 1 August 1972 a number of special patrols were set up, divisional commanders were encouraged to take action, and a crime prevention campaign was begun. The Manchester police also reported that they had introduced special measures, such as plain clothes patrols, during 1972 (though they gave no exact date). In Birmingham, similar changes were introduced, including uniformed and plain clothes patrols sometimes using dogs (again, no exact date was given).

Although the trial of Storey in March 1973 had no apparent impact on the level of robbery offences, there was a significant change (in Liverpool and Manchester, at least) in this rate during the two year period. In Liverpool it began to drop substantially in October 1972, the decline accelerated during December 1972 and early January 1973; and the rate remained reasonably level thereafter. Once the offence rate had stabilised early in 1973, there were few significant variations in it. Manchester bears some similarity to Liverpool, though

New Society 2 January 1975

the crime rate was substantially lower in both years. The level began to fall slightly in late September 1972 and again at the end of January 1973; and the overall decline from 1972 to 1973 was of a similar proportion to Liverpool. The rate was 44 per cent lower in 1973 than in 1972 in Manchester while it was 43 per cent lower in Liverpool. The pattern in Birmingham differs from the two northern cities. This was partly because the robbery rate was never as serious and partly because it did not fall substantially in 1973—the decline was only 12 per cent below 1972. Apart from an undulating pattern, there does not seem to be anything particularly remarkable in the movement of the robbery level in Birmingham.

It is difficult to measure the impact (if any) of a single deterrent sentence and the problem must be approached cautiously. When we looked more closely at Liverpool, however, and divided the two year period into three parts at 1 August 1972 (the date when special police measures were introduced) and at 19 March 1973 (the date of the Storey sentence), the offence rate showed a very clear pattern. It was rising slightly between the beginning of the year and 1 August 1972; it then fell sharply, and after the court sentence remained level. Analysis established a remarkably close statistical relationship between the introduction of police measures and the decline in the offence rate and also demonstrated that the court sentence had no statistical impact at all.

Judging from when the crime rate did begin to fall in Liverpool and Manchester in the autumn of 1972, it looks as though the chief constable of Liverpool was right when he commented, in November 1972, that: "Recent figures show a slight reduction for robbery offences but this is probably due to increased police activity rather than the publicity given to certain recent sentences." His opinion seems supported by the probability that if the sentences had had an impact, there would have been a decline at that time in all the cities we looked at, and not just in Liverpool and Manchester. It is interesting to note that the police forces of Birmingham, Liverpool and Manchester told the Home Office in November 1972 that they had already introduced special measures to combat mugging; and that by the time the Home Office circular was issued on 1 May 1973 to encourage police measures in this field, the crisis had already passed.

The sentence given to Storey was not intended by the courts to be exemplary or to operate as a general deterrent. It is apparent from our study, however, that the employment of a severe sentence as a general deterrent is of questionable use. Storey's sentence appears not to have had any effect on the rate of robbery, as other research such as the work of the California Assembly Committee on Criminal Procedure might have led us to expect. There is no evidence in our study that the sentence had any impact at all; but a strong suggestion that the police measures did.

[18]

BRIT. J. CRIMINOL. Vol. 21 No. 2 APRIL 1981

POLICE CAUTIONING OF JUVENILES IN LONDON

DAVID P. FARRINGTON AND TREVOR BENNETT (*Cambridge*)*

Unresolved Questions about Police Cautions

THE last 15 years have seen a marked change in the official processing of juvenile offenders, as more and more have been officially cautioned. This development has not been produced by any change in the law, but by changes in police policies for dealing with juvenile offenders. The implementation in 1971 of most of the Children and Young Persons Act 1969 had a relatively small and transitory effect on the trends in cautions and findings of guilt of juveniles (see Farrington, 1980, pp. 275–276). It is true that this Act gave statutory recognition to police cautioning (in the non-implemented s. 5), and that the introduction of police cautioning schemes was influenced by the two White Papers which preceded it (Home Office, 1965, 1968). Nevertheless, the change in official processing has been produced by the police (albeit under Home Office instructions) rather than by the law.

Two key questions pertinent to this change in police policy are as follows:

(1) After a police force introduces a cautioning (or juvenile bureau) scheme, to what extent do recorded cautions replace court appearances, and to what extent do they replace unrecorded warnings? In other words, does the police caution divert juveniles who would previously have been taken to court, or does it widen the net and drag juveniles into the official processing system who would previously have escaped it? (or does it do both?)

(2) What are the relative effects of recorded cautions, findings of guilt and unrecorded warnings (*e.g.* on recidivism)?

There has been little research on these questions. In what is probably the major study of cautioning, Ditchfield (1976) raised the first question, and concluded (p. 8): " There seems little doubt that increased cautioning has diverted substantial numbers of juvenile offenders from court appearance. For example, only 24,256 children aged 10–13 were found guilty at court in 1973, compared with 30,029 in 1968, this despite an undoubted increase in juvenile offending in this period . . . The number found guilty at court in the 14–16 age group rose from 63,392 to 83,616 in 1974, but here again there is reason to believe that a large proportion of offenders in this age group have been diverted from court proceedings ". Ditchfield presented no evidence to support his assertion about an undoubted increase in juvenile offending. In support of his assertion that a large proportion of offenders aged 14–16 were being diverted, he pointed out that the proportion of disposals which were discharges had decreased, and concluded that some of the more minor offenders had been removed from court proceedings. An alternative interpretation is that one effect of increasing official cautions was that juveniles appearing in court for the first time had an increasing tendency to have

* Respectively lecturer and senior research associate, Institute of Criminology, University of Cambridge.

DAVID P. FARRINGTON AND TREVOR BENNETT

previous cautions, therefore tending not to be treated as first offenders, and therefore tending not to be discharged.

Ditchfield also pointed out that, considering all the different police forces, there was a significant correlation between the decrease in the proportion of recorded offenders found guilty in court and the increase in the number of recorded offenders. He concluded (1976, p. 12): " It suggests the possibility that changes in police practice brought about by the 1969 Act have resulted in a number of juveniles being officially cautioned, when previously they would have been dealt with by an informal warning or a no-further-action decision. Most considerations of the rise in juvenile crime in recent years have been based upon the official ' known offender ' rate. To the extent that a slightly higher proportion of juvenile offenders may have been included in official statistics since the Act, then this rate may also have slightly ' over-represented ' the levels of juvenile offending in comparison with earlier years ". Ditchfield's conclusions, therefore, were that 10–13 year-olds and 14–16 year-olds had undoubtedly been diverted, but at the cost of a slight net-widening effect.

There seems to have been no attempt to answer the second question, about the relative effects of recorded cautions, findings of guilt and unrecorded warnings. Perhaps the most relevant information can be found in Gawn, Mott and Tarling (1977). They showed that the recidivism rate during a two-year follow-up period was greater for juveniles taken to court (31 per cent. in a 1966–67 sample and 45 per cent. in a 1973 sample) than for those cautioned (16 per cent. and 24 per cent. respectively). They interpreted these figures as evidence of police selection rather than as evidence of any differential effects of court appearances and cautions. Because of the lack of statistical or experimental control of variables in their research, both interpretations are possible.

The purpose of this paper is to throw further light on the above two questions. The specific issues investigated here are whether the increase in police cautions produced diversion and/or a widening of the net, and whether cautions are more effective than court appearances in preventing recidivism.

Changes in Official Criminal Statistics

Table 1 shows changes in the incidence of official processing (cautions and findings of guilt) from 1964, the first year in which the age of criminal responsibility was 10, to 1978, the last year for which the Home Office *Criminal Statistics* are available. Figures are given for children (aged 10–13), young persons (aged 14–16), and young adults (aged 17–20). The young adults are included for comparison purposes, since official cautioning of this age group is relatively unusual. The rates for males are given per 100 of the population in each age group (as estimated in the *Criminal Statistics*), and for females per 1,000.

It is necessary to correct these figures for changes in legislation. Between 1964 and 1978, the two major Acts which had significant effects on the number of findings of guilt and cautions for indictable offences were the Theft Act 1968 and the Criminal Damage Act 1971. The Theft Act re-

POLICE CAUTIONING OF JUVENILES IN LONDON

TABLE 1

Changes in Official Processing for Indictable Offences, 1964–78.

	1964	1978	% Change	% Change Corrected*
Males aged 10–13				
Found guilty	1·63	1·24	−24	−30
Cautioned	0·74	2·20	+197	+168
Officially processed	2·37	3·44	+45	+32
Males aged 14–16				
Found guilty	2·91	5·26	+81	+50
Cautioned	0·54	2·60	+381	+311
Officially processed	3·45	7·86	+128	+90
Males aged 17–20				
Found guilty	2·46	6·46	+163	+114
Cautioned	0·15	0·22	+47	+41
Officially processed	2·61	6·68	+156	+110
Females aged 10–13				
Found guilty	2·04	1·54	−25	−27
Cautioned	1·41	8·33	+491	+468
Officially processed	3·45	9·87	+186	+175
Females aged 14–16				
Found guilty	4·20	7·05	+68	+60
Cautioned	1·27	9·11	+617	+589
Officially processed	5·47	16·16	+195	+181
Females aged 17–20				
Found guilty	2·77	8·78	+217	+202
Cautioned	0·25	0·48	+92	+83
Officially processed	3·02	9·26	+207	+192

Note The figures for males are given per 100 of the population, and for females per 1000.
* Correcting for the Theft Act 1968 and the Criminal Damage Act 1971.

classified the previously non-indictable offence of taking and driving away a motor vehicle as an indictable offence of unauthorised taking, while the Criminal Damage Act re-classified many previously non-indictable offences of malicious damage as indictable offences of criminal damage. Using the official *Criminal Statistics*, it is possible to estimate the effects of these acts in inflating recorded offending. For example, for 14–16 year-old males, the Theft Act led to an increase in findings of guilt for indictable offences of 13·9 per cent. between 1968 and 1969, and the Criminal Damage Act led to an increase of 6·0 per cent. between 1971 and 1972. The cumulative effect of these two Acts was to increase findings of guilt by 20·7 per cent. ($1·139 \times 1·06 = 1·207$).

Table 1 shows figures corrected for the effects of these two Acts. The incidence of findings of guilt of 14–16 year-old males increased from 2·91 per 100 in 1964 to 5·26 per 100 in 1978, an increase of about 81 per cent. However, as indicated above, the two Acts produced an increase of about 21 per cent. in findings of guilt for this age group. Therefore, the increase without the two Acts would have been about 50 per cent. ($1·81 \div 1·21 = 1·50$), and this corrected figure is shown in the right hand column. All the figures in the right hand column of Table 1 have been corrected on the same basis.

Table 1 shows that, between 1964 and 1978, the number of 10–13 year-olds found guilty decreased by about 30 per cent., while the corresponding

DAVID P. FARRINGTON AND TREVOR BENNETT

number of 14–16 year-olds increased by about 50–60 per cent., and the corresponding number of 17–20 year-olds increased by more than 100 per cent. The incidence of official processing increased in all cases, with the increases being greatest for females and for the older age groups.

The interpretation of these figures depends on the assumption made about the change in the incidence of juvenile delinquent behaviour, which is essentially unknown. It might be argued that the probability of a 17–20 year-old offender being officially processed has not changed over the years, because the police have not (to any great extent) introduced cautioning for young adult offenders. It therefore follows that the incidence of young adult delinquency has increased by about 100 per cent. for males and 200 per cent. for females. It might also be argued that the factors which tended to increase young adult delinquency (*e.g.* increased opportunity for crime, increased frustration, decreased parental control) might also tend to increase juvenile delinquency. If juvenile delinquency has increased by about 100 per cent. for males and 200 per cent. for females, it follows that juveniles have been diverted from court appearances to cautions, that 10–13 year-old males have been diverted from official processing to no recorded action, and that there has been no widening of the net for 14–16 year-olds.

Unfortunately, alternative assumptions are equally plausible (or implausible). Factors tending to increase the probability of official processing for juveniles (*e.g.* increases in police manpower, technology or efficiency) might also tend to increase the probability of official processing for young adults. The introduction of cautions might produce an increasing willingness to arrest juveniles, which in turn might produce an increasing willingness to arrest young adults, especially since at the time of arrest a police officer may not know whether someone is a juvenile or a young adult. Furthermore, it could be argued that some factors (*e.g.* increasing unemployment) tend to increase young adult delinquency but not juvenile delinquency. The figures in Table 1 could be explained by suggesting that (a) juvenile offending has stayed constant, while young adult offending has increased, and (b) the probability of an offender being officially processed has increased for juveniles and young adults. With these assumptions, it follows that 10–13 year-olds have increasingly been diverted, but not 14–16 year-olds, and that all juveniles have suffered net-widening.

Many other speculations are possible. The major point is that, without knowing how juvenile delinquent behaviour has changed, it is impossible to know whether diversion and/or a widening of the net has occurred. Because the number of officially processed juveniles has increased, it does not necessarily follow that juvenile delinquent behaviour has increased. For example, in the United States Gold and Reimer (1975) gave the same self-reported delinquency questionnaire to random samples of the juvenile population in 1967 and 1972. There was a marked increase in officially recorded delinquency during this period, but the researchers found little change in self-reported delinquency (with the exception of drug use, which rarely led to official processing). These results suggest that the likelihood of juvenile offending did not change during this period, but that there was an increase in

POLICE CAUTIONING OF JUVENILES IN LONDON

the likelihood that an offender would be officially processed. The *Criminal Statistics* might be easier to interpret in conjunction with the results of repeated self-reported delinquency studies.

Changes in Official Processing in London

One problem with the above analysis is that many events apart from the introduction of cautioning schemes occurred between 1964 and 1978. Even if it could be concluded that diversion and/or net-widening had occurred, it would be difficult to attribute this with confidence to the introduction of cautioning. Another problem is that the *Criminal Statistics* represent a combination of police policies in different areas. Different police forces introduced, modified or intensified cautioning schemes at different times, in some cases replacing existing juvenile liaison schemes (which combined cautions with police supervision). It should be easier to evaluate the introduction of cautioning by studying a single police force which introduced a new cautioning scheme rather abruptly during a short, specified time period. This was true of England's largest force, the Metropolitan Police.

Before 1969, a juvenile arrested in London was almost always taken to court in much the same way as an adult offender. During the first quarter of 1969, the Metropolitan Police introduced their juvenile bureau scheme (described by Oliver, 1973, 1978). When a juvenile is arrested for a crime, he is taken to a police station. The offence is then investigated by the station officer, who must satisfy himself that the charge is supported by credible evidence. The parents or guardians are requested to attend the police station, and in most instances the juvenile is released to their custody. The case is then referred to the juvenile bureau, which collects information about the juvenile from relevant agencies, such as the probation, education and social services. An officer from the bureau usually visits the offender's home and interviews him together with his parents or guardians. Any police records on the juvenile are also checked. On the basis of all the information collected, the Chief Inspector in charge of the bureau decides whether to prosecute the juvenile in court, to issue a formal caution, or to take no further action. A caution can only be administered if the juvenile admits the offence, if the parents agree that the juvenile should be cautioned, and if the complainant or victim is willing to leave the decision to the police. A caution is administered to the juvenile in the presence of his parents at the police station by a senior officer (Chief Inspector or Superintendent) in uniform. The juvenile is warned abut his future conduct and reminded of the likelihood that he will appear in court if he offends again.

Table 2 shows the incidence of arrests, findings of guilt, and official processing (findings of guilt plus cautions) in the Metropolitan Police District between 1966 and 1972. This table is derived from the annual *Report of the Commissioner of Police of the Metropolis* and the annual Home Office *Supplementary Statistics Relating to Crime and Criminal Proceedings*. Males and females are combined, and the figures are based on numbers of persons. Before 1973, cautions for indictable and non-indictable offences were not shown separately in the *Supplementary Statistics*. The number of cautions for

DAVID P. FARRINGTON AND TREVOR BENNETT

indictable offences for each year is estimated from the number of cautions each year and the proportion of cautions in each age group which were for indictable offences in 1973.

TABLE 2

Arrests, Findings of Guilt and Official Processing in the Metropolitan Police District

	YEAR			
	1966	1968	1970	1972
Age 10–13				
A	85	100	197	220
FG	91	100	70	68
OP	90	100	176	182
Age 14–16				
A	89	100	188	226
FG	89	100	113	124
OP	89	100	170	186
Age 17–20				
A	96	100	152	161
FG	93	100	138	142
OP	93	100	138	142

Notes: A = Arrests, FG = Findings of Guilt, OP = Official Processing (Findings of Guilt plus Cautions) for indictable offences, combining males and females. All figures are expressed as percentages of the corresponding 1968 figures, which were as follows:
age 10–13, A = 4527, FG = 3645, OP = 3742;
age 14–16, A = 7243, FG = 6254, OP = 6376;
age 17–20, A = 10809, FG = 9868, OP = 9985.

All figures in Table 2 are expressed as a percentage of those for 1968, which was the last complete year before the cautioning scheme was introduced. (The small experimental scheme which began in one division towards the end of 1968 can be discounted for all practical purposes). The most important comparison is between 1968 and 1970, which was the first complete year in which every division of the Metropolitan Police was operating the scheme. During this period it can be seen that arrests increased 97 per cent. for 10–13 year-olds, 88 per cent. for 14–16 year-olds, and 52 per cent. for 17–20 year-olds (who were outside the scheme). However, part of these increases could be attributed to the introduction of the Theft Act in 1969. After allowing for this, the increases in arrests between 1968 and 1970 were 85 per cent. for 10–13 year-olds, 44 per cent. for 14–16 year-olds, and 24 per cent. for 17–20 year-olds.

These figures suggest very strongly that, after the introduction of the cautioning scheme, there was a widening of the net of arrested juveniles, especially in the youngest (10–13) age group. It is implausible to suggest that there was anything approaching such a marked increase in juvenile offending, or any other marked change unconnected with the introduction of the cautioning scheme, during this short period. The same conclusion follows for the figures on official processing. The figures on findings of guilt suggest that 10–13 year-olds were diverted, but not 14–16 year-olds. In all cases, the introduction of the Children and Young Persons Act in 1971 had much less effect on arrests, findings of guilt and official processing of juveniles than the introduction of the juvenile bureau scheme.

These conclusions differ in emphasis from those of Ditchfield (1976) in

POLICE CAUTIONING OF JUVENILES IN LONDON

showing a very marked net-widening effect of cautions and a diversion effect only for the 10–13 year-olds (who were most affected by net-widening). How far these results can be generalised to the whole of England is not known. However, the study of the Metropolitan Police District, where there was an unusually abrupt change to a cautioning scheme, allows a much clearer test of the impact of police cautioning than the " averaged " *Criminal Statistics.*

The London Juvenile Bureau Sample

As with any official response to crime, the relative effectiveness of findings of guilt, recorded cautions and unrecorded warnings can be measured on a number of criteria, such as individual and general deterrence, rehabilitation, retribution, incapacitation and denunciation (see *e.g.* Farrington, 1978). They can also be compared on other criteria. For example, findings of guilt are clearly superior to cautions in the provision of procedural safeguards. As Priestley, Fears and Fuller (1977, p. 24) pointed out, police cautioning involved the " disappearance of decision making behind closed doors ".

The official caution was originally introduced because of the belief that a court appearance had negative, undesirable effects on juveniles, owing to stigmatisation. In agreement with this belief, there is evidence that a court appearance, in comparison with no official processing, is followed by an increase in delinquent behaviour (*e.g.* Farrington, 1977; Farrington, Osborn and West, 1978; Gold, 1970; Gold and Williams, 1969). Whether cautions are any less stigmatising is unclear. Oliver (1973) suggests that cautions are disseminated to statutory agencies (such as education and social services), and that they are cited in later juvenile court proceedings. A Home Office circular (49/1978) also recommends their later citation in court.

The present research attempts to compare the effects of cautions and court appearances on re-arrests, without being able to investigate the separate hypotheses discussed above (*e.g.* whether effects on re-arrests are consequences of individual deterrence, stigmatisation, etc.). A sample of 907 juveniles was obtained from the juvenile bureau files of one division of the Metropolitan Police (for more details of this research, see Bennett, 1977). This sample consisted of all juveniles referred to the bureau in 1973 for a first offence who were under age 15 at the time and who could be located in the bureau files when a search was made in October 1975. The age limit was set at under 15 in 1973 because bureau files are destroyed after a juvenile reaches his seventeenth birthday and becomes technically an adult. Therefore, it is likely that most juveniles who were 15 or 16 at the time of their first offence in 1973 would have had their bureau files destroyed by the time of the search in 1975.

Only juveniles whose first offences were indictable or akin to indictable were included in the sample. Of the 907, 705 (77·7 per cent.) were cautioned, and 202 were summoned to appear in court. Of those who made court appearances, 70 (34·7 per cent.) received a discharge, 51 (25·2 per cent.) an attendance centre order, 42 (20·8 per cent.) a supervision order, 29 (14·4 per cent.) a fine, six (3·0 per cent.) a care order, and four (2·0 per cent.) a detention centre order. Excluded from this sample are juveniles charged

DAVID P. FARRINGTON AND TREVOR BENNETT

directly in 1973 (rather than being summoned to appear in court), those whose arrests were followed by no further action (usually because the police did not have enough evidence to establish their guilt), those found not guilty in court, and those whose files were out in October 1975 (usually because they were currently under investigation for another offence). The exact frequency of occurrence of these categories is not known, but from other information provided by the police it is safe to say that the sample of 907 includes at least three-quarters of juveniles under 15 first arrested in 1973 for an indictable or akin to indictable offence in this division.

Of the 907, 264 (29·1 per cent.) had been re-arrested by the time of the search in October 1975. The follow-up period for each juvenile varied between one year 10 months and two years nine months. Since 95 per cent. of the re-arrests occurred within two years of the original arrest, the figures would not have been changed greatly if the follow-up period had been restricted to two years for each person. The re-arrest rate for those appearing in court (43·6 per cent.) was significantly greater than for those cautioned (25·0 per cent; $\chi^2(1) = 25·43$, $p < 0·001$).

Table 3 shows the relationship between the disposition decision (court or caution), re-arrest and six variables derived from the juvenile bureau files. These were: (1) sex; (2) age, dichotomised into 13 years six months or more and 13 years five months or less; (3) race, dichotomised into white and non-white, most of the non-whites being West Indians (39) or Asians (35); (4) class, based on the socio-economic status of the job of the parent or guardian on the Registrar General's scale, dichotomised into non-manual and manual; (5) area, dichotomised into lower and middle-class. The

TABLE 3
Large Sample Factors, Disposition and Recidivism

Variable		% Court		% Court	χ^2
Sex	Female (226)	16·8	Male (681)	24·1	4·77*
Age	13y 5m or less (413)	16·5	13y 6m or more (494)	27·1	14·16***
Race	White (826)	21·9	Non-white (81)	25·9	0·47
Class	Non-manual (113)	10·6	Manual (611)	21·6	6·55*
Area	Middle-class (315)	19·7	Lower-class (591)	23·5	1·54
Offence	Non-serious (699)	17·2	Serious (208)	39·4	44·58***

Variable		% Re-arrest		% Re-arrest	
Disposition	Caution (705)	25·0	Court (202)	43·6	25·43***
Sex	Female (226)	10·6	Male (681)	35·2	48·67***
Age	13y 5m or less (413)	29·8	13y 6m or more (494)	28·5	0·11
Race	White (826)	28·9	Non-white (81)	30·9	0·06
Class	Non-manual (113)	18·6	Manual (611)	29·3	4·95*
Area	Middle-class (315)	22·9	Lower -class (591)	32·5	8·77**
Offence	Non-serious (699)	25·2	Serious (208)	42·3	21·97***

Note: Significance test based on χ^2 from 2 × 2 table.
* $p < 0·05$, ** $p < 0·01$, *** $p < 0·001$
The number of juveniles categorised on area was 906 because this information was missing for one case. The 183 missing cases on class consisted of 74 from fatherless families, 43 with unemployed fathers, and 66 with no information about the father's occupation.

POLICE CAUTIONING OF JUVENILES IN LONDON

division covered three London boroughs, one of which was considered to be middle-class, as indicated by its high percentage of owner-occupied dwellings (66 per cent. in the 1971 Census), and the other two lower-class, with much lower percentages of owner-occupation (33 and 25 per cent.); (6) offence seriousness, as rated by the Chief Inspector in charge of the juvenile bureau, who made the final decision about whether to caution each juvenile or summon him or her to court. This Chief Inspector considered all offences involving an actual or potential threat to the person (primarily burglary, taking and driving away motor vehicles, robbery, assault and carrying an offensive weapon) to be relatively serious, and all other offences (primarily theft, damage and handling) to be relatively non-serious, so his ordering of offences was collapsed into these two categories.

As shown in Table 3, offence seriousness was the variable which was most closely related to the disposition decision, followed by age, with the older juveniles being more likely to be taken to court. A loglinear analysis (see, *e.g.* Fienberg, 1977) showed that seriousness and age were independently related to disposition. In other words, the disposition × age term was needed in the equation ($G^2(1) = 15 \cdot 04$, $p < 0 \cdot 001$) after the disposition × seriousness term was entered ($G^2(1) = 40 \cdot 36$, $p < 0 \cdot 001$).

The most important predictors of re-arrest were sex, disposition and offence seriousness (see Table 3), with males, those taken to court, and more serious offenders being more prone to re-arrest. A loglinear analysis showed that each of the three variables was related to re-arrest independently of all other relationships among the four variables. In other words, after entering all other two-way terms in the equation, the re-arrest × sex term was still needed ($G^2(1) = 44 \cdot 59$, $p < 0 \cdot 001$), and the same was true for re-arrest × disposition ($G^2(1) = 15 \cdot 94$, $p < 0 \cdot 001$) and re-arrest × seriousness ($G^2(1) = 4 \cdot 75$, $p < 0 \cdot 05$).

It is clear that, independently of sex, age, race, class, area and offence seriousness, disposition predicted re-arrest, with the cautioned juveniles having the lower re-arrest rate.

A More Detailed Analysis

The problem with the above analysis of juvenile bureau files is the small number of measured variables. It could always be argued that cautions might not prove to be superior to court appearances after allowing for other, more pertinent, variables. It was possible to measure a wider range of factors in a more detailed analysis of 47 juveniles. These were chosen basically by taking every twentieth home visit report, with the restriction that only juveniles from the two lower-class areas who had committed offences of medium seriousness were selected, and that cases adjacent to the twentieth were selected if they were members of groups seriously under-represented in the main sample (*i.e.* non-white race and non-manual class). Therefore, the sample of 47 includes disproportionate numbers of non-manual class (24) and non-white race (17).

For each of these cases, the complete home visit report (a discursive, unstructured account) was transcribed word by word, and each factor which

DAVID P. FARRINGTON AND TREVOR BENNETT

was frequently mentioned in it was coded subsequently. Since the home visit report usually included a disposition recommendation, the coder was not blind to disposition, but he had no way of knowing whether or not the juvenile was re-arrested. Thirteen of the cases were taken to court (27·7 per cent.) and the remainder cautioned.

Apart from those factors discussed before, five variables were mentioned in most or all home visit reports, namely the number of children in the family, the attitude of the parents, the attitude of the juvenile, the juvenile's academic performance in school, and his or her behaviour in school. Each of these was dichotomised. The number of children in the family was divided into one or two children versus three or more, while each of the other four factors was coded as good or bad. This coding was relatively objective, since each factor was usually mentioned in a clearly positive or clearly negative fashion, as the following examples indicate:

" I was very impressed with the attitude of the parents who obviously care a lot for their family " (parental attitude good).

" The television was on during the time I was speaking to Mr. . . . and, though on two separate occasions I asked him to turn it off, he merely turned it fractionally down " (parental attitude bad).

" I found him to be a very polite and well-mannered lad who apologised for all the trouble he has caused and stated that he would never do wrong again " (juvenile attitude good).

" I found him shifty, sullen, little or no conversation, and a sly smile on his face the whole of the time I was in the house " (juvenile attitude bad).

" The school reports have always been good as far as academic subjects are concerned " (school performance good).

" He could not care less whether he attended school, and at school is not the slightest concerned in learning anything " (school performance bad).

" He does not play truant and is amenable to class discipline " (school behaviour good).

" A letter sent to the parents stated that the girl's conduct was deplorable; she was arrogant and she swore at the teachers " (school behaviour bad).

Table 4 displays the relationship between each of the variables measured in this small sample and disposition (showing the percentage taken to court as opposed to cautioned) and re-arrest (showing the percentage re-arrested). Because of the small numbers, it was difficult to achieve statistical significance in a χ^2 test, and several of the tests were invalid. In view of this, phi correlations are given rather than χ^2 values. A phi correlation of 0·065 in a sample of 907 is statistically significant, in comparison with one of 0·286 in a sample of 47. Only three of the relationships shown in Table 4 were statistically significant in a valid χ^2 test. A bad juvenile attitude was significantly related to disposition (57·9 per cent. of 19 with a bad attitude going to court, in comparison with 7·7 per cent. of 26 with a good attitude: $\chi^2(1) = 14·13$, $p < 0·001$) and to re-arrest (47·4 per cent. of 19 with a bad attitude being re-arrested, in comparison with 11·5 per cent. of 26 with a good attitude:

POLICE CAUTIONING OF JUVENILES IN LONDON

$\chi^2(1) = 5 \cdot 49$, $p < 0 \cdot 025$). Also, repeating a significant result in the large sample (see also Bennett, 1979), those with parents in manual occupations were more likely to be taken to court ($47 \cdot 8$ per cent. of 23 with manual parents going to court, in comparison with $8 \cdot 3$ per cent. of 24 with non-manual parents: $\chi^2(1) = 7 \cdot 29$, $p < 0 \cdot 01$).

TABLE 4
Small Sample Factors, Disposition and Recidivism

Variable	% Court	phi	% Re-arrest	phi
Number of children	12 (0·0) 3+ (36·8)	0·445	12 (14·3) 3+ (47·4)	0·347
Parental attitude	G (18·9) B (62·5)	0·377	G (24·3) B (37·5)	0·114
Juvenile attitude	G (7·7) B (57·9)*	0·547	G (11·5) B (47·4)*	0·400
School performance	G (15·4) B (25·0)	0·107	G (15·4) B (50·0)	0·346
School behaviour	G (16·0) B (44·4)	0·296	G (20·0) B (44·4)	0·244
Sex	F (18·2) M (30·6)	0·117	F (27·3) M (27·8)	0·005
Age	Y (17·4) O (37·5)	0·225	Y (30·4) O (25·0)	−0·061
Race	W (30·0) NW (23·5)	−0·070	W (23·3) NW (35·3)	0·128
Class	NM (8·3) M (47·8)*	0·441	NM (20·8) M (34·8)	0·156
Disposition	—	—	Ca (23·5) Co (38·5)	0·149

* Significant on a valid 2 × 2 χ^2 test.

Court appearances were followed by a somewhat higher re-arrest rate than cautions in the small sample ($38 \cdot 5$ per cent. as opposed to $23 \cdot 5$ per cent., phi = $0 \cdot 149$, n.s.). Apart from the significance level, these figures are consistent with those in the large sample ($43 \cdot 6$ per cent. as opposed to $25 \cdot 0$ per cent., phi = $0 \cdot 170$, $p < 0 \cdot 001$). Partial correlations were used to investigate whether the relationship between disposition and re-arrest held in the small sample independently of the other variables. With two exceptions, the partial correlation between disposition and re-arrest was similar to the zero-order correlation. These were number of children (partial r = −0·006) and juvenile attitude (partial r = −0·091).

The result with juvenile attitude is the more interesting, with the negative partial correlation showing that, after controlling for juvenile attitude, cautions were followed by a higher re-arrest rate. Of the 19 with a bad juvenile attitude, $50 \cdot 0$ per cent. of the eight cautioned were re-arrested, in comparison with $45 \cdot 5$ per cent. of the 11 taken to court. Almost all of those with a good juvenile attitude were cautioned, so not much should be made of their higher re-arrest rate ($12 \cdot 5$ per cent. of 24 as opposed to neither of the two taken to court).

The numbers in this analysis are very small, and so any conclusions must be tentative. However, the clear indication is that, after allowing for juvenile attitude, which was the factor most closely related to both disposition and to re-arrest, cautions were not followed by lower re-arrest rates than court appearances. Therefore, there is no suggestion in this analysis of juvenile bureau files that cautions are more effective in preventing re-offending.

It would have been possible to draw more definite conclusions about the effectiveness of police cautions, at least in relation to recidivism, if research had been carried out in which juvenile offenders were randomly allocated to

DAVID P. FARRINGTON AND TREVOR BENNETT

receive court appearances, official cautions or unrecorded warnings. For ethical and practical reasons, this kind of research is difficult to arrange. It may be necessary to ensure that no offenders who would normally receive cautions or warnings are taken to court because of the experiment. In an experiment, offenders who would normally be taken to court could be randomly allocated to court appearances, cautions or unrecorded warnings. Random allocation experiments have been carried out in this country to compare different kinds of court processing (Berg, Hullin and McGuire, 1979) and different kinds of police processing (Rose and Hamilton, 1970). Furthermore, random allocation experiments have been carried out in the United States to investigate the effectiveness of juvenile diversion schemes (*e.g.* Baron, Feeney and Thornton, 1973; Binder and Newkirk, 1977; Quay and Love, 1977). Our knowledge about the effect of police cautioning in England is greatly hindered by the absence of any random allocation experiment comparing it with court appearances.

Conclusions

Insofar as it is possible to draw any conclusions, in view of the lack of information about changes in juvenile delinquent behaviour and the lack of random allocation experiments, our research in London suggests that (a) the introduction of the police caution caused a great increase in the number of officially processed juveniles, and (b) after allowing for the important factor of juvenile attitude, police cautions were no more successful than findings of guilt in preventing recidivism. Cautions probably succeeded in diverting 10–13 year-olds from court appearances, but diversion of 14–16 year-olds probably has not happened. Taking all these results into account, the adoption of police cautions seems to have had more undesired than desired effects.

Because so little is known about the effects of police cautions (or court appearances for that matter) on juvenile delinquency, it is difficult to come to any firm conclusion other than that there should be more adequate research, especially using random allocation experiments of the kind discussed above to compare disposals, and using self-reports as well as official records to measure delinquency. If the Home Office wishes to divert juveniles from court appearances, it would be desirable to choose a method of diversion which has been proved to be effective. A diversion scheme which has had some success in reducing recidivism is that carried out in California by Binder, Monahan and Newkirk (1976), largely based on contingency contracting within the families of arrested juveniles. Ideally, changes in official responses to delinquency should be made in the light of well-designed research.

The present research, admittedly based on small numbers, suggests that the introduction in London of police cautioning for juveniles produced a widening of the net rather than diversion, and that police cautions were no more effective than court appearances in preventing rearrest.

REFERENCES

BARON, R., FEENEY, F. and THORNTON, W. (1973). " Preventing delinquency through diversion ". *Federal Probation*, **37**, (1), 13–18.

POLICE CAUTIONING OF JUVENILES IN LONDON

BENNETT, T. H. (1977). *Labelling Theory, the Police and Juvenile Delinquency.* (Unpublished Ph.D. thesis, University of Kent at Canterbury).

BENNETT, T. H. (1979). " The social distribution of criminal labels ". *British Journal of Criminology,* **19,** 134–145.

BERG, I., HULLIN, R. and McGUIRE, R. (1979). "A randomly controlled trial of two court procedures in truancy ", in: Farrington, D. P., Hawkins, K. and Lloyd-Bostock, S. M. (eds.) *Psychology, Law and Legal Processes.* London: Macmillan.

BINDER, A., MONAHAN, J. and NEWKIRK, M. (1976). " Diversion from the juvenile justice system and the prevention of delinquency ", in: Monahan, J. (ed.) *Community Mental Health and the Criminal Justice System.* New York: Pergamon.

BINDER, A. and NEWKIRK, M. (1977). " A program to extend police service capability ". *Crime Prevention Review,* **4,** 26–32.

DITCHFIELD, J. A. (1976). *Police Cautioning in England and Wales.* London: H.M.S.O.

FARRINGTON, D. P. (1977). " The effects of public labelling ". *British Journal of Criminology,* **17,** 112–125.

FARRINGTON, D. P. (1978). " The effectiveness of sentences ". *Justice of the Peace,* **142,** 68–71.

FARRINGTON, D. P. (1980). " La déjudiciarisation des mineurs en Angleterre ". *Déviance et Société,* **4,** 257–277.

FARRINGTON, D. P., OSBORN, S. G. and WEST, D. J. (1978). " The persistence of labelling effects ". *British Journal of Criminology,* **18,** 277–284.

FIENBERG, S. E. (1977). *The Analysis of Cross-Classified Categorical Data.* Cambridge: MIT Press.

GAWN, J., MOTT, J. and TARLING, R. (1977). " Dealing with juvenile offenders in a new town, 1966/67 and 1973 ". *Justice of the Peace,* **141,** 279–280.

GOLD, M. (1970). *Delinquent Behaviour in an American City.* Belmont: Brooks/Cole.

GOLD, M. and REIMER, D. J. (1975). " Changing patterns of delinquent behaviour among Americans 13 through 16 years old: 1967–72 ". *Crime and Delinquency Literature,* **7,** 483–517.

GOLD, M. and WILLIAMS, J. R. (1969). " National Study of the aftermath of apprehension ". *Prospectus: A Journal of Law Reform,* **3,** 3–12.

HOME OFFICE (1965). *The Child, the Family and the Young Offender.* London: H.M.S.O. (Cmnd. 2742).

HOME OFFICE (1968). *Children in Trouble.* London: H.M.S.O. (Cmnd. 3601).

OLIVER, I. T. (1973). " The Metropolitan Police juvenile bureau scheme ". *Criminal Law Review,* 499–506.

OLIVER, I. T. (1978). *The Metropolitan Police Approach to the Prosecution of Juvenile Offenders.* London: Peel Press.

PRIESTLEY, P., FEARS, D. and FULLER, R. (1977). *Justice for Juveniles.* London: Routledge and Kegan Paul.

QUAY, H. C. and LOVE, C. T. (1977). " The effect of a juvenile diversion program on rearrests ". *Criminal Justice and Behaviour,* **4,** 377–396.

ROSE, G. and HAMILTON, R. A. (1970). " Effects of a juvenile liaison scheme ". *British Journal of Criminology,* **10,** 2–20.

[19]

Crim.L.R.

Feminists' Extravaganzas

By Nigel Walker

This is a small but choice collection of the strange things that have been written in recent years with the aim of demonstrating the bias of our criminal justice against women. In order to avert the Furies, I had better make it clear that this is not an attack on sensible feminism. I too believe:

1. that even in Western societies women suffer from many disadvantages, most of them subtler than those of Islam and therefore harder to rectify by direct measures;

2. that there is sex-discrimination in the English criminal justice system, though less than is sometimes asserted, and sometimes in favour of women.

All that I am doing is drawing attention to one or two very strange arguments that have been used by people who have paid special attention to these two points.

Nor am I saying that all these arguments are women's work. I shall begin—as I end—with a male academic, who wrote that

". . . when previous record is taken into consideration, females are more likely to be imprisoned than males. More precisely, for adults, females with no previous convictions make up five times the proportion of receptions than do males with no previous convictions." [1]

The second sentence is supported by his figures: the first is not. Here are the crucial statistics from his table of percentages of receptions into prisons in 1975 (excluding fine-defaulters)

	Men	Women
No previous convictions	7·4	37·5
1–2 previous convictions	8·5	11·0
3 previous convictions	84·1	51·6

But it does not follow that women with no previous convictions are more likely to get a sentence of immediate imprisonment. The clearest way to demonstrate this is to turn these percentages into two imaginary samples of 100 each. Seven of the men and 38 of the women would have no previous convictions. But the seven men might represent say 4 per cent. of all men with no previous convictions sentenced in 1975, while the 38 women might represent, say, 2 per cent. of women in a similar situation. The point is that the ratio between receptions with and receptions without previous convictions tells us nothing about the numbers *at risk* of being so sentenced.

This extraordinary confusion has been repeated in a well-known book

---

[1] See R. Mawby, "Sexual Discrimination in the Law," in (1977) 24 *Probation Journal* 42.

on British prisons: " Women are five times as likely as men to be sent to prison for their first offence. . . ." [2] Fortunately, since the original article was written, the publication of the *Criminal Statistics for England and Wales, 1978,* has provided for the first time a sentencing table based on a national sample which distinguishes " first offenders " and others. Admittedly it is a sample (2 per cent. of those sentenced in 1977 for certain groups of standard list offences). Admittedly also the only fairly specific offence group for which female figures are given is shoplifting. But what it shows is this:

Women aged 21 or older sentenced (with figures for men in brackets)

Offence group	Previous convictions	Ns	Sentenced to immediate imprisonment
Shoplifting	0	19,300 (12,500)	— (1%)
	1+	8,300 (15,700)	2% (17%)
Other theft	0	6,100 (21,800)	2% (4%)
or handling			
stolen goods	1+	3,400 (38,500)	7% (17%)

There is no support here for Mawby's fallacious inference. In fact, the figures for " other theft and handling stolen goods " show how it is posssible in practice as well as theory for women without previous convictions to be *less* likely than men to be sent to prison under sentence, although, when they are, they account for a *larger* fraction of those who are so sentenced:

$$\frac{2\%}{2\% + 7\%} \quad \text{compared with} \quad \frac{4\%}{4\% + 17\%}$$

Another strange confusion appears in a well-known book on women and the criminal justice system.[3] The author is arguing against the usual view that the system of police cautioning favours women. She realises that the Tables in the *Criminal Statistics, England & Wales* show that, when the police have a choice between prosecuting and cautioning people, women are more likely than men to be let off with a caution. For example

Offenders cautioned as a percentage of those cautioned or found guilty of indictable offences in 1961

Age-group	Males	Females
8–13 years	28	40
14–16	14	22
17–20	6	8
21 and over	3	8

---

[2] M. Fitzgerald and J. Sims, *British Prisons* (1979).
[3] C. Smart, *Women, Crime and Criminology* (1977) pp. 137 *et seq.* The book is based on a Master's dissertation: I wonder whether the examiners allowed this fallacy to pass.

But she says these figures are misleading, and points to a table which shows

	Persons cautioned for indictable offences per 100,000 of the population in the age-group, 1971	
	Males	Females
8–13	1,962	479
14–16	2,060	586
17–20	283	41
and so on.		

This table she says, contradicts the statement that female offenders are more likely to be cautioned than their male counterparts. It does nothing of the sort. The first table shows what happens if you are detected. The second table merely reflects the fact that so few women are detected in offences.

In a recent article [4] the same author tries to play down the sharp rise in women's convictions for violence between 1965 and 1975, which is sharper than the male increase, by arguing.

1. that expressing increases in percentages is misleading when numbers are very small. She points out that there was a 500% increase in women convicted of murder because only one woman was convicted of murder in 1965. True, but the fuss is not simply about murder, it is about manslaughter, grievous bodily harm and other serious and deliberate injuries. On her own showing, 857 females were found guilty of such offences in 1965 but 2,785 in 1975. These are *not* small numbers, and the increase is 320 per cent., twice the percentage increase for males.

2. that anyway convictions for violent crimes by women are not a new phenomenon. But the very figures she cites herself show much smaller increases—and even one decrease—in earlier decades.

The moral seems to be that if the statistics don't prove what you want, don't be too discouraged: see what you can do with them.

Another kind of misrepresentation can be found in a recent article by Greenwood and Young.[5] Writing about the effect of the Street Offences Act 1959, they say " the increase in the punitive nature of sentences was immediately apparent . . ." Their evidence for this was mainly that in 1958, the year before the Act, only 0·8 per cent. of prostitutes [*sic*] were imprisoned: but in 1960, the first complete year after the Act came into operation, the percentage was 16·3 per cent. True: but they do not give the whole picture. First, they ignore the fact that police were instructed, just after the Act came into operation, not to prosecute but to caution women on the first and second occasions on which they were detected in soliciting. The effect of this was a spectacular drop in numbers brought to court: from above 19,000 to below 3,000.

---

[4] " The New Female Criminal: reality or myth? " in (1979) 19 Brit.J.Criminol. 50 *et seq.*

[5] " Ghettos of Freedom " in *Permissiveness and Control,* edited by the National Deviancy Conference (1980).

Secondly, what the figures showed was this:

Offences by prostitutes

	1958	%	1960	%
Brought to court	19,663		2,821	
Charge dismissed etc.	125	0·6	94	3·3
Convicted	19,536	100·0	2,726	100·0
and given discharges or probation	337	1·7	329	12·0
fined	19,049	97·5	1,953	71·7
sentenced to prison	148	0·8	443	16·3

Certainly this shows an increase in numbers sentenced to imprisonment; but when only 2,726 women were convicted instead of 19,536 it should be obvious that the courts were dealing with a very different " population." What is more, there was a sharp rise in (a) percentages not convicted and (b) percentages of convicted women who were given discharges or probation. Clearly the courts had switched from a policy of more or less wholesale fining to one of " individualisation," and were dealing with women whom they knew to have failed to respond to cautions, and in some cases to earlier fines.

The rapist next door

Statistical perversity is tedious, however serious. There is no shortage, however, of more exciting atrocities. The subject of rape seems to generate these, a notorious example being Susan Brownmiller's assertion that rape " . . . is nothing more or less than a conscious process of intimidation by which *all men* keep *all women* in a state of fear " [6] One is forced to admire her rejection of safe ambiguity. Not just " men " and " women," but " all men " and " all women." Not " conscious or unconscious " but " conscious."

Subtler and less well-known is an item which is on loan to my collection:

> " Most men in [the United States] are potential rapists. But you might ask, doesn't something have to snap in a man, doesn't something have to go dreadfully wrong with his mind for him to become a rapist? Isn't the rapist really sick, a sexual deviant whose actions are universally condemned by other men and who rapes in spite of all the best efforts of society to stop him? Perhaps the potential for rape lies in all men in our society, but, you ask yourself, isn't it a potential which must be aggravated and exaggerated to the point of sickness before a man actually rapes? If you believe that, you are in for a shock. The rapist is the man next door." [7]

Professor Geis has neatly dealt with this piece of rhetoric:

> " . . . the difficulty inheres in a violation of fundamental rules of fairness and logic, rules which insist that a person should not be accused of meretricious actions only on the basis of the fact that he possesses

---

[6] In *Against Our Will* (1975). p. 15 (Her italics).
[7] A. Medea and K. Thompson, *Against Rape* (1974). p. 29, *cit. Geis*, r. 8 *infra*.

the potentiality for engaging in them. Rapists, similar to other kinds of persons who perform distinctive acts, tend to be distinctive kinds of persons. That prediction is highly inexact and provides no rationale for confusing potentiality with likelihood of performance. It is known, for example, that forcible rape rates vary dramatically with age. [The author's] sweeping generalization is not far different from suggesting that the woman next door is a potential perpetrator of infanticide because other women have killed their children and all mothers are capable of doing so." [8]

Prostitution

Prostitution is another subject which generates extreme statements. An otherwise excellent article concludes [9] that " As long as women are socialised into the traditional female role and see their alternatives limited by that role, prostitution will remain an attractive occupational option."

Yet a couple of pages earlier the author has a summary of her observations which includes

1. There are virtually no other occupations available to unskilled or low-skilled women with an income (real or potential) comparable to prostitution.

2. There are virtually no other occupations available to unskilled or low-skilled women that provide the adventure or allow the independence of the prostitution life-style.

3. The traditional " woman's role " is almost synonymous with the culturally defined female sex role, which emphasises service, physical appearance, and sexuality.

4. The discrepancy between accepted male and female sex roles creates the " Madonna-whore " syndrome of female sexuality, such that women who are sexually active outside the limits of their " normal " sex-role expectations are labelled " deviant " and lose social status.

5. The cultural importance of wealth and material goods leads some women to desire " advantages to which [they are] not entitled by [their] position " in the socioeconomic stratification.

Most of these observations are probably true of most industrialised societies. What they do not add up to is the conclusion that the blame must be put on " the traditional female role." Indeed, the first two observations make it likely that it will take a lot more than a change in female roles to remove the attractions of prostitution: it will need an economic revolution. It is instructive to substitute " men " for " women " and " robbery " for " prostitution " in each of these observations (a bit of rewriting would be needed for Nos. 3 and 4, but can be imagined). They would all make sense: indeed No. 5 would read very like a sentence by Merton himself. Then try to infer from them what change in the male role would get rid of robbery.

[8] G. Geis. " Forcible Rape: Introduction " (1977), in *" Forcible Rape: The Crime, The Victim and the Offender* (Chappell, D., Geis, G. eds. 1977).

[9] Jennifer James. " Motivations for entrance into prostitution." in *The Female Offender* (ed. L. Crites. 1976).

Another interesting aspect of prostitution is the belief that English criminal law discriminates against women because prostitutes' clients are not prosecuted. It does not seem sufficient to point out that in England (unlike the USA) it is not the act of prostitution which is prohibited, but certain ways of pursuing or assisting in the occupation, the most frequently prosecuted being soliciting. What has to be granted is that men who offensively proposition women (the phrase is that of the Home Office's Working Party [10]) have not been the focus of much police attention, and that the state of the law as well as the attitudes of police has been partly responsible for this. On the credit side, it can be pointed out that the tough penalties for " living on immoral earnings," intended to protect women from coercive exploitation by men, do not seem to have a female counterpart, in spite of the fact that wives and girl-friends of acquisitive criminals knowingly live on *their* immoral earnings (" dishonest handling " is narrower in scope). Members of either sex can be—and are—convicted of brothel-keeping and procuring: if more women are so convicted it is almost certainly because more women do it.

Monocular vision

But prostitution does not merely give rise to complaints about bias in the law-enforcement system. The very practice is seen by some as a degrading exploitation of women by men. This is not rebutted by pointing to the existence of male prostitutes, both heterosexual and homosexual: they merely seem to accentuate the greater tolerance with which female heterosexual prostitution is treated.

The central issue seems to be whether prostitution involves exploitation, and if so of which partner. A definition of exploitation is obviously needed, and in more precise terms than those of the dictionary. I suggest that when we say " A is exploiting B " we mean that A is inducing or allowing B to do something that benefits or pleases A but is—in the long or short run—detrimental to B. The fact that B may be willingly induced, or even offer spontaneously, to do whatever it is would, in many people's usage, still be consistent with calling the relationship or transaction exploitative. So would the fact that A may not be aware of the detriment to B: we would simply distinguish " conscious " from " unconscious " exploitation. It is sufficient if A shows no interest in or concern for B's welfare.

Thus promoters of matches between professional boxers can fairly be

---

[10] See the Report of the Working Party on *Vagrancy and Street Offences* (1976), para. 96. The Working Party found that as a result of the judgment in *Crook* v. *Edmondson* ([1966] 2 Q.B. 81), s. 32 of the Sexual Offences Act 1956 could no longer be used to prosecute soliciting or importuning for ordinary heterosexual intercourse (apparently because this was not an " immoral purpose "). While some police forces relied on s. 5 of the Public Order Act 1936 (which prohibits *inter alia.* " insulting words or behaviour " in a public place), or traffic legislation on obstruction, or " binding over to keep the peace " or various local enactments, success had been only partial. The Working Party suggested a definition of a new offence to deal with the problem, but drew attention to the problems that must be faced.

called exploiters, once the likelihood of cerebral damage from repeated punches becomes generally known.

There seems to be an equally strong prima facie case for saying that clients (as well as pimps and " madams ") exploit prostitutes, since a prostitute is in danger of several kinds of harm (from disease, physical abuse or psychological damage). What may be overlooked is the case for saying that prostitutes also exploit clients, though from different motives, so that the transaction is mutually exploitative.

It is possible of course to grant this, but to argue that the exploitation of the prostitute is worse. This could be argued on two grounds: that her role is the more degrading, although why this should be so is not obvious, at least if ordinary sexual intercourse is all that is involved. It is arguable that a man is equally degraded by having to pay for intercourse (and that many prostitutes in fact despise their clients for this reason). Secondly, it is arguable that in some societies, or in earlier stages of our society, the prostitute, unlike the client, is forced into her role by the need to earn enough to live. When true, this would make the client more exploitative then the prostitute. But it is not true of modern Europe or North America. It seems sounder, if one must generalise in this way about an institution with so many branches, to say that it is *mutually* exploitative, and leave it at that.

Female homosexuals

There is a lot of hard sense about prostitution in Professor Honoré's *Sex Law*.[11] But in his chapter on homosexual behaviour he defends laws which are limited to men, even when he is proposing redefinitions of the relevant offence:

> " Like our present laws those suggested here offend against the claim for equal treatment of men and women. This is unfortunate, but should be accepted. The sexes are very different in their attitudes to sex. Men are far more adventurous. There are more male than female homosexuals. The ways of women arouse less feeling than those of men. The objections to homosexuality apply more strongly to men than to women. It is a bad legislative policy to create new offences unless they are absolutely necessary in the interests of the peace of society. Most societies manage without making lesbian conduct criminal. If this is thought to make life too easy for lesbians, it should be remembered that from a social point of view they are often in a worse situation then homosexual men. It is less easy for them than for men to meet one another in pubs, clubs and other places where they will feel at home."

It is worth considering his arguments one by one:

a. " The sexes are very different in their attitudes to sex. . . " The same could be said of personal violence, drunkenness and other sorts of behaviour.

b. " There are more male than female homosexuals. . . . The same could be said of bad driving, drunks, and so forth.

---

[11] A. M. Honoré, *Sex Law* (1978), p. 110.

c. " The ways of women arouse less feeling than those of men." This seems on all fours with saying " The ways of car-drivers arouse less feeling than the ways of taxi-drivers" in order to justify discrimination between them.

d. " The objections to homosexuality apply more strongly to men than to women." Earlier, he has dealt with these objections, which are

    i. male homosexuality lowers the birth-rate to a greater extent (but he concedes that in most societies birth-control is desirable);

    ii. male homosexuality " tends to undermine the economic position of women, most of whom look for support to husbands " (but he admits that this is decreasingly true);

    iii. " the third argument against homosexuality is that it is unnatural and disgusting " (especially buggery). He does not make it clear whether he regards this as a compelling argument or not: coprophagy is unnatural and disgusting but not illegal.

e. " It is . . . bad . . . policy to create new offences unless they are absolutely necessary in the interests of the peace of society." But Professor Honoré's proposed reforms of the law involve the replacement of the present law of male buggery and gross indecency with the offence *by a male* of committing a sexual act with or in the presence of *a male under 18* or inviting him to commit a sexual act with or in the presence of the person inviting or a third person; and adding the commission of a similar offence by a parent, guardian, teacher or other person in charge or control of a *man* under 18. This may well be an improvement; but if it is arguable that it is necessary to have such offences " in the interests of the peace of society "—which could at most be true of *some* cases—it seems also arguable that in *some* cases the peace of society could be threatened by similar female behaviour.

f. " Most societies manage without making lesbian conduct criminal." True; but the implication is that they wouldn't " manage " without making male homosexuals criminals, although some have done, and California seems on the way to doing so.

g. " If this is thought to make life too easy for lesbians, it should be remembered that from a social point of view they are often in a worse situation than homosexual men. It is less easy for them to meet one another in pubs, clubs and other places where they will feel at home." If this amounts to saying " life is hard enough for them anyway " it seems to be an argument which points more strongly in the direction of decriminalising male homosexuals than in the direction of penalising one group but not the other.

I had better make it clear that I am not arguing in favour of legislation directed at female homosexuals. Nor am I implying that Professor Honoré's arguments are as wrong-headed as some of my other examples. What is interesting about them is that they involve no less than seven independent reasons for discrimination of which none is really compelling. It seems fair to say that he is trying to tip the scales with a lot of short-weight counters.

Letters to the Editor

Feminists' Extravaganzas

Dear Sir,

In a footnote to my article " Feminists' Extravaganzas " [1981] Crim.L.R. 379 I " wondered " whether Ms. Smart's examiners had let her pass her use of certain statistics. I have now been told that the thesis which she expanded into her book did not contain the passage in question; and I would like to apologise for the footnote in question.

Yours faithfully,
NIGEL WALKER.

Crim.L.R.

Letters to the Editor

Feminists' Extravaganzas

Dear Sir,

Nigel Walker's article in the June issue, " Feminists' Extravaganzas " perplexed and disturbed us. We had difficulty in understanding the purpose of the article since it seemed to be such a hotch-potch of different issues whose only unifying theme was that they related to women. It is important surely to differentiate between women as victims and as offenders in the criminal process. We would make the following points.

1. Whilst it is important to highlight errors in statistical interpretation (although we wonder if the slur implied in footnote 3 was necessary), Walker does not really give a full picture of the context of Smart's statistics. For Smart fully recognises the " unfinished " nature and problem of statistical interpretation in understanding the treatment of female offenders, and indeed makes strong pleas for more empirical data and analysis on this issue. He does not inform us of Smart's own critique of Walker's statistical evidence when she reminds us of the bias in the statistics.

Moreover, he uses this criticism as an apéritif to a devastatingly brief dismissal of Brownmiller's " Against our Will " and his other highly selective comments on prostitution and female homosexuality.

2. Brownmiller, far from writing for the academic criminology market has produced an historical and socio-political book on rape. Under the heading " The Rapist Next Door " one sentence from the book is subjected to (justifiable) criticism. Some of Brownmiller's assertions may seem extreme or exaggerated but in her grand attempt to examine rape within its social context, she has made a valuable contribution to the growing body of literature on rape. We do not think that our next-door neighbours are rapists. But we think that they could be. The experiences of women in West Yorkshire recently surely highlight the rational fear of sexual attack that women in our culture have to cope with in their daily lives and we think that it is important that the sooner the popular stereotype of the rapist as the sex-starved psychopathic stranger is eradicated, the sooner rape within the family/friendship/neighbourhood network will cease to be hidden from view and unreported. Is the whole of the argument to be dismissed out of hand because one sentence is too imprecise? Is Walker dismissing the whole argument?

3. The article then moves on to a slightly larger snippet on prostitution. Walker writes that it makes as much sense to suggest that prostitution will disappear with the eradication of women's traditional female role as to assert that a change in the male role would eliminate robbery. We did not find it particularly instructive to do as Walker suggests and substitute " men " for " women " and " robbery " for " prostitution " in James' summary. While we might agree that a change in sex roles would not be *sufficient* to eradicate prostitution (we might need an economic revolution too) it would certainly be a necessary step in giving women greater equality before the law.

4. The next Aunt Sally set up to be knocked down is the argument that English criminal law discriminates against women because the clients of prostitutes are not prosecuted. Walker says that this (uncredited) argument cannot hold water because in England it is not the act of prostitution which is prohibited. Perhaps this is what is meant by the " English criminal law discriminates against women." Admittedly, if the argument is put rather loosely in terms of " lack of prose-cution " then Walker's reply has some validity. However, if he examined Greenwood's argument further, he would discover her thesis that, for the majority, the Act led to a period of " virtual decriminalisation " but, for the minority, there has been a " rapid escalation of criminalisation." This is borne out in statistics relating to the length of prison sentences given to women who have been

convicted since the Street Offences Act 1959. Moreover, this minority is likely to comprise working-class women with low economic and social status. As Greenwood says, " it was by the continual coercion of this minority that the invisible majority were socially controlled, that is, prevented from returning to the streets " (V. Greenwood: " Ghettos of Freedom " in " Permissiveness and Control," edited by National Deviancy Conference (1980), p. 161).

There is an argument that, in punishing the prostitute rather than the client, the law is unequal in its condemnation of prostitution, and this must be seen within its wider backdrop of the double standard of sexuality dominant in our society. The " madonna-whore " syndrome is the epitome of this discrimination: prostitutes are thus stigmatised not merely for having transgressed the law but also for publicly deviating so far from the traditional expectations of passive female sexuality. In contrast their male clients are socially and legally permitted to express their sexuality with prostitutes since this accords with prevailing notions of active male sexuality. Certainly, Walker does " grant " (to whom?) that " men who offensively proposition women . . . have not been the focus of much police attention." But, as the new apologist of the criminal justice system, he quickly finds " credit " in the fact that men " living off immoral earnings " are given tough penalties whereas wives and girlfriends of robbers escape lightly despite also " living off immoral earnings." The offence of living off immoral earnings, Walker informs us, is intended to protect women from coercive exploitation from men. Are the wives and girlfriends " coercively exploiting " their robbing males? Are they in a position of power to demand a high rake off? Are their husbands and boyfriends dependent on them to provide a place from which to earn immorally? We would suggest that they are not. There is slight confusion because in the next section, " Monocular Vision," Walker proceeds to demolish the idea that women are, in general, exploited by prostitution. But the foregoing argument is not we think affected since he appears to accept that pimps are involved in coercive exploitation.

5. As to the last section on female homosexuality, we agree with Walker that Honoré is not convincing. However, he could have extended his argument to an analysis of why male homosexuality has been criminalised in the first place.

But our reaction to " Feminists' Extravaganzas " is more than one of failing to comprehend its purpose. Its title gives the impression that it is about feminist interpretations of women in the criminal justice system. Yet Walker claims, almost in a tone of self-congratulation, that he is not taking issue with feminism, proof of which he suggests is that he begins and ends with criticism of male academics. On whose say-so are these two feminists? Is any argument that women are discriminated against a " feminist argument "? We would suggest not, for a feminist analysis would seek to understand discriminatory practices from a position which acknowledges the unequal economic and social power distribution between men and women in our society. We are not sure that Honoré's defence of having homosexual laws limited to men has much to do with " feminism."

There is also something disturbing about his early claim that he has " no argument " with " sensible " feminism. He does not share with his readers what he means by this or what " unsensible " feminism comprises. It is never clear whether his argument is with the methodology of some feminist criminologists, or with the underlying analyses of these writers on very disparate issues.

Yours faithfully,

ANNIE HUDSON,
Lecturer in Social Work,
Sunderland Polytechnic.

CELIA WELLS,
Lecturer in Law,
University of Newcastle upon Tyne.

PROFESSOR WALKER replies: Ms. Hudson and Ms. Wells *should* be disturbed, but not, surely, quite so perplexed The aim of my article was both explicit and simple: to illustrate the sloppy reasoning which seems to strike so often in writings about women and crime. But let me deal with their specific points:

1. A plea for more statistics does not excuse the misuse of what one has.

2. To find someone in England who believes in the rapist next door is more than I had hoped for. As Geis points out, this is to accuse someone of what he might do simply because he is not physically incapable of it. What I grant of course is that rape is a very unexpected transaction: but that is different. By the way, although your correspondents claim familiarity with Ms. Brownmiller's book, they are mistaken in attributing this fantasy to her, as my footnote made clear.

3. I am glad that we are agreed on this point. As for a change in sex roles, all I meant was that it will not cure everything.

4. On the contrary, I *conceded* that, unlike soliciting women, pestering men are neglected by the law and police; and I agree that women who live off their men's immoral receipts from burglary and robbery are not as nasty to their husbands as the stereotype of the pimp is to his girls. My point was merely that " living on immoral earnings " is something women can do too, but are likely to get away with.

5. Again, I am glad we agree: but I cannot see why I should have burdened the reader with a short history of the law on homosexuality.

6. By " sensible feminists " I meant people who do not tilt at windmills, misread texts, misuse statistics, defend fallacies or slander the innocent man next door.

Dear Sir,

It is sometimes said that a good indication of academic expertise is the ability to quote selectively in criticising other authors. If so, Nigel Walker, in his " Feminists' Extravaganzas " article, is well worthy of his position in one of academic's male bastions.

When I wrote " Sexual Discrimination and the Law "[1] I was tentatively suggesting a few reasons why we should question the almost unanimously held assumption that women were treated more leniently than men by the criminal justice system (see Pollak[2] and Reckless and Kay[3]). In so doing I argued that data which suggested that females were more leniently treated was misleading, and that other evidence pointed in the opposite direction.

At the pre-court stages of law-enforcement, for example, there is no evidence to support Pollak's assertion that women are less likely to be reported to the police than are male offenders,[4] whilst evidence of cautioning patterns[5] shows that once one controls for other variables, like offence type and criminal record, the apparently more favourable treatment of females—illustrated by the official statistics—disappears.

One crucial point here, as Walker notes, is that, until 1978 Home Office figures for sentencing did not include a control for previous convictions. In contrast, prison statistics did allow a comparison of male and female inmates by previous record, and revealed that women and girls in prison service establishments had less serious records, and had committed less serious offences, than their male counterparts. Although I did conclude with the statement which Walker attributed to me, it is perhaps a little devious to quote it without its more cautious introduction, where I noted that " It thus appears that . . . females are more likely to be imprisoned than males. . . ." I then continued to affirm the tentativeness of this conclusion by stressing: " Of course, the information available is not complete enough to allow this point to be proved conclusively. For this, we would need to know how different groups of offenders were sentenced relative to their criminal records, rather than looking solely at the prison population."

I then re-emphasised the point by concluding: " The *tentative conclusion* is that the available data support the contention that males and females are handled differently . . ." (italics not in original).

Since then, as Walker observes, the Home Office has included data on sentencing, controlling for record and—to some extent—offence type. This does indeed show that males are more likely to be sentenced to imprisonment than are females, although the differences between the sexes are certainly less once this basic control is made. Moreover, the difference is less evident for younger offenders, and between males and females given a suspended prison sentence. Despite the overall finding, however, it is still true to state that first offenders comprise a far higher proportion of the population of women's prisons than of men's prisons, and that consequently there may be more scope for restricting the use of imprisonment for women, especially since, as already noted, women in prison appear to have committed less serious offences than their male counterparts.

Two points, however, need to be emphasised in concluding this review of Professor Walker's article. First, in no way do his arguments support the assumption made by people like Pollak and Reckless and Kay, which remained uncriticised for so long. Secondly, in focussing on some of the more problematic aspects of the debate, he encourages his readers to loss sight of other findings. For example, there is no evidence that females are more likely to be cautioned than males once one controls for other variables. Moreover, women are, despite recent shifts, still more likely to be inappropriately remanded in custody than are male defendants.

Yours faithfully,

DR. R. I. MAWBY,
Principal Lecturer in Social Administration,
Plymouth Polytechnic.

References

[1] R. I. Mawby " Sexual Discrimination and the Law " in (1977) *Probation Journal.*

[2] O. Pollak *The Criminality of Women* (1961).

[3] W. Reckless and B. Kay *The Female Offender* (1967).

[4] D. Steffensmeier and R. Steffensmeier " Who Reports Shoplifters? " (1977) *International Journal of Criminology and Penology* 5, R. I. Mawby " Witnessing Crime " in *Criminal Justice and Behaviour* 7.

[5] P. Priestley *et al. Justice for Juveniles* (1977) K. Carey " Police Policy and the Prosecution of Women " (undated) *University of Leeds.*

The author also found a similar pattern in a recent study of a Bradford inner city area, see: R. I. Mawby and C. J. Fisher " Gatekeeping Juvenile Crime " (1981) *Report for DHSS.*

PROFESSOR WALKER replies: You do not make a conclusion any less fallacious by calling it " tentative," or by pleading that the really relevant figures were not yet available; still less by implying that your critic " selected " simply to discredit your entire article. The only point I was making was that there seems to be a lot of odd reasoning in books and articles about women offenders; and this was an important example which had gained currency. A fallacy is a fallacy, and a good example is a good example.

P.S. In this " male bastion " three out of nine teaching or research officers are women.

[20]

Standardising prosecutions

Debbie Crisp

A recent RPU study examined CPS reasons for terminating cases. The proportion of cases dropped varied between areas from 8% to 20% of which just over half were stopped because there was insufficient evidence and almost one-third on public interest grounds. Recent initiatives are aimed at reducing differences between areas and tightening the timetable for case preparation.

Background to the study

In November 1990 a Working Group on Pre-Trial Issues[1] produced a report which scrutinised the preparation, processing and submission of files for prosecution. The Group became aware, through field visits, that the content of 'police files differed quite considerably from one police force to another'. The speed with which files were processed also appeared to vary throughout the country. The report identified areas where delays occurred regularly, and its recommendations included proposed time limits for dealing with files. The Group also examined the existing arrangements for warning witnesses, and the provision of case results and antecedent information.

As a result of the Group's report, the Crown Prosecution Service (CPS) and the police drew up a manual of pre-trial guidance which was introduced nationally in October 1992. These guidelines aimed to standardise the content and format of prosecution files, as well as the timeliness of their submission.

The CPS was set up in the mid-eighties as an independent prosecuting body as a result of the Royal Commission on Criminal Procedure Report (1981). This report had levelled a number of criticisms at the existing system of police prosecution, including the wide variation in prosecution policies and practices between forces. It was hoped that the re-formulation of the prosecution process would reduce any arbitrary geographical differences in the treatment of offenders or offences. The Code for Crown Prosecutors sets out to 'promote efficient and consistent decision-making', thereby removing any unfairness resulting from these inconsistencies. The powers of discretion granted to prosecutors under the Prosecution of Offences Act 1985 to discontinue charges against defendants are useful in this respect.

Statistics produced by the CPS show that, in the last quarter of 1991, Crown Prosecutors dropped an average of 11% of all their finalised cases either before or at court. However, the rates of the 31 areas then in existence ranged from 8% to nearly 20%. It does not necessarily follow that these differences arise from a variation in prosecution policy as applied by the CPS. The disparity may have resulted from local differences in prosecution files prepared by the police. However, for whatever reason, the figures suggest that geographical variation in prosecution policy has, to date,

---

1   The Group comprised representatives from the Home Office, the Association of Chief Police Officers, Her Majesty's Inspectorate of Constabulary, the Metropolitan Police, the Crown Prosecution Service, the Justices' Clerks' Society and the Lord Chancellor's Department.

survived the introduction of a national prosecution service.

In March 1993, the CPS introduced their National Operation Practice (NOP) initiative, which sets quality of service standards for the work carried out in all its branches. When undertaking case review, CPS lawyers are expected to comply with these standards, but this task is made more difficult if the files received from the police are not also of uniform quality throughout the country. As part of NOP the CPS is monitoring the timing, contents and quality of the files it receives from the police. It is hoped that the implementation of the recommendations of the Working Group on Pre-trial Issues will help to create greater consistency nationally.

The Code for Crown Prosecutors asserts that they 'should not hesitate to bring proceedings to an end in appropriate cases', either before or at court. In deciding whether to proceed with a case, Crown Prosecutors must apply a two-tier test. They must first consider whether the evidence is sufficient to provide a realistic prospect of conviction. If it is, the next step is to consider whether the public interest requires a prosecution. Each case is assessed on its merits, although the Code states that 'broadly speaking, the graver the offence the less likelihood there will be that the public interest will allow of a disposal that is less than prosecution'.

Whilst prosecutors generally consult the police whenever they are minded to discontinue a case, the ultimate decision whether or not to proceed rests with the CPS - a decision which they see as the most obvious demonstration of their independent discretion. The CPS performance indicators show the proportion of cases which prosecutors

2 For example, McConville, Sanders and Leng

filter out of the criminal justice process nationally, but these statistics do not include the offence breakdown of cases dropped or the grounds given for termination. In addition, whilst a number of research projects have examined discontinuance, it has rarely been the specific focus of a study and so sample sizes have been relatively small[2]. Thus only a partial picture of the exercise of prosecutorial discretion can be drawn from the information hitherto available.

The RPU study

The Research and Planning Unit study aimed to examine more closely the process whereby the CPS decides to terminate those cases judged not to merit prosecution on evidential or public interest grounds.

Information was collected on a random sample of nearly 1,300 terminated cases. A control sample of cases that had been variously disposed of by the court was also collected, along with details of cases where the police had approached the CPS for formal pre-process advice. To aid in the interpretation of these data, interviews were undertaken with prosecutors and police officers in each of the seven areas studied.

The findings

The research helped to provide an overview of the reasons why prosecutors decide not to proceed with a case - of the terminated cases:

- 54% were dropped because there was insufficient evidence to provide a realistic prospect of conviction,

- 32% were dropped because it was not felt to be in the public interest to proceed,

- 10% of defendants could not be traced (four-fifths of these cases related to minor motoring matters[3]),

- 1% for other practical reasons (such as the death of the defendant),

- 3% were dropped because the court refused a CPS request for an adjournment.

This pattern remained broadly similar for all offences, although summary motoring offences were apparently less likely to be terminated on public interest grounds.

The research examined Crown Prosecutors' perceptions of the files they received from the police in relation to the two-tier test they must apply when reviewing cases. (The data were collected before the introduction of the guidance manual).

The content of police files

Prosecutors were asked to say whether, in their opinion, there was enough information on the initial file to assess evidential sufficiency of the case against the defendant. In four-fifths of the terminated cases it was felt that there was, although this did vary quite significantly between branches. One CPS branch studied felt that the file provided enough detail in 92 per cent of cases, whereas the figure dropped to just over 67 per cent in two other branches.

Prosecutors were also asked to assess whether the public interest required a prosecution. In nine out of ten cases it was felt that adequate detail had been provided. Again, the proportions varied from branch to branch, from nearly all cases in one to only

70 per cent in another.

In just under half of the cases where prosecutors stated that they did not have enough detail to assess the evidential criteria set out in the Code for Crown Prosecutors it was still felt that they had sufficient information to decide whether the public interest criteria were satisfied. Further, of the cases where prosecutors felt that they were able to assess the evidence on file, only four per cent felt that more information would be required before a proper assessment could be made as to whether it was in the public interest to prosecute the defendant. However, the Inner London Public Interest Case Assessment project recorded a substantial increase in the number of cases dropped on public interest grounds, when the Crown prosecutors were provided with fuller details about individual defendants than was normally available from the police (Brown and Crisp, 1992). This helps to illustrate that prosecutors have no way of knowing what gaps there are in the information they receive.

The CPS contacted the police for more information in 486 cases (38% of the sample), and had direct contact with bodies other than the police in 105 cases (8%). When the CPS contacted the police for more information, the main reason for dropping the case was that the evidence was insufficient. Where the CPS had direct contact with bodies other than the police, the case was most often terminated on public interest grounds.

The guidance manual sets out the standard content of police files, and includes copies of the forms that are now being used nationally. One of these, the Confidential Information Form (MG6), is the means

---

3 A ceiling was placed on the number of motoring offences within the sample to ensure a representative sample of non-motoring offences - nearly a quarter of discontinued minor motoring offences were dropped because the defendant could not be traced.

whereby the police may inform the prosecutor of any sensitive information which is felt to be relevant[4]. This more systematic approach should enable prosecutors to make more informed decisions on both the evidential sufficiency and the relevant public interest grounds of the files that they are given to review.

The stage at which files are received

Whatever the quality of the material received, prosecutors will be hampered in their assessment of a case if they are not given the papers until the last minute. When the data were collected, there were no national guidelines setting out timescales for the provision of files by the police, although in many instances there were local guidelines. The more formalised manual of guidance now in operation recommends that the period between charge and first appearance should be four weeks for an abbreviated file, and five weeks where a full file was required. Files should then always reach the CPS two weeks before the court appearance, allowing sufficient time for an initial review.

During the period of the study, the time taken to process files usually fell well short of the manual's recommendations. The police provided the file within two weeks of charge in only seven per cent of cases, and within one month in a further 19% of cases. The later the CPS receive the papers, the more likely it is that there will be insufficient time to notify the defendant prior to the hearing of any decision to discontinue. The defendant was not notified in over a third of the terminated cases within the sample, which is clearly unsatisfactory in terms of unnecessary case preparation and attendance at court for the defence. In just under 40% of these cases, lack of time was the reason given for not contacting the defence.

Proceedings were dropped comparatively rarely at or before the first hearing (about 12% of cases). The new pre-trial timetable set out in the guidance manual may lead to diversion taking place at an earlier stage.

Consultation with the police

The Code for Crown Prosecutors states that 'it will be normal practice to consult the police whenever it is proposed to discontinue proceedings instituted by them'. Prosecutors were asked whether they had consulted the police about their decision to terminate. In 22% of cases the police were consulted both orally and in writing. In another 26% the consultation was in writing only, and in a further 24% prosecutors discussed their decision with the police, but did not put anything in writing. In the remaining 28% of cases the CPS did not consult the police about the decision to drop the case.

The overall figures conceal a wide variation between areas in the extent to which the police were consulted on the decision not to proceed. In one branch, the police were only consulted in just over a third of cases terminated, whereas in another they were consulted in over 80%. Cases were most often terminated at court rather than before the case came to court or between hearings. When the case was dropped at court, prosecutors were much less likely to consult the police either orally or in writing. The sooner the CPS receive files, the more opportunity there is for this consultation process to take place. In all areas, the most frequent reason cited for not consulting the police was insufficient time to do so.

As part of the NOP service standards, prosecutors are now expected to provide

---

4 The confidential nature of the form means that it is not disclosed to the defence.

written reasons for discontinuance to the police. Under this standard, CPS lawyers are required to consult the police before dropping the case unless it is quite impractical to do so. It is hoped that this will result in a more consistent approach by the CPS in all its branches.

CPS and witnesses

The main reason for a late collapse was that witnesses either failed to attend or changed their minds about giving evidence at the last minute. The guidance manual suggests that the police should appoint Witness Liaison Officers (WLO) who would be responsible for warning witnesses, and act as a contact point for both witnesses and the CPS. Since such a significant proportion of cases is dependent on the attendance of witnesses, it is important that the prosecutor at court has accurate and up-to-date information on witness availability. To this end, the introduction of the WLO may prove invaluable.

Previous convictions

The guidance manual stipulates that details of a defendant's criminal history should be included in any file that the police send on to the CPS. The research suggests that information on previous convictions was not always available at the time that prosecutors were reviewing the case. Of those known to have a criminal record, those whose cases were terminated tended to have fewer previous convictions on average than those whose cases proceeded to court.

Conclusion

The manual of guidance jointly produced by the CPS and the police can be seen as a major pre-trial development. Data from the RPU study on the CPS suggest that there are a number of areas that might benefit from its standardised approach. The guidelines on the content of police files may help to lead to a more uniform approach to prosecution, whilst the timetable set out in the manual may increase the degree to which the CPS is able to fulfil its undertaking to consult the police every time it is minded to discontinue a case. Where the prosecution relies heavily on evidence from witnesses, the liaison role of the WLO may result in the CPS being informed at an earlier date in cases where the witness is unable to attend.

A national implementation structure has been established by the CPS to put these pre-trial initiatives into practice and to monitor progress in this area. Preliminary results from a monitoring scheme introduced by the CPS suggest that, on average, there is a high level of compliance amongst police forces with the file content and timeliness standards specified by the guidance manual. This is an encouraging indication of improvements in the consistency of file preparation by the police as a result of pre-trial initiatives.

References

BROWN, A. J., and CRISP, D. (1992) Diverting cases from prosecution in the public interest. *Home Office Research Bulletin* No. 32. London: Home Office.

McCONVILLE, M., SANDERS, A. and LENG, R. (1991) *The Case for the Prosecution: police suspects and the construction of criminality.* London: Routledge

ROYAL COMMISSION ON CRIMINAL PROCEDURE REPORT (1981) London: HMSO.

MANUAL OF GUIDANCE FOR THE PREPARATION, PROCESSING AND SUBMISSION OF FILES (1992) Issued by the Home Office following consultation with the Crown Prosecution Service.

Debbie Crisp is a Research Officer in the Research and Planning Unit

[21]

[1971]

The Use of Suspended Sentences

R. F. Sparks

Assistant Director of Research, Cambridge Institute of Criminology

Suspended prison sentences, which were introduced into the English penal system by the Criminal Justice Act 1967,[1] have now been available to the courts for nearly three and a half years. The introduction of this new measure—which had been considered and rejected on two different occasions by the Advisory Council on the Treatment of Offenders[2]—was apparently motivated by a number of considerations. But one factor which was of obvious importance was the size of the prison population. At the end of 1967 there were nearly 22,000 men and women serving sentences of imprisonment in England and Wales; the population of the general local prisons exceeded their cellular capacity by about 40 per cent., and there were over 6,000 persons sleeping three in a cell. Even a cursory reading of the Parliamentary Debates which preceded the passing of the 1967 Act shows that this problem was clearly in the

---

[1] S. 39 of this Act provides that any court which passes a sentence of imprisonment of six months or less (in respect of one offence) *must* suspend that sentence unless the offence involves an assault or the threat of violence, the possession of a firearm, explosive or offensive weapon, or indecency with a person under 16; or it is one in respect of which a probation order or conditional discharge was made, or which was committed when the offender was subject to such an order; or unless the offender has already served a prison or Borstal sentence, or has been subject to a suspended sentence; or, of course, if he is being sent to prison immediately for another offence. This section also provides that a court which passes a prison sentence of two years or less *may* suspend that sentence, regardless of the type of offence or the offender's antecedents. The period of suspension, for both mandatory and discretionary suspended sentences, may be from one to three years. If the offender is convicted during this period of a further offence punishable by imprisonment, then by s. 40 the court dealing with him on that occasion may—and normally shall—order that the suspended sentence shall take effect with the original term unaltered; it may, however, order a shorter term of imprisonment, or extend the period of suspension, or make no order at all. These sections came into force on January 1, 1968.

[2] See the Report of the Advisory Council on the Treatment of Offenders on *Alternatives to short terms of imprisonment* (London, H.M.S.O., 1957), para. 27, and App. D. The suspended sentence was, however, supported by a number of those who gave evidence to the Royal Commission on the Penal System: see, for example, the memorandum by Mr. Bryan Leighton, J.P., in the Written Evidence from Government Departments, Miscellaneous Bodies and Individual Witnesses, Vol. IV (London, H.M.S.O., 1967), p. 36, I am indebted to Paddy Heffernan for drawing my attention to this reference.

minds of both Government and Opposition, even though other reasons for allowing or requiring the courts to suspend prison sentences were also mentioned.[3]

In the early months of 1968 there was indeed a sharp drop in receptions into prison, and in the prison population. But this relief was short-lived: in 1969 the prison population rose sharply again, and by the end of that year it was back to about the same level as it had been at the end of 1967. The increase appears to have continued throughout 1970: by July of last year, the total population of prison service establishments (that is, prisons, Borstals and detention centres) had passed 40,000, a number which according to official forecasts would not be reached until some years later.[4] It is clear, moreover, that the suspended sentence has played a large part in this increase.[5] Thus a measure which was intended (*inter alia*) to reduce the prison population has resulted in an increase in that population. In this note I shall summarise the available evidence on the use of the suspended sentence to date, and its effect on the prison population. I shall also offer an explanation of why this measure has been counter-productive, and I shall argue that—given the sentencing policies of the English courts prior to 1967—it was inevitable that this should be so.

Use of suspended sentences by the courts

Though the Criminal Justice Act itself gives little explicit guidance to the courts concerning the use of suspended sentences, it seems fairly clear that this measure was primarily intended as an alternative to imprisonment.[6] This was made explicit by the Court of Appeal (Criminal Division) in *O'Keefe*,[7] an appeal against sentence heard in December 1968. The Court said that a suspended sentence should only be imposed when, by having eliminated all other alternatives, the court decides that the case is one for imprisonment:

---

[3] Such as " avoiding sending people to prison for the first time unnecessarily " and having " a substantial deterrent effect ": see the remarks by Mr. Roy Jenkins on the Second Reading of the Criminal Justice Bill, H.C.Deb., Vol. 738, col. 66; also the Proceedings of Standing Committee A, February 22, 1967 (London, H.M.S.O.).

[4] See the White Paper *People in Prison* (Cmnd. 4214, 1969), para. 238.

[5] See the Report of the Prison Department for 1969 (Cmnd. 4486), para. 5.

[6] Thus, *e.g.*, by s. 39 (9), a suspended sentence is for most purposes treated as a prison sentence. See also the remarks of Mr. Jenkins in the Report of Standing Committee A, February 22, 1967, col. 548, where a sentencing principle virtually identical to that enunciated in *O'Keefe* (*infra*) was mentioned.

[7] [1969] 1 All E.R. 426. The court also noted that it had found many cases where suspended sentences were being given " as what one might call a ' soft option,' when the court is not quite certain what to do, and in particular . . . many cases when suspended sentences have been given when the proper order was a probation order " (*ibid.* at p. 427).

"The court must go through the process of eliminating other possible courses such as absolute discharge, conditional discharge, probation order, fines, and then say to itself: this is a case for imprisonment, and the final question, it being a case for imprisonment, is immediate imprisonment required, or can I give a suspended sentence?" [8]

This is not, however, what happened in practice in 1968 and 1969 (the only years for which statistics are now available). The way in which the courts used the suspended sentence in those years can be seen from the following table, which gives percentage distributions of sentences imposed on males aged twenty-one and over, for indictable offences, at magistrates' courts and at assizes and quarter sessions, for 1967–1969.

TABLE 1

*Sentences on Males Aged 21 and Over for Indictable Offences,
1967–1969*

Assizes and quarter sessions	1967	1968	1969
Discharge	4·8	3·2	3·7
Fine	20·1	11·0	12·0
Probation	13·5	9·1	8·2
Imprisonment (immediate)	60·0	53·9	54·5
Suspended sentence	—	21·1	20·1
Other	1·5	1·7	1·5
Total	100·0	100·0	100·0
N =	21,664	23,491	26,358

Magistrates' courts			
Discharge	9·8	10·2	10·3
Fine	64·9	55·6	57·5
Probation	8·9	6·6	6·5
Imprisonment (immediate)	15·9	10·0	10·1
Suspended sentence	—	17·1	15·1
Other	0·6	0·6	0·6
Total	100·0	100·0	100·0
N =	86,056	91,672	107,611

Source: *Criminal Statistics for 1967–69*, Tables I (b) and II (b).

[8] *Ibid.* at p. 428.

It will be seen from this table that in both 1968 and 1969 suspended sentences accounted for about one-fifth of all sentences imposed on this group of offenders at the higher courts, and about one-sixth of those imposed at the lower courts. But while the use of immediate imprisonment dropped in both 1968 and 1969, compared with 1967, the use of fines and probation also declined. To get some idea of how the courts would probably have dealt with the offenders given suspended sentences if this measure had not been available, we may apply the percentage distribution of sentences given in 1967 to the total numbers sentenced in 1968 and 1969. First, however, we must allow for the fact that the figures for immediate imprisonment in those two years include substantial numbers of cases—probably about 3,500 in 1968 and 7,500 in 1969 —in which the offenders were *re*-convicted after having been given a suspended sentence. The simplest way to account for these cases is to subtract those numbers from the totals convicted in 1968 and 1969, before comparing those years with expectations based on 1967. If this is done, it can be estimated that of the men given suspended sentences for indictable crimes in 1968, about 40 per cent. would probably have been given immediate imprisonment if the suspended sentence had not been available. But a similar proportion would probably have been fined; and about 12 per cent. would probably have been put on probation.

For 1969, the comparison is a bit more favourable; the data suggest that over 55 per cent. of those given suspended sentences would probably have been sent to prison before the Act, though nearly one-quarter would probably have been fined, and 15 per cent. put on probation. This comparison is admittedly a rough one; the statistics summarised in Table 1 may conceal some other changes in sentencing policy since 1967, and not just the introduction of the suspended sentence. Comparison of the figures for 1968 and 1969 is also complicated by the effects on the criminal statistics of the offence classification introduced by the Theft Act 1968. Nonetheless, it seems clear that in a large number of suspended sentence cases, the courts (in particular magistrates' courts) did not follow the policy mentioned in *O'Keefe*. Instead of being used as an alternative to imprisonment, a suspended sentence was often used for offenders who would not have been sent to prison before the 1967 Act.

The statutory conditions relating to the mandatory suspended sentence suggest that the courts would be more ready to use this measure for property offences than for offences of violence. Analysis of the principal convictions for which suspended sentences were imposed in 1968 and 1969 confirms that this is true: crimes of violence are under-represented, at both higher courts and magistrates' courts, in both years. Unfortunately it is not possible, on the available data, to say much about the types of offenders for whom suspended sentences have so far been used. Something about this can be inferred from a comparison of receptions into prison in 1967 with receptions in 1968 and 1969. According to the annual statistics published by the Prison Department, the proportion of first offenders received into prison under sentence without the option of a fine fell from about 8 per cent. in 1967 to about 4 per cent. in each of the succeeding two years. There was also a fall in the numbers who had not previously been in prison: from 36 per cent. in 1967 to 30 per cent. in 1968 and 22 per cent. in 1969. It thus seems clear that an initial effect of the suspended sentence was to reduce the numbers of less persistent criminals committed to prison. There was little change in the proportions received into prison with three or more previous court appearances, or with more than one previous institutional sentence. Again, however, some allowance must presumably be made in each of the latter two years for offenders who were sent to prison on reconviction after having received a suspended sentence, who are not at present distinguished in the Prison Department's statistics of receptions.

Even less can be said about the large contingent of offenders who would probably have been fined or put on probation had the suspended sentence not been available. It can safely be assumed, of course, that before 1968 offenders dealt with in these ways had, on average, fewer previous convictions than offenders sent to prison. But neither group was homogeneous in this respect; and it is likely that those given suspended sentences in 1968 and 1969 were not a random sample of those who, on the policies of earlier years, would have been put on probation or fined.

The lengths of suspended sentences imposed in 1969 on men age twenty-one and over are shown in Table 2 (This table relates to *all* offences for this age group, and not just indictable ones.) It will be seen from this table that in both years, over half of the suspended sentences imposed at magistrates' courts were in the three- to six-month range (which probably means, in most cases, six months); at the higher courts, the average sentence was about one year. It has been suggested that courts might be inclined to give longer prison sentences when suspended, than they would have given had the sentences been of immediate imprisonment.[9] To

---

[9] This is said to have happened when the suspended sentence was introduced in Israel. See D. Reifen, "New Ventures of Law Enforcement in Israel" (1967) 58 J.Crim.Law, Crim. & P.S. 70, 72. But see the paper by L. Sebba cited in note 16 below.

some extent, this suggestion is supported, at least for magistrates' courts, by a comparison of the data in Table 2 with the lengths of prison sentences imposed on men aged twenty-one and over in 1967: only about 43 per cent. of those sentences were in the three- to six-

TABLE 2

Lengths of Suspended Sentences on Males Age 21 and Over,
1968–69

	1968		1969	
Magistrates' courts	No.	%	No.	%
14 days or less	48	0·2	33	0·2
Over 14 days, up to 1 month	793	3·6	693	3·2
Over 1 month, to 2 months	738	3·4	695	3·2
Over 2 months, to 3 months	8,394	38·5	8,266	38·6
Over 3 months, to 6 months	11,713	53·7	11,694	54·5
Over 6 months	111	0·5	62	0·3
Total	21,797	100·0	21,443	100·0
Assizes and quarter sessions				
6 months or less	901	18·2	1,151	21·4
Over 6 months, to 1 year	2,287	46·2	2,440	45·3
Over 1 year, to 2 years	1,765	35·6	1,791	33·3
Total	4,953	100·0	5,382	100·0

month category.[10] But not too much weight can be put on this comparison, since, as we have seen, there is reason to believe that the majority of offenders given suspended sentences in 1968 and 1969 were probably not offenders who would have received shorter prison sentences had the suspended sentence not been available; they are offenders who would not have been sent to prison at all. It seems reasonable to suppose that the majority of suspended sentences given by magistrates' courts were of the mandatory variety; but until more data are available on the previous criminal records of offenders dealt with in this way, no firm conclusions on this point can be drawn.

---

[10] A similar comparison is not possible for the higher courts, since the only data on lengths of sentence in 1967 are for offenders of all ages. Moreover, the lengths of suspended sentences are given only within three broad categories. But it is interesting to note that a comparison of these data does not show a tendency towards the imposition of longer suspended sentences

Reconviction after suspended sentence

The *Criminal Statistics* for 1968 and 1969 contain a limited amount of information about offenders reconvicted in those years after having been given suspended sentences. It must be stressed that these data do not permit any conclusions whatever concerning the relative "effectiveness" of suspended sentences in preventing reconviction; that is, we cannot say whether the observed reconviction rates of those dealt with in this way are higher or lower than they would have been if another measure had been used instead. For present purposes, however, what matters is simply the observed reconviction rate of these offenders, and the ways in which they were dealt with on reappearing in court after having received a suspended sentence

In 1968, a total of 4,118 men over twenty-one were dealt with for fresh offences committed during the period of a suspended sentence; in 1969, the number was 9,786. The reconvictions in 1968, when related to the total number of sentences imposed in that year, give a gross reconviction rate of just under 13 per cent., in a population at risk of reconviction for rather less than six months, taking into account time spent awaiting trial. (These figures relate to sentences imposed for both indictable and non-indictable offences.) The numbers reconvicted in 1969 obviously include offenders originally given suspended sentences in both 1968 and 1969; for this reason, and because of certain limitations of the official *Criminal Statistics*, some further assumptions must be made in order to estimate the numbers given suspended sentences who are likely to be reconvicted in 1970 and subsequent years.[11] On the

---

[11] These assumptions are made necessary because of the "double-counting" in the *Criminal Statistics*; an offender convicted on the same occasion of both an indictable and non-indictable offence is counted once in each category. Thus there is no way of knowing exactly how many offenders were given suspended sentences in any year, and thus were at risk of reconviction; and the statistics of reconvictions after suspended sentence do not distinguish between indictable and non-indictable offences. The assumptions which I have made are as follows: (1) the reconviction rate of offenders given suspended sentences is independent of the length of suspended sentence, and of the length of period of suspension. It should be noted, however, that these two things are themselves positively associated; that is, there was a tendency for both higher courts and magistrates' courts to suspend longer sentences for longer periods. (2) The curve of reconviction rates was the same for those convicted in both 1968 and 1969, and followed roughly a negative exponential distribution, with about 30 per cent. of those reconvicted in five years being reconvicted within six months; 50 per cent. within one year; 65 per cent. in $1\frac{1}{2}$ years; 75 per cent. in two years; 81 per cent. in $2\frac{1}{2}$ years; and 87 per cent. in three years. (See, *e.g., The Sentence of the Court* (H.M.S.O., 2nd ed., 1969), p. 65.) This suggests that the five-year reconviction rate for those given suspended sentences in 1968 will be about 51 per cent.; for 1969, it appears to be slightly higher. These rates are broadly consistent with those found in the Home Office

basis of these assumptions—and of data contained in *The Sentence of the Court* [12] and elsewhere—it seems likely that the overall *five-year* reconviction rate for offenders given suspended sentences in 1968–69 will probably be of the order of 50 to 55 per cent. These offenders' periods of suspension are, of course, much shorter; the maximum period of suspension is three years, and in about half of all cases to date the period has been between one and two years. Thus it is likely that about 40 per cent. of those given suspended sentences in 1968 and 1969 will be reconvicted at some time during their period of suspension. These estimated reconvictions, for the calendar years 1968–71, are shown in Table 3. It must be stressed that the figures in this table (except for the totals reconvicted in 1968 and 1969) are merely estimates; while they are consistent with the available data, and are based on assumptions which I believe to be conservative, there is at present no way of knowing how accurate they are. The totals reconvicted in 1970 and subsequent

TABLE 3

Estimated Reconvictions of Males Over 21 Given Suspended Sentences in 1968 and 1969

	Reconvicted in:				
	1968	1969	1970	1971	1972
Sentenced in 1968					
Period of suspension:					
1 year	676	451	—	—	—
1–2 years	2,071	2,423	690	—	—
2–3 years	1,345	1,574	756	246	—
Total	4,092	4,448	1,446	246	—
Sentenced in 1969					
Period of suspension:					
1 year	—	571	374	—	—
1–2 years	—	2,531	2,915	748	—
2–3 years	—	1,443	1,660	766	281
Total	—	4,545	4,949	1,514	281
Grand total	4,092	8,993	6,395	1,760	281

study reported in *The Sentence of the Court, op. cit.*, pp. 65–69. (3) I have calculated these rates on the basis of the numbers of suspended sentences passed in 1968 and 1969, ignoring the " double-counting " mentioned in the text. The true population at risk is lower than I have assumed; thus the true reconviction rate is higher. This should not make any difference, however, to my estimates of the numbers likely to be reconvicted in future years.

[12] London, H.M.S.O., 2nd ed., 1969.

years will of course include offenders given suspended sentences in those years, as well as offenders dealt with in that way in 1968 and 1969. The table does bring out, however, an important point which must be borne in mind in assessing the working of the suspended sentence. This is that, because the period of suspension may be up to three years, some offenders dealt with in this way in 1968 will continue to be at risk of having their suspended sentences activated on reconviction throughout 1971. It will not, therefore, be possible to assess accurately the full effect of this measure on receptions into prison for at least another two years

Not all of those reconvicted during the period of suspension have their suspended sentences activated in full; as is provided by section 40 (1) of the 1967 Act, some go to prison for a shorter period, and for some the court makes no order. The *Criminal Statistics* show that in 1968 just over 90 per cent. of those reconvicted during their periods of suspension were committed to prison (for the original or a shorter term); in 1969, the proportion committed to prison fell to 84 per cent. Thus a total of 4,001 offenders were committed to prison under suspended sentences in 1968, and 8,321 in 1969. The *total* numbers of adult males received into prison under sentence (without the option of a fine) were 31,565 in 1967, 24,760 in 1968 and 27,695 in 1969. There was thus a reduction in receptions into prison in the first year in which the courts could impose suspended sentences; but this reduction was much smaller in 1969, and may well disappear completely in 1971, if reconvictions after suspended sentences continue to rise.

As we have seen, a large proportion of the suspended sentences imposed in 1968–69 were imposed on offenders who before 1967 would probably have been dealt with by non-institutional measures (in particular by fines). Of course some of the latter group of offenders would have been reconvicted in any case, and some would have been sent to prison on reconviction. But these offenders' chances of imprisonment on reconviction would certainly have been much less if they had not received suspended sentences. As we have seen, the probability of imprisonment on reconviction after a suspended sentence has so far been of the order of 0·85–0·90. By way of comparison, in a pre-1967 sample of prisoners for which I have data on this point, the probability of imprisonment on reconviction after a fine or probation is about 0·15 for those with three previous court appearances, rising to about 0·40 for those with five previous court appearances. These data suggest that the risk of imprisonment on reconviction has more than doubled, for those so far given suspended sentences; for those with no, one or two previous convictions, the increase has obviously been even greater. Indeed, the chance of going to prison on reconviction after a suspended sentence may well be higher, for some offenders dealt with in this way, than the chance of imprisonment after a prison sentence prior to 1968.

Length of subsequent prison sentences

The size of the prison population is a function not only of the numbers received into prison, but also of the average effective length of sentence (allowing for remission, release on parole, etc.).[13] It is here that the effect of the suspended sentence has really been most marked. In a case in 1968,[14] the Court of Appeal said that suspended sentences should normally be allowed to run *consecutive* to any prison sentence imposed on reconviction; and it seems clear that this is what has happened in most cases. As Table 4 shows, there has been a drastic shift in the lengths of sentences of men received into prison since 1968: about half of those sentences have been for over six months, compared with less than a third in 1967. It would not be surprising if implemented suspended sentences had doubled the effective lengths (allowing for remission, etc.) of offenders imprisoned after having been given a suspended sentence. The effect of this, in turn, could well be to increase the prison population by as much as 25–30 per cent., even if receptions into prison do not rise above 1967 levels.

TABLE 4

Percentage Distributions of Length of Sentence, Adult Males Received into Prison under Sentence without Option of a Fine, 1967–69

	1967	1968	1969
Length of sentence			
Not over 1 month	6·5	4·1	3·3
1 month up to 3 months	22·3	14·5	12·2
3 months up to 6 months	31·3	27·1	23·8
6 months up to 1 year	17·2	22·3	26·2
1 year up to 2 years	13·8	19·2	21·3
2 years up to 3 years	5·0	7·2	8·0
Over 3 years	4·0	5·5	5·3
Total	100·0	100·0	100·0
Numbers received	31,565	24,760	27,695

[13] For a full discussion of this point, see R. F. Sparks, *Local Prisons: The Crisis in the English Penal System* (London: Heinemann, 1971), esp. Chaps. 1, 3.
[14] *Ithell* [1969] 2 All E.R. 449, 450.

A final point about the impact of the suspended sentence on the prison system concerns the *types* of prison most affected by the initial reduction in receptions into the prison system in 1968, and the consequent increase in later years. The statutory criteria of eligibility for the mandatory suspended sentence show clearly that this measure is aimed primarily at offenders against property who have not previously been in prison or borstal; and given the nature of judicial sentencing policies, it is clear that this is also the type of offender who is most likely to be dealt with by means of the discretionary suspended sentence. But it is precisely these offenders who—as non-violent " star " prisoners—were likely, before the 1967 Act, to be sent to *open* prisons. But the serious problem of over-crowding which existed before 1967 in the English prison system was almost entirely confined to *general local* prisons; open prisons are not, and never have been, over-crowded. Thus, given the legal criteria of offenders being suitable for the suspended sentence, it could have been predicted that this measure would be most likely to reduce over-crowding in a part of the English prison system in which over-crowding does not occur.

It seems clear that this was, in fact, precisely what happened : by the end of 1968 the numbers in open prisons had fallen sharply, whereas over-crowding in general local prisons was barely affected. As the prison population increased again in 1969–70, the open prisons naturally tended to fill up again. But since over-crowding is not permitted in these prisons, the further increase in the prison population which has resulted from the suspended sentence has been confined almost entirely to the general local prisons, thus aggravating the considerable problems which these institutions must face. At the end of 1969, according to the Prison Department's annual report,[15] general local prisons contained nearly half again as many inmates as they were built to hold; over 13,000 of these inmates were sleeping three in a cell, compared with 6,000 at the end of 1967

Conclusion: explaining the malfunction

It must be repeated that it is too early to give a full and final assessment of the working of the suspended sentence or of its effects on sentencing policy. Nonetheless, there is certainly evidence that in its first two years this measure did not work in the way in which it was intended to work; it seems clear that one main objective of the suspended sentence was to reduce the numbers in prison, and this has not happened. What is the reason for this? An easy

---

[15] Cmnd. 4486, p. 9.

answer, already being heard in certain quarters, is that the courts
have simply used this measure in the " wrong " way. They did not
give suspended sentences in the way in which Parliament intended;
and they did not follow the dictum of the Court of Appeal in
O'Keefe's case. But this answer merely begs the question, which
really is: why did the courts fail to use the measure in the " right "
way? It is of interest to note that a similar " misuse " appears
to have taken place in Israel, when suspended sentences were introduced there in 1954.[16] And it may well be that the failure of the
suspended sentence to date has been a consequence of the natural
operation of the penal system, and of established sentencing policies
and practices, rather than a capricious or wilful misuse by the
courts of this new measure.[17]

A full explanation of this matter must clearly wait for further
research on the sentencing process. More data are needed on the
sentencing policies adhered to by the courts, the consistency with
which these policies are followed, and the criteria by which they are
put into effect and there is also a need for a general theory of
judicial decision-making in sentencing.[18] But as a preliminary to
this research, and as a possible starting-point for the development
of such a theory, the following explanation seems reasonable in the
light of the available evidence.

First, the relevant sections of the Criminal Justice Act 1967 offer
very little direction or guidance to the courts concerning the types
of case for which the suspended sentence should be used. It is true
that suspension is mandatory for prison sentences in certain cases;
and there are exclusionary criteria telling the courts when a case is
not one to which mandatory suspension applies. But there are no
criteria which tell the courts when a case *is* one to which the
mandatory rule applies; that is, there are no criteria which tell the
courts when a short suspended sentence (rather than, say, a fine)
should be used. Nor do the relevant sections of the 1967 Act give
the courts any guidance as to when the discretionary suspended
sentence should be used. In purely formal terms, then, the courts
have virtually unfettered discretion in this matter. This is, of course,

---

[16] See L. Sebba, " Penal Reform and Court Practice: The Case of the
Suspended Sentence " (1969) 21 *Scripta Hierosolymitana* 133. The author
found that in district courts in Israel suspended sentences were used in
1955 in lieu of fines in about half of cases.
[17] Indeed, the apparent difference in the use of the suspended sentence in
1968 and 1969 (see above, Table 1) suggests that the *O'Keefe* rule may have
had some effect in 1969.
[18] For a discussion of this problem, and for a model of the sentencing process
based on the use of information, see Roger Hood and Richard Sparks,
Key Issues in Criminology (London, Weidenfeld & Nicolson, 1970),
Chap. 5, esp. pp. 156–170.

generally true of statutes relating to sentencing; but it is not *necessarily* true, as a comparison with, *e.g.,* the First Offenders Act 1958 or the Criminal Justice Act 1961 will show. As is well known, the Court of Appeal (Criminal Division), in its judgments on appeals against sentence, has laid down a wide variety of more detailed rules and sentencing principles, and has stipulated criteria for applying other sentencing rules and policies.[19] The dictum in *O'Keefe's* case is an example of this. But it is not known how far these rules are actually followed in practice, even by the higher courts; no research has yet been done to see how consistently the sentencing policies of the Court of Appeal are applied in practice.[20] There is, moreover, good reason to believe that these rules are much less relevant to the sentencing of offenders in magistrates' courts. For one thing, they relate to cases tried at assizes or quarter sessions, most of which differ from the mine-run of cases tried summarily; for another, there are no formal or informal lines of communication whereby magistrates' courts (or magistrates' courts' clerks) can easily learn of the rules.[21]

In any case, could the courts have followed the *O'Keefe* rule, even if they had known about it? To answer this question, we must reflect briefly on the sentencing policies of the courts before the 1967 Act, so far as these can be inferred from the available data on sentencing practice. A good deal of research, in England and elsewhere, has been done on the question of disparities in sentencing; that is roughly, the extent to which courts are consistent with each other, and with themselves over time, in dealing with the same type of offender. Such disparities undoubtedly do exist, especially in magistrates' courts. But they should not be allowed to mask the fact that, over the country as a whole, the sentencing practices of the courts are fairly consistent over time. Though there are changes in the proportions of offenders dealt with in different ways from one year to the next, these changes tend to be very slight; and the

---

[19] For a discussion of these, see D. A. Thomas, *Principles of Sentencing* (London, Heinemann, 1970), esp. Chaps. 1 and 2. For examples, of course, see any issue of this *Review*.

[20] An example of the kind of research which would be necessary is E. Green, *Judicial Attitudes in Sentencing* (London, Macmillan, 1961). It is unfortunate that in the court studied by Green (Philadelphia), and indeed in most American courts, no set of rules and principles analogous to those enunciated by the English Court of Appeal exists.

[21] By contrast, puisne judges sit with the Court of Appeal (Criminal Division) on criminal appeals; the sentencing conferences instituted by the former Lord Chief Justice, Lord Parker, are an example of another means of informal communication. The same function is fulfilled only to a limited degree by training for new and experienced magistrates. For a full discussion see my article, " Sentencing by Magistrates " (1965) 9 *Sociological Review Monograph* 71.

available data (for example, on prisoners) suggest a fair degree of judical consistency in the use of the main types of measures available to the courts, at least where adult offenders are concerned. These measures—absolute and conditional discharge, fines, probation and imprisonment—can obviously be ranked according to severity, by fairly clear criteria. There is, moreover, some reason to think that these measures tend to be used sequentially: that is, that nominal penalties (discharge and fine) tend to be used early in an offender's career, with imprisonment generally being reserved for those offenders who continue to appear before the courts, despite having been dealt with by the less severe penalties for their earlier offences. There are, of course, good economic reasons for such a policy, quite apart from its consistency with a " tariff " sentencing policy based in part on recidivism.

It must be emphasised that this utilitarian policy of using measures for adults in sequence according to severity is not invariably followed by the courts, for a number of reasons. For one thing, the perceived seriousness of the current offence(s) is apparently an important constraint in the choice of sentence, and offenders do not necessarily commit crimes of increasing seriousness. Moreover, there is evidence to suggest that fines and probation are in effect separate routes to imprisonment for many types of offender, rather than being successive steps on the same route.[22] Nonetheless, it is clear that there is *some* tendency for the measures to be used in this way, so that the probability of an offender's receiving a prison sentence increases steadily, the more often he returns to court. To the extent that this is true, the penal system is rather like a ladder, with nominal penalties comprising the bottom rung and imprisonment the top rung: as offenders climb the ladder, *i.e.* continue to appear before the courts, they receive measures of increasing severity, until they reach the top rung and are sent to prison. To complete the metaphor, we may add that at each rung some offenders "fall off the ladder," *i.e.* are not reconvicted; and that the probability of staying on the ladder increases the further one goes up it. Thus there are many offenders, few of them recidivists, on the lower rungs of the ladder; and a rather smaller number, most of whom are recidivists, at the top rung.

It is also clear that in the last fifteen or twenty years, there has been a good deal of official and unofficial pressure, from a variety of sources, to limit the use of imprisonment and to use it only as a last resort. Courts have been encouraged—and in some cases

---

[22] For a discussion of this evidence see R. F. Sparks, *Local Prisons,* etc., pp. 20-23.

compelled—to use fines and probation in place of prison sentences (especially short ones). And in the years 1963–67 there was in fact a steady, though very gradual, drop in the proportions of convicted adult offenders sent to prison by magistrates' courts, especially for short periods of time. The increasing proportion of recidivists given probation is one indication of this; the increase in receptions into prison for non-payment of fines in recent years is probably another. In terms of my metaphor, courts were discouraged from allowing offenders to proceed to the top rung of the penological ladder; the result was that the rungs just below the top one tended to contain an increasing number of offenders who would, in earlier years, have been on the top rung (prison). This policy of " one last chance before prison " was, of course, not invariable; but it does seem to have been fairly widespread, and conversations with experienced magistrates suggest that it was the source of a certain amount of tension for some members of the bench.

At this point, the 1967 Act added a new rung—the suspended sentence—to the ladder, placing this immediately below the top or prison rung. The intention of Parliament (and, presumably, of the Court of Appeal) was that the suspended sentence should be an alternative to imprisonment (rather than, say, to fines): that is, to pursue our metaphor, it was intended that some of those offenders allocated to the top rung of the ladder should instead be placed on the one just below it. But given sentencing practices of the courts up to 1967, it is likely that there were already many offenders on the rungs just below the suspended sentence rung, who should (in the opinion of the courts) ideally have been moved up instead. These offenders may have constituted only a fairly small proportion of the numbers fined or put on probation before 1967. But because the *absolute numbers* fined were much greater, a large number of those who received suspended sentences would have come from that group rather than from the group who would have previously been given imprisonment; and as we have seen, this is precisely what happened.

The characterisation of the suspended sentence as an alternative to imprisonment had another important consequence. This is that the natural sentence to be given to those offenders who were reconvicted after having been given a suspended sentence was a sentence of immediate imprisonment; in metaphorical terms, there was only one higher rung to which these offenders could advance. This could conceivably be true, because of the structure of the sentencing system, even if section 40 (1) of the 1967 Act had not virtually directed the courts to order suspended sentences to take effect on reconviction. And their probability of making that jump, as we have seen, is very much greater than if they had been fined or put on probation on the previous court appearance. The increase in the prison population in 1969 and 1970 followed inevitably in this situation.

It may be thought, nonetheless, that a rigorous application of the rule enunciated in *O'Keefe's* case could have prevented this situation; but I think this is a mistake. For what the dictum says, in effect, is that the court should first decide whether or not an offender is suitable for imprisonment, on the assumption that the suspended sentence is not available; and then should decide whether or not to suspend the prison sentence. But it is one thing to decide that an offender is (or is not) suitable for imprisonment if that prison sentence *cannot* be suspended; and another (and very differ-ent) thing to decide that the same offender is suitable for a prison sentence, given that that sentence *can* be suspended. In the first case, utilitarian considerations of economy may quite properly be taken into account in deciding to use a fine or probation instead of imprisonment. In the second case, these considerations will naturally be less important, given that there is a chance that the prison sentence will not in fact be implemented. Moreover, if the offender is one whom the court feels really ought (because of his previous record, type of crime, etc.) to receive " something more " than a fine or probation, then the suspended sentence becomes a natural choice. It allows the court to do something which *looks* sufficiently severe in such a case, but which may cost nothing; as a matter of judicial psychology, the measure must often have been virtually irresistible.

I would repeat that much further research is necessary, to show how far this general model of sentencing behaviour is a correct one, either in general or in the particular case of suspended sentences. Nonetheless, it seems clear that if the description which I have sketched is even approximately correct, then the counter-productivity of the suspended sentence was not merely likely but inevitable. More importantly, it was not, strictly speaking, a consequence of the misuse by the courts of a new form of sentence; on the contrary, it was a natural consequence of the policies and general objectives which the courts have quite properly followed in recent years.

Given this situation, it is not at all easy to see what can be done to remedy matters. It may be, of course, that it will be unnecessary to do anything; the courts' use of suspended sentences may well change in the next two or three years, so as to avoid the need to make any further alterations to the system, and in any case this should not be done until further data on the working of the system are available. But if further changes do prove necessary, it is difficult to see what form they should take. Abolition of the suspended sentence, by repeal of the relevant sections of the Criminal Justice Act 1967, is of course the simplest solution. But it is not necessarily the best solution; and it certainly would not necessarily mean an automatic reversion to the pre-1967 position. Another possibility, theoretically more promising, is the introduction of further non-institutional measures; this has recently been recommended by, among others, the Advisory Council on the Penal System.[23] It seems clear, however, that these new measures should be ones which can be used by the courts at the earlier stages of offenders' careers, rather than being " alternatives to imprisonment ": that is, to revert to my metaphor, they should aim to lengthen the penological ladder by putting new rungs in at the bottom end, rather than near the top. Otherwise there is a danger that the experience of the suspended sentence will merely be repeated with these measures. It must also be admitted that it is very difficult to think of suitable new non-institutional measures; what *can* one do with the majority of adult offenders, other than admonition (with or without court appearance), a financial penalty, supervision, or deprivation of liberty?

Perhaps the most promising course of action, in the long run, would be a considerable increase in legislative control over sentencing practice; that is, the introduction of further statutory limitations on the discretionary power of the courts (in particular, magistrates' courts), and a more clear enunciation—again perhaps by statute—of the discretionary principles which the courts are to apply, and the criteria which they are to use in doing so. Another possibility is the creation of a more adequate system for appeals against sentences passed by magistrates' courts—perhaps through the Crown Courts to the Court of Appeal (Criminal Division). But this may not help, unless those appellate courts give more positive direction and guidance than has so far been given concerning suspended sentences.[24]

In any case, a general lesson to be learned from the experience of the suspended sentence is surely that the established sentencing policies and practices of the courts must be understood, and taken into account, when a structural change in the penal system or in sentencing policy is contemplated. The measures which collectively comprise the English penal system do not function in isolation

---

[23] Advisory Council on the Penal System, Report on *Non-Custodial and Semi-Custodial Penalties* (London, H.M.S.O., 1970).
[24] I owe this point to David Thomas.

from one another, and allocation of offenders to these measures is in no sense random; the courts' own perceptions of their objectives, and of offenders, will in the last resort largely determine the use which they make of any new form of sentence which is introduced. Experience with the suspended sentence to date suggests that these elementary penalogical facts cannot be ignored, when attempts to change the penal system are made.

[22]

Journal of Criminal Justice, Vol. 8, pp. 221–231 (1980).
Pergamon Press. Printed in the U.S.A.

0047-2352/80/040221-11$02.00/0

PRISON SIZE, OVERCROWDING, PRISON VIOLENCE, AND RECIDIVISM

DAVID P. FARRINGTON

University of Cambridge
Institute of Criminology
7 West Road
Cambridge CB3 9DT,
England

CHRISTOPHER P. NUTTALL

Research Division
Ministry of the Solicitor General
340 Laurier Avenue West
Ottawa, Ontario KIA OP8
Canada

ABSTRACT

Contrary to a widespread belief about the undesirability of relatively large prisons, a review of the criminological literature yields no empirical evidence that prison size influences behavior inside or after leaving prison. The English prison statistics show that prison offenses, and more specifically assaults, are less likely in larger prisons. However, it was impossible in these analyses to control for the kinds of inmates in each prison. In a more controlled analysis of correctional effectiveness (defined as the difference between predicted and actual reconviction rates), there was a strong tendency for the more overcrowded prisons to be less effective. Size was only weakly related to effectiveness, and this association was reduced further after controlling for overcrowding. It was concluded that an important priority for governmental agencies should be to reduce overcrowding in prisons.

There seems to be a widespread belief among criminologists and criminal justice personnel that prisons containing smaller numbers of inmates are more desirable than those containing larger numbers. It has been argued that large prison size per se has a deleterious effect on the behavior of inmates inside the prison and on their behavior after leaving it. Several governmental advisory committees have recommended that prisons should be smaller, including the National Advisory Commission on Criminal Justice Standards and Goals (1973) in the United States and the Solicitor General's working group on federal maximum security institutions design (1971) in

Canada. However, none of these committees has ever provided any empirical evidence to back up their recommendations. The purpose of this article is to investigate whether it is possible to obtain empirical evidence at the present time proving that large prison size has undesirable effects on behavior inside or after leaving prison. Special attention will be given to violence within the prison and to recidivism after leaving it.

PRISON SIZE

While most writers on correctional issues have agreed that small prisons are generally more desirable, they have disagreed over the operational definition of "small." The recommended optimal sizes in different countries or states always seem to be less than the existing sizes, but otherwise have little in common. More than twenty-five years ago, R.D. Barnes, then senior architect of the United States Federal Bureau of Prisons, argued that, "For a really effective program of reformation, no institution should try to house more than 1,200 inmates" (1951: 270). On the other hand, the Canadian Solicitor General's (1971) working group concluded that "an institution for about 150 inmates represents the maximum number for a viable program." Most other recommendations fall between these two extremes.

Prisons in the United States have generally been much larger than those in Canada or England. The report on corrections of the National Advisory Commission on Criminal Justice Standards and Goals (1973) shows that the average number of inmates housed in each state maximum security prison was about 970. In England and Wales, the Home Office prison statistics for 1978 show that the average population of closed prisons for males (approximately equivalent to maximum and medium security prisons in North America) was just under 500 (Home Office, 1979a).

To some extent, the large sizes of prisons in the United States are a function of the large numbers of persons sent to prison. After an illuminating discussion of the difficulties of obtaining comparable definitions of "prisons" and "prisoners" in different countries, Waller and Chan (1977) concluded that the United States had the highest

imprisonment rate of all fifteen countries that they had surveyed. During the last decade, the prison population of the United States has increased dramatically. Rutherford et al. (1977) showed that the number of prisoners in state and federal institutions increased from 187,000 in 1968 to 283,000 in 1977. The 1977 prison population was higher than the total rated capacity for institutions of 262,000, suggesting that many prisons were overcrowded. Overcrowding is also a serious problem in England at the present time.

SIZE AND BEHAVIOR INSIDE PRISON

It is almost impossible to locate research in which the factor of prison size has been related to behavior inside or after leaving the prison. Perhaps the most relevant studies were carried out by the South Carolina Department of Corrections (1973) and by Sylvester, Reed, and Nelson (1977). Both were based on questionnaires sent to state and federal institutions in the United States, although Sylvester et al. supplemented their questionnaire data with information from criminal justice records and from the Bureau of the Census. The South Carolina Department of Corrections was interested in prison riots, defining these as incidents involving fifteen or more inmates with damage to property or physical injury. Sylvester et al. were interested in homicides in prison.

The South Carolina researchers found that prisons that had experienced riots tended to be larger than those that had not. In fact, 66 percent of riot prisons had a population of more than 500, in comparison with only 33 percent of nonriot prisons. Sylvester et al. found that homicides were more likely to occur in the larger prisons. Just over half (51 percent) of prisons containing 1,000 or more inmates had experienced a homicide, in comparison with 31 percent of those containing between 500 and 999, and 9 percent of those containing fewer than 500. However, neither group of researchers expressed their riot or homicide rates in relation to the number of prisoners. Even if any given prisoner was just as likely to be involved in a riot or a homicide in a larger institution as in a smaller one, more riots or homicides would occur in larger institutions, because more prisoners were at risk. To draw conclusions about whether the total number of riots or homicides would be less if all prisoners were held in smaller institutions than if all prisoners were held in larger ones, it is essential to know the riot or homicide rate per 100 prisoners in each kind of institution.

Another problem with these two researches is that the factor of size was confounded with many others. Sylvester et al. reported that the larger prisons tended to be maximum security institutions and that the security level of a prison was more closely related to the homicide rate than was its size. Furthermore, the larger prisons tended to be older, to have higher inmate/staff ratios, to be more overcrowded, and to be in urban areas. Sylvester et al. did not show that size was related to the homicide rate independently of each of these other factors. Since there was a very marked tendency for both assailants and victims to have criminal records of violence, they concluded that individual factors weighed more heavily in the aetiology of prison violence than environmental factors.

The South Carolina researchers found that the riot prisons differed from the nonriot prisons in many respects other than size, for example, in being maximum security institutions, in being at least sixty years old, in having higher inmate/staff ratios, and in having inmates who were younger and who had more previous convictions. Because of the failure to isolate the factor of size and control for other factors, it cannot be concluded from this study that large size was a contributory or causal factor in prison riots. It may be that riots are more likely where the prisoners are younger or more criminal, or in older or maximum security institutions; any of these causal relationships would produce an artefactual association between riots and large prison size. However, in the absence of some kind of multivariate analysis in which other factors were controlled statistically while each factor was studied, it is difficult to draw any conclusions about the causes of prison riots from this research.

The research of Megargee (1976, 1977) was more sophisticated, but on a much smaller scale. He investigated the relationship between prison offenses and population size in one Florida medium security institution for male offenders between the ages of eighteen and twenty-five. Over a three-year period, the population of this institution fluctuated between 524 and 628, and the available living space also fluctuated, because of renovation work. Megargee related fluctuations in these two factors to monthly incident reports of offenses ranging from refusing to work and insolence to assault with a deadly weapon and attempted escape. He found that the violation rate per 100 inmates was only weakly correlated with the population size, but strongly correlated (negatively) with the available living space. The available living space was significantly and negatively correlated with the population size, because more inmates happened to be in the institution during the renovation periods.

Megargee demonstrated that the population size was not related to the violation rate independently of the available living space, whereas the available living space was significantly and negatively related to the violation rate independently of the population size. These results indicate that the population size only appeared to be related to the violation rate because it happened to be related to the available living space, which was the more important factor. Megargee concluded that population density was related to disruptive behavior in prison. However, as he pointed out, variations in personal living space were associated with changes in other factors. When the available living space was reduced, individuals moved from a dormitory undergoing renovation to other areas within the institution. This involved territorial intrusions and disruptions of friendship ties as well as reductions in personal living space, and the first two factors might have been more important in producing disruptive behavior than the space reduction or change in population density.

None of these three studies, which are probably the most directly relevant to the topic of prison size, shows that it is a contributory or causal factor in prison violence. Other researches are of more marginal relevance. For example, Moos (1975) investigated aggression in living units in juvenile correctional institutions in the United States. He found that there was more aggression in units with lower inmate/staff ratios, which also tended to be the smaller units. In agreement with Megargee's conclusion about the importance of population density, Nacci, Teitelbaum, and Prather (1977) reported that overcrowding (the ratio of average population to capacity) was significantly related to assault rates in thirty-seven federal prisons. Paulus, McCain, and Cox (1978) also pointed to the importance of overcrowding in prison, in linking it to high stress, psychological impairment, and high mortality rates.

PRISON SIZE AND BEHAVIOR AFTER LEAVING PRISON

There are even fewer researches in which prison size is related to behavior after leaving the prison, and all have been carried out in juvenile institutions. Millham, Bullock, and Cherrett (1975) and Dunlop (1974) both studied a number of English juvenile correctional institutions for males, but neither set of results shows that size is correlated with the reconviction rate. No researcher has ever tried to investigate the effects of size by randomly allocating offenders to prisons differing only in size. The nearest to this is the research of Jesness (1965, 1971), who randomly allocated juvenile offenders to living units of different sizes within the same institution. He found that boys housed in the larger (fifty-bed) unit had a higher incidence of parole revocations than those housed in the smaller (twenty-bed) unit during the first year after leaving the institution. However, the cumulative revocation rates in a five-year follow-up were very similar. It is not possible to attribute the short-lived difference to the effects of size, because the larger unit had a larger inmate/staff ratio and a different (more punitive) regime.

Perhaps rather surprisingly, this review of existing research relevant to prison size has failed to unearth any empirical evidence that prison size influences behavior inside or after leaving the prison. The following pages document our own research on this topic, using the English prison statistics. We were able to investigate prison offenses in general, more specifically assaults, and reconviction rates.

THE ENGLISH PRISON STATISTICS

Prison Offenses

In England and Wales, the Home Office prison statistics for 1978 give details of the number of offenses punished in each prison, and of the average daily population (Home Office, 1979a).

It is therefore possible to investigate whether there are more recorded offenses against prison rules in larger prisons than in smaller ones. Table 1 shows the results of this analysis, for closed prisons only (i.e., those surrounded by a wall or a fence as a barrier to escapes; these are roughly equivalent to maximum and medium security institutions in North America). It can be seen that, as the size of the institution increases, the average number of offenses per prison also tends to increase. However, the average number of offenses per prisoner was less in the larger institutions (containing over 400 men) than in the smaller ones. This was a statistically significant difference (mean offenses per prisoner in thirty-one smaller prisons = 1.62, and in twenty-four larger ones = 0.94; t = 3.52 with 53 d.f., p <0.001).

One problem in interpreting these results is that the fifty-five closed prisons listed in Table 1 include a number of different types. The major distinction is between the local prisons, which take prisoners direct from the courts and those serving short sentences, and the training prisons, which take longer-term prisoners after their initial assessment in a local prison. This distinction is by no means absolute. Several institutions classified as local prisons by the Home Office have training parts (e.g., Exeter, Norwich, Wormwood Scrubs). Wormwood Scrubs, in particular, is a heterogeneous prison, and its four self-contained cell blocks house prisoners as different as fifteen-year-old borstal boys and men serving life imprisonment.

The local prisons tend to be larger than the training ones. In fact, fifteen of the twenty-four larger prisons were local, while twenty-two of the thirty-one smaller ones were training. The association between large size and low average offenses per prisoner was statistically significant for the training prisons only (mean offenses per prisoner in twenty-two smaller institutions = 1.82, and in nine larger = 0.99; t = 2.50 with 29 d.f., p. <0.02). It was not significant for the local prisons only (mean in nine smaller institutions = 1.12, and in fifteen larger ones = 0.91).

Another problem is that many of the offenses are comparatively trivial rule infractions. It may be that these kinds of offenses occurring in a smaller prison are more likely to be observed, recorded, and punished than these kinds of

TABLE 1

OFFENSES PUNISHED IN CLOSED PRISONS IN ENGLAND AND WALES IN 1978 (MALES ONLY) VERSUS SIZE OF INSTITUTION

Size of Prison*	Number of Prisons	Total Population	Average Population per Prison	Total Offenses	Average Offenses per Prison	Average Offenses per Prisoner
200 or less	7	1,111	158.7	2,010	287.1	1.81
201–300	10	2,486	248.6	4,002	400.2	1.61
301–400	14	4,764	339.0	7,429	530.6	1.57
401–500	6	2,699	449.8	2,284	380.7	0.85
501–750	8	4,566	570.8	4,480	560.0	0.98
751 or more	10	11,768	1,176.8	11,431	1,143.1	0.97
Total	55	27,394	498.1	31,636	575.2	1.15

SOURCE: Home Office, 1979a, Table 9.2.
*Size of prison refers to average daily population. Offenses punished at one establishment but committed at another are excluded. Three closed prisons are excluded: Chelmsford (which ceased operations because of a fire part-way through 1978), Grendon (a special psychiatric prison), and Standford Hill (which, although classified as a closed prison, is a secure unit within an open prison). The 31,636 offenses were as follows:

Disobedience	11,252
Unauthorized transactions/articles	4,908
Disrespect/impropriety	4,244
Willful damage to property	1,406
Assault/gross personal violence to officer	1,067
Escape/attempted escape	235
Mutiny	7
Other offenses	8,517

offenses occurring in a larger one. Fox (1970) argued that, in institutions with high inmate/staff ratios, the staff turned a blind eye to all except the most flagrant violations. The next analysis is restricted to offenses that are especially likely to be recorded and punished, namely, assaults and gross personal violence to officers.

Assaults

Table 2 shows that, for the training prisons, the average number of assaults per 100 prisoners decreased with the size of the prison. However, there seemed to be little relationship between size and the assault rate for the local prisons (since only three local prisons contained fewer than 300 inmates, the categories 300 or less and 301–500 have been amalgamated for the local prisons in Table 2).

On the face of it, this appears to confirm the earlier results obtained with prison offenses in general, showing relatively fewer offenses in larger training prisons but not in larger local ones. Unfortunately, the differences in assault rates between larger and smaller training prisons were not statistically significant (mean assault rate per 100 inmates in twenty-two institutions containing 400 or fewer inmates = 4.28, and in nine larger institutions = 2.00; $t = 1.56$ with 29 d.f., n.s.). Furthermore, the correlation between size and the assault rate for training prisons was not significant (Spearman $r = -0.11$). These findings make it impossible to discard the hypothesis that the earlier results for offenses in general were produced at least to some extent by the underrecording of trivial offenses in larger prisons.

Despite the absence of significant findings in this section, all the results quoted so far indicate

226   DAVID P. FARRINGTON and CHRISTOPHER P. NUTTALL

TABLE 2

ASSAULTS PUNISHED IN CLOSED PRISONS IN ENGLAND AND WALES IN 1978 (MALES ONLY) VERSUS SIZE
OF INSTITUTION

Size of Prison*	Number of Prisons	Total Population	Average Population per Prison	Total Assaults	Average Assaults per Prison	Average Assaults per 100 Prisoners
Training Prisons						
300 or less	14	2,895	206.8	136	9.7	4.70
301–500	11	4,088	371.6	144	13.1	3.52
501 or more	6	3,592	598.7	82	13.7	2.28
Total	31	10,575	341.1	362	11.7	3.42
Local Prisons						
500 or less	12	4,077	339.8	165	13.8	4.05
501 or more	12	12,742	1,061.8	540	45.0	4.24
Total	24	16,819	700.8	705	29.4	4.19

SOURCE: Number of assaults (including gross personal violence to officers) and average daily population (Home Office,
1979a, Table 9.2).
*Three closed prisons are excluded, as described in the notes to Table 1. Local prisons with training parts are classified as
local.

that the relationship between size and prison
offenses is different in the training prisons from
the local prisons. Why should this be so? One of
the principal differences between local and training prisons is in the degree of overcrowding. For
all local prisons in 1978, the average daily
population exceeded the certified normal population, defined as the number of offenders the
institution can hold without overcrowding (see
Home Office, 1979b, Appendix 3). Most of the
accommodations in English closed prisons take
the form of cells designed (usually according to
nineteenth century standards) to house one man.
If a prison is overcrowded, this means in practice
that two or three men are sleeping in some of
these single cells, often without proper sanitation.
The degree of overcrowding in local prisons is
intense. In 1978, the twenty-four local prisons had
a total capacity of 11,787, but were housing
16,819 inmates. In contrast, the thirty-one training prisons had a total capacity of 11,103 and were
housing 10,575 inmates.

While all the twenty-four local prisons were
overcrowded by Home Office standards, this was

true of only eight of the thirty-one training
prisons. The eight overcrowded training prisons
were similar to local prisons in that the assault
rate was slightly higher in the larger prisons than
in the smaller ones. In the nonovercrowded
training prisons, the average assaults per 100
prisoners decreased from 5.77 in nine prisons
holding 300 men or less to 3.12 in ten prisons
holding 301–500 men and 1.63 in four prisons
holding 501 men or more (cf. Table 2). However,
even in the nonovercrowded training prisons, the
correlation between size and the assault rate was
not statistically significant (Spearman $r = -0.28$).

A major problem in interpreting any relationship between size and the assault rate is that the
Home Office prison statistics give no detailed
information about the characteristics of the intake
to each prison. It may be that the assault rate
reflects the kinds of inmates allocated to each
institution rather than any aspect of the prison
itself. For example, the four prisons specifically
for offenders under age twenty-one were all
among the top ten training prisons in assault
rates. It seems plausible that this is because

TABLE 3

ASSAULTS PUNISHED IN DISPERSAL PRISONS IN ENGLAND AND WALES IN 1977 VERSUS SIZE OF
INSTITUTION AND PERCENTAGE OF CATEGORY A PRISONERS

Dispersal Prison	Average Daily Population	Percent Category A Prisoners*	Total Assaults	Assaults per 100 Prisoners
Gartree	250	14	18	7.20
Albany	294	13	25	8.50
Long Lartin	337	11	10	2.97
Parkhurst	411	10	17	4.14
Wakefield	724	8	24	3.31
Wormwood Scrubs	1,400	3	57	4.07

SOURCE: Home Office, 1978, Tables 4(c) and 9.2.
*The seventh dispersal prison, Hull, contained no Category A prisoners on the date the census was taken (June 30, 1977), because all these prisoners had been removed to other institutions while repairs were being carried out following a riot in 1976.

younger prisoners are more likely to be violent than older ones.

It was notable that three of the five training prisons with the highest assault rates were drawn from the seven "dispersal" institutions with the highest degree of security. About 1 percent of inmates are placed in the highest category (A) for security purposes, and these are prisoners whose escape would be highly dangerous to the public or the police or to the security of the country. Most of the Category A prisoners are serving life sentences, predominantly passed for murder or other violent acts, including terrorism and robberies. It is the policy of the Home Office to house these prisoners in the "dispersal" prisons.

The Home Office prison statistics for 1977 (but not for 1978) gave the percentage of inmates in each dispersal prison who were Category A prisoners. Table 3 relates these figures to the size and assault rate for each institution in 1977. It can be seen that the assault rates were highest in the two smallest dispersal prisons, Gartree and Albany, which also had the highest percentage of Category A prisoners. Both are relatively modern prisons, and neither was overcrowded by Home Office standards in 1977. One possible interpretation of these results is that the kinds of prisoners who are allocated to a prison are important in

relation to its assault rate, although there is no way of knowing how many of the assaults in the dispersal prisons can be attributed to the Category A prisoners. Albany and Gartree had the highest assault rates of all thirty-one training prisons in 1978.

Recidivism

The interpretation of the above analyses of prison offenses and assaults is made difficult by the lack of information about the kinds of inmates allocated to each class of prison. It was possible to control for intake in an analysis of reconviction rates. As a criterion of correctional effectiveness, reconviction is not ideal. For example, offenses leading to convictions in England are a biased and underrepresentative sample of all offenses committed (West and Farrington, 1977). Despite the problems of reconviction, it was the best measure of behavior after leaving prison that we had available.

The annual Home Office prison statistics do not give reconviction rates for each prison, and these figures are not available in any other official document. However, reconviction rates for specified prisons were calculated during parole research by the Home Office. These were based on all male prisoners serving sentences over eighteen

228 DAVID P. FARRINGTON and CHRISTOPHER P. NUTTALL

TABLE 4

SIZE, OVERCROWDING AND EFFECTIVENESS IN NINETEEN CLOSED PRISONS

Prison	Type[a]	Size[b]	Over-crowding[c]	Number Released[d]	Predicted % Reconviction[e]	Actual % Reconviction[e]	Effectiveness[f]
1	T	169	96.0	56	66	59	7
2	T	219	94.8	66	44	45	−1
3	T	262	75.7	77	46	34	12
4	T	307	93.0	92	63	64	−1
5	T	372	100.5	88	42	34	8
6	T	385	157.8	81	63	74	−11
7	L	518	141.9	40	58	65	−7
8	T	564	90.1	51	66	67	−1
9	T	572	85.6	87	59	57	2
10	T	591	130.5	41	59	73	−14
11	T	656	104.0	93	42	41	1
12	T	773	115.9	65	38	38	0
13	L	802	143.5	41	61	66	−5
14	L	830	137.2	58	65	72	−7
15	L	993	108.8	82	36	32	4
16	L	1039	130.2	71	66	69	−3
17	L	1069	111.8	69	60	57	3
18	L	1309	122.3	80	69	75	−6
19	L	1409	130.5	172	61	64	−3

[a] *Type:* T = Training, L = Local.
[b] *Size* refers to the average daily population of inmates in 1964 (according to Appendix 8C of Home Office, 1965).
[c] *Overcrowding* is derived by expressing the average daily population as a percentage of the capacity (as stated in Appendix 3 of Home Office, 1965).
[d] *Number released* refers to those serving over eighteen months who were released between January and June 1965, before parole was introduced.
[e] *Predicted and actual reconviction rates* are explained in the text, and are based on two-year follow-up periods.
[f] *Effectiveness* is the predicted-minus-the-actual reconviction rate.

months and released during the first six months of 1965. More than 2,000 men were followed up for two years after release. The researchers were interested in predicting recidivism, and so they randomly divided the sample into two halves. One half was used to construct a prediction index, and the other half to investigate its validity. The prediction index was based on such factors as the offender's previous criminal history (the type of offense he had committed, his number of previous convictions and previous prison sentences, his interval at risk since his last conviction, the age at which he was first convicted), and also his age, marital status, living arrangements, and employment history.

There was a very close correspondence be-tween predicted and actual reconviction rates in the construction and validation samples (mean cost rating = 0.50 and 0.56, respectively). The fact that there was no decline in predictive power in the validation sample showed that the high predictive power in the construction sample did not result from capitalizing on chance variations. In many cases, the factors used in predicting reconviction were ones that had proved to be efficient in previous Home Office research on prison samples (see, e.g., Hammond and Chayen, 1963; for a fuller description of the parole research see Nuttall et al., 1977).

Table 4 shows the predicted and actual recon-viction rates for nineteen closed prisons releasing at least forty of these medium- and long-term prisoners during the specified six-month period. A comparison of the two rates gives some indication of the relative effectiveness of each institution in preventing reconviction, making allowance for the kinds of prisoners allocated to it. For example, Prison 10, with an expected rate of 59 percent and an actual rate of 73 percent, seemed to have rather worse results than predicted on the basis of the prisoners in it. On the other hand, Prison 1, with an expected rate of 66 percent and an actual rate of 59 percent, seemed to be rather better than expected. The difference between predicted and actual reconviction rates was used as an index of correctional effectiveness for each prison.

Table 4 also shows the size and overcrowding of each prison in 1964. Since the prisoners were all serving sentences over eighteen months and were released between January and June 1965, most of them would have been in prison for the whole of 1964. (These figures were collected before the English parole system was introduced in 1968.) In investigating the effects of different prisons, therefore, 1964 is the most relevant year. There is no guarantee that an inmate released from a certain institution early in 1965 would have spent the whole of 1964 in that particular institution. To the extent that this was not true, it should blur differences between prisons.

The size of the institutions was weakly, and not significantly, correlated with their effectiveness (Spearman $r = -0.29$). The negative correlation indicates that the larger institutions tended to have slightly higher reconviction rates than expected. There was a much closer relationship between effectiveness and overcrowding ($r = -0.76$, $p < 0.001$) with the more overcrowded institutions being less effective.

In general, the larger institutions were more overcrowded, since size correlated 0.48 ($p < 0.05$) with overcrowding. The partial correlation between size and effectiveness, controlling for overcrowding, was 0.12. In other words, after controlling for overcrowding, the correlation between size and effectiveness was much reduced and, if anything, the larger institutions were more effective. This suggests that size appeared to be negatively correlated with effectiveness only because of the tendency for larger institutions to be overcrowded. Overcrowding was the factor that was clearly negatively related to effectiveness, not size.

The average overcrowding rate for each of these nineteen prisons was 114.2, while their average effectiveness was -1.2. *Every one* of the eight institutions with an overcrowding rate of 116 or greater had an effectiveness of -2 or less, and *every one* of the eleven institutions with an overcrowding rate of 115 or less had an effectiveness of -1 or greater. Thus, on the basis of their overcrowding, it was possible to split these nineteen institutions into two groups that did not overlap in effectiveness.

To some extent, the factor of overcrowding was confounded with the classification of the prison as local or training. Nine of the eleven institutions with an overcrowding rate of 115 or less were training prisons, while six of the eight with an overcrowding rate of 116 or more were local prisons. However, overcrowding and effectiveness were highly correlated in both kinds of institutions. The correlation was significant in the eight local prisons ($r = -0.72$, $p < 0.05$). Although it was substantial, it was not statistically significant in the eleven training prisons, no doubt because of the small numbers involved ($r = -0.50$). These results indicate that the negative relationship between overcrowding and effectiveness held independently of any differences between local and training prisons.

It was possible to investigate the relationship between the rate of violent offenses in these prisons in 1964 and their effectiveness, but this proved to be insignificant ($r = -0.16$). The age of these institutions was also insignificantly related to their effectiveness ($r = -0.24$, indicating that the older institutions were slightly less effective). Apart from age and size, it was not possible to investigate the relationship between any other aspect of these prisons and their effectiveness. However, in view of the high negative correlation between overcrowding and effectiveness, it seems unlikely that this relationship could be explained away by the operation of some third variable. It seems more likely that in some direct way overcrowding produces ineffectiveness.

CONCLUSIONS

Contrary to a widespread belief about the undesirability of larger prisons, neither our review of the research literature nor our analysis of

English prison statistics has produced conclusive empirical evidence that prison size influences behavior inside or after leaving prison. This does not necessarily mean that the widespread belief is incorrect, since there is an absence of evidence rather than evidence that size has no effect. However, it does mean that the widespread belief is not based on empirical evidence. There were some suggestions in the literature that overcrowding produced violent or disruptive behavior inside the prison.

One possible reason why the widespread belief about size may have arisen is because of the failure to separate the effects of size from the effects of other factors that may be associated with it in practice but not in principle. In practice, larger institutions in England and Wales are more overcrowded, but there is no necessary reason why this should be so. In practice, larger institutions in the United States tend to be maximum security institutions and tend to have higher inmate/staff ratios, but again there is no necessary reason why size should be associated with these factors. It seems likely to us that these other factors are more important than size, but some kind of multivariate or partial correlation analysis is needed to establish whether this is true, and indeed whether any of these factors influences behavior inside and after leaving a prison independently of the kinds of inmates allocated to it.

Our analysis of the English prison statistics showed that offending rates and assault rates were greater in the smaller prisons. It is possible that offenses were less likely to be observed or recorded in larger prisons and that the kinds of prisoners who were allocated to a prison were more important in relation to its assault rate than was its size. However, these results did not suggest that increasing the size of a prison produced a disproportionate increase in violent and disruptive behavior within it.

Unlike our analysis of prison offenses, it was possible in our analysis of recidivism rates to control for the kinds of inmates incarcerated in each institution. After doing this, it was found that size was not significantly correlated with correctional effectiveness. However, there was a high negative relationship between overcrowding and effectiveness. This relationship was discovered by using data collected in England in the 1960s. It is important to investigate the extent to which it holds today in England or in North America.

It is also important to try to establish the reasons why overcrowding and effectiveness might be negatively related. It may be that prisoners are more likely to become contaminated by other prisoners in overcrowded conditions, or that it is more difficult to attempt rehabilitative activities in overcrowded conditions, or that the experience of living in an overcrowded prison produces stress and aggression. The strength of the relationship suggests that it cannot be explained away by the operation of some third variable. If there is indeed a direct relationship between overcrowding and ineffectiveness, it follows that an important priority for governmental agencies should be to reduce overcrowding in prisons. This could be achieved by providing more prison accommodation, by sending fewer people to prison, or by reducing the effective lengths of prison sentences.

ACKNOWLEDGMENT

This paper was written while Dr. Farrington was on sabbatical leave with the Solicitor General of Canada. The views expressed are those of the authors and are not necessarily those of the Solicitor General of Canada.

REFERENCES

Barnes, R.D. (1951). Modern prison planning. In *Contemporary correction*, P.W. Tappan, ed. New York: McGraw-Hill.

Dunlop, A.B. (1974). *The approved school experience.* London: Her Majesty's Stationery Office.

Fox, V. (1970). Prison disciplinary problems. In *The sociology of punishment and correction*, second edition, N. Johnston; L. Savitz; and M.E. Wolfgang; eds. New York: Wiley.

Hammond, W.H., and Chayen, E. (1963). *Persistent criminals.* London: Her Majesty's Stationery Office.

Home Office (1965). *Report on the work of the prison department 1964.* London: Her Majesty's Stationery Office.

———(1978). *Prison statistics, England and Wales, 1977.* London: Her Majesty's Stationery Office.

———(1979a). *Prison statistics, England and Wales, 1978.* London: Her Majesty's Stationery Office.

———(1979b). *Report on the work of the prison department 1978.* London: Her Majesty's Stationery Office.

Jesness, C.F. (1965). *The Fricot Ranch study.* California Youth Authority, Report No. 47.

————(1971). Comparative effectiveness of two institutional treatment programs for delinquents. *Child care quarterly* 1:119–30.

Megargee, E.I. (1976). Population density and disruptive behavior in a prison setting. In *Prison violence*, A.K. Cohen; A.F. Cole; and R.G. Bailey, eds. Lexington, MA: D.C. Heath.

————(1977). The association of population density, reduced space and uncomfortable temperatures with misconduct in a prison community. *American journal of community psychology* 5: 289–98.

Millham, S.; Bullock, R.; and Cherrett, P. (1975). *After grace—teeth.* London: Human Context Books.

Moos, R.H. (1975). *Evaluating correctional and community settings.* New York: Wiley.

Nacci, P.L.; Teitelbaum, H.E.; and Prather, J. (1977). Population density and inmate misconduct rates in the federal prison system. *Federal probation* 41 (2): 26–31.

National Advisory Commission on Criminal Justice Standards and Goals (1973). *Corrections.* Washington: U.S. Government Printing Office.

Nuttall, C.P., et al. (1977). *Parole in England and Wales.* London: Her Majesty's Stationery Office.

Paulus, P.B.; McCain, G.; and Cox, V.C. (1978). Death rates, psychiatric commitments, blood pressure, and perceived crowding as a function of institutional crowding. *Environmental psychology and nonverbal behavior* 3: 107–116.

Rutherford, A., et al. (1977). *Prison population and policy choices.* U.S. Department of Justice: Law Enforcement Assistance Administration, National Institute of Law Enforcement and Criminal Justice.

Solicitor General of Canada (1971). *Report of the working group on federal maximum security institutions design.* Ottawa: Solicitor General of Canada.

South Carolina Department of Corrections (1973). *Collective violence in correctional institutions.* Columbia, SC: South Carolina Department of Corrections.

Sylvester, S.F.; Reed, J.H.; and Nelson, D.O. (1977). *Prison homicide.* New York: Spectrum.

Waller, I., and Chan, J. (1977). Prison use: An international comparison. In *Correctional institutions,* R.M. Carter, D. Glaser, and L.T. Wilkins, eds. Philadelphia: Lippincott.

West, D.J., and Farrington, D.P. (1977). *The delinquent way of life.* London: Heinemann.

[23]

DOES CORRECTIONAL TREATMENT WORK? A CLINICALLY RELEVANT AND PSYCHOLOGICALLY INFORMED META-ANALYSIS*

D.A. ANDREWS
IVAN ZINGER
ROBERT D. HOGE
  Carleton University

JAMES BONTA
  Ottawa–Carleton Detention Centre

PAUL GENDREAU
  Centracare Saint John, New Brunswick

FRANCIS T. CULLEN
  University of Cincinnati

Careful reading of the literature on the psychology of criminal conduct and of prior reviews of studies of treatment effects suggests that neither criminal sanctioning without provision of rehabilitative service nor servicing without reference to clinical principles of rehabilitation will succeed in reducing recidivism. What works, in our view, is the delivery of appropriate correctional service, and appropriate service reflects three psychological principles: (1) delivery of service to higher risk cases, (2) targeting of criminogenic needs, and (3) use of styles and modes of treatment (e.g., cognitive and behavioral) that are matched with client need and learning styles. These principles were applied to studies of juvenile and adult correctional treatment, which yielded 154 phi coefficients that summarized the magnitude and direction of the impact of treatment on recidivism. The effect of appropriate correctional service (mean phi = .30) was significantly (p < .05) greater than that of unspecified correctional service (.13), and both were more effective than inappropriate service (−.06) and nonservice criminal sanctioning (−.07). Service was effective within juvenile and adult corrections, in studies published before and after 1980, in randomized and nonrandomized designs, and in diversionary, community, and residential programs (albeit, attenuated in residential settings). Clinical sensitivity and a psychologically informed perspective on crime

---

* This paper is dedicated to Daniel Glaser, Ted Palmer, and Marguerite Q. Warren.

370   ANDREWS ET AL.

may assist in the renewed service, research, and conceptual efforts that are
strongly indicated by our review.

During the 1970s, the ideological hegemony of the individualized treatment ideal suffered a swift and devastating collapse (Rothman, 1980). Previously a code word for "doing good," rehabilitation came to be seen by liberals
as a euphemism for coercing offenders and by conservatives as one for letting
hardened criminals off easily. Although the public's belief in rehabilitation
was never eroded completely (Cullen et al., 1988), defenders of treatment
were branded scientifically and politically naive apologists for the socially
powerful, self-serving human service professionals, or curious relics of a posi-
tivistic past. Thus, a number of jurisdictions in the United States (Cullen and
Gilbert, 1982) and Canada (Andrews, 1990; Leschied et al., 1988) embarked
on sentencing reforms that undercut the role of rehabilitation in justice and
corrections.

The decline of the rehabilitative ideal cannot be attributed to a careful
reading of evidence regarding the effectiveness of rehabilitative treatment. As
will be shown, reviews of the effectiveness literature routinely found that a
substantial proportion of the better-controlled studies of rehabilitative service
reported positive effects, and did so for programs that operated within a variety of conditions established by criminal sanctions, such as probation or
incarceration. We will also show that criminal sanctions themselves were
typically found to be only minimally related to recidivism. Thus, rather than
a rational appreciation of evidence, the attack on rehabilitation was a reflection of broader social and intellectual trends. This is evident upon consideration of the particular historical timing and intensity of the attack on
rehabilitation.

First, the rapidly changing sociopolitical context of the decade preceding
the mid-1970s propelled conservatives to seek "law and order," while liberals
attached to class-based perspectives on crime became discouraged about the
benevolence of the state and the promise of direct intervention (Allen, 1981;
Cullen and Gendreau, 1989). Second, an emerging social science, informed
by labelling and critical/Marxist approaches, embraced antipsychological and
often anti-empirical themes (Andrews, 1990; Andrews and Wormith, 1989).
These emergent perspectives played an important role in legitimating the
decision of many academic criminologists and juridical policymakers to
declare rehabilitation fully bankrupt. Most noteworthy was Robert Martinson's (1974:25) conclusion that "the rehabilitative efforts that have been
reported so far have had no appreciable effect on recidivism." In short order,
with the blessing of a major academy of science (Sechrest et al., 1979), the
notion that "nothing works" became accepted doctrine (Walker, 1989).
"Nothing works" satisfied conservative political reactions to the apparent disorder of the 1960s, liberal sorrow over perceived failures of the Great Society,

CORRECTIONAL TREATMENT META-ANALYSIS 371

and the ideological persuasions of those academicians whose truly social visions of deviance asserted that only radical social change could have an impact on crime.

In the 1980s, however, rehabilitation and respect for evidence made at least a modest comeback. As will be noted, a number of revisionist scholars have observed that the marriage of conservative politics and leftist social science—in both its "discouraged liberal" and "critical/Marxist" versions—has neither improved justice nor increased crime control. In any case, it is our thesis that evidence of effective treatment was there from the earliest reviews, now is mounting, and constitutes a persuasive case against the "nothing works" doctrine.

Even so, criticisms of rehabilitation are not in short supply. As Walker (1989:231) comments: "It is wishful thinking to believe that additional research is going to uncover a magic key that has somehow been overlooked for 150 years." Other scholars—as exemplified most notably and recently by Whitehead and Lab (1989; Lab and Whitehead, 1988)—continue to participate in the scientific exchange on intervention and to present evidence ostensibly bolstering the "nothing works" message.

Whitehead and Lab's (1989) report is very much in the tradition of the reviews and conclusions that are challenged in this paper. Before detailing our position, however, we note that the Whitehead and Lab review is important for several reasons. First, having searched the psychological, sociological, and criminological journals, they produced an impressively complete set of controlled evaluations of juvenile treatment for the years 1975 to 1984. They coded the setting of treatment and distinguished among diversion programs (within and outside the juvenile justice system), probation and other community-based programs, and residential programming. Moreover, they coded type of treatment within these settings as either behavioral or nonbehavioral and considered recency (year of publication) and quality of research design. Focused exclusively upon evaluations employing recidivism as an outcome variable, their conclusions actually had to do with crime control. Clearly then, the negative conclusion of Whitehead and Lab is worthy of serious consideration by those in criminal justice.

Most serious, and unlike most earlier reviews—including the Martinson (1974) review—portions of the Whitehead and Lab (1989) paper support a very firm version of "nothing works." That is, the methodological, clinical, and sampling caveats typically listed by earlier reviewers were discounted systematically in Whitehead and Lab (1989). Regarding quality of the research, the more rigorous studies were reported to find correctional treatment to have effects even more negative than did the less rigorous studies. As to standards of effectiveness, Whitehead and Lab advised that their standard (a phi coefficient of .20 or greater) was so generous that evidence favorable to treatment would certainly have emerged had positive evidence, in fact, existed. In

372   ANDREWS ET AL.

regard to type of treatment, they admitted that behavioral forms of intervention may be effective with outcomes other than recidivism, but they found behavioral treatment to be no more effective than nonbehavioral approaches in the control of recidivism.

Our meta-analysis includes, but is not confined to, the Whitehead and Lab (1989) sample of studies. Challenging sweeping conclusions regarding program ineffectiveness, we reaffirm a line of analysis for developing meaningful conclusions on the conditions under which programs will work. Our challenge is informed by considerations of research and theory on the causes of crime and by research and theory on behavioral influence processes. In particular, a growing number of scholars and practitioners now agree with what was always the starting point of the Gluecks (1950), the Grants (1959), Glaser (1974), and Palmer (1975): The effectiveness of correctional treatment is dependent upon what is delivered to whom in particular settings. Certainly that has been our view[1] and the view of many other reviewers and commentators.[2]

CLINICALLY RELEVANT AND PSYCHOLOGICALLY INFORMED PROGRAMMING, EVALUATION, AND META-ANALYSIS

The psychology of criminal conduct recognizes multiple sources of variation in criminal recidivism (Andrews, 1980, 1983; Andrews and Kiessling, 1980; Andrews et al., 1990; Cullen and Gendreau, 1989; Hoge and Andrews, 1986; Palmer, 1983; Warren, 1969). These major sources of variation are found through analyses of the main and interactive effects of (a) preservice characteristics of offenders, (b) characteristics of correctional workers, (c) specifics of the content and process of services planned and delivered, and (d) intermediate changes in the person and circumstances of individual offenders. Logically, these major sources of variation in outcome reside within the conditions established by the specifics of a judicial disposition or criminal sanction. Thus, there is little reason to expect that variation among settings or sanctions will have an impact on recidivism except in interaction with offender characteristics and through the mediators of intervention process and intermediate change. We develop this "criminal sanction" hypothesis first and then compare it with hypotheses regarding the effectiveness of a correctional service approach that attends to preservice case characteristics, to

---

1.   Andrews (1980, 1983, 1990), Andrews and Kiessling (1980), Andrews et al. (1990), Cullen and Gendreau (1989), Gendreau and Ross (1979, 1981, 1987).

2.   Basta and Davidson (1988), Currie (1989), Garrett (1985), Geismar and Wood (1985), Greenwood and Zimring (1985), Izzo and Ross (1990), Lipsey (1989), Martinson (1979), Mayer et al. (1986), Palmer (1983), Ross and Fabiano (1985).

CORRECTIONAL TREATMENT META-ANALYSIS 373

the process and content of intervention, and to intermediate change within particular sanctions.

IN THEORY, WHY SHOULD CRIMINAL SANCTIONING WORK?

A focus upon variation in official disposition is a reflection of one or more of the three sets of theoretical perspectives known as *just deserts, labelling,* and *deterrence*. The just deserts or justice set is not overly concerned with recidivism, but on occasion the assumption surfaces that unjust processing may motivate additional criminal activity (Schur, 1973:129). It appears, however, that the devaluation of rehabilitation—in the interest of increasing "just" processing—has been associated with increased punishment and decreased treatment but not with reduced recidivism (Cullen and Gilbert, 1982; Leschied et al., 1988).

The labelling and deterrence perspectives actually yield conflicting predictions regarding the outcomes of different dispositions (Rausch, 1983). Labelling theory suggests that less involvement in the criminal justice system is better than more (because the stigma is less), while deterrence theory suggests the opposite (because fear of punishment is greater). The assumptions of both labelling (Andrews and Wormith, 1989; Wellford, 1975) and deterrence (Gendreau and Ross, 1981) have been subjected to logical and empirical review, and neither perspective is yet able to offer a well-developed psychology of criminal conduct. Basic differentiations among and within levels and types of sanctions have yet to be worked out (Smith and Gartin, 1989), type of offender is likely a crucial moderating variable (Klein, 1986), and the social psychology of "processing" is only now being explored (Link et al., 1989).

IN FACT, DOES CRIMINAL SANCTIONING WORK?

To our knowledge, not a single review of the effects of judicial sanctioning on criminal recidivism has reached positive conclusions except when the extremes of incapacitation are tested or when additional reference is made to moderators (e.g., type of offender) or mediators (e.g., the specifics of intervention). Reading Kirby (1954), Bailey (1966), Logan (1972), and Martinson (1974) reveals the obvious but unstated fact that their negative conclusions regarding "treatment" reflected primarily the negligible impact of variation in sanctions such as probation and incarceration. Thus, we agree with Palmer (1975): The main effects of criminal sanctions on recidivism have been slight and inconsistent.

This hypothesis is extended to judicial "alternatives," because there are no solid reasons for expecting alternative punishments, such as community service or restitution, to have an impact on recidivism. Any anticipated rehabilitative benefit of "alternatives" is based on the hope that offenders will learn that crime has negative consequences, and yet the enhancement of cognitive

374   ANDREWS ET AL.

and interpersonal skills (e.g., future-orientation and perspective-taking) are dependent upon systematic modeling, reinforcement, and graduated practice (Ross and Fabiano, 1985). Given little reason to expect much from the incidental learning opportunities provided by such sanctions as restitution, correctional treatment service is a crucial supplement to a criminal justice approach that is preoccupied with avoiding stigma while delivering "just" and "innovative alternative" punishment.

CORRECTIONAL TREATMENT SERVICES

Reviewers of the literature have routinely found that at least 40% of the better-controlled evaluations of correctional treatment services reported positive effects (Andrews et al., 1990). For example, considering only the better-controlled studies, the proportion of studies reporting positive evidence was 75% ($^3/_4$) in Kirby (1954), 59% ($^{13}/_{22}$) in Bailey (1966), 50% ($^9/_{18}$) in Logan (1972), 78% ($^{14}/_{18}$) in Logan when Type of Treatment $\times$ Type of Client interactions are considered, 48% ($^{39}/_{82}$) in Palmer's (1975) retabulation of studies reviewed by Martinson (1974), 86% ($^{82}/_{95}$) in Gendreau and Ross (1979), and 47% ($^{40}/_{85}$) in Lab and Whitehead (1988). This pattern of results strongly supports exploration of the idea that some service programs are working with at least some offenders under some circumstances, and we think that helpful linkages among case, service, and outcome are suggested by three principles known as risk, need, and responsivity (Andrews et al., 1990).

THE RISK PRINCIPLE AND SELECTION OF LEVEL OF SERVICE

The risk principle suggests that higher levels of service are best reserved for higher risk cases and that low-risk cases are best assigned to minimal service. In the literature at least since the Gluecks (1950), the risk principle has been restated on many occasions (e.g., Glaser, 1974). Although the parameters remain to be established, evidence favoring the risk principle continues to grow (Andrews et al., 1990). In brief, when actually explored, the effects of treatment typically are found to be greater among higher risk cases than among lower risk cases. This is expected unless the need and/or responsivity principles are violated.

THE NEED PRINCIPLE AND SELECTION OF APPROPRIATE INTERMEDIATE TARGETS

Risk factors may be static or dynamic in nature, and psychology is particularly interested in those dynamic risk factors that, when changed, are associated with *subsequent* variation in the chances of criminal conduct. Clinically, dynamic risk factors are called *criminogenic needs*, and guidelines for their assessment are described elsewhere (Andrews, 1983; Andrews et al., 1990).

CORRECTIONAL TREATMENT META-ANALYSIS 375

The most promising intermediate targets include changing antisocial attitudes, feelings, and peer associations; promoting familial affection in combination with enhanced parental monitoring and supervision; promoting identification with anticriminal role models; increasing self-control and self-management skills; replacing the skills of lying, stealing, and aggression with other, more prosocial skills; reducing chemical dependencies; and generally shifting the density of rewards and costs for criminal and noncriminal activities in familial, academic, vocational, and other behavioral settings.[3] Theoretically, modifying contingencies within the home, school, and work by way of an increased density of reward for noncriminal activity may reduce motivation for crime and increase the costs of criminal activity through having more to lose (Hunt and Azrin, 1973).

Less-promising targets include increasing self-esteem without touching antisocial propensity (e.g., Wormith, 1984), increasing the cohesiveness of antisocial peer groups (e.g., Klein, 1971), improving neighborhood-wide living conditions without reaching high-risk families (the East Side, Midcity, and other community projects in Klein, 1971, and Schur, 1973), and attempts to focus on vague personal/emotional problems that have not been linked with recidivism (Andrews and Kiessling, 1980).

THE RESPONSIVITY PRINCIPLE AND SELECTION OF TYPE OF SERVICE

The responsivity principle has to do with the selection of styles and modes of service that are (a) capable of influencing the specific types of intermediate targets that are set with offenders and (b) appropriately matched to the learning styles of offenders. We begin with the general literature on the treatment of offenders and then turn to specific Responsivity × Service interactions.

Responsivity: General principles of effective service. Drawing upon our earlier review (Andrews et al., 1990), appropriate types of service typically, but not exclusively, involve the use of behavioral and social learning principles of interpersonal influence, skill enhancement, and cognitive change. Specifically, they include modeling, graduated practice, rehearsal, role playing, reinforcement, resource provision, and detailed verbal guidance and explanations (making suggestions, giving reasons, cognitive restructuring). Elsewhere (Andrews and Kiessling, 1980), we describe the applications of these practices as (a) use of authority (a "firm but fair" approach and definitely not interpersonal domination or abuse), (b) anticriminal modeling and reinforement (explicit reinforcement and modeling of alternatives to procriminal styles of thinking, feeling, and acting), and (c) concrete problem solving and

---

3. For example, Andrews et al. (1990), Andrews and Wormith (1989), Glueck and Glueck (1950), Johnson (1979), Loeber and Stouthamer–Loeber (1987), Wilson and Herrnstein (1985).

376   ANDREWS ET AL.

systematic skill training for purposes of increasing reward levels in anticriminal settings. High levels of advocacy and brokerage are also indicated as long as the receiving agency actually offers appropriate service. Finally, Andrews and Kiessling (1980) recommended that service deliverers relate to offenders in interpersonally warm, flexible, and enthusiastic ways while also being clearly supportive of anticriminal attitudinal and behavioral patterns. Interestingly, social learning approaches receive strong, albeit indirect, support from the prediction literature on the causal modeling of delinquency (Akers and Cochran, 1985; Jessor and Jessor, 1977).

Responsivity: Ineffective service. Some types and styles of services should be avoided under most circumstances (Andrews et al., 1990). Generally, programming for groups is to be approached very cautiously because the opening up of communication within offender groups may well be criminogenic (Andrews, 1980). In group and residential programming, clinicians must gain control over the contingencies of interaction so that anticriminal, rather than procriminal, patterns are exposed and reinforced (Buehler et al., 1966). For example, Agee's (1986) programmatic structures supporting positive change may be contrasted with the failure of unstructured, peer-oriented group counseling and permissive, relationship-oriented milieu approaches. The failure of these unstructured approaches is well documented in open community settings (e.g., Faust, 1965; Klein, 1971), in group homes operating according to the essentially nondirective guidelines of "guided group interaction" (Stephenson and Scarpitti, 1974:Ch. 8), in hospitals (Craft et al., 1966), and in prisons (Kassebaum et al., 1971; Murphy, 1972). There are also no convincing theoretical grounds for believing that young people will be "scared straight" (Finckenauer, 1982). Fear of official punishment is not one of the more important correlates of delinquency (Johnson, 1979), and yelling at people is counter to the relationship principle of effective service (Andrews, 1980).

Finally, traditional psychodynamic and nondirective client-centered therapies are to be avoided within general samples of offenders (Andrews et al., 1990). These therapies are designed to free people from the personally inhibiting controls of "superego" and "society," but neurotic misery and overcontrol are not criminogenic problems for a majority of offenders. Authorities such as Freud (in his introductory lectures on psychoanalysis, 1953) and the Gluecks (in their classic *Unraveling*, 1950) warned us about evocative and relationship-dependent psychodynamic approaches with antisocial cases.

Specific responsivity considerations. The success of highly verbal, evocative, and relationship-dependent services seems to be limited to clients with high levels of interpersonal, self-reflective, and verbal skill. The "I-Level" (Harris, 1988) and "Conceptual Level" (Reitsma–Street and Leschied, 1988) systems

CORRECTIONAL TREATMENT META-ANALYSIS 377

provide guidance regarding the types of offenders who may respond in positive ways to services that are less structured than those we have been describing as appropriate for antisocial samples in general.

SUMMARY

Our clinically relevant and psychologically informed principles of treatment predict that criminal sanctioning without attention to the delivery of correctional service will relate to recidivism minimally. Additionally, we suggest that the delivery of services, regardless of criminal sanction or setting, is unproductive if those services are inconsistent with the principles of risk, need, and responsivity. Positively, we predict that appropriate treatment—treatment that is delivered to higher risk cases, that targets criminogenic need, and that is matched with the learning styles of offenders—will reduce recidivism.

METHOD

SAMPLES OF STUDIES

We subjected 45 of the 50 studies included in the Whitehead and Lab (1989) review to content and meta-analysis.[4] The Whitehead and Lab sample included only studies of juvenile treatment that appeared in professional journals between 1975 and 1984 and that presented effects of treatment on binary (less–more) measures of recidivism. Studies that focused on imprisonment or the treatment of substance abuse were not included.

We also explored a second sample of studies in order to check on the generalizability of any findings based on the Whitehead and Lab sample. Sample 2 included 35 studies in our research files as of February 1989 that were not included in the Whitehead and Lab set but had employed binary measures of recidivism. Studies in sample 2 date from the 1950s through 1989, but they are not purported to be a representative sample of any particular time period. Sample 2 provides a convenient means of exploring, albeit tentatively, how well conclusions based on the Whitehead and Lab sample may generalize to adult samples.

ESTIMATES OF TREATMENT EFFECT

The Whitehead and Lab sample yielded a total of 87 2 × 2 contingency

---

4. Douds and Collingwood (1978) and Collingwood and Genthner (1980) were excluded because their samples appeared to overlap those of either Collingwood et al. (1976) or Williams (1984). Similarly, Fo and O'Donnell (1975) was dropped because of overlap with O'Donnell et al. (1979). The Baer et al. (1975) report on Outward Bound was excluded because the independent variable did not involve variation in service. Beal and Duckro (1977) was dropped because the outcome seemed to be court proceedings on the offense that led to a program referral.

378   ANDREWS ET AL.

tables reflecting the strength and direction of the association between two levels of treatment and recidivism-nonrecidivism. Whitehead and Lab, on the other hand, tabled a single phi coefficient for each study. With our approach, distinct phi coefficients were computed when distinct samples and distinct treatments were reported in a paper (e.g., Klein et al., 1977), and rather than compare two "appropriate" styles of service, we compared each service with its respective control (e.g., Jesness, 1975; Mitchell, 1983; in the latter study we estimated that the experimental recidivists were averaging twice the number of new offenses found among control recidivists). Tests of Type of Offender × Type of Treatment interactions were represented only incidentally in Whitehead and Lab. In our report, services to higher and lower risk cases yield separate estimates of treatment effects.

Sample 2 yielded 67 treatment-recidivism tables, 44 based on studies of juveniles and 23 based on adults. (Romig's 1976 analysis of parole supervision is entered as part of the Whitehead and Lab sample, and the analysis of months incarcerated is entered as part of sample 2). The studies and treatment comparisons are outlined in detail in the appendix (Table A1) for readers who may wish to reconstruct our analyses. Phi was employed as the measure of treatment effect because it provides a convenient summary of the direction and magnitude of the association between two binary variables, is equivalent to the Pearson product-moment coefficient, is more conservative than gamma, and was used by Whitehead and Lab.

CONTENT ANALYSIS

The potential covariates of phi estimates were coded as follows:

1. Setting: The Whitehead and Lab codes for setting were accepted uncritically: nonsystem diversion, system diversion, probation/ parole/community corrections, and institutional/residential. Preliminary analyses confirmed that the effects on phi coefficients of the three different community settings were statistically indistinguishable. Hence, setting was employed as a two-level, community-residential factor in further analyses. Table A1, however, includes the elaborate code.
2. Year of publication: before the 1980s/in the 1980s.
3. Quality of research design: Studies employing random assignment were coded "stronger design." Nonrandom assignment was coded "weaker design," except when information on risk factors (e.g., prior offense or "bad attitude") allowed the computation of separate treatment comparisons for lower and higher risk cases. When risk was so controlled, the design was coded "stronger."
4. Sample of studies: Whitehead and Lab/sample 2.
5. Justice system: Juvenile system/adult system.

CORRECTIONAL TREATMENT META-ANALYSIS   379

6. Behavioral intervention: Programs described as behavioral by the authors of an evaluation study were coded "behavioral," as were those that systematically employed behavioral techniques.[5]

7. Type of treatment: Following the principles discussed above, the four levels of type of treatment were as follows:

    a. Criminal sanctions: This code involved variation in judicial disposition, imposed at the front end of the correctional process and not involving deliberate variation in rehabilitative service (e.g., restitution, police cautioning versus regular processing, less versus more probation, and probation versus custody).

    b. Inappropriate correctional service: Inappropriate service included (1) service delivery to lower risk cases and/or mismatching according to a need/responsivity system, (2) nondirective relationship-dependent and/or unstructured psychodynamic counseling, (3) all milieu and group approaches with an emphasis on within-group communication and without a clear plan for gaining control over procriminal modeling and reinforcement, (4) nondirective or poorly targeted academic and vocational approaches, and (5) "scared straight."

    c. Appropriate correctional service: Appropriate service included (1) service delivery to higher risk cases, (2) all behavioral programs (except those involving delivery of service to lower risk cases), (3) comparisons reflecting specific responsivity-treatment comparisons, and (4) nonbehavioral programs that clearly stated that criminogenic need was targeted and that structured intervention was employed.[6]

---

5. The interventions of Hackler and Hagan (1975) were coded as nonbehavioral. William's (1984) Dallas program was coded behavioral in our study, in line with Whitehead and Lab's coding of the Collingwood et al. (1976) report on the same program as behavioral. Both studies of restitution were coded nonbehavioral in our study (only one of which was coded nonbehavioral by Whitehead and Lab). The Ross and Fabiano behavioral skills program was coded as unspecified because it was a comparison condition for a more appropriate program.

6. Treatments admitted to the "appropriate" category by criterion "4" were appropriate according to the principles of need and responsivity (although some readers might disagree): Kelly et al. (1979) encouraged delinquents to explore alternative values and behavior patterns; the transactional program (Jesness, 1975) established individualized targets based on criminogenic need; the family counseling program of McPherson et al. (1983) targeted discipline and self-management; Bachara and Zaba (1978) focused on specific learning problems; Shore and Massimo (1979) studied very intensive, highly individualized, vocationally oriented counseling. Some difficult calls, which we ultimately coded as unspecified, included the following: Druckman's (1979) family counseling, which hinted at a nondirective client-centered approach but lacked a clear statement of same; the paraprofessional advocacy program of Seidman et al. (1980), Wade et al.'s (1977) family program, and Sowles and Gill's (1970) counseling programs all included references to both

    d. Unspecified correctional service: Unspecified service was a residual set for those comparisons involving treatments that we could not confidently label appropriate or inappropriate.

HYPOTHESES

Our first hypothesis is that Type of Treatment is the major source of variation in estimates of effect size (phi coefficients).[7] Specifically, the contributions of Type of Treament to the prediction of effect size will exceed the predictive contributions of year of publication, quality of design, setting, behavioral-nonbehavioral intervention, justice system (juvenile or adult), and sample of studies examined.

Our second hypothesis is that appropriate correctional service will yield an average estimate of impact on recidivism that is positive and exceeds those of criminal sanctions, unspecified service, and inappropriate service.

RESULTS AND DISCUSSION

A preliminary comparison of the two samples of studies was conducted on various control variables. The comparisons reflected an obvious concern that any systematic differences between the Whitehead and Lab sample and sample 2 be documented. Overall, apart from the inclusion of studies of adult treatment in sample 2, the two samples of studies were found to be reasonably comparable across the various potential predictors of treatment effect size explored in this paper (see row 2 of the intercorrelation matrix in Table 1).[8]

---

appropriate and inappropriate elements. Some "treatments" in Rausch (1983) may have involved unspecified service components, but they were assigned to the criminal sanction set in the spirit of the Rausch analysis of labelling and deterrence theory.

    7. Reliability and validity in coding the type of treatment are obvious concerns. One of our ongoing research efforts involves building a psychometrically sound instrument that can be used to assess the correctional appropriateness not simply of printed program descriptions but also of ongoing programs. The psychometrics of this instrument will be the focus of future reports. For now, we have indicated in Table A1 what comparisons were assigned to what categories, and they are thereby appropriately and easily the focus of critical review.

    8. The Whitehead and Lab sample ($n = 87$) and sample 2 ($n = 67$) were virtually identical in the proportion of tests falling in the three categories of treatment services: inappropriate ($20/87$ vs. $16/67$), unspecified ($16/87$ vs. $16/67$), appropriate ($30/87$ vs. $24/67$). The nonsignificant trend was an underrepresentation of comparisons involving criminal sanctions in sample 2 ($21/87$ vs. $9/67$, $r = .08$). Because the Whitehead and Lab sample was limited to studies of juveniles, there was an expected and substantial correlation between Justice System and Sample of Studies (phi $= .48$, $p < 0.01$). Not as obviously deducible from the descriptions of the samples provided in the methods section, sample 2 included a statistically significant overrepresentation of institution-based treatments (phi $= .21$, $p < .05$).

CORRECTIONAL TREATMENT META-ANALYSIS 381

Table 1. Intercorrelation Matrix, Correlations with Phi Coefficients (N = 154), and Mean Phi Coefficients at Each Level of Each Variable

	A Type of Treatment	B Sample of Studies	C Justice System	D Year of Publication	E Quality of Design	F Setting
A.		.08	.01	−.14	.10	.11
B.			.48**	.11	.14	.21*
C.				.23*	.15	−.01
D.					−.10	−.33**
E.						−.17

Simple Unadjusted Correlation with Phi (Mean Phi = .104, SD = .234)

.69**	.18*	.02	.09	−.03	−.07

Unadjusted Mean Phi Coefficient (n) at Each Level of Each Variable

1.	−.07 (30)	.07 (87)	.10 (131)	.08 (76)	.11 (81)	.11 (119)
2.	−.06 (38)	.15 (67)	.11 (23)	.13 (78)	.10 (73)	.07 (35)
3.	.13 (32)					
4.	.30 (54)					

F Values for Unadjusted Effects

45.62**	5.27*	0.49	1.33	0.11	0.74

Partial Correlation with Phi, Controlling for Other Variables

.72**	.15*	.02	.18*	−.07	−.16*

Adjusted Mean Phi Coefficient (n) at Each Level of Each Variable

1.	−.08 (30)	.07 (87)	.10 (131)	.06 (76)	.11 (81)	.12 (119)
2	−.07 (38)	.14 (67)	.11 (23)	.14 (78)	.08 (73)	.03 (35)
3.	.10 (32)					
4.	.32 (54)					

F Values for Adjusted Effects

57.15**	6.99*	0.33	9.80**	1.18	7.43**

* p < .05   ** p < .01

Note: The levels of the variables are as follows: Type of Treatment (criminal sanctions, inappropriate service, unspecified service, appropriate service), Sample of Studies (Whitehead and Lab, sample 2), Justice System (juvenile, adult), Year of Publication (before 1980, 1980s), Quality of Research Design (weaker, stronger), and Setting (community, institutional/residential).

A qualitative and nonparametric summary of findings is appended, but here the hypotheses are tested directly.

HYPOTHESIS 1: RELATIVE PREDICTIVE POTENTIAL OF TYPE OF TREATMENT

Inspection of the first column of Table 1 reveals that the correlation between Type of Treatment and phi coefficients was strong (Eta = .69) and, with simultaneous control introduced for each of the other variables through

382   ANDREWS ET AL.

analysis of covariance techniques in a multiple classification analysis, the correlation increased to .72 (Beta). The only other significant unadjusted predictor of phi coefficients was Sample of Studies (.18, unadjusted; .15, adjusted). With controls for Type of Treatment introduced, the magnitude of correlation with phi coefficients increased to significant levels for Year of Publication (from .09 to .18) and for Setting (from −.07 to −.16).

Comparisons from sample 2, recency of publication and community-based treatment, were each associated with relatively positive effects of treatment. These trends, however, were overwhelmed by Type of Treatment. In a stepwise multiple regression, the only variables contributing significantly ($p < .05$) to variation in phi estimates were Type of Treatment (beta = .69) and Year of Publication (beta = .19), $F(^2/_{151}) = 68.01$, $p < .000$, adjusted R square = .47. In summary, our first hypothesis was strongly supported: Type of Treatment was clearly the strongest of the correlates of effect size sampled in this study.

HYPOTHESIS 2: THE IMPORTANCE OF APPROPRIATE CORRECTIONAL SERVICE

As described above, the main effect of Type of Treatment on phi estimates was strong and positive, with or without adjustment for control variables. Scheffe tests confirmed that the mean phi coefficient for appropriate correctional service (.30, n = 54) was significantly ($p < 0.05$) greater than that for criminal sanctions (−.07, n = 30), inappropriate service (−.06, n = 38), and unspecified service (.13, n = 32). In addition, Scheffe tests revealed that the average effect of unspecified correctional service significantly exceeded the mean phi coefficients for criminal sanctions and inappropriate service.

Mean phi coefficients for each of the four types of treatment are presented in Table 2 at each of the two levels of the various control variables. Inspection reveals a robust correlation between Type of Treatment and effects on recidivism at each level of Sample of Studies, Justice System, Year of Publication, Design, and Setting.

The only variable to interact significantly ($p < 0.05$) with Type of Treatment was Year of Publication. It appears that criminal sanctions yielded more negative phi estimates in the earlier literature than in the more recent literature (−.16 versus −.02, $F[^1/_{28}] = 8.98$. $p < .006$). This reflects a greater representation of residential studies in the earlier years (the negative implications of residential programs will be discussed below). More interestingly, studies of appropriate correctional treatment in the 1980s yielded a much higher mean phi estimate than did earlier studies of appropriate treatment (.40 versus .24, $F[^1/_{52}] = 8.40$, $p < .005$). Most likely, this reflects three trends. First, the earlier studies included what are now recognized to be unsophisticated applications of token economy systems (see Ross and

CORRECTIONAL TREATMENT META-ANALYSIS 383

McKay, 1976). Second, studies of the 1980s paid greater attention to cognitive variables (Ross and Fabiano, 1985). Third, the positive effects of short-term behavioral family counseling have been replicated in the 1980s (Gordon et al., 1988). In summary, Hypothesis 2 was supported to a stronger degree than was initially anticipated: Both appropriate and unspecified correctional services were significantly more effective in reducing recidivism than were criminal sanctions and inappropriate service.

NOTE ON BEHAVIORAL INTERVENTION

The use of behavioral methods was a major element in the coding of appropriateness according to the principle of responsivity. Not surprisingly, in view of our coding rules, 95% ($^{38}/_{41}$) of the behavioral treatments were coded as appropriate treatment and 70% ($^{38}/_{54}$) of the appropriate treatments were behavioral. Thus, the correlation between Behavioral Intervention and Type

Table 2. The Effect of Type of Treatment on Recidivism at Each Level of the Control Variables: Mean Phi Coefficients (N)

	Criminal Sanctions	Correctional Service		
		Inapp.	Unspec.	Appropriate
Sample of Studies				
Whitehead and Lab	−.04 (21)	−.11 (20)	.09 (16)	.24 (30)
Sample 2	−.13 (9)	−.02 (18)	.17 (16)	.37 (24)
Justice System				
Juvenile	−.06 (26)	−.07 (31)	.13 (29)	.29 (45)
Adult	−.12 (4)	−.03 (7)	.13 (3)	.34 (9)
Year of Publication				
Before the 1980s	−.16 (10)	−.09 (22)	.17 (11)	.24 (33)
1980s	−.02 (20)	−.03 (16)	.11 (21)	.40 (21)
Quality of Research Design				
Weaker	−.07 (21)	−.04 (10)	.15 (18)	.32 (26)
Stronger	−.07 (9)	−.08 (22)	.11 (14)	.29 (28)
Setting				
Community	−.05 (24)	−.14 (31)	.12 (27)	.35 (37)
Institution/Res.	−.14 (6)	−.15 (7)	.21 (5)	.20 (17)
Behavioral Intervention				
No	−.07 (30)	−.06 (36)	.13 (31)	.27 (16)
Yes	—	−.09 (2)	.23 (1)	.31 (38)
Overall Mean Phi	−.07 (30)	−.06 (38)	.13 (32)	.30 (54)
S.D.	.14	.15	.16	.19
Mean Phi Adjusted for Other Variables	−.08 (30)	−.07 (38)	.10 (32)	.32 (54)

384   ANDREWS ET AL.

of Treatment was substantial ($r = .62$). As expected, Behavioral Intervention, on its own, yielded a significantly greater mean phi coefficient than did non-behavioral treatment. The mean phi coefficients were .29 (SD = .23, n = 41) and .04 (SD = .20, n = 113) for behavioral and nonbehavioral interventions, respectively ($F[^1/_{152}] = 46.09$, $p < .000$, Eta = .48). Once controls were introduced for Type of Treatment, however, the contribution of Behavioral Intervention was reduced to nonsignificant levels, $F(^1/_{151}) < 1.00$, Beta = .07. It appears, then, that use of behavioral methods contributes to the reduction of recidivism, but those contributions are subsumed by the broader implications of risk, need, and responsivity as represented in our Type of Treatment variable.

NOTE ON RESIDENTIAL PROGRAMMING

The minor but statistically significant adjusted main effect of setting is displayed in column six of Table 1. This trend should not be overemphasized, but the relatively weak performance of appropriate correctional service in residential facilities is notable from Table 2 (mean phi estimate of .20 compared with .35 for treatment within community settings, $F[^1/_{52}] = 5.89$, $p < .02$). In addition, inappropriate service performed particularly poorly in residential settings compared with community settings ($-.15$ versus $-.04$, $F[^1/_{36}] = 3.74$, $p < .06$). Thus, it seems that institutions and residential settings may dampen the positive effects of appropriate service while augmenting the negative impact of inappropriate service. This admittedly tentative finding does not suggest that appropriate correctional services should not be applied in institutional and residential settings. Recall that appropriate service was more effective than inappropriate service in all settings.

CONCLUSIONS

The meta-analysis has revealed considerable order in estimates of the magnitude of the impact of treatment upon recidivism. As predicted, the major source of variation in effects on recidivism was the extent to which service was appropriate according to the principles of risk, need, and responsivity. Appropriate correctional service appears to work better than criminal sanctions not involving rehabilitative service and better than services less consistent with our a priori principles of effective rehabilitation. This review has convinced us that the positive trends that we and others detected in the literature of the 1960s and early 1970s were indeed worthy of serious application and evaluation. There is a reasonably solid clinical and research basis for the political reaffirmation of rehabilitation (Cullen and Gilbert, 1982).

The importance of clinical and theoretical relevance in programming and in meta-analysis has been demonstrated—the sanction and treatment services should be differentiated, and the action in regard to recidivism appears to

CORRECTIONAL TREATMENT META-ANALYSIS 385

reside in appropriate treatment. Much, however, remains to be done. We look forward to critiques and revisions of the principles of risk, need, and responsivity as stated and applied herein. What comparisons were assigned to what analytic categories is described in our report and is thereby easily and appropriately the focus of critical review (see note 7). Reserved for future reports are the many issues surrounding therapeutic integrity (Gendreau and Ross, 1979), the measurement of recidivism (Andrews, 1983), and methodological issues such as sample size (Lipsey, 1989). Similarly, we anticipate exploring in detail the value of alternatives to ordinary least squares analyses (for now, nonparametric tests of Type of Treatment are appended). Gender effects and the treatment of sex offenders, substance abusers, and inmates of long-term institutions require detailed analyses. Toward these ends, our meta-analytic data base is being extended. Our focus here, however, remains on type of service and effect size.

Of immediate concern is the meaning of an average phi coefficient of .30 for comparisons involving appropriate correctional service. First, until convinced otherwise, we will assume that an average phi of .30 is more positive, clinically and socially, than the mean effects of the alternatives of sanctioning without regard for service or servicing without regard to the principles of effective correctional service. Casual review of recidivism rates will reveal that, on average, appropriate treatment cut recidivism rates by about 50% (in fact, the mean reduction was 53.06%, SD = 26.49). Thus, we do not think that the positive effects are "minimal". Second, the correlation between effect size estimates and type of treatment approached .70. Correlations of this magnitude are unlikely to reflect "lucky outliers" (Greenwood, 1988), although more systematic sources of error may indeed inflate correlation coefficients. Third, issues surrounding the assessment of the clinical and social significance of diverse measures of effect size are indeed worthy of ongoing research. Future reports on our expanding data bank will compare various estimates of effect size, including some direct estimates of clinical/ social significance. For now, we are interested in discovering ethical routes to strengthened treatment effects, but we are not talking about magical cures.

Critics of rehabilitation are correct when they note that the average correlation between treatment and recidivism is not 1.00. At the same time, critics might be asked to report on the variation that their "preferred" variable shares with recidivism. For example, if their preferred variable is social class, they may be reminded that some reviewers have estimated that the average correlation between class and crime is about −.09 (Tittle et al., 1978). If their preferred approach is incapacitation or community crime prevention, they may be reminded of the minimal effects so far reported for these strategies (Rosenbaum, 1988; Visher, 1987). Critics, be they supporters of social class or incapacitation, likely will respond with examples of particular studies that yielded high correlations with indicators of crime. We remind them that

386   ANDREWS ET AL.

the largest correlations are no better estimates of the average effect than are the least favorable estimates. We also remind them that the positive evidence regarding appropriate rehabilitative service comes not from cross-sectional research—the typical research strategy of critics of rehabilitation—but from deliberate and socially sanctioned approximations of truly experimental ideals. Finally, we remind the critics that one can be interested in the effects of class, punishment, and prevention programs on individual and aggregated crime rates while maintaining multiple interests and without letting one interest justify dismissal of the value of another.

This meta-analysis has done more than uncover evidence that supported our a priori biases regarding the importance of appropriate correctional service. The finding that the effects of inappropriate service appeared to be particularly negative in residential settings while the positive effects of appropriate service were attenuated was something of a surprise. While sensitive to the difficulties of working with antisocial groups, we did not predict this incidental affirmation of a widely shared preference for community over residential programming. Institutions and group homes, however, remain important components of correctional systems and hence active but thoughtful service is indicated. The literature should be carefully scrutinized in order to avoid inappropriate service, and follow-up services in the community may be necessary in order to maximize effectiveness. Finally, the suppressive impact of residential programming suggests that the negative effects of custody are better established than we anticipated.

The effect of the quality of the research design on estimates of effect size was relatively minor. Even if some design problems do inflate effect size estimates (Davidson et al., 1984; Lipsey, 1989), the interesting finding was that comparisons involving more and less rigorous research designs agreed as to what types of treatment were most effective. Program managers and frontline clinicians who find truly randomized groups to be practically or ethically impossible may consider conducting an evaluation that approximates the ideals of a true experiment. In particular, we strongly endorse the use of designs that introduce controls for the preservice risk levels of clients and that actually report on risk × service interactions. In addition, even evaluations that rely upon comparisons of clients who complete or do not complete treatment may be valuable.

Finally, the number of evaluative studies of correctional service should increase dramatically over the next decade. Although millions of young people were processed by juvenile justice systems during the past decade, the total number of papers in the Whitehead and Lab (1989) set that involved systematic study of appropriate service was 21. Were it not for behavioral psychologists, the number of papers involving appropriate service would have been nine. From a positive perspective, there is renewed interest, vigor, and sensitivity in the study of the psychology of criminal conduct (Andrews and

CORRECTIONAL TREATMENT META-ANALYSIS 387

Wormith, 1989; Loeber and Stouthamer–Loeber, 1987; Wilson and Herrn-stein, 1985) and of correctional service and prevention (e.g., Andrews et al., 1990; Cullen and Gendreau, 1988; Currie, 1989; Gendreau and Ross, 1987). There are solid reasons to focus in ethical and humane ways on the client and the quality of service delivered within just dispositions.

REFERENCES

Adams, R. and H.J. Vetter
  1982   Social structure and psychodrama outcome: A ten-year follow-up. Journal of Offender Counseling, Services, and Rehabilitation 6:111–119.

Agee, V.L.
  1986   Institutional treatment programs for the violent juvenile. In S. Apter and A. Goldstein (eds.), Youth Violence: Program and Prospects. Elmsford, N.Y.: Pergamon.

Akers, R.L. and J.K. Cochran
  1985   Adolescent marijuana use: A test of three theories of deviant behavior. Deviant Behavior 3:323–346.

Alexander, J.F., B. Cole, R.S. Schiavo, and B.V. Parsons
  1976   Systems-behavioral intervention with families of delinquents: Therapist characteristics, family behavior, and outcome. Journal of Consulting and Clinial Psychology 44:556–664.

Allen, F.A.
  1981   The Decline of the Rehabilitative Ideal: Penal Policy and Social Purpose. New Haven: Yale University Press.

Andrews, D.A.
  1980   Some experimental investigations of the principles of differential association through deliberate manipulations of the structure of service systems. American Sociological Review 45:448–462.
  1983   The assessment of outcome in correctional samples. In M.L. Lambert, E.R. Christensen, and S.S. DeJulio (eds.), The Measurement of Psychotherapy Outcome in Research and Evaluation. New York: John Wiley & Sons.
  1990   Some criminological sources of antirehabilitation bias in the Report of the Canadian Sentencing Commission. Canadian Journal of Criminology. Forthcoming.

Andrews, D.A. and J.J. Kiessling
  1980   Program structure and effective correctional practices: A summary of the CaVIC research. In R.R. Ross and P. Gendreau (eds.), Effective Correctional Treatment. Toronto: Butterworth.

Andrews, D.A. and J.S. Wormith
  1989   Personality and crime: Knowledge destruction and construction in criminology. Justice Quarterly 6:289–309.

Andrews, D.A., J.J. Kiessling, D. Robinson, and S. Mickus
  1986   The risk principle of case classification: An outcome evaluation with young adult probationers. Canadian Journal of Criminology 28:377–396.

388   ANDREWS ET AL.

Andrews, D.A., J. Bonta, and R.D. Hoge
  1990   Classification for effective rehabilitation: Rediscovering psychology. Crimi-
          nal Justice and Behavior 17:19–52.

Bachara, G.H. and J.N. Zaba
  1978   Learning disabilitites and juvenile delinquency. Journal of Learning Disabili-
          ties 11:242–246.

Baer, D.J., P.J. Jacobs, and F.E. Carr
  1975   Instructors' ratings of delinquents after Outward Bound survival training
          and their subsequent recidivism. Psychological Reports 36:547–553.

Bailey, W.C.
  1966   Correctional outcome: An evaluation of 100 reports. Journal of Criminal
          Law, Criminology and Police Science 57:153–160.

Baird, S.C., R.C. Heinz, B.J. Bemus
  1979   Project Report #14: A Two Year Follow-up. Bureau of Community
          Corrections. Wisconsin: Department of Health and Social Services.

Barkwell, L.J.
  1976   Differential treatment of juveniles on probation: An evaluative study.
          Canadian Journal of Criminology and Corrections 18:363–378.

Barton, C., J.F. Alexander, H. Waldron, C.W. Turner, and J. Warburton
  1985   Generalizing treatment effects of functional family therapy: Three replica-
          tions. The American Journal of Family Therapy 13:16–26.

Basta, J.M. and W.S. Davidson
  1988   Treatment of juvenile offenders: Study outcomes since 1980. Behavioral
          Sciences and the Law 6:355–384.

Beal, D. and P. Duckro
  1977   Family counseling as an alternative to legal action for the juvenile status
          offender. Journal of Marriage and Family Counseling 3:77–81.

Berman, J.J.
  1978   An experiment in parole supervision. Evaluation Quarterly 2:71–90.

Buckner, J.C. and M. Chesney–Lind
  1983   Dramatic cures for juvenile crime: An evaluation of a prisoner-run
          delinquency prevention program. Criminal Justice and Behavior 10:227–247.

Buehler, R.E., G.R. Patterson, and J.M. Furniss
  1966   The reinforcement of behavior in institutional settings. Behavioral Research
          and Therapy 4:157–167.

Byles, J.A.
  1981   Evaluation of an attendance center program for male juvenile probationers.
          Canadian Journal of Criminology 23:343–355.

Byles, J.A. and A. Maurice
  1979   The Juvenile Services Project: An experiment in delinquency control.
          Canadian Journal of Criminology 21:155–165.

Clarke, R.V.G. and D.B. Cornish
  1978   The effectiveness of residential treatment for delinquents. In L.A. Hersov,
          M. Berger, and D. Shaffer (eds.), Aggression and Anti-social Behavior in
          Childhood and Adolescence. Oxford: Pergamon.

CORRECTIONAL TREATMENT META-ANALYSIS 389

Collingwood, T.R. and R.W. Genthner
1980   Skills trainings as treatment for juvenile delinquents. Professional Psychology 11:591–598.

Collingwood, T.R., A.F. Douds, and H. Williams
1976   Juvenile diversion: The Dallas Police Department Youth Services Program. Federal Probation 40:23–27.

Craft, M., G. Stephenson, and C. Granger
1966   A controlled trial of authoritarian and self-governing regimes with adolescent psychopaths. American Journal of Orthopsychiatry 34:543–554.

Cullen, F.T. and P. Gendreau
1989   The effectiveness of correctional rehabilitation. In L. Goodstein and D.L. MacKenzie (eds.), The American Prison: Issues in Research Policy. New York: Plenum.

Cullen, F.T. and K.E. Gilbert
1982   Reaffirming Rehabilitation. Cincinnati: Anderson.

Cullen, F.T., J.B. Cullen and J.F. Woznick
1988   Is rehabilitation dead? The myth of the punitive public. Journal of Criminal Justice 16:303–317.

Currie, E.
1989   Confronting crime: Looking toward the twenty-first century. Justice Quarterly 6:5–25.

Davidson, W.S. and T.R. Wolfred
1977   Evaluation of a community-based behavior modification program for prevention of delinquency. Community Mental Health Journal 13:296–306.

Davidson, W.S., L. Gottschalk, L. Gensheimer, and J. Mayer
1984   Interventions with Juvenile Delinquents: A Meta-analysis of Treatment Efficacy. Washington, D.C.: National Institute of Juvenile Justice and Delinquency Prevention.

Davidson, W.S., R. Redner, C. Blakely, C. Mitchell, and J. Emshoff
1987   Diverson of juvenile offenders: An experimental comparison. Journal of Consulting and Clinical Psychology 55:68–75.

Douds, A.F. and T.R. Collingwood
1978   Management by objectives: A successful application. Child Welfare 57:181–185.

Druckman, J.M.
1979   A family-oriented policy and treatment program for female juvenile status offenders. Journal of Marriage and the Family 41:627–636.

Dutton, D.G.
1986   The outcome of court-mandated treatment for wife assault: A quasi-experimental evaluation. Violence and Victims 1:163–175.

Empey, L.T. and M.L. Erickson
1972   The Provo Experiment: Evaluating Community Control of Delinquency. Lexington, Mass.: Lexington Books.

Farrington, D.P. and T. Bennett
1981   Police cautioning of juveniles in London. British Journal of Criminology 21:123–135.

390   ANDREWS ET AL.

Faust, D.
  1965   Group counseling of juveniles by staff without professional training in group
           work. Crime and Delinquency 11:349–354.

Finckenauer, J.O.
  1982   Scared Straight! and the Panacea Phenomenon. Englewood Cliffs, N.J.:
           Prentice-Hall.

Fo, W.S.O. and C.R. O'Donnell
  1975   The buddy system: Effect of community intervention on delinquent offenses.
           Behavior Therapy 6:522–524.

Freud, S.
  1953   A General Introduction to Psychoanalysis. Reprint ed. New York:
           Permabooks.

Garrett, C.J.
  1985   Effects of residential treatment of adjudicated delinquents: A meta-analysis.
           Journal of Research in Crime and Delinquency 22:287–308.

Geismar, L.L. and K.M. Wood
  1985   Family and Delinquency: Resocializing the Young Offender. New York:
           Human Sciences Press.

Gendreau, P. and R.R. Ross
  1979   Effectiveness of correctional treatment: Bibliotherapy for cynics. Crime and
           Delinquency 25:463–489.
  1981   Correctional potency: Treatment and deterrence on trial. In R. Roesch and
           R.R. Corrado (eds.), Evaluation and Criminal Justice Policy. Beverly Hills,
           Calif.: Sage.
  1987   Revivification of rehabilitation: Evidence from the 1980s. Justice Quarterly
           4:349–408.

Gensheimer, L.K., J.P. Mayer, R. Gottschalk, and W.S. Davidson
  1986   Diverting youth from the juvenile justice system: A meta-analysis of
           intervention efficacy. In S.J. Apter and A. Goldstein (eds.), Youth Violence:
           Programs and Prospects. Elmsford, N.Y.: Pergamon.

Gilbert, G.R.
  1977   Alternate routes: A diversion project in the juvenile justice system.
           Evaluation Quarterly 1:301–318.

Glaser, D.
  1974   Remedies for the key deficiency in criminal justice evaluation research.
           Journal of Research in Crime and Delinquency 11:144–153.

Glueck, S. and E.T. Glueck
  1950   Unraveling Juvenile Delinquency. Cambridge, Mass.: Harvard University
           Press.

Gordon, D.A., J. Arbuthnot, K.E. Gustafson, and P. McGreen
  1988   Home-based behavioral systems family therapy with disadvantaged juvenile
           delinquents. Unpublished paper, Ohio University.

Grant, J.D.
  1965   Delinquency treatment in an institutional setting. In H.C. Quay (ed.),
           Juvenile Delinquency: Research and Theory. Princeton, N.J.: Van Nos-
           trand.

CORRECTIONAL TREATMENT META-ANALYSIS 391

Grant, J.D. and M.Q. Grant
1959   A group dynamics approach to the treatment of nonconformists in the navy. Annals of the American Academy of Political and Social Science 322:126–135.

Greenwood, P.W.
1988   The Role of Planned Interventions in Studying the Desistance of Criminal Behavior in Longitudinal Study. Santa Monica, Calif.: Rand.

Greenwood, P.W. and F.E. Zimring
1985   One More Chance: The Pursuit of Promising Intervention Strategies for Chronic Juvenile Offenders. Santa Monica, Calif.: Rand.

Gruher, M.
1979   Family counseling and the status offender. Juvenile and Family Court Journal 30:23–27.

Hackler, J.C. and J.L. Hagan
1975   Work and teaching machines as delinquency prevention tools: A four-year follow-up. Social Service Review 49:92–106.

Harris, P.W.
1988   The interpersonal maturity level classification system: I-level. Criminal Justice and Behavior 15:58–77.

Hoge, R.D. and D.A. Andrews
1986   A model for conceptualizing interventions in social service. Canadian Psychology 27:332–341.

Horowitz, A. and M. Wasserman
1979   The effect of social control on delinquent behavior: A longitudinal test. Sociological Focus 12:53–70.

Hunt, G.M. and N.H. Azrin
1973   A community-reinforcement approach to alcoholism. Behavior Research and Therapy 11:91–104.

Izzo, R.L. and R.R. Ross
1990   Meta-analysis of rehabilitation programs for juvenile delinquents. Criminal Justice and Behavior 17:134–142.

Jackson, P.C.
1983   Some effects of parole supervision on recidivism. British Journal of Criminology 23:17–34.

Jesness, C.F.
1975   Comparative effectiveness of behavior modification and transactional analysis programs for delinquents. Journal of Consulting and Clinical Psychology 43:758–779.

Jessor, R. and S.L. Jessor
1977   Problem Behavior and Psychosocial Development: A Longitudinal Study of Youth. New York: Academic Press.

Johnson, R.E.
1979   Juvenile Delinquency and Its Origins: An Integrative Theoretical Approach. New York: Cambridge University Press.

392   ANDREWS ET AL.

Johnson, B.D. and R.T. Goldberg
   1983   Vocational and social rehabilitation of delinquents. Journal of Offender
            Counseling, Services, and Rehabilitation 6:43–60.

Kassebaum, G., D. Ward, and D. Wilner
   1971   Prison Treatment and Parole Survival: An Empirical Assessment. New
            York: John Wiley & Sons.

Kelley, T.M., A.K. Havva, and R.A. Blak
   1979   The effectiveness of college student companion therapists with predelinquent
            youths. Journal of Police Science and Administration 7:186–195.

Kirby, B.C.
   1954   Measuring effects of treatment of criminals and delinquents. Sociology and
            Social Research 38:368–374.

Kirigin, K.A., C.J. Braukman, J.D. Atwater, and M.W. Montrose
   1982   An evaluation of Teaching Family (Achievement Place) Group Homes for
            juvenile offenders. Journal of Applied Behavior Analysis 15:1–16.

Klein, M.W.
   1971   Street Gangs and Street Workers. Englewood Cliffs, N.J.: Prentice-Hall.
   1986   Labeling theory and delinquency policy: An experimental test. Criminal
            Justice and Behavior 13:47–79.

Klein, N.C., J.F. Alexander, and B.V. Parsons
   1977   Impact of family systems intervention on recidivism and sibling delinquency:
            A model of primary prevention and program evaluation. Journal of
            Consulting and Clinical Psychology 3:469–474.

Kratcoski, P.C. and L.D. Kratcoski
   1982   The Phoenix Program: An educational alternative for delinquent youths.
            Juvenile and Family Court Journal 33:17–23.

Kraus, J.
   1978   Remand in custody as a deterrent in juvenile jurisdiction. British Journal of
            Criminology 18:17–23.
   1981   Police caution of juvenile offenders: A research note. Australian and New
            Zealand Journal of Criminology 14:91–94.

Lab, S.P. and J.T. Whitehead
   1988   An analysis of juvenile correctional treatment. Crime and Delinquency
            34:60–83.

Leschied, A.W., G.W. Austin, and P.G. Jaffe
   1988   Impact of the Young Offenders Act on recidivism rates of special needs
            youth: Clinical and policy implications. Canadian Journal of Behavioural
            Science 20:322–331.

Lewis, R.V.
   1983   Scared straight—California style: Evaluation of the San Quentin Program.
            Criminal Justice and Behavior 10:209–226.

Link, B.G., F.T. Cullen, E. Struening, P.E. Shrout, and B.P. Dohrenwend
   1989   A modified labeling theory approach to mental illness. American Sociologi-
            cal Review 54:400–423.

CORRECTIONAL TREATMENT META-ANALYSIS 393

Lipsey, M.W.
  1989   The efficacy of intervention for juvenile delinquency: Results from 400
          studies. Paper presented at the 41st annual meeting of the American Society
          of Criminology, Reno, Nev.

Lipsey, M.W., D.S. Cordray, and D.E. Berger
  1981   Evaluation of a juvenile diversion program using multiple lines of evidence.
          Evaluation Review 5:283–306.

Loeber, R. and M. Stouthamer–Loeber
  1987   Prediction. In H.C. Quay (ed.), Handbook of Juvenile Delinquency. New
          York: John Wiley & Sons.

Logan, C.H.
  1972   Evaluation research in crime and delinquency: A reappraisal. Journal of
          Criminal Law, Criminology and Police Science 63:378–387.

Martinson, R.
  1974   What works? Questions and answers about prison reform. The Public
          Interest 35:22–54.
  1979   New findings, new views: A note of caution regarding prison reform.
          Hofstra Law Review 7:243–258.

Maskin, M.B.
  1976   The differential impact of work vs communication-oriented juvenile correc-
          tion programs upon recidivism rates in delinquent males. Journal of Clinical
          Psychology 32:432–433.

Mayer, J.P., L.K. Gensheimer, W.S. Davidson, and R. Gottschalk
  1986   Social learning treatment within juvenile justice: A meta-analysis of impact
          in the natural environment. In S.J. Apter and A. Goldstein (eds.), Youth
          Violence: Programs and Prospects. Elmsford, N.Y.: Pergamon.

McPherson, S.J., L.E. McDonald, and C.W. Ryder
  1983   Intensive counseling with families of juvenile offenders. Juvenile and Family
          Court Journal 34:27–33.

Mitchell, C.M.
  1983   The dissemination of a social intervention: Process and effectiveness of two
          types of paraprofessional change agents. American Journal of Community
          Psychology 11:723–739.

Mott, J.
  1983   Police decisions for dealing with juvenile offenders. British Journal of
          Criminology 23:249–262.

Murphy, B.C.
  1972   A Test of the Effectiveness of an Experimental Treatment Program for
          Delinquent Opiate Addicts. Ottawa: Information Canada.

O'Donnell, C.R., R. Lydgate, and W.S.O. Fo
  1979   The buddy system: Review and follow-up. Child Behavior Therapy
          1:161–169.

Ostrum, T.M., C.M. Steele, L.K. Resenblood, and H.L. Mirels
  1971   Modification of delinquent behavior. Journal of Applied Social Psychology
          1:118–136.

394   ANDREWS ET AL.

Palmer, T.
    1975   Martinson revisited. Journal of Research in Crime and Delinquency
              12:133–152.
    1983   The effectiveness issue today: An overview. Federal Probation 46:3–10.

Palmer, T. and R.V. Lewis
    1980   A differentiated approach to juvenile diversion. Journal of Research in
              Crime and Delinquency 17:209–227.

Persons, R.
    1967   Relationship between psychotherapy with institutionalized boys and subse-
              quent adjustments. Journal of Consulting Psychology 31:137–141.

Petersilia, J., S. Turner, and J. Peterson
    1986   Prison versus Probation in California: Implications for Crime and Offender
              Recidivism. Santa Monica, Calif.: Rand.

Phillips, E.L., E.A. Phillips, D.L. Fixen, and M.W. Wolf
    1973   Achievement Place: Behavior shaping works for delinquents. Psychology
              Today 6:75–79.

Quay, H.C. and C.T. Love
    1977   The effect of a juvenile diversion program on rearrests. Criminal Justice and
              Behavior 4:377–396.

Rausch, S.
    1983   Court processing vs. diversion of status offenders: A test of deterrence and
              labeling theories. Journal of Research in Crime and Delinquency 20:39–54.

Redfering, D.L.
    1973   Durability of effects of group counseling with institutionalized females.
              Journal of Abnormal Psychology 82:85–86.

Regoli, R., E. Wilderman, and M. Pogrebin
    1985   Using an alternative evaluation measure for assessing juvenile diversion.
              Children and Youth Services Review 7:21–38.

Reitsma–Street, M. and A.W. Leschied
    1988   The conceptual level matching model in corrections. Criminal Justice and
              Behavior 15:92–108.

Romig, D.A.
    1976   Length of institutionalization, treatment program completion, and recidivism
              among delinquent adolescent males. Criminal Justice Review 1:115–119.

Rosenbaum, D.P.
    1988   Community crime prevention: A review and synthesis of the literature.
              Justice Quarterly 4:513–544.

Ross, R.R. and E.A. Fabiano
    1985   Time to Think: A Cognitive Model of Delinquency Prevention and Offender
              Rehabilitation. Johnson City, Tenn.: Institute of Social Sciences and Arts.

Ross, R.R. and H.B. McKay
    1976   A study of institutional treatment programs. International Journal of
              Offender Therapy and Comparative Criminology 21:165–173.

Ross, R.R., E.A. Fabiano, and C.D. Ewles
    1988   Reasoning and rehabilitation. International Journal of Offender Therapy and
              Comparative Criminology 32:29–35.

CORRECTIONAL TREATMENT META-ANALYSIS   395

Rothman, D.J.
   1980   Conscience and Convenience: The Asylum and Its Alternatives in Progres-
            sive America. Boston: Little, Brown.

Sarason, I.G. and V.J. Ganzer
   1973   Modeling and group discussions in the rehabilitation of juvenile delinquents.
            Journal of Counseling Psychology 20:442–449.

Schneider, A.L. and P.R. Schneider
   1984   A comparison of programmatic and ad hoc restitution in juvenile court.
            Justice Quarterly 1:529–547.

Schur, E.M.
   1973   Radical Nonintervention: Rethinking the Delinquency Problem. Englewood
            Cliffs, N.J.: Prentice-Hall.

Sechrest, L., S.O. White, and E.D. Brown
   1979   The Rehabilitation of Criminal Offenders: Problem and Prospects. Wash-
            ington, D.C.: National Academy Press.

Seidman, E., J. Rappaport, and W.S. Davidson
   1980   Adolescents in legal jeopardy: Initial success and replication of an
            alternative to the criminal justice system. In R.R. Ross and P. Gendreau
            (eds.), Effective Correctional Treatment. Toronto: Butterworth.

Shichor, D. and A. Binder
   1982   Community restitution for juveniles: An approach and preliminary investi-
            gation. Criminal Justice Review 7:46–50.

Shore, M.F. and J.L. Massimo
   1979   Fifteen years after treatment: A follow-up study of comprehensive vocation-
            ally-oriented psychotherapy. American Journal of Orthopsychiatry
            49:240–245.

Shorts, I.D.
   1986   Delinquency by association. British Journal of Criminology 26:156–163.

Smith, D.A. and P.R. Gartin
   1989   Specifying specific deterrence. American Sociological Review 54:94–105.

Sorenson, J.L.
   1978   Outcome evaluation of a referral system for juvenile offenders. American
            Journal of Community Psychology 6:381–388.

Sowles, R.C. and J. Gill
   1970   Institutional and community adjustment of delinquents following counseling.
            Journal of Consulting and Clinical Psychology 34:398–402.

Stephenson, R.M. and F.R. Scarpitti
   1974   Group Interaction as Therapy: The Use of the Small Group in Corrections.
            Westport, Conn.: Greenwood Press.

Stringfield, N.
   1977   The impact of family counseling in resocializing adolescent offenders within
            a positive peer treatment milieu. Offender Rehabilitation 1:349–360.

Stuart, R.B., S. Jayaratne, and T. Tripodi
   1976   Changing adolescent deviant behaviour through reprogramming the beha-
            viour of parents and teachers: An experimental evaluation. Canadian
            Journal of Behavioural Science 8:132–143.

396   ANDREWS ET AL.

Tittle, C.R., W.J. Villimez, and D.A. Smith
    1978   The myth of social class and criminality: An empirical assessment of the
            empirical evidence. American Sociological Review 43:643–656.

Viano, E.C.
    1976   Growing up in an affluent society: Delinquency and recidivism in suburban
            America. Journal of Criminal Justice 3:223–236.

Vinglis, E., E. Adlap, and L. Chung
    1982   The Oshawa Impaired Drivers Programme: An evaluation of a rehabilita-
            tion programme. Canadian Journal of Criminology 23:93–102.

Visher, C.A.
    1987   Incapacitation and crime control: Does a "lock 'em up" strategy reduce
            crime? Justice Quarterly 4:513–544.

Vito, G.V. and H.E. Allen
    1981   Shock probation in Ohio: A comparison of outcomes. International Journal
            of Offender Therapy and Comparative Criminology 25:70–76.

Wade, T.C., T.L. Morton, J.E. Lind, and N.R. Ferris
    1977   A family crisis intervention approach to diversion from the juvenile justice
            system. Juvenile Justice Journal 28:43–51.

Walker, S.
    1989   Sense and Nonsense about Crime: A Policy Guide. Pacific Grove, Calif.:
            Brooks/Cole.

Walsh, A.
    1985   An evaluation of the effects of adult basic education on rearrest rates among
            probationers. Journal of Offender Counseling, Services and Rehabilitation
            9:69–76.

Walter, T.L. and C.M. Mills
    1980   A behavioral-employment intervention program for reducing juvenile delin-
            quency. In R.R. Ross and P. Gendreau (eds.), Effective Correctional
            Treatment. Toronto: Butterworth.

Warren, M.Q.
    1969   The case for differential treatment of delinquents. Annals of the American
            Academy of Political and Social Science 381:47–59.

Wellford, C.
    1975   Labelling theory and criminology: An assessment. Social Problems
            22:332–345.

Whitaker, J.M. and L.J. Severy
    1984   Service accountability and recidivism for diverted youth: A client- and
            service-comparison analysis. Criminal Justice and Behavior 11:47–74.

Whitehead, J.T. and S.P. Lab
    1989   A meta-analysis of juvenile correctional treatment. Journal of Research in
            Crime and Delinquency 26:276–295.

Williams, L.
    1984   A police diversion alternative for juvenile offenders. Police Chief (Feb),
            54–56.

CORRECTIONAL TREATMENT META-ANALYSIS 397

Willman, M.T. and J.R. Snortum
1982   A police program for employment and youth gang members. International Journal of Offender Therapy and Comparative Criminology 26:207–214.

Wilson, J.Q. and R.J. Herrnstein
1985   Crime and Human Nature. New York: Simon & Schuster.

Winterdyk, J. and R. Roesch
1982   A Wilderness Experimental Program as an alternative for probationers. Canadian Journal of Criminology 23:39–49.

Wormith, J.S.
1984   Attitude and behavior change of correctional clientele: A three year follow-up. Criminology 22:595–618.

Wright, W.E. and M.C. Dixon
1977   Community prevention and treatment of juvenile delinquency. Journal of Research in Crime and Delinquency 14:35–67.

Zeisel, H.
1982   Disagreement over the evaluation of a controlled experiment. American Journal of Sociology 88:378–389.

D.A. Andrews is a professor of psychology at Carleton University and co-director of the Laboratory for Research on Assessment and Evaluation in the Human Services. His research interests include the assessment of risk, need, and responsivity factors among clients of correctional, youth, family, and mental health agencies, as well as the analysis and evaluation of effective treatment services. Additionally, he is interested in the social psychology of criminological knowledge.

Ivan Zinger, a recent graduate from Carleton University, is currently a student of law at the University of Ottawa. His research interests include the clinical/community psychology of crime and the social psychology of law and justice.

Robert D. Hoge is a professor of psychology at Carleton University and co-director of the Laboratory for Research on Assessment and Evaluation in the Human Services. His major areas of research interest concern problems in psychological assessment, with a particular concern for educational and criminal justice settings.

James Bonta is Chief Psychologist at the Ottawa–Carleton Detention Centre, clinical associate professor at the University of Ottawa, and research adjunct professor at Carleton University. His research interests include the assessment of offenders, the effectiveness of correctional rehabilitation, and the effects of incarceration.

Paul Gendreau is a professor of psychology at the University of New Brunswick (Saint John), consultant and past-director of research at Centracare Saint John, and consultant to Saint John Police Services. His research interests include assessment, treatment, and consultation.

Francis T. Cullen is a professor of criminal justice at the University of Cincinnati. His research interests include theories of crime and deviance, white-collar crime, correctional policy, and the attitudes of the public and professionals toward deviance and official processing.

APPENDIX: NONPARAMETRIC SUMMARY AND OVERVIEW OF THE STUDIES

Descriptions of the 154 explorations of treatment and recidivism are presented in Table A1. The major subheadings in the table identify Type of Treatment. Levels of the remainder of the variables are indicated in the columns labeled Sample, System, Design, Setting, Beh., and Phi. As noted at the bottom of the table, numeric codes reflect the levels for each Sample of Studies, Justice System, Quality of Research Design, Setting, and Behavioral Intervention. The minor subheadings in Table A1 enhance descriptions of type of treatment but did not enter into the analyses. The Comments column is intended as a guide for readers who wish to recreate the 2 × 2 tables that we drew from the original studies. Many of the comments will make little sense without reference to those original studies.

CRIMINAL SANCTIONS

Inspection of Table A1 provides an overview of the 30 "criminal justice" comparisons. Phi coefficients were signed positive when lower recidivism rates were found under "more" processing conditions. The first eight comparisons were culled from four studies of diversion through police cautioning versus regular processing, and only one phi estimate, a negative one, reached the .20 level (the standard of effectiveness in Whitehead and Lab was a positive phi coefficient of at least .20). The next set of 20 comparisons involved less versus more severe judicial dispositions, and six of the phi coefficients, all negative, equaled or exceeded .20. The final two studies in the criminal justice set reveal that completion of restitution contracts was only mildly associated with reduced recidivism rates. One might expect that the confound with selection factors would have had a stronger inflationary effect on the phi estimates. Overall, the findings of the 30 criminal justice comparisons were consistent with expectations: Only seven (20%) phi coefficients reached the criterion of .20 and, more consistent with labelling than deterrence theory, they were each negative in sign.

INAPPROPRIATE CORRECTIONAL SERVICE

Thirty-eight comparisons involved "inappropriate" treatments—treatments that we predicted would be either unrelated to recidivism or have a negative effect. Inspection confirms that only five phi coefficients reached the .20 level, and each was negative in sign. The mean phi coefficient was −.06. The only surprises in this set of comparisons were the positive phi coefficients, albeit statistically insignificant, yielded by Davidson et al.'s (1987) paraprofessional relationship-oriented program. Overall, the hypothesized ineffectiveness of inappropriate service was supported.

CORRECTIONAL TREATMENT META-ANALYSIS 399

UNSPECIFIED CORRECTIONAL SERVICE

Table A1 provides an overview of 32 comparisons involving unspecified correctional service. The number of positive phi coefficients equaling or exceeding .20 was 10 (34%), and the mean phi was clearly positive but low (.13). In regard to our hypothesis, we now begin to uncover evidence of the effectiveness of rehabilitative service. Note, in addition, the many significant but low phi estimates. Obviously, many weak effects emerged significant statistically because of the large samples studied. Not as obvious, except upon a reading of the original papers (e.g., Palmer and Lewis, 1980), several Type of Client × Type of Service interactions were found in this set of studies. Hence, some of the tabled effect size estimates are misleading because they reflect an averaging of what were actually positive and negative effects dependent upon type of case. For example, Palmer and Lewis (1980) reported that nonspecific family counseling for female first offenders was associated with clearly negative effects, apparently replicating the Druckman (1979) study. Unfortunately, these interactions were not reported in a manner that allowed the simple effects of treatment to be coded by type of case. Klein (1986) also reported some intriguing interactions that suggest weak or negative effects with low-risk cases. This pattern would be consistent with those tests of treatment in the inappropriate service set that involved the delivery of services to low-risk cases (studies 58-66 in Table A1).

APPROPRIATE CORRECTIONAL SERVICE

The overall pattern here reveals that 70% ($^{38}/_{54}$) of the comparisons within the appropriate service set yielded a positive phi of at least .20, and the overall mean phi coefficient was .30. In every comparison but two, which involved token economy programs in residential settings, the phi coefficients were positive. Appropriate treatment appears to work at least moderately well. Note that many of the studies in the appropriate set involved small samples (and sample size is inversely correlated with effect size: Lipsey, 1989). Future research will explore the relative contributions of methodological, statistical, and therapeutic integrity factors to this correlation between sample size and effect size. Preliminary explorations, however, have revealed that the effect of Type of Treatment on phi estimates is found in both smaller and larger sample studies. For example, 30 of the 54 tests of appropriate service involved a control group with 30 or fewer cases, compared with only 28 of the 100 other tests of treatment. Among the small sample tests, 77% ($^{23}/_{30}$) of the tests of appropriate treatment yielded a positive phi of at least .20 compared with 21% ($^{6}/_{28}$) of the tests of less appropriate treatments. The corresponding figures among the tests based on larger samples were 63% ($^{15}/_{24}$) for appropriate treatment and 7% ($^{5}/_{72}$) for other treatments.

400   ANDREWS ET AL.

NONPARAMETRIC SUMMARY

The proportion of coefficients within each of the four levels of Type of Treatment reaching or exceeding the Whitehead and Lab (1989) standard of effectiveness were .00, .00, .34, and .70 for the criminal sanction, inappropriate service, unspecified service, and appropriate service sets, respectively; chi-square = 68.83, $p < .000$, Eta = .67, r = .64, gamma = .92.

Table A1.   Summary of 154 Tests of Correctional Treatment

ID Author (Year)	Sample	System	Design	Setting	Beh	Phi	Rec Rate: % (n) Treat		Control		Comments
TYPE OF TREATMENT: 1) CRIMINAL SANCTIONS											
Sanctioning vs Cautioning											
1 Kraus (81)	1	1	1 1NSD		1	−15	41	(78)	27	(78)	
2 Klein (86)	2	1	2 1NSD		1	−25*	73	(81)	49	(82)	Release vs Petition
Studies with Higher Risk Cases											
3 Mott (83)	1	1	2 1NSD		1	−08	58	(167)	46	(26)	
4	1	1	2 1NSD		1	19	53	(30)	80	(5)	(girls)
5 Farrington & P (81)	1	1	2 1NSD		1	04	45	(11)	50	(8)	
Studies with Lower Risk Cases											
6 Mott (83)	1	1	2 1NSD		1	−03	33	(57)	30	(174)	
7	1	1	2 1NSD		1	−05	14	(7)	9	(75)	(girls)
8 Farrington & P (81)	1	1	2 1NSD		1	10	0	(2)	12	(24)	
More vs Less Severe Disposition											
9 Viano (76)	1	1	1 1 SD		1	−08	26	(35)	19	(21)	
10	1	1	1 1 SD		1	−20	26	(35)	10	(38)	Informal adjustment
11	1	1	1 1 SD		1	−12	19	(21)	10	(38)	Dismissal
12 Rausch (83)	1	1	1 1 SD		1	−01	47	(196)	44	(18)	
13	1	1	1 1 SD		1	−02	47	(196)	45	(91)	Probation
14	1	1	1 1 SD		1	−05	47	(196)	47	(45)	Maximum Community
15	1	1	1 1 SD		1	04	40	(45)	44	(18)	Community agent
16	1	1	1 1 SD		1	05	40	(45)	45	(91)	Probation
17	1	1	1 1 SD		1	00	45	(91)	44	(18)	Community agent
18 Kraus (78)	1	1	1 1PPC		1	−28*	64	(90)	37	(90)	
19 Horowitz & W (79)	1	1	2 1PPC		1	−22	91	(196)	75	(67)	
20	1	1	2 1PPC		1	−32*	83	(29)	43	(106)	Lower risk
21 Stephenson & S (74)	2	1	1 2		1	−23*	61	(44)	39	(44)	Prob vs Group Home
22	2	1	1 2		1	−20*	59	(44)	39	(44)	Inst vs Prob
23	2	1	1 2		1	02	59	(44)	61	(44)	Inst vs Group Home
24 Phillips P F & W (73)	2	1	1 1PPC		1	01	53	(15)	54	(13)	Inst vs Prob
25 Vito & A (81)	2	2	1 1PPC		1	−07*	17	(585)	12	(938)	Shock Incar vs Prob
26 Petersilia T & P (86)	2	2	1 2		1	−07	41	(162)	34	(162)	I vs P (viol offs)
27	2	2	1 2		1	−18*	61	(219)	43	(219)	I vs P (prop offs)
28	2	2	1 2		1	−17*	35	(130)	20	(130)	I vs P (drug offs)
Restitution (Successful Completion of)											
29 Schicor & B (82)	1	1	1 1NSD		1	14	7	(59)	15	(55)	
30 Schneider & S (84)	1	1	1 1PPC		1	18*	60	(190)	80	(61)	

CORRECTIONAL TREATMENT META-ANALYSIS   401

Table A1. (continued)

ID Author (Year)	Sample	System	Design	Setting	Beh	Phi	Rec Rate: % (n) Treat		Control	Comments

TYPE OF TREATMENT: 2) INAPPROPRIATE CORRECTIONAL SERVICE

Intensive Non-Behavioral Group Interaction (including Recreation)

31 Byles (81)	1		1	1	1PPC	1 −11	71	(31)	60	(35) Attendance Centers
32	1		1	1	1PPC	1 08	68	(25)	76	(49)
33 Shorts (86)	2		1	1	1NSD	1 −01	48	(43)	47	(19)
34	2		1	1	1NSD	1 03	10	(31)	12	(17)
35 Winterdyk & R (82)	2		1	2	1 SD	1 00	20	(30)	20	(30) Wilderness Program

Non-Directive Client-Centered/Psychodynamic Counselling

36 Klein A & P (77)	1		1	2	1 SD	1 −11	60	(30)	49	(56)
37	1		1	2	1 SD	1 −17	61	(30)	40	(10) (Sibs)
38 Adams & V (82)	1		1	2	2	1 −44*	100	(14)	69	(13) Group Psychodrama
39 Davidson R B M & E (87)	2		1	1	1NSD	1 06	33	(12)	43	(112) Rel vs Beh/Adv/Act
40	2		1	1	1NSD	1 16	33	(12)	58	(89) Rel vs Controls
41 Berman (78)	2		2	2	1PPC	1 00	25	(16)	25	(16) Non-Bev Para-prof

Non-Behavioral Milieu Therapy/Guided Group Interaction

42 Stringfield (77)	1		1	1	1PPC	1 −31*	56	(32)	25	(20) Milieu vs Fam
43 Clarke & C (78)	1		1	2	2	1 −01	70	(86)	69	(87)
44 Stephenson & S (74)	2		1	1	1PPC	1 −20*	59	(44)	39	(44) GGI vs Prob
45	2		1	1	2	1 00	59	(44)	59	(44) GGI vs Inst
46	2		1	1	2	1 02	59	(44)	61	(44) GGI vs Group Home
47 Empey & E (72)	2		1	2	1PPC	1 −03	58	(71)	54	(79) GGI vs Prob
48	2		1	1	1PPC	1 16*	64	(44)	79	(132) GGI vs Incar
49 Craft S & G (64)	2		1	2	2	1 −13	58	(24)	46	(24) Milieu vs Auth

Non-Behavioral Weakly-Focused Academic/Vocational Approaches

50 Willman & S (82)	1		1	1	1 SD	1 −11	71	(68)	60	(68)
51 Maskin (76)	1		1	2	2	1 −39*	50	(30)	13	(30)
52 Hackler & H (75)	1		1	2	1NSD	1 −05	33	(85)	29	(70)
53	1		1	2	1NSD	1 07	25	(67)	32	(131)
54 Zeisel (82)	2		2	2	1PPC	1 00	49	(???)	49	(???) (TARP)

Confrontational Groups (Scared Straight)

55 Buckner & C-L (83)	1		1	1	1 SD	1 −04	41	(100)	37	(100)
56	1		1	1	1 SD	1 11	22	(50)	32	(50) (female)
57 Lewis (83)	1		1	2	1 SD	1 −16	67	(55)	81	(53)

Mismatched According to Risk or Responsivity/Need Systems

58 Sorenson (78)	1		1	2	1NSD	1 −35*	30	(30)	4	(45)
59 Byles & M (79)	1		1	2	1 SD	1 −12	57	(94)	43	(114)
60 Gruher (79)	1		1	2	1 SD	1 06	32	(38)	38	(40)
61 Quay & L (77)	1		1	2	1NSD	1 07	28	(268)	36	(92)
62 O'Donnell L & F (79)	1		1	2	1NSD	2 −07	25	(169)	19	(130)
63	1		1	2	1NSD	2 −10	18	(116)	11	(65) (female)
64 Baird H & B (79)	2		2	2	1PPC	1 −13	10	(58)	3	(58)
65 Andrews & K (80)	2		2	2	1PPC	1 −09	17	(58)	11	(62) Para-prof prog
66 Andrews K M & R (86)	2		2	2	1PPC	1 −09	14	(98)	2	(28) Para-prof prog
67 Grant & G (59)	2		2	2	2	1 −14*	52	(91)	38	(144) Low maturity
68 Andrews & K (80)	2		2	2	1PPC	1 11	42	(23)	48	(13) Low Emp/High Risk

402 ANDREWS ET AL

Table A1. (continued)

ID Author (Year)	Sample	System	Design	Setting	Beh	Phi	Rec Rate: % (n) Treat		Control		Comments

TYPE OF TREATMENT: 3) UNSPECIFIED CORRECTIONAL SERVICE

Service-Oriented Diversion

ID Author (Year)	Sample	System	Design	Setting	Beh	Phi	Treat %	Treat (n)	Control %	Control (n)	Comments
69 Regoli W & P (85)	1	1	1 1NSD	1	19*	2	(52)	11	(52)	Complete prog vs pre-program controls
70	1	1	1 1NSD	1	16*	8	(98)	21	(98)	
71	1	1	1 1NSD	1	31*	6	(61)	32	(61)	
72	1	1	1 1NSD	1	12	10	(72)	18	(72)	
73	1	1	1 1NSD	1	−06	29	(119)	24	(119)	
74	1	1	1 1NSD	1	−05	26	(107)	24	(107)	
75 Lipsey C & B (81)	1	1	1 1 SD	1	18*	26	(776)	44	(476)	Complete vs Incomplete
76	1	1	1 1 SD	1	10*	27	(870)	37	(533)	
77	1	1	1 1 SD	1	10*	35	(543)	45	(333)	
78 Whitaker & S (84)	1	1	1 1NSD	1	10*	33	(???)	46	(???)	More vs Less Diverse
79 Palmer & L (80)	1	1	1 1 SD	1	07*	25	(1345)	31	(1192)	Unspec quasi control
80 Gilbert (77)	1	1	1 1 SD	1	30*	34	(58)	65	(78)	Assign vs Preprog conts
81 Klein (86)	2	1	2 1NSD	1	17*	57	(88)	73	(81)	Ref vs Petition
82	2	1	2 1NSD	1	12	62	(55)	73	(81)	Ref+ vs Petition
83	2	1	2 1NSD	1	−08	57	(88)	49	(82)	Ref vs Release
84	2	1	2 1NSD	1	−13	62	(55)	49	(82)	Ref+ vs Release

Appropriateness Uncertain On Targets/Style

ID Author (Year)	Sample	System	Design	Setting	Beh	Phi	Treat %	Treat (n)	Control %	Control (n)	Comments
85 Romig (76)	1	1	1 1PPC	1	15*	14	(301)	27	(127)	Parole Supervision
86 Jackson (83)	1	1	2 1PPC	1	03	82	(198)	84	(98)	Parole Supervision
87 Barkwell (76)	1	1	2 1PPC	1	−16	88	(16)	75	(16)	Prob Serv vs Surveill
88 Druckman (79)	1	1	1 1NSD	1	−17	50	(14)	33	(15)	Family Counseling
89 Seidman R & D (80)	2	1	2 1NSD	1	46*	50	(12)	90	(12)	Parapro Advocacy
90 Wade M L & F (77)	2	1	1 1NSD	1	51*	15	(34)	70	(77)	Family crisis
91 Romig (76)	2	1	1 2	1	10*	12	(177)	20	(251)	Mths served/rel order
92 Johnson & G (83)	2	1	2 1PPC	1	05	3	(87)	5	(87)	State Vocational Serv
93 Sowles & G (70)	2	1	2 2	1	22	37	(30)	60	(15)	Ind/Group (boys)
94	2	1	2 2	1	38	0	(10)	20	(5)	(girls)
95 Ostrum S R & M (71)	2	1	2 1 SD	1	22	26	(19)	48	(19)	Mixed socio-psych prog
96 Redfering (73)	2	1	1 2	1	29	35	(17)	64	(14)	Cl-Ce Group (appro tar)
97 Jesness in grant (65)	2	1	2 2	1	05	73	(11)	77	(13)	Small vs Large Units
98 Ross F & E (88)	2	2	2 1PPC	2	23	47	(17)	70	(23)	Life Skill vs Reg Prob
99 Vinglis A & C (82)	2	2	2 1PPC	1	−05	15	(58)	19	(62)	Impaired Driving
100 Walsh (85)	2	2	1 1PPC	1	21*	24	(50)	44	(50)	Gen Equiva Prog

CORRECTIONAL TREATMENT META-ANALYSIS   403

Table A1. (continued)

ID Author (Year)	Sample	System	Design	Setting	Beh	Phi	Rec Rate: % (n) Treat	Control	Comments
TYPE OF TREATMENT: 4) APPROPRIATE CORRECTIONAL SERVICE									
Short-Term Behavioral/Systems Family Counseling									
101 Alexander C S P (76)	1	1	1	1 SD	2	64*	0 (12)	56	(9)
102 Klein A & P (77)	1	1	2	1 SD	2	23*	26 (46)	48	(56)
103	1	1	2	1 SD	2	18	20 (46)	40	(10) (sibs)
104	1	1	2	1 SD	2	31*	26 (46)	57	(30)
105	1	1	2	1 SD	2	41*	20 (46)	60	(30) (sibs)
106 McPherson M & R (83)	1	1	2	1 SD	1	20*	33 (15)	58	(60) (target = discipline)
107 Gordon A G & M (88)	2	1	1	1 SD	2	83*	0 (12)	75	(4) (girls)
108	2	1	1	1 SD	2	44*	20 (15)	65	(23) (boys)
109 Stuart J & T (76)	2	1	2	1NSD	2	19	0 (30)	7	(30)
110 Barton A W T & W (85)	2	1	1	2	2	41*	60 (30)	93	(44)
Structured One-on-One Paraprofessional/Peer Program									
111 Kelly H & B (79)	1	1	1	1NSD	1	26*	0 (65)	12	(63) (target = thinking)
112 Mitchell (83)	1	1	1	1PPC	2	29*	14 (29)	43	(63)
113 Ross & M (77)	1	1	1	2	2	33	7 (15)	33	(15)
114	1	1	1	2	2	46*	7 (15)	60	(45)
115 Seidman R & D (80)	2	1	2	1NSD	2	51*	48 (25)	100	(12) Beh/adv vs Controls
116	2	1	2	1NSD	2	60*	25 (12)	92	(12) Beh vs Controls
117	2	1	2	1NSD	2	17	25 (12)	50	(12) Beh vs Advocacy
118 Davison R B M & E (87)	2	1	1	1NSD	2	15*	43 (112)	58	(89) Beh/Adv/Action vs C
119 Andrews (80)	2	2	2	1PPC	2	15*	15 (72)	28	(116) Hi Emp Hi So Officers
Specialized Academics/Vocational Services									
120 Bachra & Z (78)	1	1	1	1NSD	1	38*	7 (31)	42	(48) (specific focus)
121 Kratcoski & K (82)	1	1	1	1PPC	2	65*	42 (38)	100	(83)
122 Walter & M (80)	2	1	1	1PPC	2	62*	9 (53)	70	(23)
123 Shore & M (79)	2	1	2	1NSD	1	52*	40 (10)	90	(10) (intense/ individualized)
Intensive Structured Skill Training									
124 Collingwood D & W (76)	1	1	1	1 SD	2	41*	11 (813)	51	(196) Participants vs Nonpar
125 Williams (84)	1	1	1	1 SD	2	33*	21 (564)	64	(77) Participants vs Nonpar
126 Sarason & G (73)	2		2	2	2	18*	19 (64)	34	(64) Modeling vs Contr
127	2	1	2	2	2	24*	14 (64)	34	(64) Discuss vs Control
128 Ross F & E (88)	2	2	2	1PPC	2	52*	18 (22)	70	(23) Cog-Bch vs Reg Prob
129	2	2	2	1PPC	2	31*	18 (22)	47	(17) Cog-Beh vs Life Skill
130 Dutton (86)	2	2	1	1PPC	2	43*	4 (50)	40	(50) Cog-beh (wife batter)
Introduction of Individualized Rehabilitative Regime									
131 Jesness (75)	1	1	1	2	2	10*	32 (398)	42	(499) Token Eco vs Pre-Prog

404

ANDREWS ET AL

Table A1. (continued)

ID Author (Year)	Sample	System	Design	Setting	Beh	Phi	Treat % (n)	Control % (n)	Comments
132	1	1	1	2	1	14*	33 (453)	47 (660)	(target=ind crimino need)
133 Ross & M (76)	1	1	1	2	2	27	10 (10)	33 (15)	
134	1	1	1	2	2	38*	10 (10)	60 (45)	
Token Economy									
135 Kirigin B A & W (82)	1	1	1	2	2	21	27 (38)	47 (30)	(girls)
136	1	1	1	2	2	12	57 (102)	73 (22)	(boys)
137 Davidson & W (77)	1	1	1	2	2	−26*	?? (??)	?? (??)	
138 Ross & M (77)	1	1	1	2	2	−23	60 (45)	33 (15)	
139 Phillips P F & W (73)	2	1	1	2	2	36*	18 (16)	53 (15)	Ach Place vs Inst
140	2	1	1	2	2	37*	18 (16)	54 (13)	Ach Place vs Prob
Individual/Group Counselling									
141 Persons (67)	2	1	2	2	2	29*	32 (41)	61 (41)	Ind + Group
Appropriately Matched According to Risk or Responsivity/Need Systems									
142 Sorenson (78)	1	1	2	1NSD	1	06	25 (44)	31 (26)	
143 Byles & M (79)	1	1	2	1 SD	1	27*	68 (60)	92 (37)	
144 Gruher (79)	1	1	2	1 SD	1	07	56 (16)	63 (30)	
145 Quay & L (77)	1	1	2	1NSD	1	23*	36 (164)	65 (40)	
146 O'Donnell L & F (79)	1	1	2	1NSD	2	20	62 (37)	81 (21)	(boys)
147	1	1	2	1NSD	2	08	38 (13)	50 (2)	(girls)
148 Barkwell (76)	1	1	2	1PPC	1	35*	56 (16)	88 (16)	
149	1	1	2	1PPC	1	20	56 (16)	75 (16)	
150 Baird H & B (79)	2	2	2	1PPC	1	17*	16 (184)	30 (184)	
151 Andrews K M & R (86)	2	2	2	1PPC	1	31*	33 (54)	75 (12)	Para-prof prog
152 Andrews & K (80)	2	2	2	1PPC	1	82*	0 (11)	80 (10)	(Hi Emp & Risk)
153 Grant & G (59)	2	2	2	2	1	09	29 (135)	38 (141)	(High Maturity)
154 Andrews & K (80)	2	2	2	1PPC	1	27*	31 (34)	58 (23)	Para-prof prog

* $p < .05$ (Chi square)

Note: The value labels for codes "1" and "2" are as follows: Sample of Studies (Whitehead & Lab, Sample 2), Justice System (juvenile, adult), Quality of Research Design (weaker, stronger), Behavioral Intervention (no, yes) and Setting (community, institutional/residential). The letters beside code "1" for Setting refer to different types of community settings (NSD: nonsystem diversion; SD: system diversion; PPC: probation, parole, community).

Name Index